M

Chapter 5   **BASIC ELECTRONICS AND DIGITAL LOGIC**   151

ASSEMBLY LANGUAGE AND COMPUTER ARCHITECTURE
Using C++ and Java

ANTHONY J. DOS REIS
State University of New York at New Paltz

• •

THOMSON
★
COURSE TECHNOLOGY

Australia • Canada • Mexico • Singapore • United Kingdom • United States

Assembly Language and Computer Architecture Using C++ and Java
by Anthony J. Dos Reis

Managing Editor:
Jennifer Muroff

Associate Product Manager:
Mirella Misiaszek

Cover Design:
Roy Neuhaus

Editorial Assistant:
Amanda Piantedosi

Designer:
Roy Neuhaus

Compositor:
WestWords, Inc.

Manufacturing Coordinator:
Trevor Kallop

CONTENTS

To my parents

Chapter 6   MICROLEVEL OF H1 AND V1   210

Chapter 12   **OPTIMAL INSTRUCTION SET**   490

Chapter 13   **USING, EVALUATING, AND IMPLEMENTING THE OPTIMAL AND STACK INSTRUCTION SETS**   **528**

• •

Chapter 14   **MEMORY SYSTEMS**   **612**

• •

Chapter 15   **SOME MODERN ARCHITECTURES**   647

PREFACE

FEATURES OF THE BOOK

• •

Assembly language and computer architecture are tough subjects to learn. The typical assembly language is so complex and idiosyncratic that learning even basic concepts can be a difficult task. The same problem is present with architecture, but worse. With assembly language, one deals with one complex system; with architecture, one deals with a multitude of complex systems.

How then can assembly language and computer architecture be most effectively presented? The approach taken by this book is to use a simple computer model called H1. H1 is so easy to learn that students can quickly accomplish a great deal with it. Moreover, they can focus on learning important system concepts rather than idiosyncratic details.

The use of a simple computer model to present fundamental concepts is hardly an innovative technique. This book, however, uses its H1 model in two innovative ways. First, H1 is in almost every chapter. The result is a coherent development of a computer system rather than a collection of disconnected topics. Second, H1 is not a static model. It has flaws (major flaws, in fact) that *students fix.* Thus, the flaws in H1 are not flaws in the book. Rather, they are assets the book uses to engage students in the design and implementation process.

One of the most important features of the book is the large number of activities it provides that promote greater understanding. For example, students can write a linker in C++ or Java; or they can implement a stack-oriented architecture for H1 and evaluate its performance.

Because of its emphasis on important system concepts, the book provides excellent preparation for advanced courses in computer science and engineering. Students using this book will be prepared to do serious work in advanced programming, compiler design, the design of programming languages, operating systems, advanced architecture, and computer engineering.

H1 admirably demonstrates the basics of computer architecture and organization. However, it cannot demonstrate some of the advanced features found in modern computers. To this end, I have included material in Chapters 14, 15, and 16 on modern systems. These chapters cover memory systems, RISC, CISC, pipelining, the SPARC, the Pentium, and the Java Virtual Machine (JVM).

The book's chapters can be covered in a variety of orders, and some chapters can be skipped (see the chapter prerequisite structure on page xv). For example, Chapter 5 (digital logic) can be covered any time after Chapter 1, or skipped; Chapter 16 (the Java Virtual Machine) can be covered any time after Chapter 7, or skipped.

AUDIENCE

· ·

The book is for a one-semester undergraduate course that combines assembly language with architecture. However, it will also work well for courses that cover only assembly language or only architecture. Because of its balanced treatment of hardware and software, it is suitable for both computer science and engineering curricula. The book is also excellent for a first course in a graduate computer science program, particularly for students without strong computer science or engineering backgrounds.

PREREQUISITES FOR THE BOOK

· ·

Although the book uses C++ *and* Java, its only prerequisite is C++ *or* Java. The C++ examples start simply, become more complex slowly, and are thoroughly explained. This gentle treatment of C++, combined with C++'s similarity to Java, makes the book entirely suitable for a student who knows only Java. Indeed, such a student will derive an additional benefit from the book: an almost painless introduction to C++. If, in a crowded curriculum, there is no room for C++, the book makes it possible to include C++, as well as assembly language and architecture, in a single course.

Although the book's treatment of C++ is gentle, it will nevertheless provide many insights into C++ in particular, and programming languages in general. For example, the book shows precisely how an object is implemented. Even a student who is highly skilled in C++ will find this material informative and engaging.

The material on Java should not pose any problems for a student who knows only C++. Chapter 1 presents several Java programs that illustrate floating point errors. Chapter 4 discusses a problem with endianness that can occur with Java programs. Chapter 8 discusses pointers and arrays in Java. Chapter 9 discusses Boolean operators in Java. Chapter 11 shows students how to implement an assembler and linker in Java (or in C++). Chapter 13 discusses some of the ramifications of a stack architecture with respect to the JVM. All of Chapter 16 is devoted to the JVM's structure and operation. The book also contains plenty of generic material that applies to both Java and C++. Students who already know Java will gain a deeper and more comprehensive understanding of the language.

SUPPLEMENTS

· ·

The software package, lecture slides, and other supplements are available on the Course Technology/course website at **www.brookscole.com.** An instructor's manual with answers to problems, extra problems, microcode, C++ and Java source code for an assembler and a linker, and teaching suggestions is also available.

The software package runs on Microsoft Windows, Microsoft DOS, SPARC Solaris, X86 Linux, and Macintosh OS X. Support for additional platforms is planned. The package includes a simulator/source-level debugger/profiler (`sim`); an assembler (`mas`); a linker (`lin`); a library program (`lib`); three programs (`pic`, `mex`, and `see`) for examining object, executable, and library modules; a horizontal microcode assembler (`has`); a vertical microcode assembler (`vas`); a microcode encrypter (**enc**); several utility programs; complete documentation; and all the example programs in the text. **sim**, **mas**, **has**, and **vas** are reconfigurable to accommodate new instruction sets.

sim supports a large variety of commands that are useful for tracing or debugging machine language programs or microcode. A particularly useful feature is its ability to display microlevel activity on a per machine instruction basis. With this facility, a student can clearly see the microlevel activity corresponding to the execution of any single machine instruction.

sim can use either unencrypted or encrypted microcode. This feature allows students to use, but not examine, the encrypted microcode in the software package. Students can then write their own versions, without the "benefit" of seeing my versions.

All the software uses a simple command line interface. The command line interface is completely satisfactory for the type of programs in the software package, and it is the easiest to learn to use. Moreover, it does not change from one platform to another. All the programs can be invoked without any command-line arguments (in which case the programs prompt for arguments). Thus, they can be conveniently invoked via an icon in a graphical user interface.

Instructions on using the software package are integrated into the textbook. This approach makes learning how to use the software easier. Students never have to wade through reams of documentation, and instructors do not have to waste class time teaching students how to use the software. Complete documentation is available in file form in the software package for those who want it.

ESSENTIAL CHAPTER PREREQUISITES

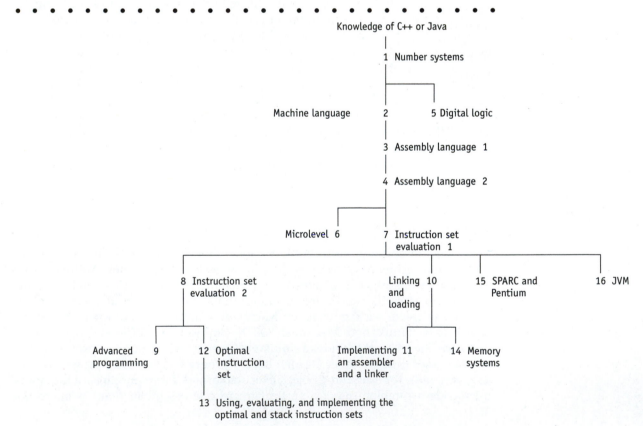

CHAPTER SUMMARIES

• •

Chapter 1 is mostly an introduction to number systems. However, it does cover some subtle points on the carry and overflow flags, and on signed and unsigned comparisons that are needed later in the text. Using several Java programs, it also illustrates various types of computational errors that can occur with floating-point numbers.

Chapter 2 introduces H1, machine language, and `sim`.

Chapter 3 introduces assembly language, assemblers, the assembly process, and the mechanism for the sequential execution of instructions.

Chapter 4 completes the presentation of assembly language basics for H1. It also discusses an endianness problem that can occur with Java programs. Because H1 is so simple, Chapters 2, 3, and 4 require little class time.

Chapter 5 provides the foundation in digital logic that is needed for a complete understanding of the internal organization of H1. In addition, it introduces some important principles of electronics. Chapter 6 depends on this chapter, but only minimally. Thus, this chapter can be skipped if the instructor provides descriptions of a few logic circuits in class.

Chapter 6 presents the internal organization of H1 and V1 (V1 is similar to H1, but vertically microprogrammed), and the fundamentals of microprogramming. It implements a basic instruction set in both horizontal and vertical microcode. It also discusses hardwired control. This chapter can be skipped in a course covering assembly language only.

Chapters 7 and 8 are important chapters that expose the weaknesses of the standard instruction set. By examining compiler-generated code, students develop a sense of what a good instruction set should do. These chapters also provide an invaluable look at C++ from an "under the hood" perspective.

Chapter 9 covers several advanced topics in programming, at both the assembler and C++ levels. Topics include pointers to pointers, a potential bug in call by reference (if it is implemented in the "obvious" way), call by value-result, and variable-length argument lists. Most instructors will want to cover at least part of this chapter. However, the entire chapter can be skipped.

Chapter 10 presents the loading and linking mechanisms. It uses the `pic`, `mex`, and `see` programs to simplify the examination of object, executable, and library modules. It also examines start-up code at the assembler level.

Chapter 11 provides guidance on implementing an assembler and a linker— two appropriate programming projects for students at this point in the text. Guidance is provided for both C++ and Java implementations. Students typically enjoy these projects and learn a great deal from them. They provide a rare opportunity to do systems programming in Java. Most instructors will find that this chapter requires very little, if any, discussion in class.

Chapter 12 introduces the optimal instruction set, an improvement of the standard instruction set that fixes the weaknesses in H1 exposed mostly in Chapters 7 and 8.

Chapter 13 determines how well the optimal instruction set can support sophisticated programming entities and mechanisms, such as objects, virtual functions, and call by name. Using multiplication as an example, this chapter also discusses the various levels—circuit, micro, and machine—at which computational function can be placed. It introduces a stack instruction set for H1 and compares it with the optimal instruction set. It also provides guidance on how to implement the optimal and stack instruction sets (two worthwhile projects students can do at this time).

Chapter 14 uses H1 as a vehicle to explain the ramifications of program relocation, leading to an investigation of a variety of memory systems. Topics include paging, demand paging, associative memory, interrupts, page replacement policies, memory protection, segmentation, and cache memory.

Chapter 15 uses the SPARC and the Pentium to cover some important topics (for example, RISC, pipelining, code optimization) for which H1 is not a suitable vehicle.

Chapter 16 presents Java and the JVM in the same way earlier chapters present C++ and H1 assembly language (although in a more condensed form).

ACKNOWLEDGEMENTS

• •

My design of H1 and V1, at both the micro and machine levels, was influenced by similar models in *Principles of Computer Architecture* by Miles Murdocca and Vincent Heuring, Prentice-Hall, 2000; in *Computer Systems Design and Architecture* by Vincent Heuring and Harry Jordan, Addison Wesley Longman, 1997; and particularly in *Structured Computer Organization Third Edition,* by Andrew Tanenbaum, Prentice-Hall, 1990.

Reviewers during the editing process can significantly contribute to making a book better. This was, indeed, the case for my reviewers. Their input provided me with essential guidance during the extensive revision of the manuscript. I am grateful to Mahdi Abdelguerfi of the University of New Orleans, Ming Hsing Chiu of the University of New Orleans, Annie Groeninger of Western Washington University, Lubomir Ivanov of Iona College, and Gene Sheppard of Georgia Perimeter College.

I would like to thank my students for their helpful feedback on early versions of the manuscript; John Collier and Brian Chickery at Vassar College for their assistance with the Macintosh; Andy Pletch in my department for his expertise on UNIX; Addie Haas for her advice and encouragement; Merrill Peterson at Matrix Productions who coordinated the production of the book; and Kallie Swanson at Brooks/Cole who recognized the value of this project when it still had many rough edges.

Anthony J. Dos Reis

Chapter One

NUMBER SYSTEMS

1.1 INTRODUCTION

In a well-known joke, a graduate of a speed-reading course proudly announces that he was able to read Tolstoy's *War and Peace* in 10 minutes. When asked what the book was about, the graduate replied, "I think it was about Russia." Students completing computer courses—particularly courses in assembly language and computer architecture—often have similarly inadequate answers about their courses. Computers, after all, are complex systems that span a multitude of technologies. To thoroughly understand even one computer system can take years of diligent study. There is, however, one way to quickly acquire an understanding of the fundamental concepts of computers: study a computer that is well suited for learning these concepts. We will do precisely that in this book. We will study a computer that is simple enough that it can be mastered quickly, but realistic enough that it accurately models the essential features of modern computers.

In this chapter, we start with the study of number systems. We humans use the *decimal* number system. Computers, however, use a different number system, called *binary*. Decimal numbers use 10 symbols (0, 1, 2, . . . , 9) called *digits*. Binary numbers use only two symbols (0 and 1), called *bits*. A third number system, *hexadecimal* (or *hex*, for short), can be used as a convenient shorthand representation of the binary numbers inside a computer. For this reason, hexadecimal as well as binary numbers are important in the computer field. Hexadecimal numbers use 16 symbols (0, 1, 2, . . . , 9, A, B, C, D, E, F) called *hex digits* or, when the context implies hex, simply *digits*.

1.2 POSITIONAL NUMBER SYSTEMS

Decimal, binary, and hexadecimal are all *positional number systems*. In a positional number system, each position is associated with a different weight. For example, in the decimal number 25.4, the weights of the three positions, from right to left, are $\frac{1}{10}$, 1, and 10:

$$
\begin{array}{ccc}
2 & 5 & \cdot \quad 4 \\
\hline
10 & 1 & \frac{1}{10} \quad \text{weights}
\end{array}
$$

The weight of each position determines how much the digit in that position contributes to the value of the number. For example, because the "2" in 25.4 occupies the 10's position (i.e., the position with weight 10), it contributes $2 \times 10 = 20$ to the value of the number. The value of a decimal number is the sum of each digit times its weight. Thus, the value of 25.4 is

$$2 \times 10 + 5 \times 1 + 4 \times \frac{1}{10}$$

In a decimal number, weights increase by a factor of 10 from right to left from one position to the next. The weight of the position to the immediate left of the decimal point is always 1. Because decimal numbers have 10 symbols (0 to 9), and have weights that increase by a factor of 10, we call decimal a *base 10* or *radix 10* positional number system.

We call the period in a number that divides the whole part from the fractional part the *radix point*. When we are dealing with decimal numbers, we usually call the radix point a *decimal point*. In binary and hexadecimal numbers, we can similarly call the radix point the *binary point* and the *hexadecimal point*, respectively.

Binary is the base 2 positional number system. Thus, in the binary number 1011.1, the weights of each position increase by a factor of 2 from right to left. As in decimal, the position to the immediate left of the radix point has weight 1. Thus, in the binary number 1011.1, the weights are

$$
\begin{array}{ccccc}
1 & 0 & 1 & 1 & \cdot & 1 \\
\hline
8 & 4 & 2 & 1 & & \frac{1}{2}
\end{array}
\quad \text{weights (in decimal)}
$$

and its value in decimal is

$$1 \times 8 + 0 \times 4 + 1 \times 2 + 1 \times 1 + 1 \times \frac{1}{2} = 11.5$$

Because bits are either 1 or 0, the value of a binary number is simply the sum of the weights whose corresponding bits are 1.

Hexadecimal is the base 16 positional number system. For its 16 symbols, we use 0 to 9 and A to F. The symbols 0 to 9 have the same values as they do in decimal. The symbols A, B, C, D, E, and F have values equal to decimal 10, 11, 12, 13, 14, and 15, respectively (see Figure 1.1).

FIGURE 1.1

Decimal	Binary	Hexadecimal
0	0000	0
1	0001	1
2	0010	2
3	0011	3
4	0100	4
5	0101	5
6	0110	6
7	0111	7
8	1000	8
9	1001	9
10	1010	A
11	1011	B
12	1100	C
13	1101	D
14	1110	E
15	1111	F

The weights in a hexadecimal number increase by a factor of 16. As in decimal and binary, the weight of the position to the immediate left of the radix point is 1. For example, in the hexadecimal number 1CB.8, the weights are

$$\frac{1 \quad C \quad B \; \cdot \; 8}{256 \quad 16 \quad 1 \qquad \frac{1}{16}} \quad \text{weights (in decimal)}$$

and its value is

$$1 \times 256 + C \times 16 + B \times 1 + 8 \times \frac{1}{16}$$

Substituting the decimal equivalents for the symbols B (11 decimal) and C (12 decimal), we get an all-decimal expression from which we can compute its decimal value:

$$1 \times 256 + 12 \times 16 + 11 \times 1 + 8 \times \frac{1}{16} = 459.5$$

Because the leftmost position in a positional number has the most weight, we call the symbol in that position the *most significant*. The symbol in the rightmost position is the *least significant*. For example, in the binary number 0101, the 0 in the leftmost position is the *most significant bit* (*MSB*), and the 1 in the rightmost position is the *least significant bit* (*LSB*). In decimal and hexadecimal numbers, we use the terms *most significant digit* (*MSD*) and *least significant digit* (*LSD*).

The *complement* of a symbol s in the base b positional number system is the symbol whose value is $(b - 1) - s$. For example, the complement of 3 in decimal is $(10 - 1) - 3 = 6$. In binary, the complement of 1 is $(2 - 1) - 1 = 0$; the complement of 0 is $(2 - 1) - 0 = 1$. A symbol in base b plus its complement always equals the value of the symbol in base b with the largest value. For example, in decimal, 3 plus its complement, 6, equals 9; in hexadecimal, 3 plus its complement, C, equals F.

To complement a symbol means to change it to its complement. For example, if we complement 1 binary, 1 decimal, and 1 hexadecimal, we get 0, 8, and E, respectively. In binary, to *flip* a bit means to complement it. Thus, if we flip 1, we get 0; if we flip 0, we get 1.

Let's determine how many distinct numbers can be represented in base b using three positions. Because there are b possible symbols for each of the three positions, combinatorial mathematics tells us that there are $b \times b \times b = b^3$ possible numbers. For example, in a decimal number, there are 10 possible symbols for each position. Thus, with three digits, there are $10 \times 10 \times 10 = 10^3 = 1000$ possible decimal numbers. Similarly, with three bits, there are $2 \times 2 \times 2 = 2^3 = 8$ possible binary numbers. Generalizing, we can state that with n positions, there are b^n possible base b numbers. Figure 1.2 shows a table containing the number of distinct binary numbers for various sizes that commonly appear in computers. You should familiarize yourself with this table—it will prove useful as you study the rest of the book.

A *byte* is a sequence of 8 bits. One byte can represent $2^8 = 256$ numbers. Thus, if we use all 8 bits to hold consecutive positive binary numbers starting from zero, numbers can range from 0 to $2^8 - 1 = 255$. Similarly, with 16 bits, numbers can range from 0 to $2^{16} - 1 = 65,535$. With n bits, numbers can range from 0 to $2^n - 1$.

Computer circuits are designed to operate on chunks of data of a specific length. These chunks of data are called *words*. A word typically contains some

FIGURE 1.2   Distinct Binary Numbers

Number of Bits		Decimal		Hex
4	$2^4 =$		$16 =$	10
7	$2^7 =$		$128 =$	80
8	$2^8 =$		$256 =$	100
10	$2^{10} =$	1K =	$1{,}024 =$	400
12	$2^{12} =$	4K =	$4{,}096 =$	1000
15	$2^{15} =$	32K =	$32{,}768 =$	8000
16	$2^{16} =$	64K =	$65{,}536 =$	10,000
20	$2^{20} =$	1M =	$1{,}048{,}576 =$	100,000
30	$2^{30} =$	1G $= 1{,}073{,}741{,}824 =$		40,000,000

integral multiple of bytes, and holds a single binary number. Common word sizes for modern computers are 32 bits (4 bytes) and 64 bits (8 bytes).

We have been using the term *positive* for a number greater than or equal to zero. However, if you are a mathematician, you know that zero is not considered a positive number. Only numbers that are greater than zero are positive. To be mathematically correct, we should designate the numbers greater than or equal to zero as the *non-negative* numbers. However, in the computer field the term *positive* usually includes zero, and we will use it in that way in this chapter.

When we specify the memory size of a computer, we use the prefixes *kilo* (abbreviated with K), *mega* (abbreviated with M), and *giga* (abbreviated with G) to designate, respectively, 2^{10} (1024), 2^{20} (1,048,576), and 2^{30} (1,073,741,824). For example, we can refer to a computer memory that contains 512×2^{20} bytes as a 512 megabyte memory. Note that this usage of "kilo," "mega," and "giga" is contrary to their usual meanings, namely, 1000 for "kilo," 1 million for "mega," and 1 billion for "giga." A kilometer, for example, means 1000 meters, not 1024 meters.

Numbers inside a computer are binary. Because we use decimal in our everyday lives, one would expect a computer to use decimal, too. The reason that computers use binary instead of decimal is an engineering one: Binary numbers can be stored more cheaply and reliably than decimal. Each bit of a binary representation can be stored by a simple electronic off/on switch. The off position represents 0; the on position represents 1 (or vice versa). Electronic off/on switches are reliable and cheap. Now consider how a decimal number would be stored. Each position has 10 possible values. Thus, we would need an electronic 10-position switch for each position in the number. But a 10-position switch is far more complicated and costly than a simple off/on switch.

To get a sense of the superiority of off/on switches, consider a light in a room that is controlled by an off/on switch. It is easy to tell from the light if the switch is off or on. We can easily distinguish the two extremes—completely off or completely on. Now consider a light controlled by a 10-position dimmer switch whose settings are numbered from 0 to 9. We would find it difficult to distinguish between adjacent switch settings because the light levels for adjacent settings are so similar. For example, the light produced by a setting of 5 would be nearly indistinguishable from a setting of 4 or 6. Moreover, during a power brown-out, a 6 setting might produce the same amount of light that a 5 or 4 setting would during periods of normal power. As with a 10-position light switch, 10-position switches within a computer would not be able to reliably indicate their settings.

There is one way, however, to make a 10-position electronic switch usable in a computer: Use an array of 4 off/on switches. Such an array can hold 4 bits with which we can represent a single decimal digit. We can use the binary numbers 0000, 0001, 0010, . . . , 1001 to represent the decimal digits 0, 1, 2, . . . , 9, respectively. This representation of decimal digits using 4-bit numbers is called *binary coded decimal (BCD)*. With BCD, computers can reliably store and process decimal numbers.

1.3 ARITHMETIC WITH POSITIONAL NUMBERS

• •

The rules for performing arithmetic with positional numbers are essentially the same for all bases. For example:

- In addition, whenever a column sum is greater than or equal to the number base, a carry is added to the next column. The column result is the rightmost symbol of the column sum; the carry is the left symbol(s) of the column sum. For example, in the decimal addition,

$$
\begin{array}{r}
1 \longleftarrow \text{carry} \\
28 \\
+\ 39 \\
\hline
67
\end{array}
$$

the right column sum is 17. Thus, the result digit in the right column is 7 with a carry of 1 into the next column.

- In subtraction, a borrow into a column is equal to the number base. For example, in the decimal subtraction

$$
\begin{array}{r}
34 \\
-\ \ 8 \\
\hline
26
\end{array}
$$

we borrow 1 from the 3 in the left column. This borrow is worth 10 in the right column. Thus, we subtract 8 from the sum of 10 (the borrow) and 4 to get 6. We borrow whenever the bottom symbol in a column is greater than the effective top symbol (the top symbol less any borrows from it).

- A borrow from 0 propagates to the left. For example, in the subtraction

$$
\begin{array}{r}
3000 \\
-\ \ \ \ 2 \\
\hline
2998
\end{array}
$$

the rightmost column requires a borrow from the second column. But because this and the next column contain 0, the borrow request propagates to the left, until it reaches 3 in the fourth column, from which 1 is borrowed. The borrowed value then propagates back to the right, satisfying the borrow requests from those columns. Thus, the 10 borrowed into the third column becomes 9 because of the borrow from the second column. Similarly, the second column becomes 9 because of the borrow from the first column. Finally, the borrow into the right-most column, whose value in this column is 10, becomes 8 when 2 is subtracted from it.

- Each position the radix point is moved to the right multiplies the number by its base. Each position the radix point is moved to the left divides the number by its base.

Let's do a few examples with binary and hexadecimal numbers. Once you become comfortable doing arithmetic in binary and hex, you should be able to do arithmetic in any number base. Let's start by adding the binary numbers 01100 and 11110:

```
  111     ⟵── carries
  01100
+ 11110
 ───────
 101010
```

In the rightmost column, the sum is 0 with no carry out. In the next column, the sum is 1 with no carry out. In the third column, the sum is 10 binary (2 decimal). Thus, we enter 0 (the right bit of the sum) into the result for this column. The left bit of the sum is the carry into the next column. The sum of the fourth column is 11 binary (3 decimal). We enter 1 into the result and carry 1. In the fifth column, the sum is 10 binary (2 decimal). We enter 0 into the result and carry 1 into the sixth column. In the sixth column, the sum is 1 with no carry out. This addition problem illustrates the four possible cases that can occur when adding one column from two binary numbers:

1. There are no 1's, in which case the result bit is 0 with no carry out (column 1).
2. There is exactly one 1, in which case the result bit is 1 with no carry out (columns 2 and 6).
3. There are exactly two 1's, in which case the result bit is 0 with a carry out into the next column (columns 3 and 5).
4. There are three 1's, in which case the result bit is 1 with a carry out into the next column (column 4).

Let's now consider the subtraction of binary numbers. Subtracting 011 from 101, we get:

```
  2  decimal⟵── borrow into second column
  101
− 011
 ─────
  010
```

In the right column, the result is 0 with no borrow. In the middle column, we cannot subtract 1 from 0 (because 0 is smaller than 1). Thus, we borrow 1 from the third column (this borrow is worth 2—the number base—in the second column), from which we subtract 1. Every unit borrowed from one column is worth the number base in the column to the right. In the left column, we subtract 0 from the top value (now 0 because of the borrow into the middle column) to get 0.

Let's move the binary point in the binary number 110.0 (6 decimal) one position to the right. We get 1100 (12 decimal), the original number multiplied by the base 2. Each right move multiplies by 2; each left move divides by 2.

Let's now add and subtract in hexadecimal. In the following hexadecimal addition,

```
  1   ⟵── carry
  A9
+ 19
 ────
  C2
```

the sum of the right column is 12 hexadecimal (18 decimal). Thus, we enter 2 (the right digit of the sum) into the result for this column. The left digit of the column sum, 1, is the carry into the next column. The left column sum is C with no carry into the next column. In the following hexadecimal subtraction,

$$
\begin{array}{r}
16 \text{ decimal} \longleftarrow \text{ borrow into right column} \\
A5 \\
+ \ 2B \\
\hline
7A
\end{array}
$$

B, the bottom digit in the right column, is greater than 5, the top digit. Thus, we borrow 1 from the A in the left column. This borrow is worth 16 decimal—the base for hexadecimal—in the right column. Thus, the result digit for the right column is the sum of 16 decimal (the borrow) and 5 (the top digit) minus B (the bottom digit). Converting to decimal, we get $16 + 5 - 11 = 10$ decimal = A hex. In the left column, we subtract 2 from the top digit—now 9 because of the borrow—to get 7.

1.4 NUMBER BASE CONVERSIONS

• •

Suppose

$$s_n \ldots s_2 s_1 s_0$$

is a whole number in base b. If we represent the weight of its symbols as powers of the base b ($b^0 = 1$, b^1, b^2, b^3, etc.), then the value of the number is given by

$$s_n \times b^n + \cdots + s_2 \times b^2 + s_1 \times b^1 + s_0$$

If we divide the summation above by the base b, the base divides into every term except for the rightmost, whose value is always less than b (any single symbol is always less than the base in a positional number system). Thus, the quotient is

$$s_n \times b^{n-1} + \cdots + s_2 \times b^1 + s_1$$

and the remainder is s_0 (the rightmost symbol in our number). If we now divide the quotient above by the base b, we get a second quotient

$$s_n \times b^{n-2} + \cdots + s_2 \times b^0$$

and a second remainder s_1 (the second symbol in our original number). Each time we divide a quotient by the base, we get a remainder that is equal to the next symbol (from right to left) in the original number. Let's try this with the decimal number 905. By repeatedly dividing by the base 10, we get:

$$
\begin{array}{ll}
& \text{remainders} \\
\underline{\ 0} & \quad 9 \\
10 \overline{)\ \ 9} & \quad 0 \\
10 \overline{)\ 90} & \quad 5 \\
10 \overline{)905} & \longleftarrow \text{ start with this division and work up}
\end{array}
$$

The three divisions produce the remainders 5, 0, and 9, which are the digits of the original number from right to left.

The foregoing analysis leads us to the following conclusion: Dividing a number repeatedly by b yields remainders equal to the symbols of that number written as a base *b* number. In other words, if you divide repeatedly by 10, the remainders are equal to the digits of the number in decimal; if, instead, you divide by 2, the remainders are equal to the bits of the number in binary; and if you divide by 16, the remainders are equal to the digits of the number in hexadecimal. Thus, to convert a number to base *b*, simply divide the number repeatedly by *b*. The remainders then are the symbols that make up the number in base *b*.

Let's use this technique to convert 11 decimal to binary. We divide repeatedly by 2:

```
                remainders
        0           1
     2) 1           0                    ↑
     2) 2           1                    |
     2) 5           1                    |
     2)11                    ←——— start with this division and work up
```

The remainders read from top down (1011) are the bits from left to right of the binary number that is equal to 11 decimal. Thus, 11 decimal equals 1011 binary.

Let's now do an example with hexadecimal. To convert 30 decimal to hexadecimal, we divide repeatedly by 16:

```
                remainders
        0           1
    16) 1          14 = E                ↑
    16)30                    ←——— start with this division and work up
```

Thus, 30 decimal is equal to 1E hexadecimal. To get a hexadecimal number from the remainders, the remainders must be represented in hex. Thus, in the conversion above, we substituted the digit E for its decimal equivalent 14.

To convert a fraction to a different base, we repeatedly multiply by the target base, stripping off the whole part of the product at each step. We continue multiplying until a fractional part equal to zero occurs. For example, to convert 0.6875 decimal to binary, we multiply repeatedly by 2:

```
whole
parts
                 .6875      ←——— start with this multiplication and work down
              ×      2
     1           .3750                       |
              ×      2                       |
     0           .7500                       |
              ×      2                       |
     1           .5000                       ↓
              ×      2
     1           .0000
```

The whole parts read from top down are the bits from left to right of the binary fraction that is equal to 0.6875. Thus, 0.6875 decimal equals 0.1011 binary.

To convert a number that has both a whole part and a fractional part, we simply do each part separately. For example, to convert 14.6875 decimal to binary, we convert its whole part, 14 (to get 1110), we convert its fractional part, 0.6875 (to get .1011), and we then put the two results together (to get 1110.1011).

The conversion of the decimal number 0.1 to binary is particularly interesting. Let's do the conversion and see what happens:

whole
parts

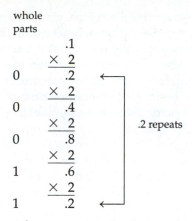

.2 repeats

After executing the first multiplication, we get .2 as the fractional part. After executing four more multiplications (during which the sequence of whole parts produced is 0011), we again get .2 as the fractional part. Thus, if we again multiply four times, we will again get the same sequence of whole parts (0,0,1,1) and .2 as the last fractional part. Our procedure is clearly in an unending loop. No matter how many times we multiply, we will never get a zero fractional part. Each group of four multiplications after the first produces the sequence 0, 0, 1, 1 of whole parts. There is nothing wrong with our procedure. That it never ends for this example simply reflects the fact that there is no finite-length binary fraction equal to 0.1 decimal. Our procedure tells us that 0.1 decimal is equal to the infinite-length binary fraction

0.0 0011 0011 0011 0011 . . .

In Section 1.18, you will see that the preceding example has an important ramification for computations with floating point numbers in Java and C++.

There is a particularly easy technique for converting between binary and hexadecimal. Suppose we wish to convert the binary number 11110101100.111 to hexadecimal. First, we break up the binary number into 4-bit groups, working outward in both directions from the binary point. If necessary, we extend the last group to the left of the binary point with zeros to make it a 4-bit group. Similarly, if necessary, we extend the last group to the right of the binary point with zeros to make it a 4-bit group. Breaking up the binary number 11110101100.111 in this way, we get

0111 1010 1100 . 1110

Next, we replace each 4-bit group with its hexadecimal equivalent given in Figure 1.1:

0111 1010 1100 · 1110

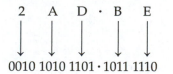

7   A   C · E

The resulting hexadecimal number, 7AC.E, is equal in value to the original binary number, 11110101100.111. To convert a hexadecimal number to binary, we simply replace each digit with its 4-bit equivalent. For example, to convert 2AD.BE to binary, we replace its digits as follows:

2   A   D · B   E

0010 1010 1101 · 1011 1110

Because it is so easy to convert between binary and hexadecimal, we often use hexadecimal as a shorthand representation of binary numbers. For example, if we say that a byte contains F6 hex, we really mean that it contains the binary equivalent of F6 hex (i.e., 11110110 binary). Be sure to memorize the table of equivalents in Figure 1.1 so that you can quickly convert between binary and hexadecimal.

You will probably find it easier to do computation involving binary numbers if you first convert them to hexadecimal. For example, the easiest way to convert the binary number 10100111 to decimal is to first convert it to its hexadecimal equivalent A7 (this is simple), and then to convert the hexadecimal to its decimal equivalent 167 (this is also simple). These two steps are easier than working directly with the original binary number. Similarly, the easiest way to convert a decimal number to binary is to first convert it to hexadecimal, and then convert the hexadecimal to binary.

1.5   HORNER'S METHOD

Suppose we wish to compute the value of the hexadecimal number 2CD5. We can, of course, multiply each digit by its weight, and add up all the products. That is, we can compute

$$2 \times 16^3 + 12 \times 16^2 + 13 \times 16 + 5$$

A straightforward, but inefficient, way to evaluate the above expression is to

1. Compute 16^3 (two multiplications) and multiply by 2.
2. Compute 16^2 (one multiplication) and multiply by 12.
3. Multiply 13 by 16.
4. Add the preceding three products along with 5, the least significant digit.

The preceding computation uses six multiplications and three additions. A more efficient approach is to use *Horner's method*. With Horner's method, we start with the most significant digit, multiply by 16, and then add the next digit. We then multiply this result by 16 and add the next digit. We continue in this fashion until we reach the point where we add the least significant digit. For example, to evaluate 2CD5, we compute as follows:

```
              2
  ×          16      multiply MSD (2) by 16
             32      product
  +          12      add next digit (C)
             44
  ×          16      multiply result by 16
            264
             44
            704      product
  +          13      add next digit (D)
            717
  ×          16      multiply result by 16
           4302
            717
          11472      product
  +           5      add LSD (5)
          11477      final result
```

Our final result, 11477 decimal, equals 2CD5 hex. With Horner's method, converting 2CD5 hex requires only three (instead of six) multiplications and three additions. Let's write horizontally the computation that we perform with Horner's method when converting 2CD5:

$$((2 \times 16 + 12) \times 16 + 13) \times 16 + 5$$

2 multiplied by 16 three times

In this form, it is easy to see that the digit 2 is effectively multiplied by 16 three times; that is, it is given the weight 16^3. Similarly, the digits C (12) and D (13) are multiplied by 16 twice and once, respectively. Thus, the final result is the sum of the digits, properly weighted.

Horner's method can be used to convert a number of any base—simply multiply by that base when using Horner's method. Moreover, the value of the number that is computed is in whatever base we use for the computation. For example, if we apply Horner's method to a decimal number but perform the computation in binary, the result is the binary value of the number. This is precisely what occurs when the C++ statement

```
cin >> z;
```

is executed, where **z** is of type **int**, when the user enters a positive decimal number on the keyboard. The **cin** object applies Horner's method to the number, *performing the computation in binary*. It then places the final result, which is the value of the inputted number in binary, in **z**. For example, suppose the user enters 38. The **cin** object would perform the following computation:

```
          0011        = 3 decimal
 ×        1010        = 10 decimal
          0000
         0011
        0000
       0011
       0011110        product
 +       1000         = 8 decimal
       0100110        = 38 decimal
```

1.6 SIGNED BINARY NUMBERS

Signed binary numbers are binary numbers that use a representation that can accommodate both positive and negative numbers. *Unsigned binary numbers,* on the other hand, are binary numbers in which all bits are used to hold the magnitudes of the numbers. Thus, unsigned numbers can represent positive numbers only.

We will study four types of signed numbers: sign-magnitude, two's complement, one's complement, and excess-*n*.

1.6.1 Sign-Magnitude Representation

In mathematics, we use a minus sign to designate a negative number. We can do essentially the same thing within a computer. Numbers are stored inside a computer in binary in fixed-length sizes. We can use the leftmost bit of a binary number to represent its sign: 0 for "+" and 1 for "−". For example, assume numbers are represented in a computer using 16 bits. We can use the leftmost bit for the sign and the remaining 15 bits for the magnitude of the number. With this scheme, −5 and +5 become

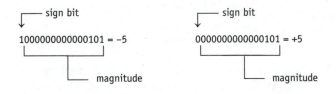

This number representation is called *sign-magnitude representation.* The leftmost bit is the *sign bit;* the remaining bits to the right hold the magnitude of the number.

The principal shortcoming of sign-magnitude representation is that it requires the computer to analyze the signs of the numbers when it performs a computation. For example, suppose +5 and −5 are to be added. The computer must first examine the sign bits of the two numbers. Because the sign bits differ in this example, the computer must subtract the two magnitudes in order to add the two numbers. If, on the other hand, the sign bits were the same, then the computer must add the magnitudes. The particular computation that the computer has to perform *depends on the signs of the numbers.*

1.6.2   Two's Complement Representation

Before we discuss two's complement representation, let's make an observation that we will use later. Suppose a binary number contains 16 bits that are all equal to 1. If we add 1 to this number and discard the carry out of the leftmost column, we get a zero result:

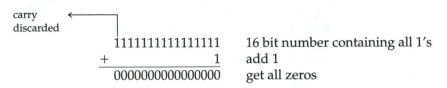

Two's complement representation is another representation that can accommodate both positive and negative numbers. The advantage of two's complement representation is that, unlike sign-magnitude representation, it does not require a computer to perform sign analysis when adding or subtracting. To understand this representation, consider what −5 means mathematically: −5 *is the number that when added to +5 results in zero.* Let's write +5 in binary and see which number produces zero when added to it. This number—the binary number that yields zero when added to the binary for +5—is called the *two's complement* of +5. For our first guess at the two's complement of +5, let's take +5 in binary and flip all its bits. We then add the result to +5 and check if the result is zero:

```
  0000000000000101 = +5
+ 1111111111111010 = +5 flipped
  1111111111111111    should be zero
```

Clearly, the flipped version of +5 is not −5 because it does not yield zero when added to +5. However, recall our earlier observation that adding 1 to a binary number of all 1's results in zero. Because the flipped version of +5 produces all 1's when added to +5, *the flipped value plus one more should produce zero.* Let's add one to the flipped version of +5:

```
   1111111111111010  = +5 flipped
+                 1
   1111111111111011  = +5 flipped + 1
```

Now let's see if this new value, +5 flipped + 1, yields zero when added to +5:

carry ⟵⎤

$$
\begin{array}{r}
0000000000000101 = +5 \\
+\ 1111111111111011 = +5\ flipped + 1 \\
\hline
0000000000000000
\end{array}
$$

Indeed, it does, assuming the carry out of the leftmost column is not included in the result. But this is precisely what happens in a computer because numbers are held in fixed-length areas. Thus, when "+5 flipped + 1" is added to +5 in a computer, the result is zero. We have, indeed, found the two's complement of +5. More important, we have determined the procedure for computing the two's complement of any binary number: simply flip its bits and add one. When we flip the bits of a binary number and add one, we say that we are *taking the two's complement* of the number, or, more simply, that we are *complementing* the number. Beware that we will use the term *complement* in three different ways when dealing with binary numbers:

1. To *complement a bit* means to flip the bit.
2. To *complement a number* means to take its two's complement (i.e., flip its bits and add one).
3. To *bitwise complement a number* means to flip each of its bits but *not* add one. The bitwise complement of a number is sometimes called the *one's complement* of the number (see the next section).

Taking the two's complement of a binary number is, in effect, negating the number. If we take the two's complement of +5, we get −5. If we then take the two's complement of −5, we get +5 (try it).

We can find the two's complement of any number using the procedure that we used on +5: Flip all the bits and then add one. For example, the computation of the two's complement of

```
0000000000000001  = +1
```

is:

```
   1111111111111110  = +1 flipped
+                 1
   1111111111111111  = −1
```

In the two's complement system, the leftmost bit of a number indicates its sign. A 1 bit indicates a negative number; a 0 bit indicates a positive number. For example, with 3-bit numbers, we get the range of values given in Figure 1.3.

Notice that the maximum absolute value of the negative numbers, −4, is one more than the maximum positive number (+3). In the two's complement system, we refer to positive numbers as numbers in *true form*, and negative numbers as numbers in *complement form*.

Although the leftmost bit is the sign bit in both the sign-magnitude and the two's complement systems, the two systems are quite different. For example, in the sign-magnitude system, the 16-bit number

1111111111111111

FIGURE 1.3

```
                            ── sign bit

        011 = +3 ┐
        010 = +2 │  Positive Numbers
        001 = +1 │
        000 =  0 ┘


        111 = -1 ┐
        110 = -2 │  Negative Numbers
        101 = -3 │
        100 = -4 ┘
```

is equal to $-32{,}767$ decimal. In the two's complement system, it is equal to -1 decimal. Furthermore, in the sign-magnitude system, sign analysis is necessary when adding (or subtracting), but in the two's complement system sign analysis is not necessary. That is, regardless of the signs of the two numbers, to compute their sum (or difference), we simply add (or subtract) the two numbers. If the value of the result is positive, it will appear in true form; if the result is negative, it will appear in complement form. Let's demonstrate this with an example. First, add $+5$ and -1:

```
    0000000000000101 = +5
  + 1111111111111111 = -1
    0000000000000100 = +4
```

The result is $+4$ in true form. Now let's add $+2$ and -5.

```
    0000000000000010 = +2
  + 1111111111111011 = -5
    1111111111111101 = -3
```

The result is -3 in complement form.

Computer circuits designed for the two's complement system are cheaper and less complex than circuits designed for the sign-magnitude system because the former does not require sign analysis. It is for this reason that most computer systems today use the two's complement system.

1.6.3   One's Complement Representation

The *one's complement* of a number is its bitwise complement. That is, it is the number that is obtained by flipping all the bits in the original number. For example, the one's complement of

0000000011111110

is

1111111100000001

If we add a number and its one's complement, we get a sum in which all the bits are one. For example, if we add the two numbers above, we get

1111111111111111

Adding a number with its one's complement does not yield zero. Thus, we can conclude that the one's complement of a number is *not* the negative of that number. But suppose we let the value zero be represented by *two* bit patterns: all zeros and all ones. Then adding a number with its one's complement would, indeed, yield zero. Specifically it would yield 111 . . . 1, one of our two forms of zero.

If we interpret both "000 . . . 0" and "111 . . . 1" as zero, we can use one's complement numbers in very much the same way that we use two's complement numbers, but with one additional twist: For addition, we must add the *end-around carry* to the LSB of the sum. That is, we must add the carry out, if any, of the leftmost column to the LSB of the sum. For example, consider the following addition in which we add -1 with -1:

```
carry out
 ┌──────┐
 │      │  1111111111111110 = −1 in one's complement
 │ +    │  1111111111111110 = −1 in one's complement
 │         1111111111111100      intermediate sum
 └──────────────→  + 1           end-around carry
           1111111111111101 = −2 final sum
```

When we add the end-around carry to the intermediate sum, we then get the correct sum, -2.

One's complement representation has the advantage that the negation of a number is simple and fast. We simply flip its bits. Negation in two's complement representation, on the other hand, takes considerably longer because it requires an addition operation. One's complement representation, however, has two disadvantages. First, there are two representations of zero. If we input these two distinct zeros to a comparison circuit, it would incorrectly flag them as unequal because they have different bit patterns. Thus, to avoid this erroneous result, a comparison circuit would have to treat comparisons with zero as special cases. Second, one's complement addition involves the added complexity of processing the end-around carry. Processing this carry is particularly bothersome, and is the principal reason why one's complement representation is rarely used in modern computers.

1.6.4 Excess-*n* Representation

In *excess-n representation, n* is added to the value of a number to get its representation. Thus, an excess-*n* number is "in excess of" (i.e., more than) the number it represents by *n*. For example, the excess-4 representation of the value 2 is $2 + 4 = 6$ decimal. To obtain the value that an excess-*n* number represents, we subtract *n*. For example, the value of the excess-4 number 6 is $6 - 4 = 2$. Figure 1.4 shows both the 3-bit excess-4 and two's complement representations of the numbers ranging from -4 to 3.

FIGURE 1.4

Value	Excess-4	Two's Complement
−4	000	100
−3	001	101
−2	010	110
−1	011	111
0	100	000
1	101	001
2	110	010
3	111	011

An important property of excess-n numbers is that they end up in ascending order if they are sorted as unsigned integers. Two's complements numbers do not have this property. For example, the order of the excess-4 numbers in Figure 1.4 would be unchanged by an unsigned sort, but the two's complement numbers would end up in 0, 1, 2, 3, -4, -3, -2, -1 order.

As we have already discussed, to convert two values, v_1 and v_2, to excess-n representation, we add n to each value, yielding the excess-n numbers $(v_1 + n)$ and $(v_2 + n)$. If we then add these two numbers, we get $(v_1 + n + v_2 + n)$. Notice that the sum includes two n's. But, the sum of v_1 and v_2, in excess-n representation, is $(v_1 + v_2 + n)$. It has only one n. Thus, to get the correct sum in excess-n representation, we have to subtract out one n from our intermediate sum. For example, suppose we add the excess-4 representations of 1 and 2 from Figure 1.4. To get the excess-4 representation of the sum, we have to subtract 4 from the intermediate sum:

$$
\begin{array}{rl}
101 & = \text{excess-4 representation of 1} \\
+\quad 110 & = \text{excess-4 representation of 2} \\
\hline
1011 & = \text{intermediate sum} \\
-\quad 0100 & = 4 \\
\hline
111 & = \text{correct sum}
\end{array}
$$

From the preceding example, it is clear that computation with excess-n numbers is awkward because of the presence of the bias n. One, therefore, would not expect computers to use them. They are, however, used in floating-point numbers, which we will discuss in Section 1.18.

A bit pattern can represent different values, depending on the type of representation in effect. For example, 111 equals 7 decimal when viewed as an unsigned number. The same pattern, however, equals -3, -1, 0, and 3 when viewed, respectively, as a sign-magnitude, two's complement, one's complement, and excess-4 number.

1.7 SUBTRACTION BY TWO'S COMPLEMENT ADDITION

Suppose A and B are two binary numbers and we want to subtract B from A. That is, we want to compute

$A - B$

One way to subtract B from A is to use the *borrow technique* that we all learned in grade school (the technique that involves a borrow whenever the upper value is less than the lower value in any column). We demonstrated this technique in Section 1.3. We can also use the *two's complement technique* to subtract B from A. In this technique we *add* the two's complement of B to A. Because the two's complement of B is equal to $-B$, we are computing

$A + (-B)$

which, of course, equals $A - B$. For example, suppose we want to subtract $+3$ from 5. We do this by *adding* -3 to 5:

$$
\begin{array}{rl}
0000000000000101 & = +5 \\
+\quad 1111111111111101 & = -3 \\
\hline
0000000000000010 & = +2
\end{array}
$$

Computers typically perform subtraction with the two's complement technique for a very good reason: The computer then does not need a subtractor circuit. It subtracts with its adder circuit (by adding the two's complement of the number to be subtracted).

As we mentioned in the previous section, an unsigned number is a number whose bits are all used to hold the magnitude of the number. Thus, an unsigned number is always positive. We, of course, can subtract unsigned numbers using the borrow technique. But we can also use the two's complement technique. For example, to compute

$$
\begin{array}{ll}
0000000000000101 = 5 \\
-\ \underline{0000000000000011 = 3}
\end{array}
$$

where both numbers are unsigned, we complement the bottom number and then add it to the top number, exactly as we did for signed numbers:

$$
\begin{array}{ll}
0000000000000101 = & 5 \\
+\ \underline{1111111111111101 = -3} \\
0000000000000010 = & 2
\end{array}
$$

Computers use the two's complement technique to subtract *both* signed and unsigned numbers.

1.8   RANGE OF TWO'S COMPLEMENT AND UNSIGNED NUMBERS

• •

In Section 1.2, you learned that there are $2^{16} = 65,536$ distinct 16-bit numbers. In an *unsigned* 16-bit number, all 16 bits are used for positive numbers. Because unsigned numbers start from 0, the maximum number—when all 16 bits are one—is $2^{16} - 1$.

In a two's complement 16-bit *positive* number, the leftmost bit is always 0, leaving 15 bits to represent the various positive values. Thus, there are only $2^{15} = 32,768$ distinct positive numbers. Because the positive numbers start from 0, they range from 0 to $2^{15} - 1$. In a two's complement 16-bit *negative* number, the leftmost bit is always 1, leaving 15 bits to represent the various negative numbers. Thus, there are $2^{15} = 32,768$ negative numbers. Because the negative numbers start with -1, they range from -1 to -2^{15}. Thus, the complete range of 16-bit two's complement numbers is

-2^{15} to $2^{15} - 1$

or, in decimal,

$-32,768$ to $32,767$

If we extend the foregoing analysis to the general case of *n*-bit numbers, we get:

Range of unsigned *n*-bit numbers: 0 to $2^n - 1$
Range of signed *n*-bit numbers: -2^{n-1} to $2^{n-1} - 1$

Figure 1.5 gives the ranges of binary numbers for various sizes that are commonly used in computers. You should memorize the information in this table because you need to know it for our study of computers.

FIGURE 1.5   Ranges of Binary Numbers

Number of Bits	Unsigned	Two's Complement
8	0 to 255	−128 to 127
12	0 to 4095	−2048 to 2047
16	0 to 64K − 1	−32,768 to 32,767
20	0 to 1M − 1	−512K to 512K − 1
32	0 to 4G − 1	−2G to 2G − 1
n	0 to $2^n - 1$	-2^{n-1} to $2^{n-1} - 1$

1.9   EXTENDING TWO'S COMPLEMENT AND UNSIGNED NUMBERS

Suppose we want to extend an 8-bit unsigned number to 16 bits. We want the 16-bit number to have the same value as the 8-bit number. The required extension is obvious: Just add eight zeros to the left of the 8-bit number. For example, to convert 00000011 to 16 bits, we add eight zeros to the left to get 0000000000000011. The 8-bit and 16-bit versions have the same value (3 decimal). We call this type of extension *unsigned-number* or *zero extension*.

Now let's consider what we have to do to extend a two's complement number. If we use unsigned-number extension on a negative two's complement number, we will get an incorrect result. For example, let's extend the 8-bit number, 11111110 (−2 decimal), to 16 bits by adding eight zeros to the left. We get 0000000011111110, which equals +254—not −2. The correct way to extend a two's complement number is to extend it by replicating its sign bit. If the number is positive (i.e., its sign bit is 0), we add zeros. If the number is negative (i.e., its sign bit is 1), we add 1's. We call this type of extension *signed-number extension*. Let's use signed number extension on 11111110 (−2). We get 1111111111111110, which also equals −2. To confirm that the two numbers have the same value, take the two's complement of both to determine their magnitudes. We get 00000010 and 0000000000000010—both are equal to 2. Notice that all the 1's that we added to the left of the 8-bit number turn into zeros when the extended number is complemented, and, therefore, do not affect the magnitude of the number.

Sometimes a number extension that occurs during the execution of a computer program can cause problems. For example consider the C++ program in Figure 1.6. This program assigns −1 to c and then checks if c is equal to −1.

One would naturally expect c to test equal to −1, causing the message "equal" to be displayed. But, in fact, this result may not occur, depending on the

FIGURE 1.6
```
#include <iostream>
using namespace std;
int main()
{
    char c;
    c = -1;                  // -1 is truncated to fit into c
    if (c == -1)             // promote c to int
        cout << "equal\n";
    else
        cout << "not equal\n";
    return 0;
}
```

compiler. Here is why. On most computers, an `int` constant like −1 occupies 2 or 4 bytes; a `char` variable like `c` occupies only one byte. Thus, when −1 is assigned to `c`, it has to be truncated to fit into `c`. Recall that the two's complement representation of −1 is all 1's. Thus, the value of `c` and −1 are both represented with all 1's in binary, but −1 is longer:

c: 11111111   (one byte)
−1:   11 . . . 111111111   (two or four bytes)

Then in the `if` statement, the value `c` has to be extended to match the length of −1 before the comparison can be performed (in C++ terminology, the value in `c` has to be *promoted* to an `int`). If this value is signed-number extended, we get

11 . . . 111111111

which equals −1. However if it is unsigned-number extended, we get

00 . . . 011111111

which equals +255. In the latter case, `c` tests unequal to −1, and the message "unequal" is displayed.

The standard that defines the C++ language does not specify whether a variable of type `char` is signed or unsigned. Nor does it specify how a variable of type `char` should be extended. Thus, a compiler could correctly extend `c` in Figure 1.6 using either signed-number or unsigned-number extension. To avoid this compiler dependency, we can qualify `char` in the declaration of `c` with either **signed** or **unsigned**. The former forces signed-number extension; the latter forces unsigned-number extension. For example, if we declare `c` with

```
signed char c;
```

then `c` will test equal to −1, regardless of the compiler. Suppose we instead declare `c` to be type `int`. Then, we avoid the truncation of −1 when it is assigned to `c`, and its subsequent extension. Thus, `c` would test equal to −1, independently of how `char` values are extended.

Most C++ compilers allow the user to choose the type of extension—signed or unsigned—to be used for `char` values. However, for portability reasons, it is better to write programs so that any `char` values that are extended are always extended in the desired way, regardless of the option the compiler user selects. As we pointed out in our discussion of Figure 1.6, we can do this by specifying the **signed** or **unsigned** keywords. Alternatively, we can use `int` variables in place of `char` variables to avoid their truncation and subsequent extension.

1.10 OVERFLOW

In a computer, the results of computations are usually stored in areas of fixed size. Because of their fixed size, the range of values these areas can hold is limited. If a computation produces a result that is outside this range, we say *overflow* has occurred. Overflow can occur with either signed or unsigned numbers. Let's first consider overflow with signed numbers.

1.10.1 Signed Overflow

When adding two signed numbers in the two's complement system, overflow can occur only if the two numbers are both positive or both negative. If one number is

FIGURE 1.7 Overflow Cases:

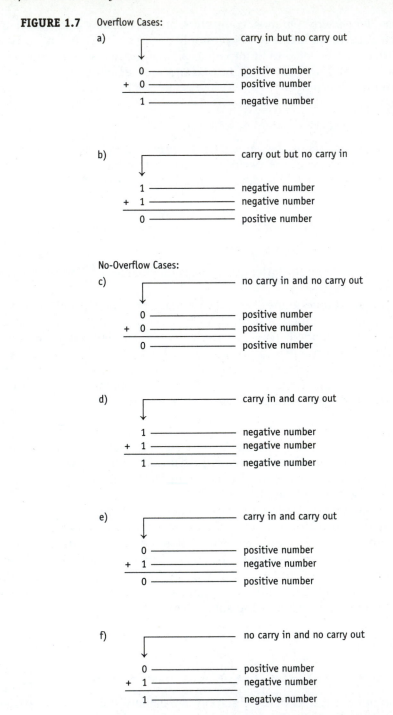

a) — carry in but no carry out

   0 ———— positive number
+ 0 ———— positive number
   1 ———— negative number

b) — carry out but no carry in

   1 ———— negative number
+ 1 ———— negative number
   0 ———— positive number

No-Overflow Cases:

c) — no carry in and no carry out

   0 ———— positive number
+ 0 ———— positive number
   0 ———— positive number

d) — carry in and carry out

   1 ———— negative number
+ 1 ———— negative number
   1 ———— negative number

e) — carry in and carry out

   0 ———— positive number
+ 1 ———— negative number
   0 ———— positive number

f) — no carry in and no carry out

   0 ———— positive number
+ 1 ———— negative number
   1 ———— negative number

positive and the other negative, then their sum cannot be bigger than the positive number (because we are adding a negative number to it) nor smaller than the negative number (because we are adding a positive number to it). Thus, the sum must lie *in between* the two numbers, which implies overflow cannot occur.

When overflow occurs during the addition of two positive numbers, a carry into the sign bit of the result occurs (because the sum is too big to fit into the bits to the right of the sign bit). Thus, the result appears negative, resulting in the pattern of sign bits in Figure 1.7a.

A carry into the leftmost column occurs but a carry out of the leftmost column does not (because the two 0 bits in the leftmost column cannot generate a carry out even with a carry in).

When overflow occurs during the addition of two negative numbers, the result looks positive, resulting in the pattern of sign bits in Figure 1.7b. A carry into the leftmost position does *not* occur (otherwise, the sign bit in the result would be 1). However, a carry out of the leftmost column does occur (because the two 1 bits in the leftmost column generate a carry).

For both cases in which overflow occurs—in the addition of two positive numbers or two negative numbers—the carry into the leftmost column *differs* from the carry out of the leftmost column. That is, if a carry in occurs then a carry out does not; if a carry in does not occur, then a carry out does. However, whenever overflow does *not* occur, a carry into and out of the leftmost column always *both* occur or *both* do not occur. To see this, examine the no-overflow cases in Figure 1.7c, d, e, and f. For every no-overflow case, either a carry in and a carry out both occur or both do not occur.

Most computers have some special 1-bit storage areas, called *flags*, that are set according to the result of a computation. For example, the *overflow flag* (V, for short) is set to 1 if overflow with signed numbers occurs, or 0 otherwise. The *sign flag* (S, for short) is set to the sign bit of the result. The *carry flag* (C, for short) is set to the carry out of the leftmost column (i.e., it is set to 1 if a carry out occurs, and 0 otherwise). The *zero flag* (Z, for short) is set to 1 if the result is zero, and 0 otherwise.

We have seen that the carry into and out of the leftmost column provide a very simple test for signed number overflow: *Overflow occurs if and only if the carry into the leftmost column does not equal the carry out of the leftmost column*. The computer hardware can easily perform this test and set the overflow flag accordingly. Similarly, the hardware can easily set the sign, carry, and zero flags.

1.10.2 Unsigned Overflow

Now let's consider overflow with unsigned numbers. When adding unsigned numbers, a carry out of the leftmost column indicates that an additional bit is needed to hold the result, and, therefore, that overflow has occurred. For example, in the 16-bit addition

$$
\begin{array}{r}
1111111111111111 = 65{,}535 \\
+\ 0000000000000001 = 1 \\
\hline
0000000000000000
\end{array}
$$

carry out of ← leftmost column

a carry out of the leftmost column occurs, indicating 17 bits are needed for the result. Notice that the carry *into* the leftmost column is irrelevant as far as *unsigned* overflow is concerned. Contrast this with the overflow test for signed numbers, in which both the carry in and carry out of the leftmost column are involved. When adding unsigned numbers, the carry flag—*not* the overflow flag—indicates whether overflow has occurred. The overflow flag is for *signed numbers only*.

Another type of unsigned overflow can occur when we subtract two unsigned numbers. If the bottom number is bigger than the top number, then the result is negative. But a negative number is smaller than 0, the smallest possible unsigned number. Thus, the computed result is outside the allowable range for unsigned numbers, which is, by definition, overflow.

Let's examine a subtraction in which unsigned overflow occurs. If we subtract 2 from 1, we get:

$$
\begin{array}{r}
0000000000000001 = 1 \\
-\ \underline{0000000000000010 = 2} \\
1111111111111111 = 65{,}535
\end{array}
$$

The result, *when viewed as an unsigned number,* is incorrect. It equals 65,535. It does not equal the correct result, -1. This type of overflow occurs in an unsigned subtraction whenever the bottom number is greater than the top number. Because the bottom number is larger, a borrow into the leftmost column will necessarily occur if we use the borrow technique for subtraction. Thus, we can use a *borrow into leftmost column* as the indicator for this type of overflow.

Because computers use the two's complement technique and not the borrow technique for subtraction, computers cannot test for unsigned overflow during subtraction by checking for a borrow. However, it turns out that a *borrow into the leftmost column occurs when subtracting with the borrow technique if and only if a carry out of the leftmost column does NOT occur when subtracting with the two's complement technique.* Thus, the indicator of overflow when subtracting unsigned numbers using the two's complement technique is *no carry out* of the leftmost column. This is a simple test, but, unfortunately, it is the exact opposite of the indicator of overflow when adding unsigned numbers (recall that a *carry out* of the leftmost column is the overflow indicator for unsigned *addition*). To avoid two separate tests for unsigned overflow (one for addition and one for subtraction), computers use this simple trick: In an addition, the carry flag is set to the carry out of the leftmost column; in a subtraction, the carry flag is set to the *complement* of the carry out of the leftmost column. Then, in both an addition and a subtraction, a 1 in the carry flag indicates that unsigned overflow has occurred. Moreover, the carry flag then functions as a borrow flag in a subtraction. That is, a 1 in the carry flag means that a borrow *would have occurred* had the borrow technique been used. It would certainly be more accurate to call the carry flag a *carry/borrow flag,* but this longer name is generally not used.

Figure 1.8 shows the circuit that drives the carry flag.

The carry out of the leftmost column is applied to its data input. This circuit then either complements its data input (if its control input is 1) or allows it to pass through unchanged (if its control input is 0). On an addition, its control input is set to 0 (allowing the carry out to pass through unchanged to the carry flag), and on a subtraction, it is set to 1 (causing the complementation of the carry out before it reaches the carry flag).

FIGURE 1.8

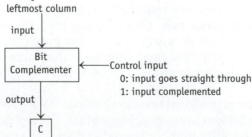

Carry out of
leftmost column

input

Bit
Complementer

Control input
0: input goes straight through
1: input complemented

output

C

1.11 ANALYZING TWO'S COMPLEMENT NUMBERS

• •

We can flip the bits in an n-bit number by subtracting it from the n-bit number that contains all 1's. For example, to flip 0101, we subtract it from 1111:

$$
\begin{array}{r}
1111 \\
-\ 0101 \\
\hline
1010
\end{array}
\quad \text{(0101 flipped)}
$$

The n-bit number containing all 1's is equal to $2^n - 1$. Thus, to take the two's complement of a positive number x, we can flip its bits by computing

$$(2^n - 1) - x$$

and then adding 1. The result is

$$((2^n - 1) - x) + 1 = 2^n - x$$

For example, the two's complement of the 4-bit number 0101 (5 decimal) is $2^4 - 5 = 11$ decimal $= 1011$ binary.

We can easily confirm that $2^n - x$ is the n-bit two's complement of x by adding it to x:

$$
\begin{array}{r}
x \\
+\ 2^n - x \\
\hline
2^n + 0
\end{array}
$$

↰——— This is a carry out of the leftmost column.

The 2^n term in the sum is represented by a 1 bit in the $(n + 1)$st column. For n-bit numbers, it is a carry out of the leftmost column, and, therefore, is not part of the n-bit result. Thus, the n-bit result of our addition is zero, confirming that $2^n - x$ is the two's complement of x.

$2^n - x$ is the n-bit two's complement number that is the negative of the positive number x. Thus, its absolute value is x. Because the maximum absolute value of a negative n-bit number is 2^{n-1} (see Figure 1.5), the maximum value of x in our formula $2^n - x$ is 2^{n-1}.

Now that we have a mathematical formulation for the two's complement of a positive number, we can use it to show that the addition of two's complement numbers behaves almost exactly like the addition of signed numbers in mathematics.

If we add two positive numbers in mathematics, the result is their sum (a positive number). If we add two negative numbers, the result is also their sum (a negative number). If we add a positive and a negative number, the result is the difference of their absolute values. For this case, the sign of the result depends on which number has the larger absolute value. If the negative number has the larger absolute value, then the sign of the result is negative; otherwise, the sign is positive. For example, if we add -5 and $+3$, we get -2, a negative number. But if we add $+5$ and -3, we get $+2$, a positive number. In both cases, the absolute value of the result is 2. The sign of the result depends on which number—the negative or positive—has the larger absolute value.

Now let's consider the addition of two's complement numbers. Let a and b be two positive n-bit numbers; let $2^n - c$ and $2^n - d$ be n-bit negative numbers. We consider four cases:

CASE 1:   Add a and b (two positive numbers)
The n-bit result equals the true value of $a + b$, as long as overflow does not occur (i.e., as long as $a + b < 2^{n-1}$).

CASE 2: Add $2^n - c$ and $2^n - d$ (two negative numbers)

$$\begin{array}{r} 2^n - c \\ + \ 2^n - d \\ \hline 2^n + 2^n - (c + d) \end{array}$$

The first 2^n term in the sum is a 1 bit in the $(n + 1)$st column (i.e., it is a carry out of the leftmost column of the n-bit result). Thus, $2^n - (c + d)$ is the n-bit result. Moreover, this result is equal to the two's complement of $c + d$ as long as overflow does not occur (i.e., as long as $c + d \leq 2^{n-1}$).

CASE 3: Add a and $2^n - d$ (a positive and a negative number) where $a < d$

$$\begin{array}{r} a \\ + \ 2^n - d \\ \hline 2^n - (d - a) \end{array}$$

Since $(d - a)$ is greater than 0, $2^n - (d - a)$ is less than 2^n, and therefore fits into n bits. In other words, there is no carry out of the leftmost column of the n-bit result. The n-bit result, $2^n - (d - a)$, is the two's complement of $d - a$.

CASE 4: Add a and $2^n - c$ (a positive and a negative number) where $a \geq c$

$$\begin{array}{r} a \\ + \ 2^n - c \\ \hline 2^n + a - c \end{array}$$

Since $a - c$ is greater than or equal to 0, the sum $2^n + a - c$ is equal to or bigger than 2^n. Thus, the sum does not fit into n bits. The term 2^n in the sum is a carry out of the leftmost column of the n-bit result. Thus, the n-bit result is equal to the positive value $a - c$.

These four cases show that the addition of two's complement numbers behaves exactly like signed numbers in mathematics, as long as overflow does not occur. If we add two positive numbers, we get their positive sum (case 1); if we add two negative two's complement numbers, we get their sum as a negative two's complement number (case 2); and if we add a positive and a negative two's complement number (cases 3 and 4), we get a sum equal to the difference of their absolute values. If the negative number has the larger absolute value (case 3), the result is a negative two's complement number; otherwise (case 4), the result is a positive number.

1.12 ADDER CIRCUIT

Let's design an adder circuit that can be used in a computer. For some types of computations, a computer uses techniques that are completely different from what humans use. For example, computers subtract with the two's complement technique; humans usually subtract with the borrow technique. For addition, however, computers and humans use the same technique. Let's analyze what we do when we add two binary numbers. We start on the right adding one column at a time. The addition for each column, except for the rightmost, involves adding up three bits: the bit from the lower number, the bit from the upper number, and the carry from the column to the right. In the rightmost column, only two bits are

FIGURE 1.9

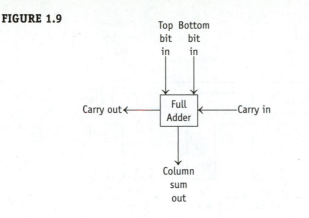

added because there is never a carry into this column. For each column, we must determine two results:

- The sum of the bits added
- The carry into the column to the left

This computation—the computation for a *single* column—is performed by the circuit shown in Figure 1.9 called a *full adder.*

A full adder has three inputs (one for each bit it has to add) and two outputs (one for the column sum and one for the carry out).

Consider the computation we must perform on the second column of the following addition:

$$\begin{array}{r} 0000000000000011 \\ + \ 0000000000000001 \\ \hline 0 \end{array}$$

We must add the carry (which equals 1) from the first column and the two bits in the second column (1 and 0). The sum and the carry out for the second column are 0 and 1, respectively. This computation is performed by a full adder whose inputs are set to the three bits to be added (see Figure 1.10).

A full adder can also be used to add the rightmost column: Just set the carry in on the rightmost full adder to 0. Then the full adder effectively adds only the rightmost bits of the top and bottom numbers.

FIGURE 1.10

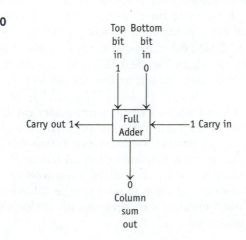

FIGURE 1.11

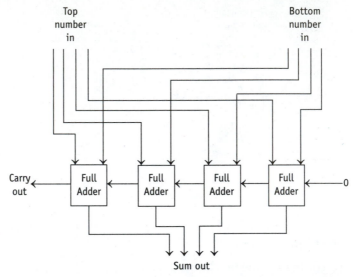

A full adder adds only one column. If we want a circuit to add two multiple-bit numbers, we simply connect multiple full adders, one for each column, with the carry out of each one connected to the carry in of the full adder to its left. If, for example, we want to add two 4-bit numbers, we connect four full adders (see Figure 1.11).

The adder circuit in Figure 1.11 has nine inputs: four inputs for each 4-bit number, and the carry in on the rightmost full adder (which should be set to 0).

When we apply two 4-bit numbers to the inputs in the adder in Figure 1.11, the rightmost full adder immediately has valid inputs on which to operate. The second (from the right) full adder does not, however, because it has to wait for the rightmost full adder to determine and place the proper value on the carry out line. Similarly, the third full adder has to wait for the second, and the fourth has to wait for the third. Thus, the additions for the various columns do not take place at the same time. Rather, the computations for the columns occur in right-to-left order, precisely the way humans perform the addition. Because each full adder has to wait for the one to its right to output a carry, each full adder contributes to the total time needed to perform a multiple-bit addition. In other words, their computations are performed *in series* (i.e., one after another) rather than *in parallel* (i.e., at the same time). Because of the serial nature of our adder circuit, the time required to compute a sum is proportional to the number of full adders it contains. A 32-bit adder, for example, will take twice the time as a 16-bit adder. Our adder circuit in Figure 1.11 is called a *ripple-carry adder* because the carries "ripple" from right to left as the full adders, from right to left, produce their outputs.

Because of its serial operation, a ripple-carry adder can be unacceptably slow. For better performance, adders can use a technique called *carry look-ahead* in which special circuits compute *in parallel* the carry-out values for each position. These values are then applied to their respective full adders *at the same time.* Thus, the full adders can compute the sum-out values in parallel as well. With this technique, each full adder does not have to wait for the full adder to its right to produce a carry out. This technique can dramatically reduce the time required to perform a multi-bit addition.

FIGURE 1.12

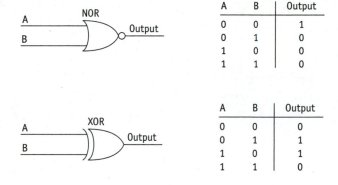

A	B	Output
0	0	1
0	1	0
1	0	0
1	1	0

A	B	Output
0	0	0
0	1	1
1	0	1
1	1	0

1.13   GATES

A *gate* is a component used in computer circuits that has one output line and one or more input lines. Each line carries only one bit—a 0 or 1. The value that a gate places on its output line depends exclusively on the current values on its input lines.

There are many different types of gates. The way the output of a gate depends on its input is a function of the type of gate. For example, a *NOR gate* can have two or more inputs. It outputs a 1 if all its inputs are 0; otherwise, it outputs a 0. "NOR" stands for "*Not-OR*". An *XOR gate* has two inputs. It outputs a 1 if its two inputs differ in value; otherwise, it outputs a 0. "XOR" stands for "*eXclusive-OR*".

A convenient way to represent the input-output relationship of a gate is with a *truth table*, which shows the output value for every possible combination of input values. Figure 1.12 provides the truth table for the NOR and XOR gates, along with the symbols used to represent them in circuit diagrams.

The NOR gate is a *zero-detecting gate* in that it outputs a 1 only when all its inputs are 0. If any of its inputs are 1, then it outputs 0. A NOR gate can have more than two inputs. For example, a 16-input NOR gate outputs a 1 only when the 16-bit number applied to its inputs is 0.

The XOR gate is a *complementing gate* in that it can selectively complement one of its inputs. To see this, let's examine the operation of the XOR gate in detail. An XOR gate consists of two inputs and one output. Examining all four rows for the XOR gate in Figure 1.12, we see that its output is 1 only when the two inputs differ.

An important question to consider is what happens to data applied to one input of an XOR gate if the other input is set to 0. Figure 1.13a and 1.13b shows the two cases we have to consider.

In Figure 1.13a, the first input is held at 0 and the data (equal to 0) is applied to the second input. For this case, the output is 0, which happens to equal the data value. In Figure 1.13b the first input is again held at 0 and the data (equal to 1 this time) is applied to the second input. For this case, the output is equal to 1, which again equals the data value applied to the second input. Thus, whenever one input to an XOR gate is held at 0, the data (0 or 1) on the other input "goes right through" the gate and appears on the output. This behavior is what we mean by Figure 1.13c—the data (0 or 1) on the second input goes right through the gate and appears *unchanged* on the output. A common and more concise way of describing this action of the XOR gate is with the mathematical equation

$$\text{data XOR } 0 = \text{data}$$

FIGURE 1.13

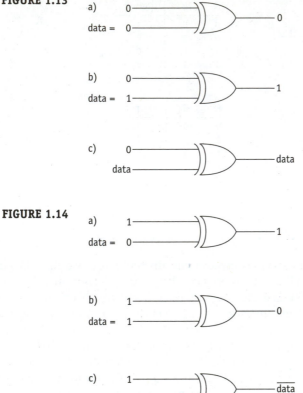

a)   0 —
data =   0 —   0

b)   0 —
data =   1 —   1

c)   0 —
data —   data

FIGURE 1.14

a)   1 —
data =   0 —   1

b)   1 —
data =   1 —   0

c)   1 —
data — $\overline{data}$

That is, the exclusive OR of data with 0 always equals the data.

Now let's see what happens to the data signal applied to an XOR gate when the first input is held at 1. If the data is 0, then the output is 1 (see Figure 1.14a).

If the data is 1, then the output is 0 (see Figure 1.14b). We see that the output in both cases is *equal to the complement of the data input.* This behavior is what we mean by Figure 1.14c—the data applied to the second input appears on the output in complemented form. In Figure 1.14c, $\overline{data}$ represents the complement of the input data. Thus, if the input data equals 0 then $\overline{data}$ equals 1; if the input data equals 1 then $\overline{data}$ equals 0. We can describe the action of the XOR gate in Figure 1.14c with the equation

$$data \text{ XOR } 1 = \overline{data}$$

That is, the exclusive OR of data and 1 is always equal to the complement of the data.

In the next section, we explore how we can use the XOR gate to give an adder circuit the ability to subtract as well as add.

1.14   SUBTRACTING USING AN ADDER

The advantage of using the two's complement technique of subtraction in a computer is that it does not require a subtractor circuit. Thus, for both addition and subtraction, the computer can use its adder circuit. Because the computer does not need a subtractor circuit, it is less expensive. However, there is one potential problem with two's complement subtraction: Determining the two's complement of the number to be subtracted requires time. The first step in determining the two's complement—flipping the bits—is easy. As we discussed in the previous section, we can use an XOR gate with one input held at 1 to flip a bit. To flip multiple bits, we simply use multiple XOR gates. The second step in complementing a number—adding 1—is not, unfortunately, a simple operation. Adding 1 takes as much time as adding any other number. Thus, it appears that subtraction by the two's complement technique requires *two* additions—one addition (of +1) to determine the complement of the bottom number, and a second addition to add the complement to the top number. We therefore expect subtraction by complement addition to take twice as long as addition. This reasoning, however, is not correct. We can, in fact, perform both additions in the two's complement technique in one step. Figure 1.15 shows how. We simply

1. Input the bottom number to the adder through XOR gates, which flip the bottom number.
2. Set the carry input of the rightmost full adder to 1.

The 1 on the carry input of the rightmost full adder adds 1 to the flipped bottom number, producing the correct two's complement. Thus, the complementation process and the addition of the complement are done in one step.

FIGURE 1.15

Adder/Subtracter

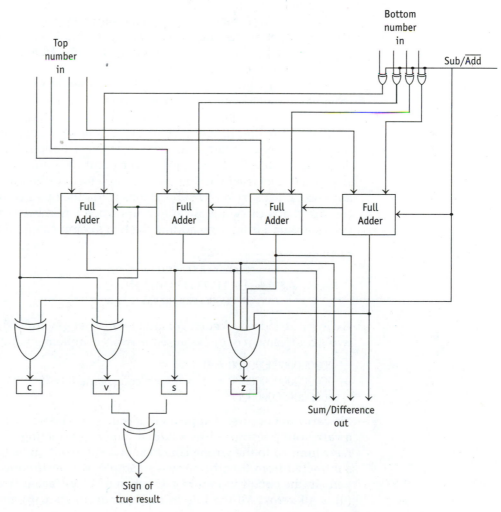

We call the input line that drives the carry input of the rightmost full adder a *control line* because it controls the operation of the circuit. A 1 on this line drives the carry in of not only the rightmost full adder, but also the XOR gates, causing them to flip the bottom number. Thus, the circuit functions as a subtractor. A 0 on the control line, on the other hand, causes the XOR gates to pass the bottom number unchanged. Thus, for this case, the circuit functions as an adder.

The control line in Figure 1.15 is labeled with SUB/$\overline{\text{ADD}}$ to indicate its effect on the circuit. By convention, we use a label without an overscore to designate the action triggered by 1, and we use a label with an overscore to designate the action triggered by 0. Thus, our label indicates that the subtract and add functions are triggered by 1 and 0, respectively.

Recall from Section 1.10 that on an addition, the carry flag is set equal to the carry out of the leftmost full adder. However, on a subtraction, the carry flag should be set to the *complement* of the carry out of the leftmost full adder. To perform this complementation, we can again use an XOR gate. We drive this gate with the SUB/$\overline{\text{ADD}}$ control line so that it lets the carry out pass through unchanged on an addition, but complements it on a subtraction.

Another XOR gate is used to set the overflow flag. Its inputs are the carry in and carry out of the leftmost full adder. Its output goes to the overflow flag. Thus, the overflow flag is set to 1 if the carry in and the carry out of the leftmost full adder differ.

The sign flag is set directly from the sum output of the leftmost full adder. The zero flag is set by the output of a NOR gate. Notice in Figure 1.15 that the NOR gate is driven by all the bits of the result. Thus, the NOR gate outputs 1 if and only if all the bits of the result are zero.

In Section 1.10.2, we learned that a borrow into the leftmost column occurs when subtracting with the borrow technique if and only if a carry out *does not occur* when subtracting with the two's complement technique. When a number is subtracted from itself with the borrow technique, a borrow into the leftmost column should *never* occur. This is because every bottom bit is equal to its corresponding top bit—thus, borrows never occur. It follows that when a number is subtracted from itself with the two's complement technique, a carry out should *always* occur. Let's try a few subtractions using the two's complement technique to confirm that a carry out always occurs when a number is subtracted from itself. Let's subtract 5 from 5 (by adding the two's complement of 5):

```
carry out ←
          0000000000000101 = +5
        + 1111111111111011 = −5
          0000000000000000
```

A carry out, indeed, occurs. For another test, let's subtract 0 from 0 (by adding the two's complement of 0). Because the two's complement of 0 is also 0, we get

```
  0000000000000000 = 0
+ 0000000000000000 = 0  ≠ two's complement of 0
  0000000000000000
```

No carry out occurs! It appears that our rule—a borrow in occurs if and only if a carry out does not—breaks down when subtracting 0 from 0. We, however, have jumped to the wrong conclusion. A carry out, in fact, does occur when 0 is subtracted from 0 with the two's complement technique. Consider what happens in the circuit in Figure 1.15 when 0 is subtracted from 0. The top number (0) is all zeros. All the bits in the bottom number (0) are flipped by the XOR gates before they are applied to the full adders. Thus, the circuit performs the following summation:

carry out ←

$$
\begin{array}{ll}
0000000000000000 & = 0 = \text{top number} \\
1111111111111111 & = \text{bottom number with all its bits flipped} \\
+ \qquad\qquad\qquad 1 & = \text{carry in on rightmost full adder} \\
\hline
0000000000000000 &
\end{array}
$$

which does, indeed, generate a carry out of the leftmost column. The carry out originates from the two's complementation of zero (when +1 is added), and not from the addition of the two's complement of the bottom number to the top number (and that is the reason for our incorrect conclusion).

1.15 COMPARING SIGNED NUMBERS

When comparing signed numbers, a computer subtracts the numbers and then examines the flags. A 1 in the zero flag indicates a zero result, which, in turn, indicates that the two numbers are equal. A 1 in the sign flag indicates a negative result, which, in turn, indicates that the top number is less than the bottom number. The foregoing analysis, however, is not quite correct because it does not consider the possibility of overflow. When two signed numbers are subtracted, overflow can occur. When overflow occurs, the sign flag is the *complement* of what it should be. Thus, the sign flag indicates just the opposite of what it implies when overflow does not occur. To correctly compare signed numbers, a computer must always use the sign of the *true result*. The sign of the true result and the sign of computed result are the same if overflow does not occur, but they are different if overflow does occur. Let's see how we can determine the sign of the true result from the S and V flags. Recall from Section 1.13 that

$$\text{data XOR } 0 = \text{data}$$

and

$$\text{data XOR } 1 = \overline{\text{data}}$$

Using this relationship, let's determine what we get when we apply S and V to an XOR gate. If $V = 0$ (i.e., if signed overflow does not occur) then

$$S \text{ XOR } V = S \text{ XOR } 0 = S = \text{sign of true result}$$

But for this case, S, the sign of the computed result, is also the sign of the true result. Now let's consider the case when $V = 1$ (i.e., signed overflow occurs), then

$$S \text{ XOR } V = S \text{ XOR } 1 = \overline{S} = \text{sign of true result}$$

For this case, S is the complement of the sign of the true result. But then $\overline{S}$ is the sign of the true result. Thus, for both the no overflow and overflow cases, the *value of S XOR V is equal to the sign of the true result*. It follows that a computer can compare two signed numbers by subtracting them and then applying S and V to an XOR gate (see Figure 1.15). An output of 1 from this gate indicates that the true result is negative—that is, that the top number is less than the bottom number. An output of 0 indicates that the true result is positive—that is, that the top number is greater than or equal to the bottom number. The zero flag, as usual, indicates equality (if set to 1) or inequality (if set to 0).

1.16   COMPARING UNSIGNED NUMBERS

Now let's consider the comparison of unsigned numbers. When comparing two unsigned numbers, a computer subtracts them. The result of the comparison is then determined from the setting of the carry flag. Recall from Section 1.10.2 that in a subtraction (and, therefore, in a comparison), the carry flag functions as a borrow flag. Thus, a 1 in the carry flag after an unsigned subtraction indicates that a borrow into the leftmost column occurred, which, in turn, indicates that the top number is smaller than the bottom number. A 0 in the carry flag indicates that a borrow did not occur, which, in turn, indicates that the top number is greater than or equal to the bottom number. The zero flag, as usual, indicates equality (if set to 1) or inequality (if set to 0).

1.17   UNIFORM TREATMENT OF POSITIVE, NEGATIVE, AND UNSIGNED NUMBERS

When a computer uses the two's complement system for signed numbers, the way it adds or subtracts does *not* depend on whether the numbers are signed or unsigned. The computer adds signed positive numbers, signed negative numbers, and unsigned numbers in exactly the same way using the same circuit (the circuit shown in Figure 1.15). Similarly, the computer subtracts signed positive numbers, signed negative numbers, and unsigned numbers in exactly the same way using the same circuit. The distinction among the various types of operands appears in the tests that occur *after* the addition or subtraction. For example, if we use the "$C = 1$" test after a subtraction to determine if the top number is less than the bottom number, then we are treating the numbers as unsigned numbers. If, instead, we use the "S XOR $V = 1$" test, then we are treating the numbers as signed numbers.

When a computer adds or subtracts, it *always* sets its flags. For example, the V flag in Figure 1.15 is *always* set (to the exclusive OR of the carry in and carry out of the leftmost column) *even when unsigned numbers are involved*. However, $V = 1$ indicates overflow only for signed computations. For example, in the following addition of *unsigned* numbers

```
  0111111111111111
+ 0000000000000001
  1000000000000000
```

unsigned overflow does *not* occur, but V, nevertheless, is set to 1 because there is a carry into the leftmost column but no carry out. The important point here is that computers add, subtract, and set flags in only one way. The setting of flags does not depend on the type—signed or unsigned—of numbers involved. The distinction between signed and unsigned numbers comes from the different tests that we perform on the flags after a computation is done.

1.18   FLOATING-POINT REPRESENTATION

Floating-point numbers are the numbers we get when we declare `float` or `double` variables in a C++ or Java program. Unlike two's complement numbers, floating-point numbers can represent numbers with fractional parts. Moreover, floating-point numbers have a much broader range than two's complement numbers of the same size. For example, the range of 32-bit two's complement numbers is from approximately -2×10^9 to $+2 \times 10^9$; the range of 32-bit floating-point numbers, on the other hand, is from approximately -3×10^{38} to $+3 \times 10^{38}$.

Floating-point numbers appear to be superior to two's complement numbers. They have a broader range and the ability to hold fractional numbers. There is, however, one important limitation of floating-point numbers: They cannot exactly represent every possible number within their range. There is, in fact, an infinite set of numbers within their range. Thus, with 32 bits (or with any other finite number of bits), we cannot possibly represent every number in this infinite set. Two's complement numbers, on the other hand, can exactly represent *every* integer number within their range.

1.18.1 Scientific Notation

Because floating-point numbers are similar to numbers written in scientific notation, let's start by examining scientific notation. In scientific notation, nonzero decimal numbers are written in the form

Significand $\times$ power of ten

where *Significand* is a number in which the decimal point has exactly one nonzero digit to its left. Let's convert 967.89 to scientific notation. In this number, the decimal point is not in the required position. To correctly position the decimal point, we have to move it two positions to the left, the effect of which is to divide the number by 10^2. To compensate for this division, we multiply by 10^2. The result is 9.6789×10^2, a number in scientific notation equal in value to the original number. We call the process of moving the decimal point to the required position and compensating by multiplying by the appropriate power *normalization*.

Before we can add two numbers in scientific notation, we have to make their powers of 10 equal. We usually do this by increasing the power of 10 in the smaller number. For example, to add 9.6789×10^2 and 6.789×10^1, we change the power of 10 in the second number (the smaller number) to 10^2. We then compensate for this change by shifting the decimal point one position to the left (we are *unnormalizing* it to increase its exponent to 2). We can then add our unnormalized number to the first number:

$$
\begin{array}{r}
9.6789 \times 10^2 \\
+\ \ 0.6789 \times 10^2 \\
\hline
10.3578 \times 10^2
\end{array}
$$

In this example, the sum needs normalization (this is not always the case), after which we get 1.03578×10^3. Subtraction is handled similarly.

To multiply two numbers in scientific notation, we multiply their significands and add their exponents. We then normalize the result if necessary. For example, multiplying 9.6789×10^2 and 6.789×10^1, we get $(9.6789 \times 6.789) \times 10^{(2+1)} = 65.7100521 \times 10^3$, which, after normalization, is 6.57100521×10^4. To divide two numbers in scientific notation, we divide their significands, subtract their exponents, and normalize the result if necessary.

We can also use scientific notation with binary numbers. In decimal scientific notation, we use powers of 10; in binary scientific notation, we use powers of 2. For example, let's normalize the binary number 1110.11. To correctly position the binary point, we have to shift it three positions to the left, effectively dividing the

FIGURE 1.16

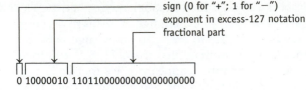

number by 2^3. Thus, we compensate by multiplying by 2^3 to get 1.11011×2^3. Note that for nonzero binary numbers in scientific notation, the initial bit of the significand (i.e., the bit to the left of the binary point) is always 1.

1.18.2   32-Bit IEEE 754 Floating-point Format

There are a variety of formats for floating-point numbers. The one we will describe is the 32-bit IEEE 754 format, the standard supported by most modern computers.

The floating-point representation of a number is essentially a shorthand representation of the binary scientific notation for that number. For example, consider the number 1.11011×2^3. The 32-bit floating-point representation of this number has three components (see Figure 1.16):

1. 0, the sign of the number (0 for "+", 1 for "−")
2. 10000010, the exponent 3 as an excess-127 8-bit number
3. 11011000000000000000000, the 23-bit fractional part of the significand

The bit to the left of the binary point in the significand is not included in the floating-point representation. This bit is omitted because it is 1 for *every* nonzero binary number in scientific notation. Thus, there is no need to store it. Nor does the floating-point representation include the binary point itself. Thus, when converting a floating-point number back to its equivalent value in binary scientific notation, we should always prefix the missing "1." to the front of the fractional part.

Because the initial 1 bit in the significand of a binary number in scientific notation does not appear in its floating-point representation, we call it the *hidden bit*.

We call the field in a floating-point number that holds the fractional part of the significand the *significand field*. Be sure to keep in mind that this field does not hold the complete significand—it holds only its fractional part.

1.18.3   Underflow, Overflow, and Special Values

Floating-point numbers in which the exponent field contains all zeros or all ones represent special values. Thus, only the intermediate 254 values—00000001 (-126 decimal) to 11111110 (127 decimal)—represent exponents. A computation that produces a result whose normalized exponent is less than -126 or greater than 127 is an *exceptional event* (i.e., it is an "exception" that may require special treatment). If its exponent is less than -126, we have *underflow*; if the exponent is greater than 127, we have *overflow*. In underflow, the result is so close to zero, on either the positive or negative side, that it cannot be represented by a normalized floating-point number. In overflow, the result is outside the range of numbers, on either the positive or negative side.

Figure 1.17 shows the special values represented by floating-point numbers in which the exponent field is all zeros or all ones.

FIGURE 1.17

Exponent	Significand Field	Value
all zeros	zero	zero
all ones	zero	∞ (infinity)
all ones	nonzero	NaN (Not a Number)
all zeros	nonzero	denormal number

Because the number zero does not have any nonzero bits, it cannot be converted to a normalized number in scientific notation. We represent it with a floating-point number in which both the exponent and significand fields are all zeros. The sign field can be either "+" or "−".

Infinity, ∞, is the result when a number other than zero is divided by zero. It is represented by a floating-point number that has all ones in the exponent field and zero in the significand field. The sign field indicates the sign of the infinity. Dividing a negative number by 0 produces −∞; dividing a positive number by 0 produces +∞.

NaN (Not a Number) is used to represent results that are neither numbers nor infinity. For example, if we divide 0 by 0, or take the square root of a negative number, or use NaN in a computation, the result is mathematically undefined, and is, therefore, appropriately set to NaN.

The inclusion of NaN and infinity in the IEEE 754 floating-point standard ensures that the result of any floating-point computation will be both well-defined and uniform across all computer platforms supporting the standard.

The normalized number with the smallest possible magnitude has 00000001 in its exponent field, representing −126 (the smallest possible exponent). It also has all zeros in its significand field, representing the significand 1.0 (remember the hidden bit). It has either 0 or 1 in its sign bit. Thus, its value is $\pm 1.0 \times 2^{-126}$. These two numbers are the two normalized numbers—one on the positive side, and one on the negative side—that are the closest to zero.

A *denormal* number is one whose exponent field is all zeros, but whose significand field is nonzero. For denormal numbers, the exponent is assumed to be −126. Moreover, the hidden bit is assumed to be 0. For example, the exponent and significand fields in the following denormal number

0 00000000 00000000000000000000001

represent −126 and 0.00000000000000000000001, respectively. Thus, its value is

$$0.00000000000000000000001 \times 2^{-126}$$

which equals 2^{-149}. This number is considerably smaller than the smallest positive normalized number (2^{-126}).

All the denormal numbers lie in the region around zero that is bracketed by the two normalized numbers that are closest to zero (-1.0×2^{-126} and $+1.0 \times 2^{-126}$). Thus, they allow the representation of numbers in this range that otherwise would not be representable, albeit with less precision (i.e., with fewer significant bits).

1.18.4 Computational Error in Some Java Programs

We will illustrate a variety of computational errors using several Java programs (we use Java programs because they yield the same results regardless of the computer on which they are run).

FIGURE 1.18   a)

```
 1 class E1 {
 2    public static void main(String[] s)
 3    {
 4        float sum = 0.0f, z = 0.001f;
 5        for (int i = 1; i <= 1000; i++)
 6            sum = sum + z;
 7        System.out.print("sum = ");
 8        System.out.println(sum);
 9    }
10 }
```

b)

```
 1 class E2 {
 2    public static void main(String[] s)
 3    {
 4        float sum = 0.0f, z = 1.0f/1024.0f;
 5        for (int i = 1; i <= 1024; i++)
 6            sum = sum + z;
 7        System.out.print("sum = ");
 8        System.out.println(sum);
 9    }
10 }
```

The program in Figure 1.18a adds z (which contains 0.001) to **sum** 1000 times. Because **sum** is initially zero, its final value should be exactly 1.0. Recall from Section 1.4 that 0.1 cannot be represented exactly with a finite-length fraction in binary. Another number that has no finite-length representation in binary is 0.001. The infinite-length binary fraction equal to 0.001 decimal has to be truncated to fit into the significand field of z. Thus, the value in z is not exactly equal to 0.001 (it is slightly less). As z is repeatedly added to **sum**, the error in **sum** accumulates. Thus, at the end of the loop, the value in **sum** is noticeably less than the correct result, 1.0 (try it).

The program in Figure 1.18b is like the program in Figure 1.18a, except that it repeatedly adds 1.0/1024.0 — a value that can be represented exactly as a floating-point number. The final value in **sum** for this program equals the true sum (1.0).

The programs in Figure 1.18 give us two rules for floating-point computations:

RULE 1   Not all numbers can be represented exactly as floating-point numbers.

RULE 2   Errors can accumulate.

Because of the error inherent in floating-point computations, a computed result is often not equal to the true result. For this reason, it is dangerous to test for equality. For example, from a mathematical point of view, the program in Figure 1.19a is quite reasonable.

It increases **x** in increments of 0.1 until its value reaches 1.0. However, in the real world of computing, **x** never reaches 1.0. It gets very close to 1.0 (on the tenth

FIGURE 1.19 a)

```
 1 class E3 {
 2   public static void main(String[] s)
 3   {
 4      float x = 0.0f;
 5      while (x != 1.0f)     // infinite loop
 6         x = x + 0.1f;
 7      System.out.print("x =");
 8      System.out.println(x);
 9   }
10 }
```

b)

```
 1 class E4 {
 2   public static void main(String[] s)
 3   {
 4      float x = 0.0f;
 5      while (Math.abs(x - 1.0f) > 0.00001f)
 6         x = x + 0.1f;
 7      System.out.print("x = ");
 8      System.out.println(x);
 9   }
10 }
```

iteration), but it never equals 1.0 exactly because of the error in the internal representation of 0.1. The computed value of **x** skips over 1.0, causing an infinite loop. The program in Figure 1.19b fixes this problem by using an exit test that requires only that **x** be close to 1.0 (we are using `Math.abs`, the absolute value function, to determine if **x** is within 0.00001 of 1.0).

The programs in Figure 1.19 give us Rule 3:

RULE 3   It is dangerous to test for the equality of floating-point numbers.

When we perform a computation with floating-point numbers, not all the bits of the fractional part of the result may fit into the 23-bit significand field of a floating-point number. For example, suppose we want to add the floating-point numbers whose values are

$1.10000000000000000000000 \times 2^{30}$ (1st number)

and

$1.10101000000000000000000 \times 2^{10}$ (2nd number)

Before we can add, we have to shift the binary point in the second number 20 positions to the left to increase its exponent to 30. We can then add:

$$
\begin{array}{ll}
 1.10000000000000000000000 \times 2^{30} & \text{1st number} \\
+\ 0.00000000000000000000110101 \times 2^{30} & \text{2nd number (unnormalized)} \\
\hline
 1.10000000000000000000110101 \times 2^{30} &
\end{array}
$$

these bits are lost

FIGURE 1.20   Round to Nearest

Guard	Round	Sticky	Action	Effect
1	0	1	Add 1 to 23rd bit, then chop off extra bits.	Round away from zero.
1	1	0		
1	1	1		
0	0	0	Chop off extra bits.	Round toward zero.
0	0	1		
0	1	0		
0	1	1		
1	0	0	Add 1 to 23rd bit, but only if it is 1. Then chop off extra bits.	Depends on 23rd bit, which always ends up 0.

The fractional part of the sum has 25 bits, but the significand field can accommodate only 23 bits. Thus, the rightmost two bits of the sum are lost, causing a small error in the result. This type of error is called *round-off error.*

If a computed result falls somewhere between two representable numbers, we have to round the result to one of these two numbers. One approach is to simply use the first 23 bits of the fractional part of the result. This approach is called *rounding toward zero* because it selects the nearest representable number in the direction toward zero. *Rounding down* selects the nearest representable number in the $-\infty$ direction. *Rounding up* selects the nearest representable number in the $+\infty$ direction. Rounding down and rounding up are useful for *interval arithmetic* (i.e., computations in which we compute the lower and upper bounds of a true result). The best technique for most applications, however, is *rounding to the nearest*, because it minimizes round-off error.

All of these rounding techniques, except for round to zero, require knowledge of the bits to the right of the 23rd bit in the fractional part of the computed result. Thus, for these rounding techniques, computations have to be carried through with extra bits. The IEEE 754 standard specifies three extra bits: the *guard bit* (the 24th bit), the *round bit* (the 25th bit), and the *sticky bit* (which equals 1 if any of the bits to the right of the 25th bit are 1).

Figure 1.20 shows the actions taken by the round-to-nearest technique for various values of the guard, round, and sticky bits. The last case in Figure 1.20 (when the guard, round, and sticky bits are 1, 0, and 0, respectively) occurs when the computed result is midway between the nearest two representable numbers. An obvious action for this case is to simply chop off the extra bits. But this would introduce a bias toward zero in the round-to-nearest technique. To ensure an unbiased effect, a neutral approach is used: If the 23rd bit is 1, we round in the away-from-zero direction; if it is 0, we round in the toward-zero direction.

Round-off error can produce some unexpected results. Suppose that the exponents in two numbers to be added differ by 30. To add them, the exponent of the smaller number has to be increased by 30 by shifting its binary point 30 positions to the left. But then all of the original bits in the significand of the smaller number end up well to the right of the 23rd bit of the larger number. Thus, the computed sum of the two numbers, truncated to 23 bits, is equal to the larger number. In other words, *the smaller number would have no effect on the sum.* Try running the program in Figure 1.21. Is L + s equal to L?

FIGURE 1.21

```
1 class E5 {
2    public static void main(String[] s)
3    {
4        float L, S;
5        L = 1.0f;        // L is a Large number
6        S = 1E-30f;      // S is a Small number
7        if (L + S == L)
8            System.out.println("equal");
9        else
10           System.out.println("not equal");
11   }
12 }
```

The program in Figure 1.21 gives us Rule 4:

RULE 4   If the magnitude of the floating-point number L is sufficiently larger than the magnitude of the floating-point number S, then $L + S = L$.

With floating-point numbers, the order in which we perform additions can affect the round-off error that occurs, which, in turn, can affect the final result. Thus, the value computed for

$$(A + B) + C$$

may not be equal to the value computed for

$$A + (B + C)$$

In mathematical terminology, we describe this behavior by saying that floating-point addition is *not associative*.

Try running the two programs in Figure 1.22. They sum the same set of fractions, but in a different order. Is the computed sum for both programs the same? Which yields the larger result?

The programs in Figure 1.22 give us Rule 5:

RULE 5   Floating-point addition is not associative.

Suppose X is a floating-point number that holds the result of a computation. Because of computational error, X exceeds the true result by 0.0001. Let x represent the true result. Thus, $X = x + 0.0001$. Y is a number that holds the result of another computation. Y is smaller than the true result by 0.0001. Let y represent the true result. Thus, $Y = y - 0.0001$. If we were to compute $X - Y$ exactly, we would get:

$$X - Y = (x + 0.0001) - (y - 0.0001) = (x - y) + 0.0002$$

The error in $X - Y$ is the accumulation of the errors from X and Y (another illustration of Rule 2). Moreover, if x and y are nearly equal, then the error will be large compared with the true result. For example, assume $x = 12.0001$ and $y = 12.0$. Then, the true difference, $x - y$, is given by

$$12.0001 - 12.0 = 0.0001$$

FIGURE 1.22 a)

```
1 class E6 {
2    public static void main(String[] s)
3    {
4        float sum = 0.0f;
5        for (int i = 1; i <= 100; i++)
6            sum = sum + 1.0f / i;
7        System.out.println(sum);
8    }
9 }
```

b)

```
1 class E7 {
2    public static void main(String[] s)
3    {
4        float sum = 0.0f;
5        for (int i = 100; i >= 1; i--)
6            sum = sum + 1.0f / i;
7        System.out.println(sum);
8    }
9 }
```

which is half the size of the error in the computed difference, $X - Y$. This example gives us Rule 6:

RULE 6 Subtracting nearly equal values can produce meaningless results.

1.18.5 Longer Formats

The number of bits in the exponent field of a floating point representation determines its *range*. With 8 bits, we get a range from approximately -10^{38} to 10^{38}. With more bits, we get a bigger range. For example, with 11 bits, we get a range from approximately -10^{308} to 10^{308}.

The number of bits in the significand determines the *precision* of the representation. With more bits, we can represent more numbers exactly. We can also more accurately represent those numbers that cannot be represented exactly (like 0.001 decimal).

The floating-point format that we have been describing is the 32-bit IEEE 754 standard. There is also a 64-bit IEEE 754 standard, which consists of a sign bit, an 11-bit exponent field, and a 52-bit significand field.

The 32-bit and 64-bit formats are called, respectively, *single-precision* and *double-precision*. Single-precision is used for **float** variables in Java and C++ programs; double-precision is used for **double** variables. Double-precision variables provide more range and precision than single-precision variables; however, they require double the space. They also require more computational time, but not significantly more on most modern computers. Thus, unless space requirements are an issue, it is generally better to use double-precision variables.

As computers become more powerful, hardware support for even higher precision floating-point numbers will surely appear. Anticipating this eventuality, the

IEEE 754 standard includes a *quad-precision* format consisting of a sign bit, a 15-bit exponent field, and a 112-bit significand field.

1.19 SUMMARY

Let's summarize some of the observations we have made in this chapter. Recall that C, V, S, and Z are the carry, overflow, sign, and zero flags, respectively.

- In an addition or subtraction of *signed* numbers, $V = 1$ signals that overflow has occurred.
- In a subtraction of *signed* numbers, S XOR $V = 1$ indicates that the top number is less than the bottom number; S XOR $V = 0$ indicates that the top number is greater than or equal to the bottom number. $Z = 1$ indicates that the numbers are equal; $Z = 0$ indicates that the numbers are unequal.
- C functions as a borrow flag in a subtraction.
- In an addition or subtraction of *unsigned* numbers, $C = 1$ signals that overflow has occurred.
- In a subtraction of *unsigned* numbers, $C = 1$ indicates that the top number is less than the bottom number; $C = 0$ indicates that the top number is greater than or equal to the bottom number. $Z = 1$ indicates that the numbers are equal; $Z = 0$ indicates that the numbers are unequal.
- Z is set to 1 if a result is zero, and is set to 0 if a result is nonzero.

C is set to the carry out of the leftmost column on an addition, and to the complement of the carry out on a subtraction. V is set to 1 if the carry into the leftmost column differs from the carry out of the leftmost column, and to 0 otherwise. That is, it is set to the exclusive OR of the carry in and carry out of the leftmost column. S is set to the leftmost bit of the result in an addition or subtraction. Z is set to the NOR of all the bits in the result.

Numbers in floating-point format can span a very large range of values, but not all the values in this range can be represented. Between any two adjacent floating-point numbers lies an infinite set of numbers that cannot be represented exactly.

To minimize errors in floating-point computations, we should use the highest precision available. However, for any precision, it is possible for errors to enter, accumulate, and ultimately produce meaningless results.

PROBLEMS

1.1. Can the problem that occurred in the C++ program in Figure 1.6 also occur in a Java program?

1.2. Convert the following binary numbers to decimal using Horner's rule:

011010101   011101   010000000000001   01101.10101

1.3. Convert the binary numbers in Problem 1.2 to hex.

1.4. Convert the following decimal numbers to binary. Give your answers in both binary and hex.

234   4567   513   2.75   1.3

1.5. Convert the following hexadecimal numbers to binary:

1AB2   3CF8   90D4   576E   3BBD   69FC

1.6. Convert the hex numbers in Problem 1.5 to decimal using Horner's rule.

1.7. Convert the following hex numbers to decimal. Do the necessary computation in your head.

59   66   7A   AB   FF   82   BC   D3   9C   C9   D5   E7

1.8. Perform the following binary additions. Give your answers in binary and hex.

```
  0010101      00111000111      0011111111      00011
+ 0011101    + 00010101010    + 0011111111      00001
                                                 00001
                                                 00010
                                                 00011
                                                 00010
                                                 00011
                                               + 00011
```

1.9. Perform the following binary subtractions. Use the borrow technique.

```
  001001001      0100000000      010101010101
- 001000111    - 0000000001    - 001111111111
```

1.10. Redo Problem 1.9 using the two's complement technique.

1.11. Convert the numbers in Problem 1.9 to hex, and then subtract in hex using the borrow technique.

1.12. Convert the numbers in Problem 1.9 to hex, and then subtract in hex using the 16's complement technique.

1.13. Perform the following hex additions:

```
  0ABDEF      0AAAA       72ABCDEF      0BEEF      0BAD
+ 012345    + 09999     + 123EEEEE    + 0BEEF    + 0BAD
```

1.14. Take the two's complement of the following binary numbers. Give your answers in binary and hex.

0101010101010101   1111111111111111   0011001100110011

1.15. Bitwise complement the numbers in Problem 1.14. Convert your answers to hex.

1.16. If a `byte` variable in Java is converted to `int`, is it necessarily sign extended?

1.17. Prove that shifting the radix point to the right (left) multiplies (divides) a number by its base.

1.18. Write -50 decimal as an 8-bit sign-magnitude, two's complement, and excess-127 number.

1.19. What are the decimal values of 11001100 when viewed as an unsigned, sign-magnitude, two's complement, and excess-128 binary number?

1.20. Will taking the two's complement of a binary number and then converting to hex result in the same hex number as converting the original number to hex and taking its 16's complement? Try it both ways with

0000   1010   1111   10101100   00110011

1.21. Determine the 10's complement for the following decimal numbers:

19999   38457   20000

Determine the 16's complement for each of the following hexadecimal numbers:

1ABCD   20011   1BC10   FFFFF   00000

1.22. What is 400 hex in decimal?

1.23. What is 8K in decimal? What is 4M in decimal?

1.24. Is 1440K equal to 1.44M? Explain.

1.25. One disadvantage of sign-magnitude representation concerns the number zero. What is this disadvantage?

1.26. Prove that a borrow into the leftmost column occurs when using the borrow technique of subtraction if and only if a carry out of the leftmost column does not occur when using the two's complement technique of subtraction.

1.27. If two unsigned numbers are subtracted using the two's complement technique and the top number is greater than or equal to the bottom number, does a carry out of the leftmost column always occur? Explain.

1.28. Perform the following binary additions. Give your answers in both binary and hex. For each addition, determine the carry into and out of the leftmost column. For which does overflow occur (consider both the signed and unsigned cases)?

$$
\begin{array}{lll}
0000000000111111 & 1111111111111111 & 1111111111111111 \\
+\ 0000000000111111 & +\ 1111111111111111 & +\ 1100000000000000
\end{array}
$$

1.29. When does a decimal fraction have a finite binary representation?

1.30. Change the loop in Figure 1.18a so that it adds 0.1 to **sum** 10 times. Run the program. Is the final sum equal to 1.0?

1.31. Can overflow occur when numbers are subtracted? Explain.

1.32. Prove that dividing a decimal number by 10 yields a remainder that is equal to its LSD.

1.33. Convert the following octal (base 8) numbers to decimal:

274   05555   0651000   04000   030000

1.34. Convert the following base 9 numbers to decimal:

1234   07777   0111111   05555   0180

1.35. Perform the following octal (base 8) additions:

$$
\begin{array}{lllll}
1234 & 07777 & 04444 & 1111 & 07777 \\
+\ 1234 & +\ 01111 & +\ 04443 & +\ 1111 & +\ 07777
\end{array}
$$

1.36. Convert the following decimal numbers to octal (base 8):

999   2361   8   2000   4096

1.37. Convert the following octal (base 8) numbers to hex:

351   777   15741555634277554

1.38. What are the disadvantages of storing numbers in BCD format?

1.39. Suppose we use three 10-position switches to hold a 3-digit decimal number. How many distinct decimal numbers can be held? If each switch contains four off/on switches, how many distinct binary numbers can be held if all the switches were used to hold a binary number?

1.40. Suppose the following two *unsigned* numbers are added. Is the V flag set to 0 or 1?

$$
\begin{array}{l}
1111111111111111 \\
+\ 0000000000000001
\end{array}
$$

1.41. When 0 is subtracted from 0, is the carry flag set to 0 or 1? Explain.

1.42. Is V set to 1 when overflow occurs during the addition of two unsigned numbers? Explain.

1.43. What do $V = 1$ and $C = 0$ after an addition together imply?

1.44. Does overflow occur when any of the following pairs of binary numbers are added? Is *V* set to 1? Is *C* set to 1? Consider both the signed and unsigned cases. Assume an 8-bit word size.

01111111   10000000   11111111
00000001   11111111   11111111

1.45. What is the range of 16-bit sign-magnitude numbers?

1.46. What does *Q* XOR 1 equal, where *Q* is a single bit? What does *Q* XOR 0 equal?

1.47. What 16-bit numbers cause a carry out of the leftmost column when they are two's complemented?

1.48. Is the XOR operation associative? That is, is

$$(a \text{ XOR } b) \text{ XOR } c = a \text{ XOR } (b \text{ XOR } c)$$

for all possible values of *a*, *b*, and *c*? Justify your answer.

1.49. Why did the designers of C++ (and C) not specify whether a variable of type **char** is signed or unsigned.

1.50. What is the weight of the leftmost bit for two's complement numbers?

1.51. Show that if *y* is multiplied by the *n*-bit two's complement of *x*, the *n*-bit result is the *n*-bit two's complement of *xy*, assuming overflow does not occur.

1.52. Show that if the *n*-bit two's complement of *x* is multiplied by the *n*-bit two's complement of *y*, the *n*-bit result is *xy*, assuming overflow does not occur.

1.53. What conversions will **cin** do if the number input is negative?

1.54. What is the next (and last) number in the following sequence:

12, 13, 14, 20, 22, 101

1.55. Convert 0.001 decimal to binary and hex.

1.56. How does changing the **float** variables in Figures 1.18, 1.19, 1.21, and 1.22 to **double** affect the output from these programs?

1.57. Which version in Figure 1.22 yields a more accurate result? Why?

1.58. By running test cases, approximate the relative execution times of single- and double-precision operations.

1.59. What is the precision of denormal numbers?

1.60. Convert the following decimal numbers to 32-bit floating-point numbers. Give your answers in binary and hex.

0.0   0.1   200.5 -88.125 2^{-30}

1.61. Give the value in binary scientific notation of the following floating-point numbers:

40800000   C0C00000   80000000   FF800000   00400000

1.62. Add the following floating-point numbers. Give your answer as floating-point numbers in hex form.

41FFFFFF   C3FF0000

1.63. Same as Problem 1.62, but subtract the second number from the first.

1.64. Same as Problem 1.62, but multiply instead.

1.65. Same as Problem 1.62, but divide the first number by the second.

1.66. What is the difference between 1.0 and the nearest larger representable number in floating-point format? What is the difference between 2^{20} and the nearest larger representable number? What do you conclude about the density of floating-point numbers over their range?

1.67. Compute abs(x − nearest larger neighbor of x)/x, where x is a 32-bit floating-point number and $x = 1, 1024, 2^{15}$, and 2^{20}. Can you draw any interesting conclusions from your results?

1.68. When two floating-point numbers with unequal exponents are added, why is the smaller number unnormalized rather than the bigger number?

1.69. Construct tables like that in Figure 1.20, but for the round-up and round-down techniques.

1.70. If a set of floating-point numbers is treated as unsigned integers and sorted into ascending order, what would be the resulting order of the floating-point numbers?

1.71. Why is excess representation used for the exponent field of a floating-point number rather than two's complement? Why is the sign bit of the significand separated from the significand in floating-point format? Hint: See Problem 1.70.

1.72. What is the range of quad-precision floating-point numbers? Give your answer using powers of 10.

1.73. Would just two bits—a guard bit and a sticky bit—be sufficient for floating-point rounding? Explain.

1.74. Suppose the result of a floating-point computation is 0 10000010 11111111111111111111111 100 (the last three bits are the guard, round, and sticky bits). Round to the nearest (see Figure 1.20). Give your answer in hex.

1.75. Write a program that generates +0.0 and −0.0 and then compares them. What happens? Hint: Generate −0.0 by computing −1.0 × 0.0.

1.76. Write a program that computes the square root of −2.0. What happens?

1.77. Write a program that compares NaN with NaN. What happens?

1.78. Write a program that compares +∞ with NaN. What happens?

1.79. When two floating-point numbers are multiplied, must the hidden bit be included in the multiplication?

1.80. Write and run a program that divides 1.0 by +∞. What happens?

1.81. Write and run a program that evaluates 5 < +∞. What happens?

1.82. Write a Java program that will display in hex the representations used for
`java.lang.Float.MIN_VALUE`, `java.lang.Float.MAX_VALUE`, and
`java.lang.Float.NaN`.

1.83. In a positional numbering system in which the radix is negative, the weights of successive positions alternate sign. What is the advantage of using a negative radix?

1.84. Associate with each position of a three-digit number a distinct prime number. Let the digit in each position be equal to a given number mod the prime in that position. For example, let's use the primes 3, 5, and 7, left to right. To convert 25 decimal to a three-digit number, we determine 25 mod 3 = 1, 25 mod 5 = 0, and 25 mod 7 = 4. Thus, our three-digit representation of 25 is 104. How would you add two numbers in this system? For example, how would you add:

$$\begin{array}{r} 104 \\ + \ 104 \\ \hline \end{array}$$

Do all the three-digit numbers in this system have distinct values? What is the principal advantage of this system?

Chapter Two

MACHINE LANGUAGE

2.1 INTRODUCTION

In this chapter we start our study of a computer language called *machine language,* which is the only language that the computer hardware can use directly. Thus, computer programs written in any other language have to be translated to machine language before they can run on a computer. Because machine language is central to the operation of a computer, we must study machine language to fully understand how computers are organized and how they work.

Each different type of computer has its own machine language. Personal computers that use the Intel Pentium microprocessor have one type of machine language; Apple Mac computers have another; and big mainframe computers have their own machine languages.

In this book, we will study the machine language for the H1 computer. H1 is a good computer to study because, unlike most computers, its organization and operation are easy to understand. With H1, you will learn the fundamentals of computers, and will then be prepared to study more complex computers.

One apparent disadvantage of studying H1 is that you cannot buy one. H1 does not exist in hardware form. Nevertheless, we can still experiment with H1 by using the **sim** program that accompanies this book. **sim** is an H1 *simulator*—it makes a real computer behave exactly like H1. Using **sim** is actually *better* than using a real H1 because with **sim**, we can observe and control the activity that occurs within H1's simulated circuits. Moreover, because **sim** is software, we can easily modify H1, and then use **sim** to see how well our modifications work.

2.2 COMPONENTS OF A COMPUTER

The heart of a computer is the *central processing unit (CPU).* The CPU is the component of a computer that performs high-speed computations. It is also the control center for all the other components of the computer. The CPU is fast because it is completely electronic, and, therefore, has no moving parts to slow it down.

With the advent of personal computers, the public has become quite familiar with computer technology. Before personal computers, however, the public had little exposure to computers. This is reflected in the movies of the time. Computers were typically represented as a bank of tape drives with tape spools moving in a jerky fashion. The movies never represented the computer with a CPU. That would not be exciting—the CPU just sits there. The moving spools on a tape drive, on the other hand, suggested an alive, thinking machine. Tape drives were (and

FIGURE 2.1

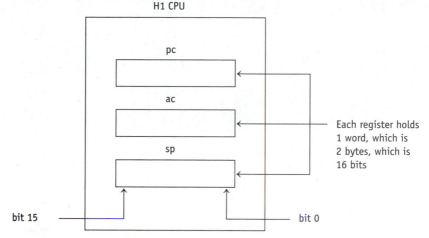

still are) a part of many computer systems, but only a peripheral (i.e., not central) part. Indeed, a computer tape drive is often called a *peripheral device.* It is ironic that moviemakers chose tape drives with their moving parts to represent computers. The computational power of a computer comes from the CPU, the component of a computer system that has no moving parts.

A CPU contains a small number of special storage areas. These storage areas are called *registers* and are usually identified by a number (e.g., register 0, register 1) or a name that suggests its function (e.g., program counter register, accumulator register). H1 has three registers: the *program counter register,* the *accumulator register,* and the *stack pointer register,* abbreviated `pc`, `ac`, and `sp`, respectively (see Figure 2.1). In H1, a *word* (i.e., the fixed-length chunk of data on which its circuits operate) is 16 bits. Each register in H1 holds one word. Modern computers typically have larger word sizes, such as 32 or 64 bits.

The bits within one word in H1 are numbered 0 to 15 from right to left. A *byte* is a grouping of 8 bits. Thus, each register in H1 holds 2 bytes.

The *clock,* another component of a computer, determines the speed at which the CPU performs its operations. A clock is a circuit that provides the CPU with a regular stream of electrical pulses (see Figure 2.2). The CPU synchronizes its operations with the clock pulses that it receives. Each pulse from the clock triggers an operation within the CPU.

The *frequency* of the clock is the number of pulses per second that it generates. The unit of frequency—one pulse per second—is the *Hertz (Hz).* A megahertz (MHz) and a gigahertz (GHz) are, respectively, 1 million and 1 billion Hertz. Modern personal computers have clock frequencies in the gigahertz range.

Because the clock determines the speed of the CPU, could we arbitrarily increase the frequency of the clock to make the CPU go faster and faster? Unfortunately, we cannot. The circuits within the CPU can operate only so fast. If the clock frequency is increased too much, the CPU will not be able to finish one operation before it has to start the next, causing it to malfunction. Even worse, the CPU might overheat, because higher clock frequencies cause the CPU to generate more heat. CPUs are designed for a specific clock frequency and usually are run at that fixed frequency. If a CPU runs at a frequency higher than it was designed for, we say the CPU is *overclocked.*

Machine language instructions are the instructions that tell the CPU what to do. Without machine language instructions, the CPU cannot do anything. The CPU

FIGURE 2.2

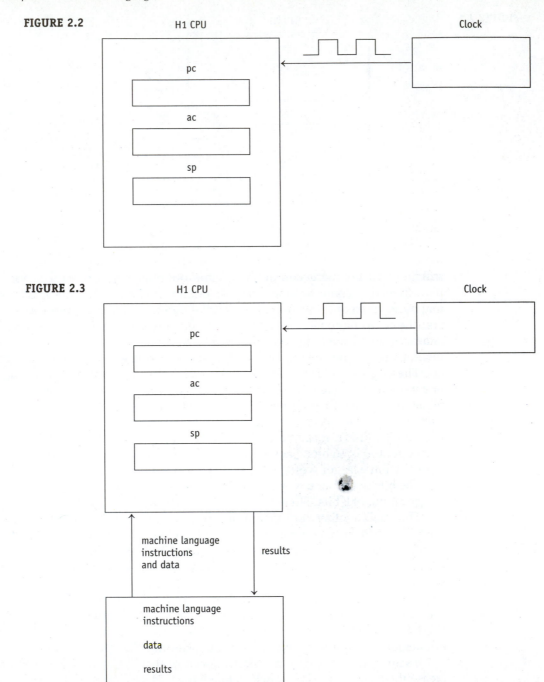

FIGURE 2.3

gets machine language instructions from *main memory,* a third component of a computer system (see Figure 2.3).

The CPU repeatedly fetches (i.e., gets) and executes machine language instructions from main memory. When the CPU *executes* an instruction, it performs the operations called for by that instruction. These machine language instructions determine what the computer does: add, subtract, compare, and so on. A *machine language program* is a sequence of machine language instructions that tell the CPU how to perform some task (like playing chess, editing a text document, or solving an algebraic equation). When we say that the CPU *executes* or *runs* a program, we mean that the CPU executes the machine language instructions that make up that program. These instructions are called *machine code.*

A machine language instruction is a binary number. For example, a typical machine language instruction for H1 is

0010000011111111

This particular instruction causes the CPU to add two numbers. In the next section, we will examine several machine language instructions for H1. Keep in mind that the CPU can use only machine language instructions. Computer programs that do not consist of machine language instructions must be translated to machine language instructions before they can be executed by the CPU.

The CPU operates on data that it obtains from main memory. After performing a computation, the CPU places the result into one of its registers or back into main memory.

Main memory is an array of memory cells, all of which are the same size (usually one byte or one word). Main memory in H1 contains 4096 one-word cells (see Figure 2.4). Each cell is given an identifying number called its *address* or *location.* Addresses are consecutive numbers that start from 0. Thus, the first cell in H1's main memory has the address 0; the last has the address 4095 decimal (FFF hex).

The size of memory is usually a power of two. For example, in H1, the size of main memory is $2^{12} = 2^2 \times 2^{10} = 4 \times 2^{10} = 4$ *kilowords.* The prefix *kilo* means $2^{10} = 1024$ when it is used to specify a memory size. However, beware that

FIGURE 2.4

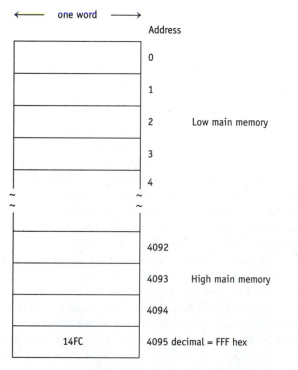

H1 Main Memory

elsewhere it usually means exactly 1000. Similarly, in memory size specifications, the prefixes *mega* and *giga* do not mean exactly 1 million and 1 billion, respectively. Instead, mega means $2^{20} = 1,048,576$, and giga means $2^{30} = 1,073,741,824$.

Most computers have many more cells in main memory than H1 does. The size of main memory in a typical personal computer currently is 512 megabytes, and is ever increasing. Although the size of main memory in H1 is too small for serious computing, it is sufficient for our purposes—that is, for learning how computers work.

The cells with the lower addresses are collectively called *low main memory;* the cells with higher addresses are collectively called *high main memory.* All the diagrams in this book will orient main memory so that low memory appears at the top. For example, in Figure 2.4, low main memory is at the top of the diagram; high main memory is at the bottom.

The information stored inside a memory cell—the binary number—is called the *contents* of the cell. Be sure to distinguish between a cell's address and its contents. Its identifying number is its *address* or *location;* the number stored inside the cell is its contents.

When a memory cell is shown in a diagram, its contents are often shown as a hexadecimal number; for example, Figure 2.4 shows the contents of the cell at location 4095 decimal as the hex number 14FC. The cell does not really contain the hexadecimal number 14FC, but rather its binary equivalent, 0001010011111100. We use hex as a convenient shorthand representation of the binary number that is actually there. Do not be misled by this book's use of hex numbers—*everything stored in the computer is in binary.*

Main memory is generally implemented with a combination of two distinct types of memory circuits: *random access memory (RAM)* and *read-only memory (ROM).* RAM is memory that can be both read from and written to. Whatever is written into a RAM cell overlays what was there previously. RAM is "random" in the sense that the CPU can directly access any cell without having to access all the preceding cells first. For example, if the CPU wants to read the contents of the cell at location 5, it can do so without first having to read the cells at locations 0 through 4. One unfortunate property of RAM is that it is *volatile*—its contents are lost whenever power is turned off.

ROM differs from RAM in two respects:

- *It is read-only:* It can be read from but not written to.
- *It is not volatile:* Its contents are not lost when power is turned off.

ROM, like RAM, can be accessed randomly (i.e., any cell can be accessed directly without first accessing its predecessors). We never call it "random access memory," however, because we reserve this term for readable/writeable random access memory. On most computers, main memory consists of a combination of RAM and ROM. On some computers, including H1, main memory consists of RAM exclusively.

To complete our computer system, we need one or more input devices and one or more output devices. An *input device* brings information from the outside world into the computer (to the CPU or main memory). An *output device* brings information from the computer (from the CPU or main memory) to the outside world (see Figure 2.5). H1 has limited but adequate input/output facilities. It can read machine language programs from a disk drive into its main memory. It can also read numbers and strings of characters from the keyboard and output the same to the monitor.

FIGURE 2.5

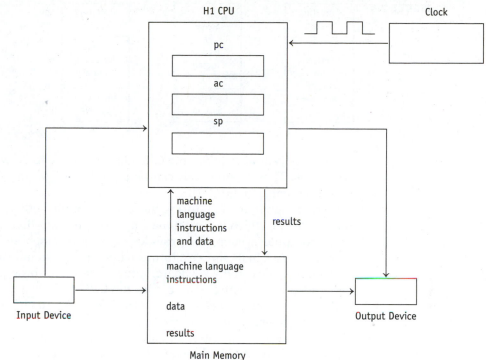

The operations performed by the computer in Figure 2.5 depends on the machine language program stored in main memory. This feature, called the *stored-program concept,* provides the computer with its enormous versatility. By loading the appropriate program into memory, we can make the computer perform virtually any computational task. This important concept was first conceived in the 1940s by three pioneers in computer design: John Von Neumann, John Mauchly, and J. Presper Eckert. In honor of Von Neumann (unfortunately neglecting Mauchly and Eckert), the basic structure illustrated in Figure 2.5—a main memory unit containing stored instructions and data accessed by the CPU—is called the *Von Neumann architecture.* Most computers today have essentially this structure.

Starting up a computer that has only RAM main memory is a tricky process. When power is first turned on, main memory contains only *garbage*—useless binary numbers—because RAM is volatile memory. Main memory initially contains no valid machine language instructions for the CPU, so the CPU (and, therefore, the whole computer) cannot do anything. The computer is stuck. It cannot even load main memory with instructions, because main memory doesn't have any instructions. What is needed on startup is some way to jump-start the computer— that is, to get a program into memory so the computer can then start functioning productively. This jump-starting process is called *booting* the computer (the term *booting* is from the expression "pulling yourself up by your bootstraps"). In a computer with only RAM in main memory, a few critical machine language instructions are permanently wired into the CPU. At the beginning of the boot process, these instructions are executed by the CPU, the effect of which is to load into main memory a small program, a *loader,* from some input device. The CPU can then execute this program because it is now in main memory. The loader, in turn, loads in the principal program to be run. Once the principal program is in memory, the CPU can execute it.

FIGURE 2.6

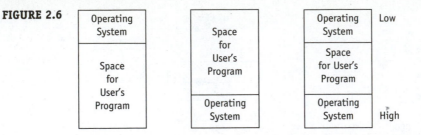

In a system with ROM, the CPU does not have to be wired with start-up instructions. These instructions can be placed in ROM and are, therefore, permanently available to the CPU.

The program read in during the last step of the boot process is usually an *operating system*, which is a machine language program that manages the resources of the computer system, and provides a convenient interface between the computer and the user. In its simplest form, an operating system reads in a program name that a user enters on the keyboard. It then locates this program, loads it into memory, and gives it control (i.e., causes the CPU to execute it). When the program ends, the operating system gets control again (i.e., the CPU starts executing the operating system again), and the cycle repeats.

Operating systems normally reside in low main memory, in high main memory, or in both low and high main memory with the intervening space for the user's program (see Figure 2.6).

The **sim** program that accompanies this book simulates not only H1's hardware, but also a simple operating system. Because this simulated operating system is part of **sim**, it does not occupy any main memory of the simulated H1 computer. Thus, all 4096 cells of memory are available for a user's program. On a real computer, the operating system would, of course, occupy some portion of main memory.

2.3 MACHINE LANGUAGE PROGRAMMING

Let's now examine several machine language instructions for H1 that together will form a simple machine language program. The first one that we will consider is called the *load* instruction because it causes the CPU to load the contents of a memory cell into the **ac** register. This instruction consists of two parts:

- The *operation code* (or *opcode,* for short), which indicates the particular type of instruction (load, in this case)
- The address of the main memory cell from which the **ac** register is to be loaded

The whole instruction is 16 bits long. A 16-bit length is the ideal size because the instruction just fits into one memory cell. Four bits are for the opcode; the remaining 12 bits are for the memory address. We call the 12-bit portion of the instruction that holds the memory address the *x field.* Its content is an unsigned number (because all memory addresses are greater than or equal to 0). An actual load instruction is shown in Figure 2.7.

Its leftmost four bits, 0000, are the opcode. These bits indicate to the CPU that this is a load instruction. The remaining 12 bits, 000000000100 (4 decimal), are the address of the cell from which the **ac** register is to be loaded. When executing this instruction, the CPU makes a copy of the number in memory location 4 and loads

FIGURE 2.7

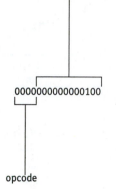

it into the `ac` register. Suppose the cell at location 4 contains the binary number 0000000000001111. Then this number is loaded into the `ac` register, overlaying whatever is already there. The action of the load instruction does not change the contents of the cell at location 4 (see Figure 2.8).

Any main memory address can be used in a load instruction. For example, the instruction 0000000000000101 would load from location 000000000101 (5 decimal).

It is awkward and tedious to read and write binary numbers, so we generally use hexadecimal notation to represent binary numbers. For example, our load machine language instruction, 0000000000000100, can be conveniently represented with the four hex digits 0004. The leftmost digit, 0, represents the 4-bit opcode; the remaining three digits, 004, represent the 12-bit address. Be sure to keep in mind that machine language instructions, register contents, and memory contents are all binary numbers. We use hexadecimal as a convenient representation of these binary numbers.

The load instruction is one of several instructions on H1 that are called direct instructions. A *direct instruction* is an instruction that contains a main memory address. The address that the load instruction contains allows the CPU to go *directly* (hence, the name "direct instruction") to the memory cell from which it loads.

Our next machine language instruction is the *add* instruction, which adds the contents of a memory cell to the `ac` register. Let's examine the add instruction 2005. It contains the opcode 2 (i.e., 0010 binary) and the address 005 (i.e., 000000000101 binary). When it is executed, the contents of location 005 are added to the `ac` register (see Figure 2.9).

After the execution of the add instruction, the result of the addition is in the `ac` register. Let's now store this result in memory. To do this, we need the instruction that does the reverse of the load instruction—that stores the `ac` register into memory instead of loading it. The instruction that does this is called the *store instruction*. Let's use a store instruction that stores the contents of the `ac` register into cell 6 of memory. Because the opcode for the store instruction is 1 and the required address is 006, the instruction we need, in hex notation, is 1006. Figure 2.10 shows its effect.

You can see in Figure 2.10 that the original contents of cell 6 are destroyed by the action of the store instruction. This is fine as long as cell 6 does not contain something we may need later.

The add and store instructions, like the load instruction, are direct instructions because they contain a main memory address. The add instruction contains the

FIGURE 2.8

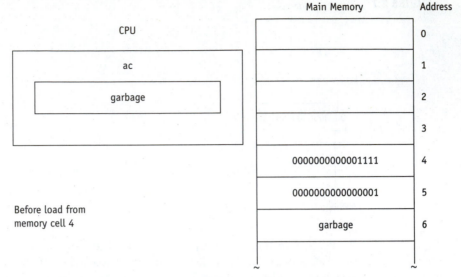

Before load from
memory cell 4

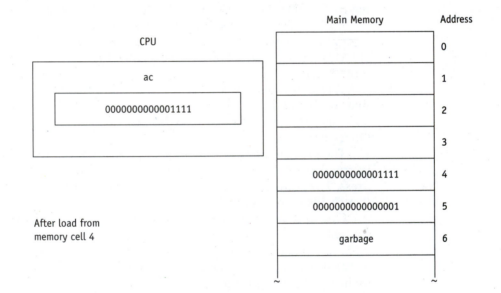

After load from
memory cell 4

address of the number to be added; the store instruction contains the address of the destination of the store.

The last instruction we need for our program is the *halt* instruction. It halts execution of the program by causing the CPU to jump back to the operating system (i.e., **sim**) and recommence executing instructions there. Without a halt instruction, the CPU would continue past the end of the program, executing whatever instructions happen to be there.

The halt instruction in H1 consists of a 16-bit opcode. The opcode takes up the whole instruction. This works fine because there is no need for the halt instruction to contain an address. In hex notation, the halt instruction is FFFF.

FIGURE 2.9

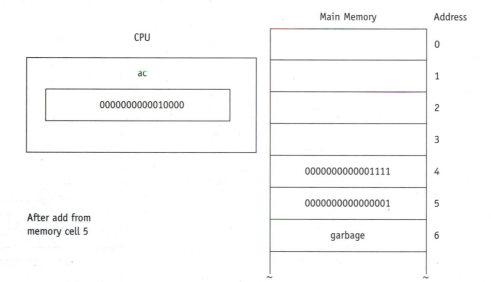

Before add from
memory cell 5

After add from
memory cell 5

Our simple machine language program that adds two numbers and stores the result consists of

- Four instructions
- The two numbers to be added
- A cell in memory for storing the result

We can place the four instructions into locations 0 through 3 in memory, followed by the two numbers and the cell to hold the result. Figure 2.11 shows the final program.

In Figure 2.11, we have specified the initial contents of the cell at location 6 as 0000. However, this initial value is not important because the store instruction will overlay it. The two numbers to be added (000F and 0001) in our machine language

FIGURE 2.10

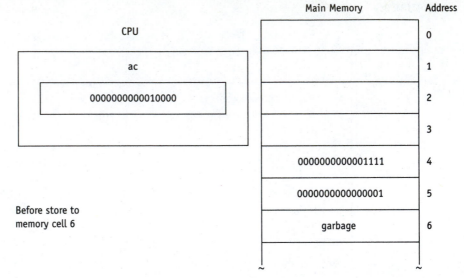

CPU

ac

0000000000010000

Before store to
memory cell 6

Main Memory   Address

	0
	1
	2
	3
0000000000001111	4
0000000000000001	5
garbage	6

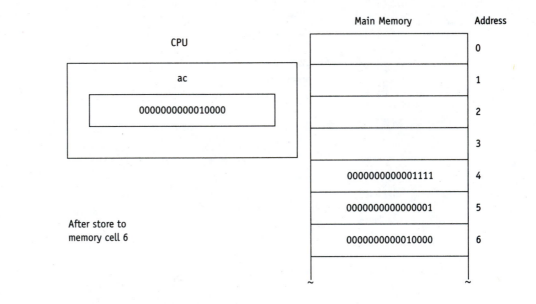

CPU

ac

0000000000010000

After store to
memory cell 6

Main Memory   Address

	0
	1
	2
	3
0000000000001111	4
0000000000000001	5
0000000000010000	6

FIGURE 2.11

Address	Machine Instructions and Data in Hex	Description
0	0004	load instruction
1	2005	add instruction
2	1006	store instruction
3	FFFF	halt instruction
4	000F	data
5	0001	data
6	0000	cell to hold the result

FIGURE 2.12

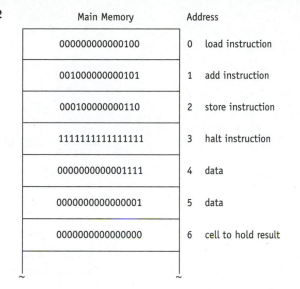

Main Memory	Address	
000000000000100	0	load instruction
001000000000101	1	add instruction
000100000000110	2	store instruction
1111111111111111	3	halt instruction
0000000000001111	4	data
0000000000000001	5	data
0000000000000000	6	cell to hold result

program are both positive, but they do not have to be. We could have added two negative numbers, or a negative and a positive number. Negative numbers are represented on H1 in two's complement form.

Remember that machine language instructions are binary numbers. We use hex notation as a convenient shorthand representation for binary numbers. To make this absolutely clear, Figure 2.12 shows what our program really looks like in main memory (i.e., as a sequence of binary numbers).

2.4 RUNNING A MACHINE LANGUAGE PROGRAM ON SIM

If we had a file in the appropriate format containing the machine language program that we developed in the preceding section, we could easily have **sim** read and run it. However, because we do not have such a file, we will instead enter our program directly into memory. To do this, we will use a part of **sim** called the *debugger,* which allows the user to do many useful things, such as loading, changing, or examining main memory of the simulated H1 computer. The debugger is a very useful tool for detecting and removing *bugs* (i.e., errors) from computer programs (hence, the name *debugger*). We can invoke any function that the debugger provides by entering a command at the debugger's prompt message. The debugger treats any number you enter as a hex number unless the number ends with the letter *t*, in which case it is treated as a decimal number (*t* stands for "base 10"). For example, the debugger treats "10" as hex 10, but "10t" as decimal 10. All numbers that the debugger displays are hex unless labeled otherwise.

Figure 2.13 shows a session with **sim** in which we create and run our machine language program. In this session, we use the following debugger commands:

e (edit memory)
d (display memory)
t (trace)
r (register display)
f (file)
q (quit)

FIGURE 2.13   ```
C:\H1>sim
Simulator Version x.x
Enter machinecode file name and/or args, or hit ENTER to quit
none

Starting session.
Enter h or ? for help.
---- [T7] 0: ld   /0 000/ e0
   0: 0000/0004   ←enter machine language program
   1: 0000/2005
   2: 0000/1006
   3: 0000/ffff
   4: 0000/000f
   5: 0000/0001
   6: 0000/0000
   7: 0000/   ←hit ENTER to exit edit mode
---- [T7] 0: ld   /0 004/ d0   ←display memory from location 0
   0: 0004 2005 1006 FFFF 000F 0001 0000 0000   ....
   8: 0000 0000 0000 0000 0000 0000 0000 0000   ....
  10: 0000 0000 0000 0000 0000 0000 0000 0000   ....
  18: 0000 0000 0000 0000 0000 0000 0000 0000   ....
---- [T7] 0: ld   /0 004/   ←hit ENTER to trace program with T7
   0: ld   /0 004/ ac=0000/000F
   1: add   /2 005/ ac=000F/0010
   2: st   /1 006/ m[006]=0000/0010
   3: halt /FFFF /
Machine inst count =   4 (hex) =   4 (dec)
---- [T7] r*   ←display all registers
     pc   = 0004   sp   = 0000   ac   = 0010
---- [T7] d6   ←display memory from location 6
   6: 0010 0000 0000 0000 0000 0000 0000 0000   ....
   E: 0000 0000 0000 0000 0000 0000 0000 0000   ....
  16: 0000 0000 0000 0000 0000 0000 0000 0000   ....
  1E: 0000 0000 0000 0000 0000 0000 0000 0000   ....
---- [T7] f 0 6   ←write locations 0 to 6 to a file
Enter file name.   [f.mac]
simple   ←file name to use
Writing locations 0 - 6 to simple.mac
---- [T7] q   ←quit sim
C:\H1>
```

In Figure 2.13, we have distinguished the items that the user enters with boldface (we will follow this convention throughout the book). All debugger commands can be in either upper- or lowercase, assuming **sim** is in the *disabled* state. If, on the other hand, **sim** is *enabled,* then all debugger commands should be in uppercase. The default state for **sim** is disabled, so you won't have to use uppercase unless you previously enabled it (we will discuss using **sim** in the enabled state in Chapter 6).

　　We start the session in Figure 2.13 by invoking **sim**. We do this by entering **sim** at the prompt that is generated by the operating system. **sim** starts by prompting
```

for the name of the file containing the machine language program (the *machinecode file*). At this point, we can

- Enter the name of a machine code file that we want to load.
- Enter **none**, in which case **sim** does not load any machine code file.
- Hit ENTER immediately, in which case **sim** will terminate.

Because we do not have a machine code file for the program in Figure 2.11, enter **none**; **sim** then activates its debugger. The debugger displays the following prompt message, which is packed full of information:

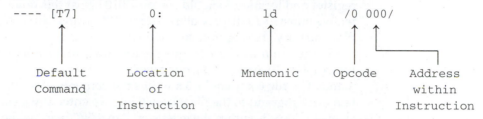

The square brackets surround the *default command*. The default command is executed if you do not enter anything before hitting the ENTER key. **T7** stands for "trace 7 instructions." To *trace* an instruction means to execute it and display its effect. Following the square brackets is the location of the instruction to be executed next. Following that is the actual instruction to be executed next, in both mnemonic and hex forms. `1d` is the *mnemonic* (i.e., a shorthand name that is easy to remember) for the load opcode. Inside the slashes is the hex form of the instruction, with the opcode separated by one space from the address.

Where did the load instruction in the prompt message that the debugger displays come from? Actually, there is no instruction at location 0. Location 0 just happens to contain 0000 initially, which looks like a load instruction. **sim** shows this bogus instruction in the prompt message that it generates.

To enter our machine language program, we must activate the edit mode of the debugger by entering **e0** ("0" is the main memory location from which we wish to start editing). The debugger then shows the current contents of location 0. We then enter in hex the first machine language instruction (0004) followed by the ENTER key. The debugger will display the contents of the next location. We then similarly enter the next instruction. We continue in this fashion until we enter the entire program. We then hit the ENTER key one more time to exit from edit mode.

When we enter data in the edit mode, we do not need to enter any leading zeros. For example, in the edit session in Figure 2.13, we could have entered the three data items as f, 1, and 0 instead of as 000f, 0001, and 0000. We can also enter data directly in decimal, if that is more convenient—just append t to the end of the number. For example, we could have entered 15t at location 4 instead of 000f. Either way, the effect is the same: The debugger places the binary number 0000000000001111 into location 4 of main memory.

To verify that our program is correctly in memory, we enter **d0** to display memory starting from location 0. The hex representation of the program is then displayed across the screen.

Next we hit ENTER to activate the default command, **T7** (trace 7 instructions). The debugger then lists the mnemonic and hex representation of the instructions as they are executed, along with their effect. For example, to the right of the add mnemonic is

`ac=000F/0010`

This shows that the add instruction changed the contents of the `ac` register from 000F to 0010 (the "before" and "after" values are on the left and right sides, respectively, of the slash). To the right of the `st` mnemonic is

```
m[006]=0000/0010
```

This shows that the store instruction wrote to location 6 in memory, changing its contents from 0000 to 0010.

When the halt instruction is executed, the program ends. `sim` displays the total number of machine instructions executed (the *machine inst count*). Both the `ac` register and location 6 should contain 0010 hex at this point. To check the `ac` register, we enter `r*` to display all registers ("*" means "all"). We then enter `d6` to display memory starting from location 6.

Because our machine language program is in memory only, it will be lost once we exit `sim`. To avoid losing our program, we save it to a file using the **f** (file) command. The file command **f 0 6** writes the contents of locations 0 to 6 (which contain our program) to the file whose name we enter. If we enter a name without an extension, `sim` assumes the extension ".mac" (".mac" is the extension we use for machine code files). If we do not enter a name but immediately hit the ENTER key, `sim` uses the default name, **f.mac**. In our session, we enter **simple**. Thus, the output file name is **simple.mac**.

To end our session, we enter **q** to quit `sim`. If we want to use our program again, we can do so because we saved it to the file **simple.mac**. We simply invoke `sim`, and specify **simple** (or **simple.mac**) instead of **none** when it prompts for a machine code file name.

To trace a program, we do not have to use the default command **T7** (which is invoked by hitting the ENTER key). Instead, we could enter any trace command. For example, we could enter **T1**, causing only one instruction to be traced. Furthermore, **T1** then becomes the new default command. Thus, each time we subsequently hit the ENTER key, only one instruction would be traced. The default command is always set to the most recently entered trace command.

To get a permanent record of our debugging activity, we can enter **L** (in upper- or lowercase) at the debugger's prompt. This command turns on a log file to which all *subsequent* activity is recorded. Thus, to record all the activity shown in Figure 2.13, we should enter the **L** command at the very beginning of the debugging session (see Figure 2.14).

The name of the log file is derived from the name entered for the machine code file when `sim` is first started. The log file name is formed by combining the

FIGURE 2.14

```
C:\H1>sim
Simulator Version x.x
Enter machinecode file name and/or args, or hit ENTER to quit.
none

Starting session.  Enter h or ? for help.
---- [T7] 0: ld   /0 000/ 1              ←the letter "L"
Log file none.log is now on
---- [T7] 0: ld   /0 000/ e0
  0: 0000/0004
          .
          .
          .
```

FIGURE 2.15   `C:\H1>`**`sim none`**
`Simulator Version x.x`

`Starting session.  Enter h or ? for help.`
`---- [T7] 0: ld   /0 000/`
.
.
.

base file name entered for the machine code file and the extension ".log". Because we entered **none** for the machine code file name in Figure 2.14, the log file name is **none.log**. Recording to the log file can be turned off at any time by entering **L-** (in upper- or lowercase), and back on again with **L**.

When **sim** is first started, it generates a *start-up prompt* that requests the name of a machine code file. If, however, we specify the name of the machine code file or **none** *on the command line* when we invoke **sim**, then **sim** does not generate the start-up prompt; instead, it goes immediately into a debugging session (see Figure 2.15).

Because we specified **none** on the command line in Figure 2.15, **sim** does not prompt for a machine code file name. Every program in the H1 software package behaves in this way—information that the program needs is prompted for unless we provide the information on the command line. If you do not remember which arguments a program requires, then do not enter any. The program will prompt you for whatever it needs. If, on the other hand, you know which arguments the program requires, you can expedite the execution of the program by entering them on the command line.

Every program in the H1 software package will display a help screen if **/h**, **-h**, **/?**, or **-?** is specified on the command line or in response to the start-up prompt. For example, to display the help screen for **sim**, enter

`sim /h`

at the operating system's prompt. On some operating systems (for example, UNIX), **/?** and **-?** will not work because of the special way **?** is interpreted when it appears on the command line. For these systems, use the argument **/h** or **-h** (these should work on any system). Another help screen—on **sim**'s debugger—is available whenever the debugger is active. To display this help screen, enter **h** or **?** at the *debugger's* prompt.

You will learn more about the programs in the H1 software package in later chapters on an as-needed basis. If you should want to consult a complete reference for any program, please see the ".txt" file in the software package for that program.

PROLEMS

• •

2.1.   Write and run on **sim** a machine language program that adds the decimal numbers 4, −35, 16, 555, and −8, and stores the result.

2.2.   Write and run on **sim** a machine language program that subtracts 15 decimal from 20 decimal using the add instruction.

2.3.   Write and run on **sim** a machine language program that computes the value of the decimal expression $(44 + 54 + 64) - (15 + 8 + 33)$.

2.4. Write and run on **sim** a machine language program that consists of a load and a halt instruction. The load instruction should load itself into the **ac** register.

2.5. Write and run on **sim** a machine language program in which an st instruction stores −1 into the location that immediately follows it. What happens?

2.6. What are the contents of the **ac** register when the following program halts? Explain what happens.

```
0004
1002
0005
2006
FFFF
0001
0002
```

2.7. Trace the following program on **sim**. What happens?

```
2002
9000
0010
```

2.8. Enter the program in Problem 2.7 on **sim**. At the debugger's prompt, enter u⁰. What happens? What is the mnemonic for the instruction at location 1?

2.9. Run the following program on **sim**. What is the effect of each instruction?

```
0003
3004
FFFF
0009
0003
```

2.10. Run the following program on **sim**. What is the effect of the first instruction? Where does the 5 in the **ac** register come from?

```
8005
FFFF
```

2.11. Run the following program on **sim**. What is the effect of the instruction at location 3?

```
8005
F300
8005
F700
FFFF
```

2.12. Run the following program on **sim**. What is the effect of the instructions at locations 1 and 2?

```
8010
FFFD
FFF9
FFFF
```

2.13. Rewrite the following program, replacing the opcodes with their mnemonics (use ld, add, st, and halt) and the addresses with their decimal equivalents (omit any leading zeros in the addresses). For example, the first instruction is rewritten as **ld 7**. Replace any constants with the decimal equivalent preceded by **dw**. For example, the constant at the end of the program should be rewritten as `dw 5`. Which version is easier to understand?

```
0007
2008
2009
200A
200B
100C
FFFF
0001
0002
0003
0004
0005
```

2.14. How many instructions are executed when the following program runs? Explain your answer.

```
0007
2008
1003
0007
2008
FFFF
FFFF
FF00
00FF
```

2.15. Run the following program on `sim`. What happens?

```
0003
2004
1000
0002
FFFD
```

2.16. What is the largest address that a load instruction can specify? Give your answer in binary, hex, and decimal. What is the address of the highest cell in main memory of H1?

2.17. How many bits would a load instruction need to hold an address if main memory in H1 had 65,536 (decimal) cells?

2.18. How many distinct opcodes can 4 bits specify?

2.19. What are the dangers of overclocking the CPU? What are the benefits?

2.20. Is there an instruction in H1 whose opcode is 1111 binary? Using only the information in Chapter 2, how can you tell?

2.21. How does H1 determine if 0001 hex is a load instruction or a data item?

2.22. Replace the halt instruction in the program described in Section 2.3 with 0000 hex. Now rerun the program on `sim`. What happens?

2.23. Create a file that contains only the word `tess` with no blanks preceding or following it. Name your file `junk.mac`. Run `sim` and enter `junk` in response to the first prompt message. What happens? Now change your file so that it contains only the word `Text`. Again run `sim`, entering `junk` at the first prompt. What happens? What *specific* difference between the two files causes the difference in behavior?

2.24.   Explain how both of these statements can be true:

ROM is RAM.
ROM is not RAM.

2.25.   During the boot process, the instructions that are wired into the CPU read in the loader program which, in turn, reads in the operating system. Could the wired instructions directly read in the operating system?

2.26.   Why is the debugger in **sim** so named?

2.27.   What is the operating system doing when a user's program is running?

2.28.   What is an advantage of having an operating system consist of two parts, one part in low main memory, the other part in high main memory?

2.29.   Why is the size of main memory usually a power of two?

2.30.   Suggest a modification to the structure in Figure 2.5 that would permit the faster execution of instructions.

Chapter Three

H1 ASSEMBLY LANGUAGE: PART 1

3.1 INTRODUCTION

• •

Assembly language is a symbolic form of machine language. Machine language consists of binary numbers; assembly language consists of symbols that represent these binary numbers. Each assembly language instruction represents one machine language instruction. Thus, an assembly language program with 10 instructions is translated to a machine language program with 10 instructions. Assembly language is symbolic, and is, therefore, easier for us humans to use; machine language is binary, and is, therefore, more difficult for us humans to use.

Because assembly language is close to machine language, it is called a *low-level language*. Languages, such as C++ and Java, that hide the details of the machine from the programmer are called *high-level languages.*

Machine language is the only language that the CPU can use directly. Thus, to execute an assembly language program, it first must be translated to machine language. An *assembler* is a program that performs this translation. Because of the close connection between assembly language and machine language, the translation of the assembly language to machine language is simple: We replace the symbols that make up an assembly language program with the binary numbers they represent. We can do this translation by hand, but it is a tedious process during which one can easily make a mistake. It is better to let a program—the assembler—do the job for us.

Programs written in high-level languages, of course, also have to be translated to machine language before they can be executed. A program that translates high-level language programs is called a *compiler.*

Assembly language gives a programmer total control over what goes into the machine language program. It is in this sense that assembly language is the most powerful programming language. When total control is important, assembly language is the language to use. Here are several areas in which assembly language is typically used:

- Most of an operating system can be written in a high-level language; for example, the data structures associated with the file system are usually handled by code written in a high-level language. However, a small portion of any operating system has to control hardware mechanisms that differ from one computer type to next. Because of the machine-independent nature of high-level languages, they are ill-suited for these machine-specific tasks. Assembly language, on the other hand, can easily handle these tasks.

- A computer's operating system cannot possibly contain the code to handle every device that might be attached to that computer. There are just too many devices, with new devices appearing all the time. Thus, attachable hardware devices, such as printers, all come with *device drivers*—code that has to be installed before the devices are usable. Because of the hardware-specific nature of device drivers, they are typically written in assembly language.

- Some high-level languages have capabilities that are implemented very inefficiently at the machine level. For some applications, these inefficiencies can result in unacceptable performance. With assembly language, however, an implementation's efficiency is limited only by the programmer's skill.
- Some computer systems have very severe main memory limitations. For example, *embedded systems*—computer chips installed in devices (such as a microwave oven) that control those devices often have such small memories that the space efficiency provided by assembly language is a necessity.
- *Application programs* (programs for the end user of a computer system) are often written and debugged entirely in a high-level language. Then, by means of a trace program, modules causing performance bottlenecks, if any, are identified. These bottlenecks are then minimized or eliminated by rewriting the modules more efficiently in assembly language. This approach makes writing, debugging, documenting, and maintaining a program easy (because we write most of it in a high-level language), yet it still yields high performance (because its critical modules are in assembly language).

Assembly language, unfortunately, has disadvantages. It is more challenging to write, understand, debug, maintain, and document programs written in assembly language than in a high-level language. Moreover, assembly language instructions are more primitive (i.e., each instruction does less) than instructions in high-level languages. Thus, assembly language programs need more lines of code to do the same thing as comparable high-level language programs. Finally, a programmer who is not highly skilled may not produce code that is smaller or faster than compiler-generated code.

Although an assembly language program usually has more lines of code than a comparable program in a high-level language, its corresponding machine language program is sometimes smaller. There are three reasons for this smaller size:

1. The machine code produced by a compiler may be less efficient than that of a hand-written assembly language program. Which is better depends, of course, on the compiler and the skill of the assembly language programmer. Modern compilers can perform a sophisticated analysis of a program's structure that allows them to generate highly optimized code. This type of analysis is often beyond the capabilities or endurance of an assembly language programmer. Thus, these compilers can, in fact, produce code that is as good as or better than code written by a skilled assembly language programmer.

2. Programs in most high-level languages are compiled to machine language programs that include an initialization module called *start-up code*. This initialization module can contain thousands of bytes of code. Thus, even a tiny program in a high-level language produces a sizable machine language program. Try compiling the following C++ program:

```
void main()
{
}
```

Even though this program contains no executable statements, the size of its machine language program can still be considerable.

3. High-level programs usually use a variety of general-purpose functions that often have all sorts of "bells and whistles." Whenever a program uses one of these functions, it gets the machine code for the whole function—not just the particular features it needs. The resulting machine language program is, therefore, far bigger than necessary. For example, suppose a C++ program contains the function call

```
printf("Hello\n");
```

printf is a complex function that can perform a variety of data conversion operations. The machine language program containing this call contains *all* the code for **printf,** including all the code for performing data conversions, none of which is needed by this particular **printf** call. In contrast, assembly language programs typically use special-purpose functions that are customized to meet only the specific requirements of the program.

Every machine language has its own unique assembly language. Because different types of computers have different machine languages, they also have different assembly languages. In this chapter, we will start our study of the assembly language for H1.

3.2 ASSEMBLY LANGUAGE BASICS

In Chapter 2 we developed a machine language program consisting of

- Four machine language instructions
- Two words of data
- One word for the computed result

Figure 3.1 shows this program in hex notation.

Once again, let's emphasize that machine language programs consist of binary numbers. We are using hex notation in Figure 3.1 as a shorthand representation of these binary numbers.

We know from Chapter 2 that machine language is the only language that the CPU can use directly. Without machine language instructions, the CPU cannot do anything. Unfortunately, machine language is not an easy language for us humans. Just reading all the 1's and 0's is likely to produce eyestrain. Even if we could read binary numbers easily, we would still have to interpret the various fields that make up a machine language instruction—a task that is laborious and error-prone. Using hex notation to represent machine language is a big help, but it still leaves us with the chore of interpreting the various fields of each instruction. We need a representation of machine language that is easy for us humans to use. Let's develop such a representation. Here is what we will do:

FIGURE 3.1
```
0004    Load ac from location 4
2005    Add to ac from location 5
1006    Store result in location 6
FFFF    Halt
000F    First number
0001    Second number
0000    Result field
```

- In place of a binary opcode, we will use a *mnemonic*—a shorthand name that is easy to remember. For example, we will use "add" in place of "0010", the opcode for the add instruction. Similarly, we will use the mnemonics "ld", "st", and "halt" in place of the opcodes for the load, store, and halt instructions, respectively.
- In place of a binary address, we will use its decimal equivalent. For example, in place of "000000000101", we will use "5", separating it from the mnemonic with at least one space.

With this representation, the machine language instruction

We also need a way to represent binary data and result fields like the last three words in the program in Figure 3.1. For these cases we will use **dw** (define word) followed by the decimal equivalent of the 16-bit binary data. For example, in place of the binary number

0000000000001111

(which equals 15 in decimal) we will use

dw 15

There is an important difference between our use of **dw** and our use of the mnemonics ld, add, st, and halt. The number that follows **dw** represents the *entire* 16 bits that make up the data word. Thus, **dw** itself does not represent any part of the machine word. In contrast, mnemonics represent the opcode part of the machine word (see Figure 3.2).

Figure 3.3 shows our machine language program rewritten using our new representation. At most one instruction or **dw** is allowed on each line.

FIGURE 3.2

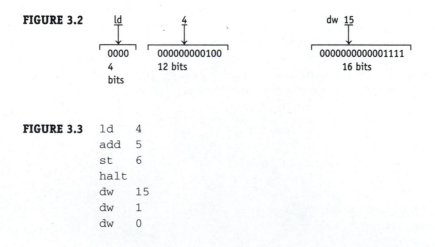

FIGURE 3.3

```
ld    4
add   5
st    6
halt
dw    15
dw    1
dw    0
```

It is, of course, much easier to remember a mnemonic like `add` than its corresponding binary opcode. Thus, the term *mnemonic* (which means something that aids memory) is, indeed, an appropriate designation for `ld`, `add`, `st`, and `halt`. Because **dw** does not represent any part of a machine language word, it is not an easier-to-remember form of something that is hard to remember. Thus, we do not call **dw** a mnemonic. Instead, we call it a *directive* because it "directs" us to do something—namely, to interpret the number that follows it as occupying a memory word.

The new form of our program (Figure 3.3) is essentially a symbolic form of our original machine language program. We are using symbols (mnemonics, directives, and decimal numbers) that are easy for us to understand. This symbolic representation of machine language is called *assembly language.*

Programs written in assembly language are much easier for us to understand than their machine language equivalents. Unfortunately, the CPU cannot use assembly language directly. Recall that the only language the CPU can use is machine language. If we want to run an assembly language program on a computer, we first have to translate the program to machine language.

Because there is such a close connection between machine and assembly languages, it is not difficult to translate assembly language into machine language. For example, consider the assembly language instruction

```
add    5
```

To *assemble* (i.e., translate to machine language) this instruction, we must

1. Determine the 4-bit opcode corresponding to the add mnemonic (0010).
2. Determine the 12-bit binary equivalent of 5 (000000000101).
3. Assemble (i.e., put together) these two binary components to form the 16-bit machine language instruction (0010000000000101).

We could certainly translate an assembly language program to machine language by hand; however, for large programs, this translation is a tedious, error-prone process. A better alternative is to use a computer program, called an *assembler,* that will do the translation for us (see Figure 3.4). The input to the assembler (the assembly language program) is called the *source program.* The machine language program produced by the assembler has a variety of names, depending on its form. It is often called the *object program* or, if it is a complete program ready to run, the *executable program.*

The name "assembler" is used for assembly-to-machine language translators because it emphasizes the simple nature of the translation. The translation process involves only the determination and *assembly* (i.e., putting together) of the components of the machine language instruction.

The software that accompanies this book includes two assemblers for our assembly language. The **sim** *assembler* is built into **sim**'s debugger, and is used for making minor modifications to a machine language program already in main memory. **mas** (*m*achine-level *as*sembler) is a full-featured, stand-alone assembler.

It is sometimes useful to do the reverse of an assembler—that is, to translate machine language into assembly language. A program that does this is called an

FIGURE 3.4

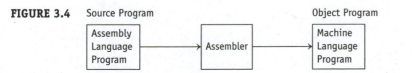

Source Program   Object Program

Assembly Language Program → Assembler → Machine Language Program

FIGURE 3.5

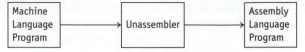

unassembler or a *disassembler* (see Figure 3.5). **sim**'s debugger has a built-in unassembler that we will use later in this chapter.

In our descriptions of the various instructions on H1, we will frequently use the term *operand* to designate an item that is used in an operation. For example, consider the instruction

```
add   5
```

When this instruction is executed, the number at location 5 is added to the **ac** register. Thus, the number at location 5 is the operand. "5" itself is *not* the operand, but the address of the operand.

3.3   COMMENTING ASSEMBLY LANGUAGE PROGRAMS

A computer program should always contain comments describing its operation. Comments are particularly important for assembly language programs because such programs tend to be difficult to understand.

When we include comments in a program, we must *delimit* (i.e., set off from the rest of the program) them in some way so that the assembler does not process them as regular statements. In H1 assembly language programs to be processed by **mas**, a comment starts with a semicolon or a slash, and continues to the end of the line. Both the semicolon and a *single* slash are inappropriate comment delimiters in C++ and Java because both can appear in C++ and Java statements. However, in our assembly language, the semicolon and slash can never appear in a statement, and therefore are suitable as comment delimiters.

Comments can, of course, greatly improve the readability of a program. We can further improve readability with the judicious use of blank lines, which are useful for separating the distinct parts of a program. When using **mas**, we can include completely blank lines anywhere within a program. The **sim** assembler, however, permits neither comments nor blank lines.

Figure 3.6 shows our simple assembly language program rewritten with comments and blank lines. Because the assembler ignores comments and blank lines, the assembler will assign addresses 0 to 3 to the instructions, and addresses 4 to 6 to the data items.

FIGURE 3.6

```
; assembly language program that adds two numbers

        ld    4      ; get first number    ←address 0
        add   5      ; add second number
        st    6      ; store sum in memory
        halt         ; return to OS         ←address 3

;       data area
        dw    15     ; first number         ←address 4
        dw    1      ; second number
        dw    0      ; store sum here       ←address 6
```

3.4   USING LABELS

• •

Let's modify the program in Figure 3.6 so that it adds three numbers instead of two. We need, of course, another **dw** for the third number. Let's place it at the very end of the program. We also need another add instruction to add the third number to the **ac** register. The new add instruction should be inserted just before the st instruction in Figure 3.6. This insertion, unfortunately, has an undesirable effect: It increases by one the addresses of everything that follows the insertion point. The address of the first number increases to 5; the address of the second number increases to 6; and the address of the result field increases to 7. Thus, the addresses contained in the ld, add, and st instructions in Figure 3.6 all have to be increased by one. The modified program is given in Figure 3.7.

We can see from Figures 3.6 and 3.7 that the insertion of a single instruction can require *many* changes to a program because an insertion changes the addresses of all the items that follow it. A deletion has a similar undesirable effect. Insertions and deletions—common editing operations that a programmer performs when writing and debugging a program—can become a clerical nightmare: A single insertion or deletion may require numerous additional changes to the program to accommodate the modified addresses. Fortunately, this problem with insertions and deletions can easily be avoided if we use labels. A *label* is a symbolic address. Consider the program in Figure 3.8, which is the program in Figure 3.6 rewritten with labels. We have placed the labels **n1**, **n2**, and **result** on the three **dw** directives. In so doing, we make **n1** the symbolic address of the first **dw**, **n2** the symbolic

FIGURE 3.7

```
; assembly language program that adds three numbers

              ld    5        ; get first number
              add   6        ; add second number
              add   8        ; add third number
              st    7        ; store sum in memory
              halt           ; return to OS

    ;                data area
                 dw   15       ; first number         ←address 5
                 dw   1        ; second number        ←address 6
                 dw   0        ; store result here    ←address 7
                 dw   4        ; third number         ←address 8
```

FIGURE 3.8

```
; assembly language program that adds two numbers

              ld     n1      ; get first number
              add    n2      ; add second number
              st     result  ; store sum in memory
              halt           ; return to operating system

    ;                 data area
    n1:          dw    15      ; first number
    n2:          dw    1       ; second number
    result:      dw    0       ; store sum here
```

address of the second **dw**, and **result** the symbolic address of the third **dw**. If we wish to refer to these **dw**'s, we can use their symbolic addresses (i.e., their labels). For example, we can write the instruction that loads from the first **dw** this way,

```
ld   n1    ; symbolic address n1 is used
```

instead of this way:

```
ld   4     ; absolute address is used
```

Because the **n1** label is attached to the first **dw**, the instruction

```
ld   n1
```

will always load from that **dw**, even if insertions or deletions are performed that change the address of the **dw**. This is *not* true, of course, for the instruction

```
ld   4
```

which always loads from location 4. A main memory address specified by a number, as in the instruction above, is called an *absolute address*. An address specified by a label is called a *symbolic address*.

When a label appears to the left of a mnemonic or a directive, it must be separated from the mnemonic or directive by a colon (:). Any number of blanks (including zero) on either side of the colon is allowed. It is advisable (but not required by **mas**) to start labels in the leftmost column to maximize the space available for the rest of the statement. A mnemonic or directive that is not preceded by a label can start in any column, including the leftmost column.

We can readily see the advantage of using labels when we modify the program in Figure 3.8 to add three numbers instead of two. The only changes needed are the insertion of the add instruction and the addition of the **dw** for the third number (see Figure 3.9). Let's insert the third number immediately after the second number instead of appending it to the end of the program.

Because we are using labels, both insertions require no additional changes. Of course, after the assembly language program is modified, it has to be reassembled to get the corresponding updated machine language program.

All of the statements in Figure 3.10a are legal, although poorly formatted.

For visual clarity, we should format an assembly language program into columns, as shown in Figure 3.10b. With this formatting, the program in Figure 3.10a becomes the considerably more readable program in Figure 3.10b.

FIGURE 3.9

```
; assembly language program that adds three numbers

        ld    n1      ; get first number
        add   n2      ; add second number
        add   n3      ; add third number    ←insertion
        st    result  ; store sum in memory
        halt          ; return to operating system

;             data area
n1:           dw    15      ; first number
n2:           dw    1       ; second number
n3:           dw    4       ; third number       ←insertion
result:       dw    0       ; store sum here
```

FIGURE 3.10   a)

```
start:ld     n1           ; A properly formatted program
st    x  ; is easy to read
        halt
   n1  : dw      5
     x:dw 0; receives copy of n1
```

b)

```
start:      ld     n1           ; A properly formatted program
            st     x            ; is easy to read
            halt
n1:         dw     5
x:          dw     0            ; receives copy of n1
```

Comments
Addresses, data
Mnemonics, directives
Labels

FIGURE 3.11

```
                    ld    x
                    ld    y
                    ld    z
                    halt
x:
y:
z:
                    dw     5
```

FIGURE 3.12

Location	Object Code		Source Code		
0	0003		ld	p	; make ac reg point to n1
1	FFFF		halt		
2	0005	n1:	dw	5	
3	0002	p:	dw	n1	; this word points to n1

The first character of a label must be a letter, the at sign (@), the dollar sign ($), or the underscore (_). After the first character, digits as well as these characters are allowed. Labels can be of any length.

A label followed by a colon can appear on an otherwise blank line, in which case it refers to the first instruction or **dw** directive that follows the label. For example, in the program in Figure 3.11, **x**, **y**, and **z** all refer to the **dw** that follows these labels. Thus, all three ld instructions load 5 into the **ac** register.

mas *translates labels to the addresses to which they correspond.* This translation applies to **dw** directives as well as assembly language instructions. For example, consider the program in Figure 3.12, which shows the location (i.e., address), object code (i.e., machine language) in hex, and source code (i.e., assembly language) for each line of the program.

FIGURE 3.13

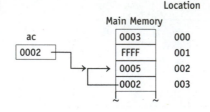

The label **p** corresponds to the location 3. Accordingly, the assembler translates the **p** that appears in the ld instruction to 003 (to be more precise, to the 12-bit binary equivalent of 003). The label **n1** corresponds to the location 2. Accordingly, the assembler translates the **n1** that appears in the *second* **dw** to 0002. Thus, the word defined by the second **dw** contains the *address* of the word defined by the first **dw**. The second **dw** is, in effect, *pointing to* the first **dw**. Figure 3.13 shows the machine language program in memory immediately after the ld instruction is executed. To emphasize that the word at location 3 is pointing to the word at location 2, Figure 3.13 shows an arrow coming out of location 3 pointing to location 2. Because the ld instruction loads the word at location 3 into the **ac** register, the **ac** register also points to location 2. The word corresponding to **n1** contains 5. Because 5 is not an address but data, this word should *not* be viewed as a pointer.

3.5   USING ASSEMBLERS

Let's learn how to use the assemblers for H1, starting with **mas**, the stand-alone assembler. We will use the extension ".mas" for assembly language files and the extension ".mac" for machine language files.

Our first step is to create a text file containing the assembly language program. You can use any text editor or word processor that can create a text file. Suppose we create a file called **fig0308.mas** that contains the program in Figure 3.8. Next, we invoke **mas**. Figure 3.14 shows the complete command line sequence. **mas** first prompts for an input file name. We can enter either **fig0308.mas** or just **fig0308** (**mas** assumes the extension ".mas" if we do not give an extension for the input file name). **mas** then assembles the program in the file **fig0308.mas** and produces two output files: **fig0308.mac** (the machine code program) and **fig0308.lst** (the list file). The latter contains the location and object code in viewable form for each statement in the assembly language program. The names of both output files are the same as the input file, but with different extensions— ".mac" for the machine code file and ".lst" for the list file. After assembling the program, **mas** displays the input, output, and list file names on the screen.

FIGURE 3.14

```
C:\H1>mas
Machine-Level Assembler Version x.x
Enter input file name and/or args, or hit ENTER to quit.
fig0308
Input file  = fig0308.mas
Output file = fig0308.mac
List file   = fig0308.lst
```

mas as initially set up treats numbers as decimal unless the base is not explicitly specified. For example, in the statement

```
dw   15
```

we do not specify a number base for 15. Thus, the assembler treats it as a decimal number. If we want the 15 to be treated as a hexadecimal number, we have to explicitly specify the hex base by appending an "h" to the end of the number, like so:

```
dw   15h ; treated as a hexadecimal number
```

Appending a "t" to the end of a number explicitly specifies the number as decimal. However, doing this is not necessary because the default number base for **mas** as shipped is decimal. Recall that numbers are treated by **sim**'s debugger as hex unless they end with a "t" (in other words, the default number base for the debugger is hex). If, for uniformity sake, you want **mas**, like the debugger, to use hex as the default, you can change **mas** either temporarily or permanently. For directions on how to do this, see the files **mas.txt** and **mod.txt** in the H1 software package.

The **mas** assembler as initially set up is case sensitive. That is, labels that differ only in case are regarded as distinct. For example, **mas** treats the labels **RESULT**, **Result**, and **result** as different labels. If, on the other hand, **mas** were *case insensitive*, then it would treat labels that differ only in case as the same. **mas** can be set to either the case sensitive or case insensitive modes, either temporarily or permanently. For directions on how to do this, see the files **mas.txt** and **mod.txt** in the H1 software package.

Case sensitivity can be adjusted for labels only. The case sensitivity for mnemonics and directives *cannot* be similarly adjusted. **mas** is always case insensitive when it processes mnemonics and directives, regardless of its case sensitivity setting. For example, LD and ld are always equivalent; DW and dw are always equivalent.

Once we assemble our program in **fig0308.mas** to produce **fig0308.mac** (the machine code program), we can then run **fig0308.mac** on **sim**. A sample session is shown in Figure 3.15. After invoking **sim**, we enter the machine code file name (i.e., the name of the ".mac" file). We can enter either **fig0308.mac** or just **fig0308** (**sim** assumes the ".mac" extension if an extension is not given). After **sim** reads in our

FIGURE 3.15
```
C:\H1>sim
Simulator Version x.x
Enter machinecode file name and/or args, or hit ENTER to quit.
fig0308
Starting session.  Enter h or ? for help.
---- [T7] 0: ld    /0 004/ u*
  0: ld  /0 004/ add  /2 005/ st   /1 006/ halt /FFFF /
  4: ld  /0 00F/ ld   /0 001/ ld   /0 000/
---- [T7] 0: ld    /0 004/       ←hit ENTER to invoke T7
  0: ld    /0 004/ ac=0000/000F
  1: add   /2 005/ ac=000F/0010
  2: st    /1 006/ m[006]=0000/0010
  3: halt /FFFF /
Machine inst count =     4 (hex) =       4 (dec)
---- [T7] q
```

FIGURE 3.16 Machine-level Assembler Version x.x

```
     LOC     OBJ     SOURCE
   hex*dec


                     ; assembly language program that adds two numbers

   0  *0    0004              ld   n1      ; get first number
   1  *1    2005              add  n2      ; add second number
   2  *2    1006              st   result  ; store sum in memory
   3  *3    FFFF              halt         ; return to operating system


                     ;           data area
   4  *4    000F    n1:        dw   15      ; first number
   5  *5    0001    n2:        dw   1       ; second number
   6  *6    0000    result:    dw   0       ; store sum here
   7  *7    ========= end of fig0308.mas ============================
```

```
                    Symbol/Cross-Reference Table

   Symbol                     Address        References
                              (hex)          (hex)


   n1                           4               0
   n2                           5               1
    result                      6               2

   Input file    = fig0308.mas
   Output file   = fig0308.mac
   List file     = fig0308.lst
   Number base   = decimal
   Label status  = case sensitive
```

program, we can confirm that it is in memory by unassembling (i.e., translating to assembly language) the program as it sits in memory. To do this, we enter **u*** (**u** is the unassemble command; "*****" means "everything"). We then hit the ENTER key to invoke the default command **T7**, which traces up to seven instructions. The program runs to completion, at which time **sim** displays the number of machine language instructions that were executed. We then quit by entering **q**.

The unassembler function in **sim** does not know which words in memory contain instructions and which contain data, so it simply treats each word as a machine instruction and unassembles it as such. We can see this in the display produced by the **u*** command in Figure 3.15. The last three words are unassembled to **ld** instructions although they are actually data words.

The **u** command does not produce assembly language in the standard form. Instead, it produces the mnemonic and hex representation (surrounded by slashes) of each machine language instruction. The hex representation is displayed with a blank between the opcode and the address.

mas produces a list file (see Figure 3.16) as well as a machine code file. A list file contains a display of each line in the assembly language program along with its corresponding machine code and location. It also includes a display of the combined symbol and cross reference tables—two tables built by **mas** as it assembles the input file. The *symbol table* contains each symbol and its corresponding address. The *cross-reference table* contains the addresses at which each symbol is referenced. We will see in Section 3.7 that the symbol table, but not the cross-reference table, is essential for the assembly process. The cross-reference table is simply a debugging aid.

Long comments in a list file are truncated on the right if there is not enough room on a line. The line containing the input file name embedded in a string of equal signs (location 7 in Figure 3.16) is generated by **mas** to mark the end of the program. It is not part of the source program input to **mas**.

Now let's examine the other assembler we have available, the one that is built into **sim**'s debugger. This assembler is less powerful than **mas**. In particular,

- Labels are not allowed. Addresses must be absolute.
- Comments are not allowed.
- Blank lines are not allowed.
- Assembly instructions are assembled directly to memory.
- An assembly listing is not generated.
- Numbers are assumed to be hexadecimal unless the decimal base is explicitly specified (by appending "t" to the end of a number).

A sample session is shown in Figure 3.17. The **a** command invokes the assembler. The "0" in the **a0** command indicates that the assembler is to use memory starting

FIGURE 3.17

```
C:\H1>sim
Simulator Version x.x
Enter machinecode filename and/or args, or hit ENTER to quit.
none
Starting session.  Enter h or ? for help.
---- [T7] 0: ld    /0 000/ a0       ←start assembling to loc 0
  0:  ld   /0 000/ ld  4            ←absolute address required
  1:  ld   /0 000/ add 5            ←absolute address required
  2:  ld   /0 000/ st 6             ←absolute address required
  3:  ld   /0 000/ halt
  4:  ld   /0 000/ dw 15t           ←"t" needed to specify decimal
  5:  ld   /0 000/ dw 1
  6:  ld   /0 000/ dw 0
  7:  ld   /0 000/                  ←hit ENTER to exit assembly mode
---- [T7] 0: ld    /0 004/ f 0 6 ←write program in memory to a file
Enter file name.   [f.mac]
simple
Writing locations 0 - 6 to simple.mac
---- [T7] 0: ld    /0 004/ u*       ←unassemble entire program
  0: ld    /0 004/ add  /2 005/ st   /1 006/ halt /FFFF /
  4: ld    /0 00F/ ld   /0 001/ ld   /0 000/
---- [T7] 0: ld    /0 004/          ←hit ENTER to invoke default command
  0: ld    /0 004/ ac=0000/000F
  1: add   /2 005/ ac=000F/0010
  2: st    /1 006/ m[006]=0000/0010
  3: halt  /FFFF /
Machine inst count =     4 (hex) =     4 (dec)
---- [T7] q
```

at location 0. We then enter the assembly language program. After we enter the program, we hit the ENTER key one more time to exit the assembly mode. The machine language program is now sitting in memory in locations 0 through 6. Because this program is in memory only, it will be lost once we exit **sim**. To avoid losing the program, we save it to a file using the **f** (file) command. Next, as a check, we unassemble (i.e., translate back to assembly language) the machine language program in memory using the **u*** command, which unassembles the entire program. ("*****" means all). Finally, we invoke the default command, **T7**, by hitting the ENTER key.

3.6   LOW-LEVEL VERSUS HIGH-LEVEL LANGUAGES

Low-level languages are languages that are "close" to machine language. The perfect example of a low-level language is assembly language. An assembly language instruction is, indeed, very close to machine language—it is just a symbolic representation of a machine language instruction. *High-level languages*, on the other hand, are not close to machine language. They do not resemble the machine language to which they are translated. A single statement in a high-level language is typically translated to several machine language statements. For example, the assignment statement in C++,

```
w = x + y + z;
```

might be translated to the four-instruction machine instruction sequence corresponding to the assembly instructions

```
ld   x
add  y
add  z
st   w
```

C++ is actually a language that has both high-level features (e.g., the loop statements) and low-level features (e.g., the shift and bitwise logical operations).

Because individual statements in high-level languages generate sequences of machine instructions, the programmer cannot specify individual machine instructions. With assembly language, on the other hand, the programmer completely determines the machine instructions that are produced. Thus, with assembly language, the programmer completely determines the machine language program. In this sense, assembly language is the most powerful programming language.

3.7   HOW AN ASSEMBLER WORKS

To translate an assembly language program, an assembler needs to know two things: the opcode for each mnemonic and the address of each label. The opcode information can be built into the assembler in the form of a table giving the opcode for each mnemonic. This table is called the *opcode table* (see Figure 3.18).

The addresses that correspond to labels have to be determined by the assembler by scanning the source program. The assembler makes a first pass over the program just to determine the address of each label. Whenever it finds a label at

FIGURE 3.18

Opcode Table
(Part of the Assembler)

Mnemonic	Opcode (hex)
ld	0
st	1
add	2
.	.
.	.
.	.

FIGURE 3.19

```
              ld    x        location_counter
              st    y        ┌───────────┐
Pass 1 scan   halt           │     3     │
is here →  x:  dw    5        └───────────┘
           y:  dw    0
           z:  dw    x
```

the beginning of a line, it enters the label and its address into a table called the *symbol table*. At the end of the first pass, the symbol table contains all the labels used in the program and their addresses. The assembler then makes a second pass, assembling each instruction using the information in the opcode and symbol tables.

Let's examine in detail the operation of a two-pass assembler as it processes the program in Figure 3.19.

The assembler starts by initializing to zero a variable within itself named `location_counter`. In pass 1, the assembler scans the program from top to bottom, one line at a time. Each time the assembler moves to the next line, it increments `location_counter` by one. Thus, the value in `location_counter` is always equal to the address of the current line. When the assembler finds a label at the beginning of a line, it enters the label and the current value in `location_counter` into the symbol table. For example, when the assembler finds **x** in the first **dw** in Figure 3.19, `location_counter` contains 3 (which is the address of **x**). The assembler enters **x** and 3 into the symbol table, increments `location_counter`, and then continues with the next line. At the end of the first pass, the assembler has built the symbol table shown in Figure 3.20.

On the second pass, the assembler "assembles" each instruction from the information in the opcode and symbol tables. For example, when processing the `ld x` instruction on pass 2, the assembler looks up the mnemonic `ld` in the opcode table, and the label **x** in the symbol table, retrieving their values (0 and 3, respectively). It then assembles these two values into the machine instruction 0003 hex, using the appropriate number of bits for each value (4 bits for the opcode; 12 bits for the address).

FIGURE 3.20

Symbol Table
(Built by the Assembler)

Symbol	Address (hex)
x	3
y	4
z	5

In Figure 3.18 we show the opcodes as hex numbers. Similarly, in Figure 3.20 we show the addresses as hex numbers. In both places, we are again using hex notation for convenience. The actual opcodes and addresses in these tables are, of course, binary numbers. Thus, to assemble an instruction like

```
ld    x
```

the assembler need only concatenate (i.e., join together) the binary opcode for `ld` obtained from the opcode table with the binary address of **x** obtained from the symbol table, using the appropriate number of bits for each. Similarly, to assemble the directive

```
dw    x
```

the assembler simply obtains the binary address corresponding to **x** from the symbol table. It then places the 16-bit form of this address into the machine language program.

If the address in an assembly language instruction or directive is an absolute address, then the assembler has to convert that address to binary. For example, for the instruction

```
ld    35
```

the assembler has to convert 35 (a decimal number) to binary and then concatenate the `ld` opcode with this binary address. Similarly, for the directive

```
dw    5
```

the assembler has to convert 5 (a decimal number) to its binary equivalent. The assembler then places the 16-bit form of this binary number into the machine language program.

3.8   USING THE DUP MODIFIER

• •

Suppose we wish to define in an assembly language program a table area that consists of five words all initialized to 0. We, of course, could use five **dw** directives:

```
table:    dw    0
          dw    0
          dw    0
          dw    0
          dw    0
```

Alternatively, we can use a single **dw** directive along with a **dup** *modifier,* which tells the assembler the number of duplicates it should generate of some item. For example, in the directive

```
table:    dw    5 dup 0
```

the **dup** modifier specifies "5 duplicates of 0." Thus, this single directive is equivalent to the preceding sequence of five **dw**'s.

The **dup** modifier becomes quite handy when we want to define large tables. For example, the directive

```
table:    dw    1000   dup 7
```

defines 1000 words, each containing 7. Without the **dup** modifier, we have to type in 1000 **dw** directives:

```
table:    dw   7      ; 1st
          dw   7      ; 2nd
               .   .
               .   .
               .   .
          dw   7      ; 1000th
```

When an assembler scans a **dw** directive with a **dup** modifier during pass 1, it must increment **location_counter** to reflect the actual number of words that are defined. For example, suppose **location_counter** contains 50 decimal when the line labeled with **table** in the following sequence is scanned during pass 1:

```
               .
               .
               .

table:    dw   1000 dup 7 ; location_counter = 50
x:        dw   22         ; location_counter = 1050
               .
               .
               .
```

The assembler would enter **table** and 50 into the symbol table and then increment **location_counter** by 1000 decimal. Then, when scanning the next line, it would enter **x** and 1050 decimal into the symbol table. 1050 is the correct address of **x** because the preceding **dup** generates 1000 words.

3.9 ARITHMETIC EXPRESSIONS IN THE OPERAND FIELD

A statement in assembly language can be thought of as consisting of distinct parts, called *fields.* The fields, from left to right, are the *label field*, the *operation field* (the mnemonic or directive), the *operand field*, and the *comment field.* For example, in the statement

```
start:  ld    x   ; hello
```

start is in the label field, **ld** is in the operation field, **x** is in the operand field, and **hello** is in the comment field. The operand field can contain the operand itself, as in

```
x:      dw  102    ; 102 is the operand
```

or the address of the operand, as in both of the following instructions:

```
ld   x     ; x is the symbolic address of the operand
st   8     ; 8 is the absolute address of the operand
```

So far we have seen either a number or a label in the operand field. We can also use arithmetic expressions in the operand field, but only the following two forms are allowed:

```
label + unsigned_number
label - unsigned_number
```

For example, the instruction,

```
st   table - 1
```

uses the "label - unsigned_number" form in the operand field. When the assembler translates this instruction, it takes the address of **table** (from the symbol table) and subtracts 1. The resulting address is then placed into the machine language instruction. Thus, when this machine instruction is executed, it stores the **ac** register contents into the location whose address is **table - 1** (that is, into the word that immediately precedes the word labeled with **table**). The subtraction in **table - 1** is *not* done by the machine language instruction but by the assembler before the machine language instruction is ever executed. Similarly, the machine language instruction to which

```
add   table + 2
```

is translated does not perform the **table + 2** addition. The assembler performs this addition and places the resulting address into the add machine language instruction. When this machine instruction is executed, it adds to the **ac** register the second word following the word labeled with **table**. Let's look at the program in Figure 3.21 that uses both the "label + unsigned_number" and the "label - unsigned_number" forms.

Because **table** in Figure 3.20 corresponds to address 6, it follows that **table + 1, table + 2,** and **table - 1** correspond to addresses 7, 8, and 5, respectively. By examining the object code shown in Figure 3.21, we can see that the assembler has, indeed, placed these addresses in the machine language instructions.

The assembly language instruction

```
st table - 1
```

specifies two operations. One operation, subtracting 1 from the address corresponding to table, is done by the assembler at *assembly time* (i.e., during the assembly of the program). The second operation, storing the contents of the **ac** register into memory, is done at *execution time* or *run time* (i.e., when the machine language instruction is executed). Let us restate this point because it is so important. When the machine language instruction for the above assembly language instruction is *executed*, a subtraction is *not* performed. The subtraction is done by the assembler when it translates the assembly language instruction. In fact, it is impossible for the subtraction in table - 1 to be specified within the st machine

FIGURE 3.21

```
            LOC     OBJ     SOURCE
            hex*dec


            0  *0    0006            ld    table
            1  *1    2007            add   table + 1
            2  *2    2008            add   table + 2
            3  *3    1005            st    table - 1
            4  *4    FFFF            halt
            5  *5    0000            dw    0
            6  *6    0008    table:  dw    8
            7  *7    0006            dw    6
            8  *8    0004            dw    4
            9  *9    ========= end of fig0321.mas ============================
```

instruction. This machine instruction contains only an opcode and an address. There is no provision within a machine instruction for specifying the three parts—"table", "-", and "1"—of `table - 1`.

The "label + unsigned_number" and "label - unsigned_number" forms are useful for accessing words that have no labels. For example, the directive

```
data:   dw  3 dup 1
```

creates three words. The label **data** is on the first word; the second and third words have no labels. We can, however, easily access them by using **data + 1** and **data + 2**, as in the following instructions:

```
add  data + 1
add  data + 2
```

3.10 SPECIFYING THE CURRENT LOCATION

• •

The following two forms in the operand field of an assembly language instruction are also allowed:

```
* + unsigned_number
* - unsigned_number
```

"*" in this context designates the current location. For example, the instruction

```
ld    * + 2
```

loads from the current location (i.e., the location of this instruction) plus 2. We can also achieve the same effect with a label. For example, an equivalent instruction constructed with a label is

```
xxx:  ld   xxx + 2
```

The latter approach, however, entails the inconvenience of labeling the current instruction.

As with the "label + unsigned_number" and "label - unsigned_number" forms, the addition or subtraction in the "* + unsigned_number" and "* - unsigned_number" forms is performed at assembly time. For example, in Figure 3.22, the operand specified in the `st` instruction (`* + 4`) is translated *at assembly time* to its corresponding address (006). Thus, the `st` instruction stores into **z** at location 6.

FIGURE 3.22

```
LOC     OBJ   SOURCE
hex*dec

0  *0   0004        ld   x
1  *1   2005        add  y
2  *2   1006        st   * + 4   ; stores into z
3  *3   FFFF        halt
4  *4   0001  x:    dw   1
5  *5   0002  y:    dw   2
6  *6   0000  z:    dw   0
7  *7         ========= end of fig0322.mas =============================
```

FIGURE 3.23

```
                              ; assume x corresponds to location 50
    dw    7                   ; 7 is a constant
    dw    x                   ; points to location 50
    dw    x + 2               ; points to location 52
    dw    x - 3               ; points to location 47
    dw    *                   ; points to this location
    dw    * - 5               ; points to first dw above
```

The asterisk can also be used by itself in the operand field of an assembly language statement, in which case it designates the current address. For example, the instruction

```
ld    *
```

loads the `ac` register with the word at the current address (i.e., it loads the `ld` machine instruction itself into the `ac` register).

If `x` is a label, then `x` and expressions with `x` are symbolic addresses. For example, if `x` is a symbolic address that corresponds to the absolute address 50, then `x + 2` is also a symbolic address (that corresponds to the absolute address 52). Similarly, expressions with "*" (the current location) also are symbolic addresses. Thus, any operand in a `dw` that includes a label or "*" is always, in effect, a pointer. If, however, the operand in a `dw` is just a number, then it is a data constant, and should not be viewed as a pointer. For example, in Figure 3.23, the first `dw` is not a pointer.

3.11   STRINGS

• •

A *string* in H1 assembly language is a sequence of characters enclosed in either single or double quotes. Each character in a string is represented in memory by a numerical code. For example, the character 'A' is represented by the binary number 1000001 (65 decimal, 41 hex). The particular set of numerical codes that H1 and most other computers use to represent characters is called *ASCII* (American Standard Code for Information Interchange). See Appendix F for a table that shows all the ASCII codes with their character equivalents.

A string is represented in memory by storing the ASCII codes of its characters in consecutive memory words. For example, the string 'ABC' appears in H1's memory as is shown in Figure 3.24a.

The ASCII codes stored in memory are, of course, binary numbers (everything in memory is in binary), although, for convenience, we will usually represent them as decimal or hexadecimal numbers. Each ASCII code requires only 7 bits (some extended versions require 8 bits). Thus, the leftmost 8 or 9 bits in each word are unused. To minimize this waste of memory, most computers use main memory that has a cell size of 1 byte (see Figure 3.24b). We call this kind of memory *byte-addressable* because each individual byte has its own address. Computers with byte-addressable memory store word items in a block of consecutive memory cells. For example, a 32-bit `int` variable would be stored in four consecutive 1-byte memory cells (see Figure 3.24c). H1's main memory is *word-addressable* because each word, but not each byte, has its own address.

Because H1 uses 12-bit addresses, it can address $2^{12} = 4096$ memory cells. Thus, if we used byte-addressable memory in H1, memory size could be at most

FIGURE 3.24   a) 'ABC' in H1's memory

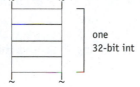

0000000001000001	ASCII for 'A' (65 decimal, 41 hex)
0000000001000010	ASCII for 'B' (66 decimal, 42 hex)
0000000001000011	ASCII for 'C' (67 decimal, 43 hex)

b) 'ABC' in byte-addressable memory

01000001	ASCII for 'A' (65 decimal, 41 hex)
01000010	ASCII for 'B' (66 decimal, 42 hex)
01000011	ASCII for 'C' (67 decimal, 43 hex)

c) A C++ 32-bit int in byte-addressable memory

one
32-bit int

d) 'ABC' in H1's memory with two characters per word

0100000101000010	ASCII for 'AB'
0100001100000000	ASCII for 'C' (padded on the right with zeros)

4096 *bytes*—half its current size of 4096 words (8192 bytes). With byte-addressable memory, we could store strings more efficiently, but at the loss of half of our memory—not a very good tradeoff. Using byte-addressable memory makes sense only on computers that use addresses with enough bits that maximum memory size is sufficiently large. For example, a computer with 32-bit addresses could address 2^{32} = 4 gigabytes of byte-addressable memory—an amount of memory that is more than enough (for now, at least).

An approach to improving the storage efficiency of strings in a word-addressable memory is to store multiple characters in each memory cell. For example, on H1, we could store two characters per memory cell (see Figure 3.24d). This approach works fine as long as the computer is capable of easily extracting the individual characters from each word. Unfortunately, H1 does not have instructions with this capability. Considering all the tradeoffs, we conclude that H1's current approach—using word-addressable memory and storing strings inefficiently (i.e., one character per word)—is the best overall approach.

Strings in assembly language can be specified with either single or double quotes. If double quotes are used, an extra code—a word containing 0—is tacked onto the end of its representation in memory. For example, the string "ABC" is represented as shown in Figure 3.25 (compare it with the string 'ABC' in Figure 3.24a).

Thus, the string "ABC" occupies four words in H1's memory, whereas 'ABC' occupies only three.

The code 0 that appears at the end of double-quoted strings (like "ABC") represents the *null character*. The null character is not really a character—it's just a special code that marks the end of a string. A string with the null character attached to its end is called a *null-terminated string*.

FIGURE 3.25   'ABC' in memory

```
┌──────────────────┐
│ 0000000001000001 │   ASCII for 'A' (65 decimal, 41 hex)
├──────────────────┤
│ 0000000001000010 │   ASCII for 'B' (66 decimal, 42 hex)
├──────────────────┤
│ 0000000001000011 │   ASCII for 'C' (67 decimal, 43 hex)
├──────────────────┤
│ 0000000000000000 │   Null Character
└──────────────────┘
```

Without a null character at the end of a string, it would not be clear where the string ends unless one knew its length. If, for example, a string of unknown length that is not null-terminated just happens to be followed by the number 65 decimal, there would be no way of knowing if this 65 (which is the code for 'A') is part of the string.

Strings usually appear in **dw** directives. For example, the directive

```
s1:    dw    'ABC'
```

defines three words in memory containing the codes for the characters 'A', 'B', and 'C'. The string

```
s2:    dw    "ABC"
```

defines four words, three for the string itself and the fourth for the null character.

During pass 1 of an assembly, the assembler must increment **location_counter** by the number of words occupied by the string. For example, when processing the directive

```
s2:    dw    "ABC"
```

the assembler would increment **location_counter** by 4, to reflect the number of words actually occupied by the string. For the directive

```
s3:    dw    10 dup "ABC"
```

the assembler would generate 10 duplicates of the 4-word string "ABC". Thus, the assembler would increment **location_counter** by $10 \times 4 = 40$ during pass 1.

Examine the program in Figure 3.26. It is not meant to be executed (it contains no instructions). We are using it simply to illustrate how string constants are trans-

FIGURE 3.26

```
LOC        OBJ    SOURCE
hex*dec

0   *0     0041   s1:     dw      'ABC'
1   *1     0042
2   *2     0043
3   *3     0041   s2:     dw      "ABC"
4   *4     0042
5   *5     0043
6   *6     0000
7   *7     0041   s3:     dw      10 dup "ABC"
8   *8     0042
9   *9     0043
A   *10    0000
2F  *47    ========= end of fig0326.mas =============================
```

FIGURE 3.27

```
\0    null character
\"    double quote
\'    single quote
\\    backslash
\a    bell
\b    backspace
\f    form feed
\n    newline
\r    carriage return
\t    horizontal tab
\v    vertical tab
```

lated to object code. You can see that the object code generated for the **s1** string consists of the ASCII codes for 'A', 'B', and 'C' (41, 42, and 43 in hex). The string at **s2** is the same except for an additional null character at its end. For the string at **s3**, the listing shows the code for only the first occurrence of "ABC", although 10 occurrences are actually generated. The address that immediately follows the ten **s3** strings is 47 decimal. Thus, **s3** occupies addresses 7 to 46 for a total of 40 bytes.

Strings can contain *escape sequences*—two-character sequences that start with "\" that represent a single character (see Figure 3.27). For example, in the string "AB\nCD" we have specified the newline character with the escape sequence "\n". Although the escape sequence "\n" contains two characters ("\" and "n"), it represents only one character (the newline character). Thus, the string "AB\nCD" requires only five words, plus one more for the null character. When this string is output, the newline character causes the "CD" portion of the string to appear on a separate line, like so:

```
AB
CD
```

The debugger's **d** command displays memory in both hex and ASCII. If there is a string in memory, it is very easy to spot in the ASCII portion of the display. For example, suppose we assemble and run on **sim** the following "program":

```
dw    'ABC'
dw    "DEF"
```

If we display memory with the **d*** command, we get

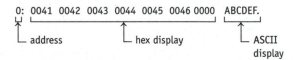

In the hex portion of the display, we see 0041 through 0046 (the ASCII codes for 'A' through 'F') and 0000 (the null character). In the ASCII portion, we see their corresponding characters. If a memory location contains a value for which there is no corresponding character, a period ('.') appears in the corresponding position in the ASCII display. Thus, the null character at the end of the second string appears as a period in the ASCII display (right after 'F').

3.12 ORG DIRECTIVE

• •

An assembly language program sometimes has a data area that is overlaid with data when the program is executed whose initial contents are unimportant. We can, of course, define such an area using either multiple **dw** directives or a single **dw** directive with a **dup** modifier. Whatever initial values we specify are unimportant because they will be overwritten when the program executes. For example, we can specify a 100-word data area with

```
dataarea:    dw     100 dup 0
```

Alternatively, we can use the **org** directive to reserve a data area. The **org** approach does not specify initial values for the data area; instead, it causes the assembler to skip over and, thereby, reserve words that make up the data area. It does this by causing **location_counter** to be reset to a new value during phase 1 of the assembly.

Examine the listing in Figure 3.28. The halt instruction is at location 4. Thus, **location_counter** within the assembler contains 5 when it starts processing the next statement, the **org** directive during phase 1:

```
dataarea:    org    1000
```

This **org** directive, however, causes the assembler to reset **location_counter** to 1000. When the assembler processes the next statement, **location_counter** contains 1000. Thus, the location that corresponds to the label **x** is 1000. Locations 5 through 999 (for a total of 995 words) are effectively skipped, and provide a data area that can be used by the program. The label **dataarea** on the **org** directive corresponds to location 5, the first word of the data area. Thus, the various words in the data area can be referenced using instructions with the "label + unsigned_number" form in the operand field, where "label" is **dataarea**.

Notice that Figure 3.28 contains no object code corresponding to the **org** directive. An **org** directive is not translated to machine code, and, therefore, has no corresponding object code.

The value specified in an **org** directive must be greater than or equal to the current location. That is, the **org** directive cannot be used to decrease the value in **location_counter**.

FIGURE 3.28

```
       LOC     OBJ     SOURCE
      hex*dec


      0  *0    03E8            ld    x              ; load from location 1000
      1  *1    1005            st    dataarea       ; store into location 5
      2  *2    1006            st    dataarea + 1   ; store into location 6
      3  *3    0004            ld    dataarea - 1   ; load from location 4
      4  *4    FFFF            halt
                     dataarea: org   1000
      3E8*1000 0005  x:        dw    5
      3E9*1001 ========= end of fig0328.mas ============================
```

FIGURE 3.29

```
          LOC       OBJ    SOURCE
          hex*dec

          0   *0    0001   x:       dw    1
          1   *1    000F   y:       dw    15
          2   *2    0000   z:       dw    0
          3   *3    0000   start:   ld    x      ; execution should start here
          4   *4    2001            add   y
          5   *5    1002            st    z
          6   *6    FFFF            halt
                                    end   start

          7   *7    ========= end of fig0329.mas =============================
```

3.13 END DIRECTIVE

In all the programs we have seen so far, execution starts at the physical beginning of the program (i.e., at location 0). There are programs, however, in which execution should *not* start at the physical beginning of the program. For example, consider the program in Figure 3.29. This program starts with data instead of instructions. Execution should start with the first instruction that follows the data (the ld instruction at the label **start**).

We call the location at which a program starts execution its *entry point*. In assembly language, we can specify the entry point of a program with the **end** directive. If an **end** directive is not used in a program, its entry point defaults to the physical beginning of the program.

In the program in Figure 3.29, the **end** directive,

```
end start
```

informs the assembler that the entry point for the program is at the label **start** (i.e., at location 3). Thus, when this program is executed, execution starts at the label **start** and not at location 0. The label on the entry point and in the end directive does not have to be **start**—any legal label is fine.

In an **end** directive, either an absolute address (i.e., a number) or a symbolic address (i.e., a label) can be specified. Notice that no object code corresponds to the **end** directive in Figure 3.29. An **end** directive is not translated to a machine language instruction, and, therefore, has no corresponding object code.

A very good question to ask at this point is this: Exactly how does the **end** directive get the CPU to start executing at the specified entry point? The CPU has to know where the entry point is. But if the **end** directive is not translated to object code, how, then, does the CPU know where the entry point is? We will defer answering this most interesting question until Chapter 10.

3.14 SEQUENTIAL EXECUTION OF INSTRUCTIONS

In all the programs we have seen so far, the CPU executes instructions from top to bottom—that is, from lower memory locations to higher memory locations, one at a time. This pattern of execution is called the *sequential execution of instructions*. It is essential (and, fortunately, easy) for you to understand the exact mechanism the CPU uses to accomplish this execution pattern.

The CPU implements the sequential execution of instructions by repeatedly performing the following four-step cycle:

1. The CPU fetches from main memory the instruction whose address is in the rightmost 12 bits of the **pc** register (only 12 bits are needed because all of main memory can be addressed with only 12 bits). When the CPU fetches this instruction, it brings a *copy* of the instruction into the CPU. The original instruction is still in memory after the fetch.
2. The CPU adds 1 to the **pc** register.
3. The CPU examines the opcode bits in the instruction that it fetched in step 1 to determine its opcode. The CPU has to know the opcode of the instruction before it can execute it. This process is called *opcode decode*.
4. The CPU executes the instruction that it fetched in step 1.

When the CPU is performing step 4 (the actual execution of the instruction), the **pc** register has *already* been incremented, so that it contains the address of the next instruction in memory. When the CPU repeats the four-step cycle, it fetches the next instruction in memory because this is the instruction whose address is now in the **pc** register. Each time through the four-step cycle, the **pc** register is incremented (in step 2) so that the next time through the cycle, the next instruction in memory is fetched and executed.

Figure 3.30 illustrates the four-step cycle in which an `ld  4` instruction is fetched and executed. The arrows shown represent instruction/data movement. In step 1, the **pc** register contains 0—the address of an `ld 4` instruction. The CPU, therefore, fetches this instruction. During a fetch, the CPU brings the instruction into a special holding area (the **ac**, **sp**, and **pc** registers are not used for this purpose). This holding area is actually a special register within the CPU called the *instruction register*, which holds an instruction during its execution by the CPU. In step 2, the CPU increments the **pc** register to 1. In step 3, the CPU determines the instruction's opcode. In step 4, the CPU executes the instruction.

To make sure you understand the four-step cycle that the CPU follows, examine the program in Figure 3.31. This is what it appears to do: The numbers at **x** (−1) and **y** (5) are added. Then the sum (4) is stored at **z**. But in fact, this program only loads **x** and then immediately halts. Here is the reason: The **pc** register contains 0 initially, causing the CPU to fetch and execute the `ld` instruction. The **pc** register is incremented to 1 in step 2 of the four-step cycle that the CPU performs. Thus, on its next cycle, the CPU fetches what is at location 1. The CPU has no way of knowing that location 1 contains data and not an instruction. The content of location 1 is the binary number 1111111111111111 (FFFF hex), which is a perfectly legitimate halt instruction. The program, therefore, halts as soon as this bogus "instruction" is executed, before it reaches the `add` instruction.

In the assembly language version of the program in Figure 3.31, it is clear that the second line of the program contains data. But in the machine language form, there is nothing that indicates this. The CPU assumes whatever it fetches during step 1 of its four-step cycle is an instruction. To prevent the CPU from executing data, it is necessary to keep the CPU from fetching data in step 1 of its four-step cycle. A simple fix to the program in Figure 3.31 is to move the second line to after the `halt` instruction. The `halt` instruction stops execution, thereby keeping the CPU from fetching and "executing" the data items that follow it.

FIGURE 3.30   Step 1: Fetch instruction addressed by pc register

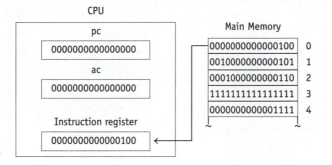

Step 2: Increment pc register

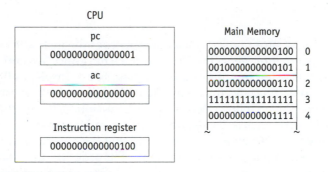

Step 3: Decode the opcode

Step 4: Execute the instruction (ld   4)

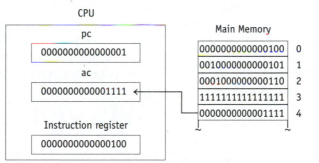

FIGURE 3.31

```
      LOC    OBJ    SOURCE
      hex*dec


      0   *0    0001           ld    x        ; load -1
      1   *1    FFFF   x:      dw    -1
      2   *2    2005           add   y        ; add 5
      3   *3    1006           st    z        ; store result
      4   *4    700B           halt
      5   *5    0005   y:      dw    5
      6   *6    0000   z:      dw    0
      7   *7    ========= end of fig0331.mas ============================
```

FIGURE 3.32

```
          LOC    OBJ    SOURCE
        hex*dec

        0  *0    0005   x:       dw   5
        1  *1    0000   epoint:  ld   x          ; need halt instruction
                                 end  epoint
        2  *2           ========= end of fig0332.mas =============================
```

FIGURE 3.33

```
1 #include <iostream>
2 using namespace std;
3 void main()
4 {
5    cout << "hello\n";
6 }
```

In a program in which data precedes the instructions, a halt instruction is still needed: It prevents the CPU from fetching and "executing" whatever is in memory following the end of the program. For example, in the program in Figure 3.32, the data precedes the instructions. The single instruction (the `ld` instruction) is incorrectly *not* followed by a `halt` instruction. After executing the `ld` instruction, the CPU will fetch and execute whatever garbage is in location 2. What about the **end** directive? Recall from Section 3.13 that the assembler does not translate it to a machine language instruction. Thus, the program in Figure 3.32 contains only two words (the 5 and the `ld` instruction). The **end** directive's only function is to indicate the program's entry point.

In high-level programming languages, we can often omit the statement that ends the execution of a module. For example, the C++ program in Figure 3.33 does not contain a **return** statement. We can get away with this omission because the compiler will automatically insert one when it translates the program. However, an assembler never performs any such automatic insertions—the assembler produces machine code *only* for the assembly language statements that you provide it. What you see is what you get.

PROBLEMS

• •

3.1. During the fetch step, the CPU in H1 fetches an entire instruction. Some CPUs, however, fetch only the opcode initially (and then later fetch the rest of the instruction). Why?

3.2. Assemble the following program with **mas**. Explain what happens.

```
    ld    x
    halt
x   dw    5
```

3.3. Assemble the following program with **mas**. Explain what happens.

```
ld ld
halt
ld:ld ld
```

3.4. Assemble the following programs by hand. Give the machine language in hex. Show the symbol table.

a.

```
        ld    add
        add   ld
st    halt
st    :halt
add :dw    2
ld   :dw    3
halt:dw     0
```

b.

```
        ld    x
        add   x
        st    * + 2
        halt
x:    dw    -3
```

c.

```
a:    dw    b
b:    dw    c
c:    dw    a
d:    dw    *
        halt
```

d.

```
        ld    x
        org   1
        halt
x:    dw    5
```

e.

```
        ld    x
        org   8
        halt
x:    dw    5
```

f.

```
        ld    6
        add   x
        add   x + 1
        add   z + 3
        add   y - 5
        add   * - 2
z:    st    y
        halt
x:    dw    3 dup 33
y:    dw    0
```

g.

```
ld    1
add   1
st    1
dw    -1
```

h.

```
      ld   x
      add  y
      st   z
      halt
x:    dw   55h
y:    dw   10h dup 22h
z:    dw   0
```

i.

```
      ld   4/2
      halt
x:    dw   3 dup 5
```

j.

```
s1:   dw    "abc"
s2:   dw    "AB\nC"
s3:   dw    'abc'
s4:   dw    5 dup "XYZ"
p1:   dw    s4
      halt
```

3.5. What is in the **ac** register when the following program halts:

```
ld    1
add   2
halt
```

3.6. What happens when the following program is run:

```
      ld   x
      dw   2006h
      dw   2007h
      st   z
      halt
x:    dw   10
      dw   20
      dw   30
z:    dw   0
```

3.7. What happens when the following program is run:

```
        ld    halt
        add   x
        st    halt
halt:halt
x:      dw    -1
```

3.8. Draw a memory diagram for the following program. Use arrows to show its pointer structure.

```
a:   dw    c
b:   dw    c - 1
c:   dw    1
     halt
```

3.9. What happens when **mas** assembles the following program?

```
     ld    x + 4096
     halt
x:   dw    5
```

3.10. Assemble and run the following program. What happens?

```
ld   1
st   -1
ld   -1
halt
```

3.11. Does **mas** accept a mnemonic as a label?

3.12. What is the largest address an `ld` instruction can specify?

3.13. What is the largest value that can be specified in a **dw** directive? The smallest value?

3.14. What happens when the following program is run?

```
ld    0
add   0
st    0
halt
```

3.15. What happens when the following program is run?

```
     halt
     ld    x
     add   x
     halt
x:   dw    5
     end   1
```

3.16. Write two programs that are identical except for a 10-word data area. One program should define the data area with **dw** directives initializing the area to zero. The other program should define the data area with the **org** directive. Assemble both programs. Compare the ".mac" files. Are they different?

3.17. What does "dissemble" mean? What does "disassemble" mean?

3.18. Assemble and run the program in Figure 3.29 without the **end** directive. What happens? What is stored in **z**?

3.19. Write, assemble with **mas**, and run on **sim** an assembly language program that computes the sum of the ASCII codes for the characters 'A', 'P', and 'Z'. Leave the sum in the **ac** register.

3.20. Write, assemble using the **sim** assembler, and run on **sim** a program that subtracts the ASCII code for 'A' from the ASCII code for 'a' and stores the result. Your program should also do the same for 'B' and 'b'.

3.21. What is loaded into the `ac` register by the first `ld` instruction below? By the second `ld` instruction?

```
        ld    s + 1
        ld    s + 5
        halt
s:      dw    "hello"
```

3.22. What is in `z` when the following program halts:

```
        dw    x
        add   y
        st    z
        dw    z
        add   z
        st    z
        halt
x:      dw    5
y:      dw    23
z:      dw    0
```

3.23. How would you store the integer 12345678 hex in a byte-addressable memory? Is there more than one way to store it? What are the advantages and disadvantages of each way?

3.24. How can a null-terminated string be defined without using double quotes?

3.25. Why does it make sense that a label may not consist exclusively of digits?

3.26. Why would anyone want to use an unassembler?

3.27. In the four-step CPU cycle, why is the incrementation of the `pc` register done in step 2? Why not in step 3 or 4?

3.28. Suppose the CPU in H1 just executed an `ld` instruction at location 4095. What would happen next?

3.29. Propose an alternative approach for representing strings that does not use the null character.

Chapter Four

H1 ASSEMBLY LANGUAGE: PART 2

4.1 INTRODUCTION

The collection of all the machine instructions available on a computer is called its *instruction set*. So far, we have studied only four machine/assembly language instructions in the instruction set for H1 (`ld`, `add`, `st`, and `halt`). In this chapter, we will study the remaining 30 instructions. You may feel that covering so many instructions in one chapter is a formidable task, but this is not the case. Most machine language instructions are very primitive—they perform only one simple operation. Thus, each instruction is quite easy to learn.

We call the set of instructions—34 instructions in all—that is built into H1 the *standard instruction set*. We can divide these instructions into nine categories: direct, stack, immediate, I/O, jump, indirect, relative, linkage, and terminating.

A summary of the standard instruction set appears in Appendix A and in the file **s.txt** in the H1 software package. You may wish to print out **s.txt** and have it available as you read this chapter.

In the preceding chapter, we displayed assembly language programs using their list files. List files show both the assembly source and the machine code for each instruction. We did this because it is important to see the connection between assembly and machine language when first learning assembly language. From now on, however, we will usually display assembly language programs using their source files, which, of course, contain only assembly language. For easy reference, we will include decimal line numbers on each line. By displaying source files instead of the list files, we will save space and eliminate unnecessary clutter.

4.2 SHORTHAND NOTATION FOR DESCRIBING INSTRUCTIONS

In assembly language, we can specify the address in an `ld` instruction with a label or an absolute address. For example, both of these `ld` instructions are legal:

```
ld    n1      ; using a label
ld    300     ; using an absolute address
```

The first instruction uses a label; the second, an absolute address. Both instructions, however, have the same form: the `ld` mnemonic followed by an address. Let's represent this single *instruction form* with

```
ld    x
```

Here **x** represents the address given by the label or absolute address that appears in the assembly instruction. We specifically use **x** because this part of the assembly instruction maps to the x field (i.e., the 12 rightmost bits) of the machine instruction.

A simple way to describe the operation of the various instructions on H1 is to use a C++-like notation. Suppose we view main memory as an array with 4096 slots. We then can represent the memory word at address **x** with **mem[x]**. With this notation, we can describe the instruction with the form

```
ld    x
```

easily and precisely with the C++-like assignment statement

```
ac = mem[x];
```

That is, **mem[x]** (i.e., the contents of memory at location **x**) is assigned (i.e., loaded into) the **ac** register. Similarly, we describe the instruction with the form

```
add   x
```

by using

```
ac = ac + mem[x];
```

That is, the contents of memory at location **x** are added to the **ac** register.

Let's now examine all the instructions on H1 category by category. We will start our discussion of each category with a list of all the instructions in that category, providing each instruction's opcode, assembly form, name, and shorthand description.

4.3   DIRECT INSTRUCTIONS

• •

Opcode (hex)	Assembly Form	Name	Description
0	ld x	Load	ac = mem[x];
1	st x	Store	mem[x] = ac;
2	add x	Add	ac = ac + mem[x];
3	sub x	Subtract	ac = ac - mem[x];

The ld, add, and st instructions all belong to a category of instructions called direct instructions. A *direct instruction* is an instruction that contains a main memory address. For example, in the load instruction,

0000000000000100

the 12 rightmost bits contain the address 000000000100 (4 decimal). When executed, this instruction does *not* load the **ac** register with 4; instead, it loads the **ac** register with the contents of location 4. In other words, the load instruction contains the address of the operand—not the operand itself.

The operand address in a direct instruction enables the CPU to go "directly" to the addressed cell in main memory (hence, the name "direct").

The fourth and last direct instruction on H1 is the *sub* (subtract) instruction. The `sub` instruction works like the `add` instruction, except that it subtracts the memory operand instead of adding it to the `ac` register. That is, it performs the operation

```
ac = ac - mem[x];
```

In the shorthand descriptions of these instructions, we use **x** to represent the address in the instruction. This address occupies the 12 rightmost bits of the machine instruction. H1 interprets this 12-bit address as an unsigned number (it would not make sense to interpret it as a signed number because addresses are never negative). Thus, the largest address that can fit into a direct instruction is the binary number consisting of 12 ones, 111111111111. This binary number equals 4095 decimal or FFF hex. The smallest address possible is, of course, 0. Thus, the range of values for **x** is

$$0 \le x \le 4095 \text{ decimal} = \text{FFF hex}$$

4.4   STACK INSTRUCTIONS

• •

Opcode (hex)	Assembly Form	Name	Description
F3	push	Push onto stack	mem[--sp] = ac;
F4	pop	Pop from stack	ac = mem[sp++];
F7	swap	Swap	temp = ac; ac = sp; sp = temp;

temp is a work register within the CPU.

A stack is a type of list. The characteristic of a stack that distinguishes it from other types of lists is that only one side of a stack (the *top* of the stack) is used when adding or removing data items. The top of the stack holds the last item added to the stack. We call the operation that places a new data item onto the top of a stack a *push* operation. We call the operation that removes the data item that is on top of the stack a *pop* operation. Only one side of a stack is used for the pop and push operations, so a pop operation always removes the item that was most recently pushed. Thus, a stack is frequently called a *last-in-first-out (LIFO)* data structure.

When a register contains the address of a memory location, we say that the register *points to* that memory location. We represent this state of affairs in diagrams by drawing an arrow emanating from the register pointing to the memory location. For example, in Figure 4.1a, the **sp** register contains FFFF. Because only its rightmost 12 bits are used for addressing purposes, it contains the address FFF, and it therefore points to the memory location with that address.

H1 implements a stack in main memory. The **sp** register points to the top of the stack. As items are pushed onto the stack, the stack grows downward (i.e., to low memory). The push and pop operations on H1 are performed by the *push* and *pop* instructions. Let's consider an example in which we use the push and pop

FIGURE 4.1 a) Before push

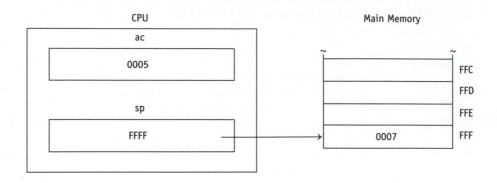

b) After push

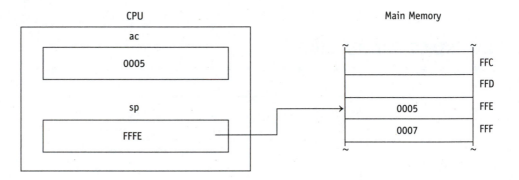

instructions. Suppose H1 is configured as shown in Figure 4.1a. If we then execute the instruction

```
push
```

the contents of the **ac** register (5) are pushed onto the stack. Specifically, the push instruction *first* decrements the **sp** register by 1, and then stores the value in the **ac** register into the new location to which **sp** points (see Figure 4.1b). Notice that we write the push assembly instruction using its mnemonic alone. The push instruction always pushes the contents of the **ac** register. Thus, it is unnecessary *and incorrect* to specify which register to push in the assembly instruction. For example, the instruction

```
push ac
```

is illegal.

If H1 is configured as shown in Figure 14.1b, and we execute

```
pop
```

the value on top of the stack (5) is first popped off the stack into the **ac** register. Then the **sp** register is incremented. Thus, H1 reverts to the configuration shown in Figure 14.1a, except that location FFE will still contain 5. However, **sp** will point above it (to location FFF). Thus, the 5 is effectively off the stack, although it is still in memory. In the pop instruction, the data movement (from memory to **ac**) occurs *before* the value in **sp** is changed (incremented). In the push instruction, the opposite occurs: The data movement (from **ac** to memory) occurs *after* the value in **sp** is changed (decremented).

The shorthand description of the push instruction is

```
mem[--sp] = ac;
```

The predecrementation construct --sp in this description means that **sp** is decremented by 1 *before* the value it contains is used to index into main memory. That is, two steps in its execution occur in the following order:

```
sp = sp - 1;
mem[sp] = ac;
```

For pop, the description is

```
ac = mem[sp++];
```

The post incrementation construct sp++ for pop means that the value in **sp** is first used to index into main memory to obtain the value to be popped, after which **sp** is incremented by 1. That is, two steps in its execution occur in the following order:

```
ac = mem[sp];
sp = sp + 1;
```

Let's determine the appropriate initial value for the **sp** register. Suppose the **sp** register contains 0 (thus, it points to the bottom of memory). What happens if we then execute a push instruction? Does the push instruction work correctly? You might expect it to fail because the stack has no room to grow downward. This reasoning, however, is not correct. During a push operation, the CPU first decrements the address in the **sp** register. It then uses this decremented address to determine where the value to be pushed is to be stored. More precisely, the CPU uses the 12 rightmost bits in the **sp** register (because addresses are only 12 bits long). If we execute a push instruction when the **sp** register contains 0, the CPU first decrements the **sp** register, leaving 111111111111111 (the binary representation of -1) whose 12 rightmost bits equal 4095 decimal. Thus, the CPU stores the value to be pushed at location 4095 decimal (at the very top of memory). The next push would then be to location 4094. Thus, the stack does not fail when it extends beyond the bottom of memory. It simply wraps around to the top of memory. If the **sp** register were initialized to 4095, then the first push would be to location 4094 (because **sp** is decremented *before* the address in it is used).

Programs on H1 normally occupy low memory. For such programs, it is advisable to put the stack as high as possible in memory to minimize the possibility of the stack growing down into the program, thereby overlaying it. Thus, the initial value in **sp** should be zero. Because **sim** initializes **sp** to zero before it gives control to a program, it is not necessary for the program itself to initialize **sp**, unless, for some reason, we need a nonzero initial value.

If we need to initialize the **sp** register, we use the *swap* instruction, which exchanges the values in **ac** and **sp**. Whatever is in the **ac** register goes into the **sp** register, and vice versa. For example, to set the **sp** register to 50, we first load the **ac** register with 50. We then execute

```
swap
```

Because the swap instruction exchanges the values in the **ac** and **sp** registers, we can also use it to obtain the current value in the **sp** register. We simply execute a swap instruction, after which the **ac** register will contain what was just in the **sp** register. Unfortunately, **sp** will similarly contain what was just in the **ac** register. By obtaining the current value in the **sp** with a swap instruction, we *necessarily corrupt the **sp*** register. We can, however, execute a second swap instruction to restore the **sp** register with its original contents. For example, suppose we execute the following sequence of instructions:

```
swap             ; corrupts sp
st @spsave
swap             ; restores sp
ld  @spsave
```

where **@spsave** is defined with

```
@spsave:  dw  0
```

The first swap loads the **ac** register with the contents of the **sp** register. It also corrupts the **sp** register by loading it with the contents of the **ac** register. The st instruction then saves in memory the stack pointer now in the **ac** register. The second swap then restores the **sp** register. Finally, the ld instruction loads the **ac** register with the saved stack pointer. At the end of this sequence, both the **sp** register and the **ac** register will contain the original stack pointer. Between the two swaps, however, the **sp** register is in a corrupted state. This presents no problem for H1. However, unlike H1, most computers have a mechanism that can trigger an *interrupt* in the middle of a program's execution. Because an interrupt makes use of the stack, the **sp** register must never be in a corrupted state when an interrupt occurs. Thus, the double-swap sequence would be a serious bug on most computers (but not on H1). We will learn more about interrupts in Chapter 14. For now, just understand that on most computers, **sp** must never be in a corrupted state when an interrupt can occur.

4.5   IMMEDIATE INSTRUCTIONS

Opcode (hex)	Assembly Form	Name	Description
8	ldc x	Load constant	ac = x;
F5	aloc y	Allocate	sp = sp - y;
F6	dloc y	Deallocate	sp = sp + y;

$0 \leq x \leq$ FFF hex = 4095 decimal
$0 \leq y \leq$ FF hex = 255 decimal

An immediate instruction is an instruction that contains the operand itself (and not the address of the operand, as in a direct instruction). When the CPU fetches an immediate-type instruction, the operand is "immediately" available—it is right there in the instruction just fetched (hence, the name "immediate"). Consider the *ldc* (load constant) instruction, which is an immediate-type instruction. An ldc instruction contains the operand in its 12 rightmost bits. For example, in the ldc machine language instruction

1000000000000001

FIGURE 4.2

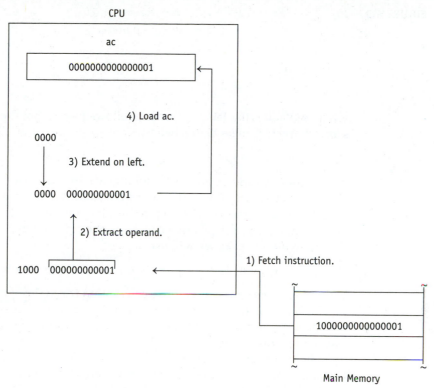

the operand (the 12 rightmost bits) is 000000000001. When this instruction is executed, its operand is extracted from the instruction, extended to 16 bits (by adding four zeros on the left), and then loaded into the **ac** register. The operand has to be extended to 16 bits because its destination, the **ac** register, contains 16 bits.

Figure 4.2 summarizes the sequence of events during the execution of an `ldc` instruction (note that all the numbers in this figure are in binary). It shows the following steps:

1. The `ldc` instruction is fetched from memory.
2. The 12-bit operand is extracted from the instruction.
3. The operand is extended to 16 bits by attaching 4 zeros on the left.
4. The 16-bit operand is loaded into the **ac** register.

The immediate value in an immediate instruction contains 12 bits. Thus, it can range from 0 to FFF hex (4095 decimal). As with the direct instructions, H1 treats the 12 rightmost bits of an `ldc` instruction as an unsigned number. Thus, the `ldc` instruction *cannot load negative numbers*. If the immediate value in an `ldc` instruction were treated as a signed number, then its range would be $-2048 \leq x \leq 2047$ decimal. `ldc` could then load negative numbers, but we would pay a price: The maximum positive number that could be loaded would be reduced from 4095 to 2047. Particularly significant is that the `ldc` instruction would not be able to load the numbers corresponding to the upper half of the addresses (2048 to 4095) on H1. This inability is far more serious than not being able to load negative numbers, so it makes sense that the `ldc` instruction works as it does. If it is necessary to load a number outside the range of the `ldc` instruction, we can always use the `ld` instruction. For example, to load -5000 into the **ac** register, we can use

```
ld      @_5000
```

FIGURE 4.3

```
1          ldc    10      ; load ac with 10
2          st     x       ; store 10 at x
3          halt
4 x:       dw     0
```

where @_5000 is the label defined as follows (recall that the at sign and the underscore character are legal in labels):

```
@_5000:   dw    -5000
```

We, of course, can use any label not already in use to define -5000. However, the label @_5000 conveys the value of the constant it defines, and, therefore, is a good choice. The underscore character in the label represents the minus sign in the constant. Thus, labels for positive constants should not have the underscore. For example, to define 5000, we will use

```
@5000:    dw    5000   ; positive, so no underscore
```

We will use this constant-naming convention throughout this book.

Let's examine the simple program in Figure 4.3. It illustrates the use of the ldc instruction. This ldc instruction loads 10 into the **ac** register. The st instruction then stores this value in **x**.

The machine instruction for the ldc instruction in Figure 4.3 is 800A. Notice that it contains the immediate operand 00A (10 decimal).

Let's review how the assembler translates the various items in an assembly language program:

- Mnemonics are translated to binary opcodes.
- Labels used within an assembly language instruction are translated to their binary addresses.
- Numbers are translated to their binary equivalents.
- Strings are translated to their binary ASCII codes.

For example, consider the following instruction:

```
ld    abc
```

where **abc** is a label corresponding to the address 9. The assembler translates the mnemonic ld to its binary opcode (0000), and it translates the label **abc** to its corresponding binary address (000000001001). Thus, the machine language instruction is 0000000000001001 (0009 hex). Now consider the instruction

```
ldc    abc
```

where **abc** is a label corresponding to the address 9. The assembler, of course, translates ldc to its binary opcode (1000), and the label **abc** to its corresponding binary address (000000001001). Thus, the machine language instruction is 1000000000001001 (8009 hex). When this instruction is executed, it loads the **ac** register with 9, *the address of abc*. Thus, this ldc instruction is, in effect, a "load address" instruction. It loads the address of **abc** into the **ac** register.

Figure 4.4 contains a short program that shows the difference between the ld and ldc instructions.

The first instruction

```
ld    w
```

FIGURE 4.4

```
 1              ld    w       ; loads 2
 2              st    x
 3              ldc   w       ; loads 7, the address of w
 4              st    y
 5              ldc   1       ; loads the constant 1
 6              st    z
 7              halt
 8 w:           dw    2
 9 x:           dw    0
10 y:           dw    0
11 z:           dw    0
```

loads from **w**. Thus, it loads 2. The first `ldc` instruction

```
ldc    w
```

loads the address of **w**. Thus, it loads 7 (8, the line number of w, is 1 more than its address). Both instructions in machine language form have 000000000111 (007 hex) in their rightmost 12 bits. The `ld` instruction loads the contents of the memory cell at this address; the `ldc` instruction loads the address itself. The second `ldc` instruction

```
ldc    1
```

loads the constant 1.

Another common form of the `ldc` instruction has a single-character string as the immediate operand. The assembler translates the string to its ASCII code and places the ASCII code in the operand field of the machine instruction. This ASCII code is then loaded into the **ac** register when the `ldc` instruction is executed. For example, the immediate operand in the instruction

```
ldc    'A'
```

is translated to 1000001 binary (41 hex), extended to 12 bits by adding zeros on the left, and placed in the machine instruction, yielding

```
1000000001000001
```

or 8041 hex. When this instruction is executed, its 12 rightmost bits, 000001000001 (041 hex), are extended to 16 bits by adding 4 zeros on the left. This 16-bit value is then loaded into the **ac** register. Thus, the **ac** register receives the ASCII code for 'A'.

Figure 4.5 shows a program with several `ldc` instructions with string operands. Notice that the immediate operand fields in the machine code contain 041, 042, and 043, the ASCII codes for 'A', 'B', and 'C', respectively. The program loads and stores in memory each of these codes.

H1 has two immediate instructions in addition to `ldc`: the `aloc` (allocate) and the `dloc` (deallocate) instructions. The opcodes for both of these instructions occupy 8 bits, leaving only 8 bits for the immediate operand. Thus, the maximum value of the operand is 11111111 binary (FF hex or 255 decimal). The operand in the `aloc` and `dloc` instructions is treated as an unsigned number.

FIGURE 4.5

```
LOC  OBJ   SOURCE
hex*dec
0    *0    8041      ldc    'A'    ; immediate operand is 041
1    *1    1007      st     x      ; store code in ac to x
2    *2    8042      ldc    'B'    ; immediate operand is 042
3    *3    1008      st     y      ; store code in ac to y
4    *4    8043      ldc    'C'    ; immediate operand is 043
5    *5    1009      st     z      ; store code in ac to z
6    *6    FFFF      halt
7    *7    0000      x:     dw     0
8    *8    0000      y:     dw     0
9    *9    0000      z:     dw     0
A    *10   ========= end of fig0405.mas ============================
```

The rightmost 8 bits of the `dloc` and `aloc` instructions hold the 8-bit immediate operand. We call this 8-bit field the *y field*.

The `aloc` instruction subtracts the immediate constant from the **sp** register; the `dloc` instruction adds the immediate constant to the **sp** register. The names of these two instructions—"allocate" and "deallocate"—requires some explanation. Suppose the **sp** register contains F201 hex. Thus, it points to location 201 in main memory because only its 12 rightmost bits are used for addressing (see Figure 4.6a). If we then execute the instruction,

```
aloc 2
```

the immediate constant 2 in the instruction is subtracted from the **sp** register, resulting in the value F1FF hex in **sp** (see Figure 4.6b).

FIGURE 4.6

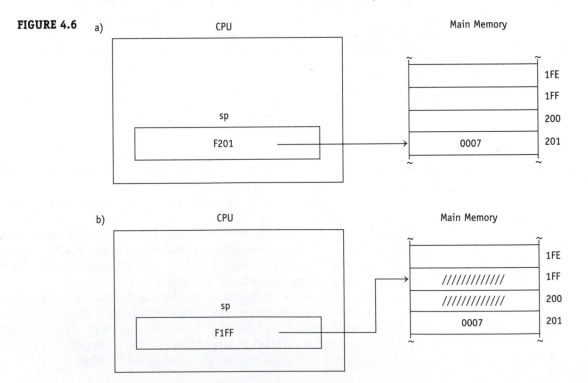

If we were now to execute a `push` instruction, the item pushed would be stored into location 1FE (recall that in a push, the **sp** register is *predecremented*). Thus, our `aloc` instruction has effectively reserved two cells on the stack (the cross-hatched cells in Figure 4.6b) that can be used by a program without the fear of being overlaid by a `push` operation. This process of reserving memory cells is called *memory allocation.* If we now execute

```
dloc 2
```

it increases the value in the **sp** register by 2, the effect of which is to unreserve the two cells reserved by the `aloc` instruction. This "unreserving" process is called *memory deallocation.* We have accordingly named these two instructions the "allocate" and "deallocate" instructions.

In the `ldc` instruction, the immediate operand can be a label, number, or string. For example, the following three instructions are all legal:

```
ldc   55    ; number 55 specified
ldc   n1    ; label n1 specified
ldc   'A'   ; string 'A' specified
```

All three forms are quite useful and will occur frequently in assembly language programs. In the `aloc` and `dloc` instructions, however, the only form that we will use is the number form. Although the assembler allows the label and string forms, it is unlikely that we would ever need either of these forms. Beware that if you were to use the label form of the `aloc` or `dloc` instruction, the address of the label must fit into the 8-bit operand field of these instructions. That is, the address must be less than 256. For example, the instruction,

```
aloc n1
```

would assemble correctly only if the address of **n1** was less than 256.

The `ld`, `aloc` , and `dloc` instructions are the only immediate instructions available in the standard instruction set. It would be useful to have more, however. For example, suppose we had an *addc* (add constant) instruction that, when executed, added the immediate operand to the **ac** register. Then the instruction

```
addc 1
```

would add one to the **ac** register. Because adding one is a very common operation in programming (e.g., to increment a counter), our nonexistent `addc` instruction would definitely be quite useful (a similar instruction that subtracts would also be useful). We do not have the `addc` instruction, however, so we have to use a less efficient approach to add one to the **ac** register: We define the constant 1 in a **dw** directive, and then add it to the **ac** register with the `add` instruction:

```
      add    @1    ; add 1 to ac register
        .
        .
        .
@1:  dw     1
```

The mnemonics for all the immediate instructions end with a "c" (for constant, as in "immediate constant"). They do not end with an "i" because we use "i" for the indirect instructions (see Section 4.8).

The `aloc` and `dloc` instructions are in the immediate category of instructions. However, because they affect the stack, it would also be correct to place them in the stack category of instructions.

4.6   I/O INSTRUCTIONS

Opcode (hex)	Assembly Form	Name	Description
FFF5	uout	Unsigned output	Output number in ac as unsigned decimal number
FFF6	sin	String input	Input string to address in ac
FFF7	sout	String output	Output string pointed to by ac
FFF8	hin	Hex input	Input hex number to ac
FFF9	hout	Hex output	Output number in ac in hex
FFFA	ain	ASCII input	Input ASCII char to ac
FFFB	aout	ASCII output	Output ASCII char in ac
FFFC	din	Decimal input	Input decimal number (signed or unsigned) to ac
FFFD	dout	Decimal output	Output number in ac as signed decimal number

The I/O instructions on H1 provide a limited input/output capability. The only I/O devices supported are the keyboard (for input) and the display monitor (for output). Except for `sin` and `sout`, each I/O instruction performs two distinct operations: it converts *and* moves data. For example, the *dout* (decimal output) instruction takes the binary number in the **ac** register, converts it to decimal, and then moves this decimal number to the monitor screen. The monitor requires the ASCII form of whatever it displays. For example, to display the number "12", the monitor must be supplied with the ASCII equivalents of the characters '1' and '2'. Thus, the `dout` instruction converts the binary number in the **ac** register to the ASCII representation of its decimal equivalent. For example, if

0000000000001100

(12 decimal) is in the **ac** register, then the `dout` instruction supplies the monitor with 0110001 and 0110010, the ASCII for '1' and '2', respectively.

The program in Figure 4.7 illustrates the use of the `dout` instruction. When the first `dout` instruction is executed, the **ac** register contains the binary number 0000000000010111 (23 decimal). The `dout` instruction converts this binary number to its decimal ASCII equivalent and outputs it to the display. The second `dout` instruction outputs 24. The opcode for `dout` (FFFD hex) occupies the entire 16 bits of the instruction.

Figure 4.8 shows the debugging session when we run this program on **sim**. In this session, we use three new debugger commands: the g (go), o (do over), and n (no display) commands. The g command causes a program to execute to completion. We use it when we do not wish to stop at intermediate points during execution. In contrast, the **T7** command executes at most seven instructions and then stops, allowing the user to examine the state of the machine. For the program in Figure 4.7, **T7** has the same effect as g because the program has only five instructions.

FIGURE 4.7
```
1          ldc     23      ; load ac with 23
2          dout            ; output 23 to display
3          add     @1      ; add 1 to ac
4          dout            ; output 24 to display
5          halt
6 @1:      dw      1
```

FIGURE 4.8
```
Starting session.  Enter h or ? for help.
---- [T7] 0: ldc  /8 017/ g       ←go to halt
   0: ldc  /8 017/ ac=0000/0017
   1: dout /FFFD / 23              ←output from dout
   2: add  /2 005/ ac=0017/0018
   3: dout /FFFD / 24              ←output from dout
   4: halt /FFFF /
Machine inst count =      5 (hex) =    5 (dec)
---- [T7] g
Now at halt. Enter o to do over, q to quit, or h or ? for help.
---- [T7] o                       ←do over
Starting session.  Enter h or ? for help.
---- [T7] 0: ldc  /8 017/ n       ←no display
No display mode
---- [T1] g
2324                              ←output from dout instructions
Machine inst count =      5 (hex) =    5 (dec)
---- [T1] q
```

In the trace output in Figure 4.8, we can see the two decimal numbers, 23 and 24, that are output for the dout instructions. If we enter the g command a second time, it does not work because the program has already terminated. Instead, sim generates a message

```
Now at halt. Enter o to do over, q to quit, or h or ? for help.
```

informing the user that the t and g commands cannot be used when at a halt instruction. If we wish to run the program again, we must enter the o (do over) command. This command resets the program execution to the beginning of the program. We now want to run the program without the trace output so that we can more easily see the output the program itself generates. To disable the trace output, we enter the n (no display) command. Then we again enter the g command. This time we see only the output generated by the program, the numbers 23 and 24. The two numbers are on the same line right next to each other because the dout instruction does not output a newline character.

If the trace output is turned off with the n command, it can be turned back on with the m (machine-level display) command. The n and m commands may be used as many times as you wish during a debugging session.

There are two ways to run a program on sim without the intervention of the debugger. One way is to use the n command within the debugger to disable trace output, as you have seen in Figure 4.8. Another way is to specify the /z argument when invoking sim. For example, if we invoke sim with

```
c:\H1>sim /z
```

sim prompts for and reads in the machine code file name, after which it immediately runs the program without any debugger intervention. Furthermore, when the program reaches a halt instruction, sim automatically terminates. The prompt for the machine code file name can be avoided by specifying it on the command line. For example, suppose the machine code version of the program in Figure 4.7 is in a file fig0407mac. Then the command

```
c:\H1>sim fig0407 /z
```

would immediately execute the program to termination without any prompts or debugger intervention, and sim would also terminate. The display would show only the following:

```
C:\H1>sim fig0407 /z
Simulator Version x.x
2324
C:\H1>
```

The *uout* (unsigned output) instruction works exactly like the dout instruction, except that it treats the number in the ac register as an unsigned number. For example, if

```
1111111111111111
```

is in the ac register, then dout would output −1, but uout would output 65535.

The *hout* (hex output) and *aout* (ASCII output) instructions are like the dout instruction except that they output the hex or ASCII character equivalent, respectively, of the binary number in the ac register. For example, suppose the ac register contains the binary number 0000000001000001 (the ASCII code for 'A'). Then dout, hout, and aout would display, respectively, 65, 0041, and the character 'A' (see Figure 4.9). Note that hout does not suppress leading zeros; dout does.

A common use of the aout instruction is to output the newline character, thereby resetting the cursor to the beginning of the next line. In the program in Figure 4.9, the outputs from the dout, hout, and aout instructions all appear on the same line producing the output

```
650041A
```

Suppose we wanted the output to look like this:

```
65
0041
A
```

```
FIGURE 4.9    1      ldc   65    ; loads ac with binary number
              2      dout        ; displays 65
              3      hout        ; displays 0041
              4      aout        ; displays A
              5      halt
```

FIGURE 4.10

```
 1      ldc  65     ; loads ac with binary number 0000000001000001
 2      dout        ; displays 65
 3      ldc  '\n'   ; load newline character
 4      aout        ; output newline—that is go to next line
 5      ldc  65      ; restore ac with 65
 6      hout        ; displays 41
 7      ldc  '\n'   ; load newline character
 8      aout        ; output newline—that is go to next line
 9      ldc  65      ; restore ac with 65
10      aout        ; displays A
11      ldc  '\n'   ; load newline character
12      aout        ; output newline—that is go to next line
13      halt
```

Figure 4.10 shows how we can use the aout instruction to create new lines. After "65" is displayed, the two-instruction sequence

```
ldc  '\n'
aout
```

on lines 3 and 4 outputs the newline character, causing the cursor to go to the beginning of the next line. Because the ldc instruction destroys the contents of the **ac** register, we reload the 65 into the **ac** register, and then execute the hout instruction, whose output now appears on the next line. On line 8, we again output a newline character, and again on line 12.

The *din* (decimal input) instruction inputs a decimal number, either signed or unsigned. When a din instruction is executed, the computer waits until a decimal number in the range −32768 to 65535 is entered on the keyboard. As the number is entered, the keyboard supplies the decimal number in ASCII form to the computer system. In particular, it supplies the ASCII code for each digit of the decimal number. Once a number is entered, the din instruction converts it to binary and places its binary form into the **ac** register. Similarly, the *hin* (hex input) instruction inputs a hexadecimal number. The *ain* (ASCII input) instruction inputs a character and places its ASCII code into the **ac** register. Commas are not allowed when inputting either decimal or hex numbers. For example, the number "3,000" must be entered without the comma. Because the din instruction can accept inputs anywhere in the range of signed numbers (−32768 to 32766) or unsigned numbers (0 to 65535), it can input either signed or unsigned decimal numbers. The dout instruction, however, outputs only signed decimal numbers. To output unsigned numbers, use the uout instruction.

The program in Figure 4.11 illustrates the use of these instructions. The din instruction reads in a decimal number, which is immediately echoed back to the screen by the dout instruction. Next, the hin instruction reads in a hex number and places its binary equivalent into the **ac** register. Next, the dout instruction on line 6 takes this binary number, converts it to decimal, and outputs it to the screen. Finally, the ain instruction inputs a character and places its binary ASCII code into the **ac** register. The dout instruction on line 10 takes this binary code, converts it to decimal, and displays it on the screen.

FIGURE 4.11

```
1     din     ; input decimal number
2     dout    ; output same decimal number
3     ldc '\n'
4     aout    ; go to next line
5     hin     ; input hex number
6     dout    ; output decimal equivalent
7     ldc '\n'
8     aout    ; go to next line
9     ain     ; input ASCII character
10    dout    ; output ASCII code in decimal
11    ldc '\n'
12    aout    ; go to next line
13    halt
```

If we run the program in Figure 4.11 and enter "12," "24," and "A," the screen will look like this (the user's inputs are in boldface):

```
12          (decimal 12 is read in)
12          (decimal 12 is echoed)
24          (hex 24 is read in)
36          (decimal equivalent of hex 24 is echoed)
A           ('A' is read in)
65          (ASCII code for 'A' in decimal is echoed)
```

The remaining two I/O instructions are for strings: *sin* (string input) and *sout* (string output). A string, in general, cannot fit into the **ac** register, so the string I/O instructions do not use the **ac** register to hold the item input or output (as do the uout, dout, din, hout, hin, aout, and ain instructions). Instead, the string instructions use the **ac** register to hold the address of the memory area from which or to which the string transfer is to take place. In other words, the **ac** register points to the memory buffer from which a string is output or to which a string is input.

A string that is read in with the sin instruction is automatically null-terminated (the null character overlays the character corresponding to the ENTER key).

Study the program in Figure 4.12. This program does not do anything useful other than illustrate how sin and sout work. At the label **inbuf** (line 14), we have defined an input buffer area. This area will receive the string that is input by the sin instruction on line 2. Before the sin instruction can be executed, the **ac** register must be loaded with the address of the input buffer area. This is the job of the ldc instruction on line 1—it loads the address of **inbuf** into the **ac** register.

Next, the sout instruction on line 3 outputs the string pointed to by the **ac** register. Because the **ac** register is still pointing to **inbuf**, the sout instruction simply echoes to the screen the string that was just read in. The aout instruction on line 5 then positions the cursor on the next line by outputting the newline character.

The remaining output instructions—the sout on line 7, the dout on line 9, and the sout on line 11—output, respectively, "x =", "5", and " (decimal)\n".

Suppose we enter the string "hello, world" when we run the program in Figure 4.12. Then the screen will look like this (the user's input is in boldface):

FIGURE 4.12

```
 1              ldc   inbuf        ; get address of input buffer
 2              sin                ; read string into inbuf
 3              sout               ; output string from inbuf
 4              ldc   '\n'         ; get newline character
 5              aout               ; go to next line
 6              ldc   msg1         ; get address of msg1
 7              sout               ; output msg1
 8              ld    x            ; load value of x
 9              dout               ; output value of x in decimal
10              ldc   msg2         ; get address of msg2
11              sout               ; output msg2
12              halt
13  x:         dw    5
14  inbuf:     dw    81 dup 0
15  msg1:      dw    "x = "
16  msg2:      dw    "(decimal)\n"
```

```
hello, world
hello, world
x = 5 (decimal)
```

When the `sout` instruction is executed, it outputs characters from memory starting at the location pointed to by the `ac` register. It stops outputting when it reaches the null character that should be at the end of the string. Thus, strings output by the `sout` instruction *must* be null-terminated. In Figure 4.12 our use of double quotes in the `msg1` and `msg2` strings automatically makes them null-terminated. If we used single quotes instead (which create strings that are not null-terminated), the `sout` instructions on lines 7 and 11 would not work correctly (try it).

When the program in Figure 4.12 is executed, it immediately waits for a string to be input via the keyboard. The program gives no indication that it is waiting, or for what it is waiting. A much better approach is to precede every input statement with a `sout` instruction that outputs an appropriate *prompt message* telling the user what should be entered. For example, we could add the instructions

```
ldc   pmsg
sout
```

to the beginning of the program in Figure 4.12, where `pmsg` is defined as

```
pmsg:  dw   "Enter a string.\n"
```

On most computers, the I/O instructions perform input/output only. They do not also perform conversions like the I/O instructions on H1. On such computers, the conversion of I/O data is the responsibility of the program that requests the I/O.

Most computer programs other than the operating system (let's call them the *users' programs*) do not execute any I/O instructions. Instead, a user's program typically passes an I/O request to the operating system. The operating system then performs the I/O (i.e., it executes the necessary I/O instructions). When the I/O operation completes, the operating system returns to the user's program. On an input operation, the user's program receives data in the form provided by the input device. For example, if input is from the keyboard, the user's program receives input data in the form of ASCII codes corresponding to the characters entered. Thus, if a user's program reads in the decimal number 123 from the keyboard, it receives the ASCII codes for the characters '1', '2', and '3'. The user's program then has to convert this string of ASCII codes to its equivalent binary number. On an output operation, the user's program must convert the data to be output to the form required by the output device. For example, to output to the monitor a binary number in decimal, the user's program must convert the binary number to a string of ASCII codes representing the digits of the equivalent decimal number. It then sends these ASCII codes to the monitor.

In C++, `cout` and `cin` provide the data conversion functions. `cout` converts data to be output to the required form. It then passes an output request to the operating system (which performs the output operation). `cin` first passes an input request to the operating system that performs the input operation. When the operating system completes the input operation, it returns to `cin`. `cin` then converts the input data to the required form.

4.7   JUMP INSTRUCTIONS

Opcode (hex)	Assembly Form	Name	Description
9	ja x	Jump always	pc = x;
A	jzop x	Jump zero or pos	if (ac $\geq$ 0) pc = x;
B	jn x	Jump negative	if (ac < 0) pc = x;
C	jz x	Jump zero	if (ac == 0) pc = x;
D	jnz x	Jump nonzero	if (ac ! = 0) pc = x;

In all the programs we have seen so far, the CPU executes instructions only once, starting at the beginning of the program. If the CPU could do no more than this, computers would not be useful tools. The time it would take to type in, assemble, and execute a program that performs a calculation would be no less (and probably more) than the time it would take to perform the calculation with a calculator. We might as well throw away our computer and buy a $10 calculator. Moreover, main memory would have to be enormous to support large computations—a billion computations would require at least a billion instructions, which would require a billion words of memory to hold the instructions.

Computers, of course, are more powerful than calculators. Their power comes from the ability of the CPU to execute instructions repeatedly. A few instructions executed repeatedly can perform millions of computations. These few instructions can be entered quickly (because there are only a few), so program creation time is short. A calculator, on the other hand, requires key operations for every computation. Thus, a million computations done on a calculator would take a very long time. In contrast, a million computations on a computer, including program creation time, might take only minutes or seconds.

FIGURE 4.13

```
1     start: ldc  5
2     again: dout
3            ja   again          ; go back to again
4            halt
```

A sequence of instructions that is repeatedly executed is called a *loop*. Loops are implemented with special instructions that alter the strictly low-to-high main memory execution of instructions. These special instructions are called *jump instructions* because they cause the CPU to "jump" to another point in the program. Let's examine the simple program in Figure 4.13 which contains a loop.

Because the **pc** register is initially 0, execution starts with the first instruction, the `ldc` instruction, which loads 5 into the **ac** register. The `dout` instruction then outputs 5. The `ja` (jump always) instruction on line 3 then causes the CPU to jump back to the instruction labeled with **again** (i.e., the `dout` instruction). The `dout` is again executed, outputting 5 (5 is still in the **ac** register). Then the `ja` instruction is again executed, causing a jump back to the `dout` instruction. Each time the `ja` instruction is executed, the CPU jumps back to the `dout` instruction. This loop results in a stream of 5's going to the screen. This program, unfortunately, has no provision for stopping. The `halt` instruction is never executed and, therefore, serves no purpose in the program. We call the loop in this program an *infinite loop* because it never ends. If you run this program on **sim** with a trace command (such as **T7**), the debugger will force a pause in execution after the specified number of instructions have been executed. If, however, you run the program with the **g** command, the program will want to run forever. After a large number of instructions have been executed, **sim** will suspect that an infinite loop is in progress, generate a warning message (which includes the current instruction count), and activate the debugger. You will see a message like the following on the screen:

```
WARNING: Possible infinite loop
Machine inst count=9C3F (hex)=39999 (dec)
Debugger activated
Enter q(quit), g(go), or other command
---- [T1]
```

You can then enter any debugger command (such as **q** or another **g**). If your infinite loop generates output (like the program in Figure 4.13) or if you are in a trace mode, **sim** will execute for a long time before it reaches the point where it generates a warning message and activates the debugger. In this situation, you can terminate **sim** immediately by entering Ctrl-Break (on a PC system) or Ctrl-c (on a UNIX system).

The `ja` instruction consists of a 4-bit opcode (9 in hex) and a 12-bit address to which the CPU jumps. As you know, the assembler translates labels to their addresses. Thus, the assembler translates the

```
ja    again
```

instruction in Figure 4.13 to a machine instruction with the address of **again** in its 12 rightmost bits. The machine instruction in hex form, 9001, contains the address of **again** (001) in the three rightmost digits. The leftmost digit is 9, the opcode for `ja`.

What happens in the CPU when the `ja` instruction in Figure 4.13 is executed? Specifically, what happens in the CPU in step 4 of the four-step cycle for this instruction (see Section 3.14)? We know that in step 2, the **pc** register is incremented so that it points to the next instruction (the `halt` instruction). But then in step 4, the CPU executes the `ja` instruction. Its execution causes the CPU to load the **pc** register with the address *in* the `ja` instruction (i.e., the address of **again**). Thus, at the end of the cycle, the **pc** register is pointing to the `dout` instruction instead of the `halt` instruction. On the next cycle, the CPU fetches and executes the `dout` instruction.

The `ja` instruction accomplishes a jump by causing the CPU to load the address in the `ja` instruction into the **pc** register. Thus, we can describe the `ja` instruction of the form

```
ja    x
```

with the C++-like statement,

```
pc = x;
```

where $0 \leq x \leq 4095$ decimal = FFF hex.

When the `ja` instruction is executed, a jump always occurs. For this reason, we call the `ja` instruction an *unconditional jump*. H1 also has four conditional jump instructions—jump instructions in which the jump occurs only if some condition is true. The `jzop` (jump zero or positive) instruction jumps only if the number in the **ac** register is greater than or equal to zero; the `jz` (jump zero) instruction jumps only if the **ac** register contains zero; the `jn` (jump negative) instruction jumps only if the number in the **ac** register is negative (i.e., if the leftmost bit is 1); and the `jnz` (jump nonzero) instruction jumps only if the number in the **ac** register is nonzero.

Notice in the descriptions of the conditional jump instructions at the beginning of this section that an action is not given for the case when the condition is not true. This is because nothing occurs during the execution of a conditional jump instruction (i.e., during step 4 of the four-step cycle) if the jump does not take place. What about the incremenation of the **pc** register (which causes the CPU to fetch the next instruction on the next cycle)? This incrementation occurs during step 2, not during the execution of the instruction (step 4). Because this incrementation *always* occurs for all instructions, we do not show it in our shorthand description of instructions.

We can use the conditional jump instructions to create loops that are not infinite. Let's examine the program in Figure 4.14, which uses a loop to compute $20 + 19 + \ldots + 1$.

The loop consists of the instructions on lines 1 to 7. The tail end of the loop consists of the instruction sequence

```
ld     count
sub    @1
st     count
jnz    loop    ; tests value in ac, which is equal to count
```

Each time this sequence is executed, the value of **count** (i.e., the value in the memory location corresponding to the **count** label) is decremented. Eventually, the value in **count** reaches 0, at which time the `jnz` instruction does not cause a jump. Instead, the instructions following the loop (which print out the sum) are executed.

count is 20 on the first pass through the loop. On the next pass, it is 19. On the last pass, it is 1. Each time through the loop, **count** is added to **sum** by the instructions on lines 1, 2, and 3.

Thus, **sum** has added to it 20, 19, . . . , and 1. Because its initial value is 0, at the end of the loop, **sum** contains $20 + 19 + \ldots + 1 = 210$.

FIGURE 4.14

```
 1 loop:    ld          sum          ; get sum
 2          add         count        ; add count to sum
 3          st          sum          ; store new sum
 4          ld          count        ; decrement count
 5          sub         @1
 6          st          count        ; put new value in count
 7          jnz         loop         ; repeat if count not zero
 8 done:    ldc         msg          ; output "Sum = "
 9          sout
10          ld          sum          ; output sum
11          dout
12          ldc         '\n'         ; output newline
13          aout
14          halt
15 @1:      dw          1
16 count:   dw          20
17 msg:     dw          "Sum = "
18 sum:     dw          0
```

4.8   INDIRECT INSTRUCTIONS

Opcode (hex)	Assembly Form	Name	Description
F1	ldi	Load indirect	ac = mem[ac];
F2	sti	Store indirect	mem[ac] = mem[sp++];

A direct instruction contains a memory address that allows the CPU to go *directly* to that address. An *indirect instruction,* on the other hand, does not contain a memory address. Thus, it requires the CPU to first go somewhere to get the address it needs (hence, the name "indirect"). H1 has two indirect instructions: `ldi` (load indirect) and `sti` (store indirect). For both of these instructions, the CPU goes to the **ac** register to obtain the address it needs.

The `ldi` instruction loads the `ac` register from the location to which the **ac** register points. In other words, it overlays the address in the **ac** register with the value from memory at that address. In shorthand notation, the `ldi` instruction performs the operation

```
ac = mem[ac];
```

The `sti` instruction stores into the location to which **ac** points. But what does it store? It does *not* store the contents of the **ac** register. Instead, it pops the stack and stores the value popped. Thus, it performs the operation

```
mem[ac] = mem[sp++];
```

The right side of this description represents the value popped from the stack. The left side is the location to which **ac** points. Notice that the contents of the **sp** register are incremented (because of the `pop` operation), but the contents of the **ac** register remain the same.

To review, the `ldi` instruction loads **ac** from the location to which **ac** points; `sti` pops the top of the stack and stores it at the location to which **ac** points.

The principal use for the indirect instructions is to dereference pointers. To *dereference a pointer* means to access the location to which the pointer points. We use the `ldi` instruction when we want to load from the location to which a pointer points; and we use the `sti` instruction when we want to store into the location to which a pointer points.

Suppose we wish to load **ac** from the location to which **p** points, and then store the value in **ac** into a variable **x**. In C++, we specify this operation with

```
x = *p;   // assign x the value to which p points
```

The dereferencing operator, *****, in this statement indicates that we should assign the value in the location to which **p** points, not **p** itself. To perform this statement, we first load **ac** with the pointer in **p**:

```
ld    p
```

causing the **ac** register to point to the same location **p** points to (see Figure 4.15a). Next, we execute

```
ldi
```

which loads the **ac** register with the contents of the memory cell to which **ac** (and **p**) point (see Figure 4.15b). Finally, we execute

```
st    x
```

to store into **x** (see Figure 4.15c),

Now let's say we wish to perform the operation,

```
*p = 5;      // store 5 where p points
```

which stores 5 at the location to which **p** points. If we know where **p** will point when we are writing the assembly language program, we could use the `st` instruction to do the necessary store operation. For example, if we know **p** will point to location 15D hex, then the sequence

```
ldc   5
st    15Dh
```

accomplishes the required task. But we cannot use this sequence if we do not know in advance where **p** will point. We also cannot use this sequence if, during the execution of the program, **p** changes. For example, suppose each time through a loop, **p** contains a new address, and 5 should be stored wherever **p** currently points. Then 5 would have to be stored to a different location on each iteration of the loop. No single `st` instruction can do this. The `st` 15Dh instruction, for example, would always store into location 15Dh. Can we use the instruction

```
st    p
```

to store in the location to which **p** points? No! This instruction does *not* do what we require—it stores into **p** rather than into the location to which **p** points.

Here is the correct way to store into the location to which **p** points. First we push the value we want to store onto the stack. For example, if we want to store 5, we use

```
ldc   5
push     ; push 5 onto the stack
```

FIGURE 4.15   a) After ld instruction

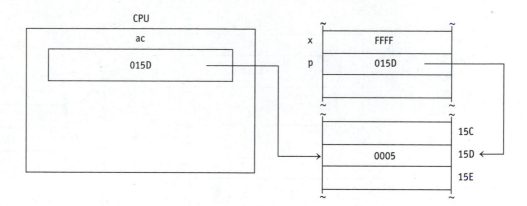

b) After ldi instruction

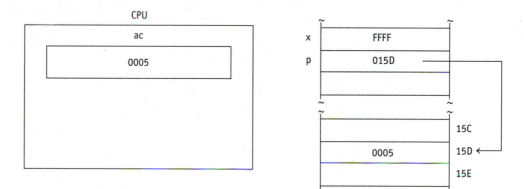

c) After st instruction

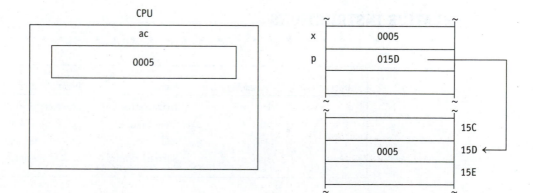

to push 5 onto the stack. We then load the pointer in **p** into the **ac** register:

```
ld    p
```

ac at this point points to the same location to which **p** points. Figure 4.16a shows the machine configuration at this point. Finally, we execute

```
sti
```

FIGURE 4.16 a) After push and ld

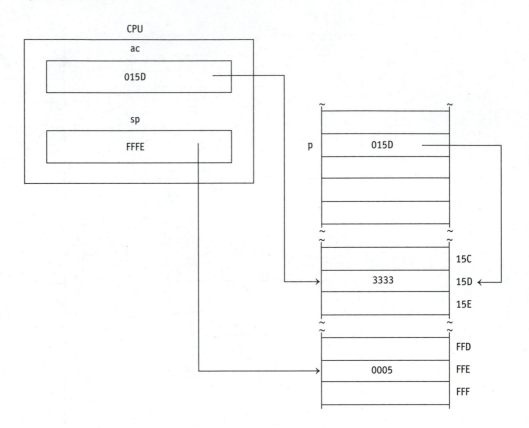

which pops the 5 off the stack into the location to which the **ac** register (and **p**) points (see Figure 4.16b)

The mnemonics for all the indirect instructions end with "i" (for indirect).

4.9 RELATIVE INSTRUCTIONS

Opcode (hex)	Assembly Form	Name	Description
4	ldr x	Load relative	ac = mem[sp + x];
5	str x	Store relative	mem[sp + x] = ac;
6	addr x	Add relative	ac = ac + mem[sp + x];
7	subr x	Subtract relative	ac = ac − mem[sp + x];

The relative instructions on H1 are instructions that contain a *relative address* in their rightmost 12 bits. For example, in the `ldr` (load relative) instruction

```
ldr   2
```

2 is a relative address rather than an absolute address. When the assembler translates this instruction, it places the binary equivalent of 2 into the rightmost 12 bits of the machine instruction. When this machine instruction is executed, this rela-

FIGURE 4.16   b) After sti instruction

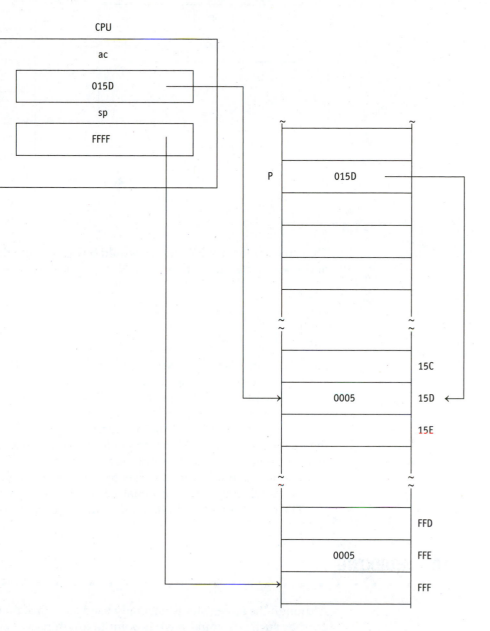

tive address and the value in the **sp** register are added together to obtain an absolute address. The load operation that the CPU then performs is from this absolute address. A relative address is dependent on the current address in the **sp** register (hence, the name "relative"). For example, suppose the current state of the computer is as shown in Figure 4.17. Then the CPU would compute an absolute address during the execution of the ldr instruction ldr 2 as follows:

```
      2   relative address in the ldr instruction
 +  F097   value in sp register
 _____
   F099   whose 12 rightmost bits (099) is the absolute address
```

FIGURE 4.17

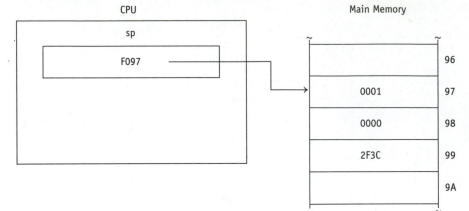

Thus, the contents of location 99 would be loaded into the **ac** register. The contents of the **sp** register are not affected. Now suppose we execute the sequence

```
push
ldr  2    ; loads from location 98
push
ldr  2    ; loads from location 97
```

Each push instruction causes the **sp** register to be decremented, so the absolute address computed during the execution of each ldr instruction is one less than that for the preceding ldr instruction. The two ldr instructions look exactly alike, but load from different locations.

As we learned earlier, relative addresses are relative to the "base" address in the **sp** register. It is for this reason that we refer to the **sp** register as a *base* register as well as the top-of-stack pointer register. Its two names reflect its dual use.

The instruction set for H1 has four relative instructions: *ldr* (load relative), *str* (store relative), *addr* (add relative), and *subr* (subtract relative).

The mnemonics for all the relative instructions end with an "r" (for relative).

4.10 INDEXING

Although the **sp** register is normally used as a stack pointer, it does not have to be used as such. We could have it point to anything we want by loading it with the proper value. For example, we could load the **sp** register with the address of the beginning of a table of numbers. Then the relative instruction

```
addr 0
```

would add the first number in the table to the **ac** register. If we then execute

```
dloc 1     ; add 1 to sp
```

the **sp** register would point to the next number in the table. Thus, another execution of

```
addr 0
```

FIGURE 4.18

```
 1                   ldc     table
 2                   swap                    ;init sp with address of table
 3 loop:             ld      sum
 4                   addr    0               ; add number pointed to by sp
 5                   st      sum
 6                   dloc    1               ; move sp to next number in table
 7                   ld      count
 8                   sub     @1              ; decrement counter
 9                   st      count
10                   jnz     loop            ; jump if counter not zero
11                   ldc     message         ; display sum
12                   sout
13                   ld      sum
14                   dout
15                   ldc     '\n'
16                   aout
17                   halt
18 message:          dw              "sum = "
19 @1:               dw              1
20 count:            dw              10
21 sum:              dw              0
22 table:            dw              56
23                   dw              -8
24                   dw              444
25                   dw              23
26                   dw              -233
27                   dw              16
28                   dw              45
29                   dw              -11
30                   dw              5
31                   dw              7
```

would add the second number in the table to the **ac** register. By repeatedly executing the instructions

```
addr 0
dloc 1
```

within a loop, we can add up all the numbers in a table. The **sp** register here is, of course, not functioning as a stack pointer. Instead, it is functioning as an *index register*—a register used to progressively index into a table.

The program in Figure 4.18 is an implementation of this table indexing technique. The program consists of a loop that is executed 10 times. The counter for the loop, **count**, is decremented each time through the loop. The **sp** register is incremented each time through the loop, causing the **addr** instruction on line 4 to add a different number in the table on each iteration of the loop. We cannot keep

FIGURE 4.19

```
 1 loop:      ldc      table      ; get address of table
 2            add      index      ; get address of table[index]
 3            ldi                 ; load table[index]
 4            add      sum        ; add sum and table[index]
 5            st       sum        ; store result back in sum
 6            ld       index
 7            add      @1         ; increment index
 8            st       index
 9            ld       count
10            sub      @1         ; decrement count
11            st       count
12            jnz      loop       ; jump if counter not zero
13            ldc      message    ; display sum
14            sout
15            ld       sum
16            dout
17            ldc      '\n'
18            aout
19            halt
20 message:   dw       "sum = "
21 @1:        dw       1
22 count:     dw       10
23 sum:       dw       0
24 index:     dw       0
25 table:     dw       56
26            dw       -8
27            dw       444
28            dw       23
29            dw       -233
30            dw       16
31            dw       45
32            dw       -11
33            dw       5
34            dw       7
```

the running sum of the numbers in the **ac** register because we need the **ac** register to decrement the loop count. Similarly, we cannot keep the loop count in the **ac** register because we need the **ac** register for the addr instruction. Thus, we use two memory locations—**sum** and **count**—to hold the running sum and the loop counter, respectively.

Most computers have either registers specifically designated for indexing or general-purpose registers that are available for indexing. H1, unfortunately, has no such registers. Because we usually need the **sp** register as a top-of-stack pointer, it is not available as an index register.

Let's rewrite the program in Figure 4.18 without using the sp register as an index register. Instead, we will use a variable index to hold the index for table. The program is given in Figure 4.19.

The instruction on line 2 adds the contents of **index** and the address of **table**, after which the **ac** register contains the address of **table[index]**. Then the ldi instruction on line 3 loads the contents of **table[index]** into the **ac** register. Next, **sum** is added to the **ac** register, and the result is stored back in **sum** on line 5. Lines 6 to 8 then increment **index** in preparation for the next iteration of the loop. Thus, lines 1 to 8 perform the operation

```
sum = sum + table[index++];
```

The remainder of the loop decrements **count** , and then performs an exit test.

In the programs in Figures 4.18 and 4.19, it would be useful to have multiple accumulator registers. Then we would not have to load and store the running sum, the loop count, and in Figure 4.19, the index on each iteration of the loop. Instead, we could keep them in the accumulator registers. Of course, multiple accumulator registers would necessitate additional instructions to access these new registers. H1's lack of an adequate number of index and accumulator registers is a major shortcoming of its design.

4.11 LINKAGE INSTRUCTIONS

Opcode (hex)	Assembly Form	Name	Description
E	call x	Call procedure	mem[--sp] = pc; pc = x;
F0	ret	Return	pc = mem[sp++];

It is important to design and implement large programs as a collection of small modules. Each module should perform an easily understood function, and be small enough to be easily written, debugged, and tested. To do otherwise—to write a large program as a single large module—usually results in a program whose structure is so complex that understanding, debugging, and testing it become very difficult tasks.

When a program consists of more than one module, it is necessary, of course, for the execution of the program to jump to and from the various modules. We call instructions that perform this function *linkage instructions*. Depending on the programming language in use, the modules that make up a large program are variously called *modules, functions, procedures,* or *subroutines.* In some languages, the module that gets control first has to have a special name. For example, in C++, the module executed first has to have the name *main*.

H1 has two linkage instructions: the *call* instruction, and the *ret* (return) instruction. The *call* instruction causes the CPU to jump to the beginning of a module. We refer to the module that is the target of this jump as the *called module.* We refer to the module that contains the call instruction as the *calling module.* A ret instruction at the end of the called module causes the CPU to jump back to the instruction that follows the *call* instruction in the calling module (see Figure 4.20).

FIGURE 4.20

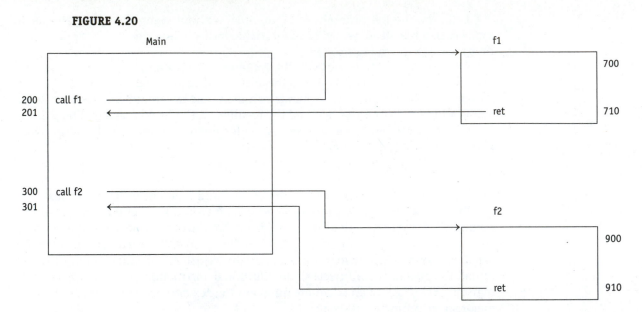

The address that the ret instruction returns to (i.e., the address of the instruction that follows the call instruction) is referred to as the *return address*. For example, in Figure 4.20, if the first call instruction is at location 200 hex, then its associated return address is 201. The effect of the ret instruction—causing the CPU to jump to the return address—is described as *returning control to the caller*.

Let's examine the mechanism used within the CPU to accomplish calls and returns. During the execution of the call instruction, the CPU

1. pushes onto the stack (and thereby saves) the contents of the **pc** register.
2. causes an unconditional jump to the address contained in the call instruction by loading the **pc** register with this address.

The value pushed onto the stack is none other than the return address. Recall that in the CPU's four-step cycle, the **pc** register is incremented (in step 2) *before* the instruction is executed (in step 4). Thus, when a call instruction is executed in step 4, the **pc** register contains the address of the instruction that follows the call instruction (i.e., the return address).

When a ret instruction is executed at the end of the called module, the return address on the stack is popped off the stack and loaded into the **pc** register. This new address in the **pc** register, of course, causes the CPU to jump back to this address and execute instructions starting from there.

Figure 4.21 shows snapshots of the computer at various points during the execution of a call and a ret instruction. In Figure 4.21a, the call instruction is about to be executed. The **pc** register has already been incremented, and, therefore, contains the return address.

In Figure 4.21b, the execution of the call instruction has been completed. The return address is now on the top of the stack. The CPU is about to fetch the first instruction in the called module.

In Figure 4.21c, the ret instruction is about to be executed. The **pc** register has already been incremented. Whatever the **pc** register is pointing to will not be executed because the ret instruction loads the **pc** register with the return address 201.

FIGURE 4.21 a) About to execute call instruction (step 4 in CPU cycle).

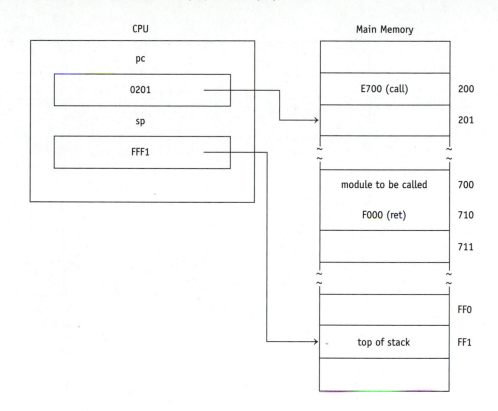

b) Execution of call instruction has been completed. The return address
has been pushed and a jump to called module has occurred.

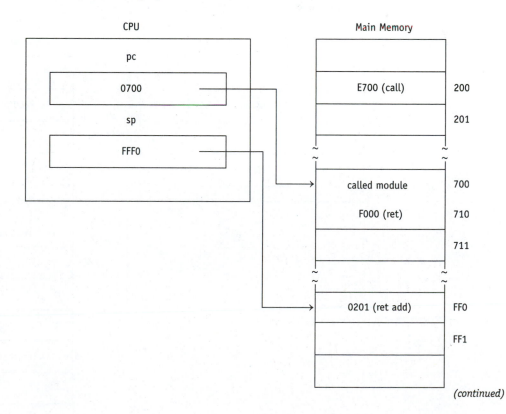

(continued)

FIGURE 4.21
(continued)

c) About to execute ret instruction (step 4 of CPU cycle).

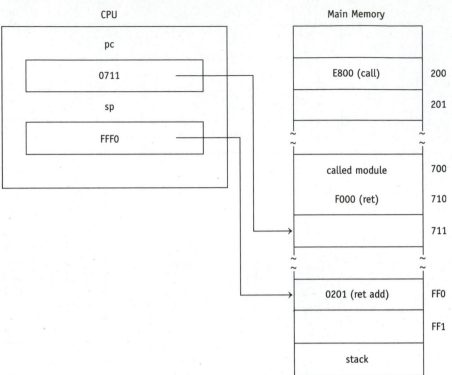

d) Execution of the ret instruction has been completed. The return address has been popped into the **pc** register. The instruction at the return address is about to be fetched and executed.

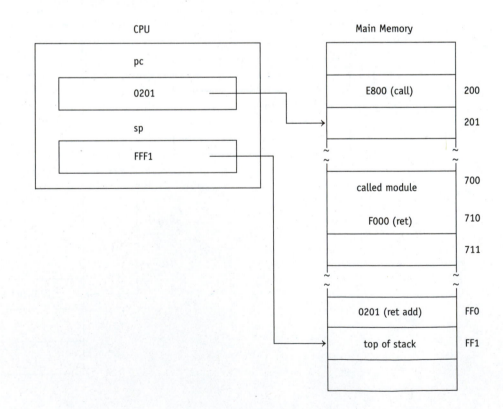

```
FIGURE 4.22   1          ;            main module -- illustrates call instruction
              2          call f1
              3 ret1:    ldc  msgmain
              4          sout
              5          call f2
              6 ret2:    halt
              7 msgmain: dw   "middle"
              8 ; =========================================================
              9          ;           module f1 -- outputs string "left"
             10 f1:      ldc  msgf1
             11          sout
             12          ret
             13 msgf1:   dw   "left"
             14 ; =========================================================
             15          ;           module f2 -- outputs string "right\n"
             16 f2:      ldc  msgf2
             17          sout
             18          ret
             19 msgf2:   dw   "right\n"
```

Figure 4.21d corresponds to immediately after the execution of the `ret` instruction. The CPU is about to fetch and execute the instruction at the return address.

Now let's look at the program in Figure 4.22, which is structured into three modules: **main**, **f1**, and **f2**. **main** first calls **f1**, which outputs "left". On return, **main** itself outputs "middle". Finally, **main** calls **f2**, which outputs "right\n". Thus, the combined output is

```
left middle right
```

Notice that each boundary between modules in Figure 4.22 is clearly identified with a comment containing equal signs. This use of comment lines is highly recommended—it greatly improves the readability of the program. In addition, each module should start with comments describing its function and providing any other information that might be useful to a programmer.

The `call` and `ret` instructions in Figure 4.22 can easily be replaced with `ja` instructions. For example, the instruction

```
call f1
```

in the **main** module can be replaced with

```
ja    f1
```

The `ret` instruction in `f1` can be replaced with

```
ja    ret1
```

where **ret1** is a label in **main** on the line following the first call. This replacement technique, however, does not always work. Consider the calling structure shown in Figure 4.23. **f1** is called from more than one point in the main module. How can the `ret` instruction be replaced with a `ja`? On the first call, the return address is 201; on the second call, the return address is 301. A `ja` instruction could jump back to only one of these addresses. Thus, it would work for one call but not the other.

FIGURE 4.23

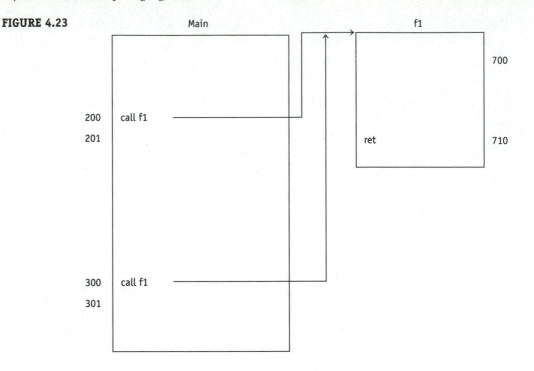

Notice that the description of the call instruction at the beginning of this section indicates that the **pc** register contents are pushed *before* the **pc** register is loaded with the address contained in the instruction. The description of the ret instruction is simple: It indicates that ret performs a pop operation, just like a pop instruction, except the pop is into the **pc** register instead of the **ac** register.

4.12 TERMINATING INSTRUCTIONS

Opcode (hex)	Assembly Form	Name	Description
FFFE	bkpt	Breakpoint	Trigger breakpoint
FFFF	halt	Halt	Trigger halt

H1 has two *terminating instructions* (i.e., instructions that stop execution): the halt instruction and the *bkpt* (breakpoint) instruction. Both instructions stop execution of the program. The bkpt instruction, however, allows a program to continue with the next instruction—just enter the **t** or **g** debugger commands. If, on the other hand, a halt instruction stops execution, then the **t** or **g** commands will not work unless you enter the **o** (do over) command first. The **o** command starts a new debugging session with program execution reset to the beginning of the program.

The bkpt instruction is typically used for debugging. A bkpt instruction is placed at every point (called a *breakpoint*) in a defective program at which the state of the computer needs to be examined. The program is then run with the **g** command. Execution stops at every breakpoint, allowing the user to examine the state of the computer at that point. When stopped at a breakpoint, execution of the program can be continued by entering the **g** or **t** commands.

If you wish to run a program that contains breakpoints without stopping at the breakpoints, enter the **z** command at the debugger's prompt. The **z** command also causes **sim** to suppress any trace output, and to terminate when a halt instruction is reached.

4.13 AUTOMATIC GENERATION OF INSTRUCTIONS IN HIGH-LEVEL LANGUAGES

In high-level languages, instructions that stop execution or return control to a calling module are not always required. For example, the C++ function

```
void f()
{
    cout << "hello\n";
}
```

is lacking a **return** statement. This function, however, works correctly because the C++ compiler automatically inserts the appropriate return instruction at the end of the function. In assembly language, no such automatic generation occurs. The machine code produced by the assembler contains *only* what the assembly language source program specifies. Thus, every assembly language module must contain the appropriate instruction (a halt or a ret) to end its execution.

One common misconception is that the **end** directive will generate a halt or ret instruction. This is not true. The **end** directive is not translated into machine code. Its only function is to inform the assembler of the program's entry point.

A halt instruction should never immediately follow a ret instruction. For example, in the sequence,

```
ret
halt
```

the ret instruction returns control to the calling module. Thus, the halt instruction will never be executed. Its inclusion just wastes memory.

4.14 DEBUGGING

The debugger that is built into **sim** is a very useful tool for debugging programs. Instruction execution can be monitored one instruction at a time or in groups. The state of the machine (i.e., register and memory contents) can be examined easily. A log file can be created recording all the activity in an entire run. A log file is invaluable when trying to find an elusive bug because it can record an entire run, if you wish, and you can print it out for offline perusal.

Here are a few commands that you will find useful when debugging. A breakpoint can be established *without* a bkpt instruction by entering the **b** (breakpoint) command at the debugger's prompt. For example, the command

b12

establishes a breakpoint at location 12 *hex*. Whenever the breakpoint is no longer needed, it can be killed (i.e., removed) by entering the **k** (kill breakpoint) command:

```
k
```

The **b** command can establish only one breakpoint at a time. To establish multiple breakpoints, you must use bkpt instructions.

The **w** (watchpoint) command is like the **b** command, except it establishes a watchpoint rather than a breakpoint at the specified address. A *watchpoint* stops execution when any instruction writes to the specified address. The **w** command makes it easy to find an instruction that is corrupting some location in your program. You simply set a watchpoint on that location and run your program. The watchpoint will stop execution immediately after the offending instruction is executed. To kill a watchpoint, enter the **kw** command.

The **mr** (machine-level display plus reads) command adds the "plus reads" option to the machine-level display mode. With this option, all the regular information plus any address read from (other than for instruction fetches) is displayed in the trace. For example, the following is the trace of a ldi instruction in this mode:

```
1: ldi   /F1 00/ [064]  ac=0064/0000
```

The number within square brackets is provided by the "plus reads" option. It is the address from which the ldi instruction reads. To cancel the "plus reads" optiom, enter the **mr-** command.

The **ms** (machine-level display plus source) command adds the "plus source" option to machine-level display mode. With this option, all the regular information plus the original source code—including labels and comments—is displayed as instructions are executed. If you want only source code displayed, then use the **mso** (machine-level display source only) command instead of the **ms** command.

Once you enter the **ms** or **mso** command, you can use labels as well as numbers in debugger commands. For example, you can enter

```
bloop
```

to set a breakpoint at the location in your program corresponding to the label **loop**. If a label spells out a hex constant, **sim** will treat it as a hex constant rather than a label. For example, the command

```
bf1
```

sets a breakpoint at location **f1** hex, even if your program contains the label **f1**. If, however, you enter

```
b'f1
```

sim will treat **f1** as a label (because the leading quote) and will set a breakpoint at the corresponding address. To cancel the "plus source" or the "source only" option, enter the **ms-** command.

The **d** command displays the contents of memory. If a starting address is not specified in the **d** command, then the block of memory displayed is the one right after the one displayed with the previous use of the **d** command. For example, to display successive blocks of memory starting from location 100 hex, enter

```
d100
d
d
d
```

To display the memory pointed to by the **sp** register (i.e., to display the stack), enter

d$

$ represents the address in the **sp** register. To display the memory pointed to by the **ac** register, enter

d@

@ represents the address in the **ac** register. To display all memory currently in use, enter

d*

* represents "all."

The debugger's prompt always shows the instruction to be executed next (i.e., the instruction pointed to by the **pc** register). However, sometimes it is handy to look at not only this instruction, but also the ones that follow it. To do this, enter

u%

This command causes the unassembly of the instruction sequence starting with the instruction pointed to by the **pc** register. % represents the address in the **pc** register.

We have used two display modes so far: machine-level display mode (activated by the **m** command) and no display mode (activated by the **n** command). A third display mode, *partial machine-level display mode* (activated by the **p** command), is also available. The partial machine-level display mode is particularly useful for identifying the location of an infinite loop within a program. It displays the contents of the **pc** register whenever an instruction is fetched. In Figure 4.24, we see the partial machine-level display of a program that contains an infinite loop. The partial machine-level display clearly shows that the program is in a loop consisting of the instructions in locations 3 to 6.

Six more commands that are useful for debugging are the **e** (edit), **a** (assemble), **r** (register), **j** (jump), **hd** (hex to decimal), and **dh** (decimal to hex) commands. We saw the **e** command in Chapter 2 and the **a** command in Chapter 3. Both the **e** and **a** commands allow the user to change the contents of any memory location. The **r** command allows the user to display and optionally change the contents of

FIGURE 4.24

```
Starting session.     Enter h or ? for help.
—  [T7] 0: ldc  /8 005/ p
Partial machine-level display mode
—  [T77]t7
0/1/2/3/4/5/6/
—  [T7]                    ←hit ENTER to invoke default command T7
3/4/5/6/3/4/5/
—  [T7]                    ←hit ENTER to invoke default command T7
6/3/4/5/6/3/4/
—  [T7]                    ←hit ENTER to invoke default command T7
5/6/3/4/5/6/3/
—  [T7] q
```

FIGURE 4.25   Starting session.   Enter h or ? for help.

```
----  [T7]  0:  1d   /0  018/ e10          ←edit from loc 10 hex
  10:  0014/003a                           ←enter new value for loc 10
  11:  0053/003b                           ←enter new value for loc 11
  12:  0075/                               ←hit ENTER to exit edit mode
----  [T7]  0:  1d   /0  018/ a3           ←assemble from loc 3
   3:  1d   /0  010/ pop                   ←assemble new inst for loc 3
   4:  sub  /3  00F/                        ←hit ENTER to exit assembly mode
----  [T7]  0:  1d   /0  018/ r*           ←display all registers
      pc   = 0000    sp   = 0000    ac   = 0000
----  [T7]  0:  1d   /0  018/ rsp          ←display/edit sp
      sp = 0000/ffff                       ←enter a new value for sp
----  [T7]  0:  1d   /0  018/ j3           ←jump to loc 3
----  [T7]  3:  pop /F4 00/ hd ffff        ←convert hex to decimal
      unsigned: 65535 (dec)  signed: -1 (dec)
----  [T7]  3:  pop /F4 00/ dh -1          ←convert decimal to hex
      FFFF (hex)
----  [T7]  3:  pop /F4 00/ q              ←quit
```

any register. If we specify an asterisk in the **r** command, all registers are displayed. If, on the other hand, we specify a register name, only that register is displayed; moreover, the user can then enter a new value for it. The **j** command causes a jump to the specified address. The **hd** command converts a hex number to its decimal equivalent; the **dh** command converts a decimal number to its hex equivalent. The **hd** command displays two decimal numbers corresponding to the signed and unsigned interpretations of the hex number. For example, if the hex number is FFFF, **hd** displays both 65535 (the value of FFFF as an unsigned number), and −1, the value of FFFF as a signed number).

In the sample session in Figure 4.25, we demonstrate a variety of commands. We use

- **e10** to put new values into locations 10 and 11 hex
- **a3** to place a new instruction (pop) at location 3
- **r*** to display all registers
- **rsp** to put FFFF hex into the **sp** register
- **j3** to jump to location 3
- **hd** to convert FFFF to decimal
- **dh** to convert −1 to hex
- **q** to quit

The **o** command (do over) reinitializes memory. Thus, if we use the **a** or **e** command to modify memory and then use the **o** command, the changes we make with the **a** or **e** command will be wiped out. To avoid this problem, use the **o#** command instead of the **o** command. The **o#** command works exactly like the regular **o** command, except that it does not reinitialize memory.

FIGURE 4.26   `C:\H1>`**`sim none`**

```
Simulator Version x.x

Starting session.   Enter h or ? for help.
---- [T7]  0: ld    /0 000/ rac
       ac = 0000/5                    ←set ac to 5
---- [T7]  0: ld    /0 000/ rsp
       sp = 0000/ffff                 ←set sp to ffff
---- [T7]  0: ld    /0 000/ efff    ←edit memory starting at loc fff
FFF: 0000/7
Now at upper limit of main memory--exiting edit mode
---- [T7]  0: ld    /0 000/ a0       ←assemble starting at loc 0
   0: ld    /0 000/ push
   1: ld    /0 000/                   ←hit ENTER to exit assembly mode
---- [T7]  0: push /F1 00/ t1        ←execute one instruction
   0: push /F3 00/ m[FFE]=0000/0005 sp=FFFF/FFFE
---- [T1]  1: ld    /0 000/ r*       ←display all registers
       pc   = 0001     sp =    FFFE    ac    = 0005
---- [T1]  1: ld    /0 000/ d$       ←display stack
FFE: 0005 0007
---- [T1]  1: ld    /0 000/ q        ←quit
```

The debugger can also be useful for simply observing the operation of H1. For example, if we want to confirm the operation of the `push` instruction as illustrated in Figure 4.1a and Figure 4.1b, we can use the debugger to configure H1 exactly as shown in Figure 4.1a. We can then execute a `push` instruction and examine the state of H1 to see if it agrees with Figure 4.1b. Figure 4.26 shows the session in which we do this. We use **r** to initialize **ac** and **sp**, **e** to initialize memory, and **a** to load the `push` instruction into location 0. Next, we use **t1** to execute just the `push` instruction. Finally, we use the **r*** (display all registers) and **d$** (display stack) commands to see its effect. Notice in Figure 4.26 that edit mode automatically exits when at the upper limit of memory.

Let's use the debugger to find the bugs in the program in Figure 4.27.

This program consists of two routines: **main** and **get_sum**. **main** pushes two numbers (2 and 3) onto the stack. It then calls **get_sum**, which accesses and adds the numbers on the stack using relative instructions. With the sum in the **ac** register, **get_sum** executes the `ret` instruction, returning control to line 10 in **main**. **main** then displays the sum in the **ac** register with a `dout` instruction. Let's run this program with the debugger to see what happens. Figure 4.28a shows the result.

From the trace, we can immediately identify a problem: The program is starting at **get_sum** instead of **main**. A quick check of the assembly program reveals that we forgot to specify the entry point with an **end main** statement.

Let's enter **o** to do over the program, and then immediately enter **j3** to jump to the correct entry point (we will correct the assembly language program later). Then enter **g** to execute to a `halt` instruction. Figure 4.28b shows the result. The execution pattern seems right, but we get the wrong answer (11 instead of 5). So

FIGURE 4.27

```
 1 get_sum: ldr   0           ; get second number
 2          addr  1           ; add first number
 3          ret               ; return sum in ac register
 4 ;===============================================
 5 main:  ld    x
 6        push              ; push first number
 7        ld    y
 8        push              ; push second number
 9        call  get_sum     ; call function which adds two numbers
10        dout              ; display number
11        ldc   '\n'        ; output newline character
12        aout
13        halt
14        x:    dw    2
15        y:    dw    3
```

let's examine the `ldr` and `addr` instructions at locations 0 and 1 in the trace in Figure 4.28b. We can see that the `ldr` is loading 8 (it's supposed to load 3 from the stack). Let's see if we can determine where this 8 is coming from. Look for an 8 in the trace. We find one in the `call` instruction—it pushes 8, the return address, onto the stack. Our `ldr 0` instruction loads this 8. Eureka! Our `ldr` instruction has the wrong relative address—we forgot to consider the return address on the stack when we determined the relative address of the stack operands. We should have used `ldr 1` and `addr 2` in **get_sum.**

Let's fix the incorrect instructions in **get_sum.** Figure 4.28c shows the commands to use. We enter the **a** command to assemble the correct instructions to locations 0 and 1. We then use **o#** to do over, but without reinitializing memory (we want to avoid wiping out our corrections). Alternatively, we could have entered **o** first, then **a**. Next, enter **j3** and **g** to run the program. It now runs correctly so we incorporate all our fixes in the assembly language program.

The **o** command allows you to rerun the current program. If, however, you use the **o&** command instead, **sim** will prompt for a new machine code file name, and will run whatever file you specify. Using this command, you do not have to exit and restart **sim** every time you want to run a different machine code file.

4.15   USING MEMORY-MAPPED I/O

● ●

The I/O instructions on H1 are somewhat unrealistic because they convert data in addition to transferring data. For example, the `dout` instruction converts the binary number in the **ac** register to the sequence of ASCII codes that represents its decimal value. `dout` then sends these codes to the monitor. Thus, if the **ac** register contains 0000000000001111 (15 decimal), `dout` converts this binary number to 00110001 00110101 (the ASCII codes for '1' and '5'). It then sends these two codes to the monitor. I/O instructions on real computers simply transfer data. Conversions have to be performed by conversion instructions (such as **System.out.println** in Java or **cout** in C++). The I/O instructions on H1 also

FIGURE 4.28   a)

```
Starting session. Enter h or ? for help.
---- [T7] 0: ldr      /4 000/            ←hit ENTER to invoke T7
   0: ldr  /4 000/   ac=0000/4000        ←wrong entry point
   1: addr /6 001/   ac=4000/A001
   2: ret  /F0 00/   pc=0003/4000  sp=0000/0001
   0: ldr  /4 000/   ac=A001/6001
   1: addr /6 001/   ac=6001/5001
   2: ret  /F0 00/   pc=4003/6001  sp=0001/0002
   1: addr /6 001/   ac=5001/500D
---- [T7] 2: ret   /F0 00/
```

b)

```
---- [T7] 2: ret   /F0 00/ o            ←do over
Starting session.  Enter h or ? for help.
---- [T7] 0: ldr      /4 000/ j3         ←jump to correct entry point
---- [T7] 3: ld       /0 00C/ g          ←go to halt
   3: ld   /0 00C/   ac=0000/0002
   4: push /F3 00/   m[FFF]=0000/0002  sp=0000/FFFF
   5: ld   /0 00D/   ac=0002/0003
   6: push /F3 00/   m[FFE]=0000/0003  sp=FFFF/FFFE
   7: call /E 000/   m[FFD]=0000/0008  pc=0008/0000   sp=FFFE/FFFD
   0: ldr  /4 000/   ac=0003/0008      ←this load not working correctly
   1: addr /6 001/   ac=0008/000B
   2: ret  /F0 00/   pc=0003/0008  sp=FFFD/FFFE
   8: dout /FFFD /   11                ←wrong answer
   9: ldc  /8 00A/   ac=000B/000A
   A: aout /FFFB /

   B:halt /FFFF /
Machine inst count =    C (hex) =    12 (dec)
---- [T7]
```

c)

```
---- [T7] a0                            ←assembly from loc 0
   0: ldr  /4 000/   ldr 1              ←correct relative address
   1: addr /6 001/   addr 2             ←correct relative address
   2: ret  /F0 00/
---- [T7] o#                            ←do over but don't reinit mem
Starting session. Enter h or ? for help.
---- [T7] 0: ldr      /4 001/ j3         ←jump to correct entry point
---- [T7] 3: ld       /0 00C/ g          ←go to halt
   3: ld   /0 00C/   ac=0000/0002
   4: push /F3 00/   m[FFF]=0002/0002  sp=0000/FFFF
   5: ld   /0 00D/   ac=0002/0003
```

(continued)

FIGURE 4.28

(continued)

```
6: push /F3 00/    m[FFE]=0003/0003   sp=FFFF/FFFE
7: call /E 000/    m[FFD]=0008/0008   pc=0008/0000   sp=FFFE/FFFD
0: ldr  /4 001/    ac=0003/0003
1: addr /6 002/    ac=0003/0005
2: ret  /F0 00/    pc=0003/0008   sp=FFFD/FFFE
8: dout /FFFD /    5                              ←correct answer
9: ldc  /8 00A/    ac=0005/000A
A: aout /FFFB /


B: halt /FFFF /
Machine inst count =    C (hex) =    12 (dec)
---0 [T7] q
```

FIGURE 4.29

Memory-Mapped Locations

Location (decimal)	Function
3000	Keyboard status (1 = ready; 0 = not ready)
3001	Keyboard data
3002	Monitor status (1 = ready; 0 = not ready)
3003	Monitor data

do not incur any of the delays that are typically associated with I/O operations on real systems. They all complete quickly in exactly the same amount of time. Because of the unrealistic nature of the I/O instructions on H1, we call them *pseudoinstructions* ("pseudo" means not real).

Real computer systems use one of two approaches for performing I/O. They use either primitive I/O instructions or *memory-mapped I/O*, neither of which performs any data conversion. In memory-mapped I/O, some memory locations correspond to I/O devices. Thus, a read or write to one of these locations is actually a read or write to an I/O device. With memory-mapped I/O, we perform I/O with ordinary load and store instructions. If we load or store to an address that is mapped to an I/O device, we access that I/O device. If, on the other hand, we load or store to an ordinary memory address, we access memory.

On H1, we will usually use the I/O pseudoinstructions to perform I/O; however, we can reconfigure H1 so that we can use memory-mapped I/O *in addition* to its I/O pseudoinstructions. The pseudoinstructions are more convenient, but memory-mapped I/O is more realistic. To configure H1 for memory-mapped I/O, we simply place the symbol "&" on a separate line at the beginning of an assembly language program. Four memory locations are then mapped to I/O devices (see Figure 4.29). To read from the keyboard, we simply load from location 3001; to write to the monitor, we simply store at location 3003. But before we perform these operations, we should check that the devices are ready. To determine their status, we read from location 3000 (for the keyboard status) or 3002 (for the monitor status). Of course, when H1 is configured for memory-mapped I/O, we cannot use locations 3000 to 3003 as ordinary memory locations. Thus, the stack should not be allowed to grow down into these locations.

Let's look at two simple examples of memory-mapped I/O on H1. Figure 4.30a shows a program that outputs 'A' to the monitor. The loop on lines 2 and

FIGURE 4.30   a)

```
1     &                    ; configure H1 for memory-mapped I/O
2     ld    3002           ; get status word from display monitor
3     jz    * - 1          ; if 0 (not ready), try again
4     ldc   'A'            ; get 'A'
5     st    3003           ; store in data word for display monitor
6     halt
```

b)

```
---- [T7] 0: ld    /0 F3A/ g
  0: ld    /0 BBA/    ac=0000/0001       ←1 indicates monitor is ready
  1: jz    /C 000/                       ←no jump because status = 1
  2: ldc   /8 041/    ac=0001/0041       ←get 'A'
  3: st    /1 BBB/    m[BBB]=0000/0041   ←output the 'A' to monitor
  4: halt  /FFFF /    A                  ←'A' displayed after a delay
Machine inst count =   5 (hex) =      5 (dec)
---- [T7] q
```

FIGURE 4.31   a)

```
1     &                    ; configure H1 for memory-mapped I/O
2     ld    3000           ; get keyboard status
3     jz    * -1           ; jump if not ready
4     ld    3001           ; get character from keyboard
5     halt
```

b)

```
---- [T7] 0: ld    /0 BB8/ g
  0: ld    /0 BB8/    ac=0000/0000  A    ←user enters 'A'
  1: jz    /C 000/    pc=0002/0000
  0: ld    /0 BB8/    ac=0000/0001       ←char now available
  1: jz    /C 000/                       ←no jump because status = 1
  2: ld    /0 BB9/    ac=0001/0041       ←read char from keyboard
  3: halt  /FFFF /
Machine inst count =   6 (hex) =      6 (dec)
---- [T7] q
```

3 repeatedly reads the status word from the monitor until the status equals 1 (which indicates that the monitor is ready to accept data). Line 5 then stores 'A' into location 3003 (monitor data).

Figure 4.30b shows the trace for this program. The monitor is ready initially. Thus, the loop immediately ends. The st instruction at location 3 then outputs the 'A' to the monitor. Notice that the output is not instantaneous—it occurs after a short delay.

Figure 4.31a shows a program that performs keyboard input using memory-mapped I/O. The loop on lines 2 and 3 repeatedly executes until data is available from the keyboard (the user has to hit a key to provide the character to be read).

When the status equals 1 (indicating a character is available), the ld instruction on line 4 reads from location 3001 (keyboard data). The trace for this program in Figure 4.31b shows that the keyboard was not initially ready. However, on the second iteration of the loop, its status changed. Thus, the loop ends. The ld instruction at location 2 then reads a character from the keyboard.

Incidentally, one of the advantages of using a simulated H1 instead of a real H1 should now be apparent. With a simulated H1, we can easily reconfigure its hardware to try out alternative designs (such as memory-mapped I/O). On a real H1, its I/O mechanism would be "wired in." Thus, we would not be able to reconfigure a real H1 by simply adding an "&" to an assembly language program.

4.16 EQU DIRECTIVE

• •

An *equ directive* tells the assembler to equate a value and a symbol. For example, the directive

```
equ  x 5
```

tells the assembler to equate **x** with 5. If a program contains this directive, the assembler will substitute 5 wherever **x** appears as an operand. For example, in the program,

```
ld    x
halt
equ   x 5
```

the assembler will substitute 5 for **x** in the ld instruction. Thus, the ld instruction will be assembled exactly as if it were written as

```
ld    5
```

equ directives are useful if we want to give a meaningful name to an absolute memory location. For example, Figure 4.32 shows the keyboard input program from Figure 4.31a rewritten with an **equ** directive. This new version assembles in exactly the same way as the old version; however, the two load instructions now reference two meaningful identifiers (**kbstatus** and **kbdata**) rather than the cryptic memory locations 3000 and 3001.

Another advantage of the **equ** directive is that it can simplify modifications. For example, suppose a program contains

```
ld kbstatus
```

FIGURE 4.32
```
&                    ; configure H1 for memory-mapped I/O
ld      kbstatus     ; get keyboard status
jz      * -1         ; jump if not ready
ld      kbdata       ; get character from keyboard
halt
equ     kbstatus 3000
equ     kbdata   3001
```

in 100 places. If we want to change the value of **kbstatus**, we have to change only the **equ** for **kbstatus**. If we used

```
ld 3000
```

instead, we would have to change all 100 occurrences of the instruction.

4.17 ENDIANNESS—A POTENTIAL PROBLEM FOR JAVA PROGRAMS

• •

In a *word-addressable* memory, successive addresses map to successive one-word memory cells. Similarly, in a *byte-addressable* memory, successive addresses map to successive 1-byte cells. H1 has a word-addressable main memory; however, most computers have byte-addressable main memories.

To store a word in a word-oriented memory, we simply store it in one cell of main memory. It is more complicated to store a word in a byte-oriented memory, however. We have to store the multiple bytes that make up the word into multiple cells in memory.

Suppose a computer uses byte-addressable memory and has 4-byte words. Such a system provides two obvious approaches for storing a word into memory. We can store the bytes that make up the word starting with the least significant byte (see Figure 4.33a), or starting with the most significant byte (see Fig 4.33b). In the former approach, we start from the "little end" (i.e., the least significant byte), and accordingly call it the *little-endian* approach. In the latter approach, we start from the "big end" (i.e., the most significant byte), and accordingly call it the *big-endian* approach. For load operations from memory, endianness is similarly observed. For example, when loading a 4-byte word that is in memory into a register on a little-endian computer, the first byte in memory goes into the "little end" (i.e., least significant part) of the register.

One disadvantage of the little-endian approach becomes immediately apparent to anyone who studies hex memory dumps. Memory dumps display bytes in increasing memory order. Thus, with the little-endian approach, a dump displays the bytes that make up a word in least-significant to most-significant order. For example, when the word 12345678 in Figure 4.33a is displayed in a hex dump, it appears as 78 56 34 12. Thus, a programmer must read the bytes from right to left rather than left to right. Although this is not a serious problem, it can be confusing to an inexperienced programmer.

Another, more serious disadvantage of the little-endian approach is that it does not lend itself to string comparisons using integer arithmetic—a technique that allows multiple bytes to be compared in parallel. In string comparisons, the first character is the most significant. If we load a string (or the initial portion thereof) into a register from memory on a little-endian computer, its first character occupies the least significant byte in the register. Thus, an integer compare of this string would not determine the correct collating order. For example, if we load the string "ABC" into a register on a little-endian computer, the first character ('A') occupies the least significant byte (see Figure 4.34). If we loaded "CBA" into another register and then performed an integer compare on the two registers, "CBA" would incorrectly appear to alphabetically precede "ABC".

On a big-endian computer, the first character of a string loaded into a register occupies the most significant byte of the register. Thus, if a second string (or initial portion thereof) were in another register, we could determine the correct collating

FIGURE 4.33   a) Little endian (store little end first)

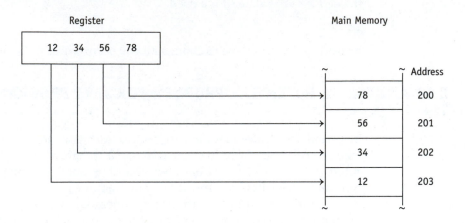

b) Big endian (store big end first)

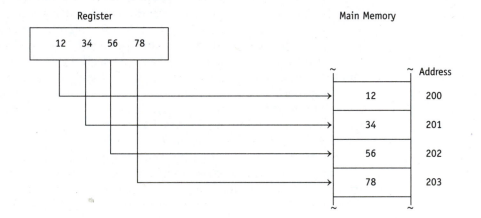

FIGURE 4.34   Loading a string on a little-endian computer

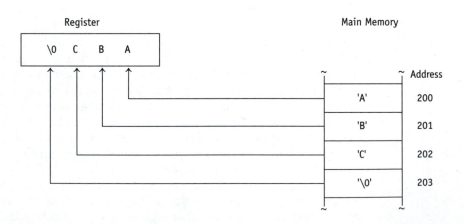

order of the multiple characters in the registers with a single integer instruction that compares the contents of the two registers.

The little-endian approach does have some advantages. One advantage is that it simplifies the conversion of a high-precision integer in memory to a lower precision. For example, suppose the types `int` and `short` map to 32- and 16-bit quantities, respectively. Now consider what happens when we execute the following sequence on a little-endian computer:

```
int x = 0x00001234;   // assume x is a 32-bit variable in memory
short y;              // assume y is a 16-bit variable in memory
y = (short)x;
```

We simply assign the halfword at the address of **x** to **y** (see Figure 4.35a). However, on a big-endian computer, we have to assign the halfword that is at the address of **x** *plus 2* (see Figure 4.35b). Thus, the precision conversion on a big-endian computer requires an address computation (we have to add 2 to the address of **x**).

Another advantage of the little-endian approach occurs when we want to process the bytes that make up a word in least-significant to most-significant order. For example, we do this when we perform multi-byte addition byte by byte. On a little-endian computer, the address of the word is also the address of the least significant byte (the byte we want to start with). However, on a big-endian machine, the address of the word is the address of the most significant byte. Thus, on a big-endian computer, we have to perform an address computation to get the address of the starting byte.

The Intel Pentium (the microprocessor in most PCs) is little endian. Its oldest predecessor was little endian (probably because of the need to do multibyte arithmetic), thus, compatibility requirements forced all its successors to be little endian as well. IBM mainframe computers and the Java Virtual Machine are big endian. The Sun SPARC workstations support both big and little endian, but default to big endian.

The endianness of a computer affects the byte order of binary data not only in main memory, but also in files the computer creates. In a file created by a big-endian computer, the most significant byte in a word is first; on a little-endian computer, it is last. Unfortunately, this effect of endianness means that a file with binary data created by a big-endian computer cannot be processed directly by a little-endian computer, and vice versa. For example, suppose a little-endian computer writes a 4-byte word whose value is 1 to a file. This word, in hex, would appear in the file as the byte sequence 01 00 00 00. When a big-endian computer reads this word from the file, it interprets the first byte as the most significant. Thus, it reads it in as the number 01000000 hex, not as the number 00000001. To obtain the correct value, the big-endian computer has to decompose the word into its component bytes and then re-form the word using the reverse byte order.

The problem that a mismatch in endianness creates when we transfer data from one computer to another does not occur with text data. Text data in a file appears in its natural order regardless of the endianness of the computer that creates it. For example, the text "Yes" would appear in memory or in a file as the byte sequence "Y", "e", and "s" on both big- and little-endian computers.

Suppose we run a program that inputs a binary file created by another program. Are there any potential endianness problems if both programs are run on the *same* system? You would expect not, but this is not the case if one of the programs is a Java program. When a Java program is compiled, it is translated to a

FIGURE 4.35   a) Precision conversion on a little-endian computer

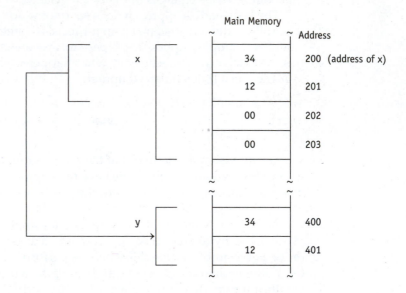

b) Precision conversion on a big-endian computer

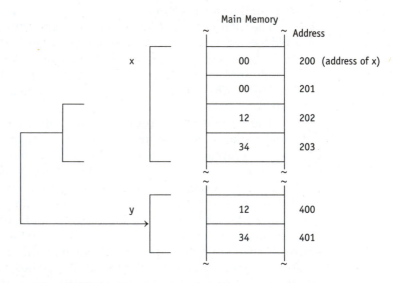

class file that contains *bytecode*—machine language for the *Java Virtual Machine (JVM)*. The JVM is not a real machine ("virtual" means not real). In contrast, when a C++ program is compiled, it is translated to *native code*—the machine language for the computer on which the C++ compiler is running.

To run a compiled Java program, we have to run a program—the Java interpreter—that makes our computer behave like the JVM. The Java interpreter is like **sim**, but without **sim**'s debugging and tracing capabilities. With **sim**, we can run H1 machine code on our computer. Similarly, with the Java interpreter, we can run JVM bytecode on our computer.

If we are running both C++ and Java programs on our computer, we are, in effect, using two computer systems: our computer itself (running native code for the

C++ programs) and the JVM (running bytecode for the Java programs). The JVM uses the big-endian approach. Thus, if our computer uses the little-endian approach, we have an endian mismatch. Binary data created by a Java program will not be directly readable by a C++ program, and vice versa. We will run into this problem (and determine a fix for it) in Chapter 11, where we implement an assembler and a linker.

Endianness normally is not a concern when porting a C++ program from one type of computer to another. However, endianness problems can occur if a program performs intricate bit manipulations. Endianness problems, in fact, did occur when **sim** (a C++ program) was ported from the Pentium (little endian) to the SPARC (big endian). Java programs, of course, never have porting problems because they always run on the same machine (the JVM), regardless of the type of the host computer.

PROBLEMS

• •

4.1. What does the output generated by the following program look like?

```
        ldc   1
        push
        ldc   2
        push
        ldc   m1
        sout
        pop
        dout
        ldc   m2
        sout
        pop
        dout
        ldc   '\n'
        aout
        halt
m1:     dw    "first pop ="
m2:     dw    "\nsecond pop ="
```

4.2. Assemble the program in problem 4.1 by hand. Show the object code in hex.

4.3. What does the following program display? Run it to check your answer

```
&
ldc   'A'
st    3003
st    3003
st    3003
halt
```

4.4. Rewrite the program in Figure 4.18 using the following approach: point the **sp** register to the first number in the table. On each iteration of the loop, pop the number to be added into the **ac** register. Is your new version better than the program in Figure 4.18?

4.5. Write and run an assembly language program that displays all the odd numbers from 1 to 99 in ascending order.

4.6. Write and run an assembly language program that displays

```
1
1 2
1 2 3
1 2 3 4
1 2 3 4 5
1 2 3 4 5 6
1 2 3 4 5 6 7
```

Use nested loops.

4.7. Write assembly language instructions that have the same effect as the following C++ statements:

```
*p = 5;
***q = 10;
x = ***q;
*(p + 1) = 6;
*p = *p + 1;
p = r;
```

4.8. What does the following program do?

```
dw   800Fh
dw   FFFDh
dw   FFFFh
```

4.9. Rewrite the program in Figure 4.14 without using the `jnz` instruction. Make as few changes as possible. Run on **sim**.

4.10. What happens when the following program is run:

```
      ldc   15
      swap
      ld    x
a:    push
      ja    a
x:    dw    -1
```

4.11. Trace the program in problem 4.10. Use the **d$** command to observe the activity on the stack.

4.12. Write and run an assembly language program that reads in a decimal number and then displays its value times 7 in decimal.

4.13. Write and run an assembly language program that displays the ASCII codes in decimal and hex for the characters 'A' to 'Z'.

4.14. Write and run an assembly language program that reads in a string and then determines and displays the frequency of occurrence of each character in the string. For example, if the string "aAbazAA??" is read in, your program would display

```
?    2
A    3
a    2
b    1
z    1
```

Hint: Place the counter for each character at the location that equals that character's ASCII code. For example, place the counter for 'A' in location 65. Then an `ld` instruction with 'A' as its address field would load the counter for 'A'.

4.15. Write and run an assembly language program that reads in 10 decimal numbers and then displays them in ascending order.

4.16. Write and run an assembly language program that reads in 10 decimal numbers and then displays them without any repeats. For example, if the input is 1, 1, 5, 1, 1, 1, 1, 1, 1, 1, then the output should be 1, 5.

4.17. Write and run an assembly language program that reads in a string, determines if it is a palindrome, and displays "yes" or "no" accordingly.

4.18. Write and run an assembly language program that reads in a number and then displays all the positive numbers divisible by 3 that are less than the input number.

4.19. Write and run an assembly language program that reads in a number and then displays all the Fibonacci numbers less than the input number.

4.20. Write and run an assembly language program that reads in 10 numbers and displays the largest and smallest.

4.21. Write and run an assembly language program that reads in a string and outputs that string in all uppercase characters.

4.22. Write and run an assembly language program that reads in a string and outputs that string with all letters removed. For example, if the input string is "A&B*", the output string should be "&*".

4.23. Write and run an assembly language program that reads in a string and displays its length (not counting the null character).

4.24. Observe that the sum of the first n positive odd integers equals n^2. For example, $1 + 3 + 5 = 3^2$. Write and run an assembly language program that uses this relationship to compute the square of a number. Your program should prompt for and read in a decimal number and then output its square, appropriately labeled.

4.25. What happens when the following program is run:

```
       ld    0
z:     ld    1
       ld    z
s:     st    x
x:     halt
       sub   z
       ja    s
```

4.26. What happens when the following program is run:

```
s:     ld    x
       sub   y
       st    x
x:     ld    y
       ja    s
y:     dw    1
```

4.27. What happens if the machine language corresponding to

```
       ld    x
       add   y
       st    z
       halt
x:     dw    2
```

```
y:  dw    3
z:  dw    0
```

is loaded into memory starting at location 400 hex. Would the program run correctly? Try it (specify the `/p400` argument on the command line when invoking **sim**). Look at the program in memory using the **u400** command.

4.28. What happens when the following program is executed:

```
    ldc  y
    swap
    call x
x:  halt
y:  dw   -1
```

4.29. What happens when the following program is executed:

```
    ldr  x
    halt
x:  dw   2
```

4.30. Replace the `call` and `ret` instructions in Figure 4.22 with `ja` instructions. Test your modification on **sim**.

4.31. Write a simple program that has the structure shown in Figure 4.23. Then replace the `call` and `ret` instructions with sequences of instructions excluding `call` and `ret` that have the same effect. Test your modification on **sim**.

4.32. In what ways is using an `add` instruction to add one to the **ac** register less efficient than using the nonexistent `addc` instruction (see Section 4.5)?

4.33. Why is an `add immediate` instruction not supported in the standard instruction set?

4.34. Why is there no instruction that loads the **sp** register directly from memory?

4.35. Assemble the following program by hand. Show the object code in hex.

```
    ldc   A
    halt
A:  ldc   'A'
```

4.36. The loop in Figure 4.14 counts down from 20 and terminates when it reaches 0. Rewrite the program so that it counts up from 0 and terminates when it reaches 20. Compare your version with Figure 4.14. Which is better?

4.37. What are some of the serious shortcomings of the standard instruction set? Hint: Consider overflow and comparisons.

4.38. The `din` and `hin` instructions perform conversions on their input. Does the `ain` instruction also perform a conversion? Explain.

4.39. Compare the total number of instructions executed by the programs in Figure 4.18 and Figure 4.19.

4.40. Give arguments for using addresses lower or higher than 3000 decimal for memory-mapped I/O.

4.41. Give arguments for and against using the addresses 4092 to 4095 decimal for memory-mapped I/O.

4.42. Write and run an assembly language program that reads in a string and echos it to the monitor using memory-mapped I/O.

4.43. Write and run an assembly language program that reads in a decimal number using memory-mapped input and displays its value in hex using `hout`.

4.44. Write and run an assembly language program that reads in a decimal number using memory-mapped input and displays its value in decimal using `dout`.

4.45. Write and run an assembly language program that
  a. Prompts for and reads in a decimal number
  b. Determines if the number of 1 bits in the binary equivalent of the decimal number is even or odd
  c. Outputs "EVEN" or "ODD" accordingly

4.46. Write and run an assembly language program that consists of four modules: **main**, **input**, **mult**, and **output**. **main** should call **input**, **mult**, and **output**, and then halt. **input** should prompt for and read in two positive decimal numbers. **mult** should multiply the two decimal numbers read in by **input** by means of a loop that repeatedly adds. **output** should output the product computed by **mult**. Assume that the product will fit into 16 bits.

4.47. Same as Problem 4.46, but handle both positive and negative numbers.

4.48. Same as Problem 4.46, but divide instead of multiplying.

4.49. The latter portion of a program is given below. Add to it its first portion (the new code you add should occupy addresses less than 1000) whose execution has the effect of executing the code at location 1001 to 1009 backwards (i.e., from locations 1009 down to 1001).

```
        org 1000
x:      dw    1
        halt
        dout
        add    x
        dout
        add    x
        dout
        add    x
        dout
        ld     x
```

4.50. The latter portion of a program is given below. Add to it its first portion (the new code you add should occupy addresses less than 1000) whose execution has the effect of executing the code starting at location 1000 and the code starting at location 2000 concurrently (i.e., in an interleaved fashion).

```
        org 1000
        ldc   1
        dout
        add   x
        dout
        add   x
        dout
        add   x
        dout
        halt
x:      dw    1
        org 2000
        ldc   'A'
        aout
        add   y
        aout
        add   y
        aout
```

```
              add   y
              aout
              add   y
              aout
              add   y
              aout
              add   y
              aout
              add   y
              aout
              add   y
              aout
              add   y
              aout
         y:   dw    2
```

4.51. Why is main memory with byte addressability more common than word address-ability?

4.52. Write a C++ program that will work correctly on a little-endian computer but not a big-endian computer.

4.53. Write a C++ program that determines the endianness of the computer on which it runs.

4.54. Write a Java program that confirms that the JVM is big endian.

4.55. Write and run a Java program that creates a binary file containing the binary values 1, 2, 3, 4, 5, 6, 7, 8, 9, and 10. Write and run a C++ program that inputs this file, sums the 10 values, and displays the sum.

BASIC ELECTRONICS AND DIGITAL LOGIC

5.1 INTRODUCTION

In the preceding chapters, we studied H1 at the *machine* and *assembly language levels*. In this chapter, we will study H1 at the *digital logic level*. In particular, you will learn the operation and implementation of all the digital logic components that make up H1. Then, in the next chapter, you will see how these components are put together and controlled to make a functioning computer. By studying the digital logic of H1, you will take one more step toward the principal goal of this book: to obtain a complete understanding of the structure and operation of H1.

We start this chapter with an examination of basic electronics. We then study the two categories of digital logic: *combinational* (a circuit whose output depends only on its present inputs) and *sequential* (a circuit whose output depends on its past as well as its present inputs).

5.2 BASIC ELECTRONICS

Before you study the circuits that are used in computers, you have to learn some basic concepts in electronics. You may feel that the material in this section is far afield from what you should be studying. It is, nevertheless, important material. In this section, we start with a quick look at the basic building block of all matter—the atom.

5.2.1 Conductors and Insulators

All matter is composed of atoms. An atom consists of a *nucleus* (a positively charged center) and *electrons* (negatively charged particles that surround the nucleus). One of the basic laws of electronics is that unlike charges attract and like charges repel. Thus, two electrons repel each other and two nuclei repel each other, but an electron and a nucleus attract each other.

In the atoms of some materials, the outermost electrons are very loosely held to the nucleus. These electrons are not "stuck" to the nucleus; instead, they can move freely from one nucleus to another. Such materials are called *conductors*. If we attach the two terminals of a battery to the two ends of a conductor, the battery will cause these free electrons to flow. This electron flow is called a *current*. Examples of conductors are gold, silver, and copper.

Some materials do not have any electrons that are free to move. Such materials are called *insulators*. When a battery is attached to an insulator, current does not flow because the electrons in an insulator are bound to their nuclei. Examples of insulators are rubber and glass.

Even the best conductors have some *resistance* (i.e., opposition) to the flow of electrons. As the free electrons flow through a conductor, they periodically crash into the nuclei. Thus, the nuclei function as barriers that oppose the flow of electrons. These collisions produce heat. If we increase the current, we increase the heat produced. This is the principle on which the standard electric light bulb works. When we turn on a light bulb, the bulb's filament (the wire that runs though the bulb) is heated by the current flowing through it. The filament becomes so hot that it emits both heat and light.

If we hold current constant, the amount of heat produced by that current is proportional to the resistance of the material through which it is flowing. Thus, a good conductor—because of its low resistance—generates little heat when carrying a normal level of current.

A common component in electrical circuits is a *resistor,* which is a device whose function is to add electrical resistance to a circuit.

5.2.2   A Simple Electrical Circuit

In Figure 5.1, we see the simple electrical circuit that represents a flashlight. It consists of two batteries that are connected to a light bulb with conducting wires. The batteries push electrons in a circle from the "−" terminal of the bottom battery through the bulb to the "+" terminal of the top battery, and then through the two batteries back to the "−" terminal of the bottom battery. We use the switch to turn the electron flow on and off. When the switch is open, no current can flow because of the barrier the open switch creates. However, when we close the switch, the circuit is completed, allowing current to flow. Because the connecting wires are good conductors, little heat is generated in them by the current. The filament in the bulb, on the other hand, has a much higher resistance. Thus, almost all of the heat generated by the current occurs in the filament.

For current to flow, we need a complete circuit from one side of the voltage source to the other. This requirement is the reason why the cord that connects a

FIGURE 5.1   Flashlight

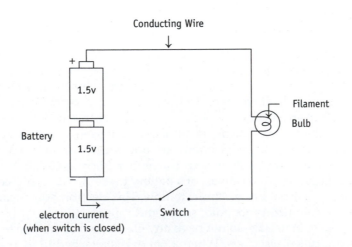

table lamp to an electrical outlet in the wall contains two wires. At any given time, one wire is carrying current from the outlet to the one end of the filament in the bulb, and the other wire is carrying current back from the other end of the filament.

The unit of current flow is the *amp*. The unit of resistance is the *ohm*. The unit of *voltage,* the electron "push" that the battery creates, is the *volt*. The relationship of these three parameters of an electrical circuit is given by *Ohm's law:*

$$I = E/R$$

where I is current in amps, E is voltage in volts, and R is resistance in ohms. From Ohm's law, we can see that current is proportional to voltage but inversely proportional to resistance. Thus, if we double the voltage, we double the current that flows; if we double the resistance, we halve the current that flows.

Suppose in the circuit in Figure 5.1 that the two batteries provide a total of 3 volts, and the resistance of the bulb is 1000 ohms. Because the connecting wires are made from a good conductor (such as copper), their resistance is small compared to the resistance of the bulb. The battery, too, has some resistance, but like the wire, its resistance is small compared to the bulb. Thus, we can take the bulb's resistance as a good approximation of the total circuit resistance. Then Ohm's law tells us that

$$I = E/R = 3/1000 = 0.003 \text{ amps}$$

will flow in the circuit. Equivalently, we can say that 3 ma will flow (*ma* is the abbreviation for *milliamp,* one-thousandth of an amp).

Given any two of the three quantities in Ohm's law, we can compute the third. For example, by rearranging terms in Ohm's law, we get that

$$E = I \times R$$

Suppose a 1000-ohm resistor has 0.1 amps flowing through it. Then the *voltage drop* across the resistor (i.e., the change in voltage from one side of the resistor to the other) is given by

$$E = I \times R = 0.1 \times 1000 = 100 \text{ volts}$$

Now suppose no current is flowing through a resistor. Then the voltage drop across it is necessarily zero because I (and, therefore IR) is zero. This is an important fact to remember: *There is no voltage drop across a resistor through which no current is flowing.*

When we draw diagrams of electrical circuits, we often use simplified pictures of the various components in the circuit. Such diagrams are called *schematic diagrams*. For example, Figure 5.2 is the schematic diagram for the flashlight circuit in Figure 5.1. In place of the bulb, we use a zigzag figure that represents the resistance in the circuit. In place of the battery, we just label the upper side of the circuit with + 3 volts (which corresponds to the "+" terminal of the top battery) and the bottom side with 0 (which corresponds to the "−" side of the bottom battery) to show the application of 3 volts.

5.2.3 Effective Voltage

The voltage that is provided by the two terminals in the electrical outlets in our homes alternates direction; that is, it first pushes electrons in one direction, then in the reverse direction. This two-direction cycle occurs 60 times a second. The

FIGURE 5.2   Schematic Diagram

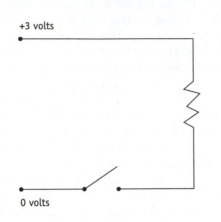

+3 volts

0 volts

current it produces correspondingly alternates and, therefore, is appropriately called *alternating current (AC)*. Current that flows in only one direction is called *direct current (DC)*.

Figure 5.3a contains a graph that shows how the voltage from an electrical outlet varies with time. It gradually increases in one direction to a peak level of 165 volts. It then gradually decreases to 0, and then increases to a peak of 165 volts in the other direction. The particular shape of this graph is called a *sine wave*.

Suppose we have two identical resistors. If we connect one resistor across the terminals of an electrical outlet and the other across the terminals of a 165-volt battery, which resistor will generate more heat? (Don't do this experiment—you may electrocute yourself.) The battery provides a constant 165 volts. The outlet, on the other hand, provides a voltage that only peaks at 165 volts. At all other times, it is less than 165 volts. It turns out that the resistor across the outlet will generate the same amount of heat that it would generate if it were across a 117-volt battery. Thus, the *effective voltage* of an outlet is only 117 volts—that is, its ability to produce heat is equivalent to that of a 117-volt battery. Effective voltage is also called *root mean square (rms)* voltage.

Effective voltage of a sine wave can be computed from peak voltage with the following formula:

$$\text{effective voltage} = 0.707 \times \text{peak voltage}$$

5.2.4 Power Supplies

For a flashlight, we use batteries as the voltage source. For nonportable devices, however, we usually use a *power supply,* a device that plugs into the wall and provides the voltage that the circuit requires. A power supply for a computer has to do three things:

- It has to transform the voltage to the level required by the circuit. Computers typically require less than 5 volts (see Figures 5.3a and 5.3b).
- It has to convert the voltage from AC to DC. This process is called *rectification* (see Figures 5.3b and 5.3c).
- Rectification produces a nonalternating voltage whose level is constantly changing. Thus, the power supply must also *filter* the rectified voltage—that is, hold it constant at the appropriate level (see Figures 5.3c and 5.3d).

FIGURE 5.3 Power Supplies

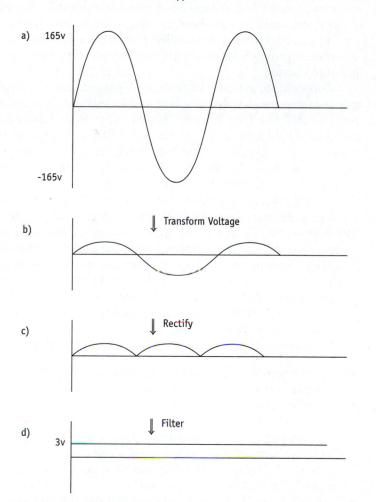

5.2.5 How to Not Electrocute Yourself

The effective voltage that is provided by the electrical outlets in most homes in the United States is about 117 volts. If you were to touch one terminal of an outlet with your forefinger and the other terminal with the thumb of the same hand (don't actually do this!), your hand would complete a circuit and current would flow. How much current depends, of course, on the resistance of your hand. If your hand is dry, its resistance is about 100,000 ohms. Using Ohm's law, we can compute the current:

$$I = E/R = 117/100,000 = 0.00117 \text{ amps} = 1.17 \text{ ma}$$

1.17 ma is probably not enough current to do any permanent harm to most individuals. However, suppose your hand is wet. Its resistance will then drop way down to about 500 ohms (or perhaps even less). Then the current is

$$I = E/R = 117/500 = 0.234 \text{ amps} = 234 \text{ ma}$$

234 ma will provide quite a jolt. But since the current will be between your forefinger and your thumb—that is, it will be confined to your hand—there is a good

chance that you will not be electrocuted. If, however, you were to touch one terminal with one hand and the other terminal with the other hand, then the current would flow across your chest, causing your heart either to shut down or to go into spasmodic contractions called fibrillations. In either case, you would likely die unless someone immediately took steps to restore your heart to its normal pumping action.

Generally, to get a shock from an electrical outlet you have to touch both terminals; however, under some circumstances if you touch only one terminal, *current can still flow (and kill you)*. Here's why: In a standard electrical outlet, one terminal is held at *ground* level (i.e., at 0 volts) and the other is *hot* (i.e., it varies between -165 volts and $+165$ volts). The hot terminal is the smaller of the two slots in an outlet (assuming the outlet is correctly wired). If you touch the hot terminal and also touch anything that is grounded (such as a water pipe), you complete the circuit and current will flow. The current coming out of the hot terminal flows through your body and then into whatever ground you are touching. Whenever this happens an imbalance occurs—the current coming out of the hot terminal does not go into the ground terminal of the outlet, but instead, goes through you and then into whatever ground you are touching. Some outlets have special safety circuitry that can detect such a current imbalance, and automatically break the circuit. These outlets (called *ground fault current interrupt outlets*) are usually used in the kitchen and bathroom, where people are often wet and, therefore, more likely to suffer a fatal electric shock.

Here are some good rules to follow when around electrical equipment:

- Do not touch any electrical equipment when any part of your body is wet; for example, never touch a radio when in the shower.
- Never open electrical equipment unless you are fully qualified to do so. Particularly dangerous are computer monitors and televisions. Internal voltages in such devices are *very* high (over 30,000 volts) and can easily electrocute.
- Keep one hand in your pocket if you must examine a circuit that may have live voltages. By doing so, you minimize the possibility that your whole body will become part of an electrical circuit.
- Never use any electrical equipment that has frayed wires.

5.2.6 Transistors

A *transistor* is an electrical switch. It can be open, in which case it does not conduct, or closed, in which case it does conduct. A transistor is similar to a light switch on a lamp. There is, however, one major difference—a lamp switch is mechanical. Because it has moving parts, its switching speed is very slow. A transistor, on the other hand, is electrical. Because it has no moving parts, its switching speed is very fast.

Transistors are made from *silicon*, an element that is in abundant supply on the earth (silicon is the principal component of sand). We call silicon a *semiconductor* because its electrical properties place it between conductors and insulators.

Among the several types of transistors, *metal-oxide semiconductor (MOS)* transistors are the most commonly used type in modern computers. MOS transistors come in two types: *PMOS (positive metal-oxide semiconductor)* and *NMOS (negative metal oxide semiconductor)*. PMOS and NMOS transistors are also called *P-type* and *N-type*, respectively. Most computer circuits with MOS transistors use *complementary metal-oxide semiconductor (CMOS)* technology. In this technology, pairs of MOS transistors are used, with each pair consisting of one transistor of each type. By

FIGURE 5.4

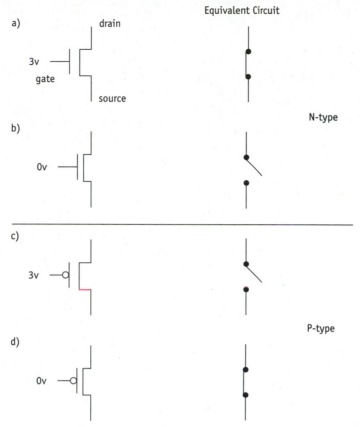

combining both types in a circuit, the power required by the circuit can be minimized. MOS transistors have several properties that make them appropriate for computer circuits: low power consumption, high noise immunity, and high *fan out* (the number of gates that the output of a single gate can drive). They are generally slower than other types of transistors, however.

MOS transistors have three leads—the *source, gate,* and *drain.* An off/on switch exists between the source and drain. The status of this switch—opened or closed—is determined by the voltage applied to the gate. For example, Figure 5.4a shows an NMOS transistor with 3 volts on its gate. Its equivalent circuit is a closed switch. Figure 5.4b shows the same transistor with 0 volts on its gate. Its equivalent circuit is an open switch.

PMOS transistors respond in the opposite way that NMOS transistors do: A zero voltage on the gate of a PMOS transistor closes its switch; a positive voltage open its switch (see Figures 5.4c and 5.4d). In schematic diagrams, we distinguish a PMOS transistor from an NMOS transistor by placing a bubble on the gate input of PMOS transistors.

If a MOS transistor's internal switch is closed, connecting the source to the drain, we say the transistor is *on.* If its internal switch is open, we say the transistor is *off.*

Figure 5.5a shows a circuit that uses CMOS transistors to implement a *NOT gate* (also called an *inverter*). A NOT gate flips its single-bit input. The symbol at the bottom of the circuit consisting of three successively smaller horizontal lines represents ground (i.e., 0 volts). The top of the circuit is connected to +3 volts. If we

FIGURE 5.5

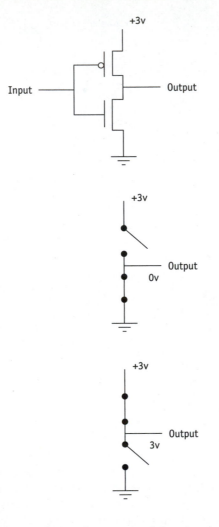

a)

b)

c)

apply 3 volts to the input of the circuit, the top transistor turns off (because it is PMOS) and the bottom transistor turns on (because it is NMOS). The effect is to connect the output directly to ground, setting it to zero volts (see Figure 5.5b). If, on the other hand, we apply 0 volts to the input, then the top transistor turns on and the bottom one turns off, connecting the output to +3 volts (see Figure 5.5c).

We call the system in which we represent the bit 0 with a lower voltage and the bit 1 with a higher voltage *positive logic*. In *negative logic*, we represent 0 with the higher voltage and 1 with the lower voltage. We can use either system in a computer, but whichever one we choose, we should use it consistently. With either positive logic or negative logic, our circuit in Figure 5.5 acts as a NOT gate (i.e., it flips its input bit). With positive logic, a 0 (i.e., 0 volt) input produces a 1 (i.e., 3 volt) output; and a 1 (i.e., 3 volt) input produces 0 (i.e., 0 volt) output. With negative logic, the circuit similarly flips its input bit.

Consider the circuit in Figure 5.6a. If either or both inputs are at +3 volts, the output is connected to ground through either or both transistors on the bottom. If, however, both inputs are 0 volts, then the top two transistors are on, connecting the output to +3 volts. The table in Figure 5.6b shows the circuit's input/output relationship. We can convert this table to a truth table by substituting 0 and 1 for their corresponding voltages. For positive logic, we get the truth table for the *NOR*

FIGURE 5.6   a)   NOR/NAND Function

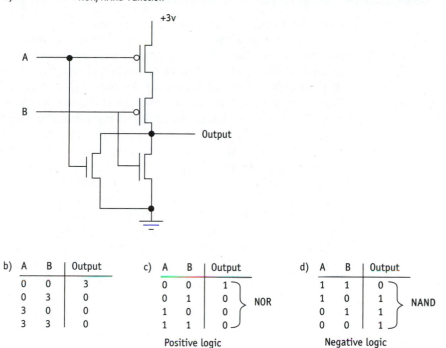

b)

A	B	Output
0	0	3
0	3	0
3	0	0
3	3	0

c)

A	B	Output
0	0	1
0	1	0
1	0	0
1	1	0

} NOR

Positive logic

d)

A	B	Output
1	1	0
1	0	1
0	1	1
0	0	1

} NAND

Negative logic

function (Figure 5.6c). But for negative logic we get the truth table for the *NAND function* (Figure 5.6d)—a different function.

With either positive or negative logic, simple CMOS circuits exist for any type of logic gate. Sometimes, we can create a new gate by combining two or more gates that we already have. For example, by attaching the output of the gate in Figure 5.6a to the input of a NOT gate, the combined circuit implements a different function.

The top two transistors in Figure 5.6a are connected *in series* (i.e., the bottom of the first is connected to the top of the second). The bottom two transistors are connected *in parallel* (i.e., the tops are connected and the bottoms are connected). An electrical path exists through a series connection only if both the top *and* the bottom transistors are on. In a parallel connection, however, an electrical path exists if left *or* right (or both) transistors are on.

We can often determine the type of connections (series or parallel) and the type of transistors (NMOS or PMOS) that are needed to implement a function directly from the truth table for a function. Let's do this for the truth table in Figure 5.6c, assuming positive logic. From this table, we see that the output should be 1 only if A *and* B are 0. The word "and" implies that we should use a series connection. That both A and B are 0 for this case implies that we should use PMOS transistors (they turn on with a 0 input). Finally, the 1 output for this case implies that our series connection should connect the output to +3 volts (implying the series connection is the top half of the circuit). Now let's determine the bottom half. Figure 5.6c shows that the output should be 0 if A *or* B (or both) are 1. The word "or" implies that we should use a parallel circuit. That A or B are 1 for these cases implies that we should use NMOS transistors (they turn on with a 1 input). The 0 output for these cases implies that this parallel circuit should connect the output to ground.

5.2.7   Capacitance, Inductance, and Impedance

Consider the circuit in Figure 5.7. A power supply is connected through a switch and a resistor to a *capacitor*—two parallel metal plates that are close to each other but are not touching. Because the plates are not touching, there is no complete circuit when the switch is thrown to the left, connecting the power supply to the circuit. One, therefore, would expect no current to flow; however, this is not the case. For a very brief period after the switch is thrown to the left, current flows, the effect of which is to charge the plates of the capacitor. Electrons flow onto the bottom plate (creating a net negative charge) and off of the top plate (creating a net positive charge). As the voltage builds on the capacitor, the voltage drop across the resistor decreases (the voltage across the resistor is equal to the power supply voltage less the capacitor voltage), and, accordingly, the current flowing through the resistor also decreases. Soon the voltage across the capacitor reaches the voltage of the battery, at which time the voltage on the two sides of the resistor are the same. Because there is no voltage drop across the resistor, no current flows.

Figure 5.8 shows a graph of current versus time, starting at the point at which we throw the switch to the left. Initially, the voltage across the capacitor is 0. Thus, the voltage drop across the resistor equals the voltage of the battery. Using Ohm's law, we get that the initial current is

$$I = E/R = 3/100 = 0.03 \text{ amps} = 30 \text{ ma}$$

The current then decays from this level to zero as the capacitor charges.

The ability of a capacitor to be charged and hold its charge is called *capacitance,* the unit of which is the *farad*. Because of capacitors, it is entirely possible to receive an electrical shock from a device that is *not* plugged in. The source of electrical energy that produces the shock is the capacitors in the circuit that were charged when the circuit was last used. Because of the possibility that capacitors in a circuit may be holding a large charge, it is dangerous to carelessly poke around in any circuit (particularly high-voltage circuits like a TV set) *even if it is unplugged*—the high voltages stored in its capacitors can be lethal.

Now suppose we throw the switch in Figure 5.7 to the right. The capacitor can then discharge through the resistor. Initially, the voltage provided by the capacitor

FIGURE 5.7   Capacitance

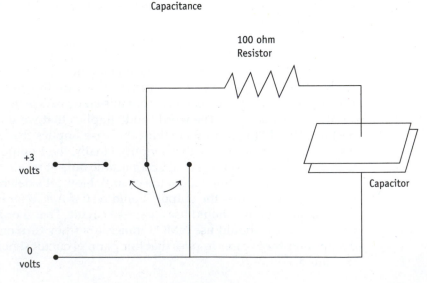

FIGURE 5.8   Resistor - Capacitor Circuit

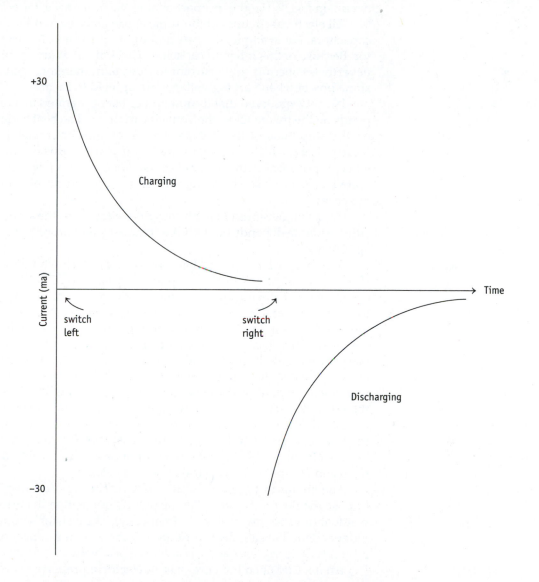

is equal to whatever voltage it received from the battery. But as the capacitor discharges, its voltage decreases, and, therefore, so does the current. The right half of Figure 5.8 shows the current for the discharging cycle (i.e., when the switch is thrown to the right). Notice that the graphs of the charging and discharging currents are on opposite sides of the *x*-axis, indicating that these two currents flow in opposite directions.

An important observation to make about our capacitor circuit is that whenever the switch is thrown to the left or right, current flows for a *brief* period *causing heat to be generated by the resistor.* The amount of heat generated depends on how frequently we alternate the switch setting. If we alternate the switch setting once an hour, then current flows briefly once an hour, generating a little heat at these one-hour intervals. If, however, we alternate the switch setting 1,000 times a second, current will be flowing *all the time*, almost as if there were a complete circuit, causing much more heat to be generated. The amount of heat generated by this circuit, in fact, is roughly proportional to the *frequency of the voltage changes*.

All electrical circuits exhibit some capacitance even if they do not contain any capacitors. For example, the gate and drain of a transistor act like a small capacitor. Because of this inherent capacitance, circuits that are essentially open circuits nevertheless permit some current to flow, and, therefore, generate heat and consume power when varying voltages are applied to them.

We have observed that the amount of heat generated in a capacitive circuit depends on the frequency of the voltage variations. The heat generated also depends on the amplitude of the voltage changes. A greater change in voltage produces more current, which, in turn, means more heat. It turns out that the heat generated is proportional to the *square of the amplitude of the voltage changes*. Thus, the generated heat increases quite rapidly as the amplitude of the voltage variations increases.

Capacitance is present in all computer circuits, so the amount of heat these circuits generate depends on both the frequency and amplitude of the applied voltage changes.

Suppose we have a CPU that is driven by a clock whose frequency is 100 Mhz. If we increase the clock frequency to 150 MHz, the CPU—because of its inherent capacitance—will generate more heat and consume more power, perhaps causing itself to overheat. If we want to drive the CPU at a higher clock frequency (assuming the circuits in the CPU are fast enough to handle the higher clock frequency), we must either dissipate the extra heat generated (with fans or other cooling devices) or redesign it to use smaller changes in voltages. For example, if we change our CPU so that the voltage levels it uses are 0 and 3 volts instead of 0 and 5 volts, then the amount of heat it generates will be substantially reduced. Unfortunately, there is a serious tradeoff in lowering the voltage diffential: It makes it harder to reliably distinguish between distinct voltage levels. For example, if a CPU used the voltage levels 0 and 0.1 volts, the heat it would generate would be minimal, but the circuits inside the CPU would not be able to reliably distinguish between the 0 and 0.1 volt levels because they are so close.

The circuit in Figure 5.7 contains a resistor and a capacitor, both of which oppose the flow of current. The capacitor's opposition to current is frequency dependent (it varies inversely with frequency). The resistor's opposition is frequency independent. We call the opposition to current that a capacitor and a resistor exhibit *capacitive reactance* and *resistance*, respectively.

An *inductor* (a coil of wire) has an electrical property called *inductance*. An inductor, like a capacitor, exhibits a frequency-dependent opposition to the flow of current. However, unlike a capacitor, an inductor's opposition to current increases with frequency (for a capacitor, the opposition decreases with frequency). We call the opposition to current that an inductor exhibits *inductive reactance*.

We saw earlier that the inherent capacitance in electrical devices like transistors results in unwanted current flow (and therefore, power consumption and heat). The inherent inductance in electrical devices also creates a problem, although of a different sort. Suppose we need to carry a signal from point A to point B in a circuit. At low frequencies, a wire will do the job nicely. However, at high frequencies, a wire (unless it is very short and straight) will have a high inductive reactance that will oppose the propagation of the signal. Thus, two problems are inherent in computer circuits and become more pronounced with increasing frequency: a decreasing capacitive reactance that allows current we do not want, and an increasing inductive reactance that opposes currents we do want.

In computer circuits, the inherent capacitance of the computer's components creates a serious problem: It results in heat that can harm the densely packed circuits. Moreover, it increases power consumption (a problem for battery-powered notebooks). Inherent inductance, on the other hand, is less of a problem. The circuits in a computer are so densely packed that their inherent inductance is minimal.

Every circuit has some resistance, capacitive reactance, and inductive reactance. We call the combination of these three circuit parameters *impedance*. When we say that a point in a circuit is *at a high impedance,* we mean that it is electrically disconnected from the rest of the circuit.

5.3 COMBINATIONAL LOGIC

Combinational logic are circuits whose outputs at any time depend only on its inputs at that time. We will start with simple combinational circuits called *gates*. We will then use gates to build more complex circuits.

5.3.1 Gates

Six circuits that are frequently used in computers are the NAND, NOR, AND, OR, XOR (exclusive OR), and NOT circuits. These circuits are often called *gates*, because of their action of allowing, blocking, or in some way modifying the propagation of binary signals. The schematic symbol and truth table for each of these circuits is given in Figure 5.9. Notice that the symbol for a NAND is the symbol for an AND gate with a "bubble" on its output. The bubble indicates a signal inversion. Thus, the picture of a NAND gate—an AND gate followed by a bubble—indicates that a NAND gate functions like an AND gate whose output is inverted. We have the same situation with the NOR and OR gates. A NAND gate is the NOT of an AND (hence, the name "NAND"). A NOR gate is the NOT of an OR (hence, the name "NOR").

We saw how to implement a NOT gate in Figure 5.5a. The circuit in Figure 5.6a implements a positive logic NOR gate. The implementation of a positive logic NAND gate is similar to that of a NOR gate (it also requires four transistors—two connected in series and two in parallel). With these three types of gates—NOT, NOR, and NAND—we can easily implement any other gate. For example, by following a NOR gate with a NOT, we get an OR gate; by following a NAND gate with a NOT, we get an AND gate (see Figure 5.10).

The use of the term "gate" to denote these circuits makes sense if we consider the action of the NAND, NOR, AND, and OR gates (see Figure 5.11). Suppose we apply a 0 to one of the inputs of a NAND gate. Then its output is forced to 1 regardless of the data on its other input. We can say the gate is "closed" to the input data. If, however, we apply a 1 to one input, then the data on the other input goes through the gate and appears on the output in complemented form. For this case, we can say the gate is "open"—it allows the data to pass through. Similarly, the NOR, AND, and OR gates are "closed" or "open" to data on one input depending on the value of the other input.

NAND, NOR, AND, and OR gates can have two or more inputs. The gates with more than two inputs operate like their two-input counterparts. For example, a three-input AND gate outputs a 1 only if all three inputs are 1. A three-input OR gate outputs a 1 whenever one or more of its inputs is 1.

FIGURE 5.9

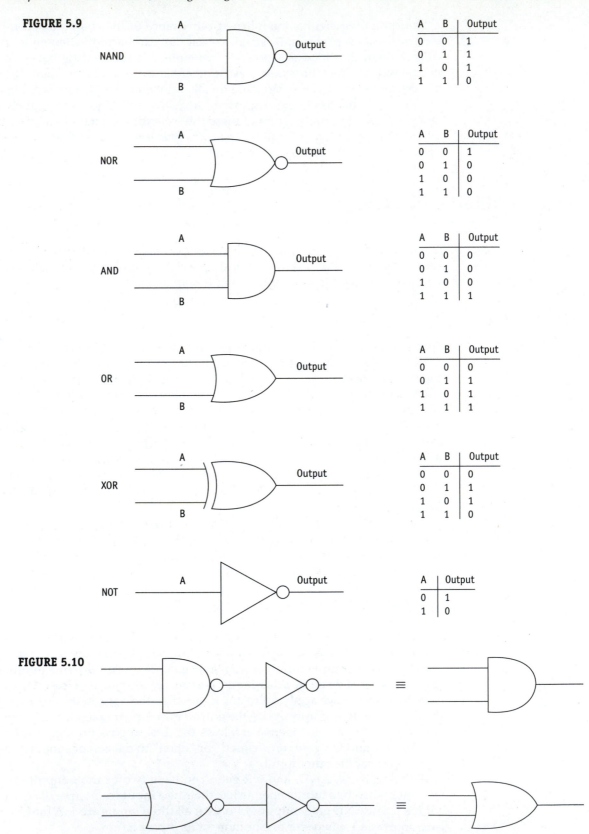

A	B	Output
0	0	1
0	1	1
1	0	1
1	1	0

A	B	Output
0	0	1
0	1	0
1	0	0
1	1	0

A	B	Output
0	0	0
0	1	0
1	0	0
1	1	1

A	B	Output
0	0	0
0	1	1
1	0	1
1	1	1

A	B	Output
0	0	0
0	1	1
1	0	1
1	1	0

A	Output
0	1
1	0

FIGURE 5.10

FIGURE 5.11   Gating Action

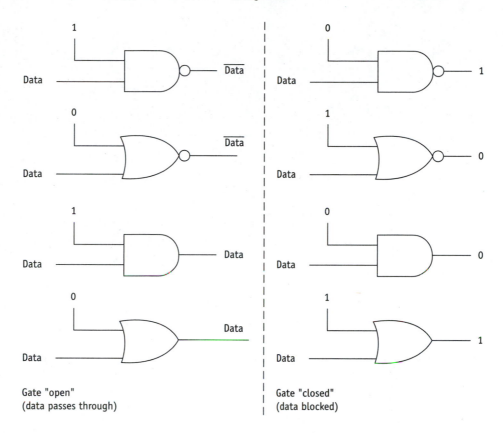

Gate "open"   Gate "closed"
(data passes through)   (data blocked)

5.3.2 Boolean Functions

Truth tables represent Boolean functions. A *Boolean function* is a function whose inputs and outputs are all two-valued. Typically the values of Boolean functions are either true/false or 1/0. Given any Boolean function in truth table form, we can easily implement it using a circuit consisting of AND, OR, and NOT gates. Let's look at the simple example in Figure 5.12—the truth table for the XOR gate. To implement this function, we select only those rows whose output column contains a 1. Thus, for this function we select only the second and third rows. For each of these rows, we create a circuit using a single AND gate that will output a 1 *only* when the inputs are as specified in that row. For example, for the second row we create the circuit in Figure 5.13a. This circuit will output a 1 if and only if its A input is 0 and its B input is 1 (the inputs for the second row). For the third row, we create a similar circuit given in Figure 5.13b. Finally, we feed the output of each of these circuits to a common OR gate and tie all the common inputs together to get the circuit in Figure 5.13c. Let's analyze

FIGURE 5.12

A	B	C
0	0	0
0	1	1
1	0	1
1	1	0

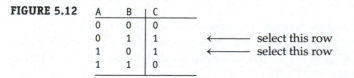

← select this row
← select this row

FIGURE 5.13   Implementing a Function

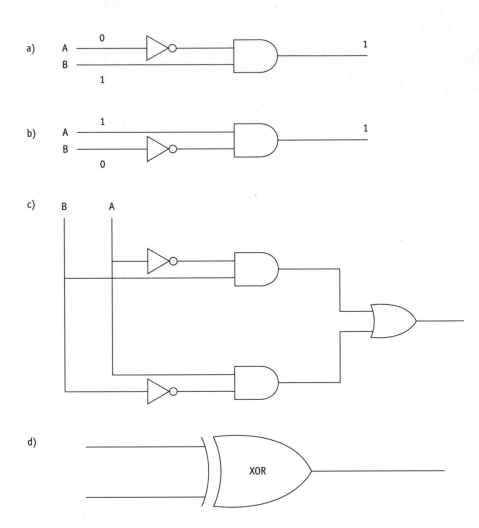

this composite circuit. If we input 0 and 1 for A and B, respectively, the top AND gate outputs a 1, causing the OR gate to also output a 1. Similarly, if we input a 1 and a 0 for A and B, respectively, then the bottom AND gate outputs a 1, again causing the OR gate to output a 1. However, all other input combinations cause both AND gates to output a 0, causing the OR gate to also output a 0. Thus, this circuit implements the truth table for the XOR function shown in Figure 5.12.

Because the XOR circuit is so important (recall we used it extensively in the adder circuit in Chapter 1), we have a special symbol for it (see Figure 5.13d).

5.3.3   A Minimal Circuit

Using the techniques given in the preceding section we can easily implement the function given by the truth table in Figure 5.14a. If we use one NOT gate to provide the $\overline{A}$ signal needed for the two AND gates, we get the circuit in Figure 5.14b.

FIGURE 5.14   Minimization

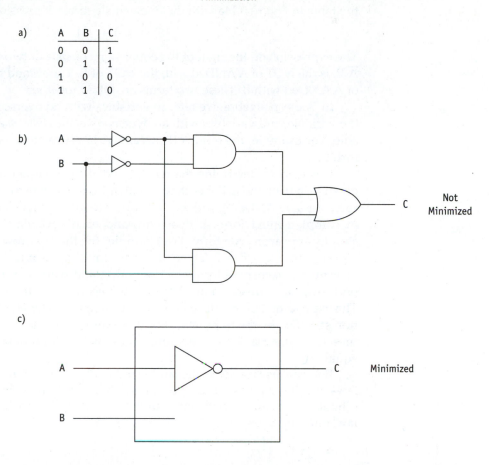

a)

A	B	C
0	0	1
0	1	1
1	0	0
1	1	0

Notice that the A column of the truth table is the complement of the C column. This property implies that C depends *only* on A. Using this fact, we can construct a much simpler circuit for this function, consisting of a single NOT gate (see Figure 5.14c). The B input is not connected to anything because it has no effect on the output for this function. Clearly, the circuit in Figure 5.14c is better than the one in Figure 5.14b. In fact, it is better in two respects. First, it uses less hardware (only a single gate). Second, it consists of only one level of circuits (the NOT gate). Thus, it produces its output more quickly than the first circuit (which consists of three levels). We call it a *minimal circuit* because it uses the fewest number of gates possible.

We can use a number of techniques to determine the minimal circuit for any Boolean function. In the next two sections, we will examine two such techniques: Boolean algebra and Karnaugh maps.

5.3.4 Circuit Minimization Using Boolean Algebra

Boolean functions can be represented using a special kind of algebra called *Boolean algebra*. Boolean algebra uses three operations: OR (represented by the plus sign), AND (represented by placing the terms next to each other), and NOT (represented by an overscore on a term). For example, we can represent the function given by the table in Figure 5.14a with the Boolean algebraic expression

$$C = \overline{A}\,\overline{B} + \overline{A}\,B$$

The expression on the right of the equal sign consists of two terms. The first term, $\overline{A}\,\overline{B}$, is the NOT of A ANDed with the NOT of B. The second term, $\overline{A}\,B$, is the NOT of A ANDed with B. These two terms are ORed together.

In Boolean algebra, we refer to variables with no overscore as the *true form* of the variable, and variables with an overscore as the *complemented form* of the variable. For example, the term $\overline{A}\,B$ contains A in complemented form and B in true form.

It is easy to determine the terms needed to represent any Boolean function given by a truth table. For each row with a 1 output, construct a term consisting of each variable ANDed together. Each variable that is 0 for that row should appear in complemented form in this term, and each variable that is 1 for that row should appear in true form. For example, for the first row of the truth table in Figure 5.14a, $A = B = 0$. Thus, the corresponding term is $\overline{A}\,\overline{B}$ (both A and B appear in complemented form because both A and B are 0 for this row). For the second row, the corresponding term is $\overline{A}\,B$ (because $A = 0$ and $B = 1$ for this row). The expression that results when we OR these terms together represents the function specified by the truth table. For those inputs for which the output is 1, the expression will equal 1; for those inputs for which the output is 0, the expression will equal 0.

Boolean algebra obeys the laws listed in Figure 5.15. Some, but not all, of these laws are the same as the laws of the algebra of numbers that we learned in high school. For example, both Boolean and number algebra have the commutative law, but only Boolean algebra has the absorption law.

FIGURE 5.15	Distributive Law	$A(B + C) = AB + AC$
		$A + BC = (A + B)(A + C)$
	Commutative Law	$AB = BA$
		$A + B = B + A$
	Absorption Law	$A + AB = A$
		$A(A + B) = A$
	Identity Law	$A1 = A$
		$A + 0 = A$
	Null Law	$A0 = 0$
		$A + 1 = 1$
	Idempotent Law	$A + A = A$
		$AA = A$
	Inverse Law	$A\overline{A} = 0$
		$A + \overline{A} = 1$
	Associative Law	$(A + B) + C = A + (B + C)$
		$(AB)C = A(BC)$
	DeMorgan's Laws	$\overline{A + B} = \overline{A}\,\overline{B}$
		$\overline{AB} = \overline{A} + \overline{B}$

Note that all the laws in Boolean algebra come in pairs. Each law in a pair can be obtained from the other by interchanging the AND and OR operations, and 0 and 1. For example, $A\overline{A} = 0$ becomes $A + \overline{A} = 1$ (the other inverse law) when we make these interchanges.

Using these laws, we can manipulate Boolean expressions into equivalent simpler expressions. For example, let's use Boolean algebra to simplify

$$C = \overline{A}\,\overline{B} + \overline{A}\,B$$

We get

$$
\begin{aligned}
C &= \overline{A}\,\overline{B} + \overline{A}\,B \\
&= \overline{A}(\overline{B} + B) \quad \text{by the distributive law} \\
&= \overline{A}(1) \qquad\quad \text{by the inverse law} \\
&= \overline{A} \qquad\qquad \text{by the identity law}
\end{aligned}
$$

This simple example illustrates an important rule. Suppose two terms are identical except for one *black sheep variable* (a variable that appears in true form in one term and in complemented form in the other). The two terms can be combined into a single term in which the black sheep variable is eliminated. For example, consider

$$ABCD + AB\overline{C}D$$

Here, both terms are identical except for the C variable. We can combine both terms and eliminate the C variable to get ABD. This rule follows directly from the distributive, inverse, and identity laws, as illustrated earlier. We will often use this rule, so let's give it a name. Let's call it the *bye, bye, black sheep rule* because the variable that differs (a "black sheep") is eliminated (goes "bye, bye").

5.3.5 Pictorial Representation of DeMorgan's Laws

DeMorgan's law at the bottom of Figure 5.15 has some interesting implications with respect to NOR and NAND gates. For example, consider the two gates in Figure 5.16a.

The gate on the left computes $\overline{A + B}$; the gate on the right computes $\overline{A}\,\overline{B}$ (the bubbles on its inputs indicate that its inputs are inverted). DeMorgan's first law,

$$\overline{A + B} = \overline{A}\,\overline{B}$$

FIGURE 5.16   De Morgan's Laws

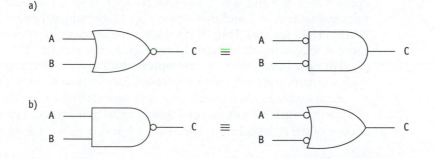

a)

b)

tells us that these gates are equivalent. Similarly, the second DeMorgan's law,

$$\overline{AB} = \overline{A} + \overline{B}$$

tells us that the two gates in Figure 5.16b are also equivalent.

For both cases in Figure 5.16, we can pictorially transform the gate on the left to the gate on the right by

1. Moving the bubble on the output back to both inputs.
2. Changing the type of the gate. Specifically, an OR gate (as in Figure 5.16a) changes to an AND gate; an AND gate (as in Figure 5.16b) changes to an OR gate.

These transformation rules are really a way to state DeMorgan's laws pictorially. In Figure 5.15, we state DeMorgan's laws using formulas; in Figure 5.16, we state DeMorgan's laws using pictures of gates.

Now consider the circuit in Figure 5.17a consisting of three NAND and two NOT gates. Let's move the bubble on the rightmost NAND gate back to its inputs, changing the AND gate to an OR gate. This gives us the circuit in Figure 5.17b. Notice that the lines connecting the gates on the left with the gate on the right each have two bubbles, representing two inversions. Because these double inversions cancel each other, we can eliminate each pair of bubbles to get the circuit in Figure 5.17c. All three circuits are equivalent by DeMorgan's laws.

We can make an important generalization from Figure 5.17. In *any* circuit consisting of AND gates driving a single OR gate, we can replace all these gates with NAND gates without affecting the function computed by the circuit. For example, in our implementation of the XOR gate in Figure 5.13c, we can replace the two AND gates and the OR gate with NAND gates.

5.3.6 Circuit Minimization Using Karnaugh Maps

At the end of the preceding section we learned a rule—the black sheep rule—for combining two terms that differ in only one variable. The repeated application of this rule is the basis of a minimization technique using Karnaugh maps.

A *Karnaugh map* is another representation of a Boolean function. A Karnaugh map is a grid, each square of which corresponds to a row in a truth table. A 1 in a square indicates a 1-output for that truth table row; a blank or 0 in a square indicates a 0-output for that truth table row. Consider the 2 by 2 (i.e., two rows, two columns) Karnaugh map in Figure 5.18a.

The first column corresponds to the A value of 0; the second column corresponds to the A value of 1. Similarly, the two rows correspond to the B values of 0 and 1. Each column and row is labeled with the variable value—0 or 1—to which it corresponds. Associated with each square is an A and B value. For example, the bottom left square corresponds to A = 0 and B = 1; the bottom right square corresponds to A = 1 and B = 1. In this Karnaugh map, a 1 appears in the squares corresponding to A = 1 and B = 0 (the upper right square) and A = 1 and B = 1 (the bottom right square). Thus, it represents the Boolean function whose value is 1 for these A, B combinations, namely, the function in Figure 5.18b.

We now have four ways to represent a Boolean function: with a truth table, with a circuit, with a Boolean expression, and with a Karnaugh map.

Each square in a Karnaugh map corresponds to the term that assumes the value of 1 for the variable values corresponding to that square. For example, the upper square of the right column (where A = 1 and B = 0) corresponds to the term $A \overline{B}$

FIGURE 5.17 NAND Gate Substitution

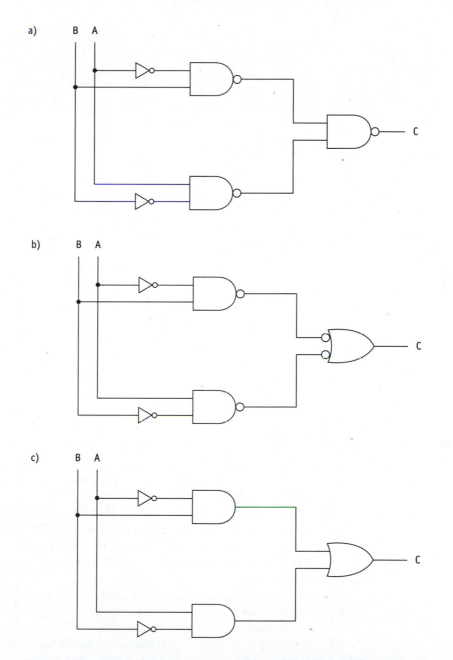

because this term equals 1 when A = 1 and B = 0. Similarly, the lower square in the right column (where A = B = 1) corresponds to the term AB. By ORing the terms that correspond to squares on the Karnaugh map containing 1's, we get the algebraic representation of the same function:

$$C = A\overline{B} + AB$$

Whenever two 1's in a Karnaugh map are adjacent in the same row or column, they necessarily represent terms that differ in only one variable. In our example,

FIGURE 5.18

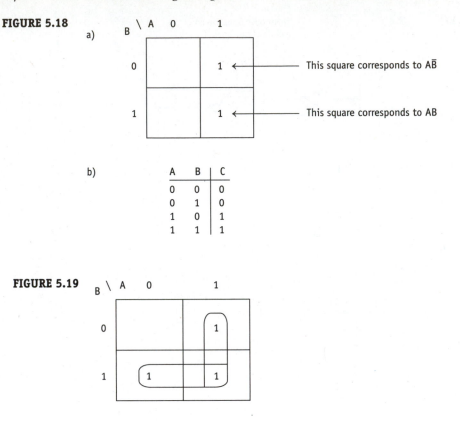

a)

This square corresponds to $A\overline{B}$

This square corresponds to AB

b)

A	B	C
0	0	0
0	1	0
1	0	1
1	1	1

FIGURE 5.19

the adjacent 1's are in the A = 1 column. Thus, A appears in true form in both of the corresponding terms. However, the adjacent 1's are in different rows (the B = 0 row and the B = 1 row). This implies that B appears in complemented form in one term and true form in the other. Using the black sheep rule, we can combine the two terms, eliminating the variable B (the variable whose value differs for the adjacent 1's), giving the simplified expression A.

Note that adjacent 1's along a diagonal do *not* combine because they correspond to terms that differ in more than one variable. For example, the upper left square corresponds to the term $\overline{A}\,\overline{B}$ whereas the lower right square corresponds to AB. These two terms differ in both A and B, and, therefore, cannot be combined using the black sheep rule.

When using a Karnaugh map, we usually circle the adjacent 1's we are combining. Now let's consider the more complicated example in Figure 5.19.

In this example, we have two adjacencies—the two 1's in the bottom row and the two 1's in the right column. You can see from the figure that we are combining both adjacencies, using the lower right square twice. The 1's in the right column combine to form A; the 1's in the bottom row combine to form B. Thus, the minimized expression is

$$C = A + B$$

If we did not combine both adjacencies in the figure, we would not get the minimal expression. Suppose, for example, we combined only the two 1's in the right column. Then the resulting expression would be

$$C = A + \overline{A}\,B$$

FIGURE 5.20

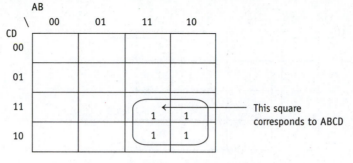

This square corresponds to ABCD

The A term results from combining the adjacent 1's in the right column. However, we still must cover the 1 in the lower left square. We do this by including its term, $\overline{A}\,B$, in the final expression. Obviously, this expression is not as minimized as the previous one in which both adjacencies were circled.

When we circle both adjacencies in this example, we are using the term corresponding to the lower right square twice—once for each circle. This multiple use of a term is justified by the idempotent law of Boolean algebra which states that

$$A + A = A$$

That is, multiple occurrences of a term ORed together always have the same value as a single occurrence. By using this law, we can perform the same minimization algebraically that we did with the Karnaugh map. Here are the steps:

$$
\begin{aligned}
C &= A\,\overline{B} + AB + \overline{A}\,B && \\
  &= A\,\overline{B} + AB + AB + \overline{A}\,B && \text{by the idempotent law}\\
  &= (A\,\overline{B} + AB) + (AB + \overline{A}\,B) && \text{by the associative law}\\
  &= A \qquad\qquad + (AB + \overline{A}\,B) && \text{by the black sheep rule}\\
  &= A \qquad\qquad + B && \text{by the black sheep rule}
\end{aligned}
$$

The algebraic approach, although more difficult to apply, yields the same minimal expression.

We can also use Karnaugh maps to minimize expressions of three or four variables. For more than four variables, however, Karnaugh maps become more than two-dimensional, and, therefore, awkward to use. Let's consider a four-variable Karnaugh map in Figure 5.20.

In this Karnaugh map, each square corresponds to a term that has four variables. For example, the square in the third column and third row corresponds to the term ABCD because it is in the column corresponding to A = 1, B = 1, and the row corresponding to C = 1, D = 1. Similarly, the other terms (in a clockwise direction) in the circled group of 1's are $A\,\overline{B}\,CD$, $A\,\overline{B}\,C\overline{D}$, and $ABC\overline{D}$. Notice how we have labeled the columns and rows. This order (00, 01, 11, 10) results in *adjacent squares differing in only one variable*. If, instead, we labeled the rows and columns using the order 00, 01, 10, 11, then an adjacency between the second and third columns (or rows) would involve the change of two variables (in which case we could not apply the black sheep rule).

In this map we can circle the top two 1's, thereby eliminating B. Doing this corresponds to the algebraic simplification

$$ABCD + A\overline{B}CD = ACD$$

FIGURE 5.21

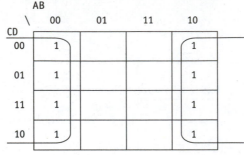

Similarly, we can circle the bottom two 1's, again eliminating B:

$$ABC\overline{D} + A\overline{B}C\overline{D} = AC\overline{D}$$

We now can combine the two resulting terms, ACD and AC$\overline{D}$, using the black sheep rule to get AC. Observe that *all four 1's combine into a single term*. This final term is the term in which all variables varying over the four terms have been eliminated. Because B varies from the third and four columns, and D varies from the third and fourth rows, both B and D are eliminated by the black sheep rule.

Rather than circling the top two 1's and the bottom two 1's, we can simply circle and combine all four 1's in one step, eliminating any "black sheep" variables in the entire grouping.

Figure 5.21 shows a Karnaugh map that illustrates an unexpected grouping.

Observe that each square in the leftmost column differs in only one variable from the corresponding square in the rightmost column. For example, the top left square corresponds to $\overline{A}\,\overline{B}\,\overline{C}\,\overline{D}$, and the top right square corresponds to $A\overline{B}\,\overline{C}\,\overline{D}$. These two terms differ only in the A variable. Thus, we can consider these two columns as adjacent, as if the right column were wrapped around and attached to the left column. The top and bottom rows are similarly adjacent, and should be viewed as attached to each other.

Because of the adjacency of the leftmost and rightmost columns, we can draw one big "circle" encompassing all eight 1's. Eliminating all variables that vary over this grouping (A, C, and D vary), we get the minimal expression $\overline{B}$.

5.3.7 Multiplexers

Earlier in this chapter, we learned how to construct logic gates (the NOT, NAND, NOR, AND, OR, and XOR gates) using transistors. We will now construct more complex circuits using these logic gates. Each of these circuits is an important building block of H1.

Let's start with the multiplexer circuit. A *multiplexer* (or *MUX* for short) is a circuit that has n control inputs, 2^n data inputs, and one output. For example, a multiplexer with three control inputs will have $2^3 = 8$ data inputs. The control inputs determine which data input reaches the single output line. Let's look at the *black box* diagram (i.e., a diagram that shows only the external connections of a circuit) of a four-input multiplexer shown in Figure 5.22a.

We can apply any of four binary numbers—00, 01, 10, 11 (0, 1, 2, or 3 in decimal)—to the C1 and C0 control inputs. The control inputs determine which of the data inputs—D0, D1, D2, or D3—are effectively connected to the output line. For example, suppose the control input is 2 (i.e., C1 = 1 and C0 = 0), then the D2 line

FIGURE 5.22   4-Input Multiplexer

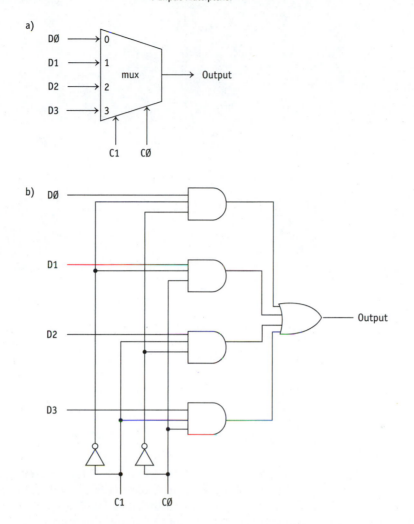

is effectively connected to the output. It is a good practice to label each data input in a multiplexer with the control input value that selects that input. For example, in Figure 5.22a, we labeled the input that is selected when the control input is 2 with 2. That way, there is never any confusion on which input corresponds to which control input value.

The implementation of a four-input multiplexer is given in Figure 5.22b. The circuit makes use of the "gating" capability of the AND gate. An AND gate with three inputs (two control and one data) allows its data input to propagate to its output only when its control inputs are both 1. Thus, D3 propagates to the OR gate only when C1 and C0 are both 1. Similarly, D2 propagates to the OR gate only when C1 = 1 and C0 = 0 (note that C0 is inverted before it is applied to the AND gate for D2).

A *bus* is a group of wires that carries information from one point in a computer to another. In circuit diagrams, we usually represent a bus with a single line, labeled with a cross-hatch and the number of wires in the bus. For example, Figure 5.23a shows a circuit with two data inputs and one output, all of which are buses that contain four wires each.

FIGURE 5.23   Two-Bus Input Multiplexer

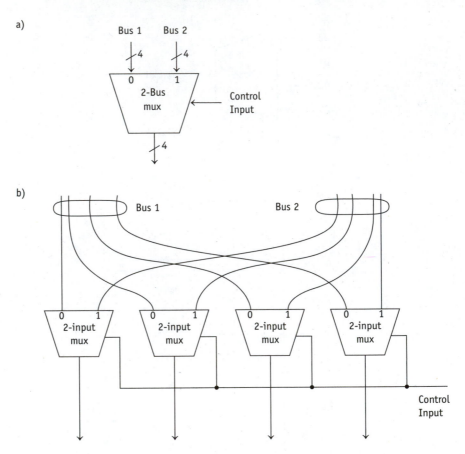

A *bus multiplexer* is a multiplexer whose data inputs are buses. Its control inputs determine which of its input buses reach its output bus. Figure 5.23a gives the black box diagram of a bus multiplexer that has two buses as inputs. When the control input is 0, the data on bus 1 reaches the output; when the control input is 1, the data on bus 2 reaches the output.

We can construct a bus multiplexer for buses with n lines by combining n regular multiplexers. For example, in Figure 5.23b we are using four two-input multiplexers to create a two-bus multiplexer for buses containing four lines.

5.3.8   Decoders and Encoders

A *decoder* is a circuit that decodes (i.e., determines the value of) the binary number placed on its input. A decoder has n input lines and 2^n output lines. For example, a three-input decoder has $2^3 = 8$ outputs. Consider the black-box diagram of a two-input decoder shown in Figure 5.24a.

In a decoder, only one output is 1 at any given time. The output with 1 is determined by the value of the number on the input. For example, suppose we input 2 (i.e., B1 = 1 and B0 = 0). A 1 will appear on output 2, indicating that the value of the input is 2; 0 will appear on all the other outputs.

A two-input decoder is essentially four combinational circuits, one for each output, in which the common inputs are tied together (see Figure 5.24b). For ex-

FIGURE 5.24   Two-Input Decoder

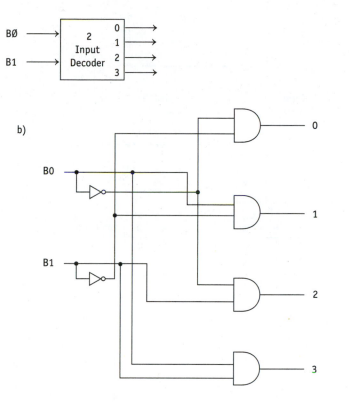

b)

ample, the circuit for output 0 is an AND gate driven by two NOT gates. Its output is 1 only when its two inputs are both 0. The circuit for output 3 is just an AND gate. Its output is 1 only when its two inputs are both 1.

An *encoder* performs the reverse function of a decoder. It has n outputs and up to 2^n inputs. At any given time, only one input should be driven with a 1. The encoder then outputs the binary number (or some other code) corresponding to the number specified by its input. Encoders sometimes have fewer than 2^n inputs. For example, a decimal-to-BCD encoder has 4 outputs and 10 (rather than 16) inputs. The 10 inputs correspond to the decimal digits 0 to 9. It outputs the 4-bit BCD encoding for each decimal digit.

5.3.9 Half and Full Adders

In Chapter 1, we learned how to construct a ripple-carry adder/subtracter circuit from multiple XOR gates and full adders. In Section 5.3.2, we learned how to construct an XOR gate. Let's now learn how to construct a full adder.

Recall that a full adder is a circuit that performs the addition needed for one column when two binary numbers are added. That is, it adds two bits and a carry in, and outputs a sum and a carry out. One way to implement a full adder is to combine two half adders. A *half adder* is a circuit that adds two bits (not including a carry in), and outputs a sum and a carry out (see Figure 5.25a). Its operation is described by the two truth tables in Figure 5.25b—one for the sum and one for the carry out.

FIGURE 5.25   Half Adder

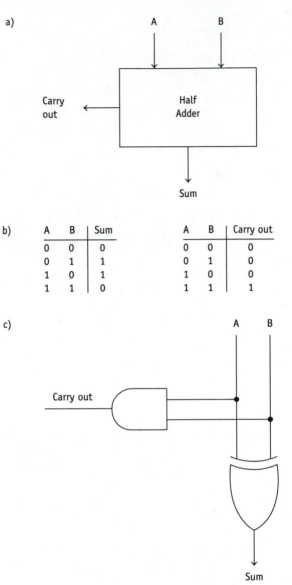

a)

b)

A	B	Sum
0	0	0
0	1	1
1	0	1
1	1	0

A	B	Carry out
0	0	0
0	1	0
1	0	0
1	1	1

c)

By examining these truth tables, we can see that the sum is the exclusive OR of the inputs A and B. The carry out is the AND of the inputs A and B. Thus, we can easily implement a half adder with an XOR gate and an AND gate (see Figure 5.25c).

Using two half adders, we can easily implement a full adder (see Figure 5.26).

We use one half adder to add the A and B inputs. We then use a second half adder to add the sum from the first adder and the carry in. If a carry out occurs for either half adder, then our full adder should also output a carry out. Thus, we route the carry-out lines from both half adders to an OR gate, the output of which is the carry out for the full adder.

The speed of a combinational circuit depends on the number of levels of gates between the inputs and outputs. In a half adder, the carry out is realized with only one level (the AND gate). An XOR gate requires three levels. Thus, the sum re-

FIGURE 5.26   Full Adder

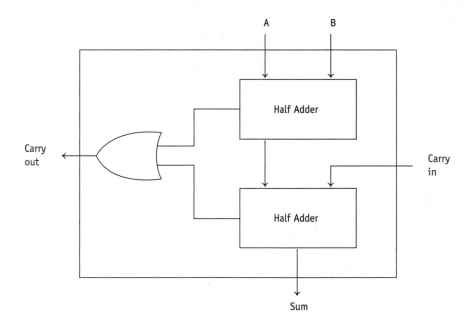

quires three levels. The sum of a full adder constructed with two half adders is realized in six levels (three from the first half adder and three from the second half adder). Its carry out depends on the carry out of both half adders, each of which is realized with one level. But the carry out of the second half adder depends on the sum out of the first half adder. Thus, four levels are needed to realize the carry out of the second half adder (three from the first half adder and one from the second half adder). These four levels plus the OR gate make a total of five levels to realize the full adder's carry out.

In a ripple-carry adder, each full adder has to wait for the full adder to its right to generate a carry out before it can compute its carry out. Thus, it is critical that each full adder generate its carry out as fast as possible. By constructing a full adder from two half adders, we get a full adder whose carry out is realized in five levels of gates. If we can reduce the number of levels, we can significantly improve the speed of the ripple-carry adder. The technique we learned in Section 5.3.2 for implementing Boolean functions yields a circuit that has *at most three levels* (a NOT driving an AND driving an OR), which is, therefore, faster. Thus, we should definitely use this technique to design the full adders for a ripple-carry adder.

5.3.10 One-Position Shifters

A *one-position shifter* is a circuit that can shift its input data one position either to the left or to the right. Because it has two possible actions (left or right), we need only one control line to specify its action. For example, with four input lines, the input 0111 appears as 0011 on the output for a right shift (a zero is shifted in from the left, and the rightmost bit is lost).

Figure 5.27a shows the black-box diagram of a four-input, one-position shifter. $R/\overline{L}$ is the control input. We use an overscore on a label to indicate that its action is triggered by a 0; no overscore indicates that the action is triggered by 1. Thus, $R/\overline{L} = 1$ triggers a right shift; $R/\overline{L} = 0$ triggers a left shift. On a right shift,

FIGURE 5.27   One-Position Shifter

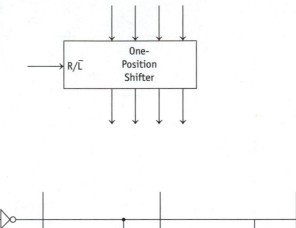

a)

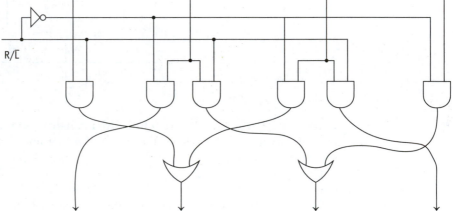

b)

the bit shifted in from the left is 0, and the rightmost bit of the input is lost. A similar action occurs on a left shift.

The idea behind the implementation of a one-position shifter is simple: Each input line, except those at the two ends, drives two AND gates. The outputs of these gates are attached through OR gates to the two possible destinations for the data: the output line to the left (for a left shift) and the output line to the right (for a right shift). Which of these AND gates is "open" (i.e., has a 1 on its control input) depends on the $R/\bar{L}$ input (see Figure 5.27b). The leftmost and rightmost input lines drive only one AND gate because these data lines have only one possible destination. The only possible destination for the leftmost line is one position to the right on a right shift. On a left shift, this bit is lost. Similarly, the only possible destination for the rightmost input line is one position to the left on a left shift.

On a left shift, the rightmost output line is necessarily 0 (because the AND gate driving it is forced to 0 by the 0 on the control line). Similarly, on a right shift, the leftmost output line is 0.

5.3.11   Multiplier Array

We do not have to consider number type—signed or unsigned—when we perform addition or subtraction with the adder/subtracter circuit in Figure 1.15 (in Chapter 1). This circuit works for both types of numbers. When we perform multiplication, can we similarly ignore the type of the numbers that we are multiplying? Let's consider some examples. To keep our examples simple, let's assume our computer has 4-bit registers. Representing -2 and -3 with 4 bits each, and multiplying -2 (the *multiplicand*) by -3 (the *multiplier*), we get

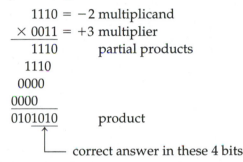

$$
\begin{array}{r}
1110 = -2 \text{ multiplicand} \\
\times\ 1101 = -3 \text{ multiplier} \\
\hline
1110 \qquad\quad \text{partial products} \\
0000 \qquad\qquad\quad \\
1110 \qquad\qquad\qquad \\
1110 \qquad\qquad\qquad\quad \\
\hline
10110110 \qquad\quad \text{product}
\end{array}
$$

correct answer in these 4 bits

The product, 10110110, is incorrect. The correct answer is 0110 ($+6$). Notice, however, that the computed product contains the correct answer in its four rightmost bits. Thus, if our computer placed the product back in a 4-bit register (truncating the excess bits on the left), we would get the *correct* answer. Let's try another example. Multiplying -2 by $+3$, we get

$$
\begin{array}{r}
1110 = -2 \text{ multiplicand} \\
\times\ 0011 = +3 \text{ multiplier} \\
\hline
1110 \qquad\quad \text{partial products} \\
1110 \qquad\qquad\quad \\
0000 \qquad\qquad\qquad \\
0000 \qquad\qquad\qquad\quad \\
\hline
0101010 \qquad\quad \text{product}
\end{array}
$$

correct answer in these 4 bits

Again, the computed product is incorrect, but its four rightmost bits contain the correct answer ($1010 = -6$).

It turns out that if the product of two *n*-bit numbers—signed or unsigned—can fit into *n* bits, the standard multiplication technique that we just used will *always* produce a product whose rightmost *n* bits are the correct answer. Thus, when multiplying *n*-bit numbers, we can ignore the type of the numbers as long as we restrict ourselves to *n*-bit products. Unfortunately, for longer products, the standard multiplication technique works with unsigned numbers and positive signed numbers, but not with negative signed numbers.

When multiplying two *n*-bit numbers, it is easy to get a product greater than *n* bits. For this reason, most computers use a *register pair* to hold the product, permitting the product to be twice as long as the multiplier and multiplicand. But then, as the earlier examples illustrate, multiplications with negative signed numbers would yield incorrect results. To avoid this problem, these computers typically have two multiplication instructions: one for unsigned numbers that uses the standard multiplication technique illustrated earlier, and a second that works for signed numbers that uses a different technique. For example, PCs that use the Intel Pentium microprocessor have two multiplication instructions: imul for signed numbers, and mul for unsigned numbers.

When we multiplied two binary numbers, we multiplied the multiplicand by each bit of the multiplier, each producing a partial product. Each partial product is either equal to the multiplicand (if the multiplying bit is 1) or zero (if

FIGURE 5.28   a)

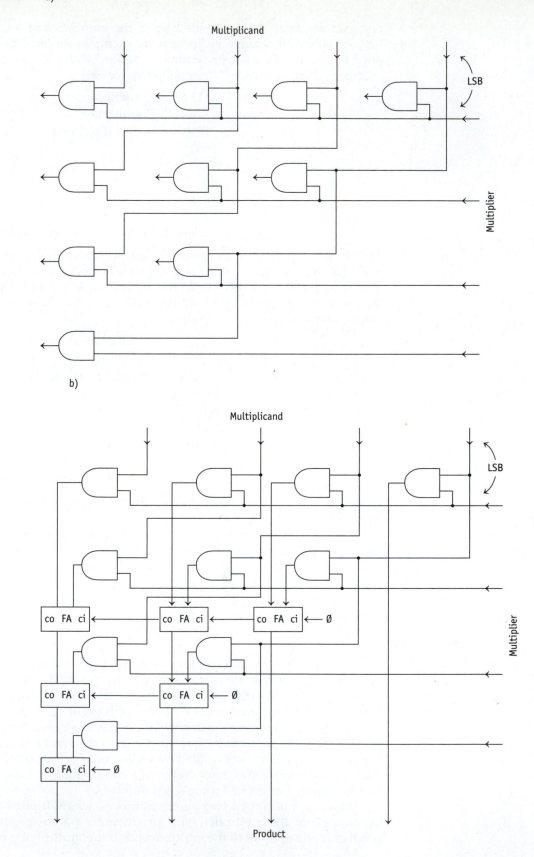

182

the multiplying bit is 0). It is easy to implement a circuit that generates these partial products. Each bit of any partial product is the AND of the corresponding bit in the multiplicand and the multiplying bit. Figure 5.28a shows the circuit for 4-bit numbers. The number on top is the multiplicand; the number to the right is the multiplier. Notice that the first row of AND gates is ANDing each bit of the multiplicand with the first bit of the multiplier. Thus, these gates generate the first partial sum. Similarly, the second, third, and fourth rows generate the second, third, and fourth partial products. Assuming we want only the four rightmost bits on the product, we don't need to generate bits beyond the fourth column.

To produce a 4-bit product, we have to sum the outputs of the AND gates in each column except for the rightmost column (the rightmost column contains only one AND gate). We can use a single full adder (with its carry in set to 0) to sum the second column. If this adder generates a carry, it must be included in the sum of the third column. Thus, we take its carry out and apply it to the carry in of the full adder in the column to its immediate left. Figure 5.28b shows the circuit with all the full adders included.

The multiplier array in Figure 5.28b computes the LSB of the product very quickly (it is the result of a single AND gate). The next bit takes more time because of the time required by the full adder. The MSB of the product requires the most time because of the multiple number of adders in column 4.

Multiplication on some computers takes considerably longer (perhaps by a factor of 100) than addition or subtraction. However, the circuit in Figure 5.28b develops its output in about twice the time as the 4-bit ripple adder in Figure 1.15 (count the number of levels in each circuit, and compare). Using a multiplier array is, in fact, a fast way to multiply. The problem with this circuit is that the total amount of logic that it requires becomes large as our number size increases. With 4-bit numbers, the triangular array in Figure 5.28b has $1 + 2 + 3 + 4 = 10$ elements. With 16-bit numbers it has $1 + 2 + \cdots + 16 = 136$ elements. And for 32-bit words (*de rigeur* for modern computers) it has 528 elements. For n elements, it has $1 + 2 + \cdots + n = n(n + 1)/2$ elements. The number of elements increases approximately with the square of the number of bits. Because of the higher cost of a multiplier array, computers sometimes use the *shift-add* technique—a technique that is slower but cheaper. We will discuss this technique in Chapter 13.

5.3.12 Arithmetic-Logic Unit

One typically first hears about an *arithmetic-logic unit (ALU)* in an introductory computer science course. We learn that an ALU is the unit within a computer that performs computations at incredible speeds. Surely, the ALU, the heart of a computer, must be awesomely complex. But this, in fact, is not necessarily the case. The ALU for H1 is actually quite simple, consisting of a straightforward combination of simple circuits, most of which we have already studied.

Let's examine the operation of the ALU in H1 from a black-box point of view (see Figure 5.29).

The ALU has two 16-bit input ports (left and right) and a 16-bit output port. Three control inputs, F0, F1, and F2, determine the function performed by the ALU, as specified in the table in Figure 5.29b. The first two and the last two functions in this table operate on the left input only. For these functions, the ALU ignores the right input. The first function (when F0 = F1 = F2 = 0) allows the left input to pass unaffected through the ALU. The S and Z outputs indicate the status

FIGURE 5.29

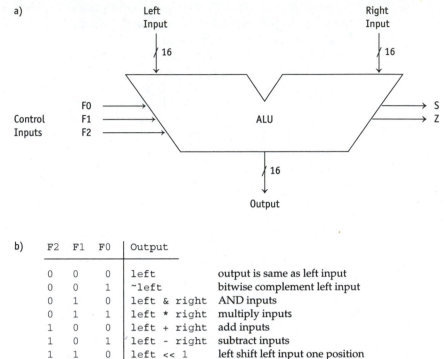

a)

b)

F2	F1	F0	Output	
0	0	0	left	output is same as left input
0	0	1	~left	bitwise complement left input
0	1	0	left & right	AND inputs
0	1	1	left * right	multiply inputs
1	0	0	left + right	add inputs
1	0	1	left - right	subtract inputs
1	1	0	left << 1	left shift left input one position
1	1	1	left >> 1	right shift left input one position

of the ALU output. S is the sign bit of the output; Z is the NOR of all the 16 output lines (thus, it equals 1 when the output is 0).

Let's now build the ALU using subcircuits to perform its various functions. We have the adder/subtracter (see Section 1.14) to perform the add and subtract functions; we have the multiplier array (see Section 5.3.11) to perform multiplication; and we have the one-position shifter to perform left and right shifts (see Section 5.3.10). We are lacking circuits for only two functions: the bitwise complement and the AND. Both are simple circuits. We build the complementer circuit with 16 NOT gates (see Fig 5.30a), and we build the ANDer circuit with 16 AND gates (see Figure 5.30b).

To keep our black box diagrams in Figure 5.30 simple, we use only a single line to represent the 16-line buses. We label these lines with a crosshatch and an adjacent "16" to indicate that they represent 16-line buses.

Now that we have a subcircuit for each ALU function, we can easily build the ALU (see Figure 5.31). An eight-bus multiplexer, controlled by F0, F1, and F2, selects which function to output. F0 also selects the subfunction in the adder/subtracter and in the shifter.

The Z output is provided by a NOR gate driven by the multiplexer's output lines (recall from Section 1.13 that a NOR gate is a zero-detecting gate). The S output is the MSB of the multiplexer's output.

5.3.13 Tri-state Buffer

Computers often use shared buses. A *shared bus* is a bus that can be driven by more than one device. Consider the circuit shown in Figure 5.32a.

Device 1 and device 2 are both attached to the same bus via AND gates. With this setup, the two devices will interfere with each other. For example, suppose de-

FIGURE 5.30   Complementer

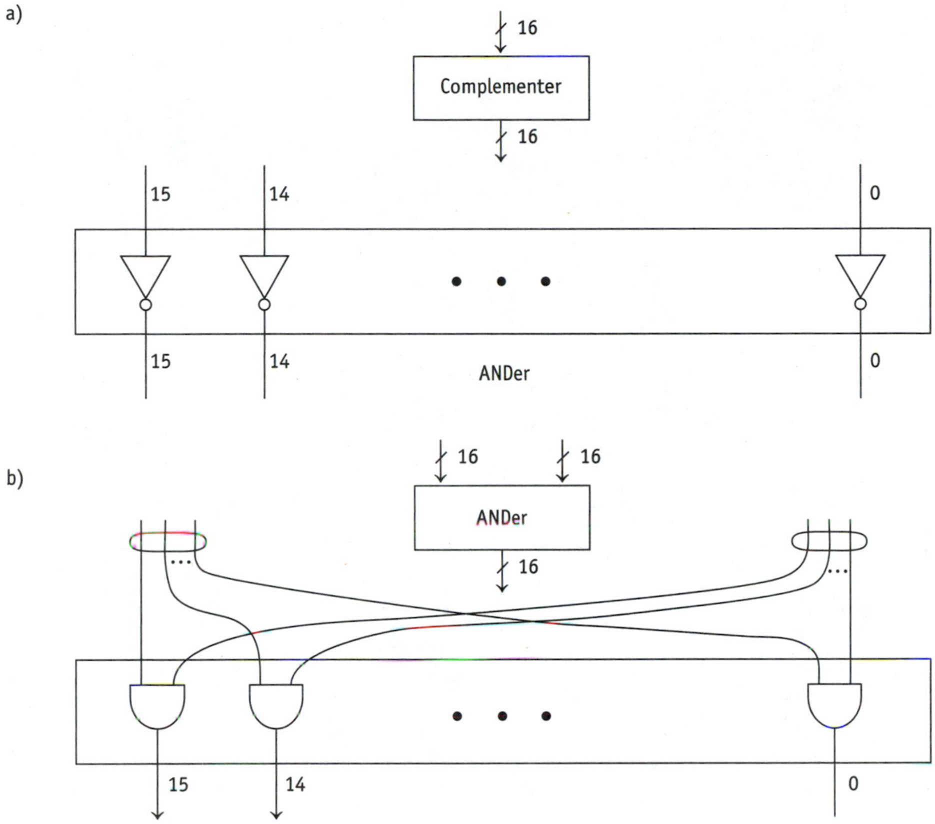

a)

b)

vice 1 is dormant and has 0 on the outputs of its AND gates. Now, suppose device 2 places data on the bus using its AND gates. The 0 outputs from device 1 will interfere with the data that device 2 is placing on the bus. Only the device that is actively driving a bus should be connected to that bus. Thus, we have to disconnect the inactive devices. It is not practical to physically connect and disconnect devices from a bus. However, we can easily *electronically* connect and disconnect devices, using a *tri-state buffer* (see Figure 5.32b). A tri-state buffer has one data input, one control input, and one output (see Figure 5.33). When the control input is 1, the output is equal to the input; however, when the control input is 0, the output is electrically disconnected from its input. It is as if we cut the wires between the input and output. We say that the output is at *high Z* (i.e., a high impedance). The output, therefore, has three possible states: 0, 1, or high Z (hence, the name "tri-state").

Using tri-state buffers, we can fix the circuit in Figure 5.32a by having each device drive the bus via tri-state buffers (see Figure 5.32b). Whenever a device is not active, it sets the control inputs of its tri-state buffers to 0, effectively disconnecting itself from the bus. Only the active device has the control inputs of its tri-state buffers set to 1.

The implementation of a tri-state buffer uses two transistors, one on top of the other (see Figure 5.33c).

If we apply a 1 to the control input, both transistors turn on (i.e., their internal switches close), connecting the output to the input. If, on the other hand, we apply a 0 to the control input, both transistors turn off (i.e., their internal switches open), disconnecting the output from the input.

FIGURE 5.31

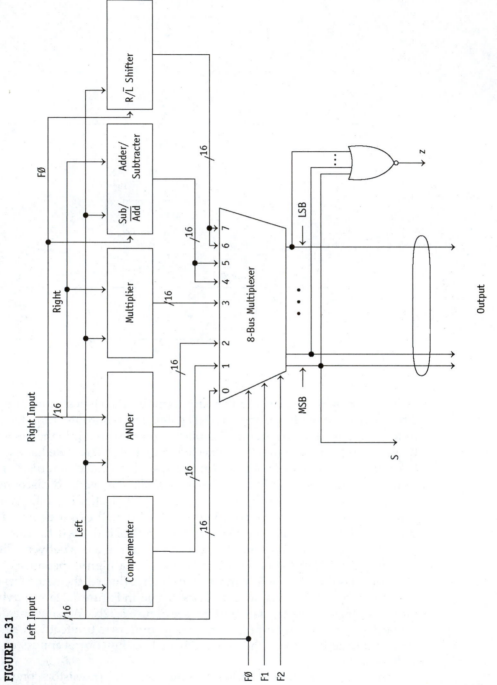

FIGURE 5.32   Shared Bus

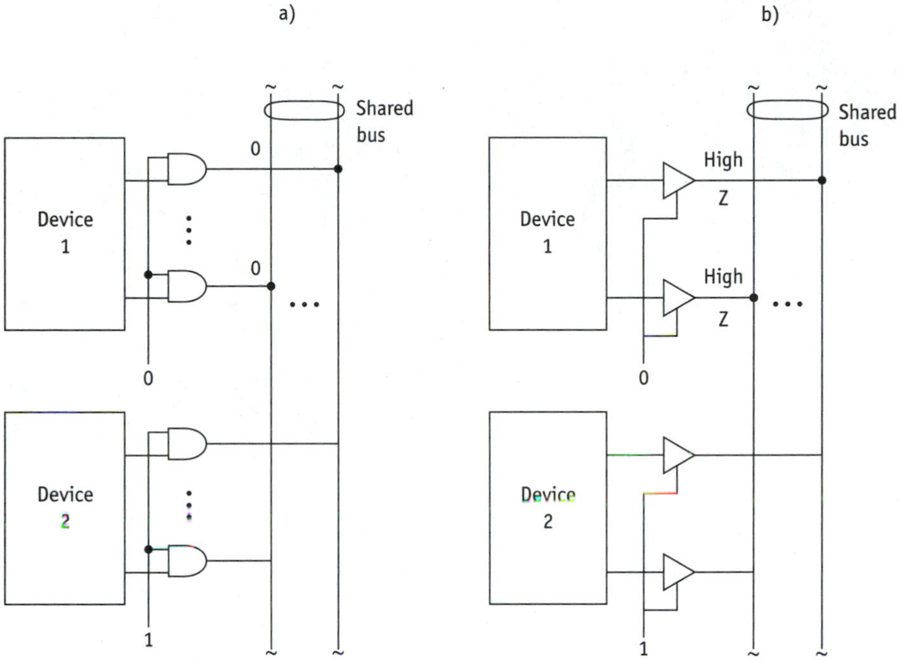

a)   b)

Arrays of tri-state buffers are used at both ends of a bidirectional bus (i.e., a bus that can carry information both ways). The state of the tri-state buffers determines the direction of the bus. For example, consider the 16-line bus in Figure 5.34a (only the top and bottom lines are drawn). When the control input is 1, the top buffer in each pair is on, creating a pathway from device 1 to 2. When the control input is 0, the bottom buffer in each pair is on, providing a pathway from device 2 to 1. Figure 5.34b shows the same bidirectional bus, but with a simplified picture (we use these simplified pictures in Chapter 6). Each tri-state buffer symbol represents a bank of 16 tri-state buffers; each line connecting their inputs and outputs represents a 16-line bus. The single left/right control line drives the upper buffers on each line; its complement drives the lower buffers.

5.3.14   Read-Only Memory

Read-only memory (ROM) is memory whose contents are permanent. We can read from it but not write to it. ROM is *nonvolatile memory;* that is, its contents are not lost when its circuits lose power.

Main memory in a computer usually contains some ROM to hold the boot, system test, and some device interfacing functions. The CPU sometimes also uses ROM—a separate ROM within the CPU itself—to hold *microinstructions* (binary numbers that specify the operations of the CPU).

We can specify the size of ROM with two numbers: the number of words and the number of bits in each word. Thus, a 512×32 (read "512 by 32") ROM has 512 32-bit words.

There are many ways to implement ROM. A particularly simple way uses NMOS transistors in a matrix configuration. Let's use this approach to construct the 4×3 ROM whose contents are given in Figure 5.35a.

FIGURE 5.33 Tri-State Buffer

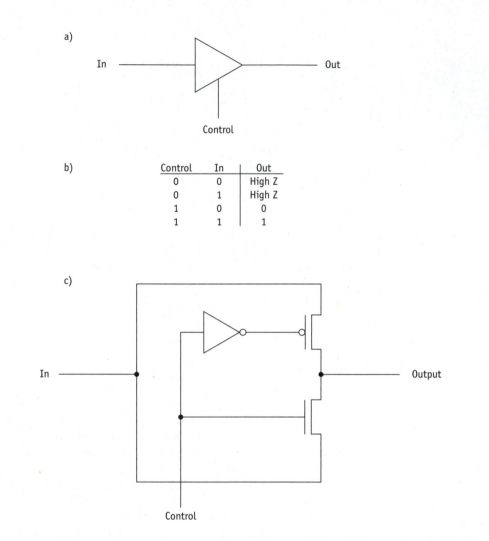

a)

In ──────▷────── Out

Control

b)

Control	In	Out
0	0	High Z
0	1	High Z
1	0	0
1	1	1

c)

In   Output

Control

We start by creating a mesh consisting of four horizontal and three vertical wires (see Figure 5.35b). We need one horizontal wire for each word in our ROM, and one vertical wire for each bit within a word. We call the horizontal wires *word lines* and the vertical wires *bit lines*. The word and bit lines are *not* connected at their intersection points. Each intersection point corresponds to a bit in our 4 × 3 ROM. For example, the intersections of the top word line and the three bit lines correspond to the three bits in the first word of our ROM. Next we connect each bit line through a resistor to the voltage level that represents 1 (let's use +3 volts). At each intersection point that corresponds to a 0 in our ROM, we connect the bit line to ground through an NMOS transistor, and we connect the word line to the gate of this transistor. Thus, whenever the word line carries +3 volts, the bit line is grounded to 0 volts through the transistor. We drive the word lines with the output from a two-input decoder.

Suppose we apply the address 2 (10 binary) to the inputs of the decoder in Figure 5.35b. The decoder then places a 1 (i.e., +3 volts) on the third word line which, in turn, causes the two transistors on this line to ground their bit lines. Thus, 0 volts appears on each of these bit lines. However, in the position in which

FIGURE 5.34   a)

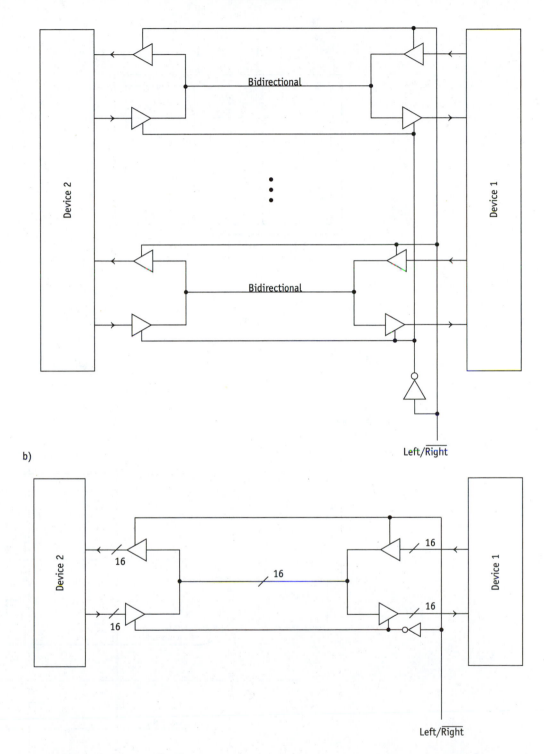

Bidirectional Bus

no transistor appears, the bit line carries +3 volts. Thus, the bit lines from left to right carry 0, 0, and +3 volts , representing the bits 0, 0, and 1 in the third word of our ROM.

FIGURE 5.35   a)   ROM

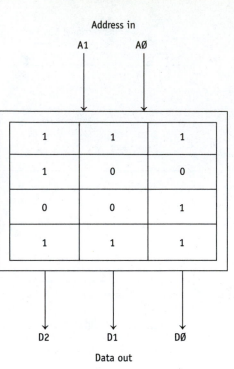

Address in

A1   AØ

1	1	1
1	0	0
0	0	1
1	1	1

D2   D1   DØ

Data out

b)

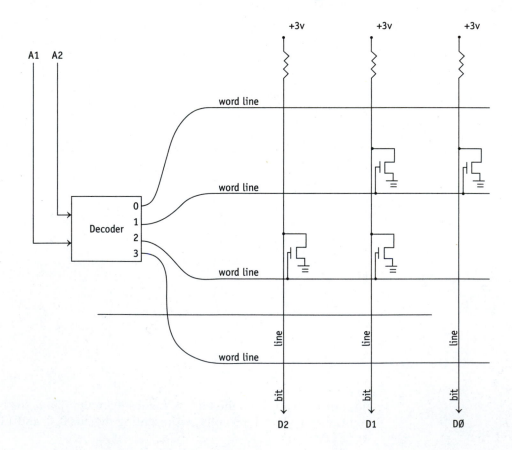

We call the resistors that connect the bit lines to +3 volts *pull-up resistors*. If we did not use them (i.e., if we were to connect the bit lines directly to +3 volts), then the transistors in the matrix, when closed, would short-circuit +3 volts directly to ground, causing excessive overcurrent.

The contents of the ROM in Figure 5.35 are fixed. However, the contents of PROM (programmable ROM) can be initialized by a customer with special equipment. Once initialized, however, the contents cannot be altered. In contrast, the contents of EPROM (erasable PROM) can be initialized and then subsequently erased. However, the erasure process is lengthy, requiring the use of ultraviolet light. In EEPROM (electrically erasable PROM) and flash memory, the contents can be repeatedly and quickly altered electrically. EEPROM allows the selective alteration of individual cells; flash memory does not. Flash memory, however, uses less power, making it well-suited for portable applications.

5.4 SEQUENTIAL LOGIC

A *sequential circuit* is a circuit that has memory. In particular, it depends on the sequence of inputs leading up to and including the present input (hence the name "sequential"). Sequential circuits, along with combinational circuits, are the building blocks of computers.

5.4.1 SR Flip-Flop

Our first sequential circuit is the *SR flip-flop*, which has two inputs labeled "S" and "R" (see Fig 5.36a). "S" stands for "set"; "R" stands for "reset." It also has two outputs, which have values that are usually (but not always) the complements of each other. Accordingly, the outputs are labeled Q and $\overline{Q}$.

Figure 5.36b shows the implementation of an SR flip-flop. Observe how the output of each NOR gate is fed back into the input of the other NOR gate. This feedback is what imparts to the circuit its memory capability.

The truth table for an SR flip-flop is unusual in that it includes two rows both corresponding to inputs S = R = 0 (see Figure 5.36c). Let's examine the circuit and confirm that this table does, indeed, describe its operation. Let's start with the first row of the truth table (S = 0, R = 1). The 1 on the R input propagates through the bottom gate but is inverted before it exits. Thus, Q, the output of this gate, is 0. The top gate has 0 on its S input and 0 (from the bottom gate) on its other input. Thus, $\overline{Q}$ is 1. A similar analysis can be done for the second row of the table. For the third row (S = R = 1), both gates necessarily output 0 because both have one input equal to 1. Now here's the interesting part. Let's assume S = 0 and R = 1. Then the output of the top gate is 1. This 1 is fed back into the bottom gate, making both inputs to the bottom gate equal to 1. If we now change R from 1 to 0, the bottom gate still has one input equal to 1 (from the output of the top gate), which holds the bottom gate's output at 0. The inputs of the upper gate do not change. Thus, its output also does not change. *Changing R from 1 to 0 does not change the outputs of the circuit.* The circuit is in a *stable state* (i.e., a state that will not change unless new inputs are applied). In this state, S = R = 0 and Q = 0 and $\overline{Q}$ = 1 (the fifth row of the table).

Now let's start with inputs S = 1 and R = 0. For this case, both inputs to the top gate are 1. If we now change S from 1 to 0, the top gate still has one input equal

FIGURE 5.36

SR Flip-Flop
(NOR Version)

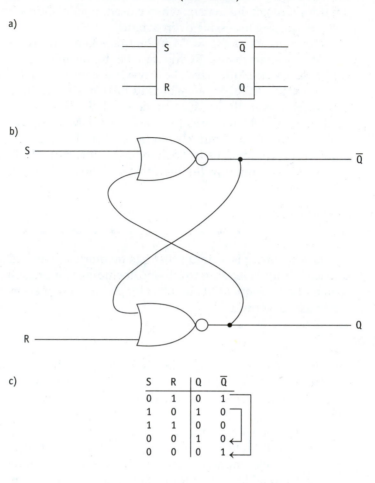

a)

b)

c)

S	R	Q	$\overline{Q}$
0	1	0	1
1	0	1	0
1	1	0	0
0	0	1	0
0	0	0	1

to 1 (from the output of the bottom gate), which holds the top gate's output at 0. The inputs of the bottom gate do not change. Thus, its output also does not change. The circuit, therefore, is in another stable state (described by the fourth row of the table). We have two possible outputs for the input S = R = 0, corresponding to the fourth and fifth rows of the truth table. Which output occurs *depends on the preceding input*. The arrows in Figure 5.36c show how to get to each state.

When Q = 1 and $\overline{Q}$ = 0, we say the flip-flop is *set*; when Q = 0 and $\overline{Q}$ = 1, we say the flip-flop is *reset*. An SR flip-flop can hold the value of a 1-bit number. Typically, the set state represents 1; the reset state represents 0.

The SR flip-flop in Figure 5. 36 uses NOR gates. We can also construct an SR flip-flop using NAND gates (see Figure 5.37). In the NOR gate version, two distinct states are possible when its two inputs are 0. To set the flip-flop, we place a 1 on its S input and a 0 on its R input. The NAND gate version works the same way, except that the roles of 1 and 0 are reversed: Two states are possible when both inputs are 1, and we set it by placing a 0 on its S input and a 1 on its R input.

We can see from the truth table in Figure 5.37c that two states are possible when S = R = 1.

FIGURE 5.37

SR Flip-Flop
(NAND Version)

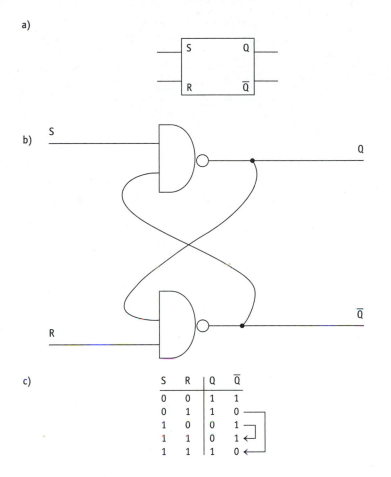

a)

b)

S

Q

Q̄

R

c)

S	R	Q	Q̄
0	0	1	1
0	1	1	0
1	0	0	1
1	1	0	1
1	1	1	0

5.4.2 Clocked D Flip-Flop

We often need a flip-flop in a computer that can be set or reset only when a synchronizing pulse (like the clock signal) is high, and which can be set with a single data input. One type of flip-flop with these properties is the *clocked D flip-flop*. Figure 5.38 shows a clocked D flip-flop constructed with NOR, AND, and NOT gates.

Notice that the two NOR gates are driven by two AND gates that are, in turn, driven by the CK input. Whenever CK = 0, both AND gates are "closed." Thus, both NOR gates are effectively isolated from the D input to the circuit. However, when CK = 1, the AND gates are "open," allowing the data on the D input and its complement to pass through to the NOR gates. By virtue of the NOT gate attached to the D input, the D input provides both the S input (the D line) and the R input (the D̄ output of the NOT gate) of the internal SR flip-flop. Because the clocked D flip-flop will respond to its D input whenever the clock input is at level 1, we call it a *level-triggered flip-flop*.

Typically, we use a clocked D flip-flop in this way. To set the flip-flop, we place a 1 on the D input, and then pulse the CK input. This combination provides the

FIGURE 5.38   Clocked D Flip-Flop

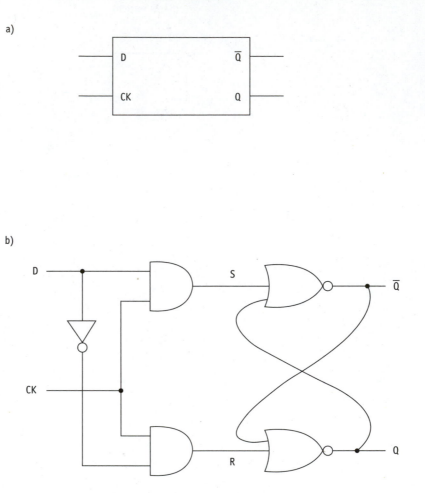

a)

b)

S = 1, R = 0 input to the internal SR flip-flop, causing it to set. Similarly, to reset the flip-flop, we place a 0 on the D line and pulse the CK input.

Sometimes it is necessary to set or reset a clocked D flip-flop when the CK signal is not available. We can do this if the flip-flop has two additional inputs—the *PR* (preset) and *CLR* (clear) inputs—that bypass the AND gates (see Figure 5.39a).

Figure 5.39b shows the connections to the PR and CLR inputs. Whenever PR becomes 1 while CLR and CK are 0, the following sequence occurs: The output of the top NOR gate becomes 0. Thus, all the inputs to the bottom NOR gate are 0, forcing its output to 1. This 1 is fed back to the top NOR gate. When PR returns to 0, the fed back 1 from the bottom NOR gate keeps the circuit in the set state. A similar sequence occurs whenever CLR becomes 1 when PR and CLR are 0, which causes the flip-flop to go into the reset state.

In Section 5.4.1, we learned that we can construct flip-flops with either NOR or NAND gates. An advantage of the NAND-gate version becomes apparent when we use it in a clocked D flip-flop: We can use NAND gates exclusively—that is, we can use NAND gates for the basic flip-flop, to gate the clock pulse, and to invert the D input (see Figure 5.40).

Note that a NAND gate with its two inputs tied together acts like a NOT gate. In this version, to preset the flip-flop, we set its PR input to 0 (not 1, as in the NOR

FIGURE 5.39   Clocked D Flip-Flop with PR & CLR
                                        (NOR Version)

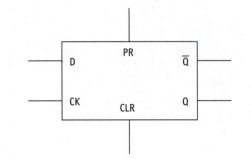

version). Similarly, to clear it, we set its CLR input to 0. We say that PR and CLR are *active low*. That is, they are activated by the lower voltage (i.e., 0 volts). In the black box diagram (see Figure 5.40a), we indicate that PR and CLR are active low in two ways: We put overscores on their labels and bubbles on their inputs.

5.4.3 Clocked JK Flip-Flop

A variation of the SR flip-flop is the JK flip-flop (see Figure 5.41). Note that the output of each NOR gate is fed back to both the other NOR gate and the driving AND gate.

The J and K inputs are like the S and R inputs, respectively, in an SR flip-flop. J = 1 and K = 0 sets the flip-flop (when CK = 1); J = 0 and K = 1 resets the flip-flop (when CK = 1). The JK flip-flop responds differently than the SR flip-flop when both its inputs are 1. Specifically, when the clock level is 1, if both J and K equal 1, *the flip-flop changes state* (if set, it resets; if reset, it sets). This behavior results

FIGURE 5.40

Clocked D Flip-Flop with PR & CLR
(NAND Version)

a)

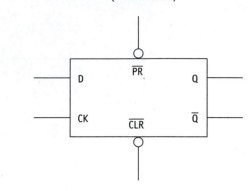

b)

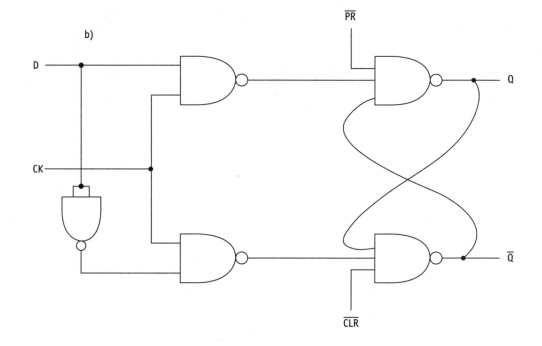

from the feedback to the AND gates. Suppose, for example, the flip-flop is reset. The feedback from the top NOR equals 1, but the feedback from the bottom NOR equals 0. This 0 keeps the bottom AND gate "closed" when a J = K = 1 input is applied. The J = 1 input propagates through the upper AND gate, but the K = 1 input is blocked by the bottom AND gate. Thus, a 1 drives the S input on the top NOR gate and a 0 drives the R input on the bottom NOR gate, causing the flip-flop to set.

5.4.4   Edge Detection

Digital circuits often form loops: One circuit drives another, which, in turn, drives—either directly or through other circuits—the first. If a flip-flop is in the loop, unwanted *oscillations* (repeated changes in signal levels) can occur. Consider

FIGURE 5.41   Clocked JK Flip-Flop

a)

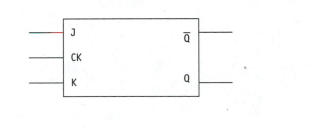

b)

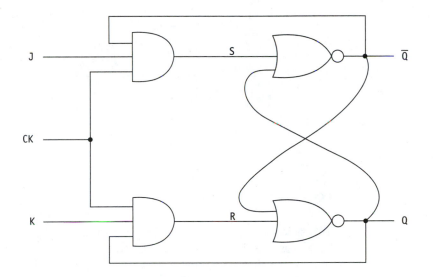

the following scenario: We apply a CK signal to the flip-flop in a loop (to set it according to its present input). Its output changes, which, because of the loop, causes its input to change. The input change, in turn, causes another output change. Each output change triggers an input change, and each input change triggers an output change. These changes in signal level at the output and input of the flip-flop occur rapidly and continue for as long as we apply a 1 to the CK input. Now suppose we replace the flip-flop in the loop with an edge-triggered flip-flop. An *edge-triggered flip-flop* is like a level-triggered flip-flop, except that it responds only during the edge of the CK signal. The *edge* of the CK signal is that portion of the signal when it is changing from 0 to 1 (or from 1 to 0). With an edge-triggered flip-flop in the loop, oscillations will not occur because by the time an output change causes an input change, the activating edge of the CK signal will be gone.

If an edge-triggered flip-flop responds to a positive-going edge of the clock, we say that it is *positive edge triggered*. If it responds to a negative-going edge, we say that it is *negative edge triggered*.

Figure 5.42 illustrates the difference between a level-triggered D flip-flop and an edge-triggered D flip-flop. Notice that the output of the level-triggered flip-flop follows the D input whenever the clock is 1. The output of the edge-triggered flip-flop, on the other hand, responds to the D input only on the positive-going edge of the clock.

You should be aware of two imprecisions in Figure 5.42. First, it shows instantaneous transitions, represented as vertical up and down lines on the graphs.

FIGURE 5.42 Edge Triggering

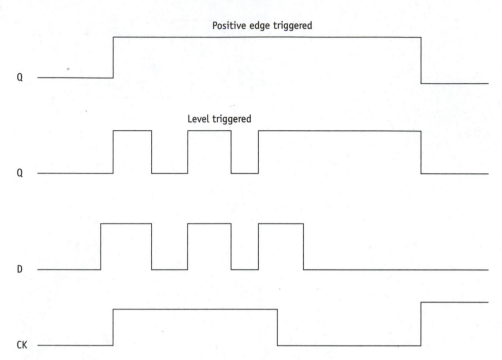

Transitions, of course, cannot be instantaneous. Transitions should be represented by almost-vertical lines. Second, it shows the Q output responding instantaneously to input changes. There is, in fact, a slight delay between an input change and a change on Q. Thus, as the CK signal goes positive, so does Q, but only after a slight delay.

Figure 5.43a shows the black box diagrams for positive and negative edge-triggered D flip-flops. Positive edge triggering is indicated by an "arrowhead" at the clock input; negative edge triggering is indicated by a bubble and an arrowhead.

The circuit for a positive edge-triggered flip-flop is given in Figure 5.43b. This circuit contains three flip-flops, two of which (the two in the boxes on the left) are *cross-coupled*—that is, each drives the other. Although this circuit is complicated, you should have little trouble understanding its operation if you understand the following two properties of two-input NAND gates:

1. A signal on one input is blocked (i.e., it has no effect on the output) whenever its other input is 0.
2. A NAND gate acts like a NOT gate for one input whenever its other input is 1.

Let's see how this circuit works. When CK is 0, the outputs of gates 1b and 2a are forced to 1, causing flip-flop 3 to stay in whatever state it is in. Moreover, the 1 out of gate 1b is fed into gate 1a, causing gate 1a to act like a NOT gate. Similarly, the 1 out of gate 2a is fed into gate 2b, causing gate 2b to also act like a NOT gate. The effect of these two "NOT" gates (1a and 2b) is to apply the complement of D to gates 1b and 2b, and D in true form to gate 2a. The input of each gate in Figure 5.43b is labeled with the value it assumes when CK = 0.

Now assume the clock makes a transition to 1. All the inputs of either gate 1b *or* 2a (but not both) will be 1, depending of the value of D. Suppose D is 1. Then gate 2a will have both of its inputs equal to 1, forcing its output, line Y, to go to 0.

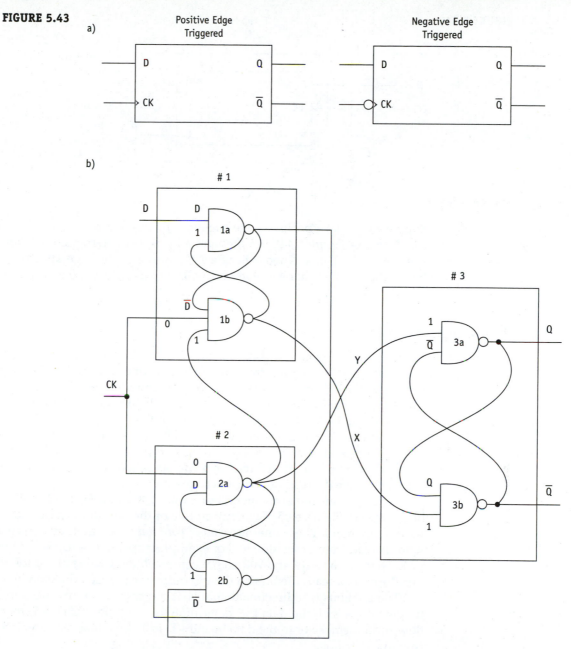

FIGURE 5.43

Line X, however, stays at 1. These values on X and Y cause flip-flop 3 to set. The 0 on line Y is fed back to gates 1b and 2b, blocking the $\overline{D}$ input. Thus, any changes in the D input occurring after the leading edge of the clock pulse have no effect on the state of flip-flop 3.

When D is 0 on a positive edge of the clock, X and Y become 0 and 1, respectively, causing flip-flop 3 to reset. Moreover, the 0 on X blocks D at gate 1a. Thus, any changes on D have no effect on the state of flip-flop 3. Thus, for this case (D = 0) and for D = 1, flip-flop 3 is set according to the value of D at the leading edge of the clock pulse. At all other times, it does not respond to the value of D.

FIGURE 5.44   T Flip-Flop

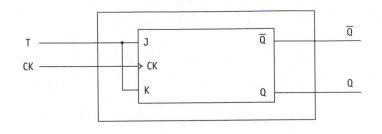

5.4.5   T Flip-Flop

Suppose we take a positive edge-triggered JK flip-flop and tie the J and K inputs together (see Figure 5.44). We then get a positive edge-triggered *T flip-flop*. Suppose we hold T at 1. Then whenever a positive-going edge appears on the CK input, the flip-flop changes state. We will use T flip-flops to construct counters in Section 5.4.7.

5.4.6   Random-Access Memory

Random-access memory *(RAM)* is memory that is both readable and writeable. It is "random" in the sense that any word can be read or written without having to access the words that precede it. ROM also has this random-access property; however, by convention, "random-access memory" refers only to readable/writeable memory.

RAM can be implemented using rows of D flip-flops, with one row for each word in memory. For example, we can implement main memory in H1 with 4096 rows of D flip-flops, each row containing 16 flip-flops. A decoder is used to determine which row is used in a read or write operation. Two control inputs, RD and WR, determine if a read or write operation occurs.

Let's examine the implementation of the 4×2 RAM (i.e, a RAM with four 2-bit words) in Figure 5.45. Each output line of the decoder is associated with one word in memory. These lines are called *word lines* because they determine which word is read from or written to. For example, suppose the top word line is equal to 1. Then, on a write, the WR signal can reach the CK inputs of the top row of flip-flops; on a read, the bits on their Q outputs can reach the data bus.

The data bus is bidirectional; that is, it can carry data in either direction. The tri-state buffers on the data bus determine its direction. If RD is 1, then data can flow from memory onto the data bus; if RD is 0, then data can flow into memory from the data bus.

The leading edge of the WR signal triggers a write operation. Thus, on a write operation, it is imperative that the address and data inputs be valid and stable *before* WR goes to 1.

5.4.7   Binary Counter

A *binary counter* is like an odometer in a car, except that it holds binary rather than decimal numbers. Each time it receives an external pulse, the number it holds increases by one. When it contains all ones and it then receives a pulse, it wraps around to all zeros.

Figure 5.46 shows the implementation of a 4-bit binary counter. The number contained in the counter at any given time is given by the Q outputs of the flip-flops.

FIGURE 5.45   4 ◊ 2 RAM

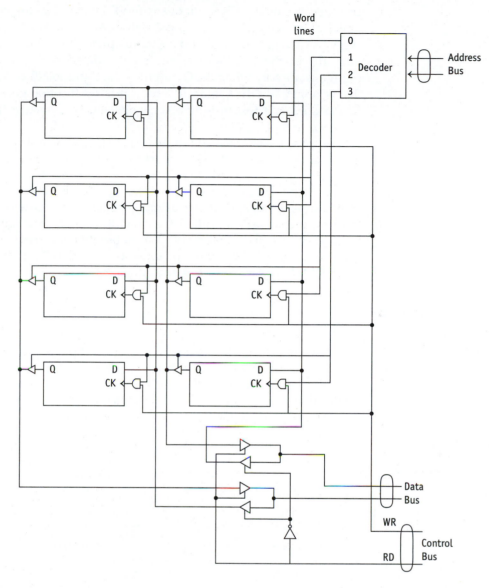

FIGURE 5.46   4-Bit Binary Counter
                                   (Asynchronous)

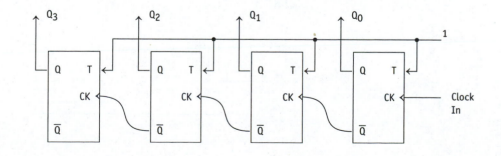

The T input of each flip-flop is fixed at 1. Thus, whenever a positive-going edge appears on the CK input of any flip-flop, that flip-flop changes state. The external pulse is applied only to the rightmost flip-flop. Thus, it changes state on every positive-going edge of the external pulse. The $\overline{Q}$ output of this flip-flop, in turn, drives the CK input of the second flip-flop. Thus, the second flip-flop changes state only when the $\overline{Q}$ output of the rightmost flip-flop goes from 0 to 1—that is, only when the Q output of the rightmost flip-flop goes from 1 to 0. Similarly, the third and fourth flip-flops change state only when the Q outputs of the flip-flops to their right go from 1 to 0.

Suppose the counter is in the 0000 state (i.e., all Q outputs are 0), and an external pulse is applied to the rightmost flip-flop. The Q output of the right flip-flop changes from 0 to 1. This change, however, does not trigger a change in the next flip-flop. Thus, the resulting state of the counter is 0001. The next external pulse again causes the Q output of the right flip-flop to change (from 1 to 0). But because this time it changes from 1 to 0, the next flip-flop also changes (from 0 to 1). Thus, the next state of the counter is 0010. As subsequent external pulses are applied, the counter continues to count up, until it reaches 1111, at which point it wraps around back to 0000, to start the cycle again.

5.4.8   Registers

A *register* is a special memory area that holds one item of information. CPUs typically have many registers that serve a variety of purposes.

Figure 5.47a shows the black box diagram of a 4-bit read/write register. When a positive-going edge appears at the CK input, the data on all four of the data inputs is simultaneously stored in four flip-flops that make up the register. Figure 5.47b gives its implementation. To make the 16-bit registers that H1 uses, we simply add more flip-flops to the register in Figure 5.47b.

FIGURE 5.47

Read/Write Register
(Synchronous)

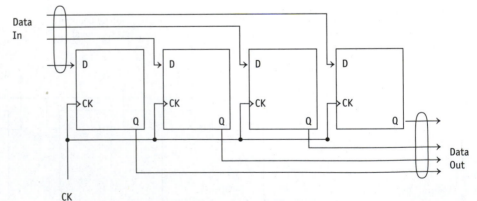

Notice that all four clock inputs in Figure 5.47 are driven by the same line. We call such a circuit a *synchronous circuit*. The operation of all its components is synchronized to a pulse on a single control line. The counter in Figure 5.46, on the other hand, is an *asynchronous circuit* ("asynchronous" means not synchronous). The clock input of each flip-flop, except for the rightmost, is driven by the output of the flip-flop to its right. The operation of each flip-flop is not synchronized to a pulse on a common control line.

To increment a regular register by 1 requires a lot of work. Specifically, the number 1 and the contents of the register have to be routed to the adder circuit. After the adder performs the addition, the result has to be routed back to the register. In contrast, incrementing a counter-register is easy. A *counter-register* is both a counter and a register. Thus, to increment it, we simply make use of its counter capabilities.

Figure 5.48 shows the black-box diagram and implementation of a 4-bit counter-register. It consists of a binary counter to which circuitry has been added to permit its loading. Its two control inputs are LD and INC. When LD is 1, the register is loaded with the data on its data input lines. When INC becomes 1, the

FIGURE 5.48   Counter-Register

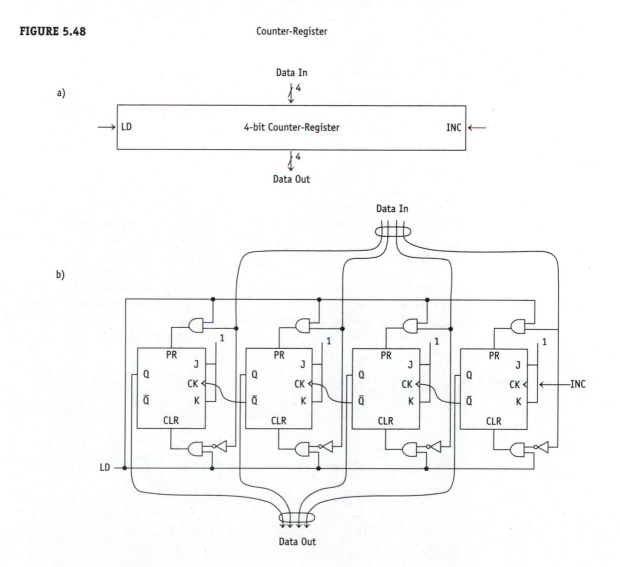

register is incremented. Because LD drives the PR and CLR inputs, the loading of the register is level-triggered; that is, whenever LD is 1, the register is loaded.

The incrementation of a counter-register occurs exactly like the incrementation of a binary counter (see Section 5.4.7). Let's now examine how it is loaded. Whenever LD = 1, all the AND gates driving the PR and CLR inputs are "open." Thus, the data input bits pass through the top row of AND gates and are applied to the PR inputs. Each data bit that equals 1 causes the flip-flop to which it is applied to set. However, a 0 data bit *has no effect when applied to a PR input*. How, then, do we ensure that the flip-flops corresponding to 0 data bits become reset? This function is performed by the bottom row of AND gates. Note that the data bits are applied to the bottom row of AND gates *through NOT gates*. Thus, the 0 data bits are first flipped to 1's, which then pass through the AND gates to the CLR inputs, resetting the corresponding flip-flops. Data bits equal to 1 are flipped to 0, and, therefore, have no effect when applied to the CLR inputs.

5.4.9   Clocks and Sequencers

The various operations that a CPU performs often require a specific sequence of suboperations. For example, to add 50 to a register, the CPU must

1. Route the number 50 and the register contents to the ALU.
2. Instruct the ALU to add.
3. Route the sum back to the register.

Ensuring the proper sequence of operations is the job of a *sequencer*.

We can construct a sequencer with a clock and a circular shift register. A *clock* is a circuit that outputs a succession of alternating 0's and 1's at a specific frequency. A simple clock can be implemented by a NOT gate whose output is fed back to its input (see Figure 5.49). Suppose the output of the NOT gate is 1. Then this 1 is fed back to its input, causing its output (after a slight delay) to change to 0. This 0 output then is fed back to the input, causing the NOT gate (after another slight delay) to again output 1, starting a new cycle. Thus, the output of the NOT gate continuously oscillates between 0 and 1. The frequency of the oscillation depends on the delay time of the NOT gate (i.e., the time it takes for a change in input to affect the output). The smaller the delay, the higher the frequency.

If the simple clock in Figure 5.49 were used in a computer, it would function erratically. Any change in ambient temperature (which would occur as the computer warms up) would affect its frequency. Moreover, with age, the delay time of the NOT gate would probably change, which would also affect the clock's frequency. A much better way to implement a clock is with a circuit that uses a

FIGURE 5.49   Clock

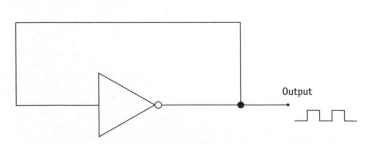

quartz crystal as the frequency-determining component. A quartz crystal is a material that exhibits the *piezoelectric effect:* Whenever the material is twisted, it outputs an electrical pulse, and whenever an electrical pulse is applied to it, it twists. In a clock circuit that uses a quartz crystal, electrical energy is continuously supplied to the crystal, causing it to continuously twist back and forth. This twisting motion then generates a stream of pulses. Quartz crystals are used in computer clocks (and wristwatches) because they are very *stable;* that is, the frequency of the pulses they generate change very little with changing environmental factors, such as temperature.

Let's now construct a *sequencer*—a circuit that can control the sequence in which other circuits operate. Figure 5.50a shows the black box diagram of a sequencer with three outputs, T1, T2, and T3. At any given time, exactly one of these outputs is 1. This 1 rotates from T1 to T2 to T3 and then back to T1, repeating the cycle. Thus, if we connect T1, T2, and T3 to the CK inputs of circuits 1, 2, and 3, respectively, circuit 1 will operate first, then circuit 2, then circuit 3. Then the cycle repeats.

Figure 5.50c shows the implementation of the sequencer. It consists of a clock that drives a circular shift register. The flip-flops form a circle with each flip-flop driving the one next to it. Thus, on each CK pulse, the bit in each register shifts circularly. If the register contains only one 1, then this 1 rotates circularly through the register as clock pulses are applied, causing one and only one output line to be high at any given time.

Before using the sequencer, we should apply a 1 to the `Init` control line of the shift register. This initializes the register so that it contains a single 1 in its leftmost flip-flop.

5.5 INTEGRATED CIRCUITS

• •

If you look inside an old radio, you will see various electronic components—vacuum tubes or transistors, resistors, capacitors, inductors, and so on—mounted on a chassis or circuit board, and connected with wires or metal traces underneath the circuit board. These electronic components are called *discrete components* because each is in its own container and is physically separate from the other components.

Transistors were introduced in the 1960s and quickly replaced vacuum tubes. Transistors are better than vacuum tubes in almost every respect: They are more reliable, are less expensive, use less power, and generate less heat. Tubes today are used only for special applications (like computer monitors) or for high-power applications (because transistors cannot handle high power as easily as tubes).

Transistors are made from silicon, which is not a good conductor. Its conductivity lies between that of conductors and insulators. It is for this reason that transistors and other devices made of silicon are called *semi-conductors*. The electrical properties of silicon, however, can be changed by *doping* (i.e., adding certain chemicals to it). With the appropriate doping, we can turn a chunk of silicon into a transistor, a resistor, a capacitor, an inductor, or connecting wires. In fact, with doping, we can fabricate in silicon virtually every type of electrical component that is used in computers. Thus, in a single chip of silicon, we can build a complete circuit. These circuits on a chip are called *integrated circuits* because they integrate all the circuit components onto a single chip.

FIGURE 5.50

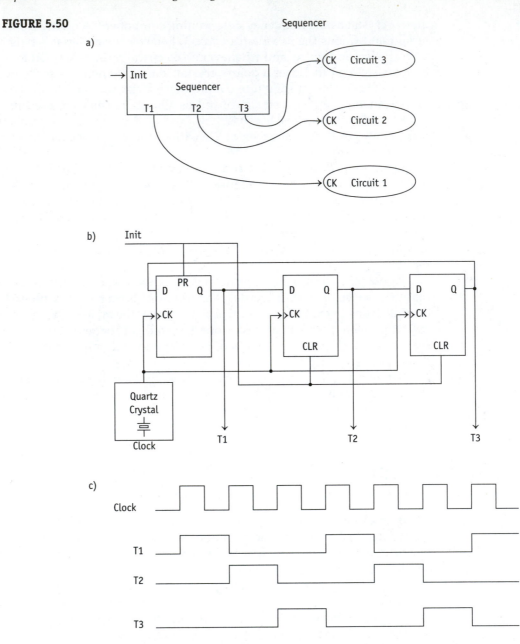

Integrated circuits are far easier and less expensive to make than circuits with discrete components. Discrete components have to be individually mounted on a chassis or circuit board, and then inter-connected. Both operations are time-consuming and costly. The components in an integrated circuit, on the other hand, are all made and interconnected by the doping mechanism—a mechanism that is fast and cheap. Moreover, because the components in an integrated circuit do not have their own containers or bulky inter-connecting wires and circuit boards, a huge number of components can be fabricated on a single, small silicon chip. With today's technology, millions of components can be fabricated on a single chip. Integrated circuits have made the computer revolution possible. Without them, the cost and size of computers would be prohibitively large. Without them, there would be no personal computers. There would be no Internet.

PROBLEMS

• •

5.1   How much current (in amps) will flow in a circuit with 100 volts and
    a. a 50-ohm resistor
    b. two 50-ohm resistors in series
    c. two 50-ohm resistors in parallel

5.2.   What is the voltage drop across a 10-ohm resistor through which 10 amps are flowing?

5.3.   Caution: do not perform the following experiment—the battery might explode. What would happen if a conductor (such as a copper wire) is connected directly across the two terminals of a battery? What is the resistance in the circuit? How much current flows?

5.4.   How much resistance is in a circuit with 100 volts through which 35 ma is flowing?

5.5.   Why are you in more danger from electrical shock if your hands are perspiring?

5.6.   How many times in one second can you switch a mechanical wall switch? How many times can a transistor switch change state?

5.7.   Implement a
    a. NAND gate using four transistors.
    b. AND gate using four transistors.
    c. OR gate using four transistors.
    d. XOR gate using eight transistors.
    e. NOR gate using only NAND gates.
    f. NOT gate using only NOR gates.
    g. NOT gate using only NAND gates.
    h. XOR gate using only NAND gates.

5.8.   If the voltage applied to a CPU were reduced from 5 to 3 volts, how much less heat would it generate due to the capacitive effect discussed in Section 5.2.7?

5.9.   If the clock frequency of a CPU were increased from 133 MHz to 166 MHz, how much more heat would it generate due to the capacitive effect discussed in Section 5.2.7?

5.10.   Implement a 4-bit shifter using four multiplexers.

5.11.   A sequencer can be implemented with a counter and a decoder. The counter outputs drive the decoder, which causes a 1 to circulate on the decoder's outputs. What is the problem with this approach? How can this problem be fixed?

5.12.   Using AND, OR, and NOT gates, implement the following Boolean functions. Do not minimize. Each question lists the output column (starting from the first row) of the truth table that defines the function.
    a. 0 0
    b. 1 1
    c. 0 1
    d. 0 0 1 1
    e. 1 1 0 0 1 1 0 0
    f. 1 1 0 0 0 0 1 1
    g. 1 1 1 1 1 1 1 1 0 0 0 0 0 0 0 0
    h. 1 1 1 1 0 0 0 0 1 1 1 1 0 0 0 0
    i. 1 1 1 1 1 0 1 0 1 1 1 1 1 0 1 0
    j. 0 0 0 0 1 1 1 1 0 0 0 0 1 1 1 1

         k. 1 0 1 0 0 0 0 0 1 0 1 0 0 0 0 0
         l. 0 0 0 0 0 1 0 1 0 0 0 0 0 1 0 1
       m. 0 0 0 0 0 0 0 0 0 0 1 1 0 0 1 0
       n. 0 0 0 0 0 0 1 1 0 1 0 1 1 1 1 1

5.13. Same as Problem 5.12, but use NAND gates only.

5.14. Same as Problem 5.12, but minimize each implementation using Karnaugh maps.

5.15. Same as Problem 5.12, but minimize each implementation using Boolean algebra. Label each step with the name of the law of Boolean algebra that you are using.

5.16. Implement a two-input multiplexer.

5.17. Implement a multiplexer with one control input that has two data inputs, each of which is a three-line bus.

5.18. Implement a 2-bit shifter.

5.19. How long does a 16-bit adder take to add two numbers? Assume each AND, OR, and NOT gate takes 1 microsecond to generate stable output once its inputs are stable. Assume each full adder is made from two half adders.

5.20. Implement a full adder directly from a truth table. Use minimization techniques. How many logic levels does your implementation have for the sum out? For the carry out? How many levels does the half adder implementation of a full adder have?

5.21. Assume a full adder uses three and two levels, respectively, to realize its sum out and carry out. How many levels do a 4-bit ripple-carry adder and a 4-bit multiplier (see Figure 5.28b) have through their longest paths?

5.22. Implement a 2-bit ALU using two 1-bit ALUs.

5.23. Implement an edge-detection circuit that converts a negative-going edge to a positive pulse.

5.24. Design a four-input "add one" circuit whose output equals one more than the input value.

5.25. Suppose an SR flip-flop has its $\overline{Q}$ output fed back into the S input, and its Q output fed back into the R input. What happens if alternating 1's and 0's are applied to the CK input?

5.26. Implement a JK flip-flop with NAND gates only.

5.27. Using two RAM units like that in Figure 5.45, implement an 8×2 RAM.

5.28. Same as problem 5.27, except implement a 4×4 RAM.

5.29. Implement a 2×4 RAM.

5.30. Implement a 4×2 ROM in which the content of location n is n.

5.31. Design a two-input decoder that has an additional control input X. When $X = 1$, the decoder should work normally; however, when $X = 0$, the decoder outputs should all be forced to 0.

5.32. Design a decimal-to-BCD encoder.

5.33. Design an 8-to-3-bit encoder whose output is the 3-bit binary number specified by the input. If more that one input is 1, your encoder should output the number corresponding to the active input with the highest number. (Encoders that work this way are called *priority encoders*.)

5.34. Design a 2-bit ALU that has one control input C. When $C = 0$, the output should be the NAND of its inputs; when $C = 1$, the output should be the AND of its inputs. Use as few gates as possible.

5.35. Design a circuit with eight data inputs and one output, P. P should be set equal to 0 if the parity of the data bits is even, and to 1, otherwise.

5.36. Add the circuitry to a register that would allow it to both input and output from the same bus. Its function—input or output—should be controlled by a new control input.

5.37. How much area would a circuit occupy that contains 200 million components (roughly the number of components in a personal computer)? Assume that each component occupies, on the average, one square centimeter. How much space would each component occupy if the total circuit space for 200 million components was 9 square centimeters.

5.38. Connect two 2×1 RAMs to create a 4×1 RAM. Connect two 2×1 RAMs to create a 2×2 RAM.

5.39. Suppose the frequency of the voltage from a wall outlet to which a computer is attached is increased from 60 to 120 Hz. Will this increase cause all the circuits in the computer to run twice as fast?

5.40. How many watts of heat are dissipated by a 100-ohm resistor connected to a sine wave with a peak value of 300 volts? Hint: power $=$ (effective voltage)^2/resistance.

5.41. When will positive and negative logic yield the same Boolean function in a single circuit?

5.42. A 64-word RAM needs a decoder with 64 outputs, one for each word. Show how the decoder with 64 outputs can be replaced by two 8-output decoders or three 4-output decoders. What is the advantage of the latter two approaches?

5.43. Implement the ROM in Figure 5.35 using a two-input decoder and four OR gates.

5.44. Is a ripple-carry adder a synchronous or an asynchronous circuit?

5.45. Design a 4-bit synchronous counter. What is its advantage over a 4-bit asynchronous counter?

5.46. Interchange the AND and OR operations in the absorption law, $A + AB = A$. Do you get the other absorption law?

5.47. Design a 3-bit counter that counts up to 6 and then wraps around to 0.

5.48. Design an edge-triggered flip-flop like that in Figure 5.43, but make it negative edge triggered.

Chapter Six

MICROLEVEL OF H1 AND V1

6.1 INTRODUCTION

In this chapter, we construct H1 using the circuits that we studied in the preceding chapter. In doing so, we will learn how all these circuits work together to form a functioning computer. We will also learn how *microinstructions,* 32-bit numbers that are stored within the CPU of H1, determine the operations that occur during the execution of machine language instructions. By changing the microinstructions within its CPU, we can change the instruction set of H1. Using the flexibility provided by microinstructions, we will replace the standard instruction set in H1 with a simple instruction set that we call the *basic instruction set.*

H1 has a similarly structured cousin named V1. The difference between H1 and V1 is that H1 uses 32-bit microinstructions but V1 uses 19-bit microinstructions. We will examine both systems and discuss their tradeoffs.

You may wish to print out the file `mic.txt` in the H1 software package and have it available as you read this chapter. `mic.txt` contains a summary of the microinstruction formats for H1 and V1. This summary also appears in Appendix B.

6.2 MICROLEVEL OF H1

6.2.1 Overview of the Organization of H1

H1 consists of five parts: the *central processing unit (CPU),* the clock/sequencer, main memory, the keyboard, and the monitor (see Figure 6.1). Let's start by briefly examining each of these parts to get an understanding of the overall structure and operation of H1. We will then examine each part in more detail. The CPU consists of two sections: a computational section and a control section. The *computational section* of the CPU contains the arithmetic-logic unit (ALU). The ALU is the circuit that performs various manipulations on data, such as addition, subtraction, and shifting. The computational section also contains a bank of 32 16-bit registers to hold data. Among these 32 registers are the pc, ac, and sp registers.

The data on which the ALU operates comes from the register bank via the A and B buses (a *bus* is a group of wires that carries a data item). The output of the ALU then goes back to the register bank via the C bus, forming a circle. We call this circle—the register bank, the ALU, and the interconnecting buses—the *datapath* of the CPU.

Main memory, the I/O devices (the keyboard and the monitor), and the circuits in the computational section have control inputs that determine their operation. The

FIGURE 6.1

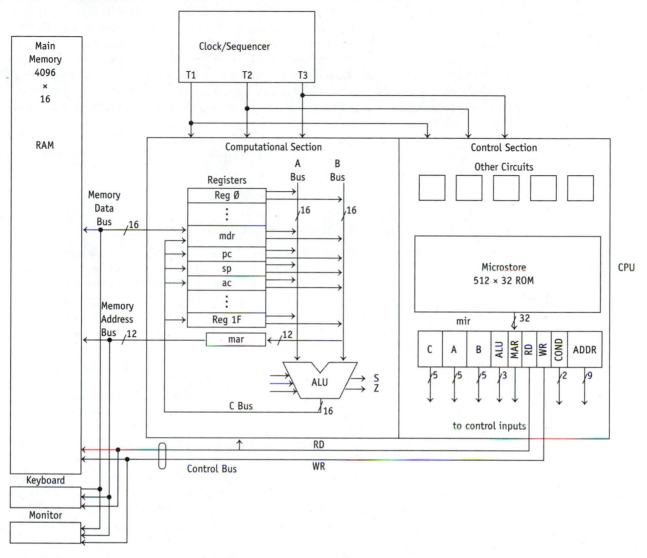

function of the *control section* of the CPU is to generate the signals that are applied to these various control inputs. These signals control the operation of these circuits (hence, the name "control section").

The bits making up the control signals that the control section generates come from *microstore,* a read-only memory (ROM) within the control section. Microstore contains up to 512 32-bit numbers. At fixed intervals, microstore deposits one of these numbers into a 32-bit register called the microinstruction register (`mir`). Wires attached to the `mir` then carry the bits it contains to the various control inputs in main memory, the I/O devices, and the control section itself.

Each time the `mir` is loaded with a number from microstore, control signals propagate from the `mir` to the various control inputs in the computer. The various circuits respond to these control inputs, performing some operation.

We call the 32-bit number in the `mir` a microinstruction because it "instructs" the various circuits in the computer via their control inputs. Each time a microinstruction is loaded into the `mir` from microstore, operations in the various circuits occur in response to the bits in that microinstruction. We call this process the *execution* of the microinstruction, and the various operations it triggers *micro-operations*. Micro-operations are primitive; that is, a single micro-operation does not do much. That is why we use the prefix "micro" in "micro-operation," "microinstruction," and "microstore"—it implies the primitive nature of a micro-operation.

The micro-operations triggered when a microinstruction is executed generally have to occur in a particular order. For example, the microinstruction that increments the `pc` register has to

1. Route the number 1 and the contents of the `pc` register to the ALU.
2. Instruct the ALU to add.
3. Place the output of the ALU into the `pc` register.

The ALU obviously cannot add before it has the numbers to add, and the `pc` register cannot be loaded with a new value until the ALU has computed it. Clearly, these three micro-operations have to be performed in the order given. A single microinstruction can specify these three micro-operations, but it cannot specify the order. Specifying the order is the job of the third section of the CPU, the clock/sequencer. The clock/sequencer generates three clock signals, T1, T2, and T3 that are offset in time. Only one of these signals is 1 at any given time. The 1 rotates from T1, to T2, to T3, and then back to T1, and so on. We use T1, T2, and T3 to impose an ordering on the micro-operations specified by each microinstruction. We use T1 to trigger the operations that goes first, T2 for the operations that are next, and T3 for the operations that are last in the cycle. We call T1, T2, and T3 *clock subcycles*.

The CPU communicates with main memory and the I/O devices via three buses: a 16-wire bidirectional *memory data bus*, a 12-wire *memory address bus*, and a two-wire *control bus*. On the CPU side, the memory data bus is connected to the memory data register (`mdr`), which is register 5 in the register bank; the memory address bus is connected to the memory address register (`mar`); and the two wires in the control bus are connected to the read (`RD`) and write (`WR`) bits of the `mir`.

To read from memory or an I/O device, the CPU first has to supply the address from which to read. It does this by loading the `mar` with this address. Once loaded into the `mar`, this address propagates to main memory and the I/O devices via the memory address bus. Next, the CPU loads the `mir` with a microinstruction whose `RD` bit is 1. This 1 then propagates to main memory and the I/O devices via the control bus, causing main memory or an I/O device to return the data via the memory data bus. The CPU then stores the data in the `mdr`.

To write to memory or an I/O device, the CPU first has to supply the address to which to write and the data to write. It does this by loading the `mar` and the `mdr` with the address and data, respectively. Once these two registers are loaded, the address and data propagate to main memory and the I/O devices via the memory address and data buses, respectively. Next, the CPU loads the `mir` with a microinstruction whose `WR` bit is 1. This 1 then propagates to main memory and the I/O devices via the control bus, causing a write at the given address.

The **mdr** can be loaded from two buses: the memory data bus (on a read from main memory or an I/O device) or the C bus (in preparation for a write to main memory or an I/O device).

6.2.2 Microinstructions

Each time H1 executes a machine language instruction, a sequence of micro-operations occurs within the CPU. Each machine language instruction triggers a different sequence. For example, the **ld** instruction causes the address it contains and a "read" signal (in that order) to be routed to main memory and the I/O devices. The "read" signal indicates that the CPU is requesting data. Main memory or an I/O device responds by sending the word at the given address back to the **mdr** in the CPU. The CPU then routes this word to the **ac** register. The **st** instruction causes a different sequence: The address in the instruction, the data in the **ac** register, and a "write" signal (in that order) are routed to main memory and the I/O devices. Main memory or an I/O device responds by writing (i.e., storing) the given data at the given address.

At the machine-language level, we see the "big" picture—the execution of each machine language instruction as a single operation. At the micro-operation level we see the "detailed" picture. We will call these two levels the *machine level* and the *microlevel*. We will sometimes call main memory—the storage we "see" at the machine level—the *machine-level store*. The machine-level assembler (**mas**) is so-called because it translates machine-level instructions in symbolic form (i.e., assembly language instructions) to binary form.

Each machine instruction has an associated sequence of microinstructions which, when executed, trigger the micro-operations needed to accomplish that machine instruction. A machine instruction is executed by loading the microinstructions in its associated sequence, one after another, into the **mir**. In other words, the *execution of a machine instruction is accomplished by the execution of the sequence of microinstructions for that machine instruction.* In a very real sense, a machine instruction is like a subroutine call of its associated microinstruction sequence.

When a microinstruction is loaded into the **mir**, it must remain there for a certain period of time before the next microinstruction is loaded. This delay between the loading of successive microinstructions provides the time that the circuits in the CPU need to respond to each microinstruction.

Where do these microinstructions come from? They are inside the CPU in microstore's read-only memory. Microstore contains the microinstruction sequence needed for fetching machine instructions, incrementing the **pc**, and decoding machine instructions, and, in addition, the microinstruction sequence for every machine instruction. Figure 6.2 shows the two principal storage areas in H1: microstore, which is within the control section of the CPU, and machine-level store (i.e., main memory), which is external to the CPU. Because the contents of microstore control the operation of the CPU, microstore is also known as *control store*.

The microinstructions within microstore are collectively called *microcode* or a *microprogram*. Not all computers have microprogrammed control sections. Some have *hardwired* control sections in which the sequence of micro-operations for each machine instruction is "wired" into the digital logic. We will further discuss the hardwired approach in Section 6.5.

As you would expect, "microprogramming" means writing microprograms. It does *not* mean, as some people think, writing high-level or assembly language programs for a microcomputer (i.e., a small, personal computer).

FIGURE 6.2

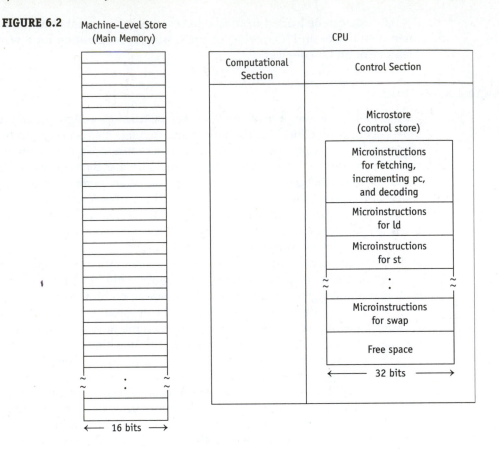

Machine-Level Store
(Main Memory)

CPU

Computational
Section

Control Section

Microstore
(control store)

Microinstructions
for fetching,
incrementing pc,
and decoding

Microinstructions
for ld

Microinstructions
for st

⋮

Microinstructions
for swap

Free space

←——— 32 bits ———→

←——— 16 bits ———→

6.2.3 Memory Data Bus

The memory data bus has a bank of tri-state buffers at each end that enable it to carry data in either direction (see Figure 6.3). These tri-state buffers and the multiplexor on the input of the **mdr** are controlled by the **RD** control line. When the **RD** is 1, a pathway is created from main memory to the **mdr**; when **RD** is 0, a pathway is created from the **mdr** to main memory. Note that each tri-state buffer symbol in Figure 6.3 represents a bank of 16 tri-state buffers, and each line connecting their inputs and outputs represents a 16-line bus.

6.2.4 Memory Address Bus

The **mar** is connected to main memory via the memory address bus (see Figure 6.4). It provides addresses to main memory during read and write operations. Its output is always enabled. Thus, as soon as an address is loaded into the **mar**, the address propagates to main memory via the memory address bus.

The **mar** is a 12-bit register that is loadable from the B bus. Its control input (called **MAR**) and T2 drive an AND gate that, in turn, drives the CK input of the **mar**. Thus, if **MAR** is 1, the **mar** is loaded from the B bus at the T2 subcycle. Don't confuse **mar** with **MAR**. The **mar** is a register; **MAR** is the control input that controls the loading of the **mar** from the B bus. The **mar** is only 12 bits wide because its only use is to hold 12-bit addresses.

FIGURE 6.3   Memory Data Bus

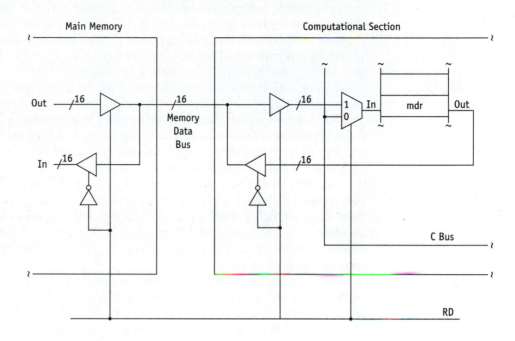

FIGURE 6.4   Memory Address Bus

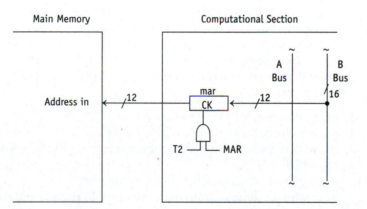

6.2.5 Register Bank

The register bank in H1 consists of 32 16-bit registers numbered in hex from 0 to 1F. The first five registers are read-only registers that hold the following constants:

```
Number Contents     Name
  0      0000
  1      0001
  2      0FFF        xmask
  3      00FF        ymask
  4      000F        zmask
```

We can refer to the registers in the register bank by their hex numbers. However, it is convenient to assign them meaningful names that reflect their content or usage. Accordingly, we have given registers 2, 3, and 4 the names "xmask," "ymask," and "zmask," respectively. Register 0 contains 0, making its hex number, 0, meaningful—it matches its contents. Thus, we did not give it a name. For the same reason, we did not give register 1 (which contains 1) a name.

Figure 6.5a shows the connection of the read-only registers to the A and B buses. Each register drives both the A and B buses, each through a bank of tri-state buffers. The control input, **EA** (enable output to A), enables output to the A bus; **EB** (enable output to B) enables output to the B bus. By applying the appropriate control signals to **EA** and **EB**, we can output any register in the register bank to the A bus, to the B bus, to both buses, or to neither bus.

Figure 6.5b shows the connections to registers 6 to 1F. They have the same connections to the A and B buses that the read-only registers do; however, in addition, the C bus drives their inputs. The **CK** inputs of the read/write registers 6 to 1F are driven by AND gates, which are, in turn, driven by T3 and an **EC** (enable input from C) control input. Thus, if **EC** is 1 on a register, the data on the C bus is loaded into that register at the T3 subcycle.

Any register in the register bank can output its contents at the same time to both the A and B buses. However, two registers should not output *at the same time to the same bus*. Thus, at any given time, at most one of the 32 **EA** control inputs should be 1. Similarly, at most, one of the 32 **EB** control inputs should be 1. On the other hand, more than one register may be loaded at the same time from the C bus; that is, more than one **EC** input can be 1 at the same time, causing all the corresponding registers to be loaded in parallel.

Figure 6.5c shows the connections to the **mdr** (register 5 in the register bank). The **mdr** interfaces with main memory through the memory data bus, and therefore requires additional connections. It drives three banks of tri-state buffers that, in turn, drive the A, B, and memory data buses. The input to the **mdr** is from a multiplexer that can select either the C bus or the memory data bus. The **mdr** has five control inputs:

1. **EA**, which enables output to the A bus
2. **EB**, which enables output to the B bus
3. **EC**, which enables the loading of the **mdr** from the C bus at T3
4. **RD**, which
   a. triggers a read operation in main memory
   b. creates a pathway from main memory to the **mdr** via the memory data bus
   c. enables the loading of the **mdr** from the memory data bus at T3
5. T3, which synchronizes the loading of the **mdr** to the T3 subcycle.

The **mdr** is a complex register whose operation is difficult to fully understand. However, for now, you need to remember only that **RD**=1 causes the loading of the **mdr** from the memory data bus, and 1 on its **EC** control input causes the loading of the **mdr** from the C bus.

Registers 6 to 1F are general purpose; register assignments among this group are completely arbitrary. For example, we can use register 6 as the **pc** register, but we can use register 1F equally well. In the standard instruction set, the **pc**, **sp**, and **ac** registers map to registers 6, 7, and 8, respectively.

The **xmask** register (register 2), the **ymask** register (register 3), and the **zmask** register (register 4) contain constants that the CPU uses to mask off the opcodes of machine instructions. For example, suppose the CPU needs to isolate the ad-

FIGURE 6.5

a)   Read-Only

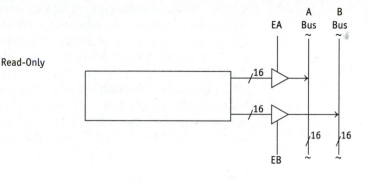

b)   Read/Write   C Bus

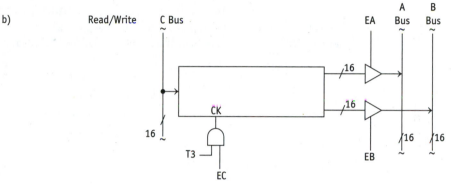

c)

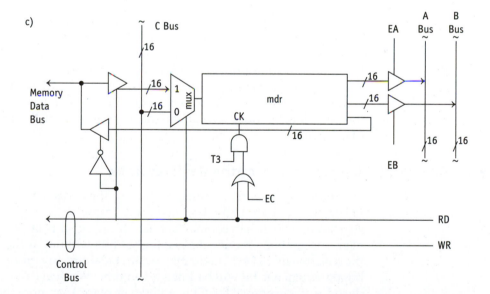

dress portion (i.e., the rightmost 12 bits) of the st instruction 12FF. To do this, the CPU performs a bitwise (i.e., column by column) AND of the instruction with the contents of the **xmask** register (0FFF hex). The four 0 bits in the leftmost positions of **xmask** zero out the opcode in the instruction, yielding 02FF, the address in the st instruction. The **ymask** and **zmask** registers are also used as masks. The **ymask** register masks out 8-bit opcodes; the **zmask** register masks out 12-bit opcodes.

To distinguish the control inputs among the registers in the register bank, we will suffix the register number to the control input. For example, we will designate the **EA**, **EB**, and **EC** control inputs of register 6 as **EA6**, **EB6**, and **EC6**, respectively.

Recall from Section 5.3.12 that "straight-through" is one of the functions of the ALU. The CPU uses the "straight-through" function whenever it needs to route data unmodified through the ALU. For example, to move the contents of register 7 to register 9 requires data to flow from register 7 down the A bus, through the ALU, and then up the C bus to register 9. To allow register 9 to receive the contents of register 7 unmodified, the CPU uses the "straight-through" function of the ALU.

6.2.6 Specifying a Micro-operation

Let's now consider how the CPU goes about adding 1 to the **pc** register. Suppose register 6 is the **pc** register. To add 1 to the **pc** register, the control section loads the **mir** with a microinstruction that sets the following control inputs as indicated:

```
Control Input                          Effect
  EA6  = 1      Places the contents of register 6 on the A bus.
  EB1  = 1      Places 1 in register 1 on the B bus.
  F2   = 1      Causes the ALU to perform function 4 (add).
  F1   = 0
  F0   = 0
  EC6  = 1      Enables the loading of register 6 from the C bus.
```

EA6=1 causes the contents of register 6 to be output to the A bus. Similarly, **EB1**=1 causes the contents of register 1 (which contains 1) to be output to the B bus. These two items propagate to the ALU, where they are added. **EC6**=1 causes the data on the C bus (the output of the ALU) to be loaded into register 6. **EC6** is blocked by the AND gate driving the **CK** input of register 6 until T3 (see Figure 6.5b). Thus, the loading of register 6 does not occur until T3. This delay is necessary to ensure that the ALU has the time it needs to add the contents of the **pc** register and 1, and place the sum on the C bus.

6.2.7 Driving the Control Inputs of the Register Bank

H1 contains 97 control inputs, excluding those driven by the clock/sequencer (32 **EA**, 32 **EB**, 27 **EC**, 1 **RD**, 1 **WR**, 1 **MAR**, and 3 **ALU**). Thus, it appears that the microinstruction on H1 has to contain 96 bits. This number is far too large. We can, however, substantially reduce the number of bits without at the same time reducing the functionality of H1. To do this, we first identify any group of controls in which no more than one bit will be 1 at a given time. We then drive these controls with a decoder. For example, the CPU will never place 1 on more than one input among the 32 **EA** control inputs (because at most one register can drive the A bus at a time). We can drive these 32 control inputs with a 5-bit decoder that has 5 input lines and 32 output lines. We can then have a field with *only 5 bits* (the *A field*) in the microinstruction drive the five inputs of the *EA decoder*, which, in turn, drives the **EA** inputs of the 32 registers in the register bank (see Figure 6.6).

By using the EA decoder, we can reduce the size of our microinstruction by 27 bits without reducing the functionality of H1. This decoder approach would not work if we needed to place 1 on more than one **EA** input at a time (recall that a decoder

FIGURE 6.6

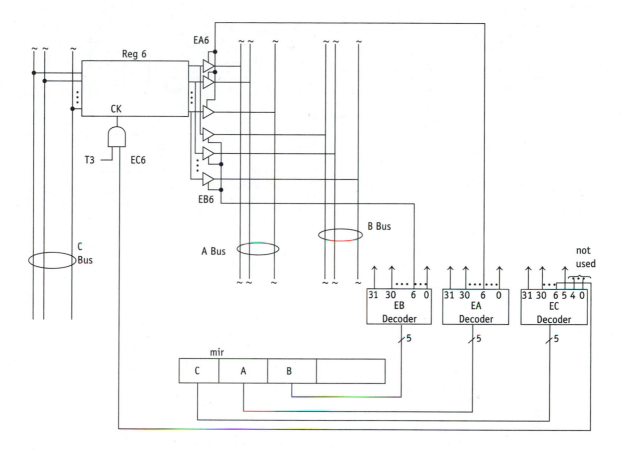

EA,EB,EC Decoders

always places 1 on only one of its outputs at any given time). But this is not the case here—we should never place 1 on more than one **EA** input at a time.

We can achieve another 27-bit reduction by driving the **EB** inputs with another 5-bit decoder (the *EB decoder*) whose inputs are from the *B field* of a microinstruction.

The CPU may want to place 1 on more than one **EC** input at a time; that is, it may want to load more than one register from the C bus at the same time. However, in practice, this will rarely occur. Thus, we can achieve another reduction in our microinstruction size by using a decoder (the *EC decoder*) to drive the **EC** inputs. We sacrifice some functionality, but only a minimal amount. This decoder has 5 inputs and 32 outputs, the first 5 of which are unconnected (these correspond to the read-only registers that have no **EC** control). Thus, inputs 0 to 4 to the **EC** decoder have no effect. Inputs 5 to 1F cause a 1 to appear on the corresponding output line, which, in turn, causes the corresponding register to be loaded from the C bus. We call the field in the microinstruction that drives the five inputs of the **EC** decoder the *C field*.

The CPU may need to perform an operation that does not include the loading of read/write registers in the register bank; for example, it may want to place 1 on **RD**, and do nothing else. Inhibiting a register load is easy. We simply drive the **EC** decoder with a number corresponding to one of the read-only registers (0 to 4) to which a write cannot occur.

FIGURE 6.7

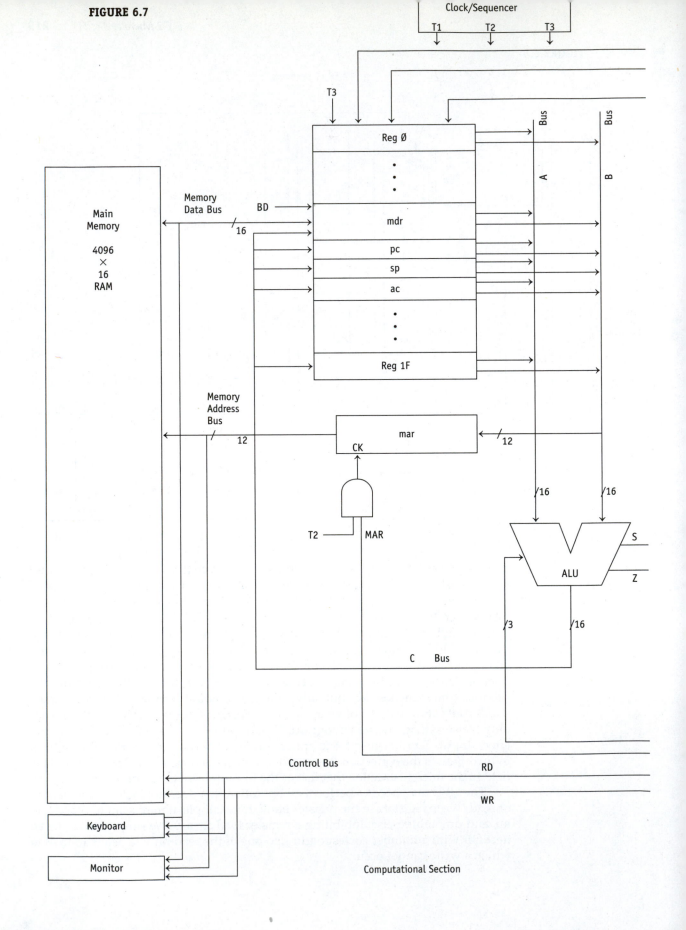

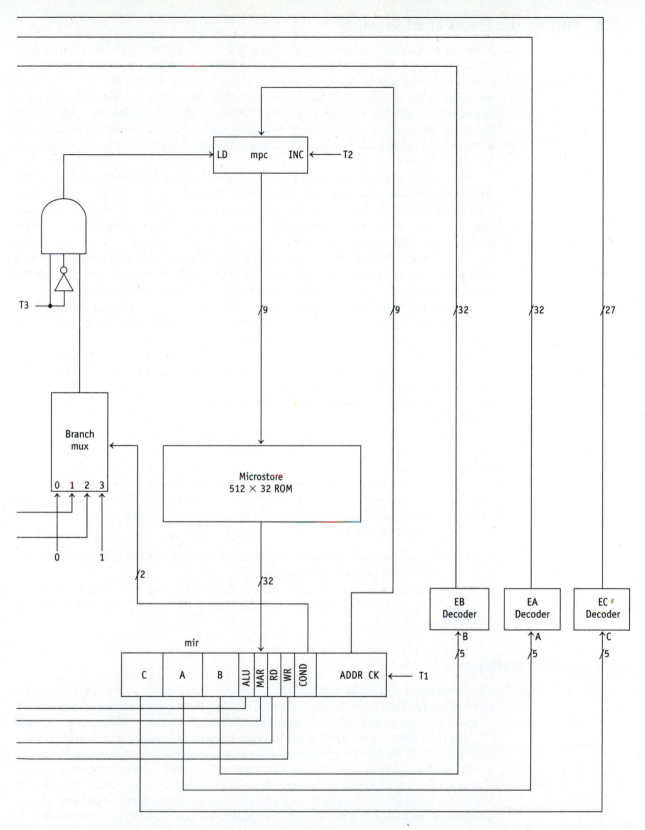

Control Section

6.2.8   Putting the Pieces of H1 Together

Now let's examine the overall structure of H1 shown in Figure 6.7. Starting at the lower right, we see the `mir`, which holds the current microinstruction. Its contents are attached via wires to the various control points in the CPU, or, in the case of the A, B, and C fields, to decoders. The 3 bits in the ALU field are connected to the F2, F1, and F0 control inputs of the ALU. The `MAR`, `RD`, and `WR` fields in the `mir` are connected to the identically named control inputs in the datapath of H1. `RD` and `WR` are also connected to main memory, the keyboard, and the monitor.

Above the `mir` is microstore (the ROM that holds all the microinstructions). Above microstore is the `mpc` (the micro program counter). The address in this register determines which microinstruction in microstore is delivered to the `mir`. The `mpc` is a 9-bit counter-register like the one in Figure 5.48 (in Chapter 5). It can be loaded with a new value or incremented.

Next to the ALU is the *branch multiplexer*. This circuit determines when a *branch* (i.e., a jump) in the execution of microinstructions occurs. We will discuss the operation of the branch multiplexer and the `mpc` in the next section.

On the top right is the clock/sequencer circuit, whose outputs, T1, T2, and T3, drive various inputs in the CPU. T1, T2, and T3 drive those circuits that need to be activated first, second, and third, respectively, in a cycle.

Each T1-T2-T3 cycle in H1 corresponds to the execution of one microinstruction. To start a cycle, the control section loads a microinstruction into the `mir` so that its bits are propagated to the various control points in the CPU. Notice that the T1 subcycle drives the `CK` input of the `mir`. Thus, the loading of the `mir` occurs first in a cycle.

Once a microinstruction is in the `mir`, its A and B fields cause the specified registers to drive the A and B buses. At T2, the `mar` is loaded if the `MAR` bit in the `mir` equals 1. The `mpc` is also incremented because its `INC` input is driven by T2, causing microstore to output the next microinstruction. However, this new microinstruction does not enter the `mir` until the next T1 subcycle, when the `mir` is again loaded. During the T2 subcycle, the ALU operates on its inputs.

A lot can happen at T3:

- The register specified by the C field in the microinstruction is loaded from the C bus unless the register is a read-only register.
- A new address may be loaded into the `mpc`, causing a branch to that address.
- The `mdr` is loaded from the memory data bus if the `RD` bit in the microinstruction equals 1.

6.2.9   Branch Multiplexer

T2 is connected to the `INC` input of the `mpc`, causing the address it holds to be incremented at T2. This incremented address drives the address inputs of microstore, causing microstore to output the microinstruction at this new address. At the next T1, this new microinstruction is loaded into the `mir`, starting a new cycle. The `mpc` is initially 0. Thus, the first microinstruction executed is the one at location 0, followed by the microinstructions at locations 1, 2, 3, and so on. Microinstructions, like machine instructions, are executed *sequentially*—that is, one after the other in the order in which they appear in memory, unless a branch occurs. A branch is a transfer of control (i.e., a jump) in the execution sequence of microinstructions. To

FIGURE 6.8

Branch Multiplexer

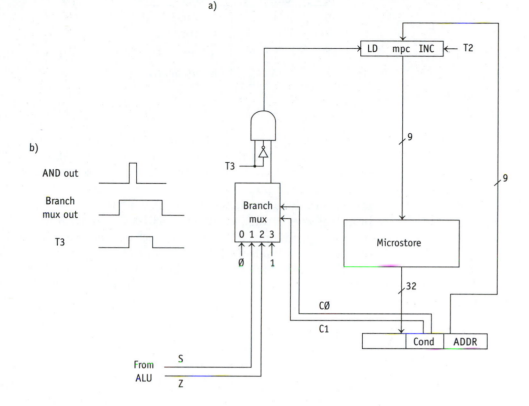

avoid confusion, we use separate terms at the machine and microlevels to denote a transfer of control: A "jump" is a transfer of control at the machine level; a "branch" is a transfer of control at the microlevel.

At the machine level, loading a new address into the `pc` register causes a jump. Similarly, at the microlevel, loading a new address into the `mpc` register causes a branch. The `mpc` is loaded whenever its **LD** (load enable) input is 1. This input is driven by the output of the branch multiplexer through an AND gate (see Figure 6.8a). If the branch multiplexer outputs a 1, this 1 passes through the AND gate to the **LD** input of the `mpc` at beginning of T3, causing it to load a new address from the **ADDR** field in the `mir`.

The AND gate that drives the **LD** input of the `mpc` and the inverter that drives this AND gate form a *pulse-narrowing circuit*. Figure 6.8b shows its effect on the T3 pulse when the output of the branch multiplexer is 1. When T3 is 0, the output of the AND gate is 0. When T3 switches to 1, the inverter's output does not change to 0 instantaneously. Thus, for the brief period, all three inputs to the AND gate are 1, causing its output to go to 1. Soon, however, the inverter's output goes to 0, causing the AND gate's output to drop back to 0, although T3 is still 1. The result is a narrow pulse on the output of the AND gate that occurs during the initial portion of the T3 subcycle. Without this pulse-narrowing circuit, timing problems can occur. In particular, if T1 becomes 1 before T3 drops to 0 (T1 and T3 do not necessarily switch at *exactly* the same time), the **ADDR** field of the microinstruction loaded at T1 might corrupt the load of the `mpc` from the previous T3 subcycle.

FIGURE 6.9

Branch Mux

C1	C0	Output	Effect
0	0	0	No branch
0	1	S	Branch if S = 1
1	0	Z	Branch if Z = 1
1	1	1	Branch always

The output of the branch multiplexer depends on the COND field of the current microinstruction and the S and Z outputs from the ALU. The **COND** field drives the two control inputs of the branch multiplexer. Thus, the **COND** field determines which of its four data inputs—0, S, Z, or 1—reaches its output. A COND field of 00 selects 0 for output; thus, no branch occurs. A COND field of 11 selects 1 for output; thus, a branch always occurs. A COND field of 01 selects the S output from the ALU; thus, the branch depends on S. If S = 1, the branch occurs; otherwise, it does not. A **COND** field of 10 is similar. It selects Z. Thus, the branch occurs if Z = 1; otherwise, it does not.

The table in Figure 6.9 summarizes the operation of the branch multiplexer.

Every microinstruction has a branch-to address (i.e., an **ADDR** field), even in microinstructions in which C1 = C0 = 0. Of course, for no-branch microinstructions, it does not matter what is in the **ADDR** field. We say the **ADDR** field for such microinstructions is a *don't care* field.

Notice that H1 has neither a sign flag nor a zero flag. If it did, these flags would be loaded from the S and Z outputs, respectively, from the ALU. Then these flags (instead of the S and Z outputs from the ALU) would drive the branch multiplexer circuit. Both approaches work, but H1's approach has one important disadvantage—a result must be tested while it is at the output of the ALU (because the S and Z outputs are driven by the *current* output of the ALU). In contrast, if the branch multiplexer were driven by a sign flag and a zero flag, H1 could perform a computation, and then *later* determine the sign and zero status of the result, even after the ALU output has changed. It could test the result as long as these flags remain unchanged.

6.2.10   Timing Problems

Suppose the microinstruction that loads the **mar** and **mdr** in preparation for a write operation also has its **WR** bit equal to 1. We would then run into a timing problem. The **mar** would be loaded at T2; the **mdr** at T3. But, main memory would receive the **WR** signal at T1. Thus, it would initiate a write operation *before* it had the data and address it needs. To avoid this problem, we use two microinstructions to perform a write. The first microinstruction loads the **mar** and **mdr** with the address and data, respectively. The second microinstruction triggers the write (i.e., has **WR** = 1). By the time the write occurs (during the execution of the second microinstruction), the contents of the **mdr** and **mar**, and the memory buses they drive are stable, ensuring a correct write (see the timing diagram in Figure 6.10a).

A timing problem can also occur when reading from main memory. If a single microinstruction both loads the **mar** and triggers a read (i.e., has its **RD** bit equal to 1), there may be insufficient time for memory to respond with the correct data. Between T2 (when the **mar** is loaded) and T3 (when the **mdr** is loaded), the address has to be loaded into the **mar** and then propagate to main memory.

FIGURE 6.10

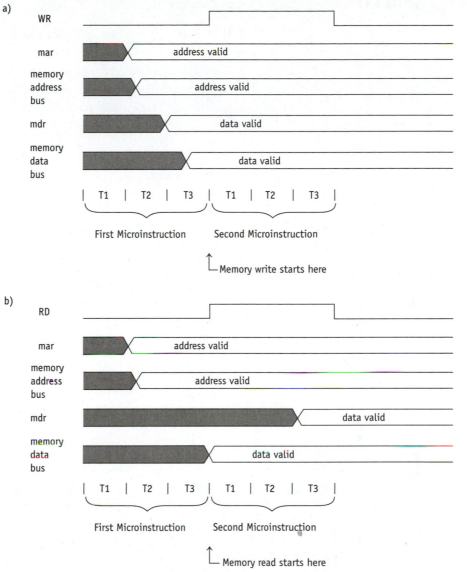

a)

First Microinstruction   Second Microinstruction

Memory write starts here

b)

First Microinstruction   Second Microinstruction

Memory read starts here

Main memory has to access the data and send it back to the **mdr**. This is too much to do in one subcycle. To avoid this problem, we use a two-microinstruction sequence to read (see Figure 6.10b). The first microinstruction loads the **mar**; the second triggers the read (i.e., has **RD**=1).

For both the read and write sequences, the **mar** and **mdr** registers should not be changed during the second microinstruction in the sequence (i.e., when **RD**=1 or **WR**=1). A change at this time in either the **mar** or **mdr** could interfere with the operation of a read or write.

6.2.11   Microinstruction Format

Figure 6.11 describes the format of a microinstruction. Let's review each field. **C** specifies which register is to be loaded from the C bus. **A** and **B** specify the registers that drive the A and B buses, respectively. **ALU** determines the operation

FIGURE 6.11 Microinstruction format:

```
C    A    B    ALU   MAR   RD   WR   COND   ADDR
5    5    5     3     1    1    1     2      9   width (bits)
```

A: Register number of register outputting to A bus

B: Register number of register outputting to B bus

C: Register number of register to be loaded from C bus

ALU

0: A (left input straight through)

1: ~A (bitwise complement)

2: A & B (bitwise AND)

3: A * B

4: A + B

5: A - B

6: Shift left one position

7: Shift right one position

MAR

0: Do not load mar

1: Load mar from B bus

RD

0: Do not read

1: Read from mem[mar]

WR

0: Do not write

1: Write mdr to mem[mar]

COND

0: No branch

1: Branch if S = 1

2: Branch if Z = 1

3: Always branch

ADDR: Branch-to address

performed by the ALU. **MAR** determines if the **mar** is loaded from the B bus. **RD** and **WR** trigger the read and write operations, respectively. On a read, the **mdr** is loaded from the memory data bus. On a write, the data in the **mdr** is stored in main memory at the location given by the **mar**. **COND** specifies the condition under which a branch is to occur. **ADDR** contains the branch-to address.

6.2.12 Sequencer-Driven Control Inputs

The microinstruction in the **mir** does not drive all of the control inputs in the CPU of H1. Some are driven by the clock/sequencer. Here is a complete list of the inputs that each output of the clock/sequencer drives:

FIGURE 6.12

Basic Instruction Set

Opcode (hex)	Assembly Form	Name	Description
0	ld x	Load	ac = mem[x];
2	st x	Store	mem[x] = ac;
4	shll z	Shift left logical	ac << z;
6	shrl z	Shift right logical	ac >> z;
8	addc x	Add constant	ac = ac + x;
A	flip	Flip ac	ac = ~ac;
C	mult x	Multiply	ac = ac * mem[x];
E	jn x	Jump on negative	if (ac < 0) pc = x;

T1: CK input of the `mir` (loads the `mir` with the next microinstruction)

T2: INC input of the `mpc` register (increments the `mpc`)

CK circuitry of the `mar` (loads the `mar` if MAR in the microinstruction is 1)

T3: EC circuitry of the read/write registers (loads the register specified by the c field in the microinstruction)

CK circuitry of the `mdr` (loads the `mdr` if the RD bit in the microinstruction is 1)

LD circuitry of the `mpc` (loads the `mpc` from the ADDR field of the current microintruction if the branch multiplexer outputs a 1)

During T2, the inputs to the ALU are stable. It is during this subcycle that the ALU performs its operation.

6.2.13 Microcode for the Basic Instruction Set

Let's now look at a sequence of microinstructions that implements a very simple instruction set that we call the *basic instruction set* (see Figure 6.12). This instruction set consists of only eight instructions (plus `bkpt`, `halt`, and all the I/O instructions), chosen to illustrate the various capabilities of H1. Three of its instructions— `ld`, `st`, and `jn`—operate in exactly the same way as the identically named instructions in the standard instruction set.

The basic instruction set contains only eight instructions, so opcodes need only 3 bits. To minimize decoding time, the instruction set uses the first 3 bits of the opcode field, with 0 in the fourth bit for all instructions. Thus, the sequence of the eight opcodes in the basic instruction set is 0000 (`ld`), 0010 (`st`), 0100 (`shll`), . . .1110 (`jn`).

Recall from Chapter 3 that the CPU performs the following four-step sequence for each machine instruction it executes:

1. Fetch the instruction whose address is in the `pc` register.
2. Increment the `pc` register.
3. Decode the opcode (i.e., determine the opcode).
4. Execute the instruction.

Our microcode must perform these four steps. We will use a C++ notation to describe the microinstructions that we need. This notation is far easier to comprehend than the 32-bit numbers that are the actual microinstructions.

The first microinstruction should load the `mar` with the address in the `pc` register, because we want to fetch the instruction pointed to by the `pc` register. In our C++ notation, our first microinstruction should be

```
mar = pc;
```

The next microinstruction should trigger a read. In our C++ notation, the next microinstruction should be

```
rd;
```

Recall from Section 6.2.10 that a read signal must be generated only *after* the **mar** is loaded. Thus, we cannot trigger a read in the same microinstruction in which we are loading the **mar**. That is,

```
mar = ir; rd;
```

is an *illegal* microinstruction.

The third microinstruction should increment the **pc**:

```
pc = pc + 1;
```

A single microinstruction can often do more than one thing. For example, either the first or second microinstructions above can also increment the **pc**. For example, in the following two-instruction sequence, the first microinstructions both loads **mar** and increments the **pc**:

```
mar = pc; pc = pc + 1;
rd;
```

How do we know that one microinstruction can both load the **mar** and increment the **pc**? It's easy if we have a mental picture of the datapath of H1. Recall that the **mar** is loaded from the B bus. Thus, the **pc** contents must be placed on the B bus. We can also put a 1 (from register 1) on the A bus, and have the ALU add the A bus data (1) and the B bus data (**pc**), and have its output (**pc** + 1) loaded back into the **pc**. In other words, the operation

```
pc = pc + 1;
```

can coexist with the operation

```
mar = pc;
```

as long as 1 and **pc** drive the A and B buses, respectively. Thus, both operations can be done by one microinstruction. The **pc** register must be incremented only after its contents are loaded into the **mar**. But this order will necessarily occur because the loading of the **mar** is from the B bus, before the ALU adds 1 to the **pc** register. Thus, it is the datapath of H1 that determines the order in which these two suboperations occur when both are specified within one microinstruction. In our C++ notation, the order in which we specify the suboperations within a single microinstruction is of *no consequence*. All possible orderings correspond to the *same* binary microinstruction. For example,

```
mar = pc; pc = pc + 1;
```

and

```
pc = 1 + pc; mar = pc;
```

both represent the *same* 32-bit binary microinstruction. In either case, the contents of the **pc** register have to be placed on the B bus in order to reach the **mar**, and, therefore, the other operand (1) has to be placed on the A bus. Thus, both forms correspond to the same 32-bit binary microinstruction.

Assume register 6 is the **pc** register. Then the microinstruction

```
mar = pc; pc = pc + 1;
```

has **C**=00110 (register 6), **A**=00001 (register 1), **B**=00110 (register 6), **ALU**=100 (add), **MAR**=1, **RD**=0, **WR**=0, **COND**=00 (no branch), **ADDR**=xxxxxxxxx (don't care). Because **COND**=00, a branch can never occur with this microinstruction. Thus, its **ADDR** field is a "don't care."

After the execution of these microinstructions, the machine instruction just fetched will be sitting in the **mdr**. We usually use the **mdr** to hold an item only temporarily, so let's move its contents to the instruction register (**ir**) with the microinstruction

```
ir = mdr;
```

Can a microinstruction do this? Easily! We simply let the contents of the **mdr** flow down the A bus, through the ALU, and up the C bus into the **ir**. If **ir** is register 9, then this microinstruction has **C**=01001 (register 9), **A**=00101 (register 5, the **mdr**), **B**=xxxxx (don't care), **ALU**=000 (straight-through), **MAR**=0, **RD**=0, **WR**=0, **COND**=00 (no branch), and **ADDR**=xxxxxxxxx (don't care).

Once we have the fetched machine instruction in the **ir** register, we can start the decoding process. To decode an opcode, we look at the bits of the opcode one at a time from left to right. To examine the leftmost bit, we use

```
dc = ir; if (s) goto L1;
```

This microinstruction passes the contents of the **ir** straight through the ALU to the decoding (**dc**) register. Thus, the ALU sets its S and Z outputs according to the contents of the **ir**. In particular, it sets S to 1 if the leftmost bit is 1. The **if** statement in the previous microinstruction tests the S bit and, if equal to 1, causes a branch to the label **L1**. If **dc** is register A and **L1** is location 7, then this microinstruction has **C**=01010 (register A), **A**=01001 (register 9), **B**=xxxxx (don't care), **ALU**=000 (straight-through), **MAR**=0, **RD**=0, **WR**=0, **COND**=01 (branch if S = 1), and **ADDR**=00000111 (7 decimal).

Before we continue, let's look at the actual microinstructions that correspond to our C++ descriptions. Figure 6.13 shows each microinstruction in C++ form and, immediately below it, in binary form. "Don't care" fields are marked with an "x". We will refer to microinstructions in the C++ form as *symbolic microinstructions*.

The binary form of a microinstruction is cumbersome, so whenever we want to represent a 32-bit microinstruction, we will use its shorter eight-digit hex

FIGURE 6.13

```
pc = 1 + pc; mar = pc;
```

C	A	B	ALU	MAR	RD	WR	COND	ADDR
00110	00001	00110	100	1	0	0	00	xxxxxxxxx

```
rd;
```

C	A	B	ALU	MAR	RD	WR	COND	ADDR
00000	xxxxx	xxxxx	xxx	0	1	0	00	xxxxxxxxx

```
ir = mdr;
```

C	A	B	ALU	MAR	RD	WR	COND	ADDR
01001	00101	xxxxx	0	0	0	0	00	xxxxxxxxx

```
dc = ir; if (s) goto L1;
```

C	A	B	ALU	MAR	RD	WR	COND	ADDR
01010	01001	xxxxx	0	0	0	0	01	000000111

FIGURE 6.14

```
 1 /    Basic Instruction Set Horizontal Microcode      b.has
 2
 3 /    The label indicates the opcode decoded up to that point.
 4 /    For example, control reaches the label L011 when opcode
 5 /    bits 011 have been decoded.
 6
 7 /*******************************************************************/
 8 /       Fetch instruction and increment pc register             /
 9 /*******************************************************************/
10 fetch: mar = pc; pc = pc + 1;                  / increment pc
11        rd;                                     / fetch mach inst
12        ir = mdr;                               / put mach inst in ir
13 /*******************************************************************/
14 /       Decode opcode                                           /
15 /*******************************************************************/
16        dc = ir; if(s) goto L1               / test 1st bit
17 L0:    dc = left(dc); if (s) goto L01;       / test 2nd bit
18 L00:   dc = left(dc); if (s) goto L001;      / test 3rd bit
19        goto L000;
20 L1:    dc = left(dc); if (s) goto L11;       / test 2nd bit
21 L10:.  dc = left(dc); if (s) goto L101;      / test 3rd bit
22        goto L100;
23 L01:   dc = left(dc); if (s) goto L011;      / test 3rd bit
24        goto L010;
25 L11:   dc = left(dc); if (s) goto L111;      / test 3rd bit
26             goto L110:
27 /*******************************************************************/
28 /    Microcode for each instruction                             /
29 /*******************************************************************/
30 L000:  /-------------------------  LD  ---------------------------
```

(continued)

representation. Using 0's in the don't care fields, we get the following hex representations for the four microinstructions in Figure 6.13:

```
304D2000
00001000
49400000
52400207
```

Figure 6.14 shows the complete microcode in our C++ symbolic form that implements the basic instruction set. For easy reference, we have added line numbers on the left. Comments start with "/". We cannot use the semicolon to delimit comments as we did in assembly language programs because we use the semicolon within the symbolic microinstructions.

FIGURE 6.14 (continued)

```
31          mar = ir;                          / get add from inst
32          rd;                                / read operand
33          ac = mdr; goto fetch;              / load ac with operand
34 L001:    /------------------------ ST ------------------------
35          mar = ir; mdr = ac;                / prepare for write
36          wr; goto fetch;                    / write
37 L010:    /------------------------ SHLL ------------------------
38          f = ir & zmask; if (z) goto fetch; / get z-field
39 lloop:   ac = left(ac);                     / shift ac left
40          f = f - 1; if (z) goto fetch;      / dec ac and test
41          goto lloop;                        / branch to lloop
42 L011:    /------------------------ SHRL ------------------------
43          f = ir & zmask; if (z) goto fetch; / get z-field
44 rloop:   ac = right(ac);                    / shift ac right
45          f = f - 1; if (z) goto fetch;      / dec ac and test
46          goto rloop;                        / branch to rloop
47 L100:    /------------------------ ADDC ------------------------
48          f = ir & xmask;                    / get const from x-field
49          ac = ac + f; goto fetch;           / add const to ac
50 L101:    /------------------------ FLIP ------------------------
51          ac = ~ac; goto fetch               / bitwise compl ac
52 L110:    /------------------------ MULT ------------------------
53          mar = ir;                          / get add from inst
54          rd;                                / read operand
55          ac = ac * mdr; goto fetch;         / mult ac by operand
56 L111:    /------------------------ JN ------------------------
57          0 = ac; if (s) goto dojn;          / branch if ac neg
58          goto fetch;                        / branch
59 dojn:    pc = ir & xmask; goto fetch;       / put new add in pc
```

The next microinstruction (line 17 in Figure 6.14),

```
L0:          dc = left(dc); if (s) goto L01;
```

shifts the machine instruction in **dc** one position to the left and places the result back in **dc**. Thus, the ALU sets its S bit according to the second bit in the machine instruction (which is now the leftmost bit because of the shift). If this bit is 1, the **if** statement causes a branch to the label L01.

In Figure 6.14, the labels indicate the opcode bits that cause control to reach that label. For example, if the first two bits of an opcode are 01, control will be routed to the label L01. If the next bit is 0, a branch to L010 would occur. If, on the other hand, the next bit were 1, a branch to L011 would occur.

The microinstructions on lines 18 to 25 continue to left shift the **dc** register and conditionally branch depending on the leftmost bit in the **dc** register after the shift.

The result is that control goes to the labels L000, L001, . . . , L111, if the first three opcode bits are 000, 001, . . . , 111, respectively.

For most machine instructions, the CPU needs the original instruction in order to execute it. That is why the microcode in Figure 6.14 saves the fetched machine instruction in the **ir**, and uses a separate register (the **dc** register) to hold the shifted machine instruction.

The microinstruction sequences for the eight machine language instructions in the basic instruction set start at the labels that correspond to the first bits of their opcodes. For example, the opcode for the ld instruction starts with 000. Accordingly, the microcode for the ld instruction starts at the label L000.

Let's examine microcode sequences in Figure 6.14 for each machine instruction. For each of these sequences, the **ir** contains the machine language instruction (by virtue of the microinstruction on line 12).

The first microinstruction (line 31) for the *ld* instruction loads the **mar** with the address in the **ir** (the **mar** is only 12 bits wide, so it receives only the 12-bit address in the **ir**). For the ld instruction, this is the address of its memory operand. The next microinstruction (line 32) then reads the operand into the **mdr**. The last microinstruction (line 33) routes the operand from the **mdr** to the **ac** register, and branches back to **fetch** (location 0 in microcode) to start another fetch-increment-decode-execute cycle.

The first microinstruction (line 35) for the st instruction loads both the **mar** and the **mdr**. The **mar** receives the address in the **ir** (which is the address in the st instruction); the **mdr** receives the contents of the **ac** register. The next microinstruction (line 36) then writes the contents of the **mdr** to the location in main memory given by the **mar** before branching back to fetch.

A *shll* instruction contains the *shift count* (i.e., the number of positions to shift) in its z-field (i.e., its rightmost 4 bits). The microinstruction on line 38 isolates this field by ANDing it with **zmask** (the read-only register that contains 000F hex). It then loads the result into the **f** register. If **f** is not zero, the microcode loops, each iteration of which shifts the **ac** register left (line 39) and decrements the count in **f** (line 40). When **f** reaches zero, the microinstruction on line 40 branches back to **fetch** to start another cycle. The code for shrl is the same, except it performs a right shift instead of a left shift.

The *addc* instruction is an immediate instruction; that is, the operand itself is in the instruction (in its rightmost 12 bits). The microinstruction on line 48 isolates this operand by ANDing it with **xmask** (the read-only register that contains 0FFF). It then loads it into the **f** register. The next microinstruction then adds the **f** register to **ac**.

The *flip* instruction uses the bitwise complement function built into the ALU; *mult* uses the hardware multiplication function in the ALU.

A *jn* instruction has its jump-to address in its x-field. The microinstruction on line 59 isolates this field by ANDing the **ir** with **xmask**. It then loads it into **pc**, causing a jump at the machine level to this memory address.

The microinstruction on line 57 appears to contain an error: an assignment to 0, a read-only register. However, this assignment is perfectly legal. It routes the number in the **ac** register through the ALU so that the **if** statement can test the leftmost bit of the number in the **ac** register. It does not affect register **0** because **0** is a read-only register. The **jn** needs only to test the leftmost bit in the **ac** register. We could have used the microinstruction

```
b = ac; if (s) goto dojn;
```

instead, but it corrupts the **b** register. Corrupting **b** would not hurt us here because we are not using this register; nevertheless, it is still better to avoid corrupting it. That way if we ever put **b** to use, we would avoid a bug that its corruption here would produce.

The pseudoinstructions (bkpt, halt, and the I/O instructions) are implemented in **sim** rather than in microcode. Thus, microcode for them does not appear in Figure 6.14.

6.2.14 Hardware/Microcode Tradeoff

The microcode for the shll instruction in the basic instruction set has to use a loop because the shifter circuit in H1 can shift only one position per operation. This loop iterates once for each position shifted. Thus, for large shift counts, the execution of a shll instruction takes a long time. For example, for a shift count of 15, the shll instruction executes 45 microinstructions (three per iteration of the loop). We have a similar situation with the shrl instruction.

We can reduce the execution time of a shift instruction considerably if we use a barrel shifter in H1 in place of the one-position shifter it currently has. A *barrel shifter* is a circuit that can shift multiple positions in one operation. With a barrel shifter, a 15-position shift would require the execution of only *one* microinstruction.

The one-position shifter in H1 has two types of inputs: the direction of the shift (one line) and the data to be shifted (16 lines). A barrel shifter for H1 would have the same two inputs, and, in addition, a four-line input for the shift count. Figure 6.15 shows how to connect a barrel shifter within the ALU. Simply connect

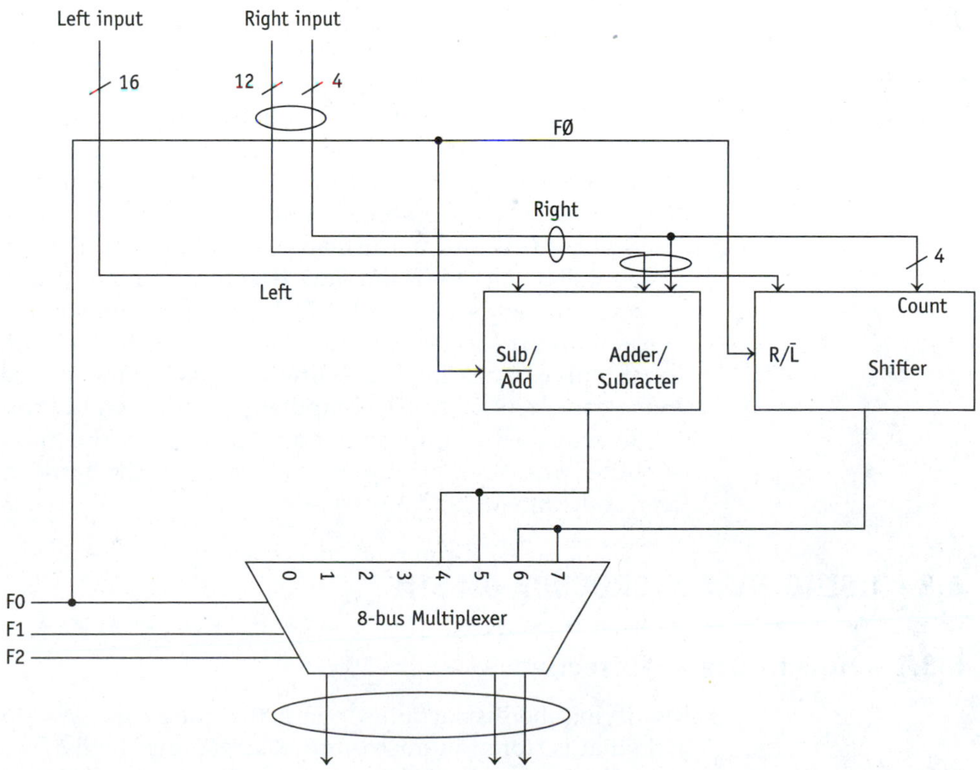

FIGURE 6.15   Barrel Shifter

its direction and data inputs exactly like the current shifter (see Figure 5.31 in Chapter 5), and connect its shift-count inputs to the four rightmost lines of the right input port of the ALU. Then, the A bus would provide the data to be shifted, and the B bus would provide the shift count (on its four rightmost bits). For example, suppose a `shll` machine instruction has been fetched, placed in the `ir`, and decoded. If we then execute the microinstruction

```
ac = left(ac, ir);
```

`ir` would drive the B bus. Thus, the rightmost four bits of the `ir` (the shift count) would drive the shift count inputs of the barrel shifter, causing it to shift the data from the `ac` register the appropriate number of positions. This single microinstruction would replace the entire loop in the microcode for the `shll` instruction. Shift instructions (particularly those with large shift counts) would then execute faster, but our computer would cost more because a barrel shifter is more expensive than a one-position shifter.

The shift instructions in the basic instruction set illustrate a choice we have to make when we design a computer: We can put function in hardware to make a faster but more expensive computer, or we can put function in microcode to make a less expensive but slower computer. With a barrel shifter, the multiple-shift capability needed by shift instructions is in the hardware. With a one-position shifter, the multiple-shift capability is in microcode (in the form of a loop that repeatedly shifts one position).

With multiplication, we have the same hardware/microcode choice that we have with shifting. H1 has a multiply circuit in its ALU that allows us to multiply with a single microinstruction. Alternatively, we can eliminate this circuit to reduce cost. To multiply, we can use a loop in microcode that multiplies by repeatedly performing shift and add operations (we will study this shift-add technique for multiplication in Chapter 13). In H1, we opted for the hardware side of the hardware/microcode tradeoff for multiplication, but we opted for the microcode side for shifting.

Because H1 is an instructional computer, its design is geared to that purpose. By placing multiplication in hardware and shifting in microcode, we get a better instructional tool: H1 illustrates both the hardware and microcode approaches. A designer of a real computer, of course, would have to make hardware/microcode choices based on cost/performance considerations. If a computer is too expensive, no one will buy it; if it is too slow, everyone will buy a faster computer.

The standard shifter in H1 is the one-position shifter. All the microcode that comes with `sim` uses this shifter. However, to further enhance H1 as an instructional tool, `sim` has the capability of replacing the standard one-position shifter with a barrel shifter. A real computer, of course, would not have both shifters.

To activate the barrel shifter on H1, simply write microcode that uses the barrel shifter. `sim` will then automatically activate the barrel shifter when it loads that microcode into microstore.

6.3   USING NEW MICROCODE ON SIM

6.3.1   How to Use a !-Directive

Modifying the instruction set on H1 is quite easy: We simply change the microcode that is stored in microstore. Redesigning the hardware is *not* necessary. For example, if we replace the sequence of microinstructions for the instruction with opcode 2 (currently the add instruction in the standard instruction set), then the new sequence of microinstructions will be executed every time a machine instruction with the opcode 2 is executed. The new sequence of microinstructions could implement a completely different instruction.

In a real computer system, all the circuits that make up the CPU, including microstore, are typically built into a single silicon chip. Such a circuit is called an *integrated circuit (IC)* or, more simply, a *chip*. Once a chip is manufactured, it generally cannot be modified. Thus, if we had H1 on a chip, we would not be able to modify its microcode; however, the chip manufacturer could easily produce new H1 chips with new microcode. This would be easy because the design and layout of H1 would not change—only the contents of microstore would be different. Thus, the manufacturer could simply produce exactly the same chip as before, except with new microcode in microstore.

On **sim**, it is even easier to use new microcode. First, you have to create a *microcode file* containing the new microcode, and a *configuration file* describing the new instruction set (we will learn how to do this in the next section). The microcode file should have the extension ".hor" (for horizontal microcode) or ".ver" (for vertical microcode); the configuration file should have the extension ".cfg"; and both files should have the same base name. For example, if the microcode file is **b.hor**, then the configuration file should be **b.cfg**. Next, you should insert a *!-directive*—a line that contains the microcode/configuration file base name preceded by "!"—at the beginning of any assembly language program that uses the new instruction set. The !-directive does not have to be the first line in the file. It may be preceded by blank lines, comment lines, or a line containing an &-directive (recall that an &-directive activates memory-mapped I/O). A !-directive may start in any column, but it must not have any non-white space to its left.

Suppose **b.hor** and **b.cfg** are the names of the microcode and configuration files that you wish to use. Then you should insert the line

    !b

at the beginning of the assembly language program. When **mas** assembles a program in which such a directive appears, it will automatically access **b.cfg**. When **sim** runs the assembled program, it will also automatically access **b.cfg**, and, in addition, load microstore from **b.hor**.

Using a !-directive is an easy way to get **mas** and **sim** to use configuration and microcode files. However, if an assembly language program does not contain a !-directive, you can still get **mas** and **sim** to use configuration and microcode files by specifying the appropriate command line arguments. A third alternative is to use the **mod** program to change the default configuration and microcode files for **mas** and **sim**.

6.3.2 Creating a Configuration File

A configuration file contains three parts, each part separated from the next with a line containing "%%". **mas** uses part 1 only; **sim** uses all three parts.

Each entry in a configuration file must be on a single line. A comment may appear either to the right of an entry or by itself on a separate line. Comments should start with ";" or "/". Completely blank lines may appear anywhere within a configuration file.

Part 1 lists all the mnemonics that we want **mas** to recognize. The mnemonics must be listed in opcode order (**mas** determines the opcode of each mnemonic from its order in the configuration file). Thus, the mnemonics for opcodes 0 to E should be listed first, then mnemonics for opcodes F0 to FE, then mnemonics for opcodes FF0 to FFE, and finally mnemonics for opcodes FFF0 to FFF4. Opcodes FFF5 to FFFF are reserved for the pseudoinstructions (bkpt, halt, and the I/O instructions). Their corresponding mnemonics should not be listed. For example, in the configuration file for the basic instruction set (see Figure 6.16), we list the ld mnemonic first because it has opcode 0. The other mnemonics follow in the appropriate positions. Opcodes with no corresponding mnemonic are represented with "?". However, we can omit "?" for the opcodes following the last mnemonic. Thus, the jn mnemonic can be the last entry in this part of the configuration file.

To the right of each mnemonic in part 1 is the number of operands (0 or 1) in the corresponding assembly language instruction. **mas** uses these numbers to check that each instruction in an assembly language program has the correct number of operands. These numbers are optional. However, if you do not include them in your configuration file, **mas** will not perform these checks.

In part 2, we list register names starting with register 6 (the names for registers 0 to 5 are fixed). If we don't list any names in part 2, we then would have to refer to registers in symbolic microcode by their hex numbers. Although this works, it makes the microcode more difficult for us to read and understand. It is better to name any register having a consistent usage with a name that reflects that usage. For example, in the microcode in Figure 6.14, we used names for all the registers that we used except for register **f** (register **f** is only a "work" register and, therefore, needs no special name).

Because we are not using and naming register 7 in the basic instruction set, its configuration file has a "?" in the position that corresponds to register 7. We skipped over register 7 so that the register mapping in the basic instruction set matches that of the standard instruction set (in the standard instruction set, registers 6 and 8 are the **pc** and **ac** registers). We did not have to do this. We did it only to be consistent with the standard instruction set.

Part 3 of the configuration file provides information that **sim**'s debugger needs. The first six entries provide three pairs of hex numbers—the first in each pair for the horizontal microcode, the second for the vertical microcode (we use a single configuration file for both horizontal and vertical microcode). The *start fetch address* is the microcode address at which fetching of a machine instruction starts (0 in **b.has**). The *pc increment address* is the address at which the **pc** register is incremented (0 in **b.has**). The *read machine instruction address* is the address of the microinstruction that triggers the read of the machine instruction (1 in **b.has**). It is essential to correctly specify these addresses. With incorrect addresses, **sim** will generate garbled trace output, and possibly go into an infinite loop.

Following the read machine instruction addresses are three hex numbers that specify the register numbers of the **pc**, **sp**, and I/O register. Our basic microcode does not use a stack pointer register, but part 3 still requires a number—so use any number between 0 and 1F. The I/O register is the register that the I/O instructions use (din, dout, etc.). For our basic microcode, we use register 8 (the **ac** register) for I/O. For microcode that uses the **sp** register, we have the option of using the top of the stack for I/O instead of a register. To do this, we should specify $ for this field instead of a register number.

The final set of hex numbers is a list of the machine-level registers—that is, registers that are visible at the machine level. When we enter the debugger command **R*** (display all machine-level registers), **sim** will display only the registers you list here. Because our microcode uses only the **pc** and **ac** registers at the machine level, we list only their numbers (6 and 8).

FIGURE 6.16

```
;                                                      b.cfg
;      Configuration file for the basic instruction set

        ; Part 1 (mnemonics in opcode order)
ld    1      ; mnemonic and number of operands for opcode 0
?
st    1      ; mnemonic and number of operands for opcode 2
?
shll  1      ; mnemonic and number of operands for opcode 4
?
shrl  1      ; mnemonic and number of operands for opcode 6
?
addc  1      ; mnemonic and number of operands for opcode 8
?
flip  0      ; mnemonic and number of operands for opcode A
?
mult  1      ; mnemonic and number of operands for opcode C
?
jn           ; mnemonic and number of operands for opcode E

%%     ; Part 2 (reg names in number order starting with reg 6)
pc           ; register 6
?            ; not using register 7
ac           ; register 8
ir           ; register 9
dc           ; register A
             ; remaining regs can be referenced by their hex numbers

%%     ; Part 3 (special addresses and numbers)
0            ; horizontal start fetch address (hex)
0            ; vertical start fetch address (hex)

0            ; horizontal increment pc address (hex)
3            ; vertical increment pc address (hex)

1            ; horizontal read machine instruction address (hex)
1            ; vertical read machine instruction address (hex)

6            ; pc register number (hex)
0            ; sp register number (hex)
8            ; I/O register number (hex)

6            ; machine-level register numbers (hex)
8
```

6.3.3   Creating Binary Microcode

In Chapter 3 we observed that working with machine instructions in symbolic form (i.e., assembly language) is much easier than working with the binary machine language. To create a machine language program, we first write the program in assembly language and then use a program (**mas**) to translate the assembly language instructions to binary form (the only form that the CPU can use). From now on, let's refer to **mas** as a *machine-level assembler,* because it translates machine-level instructions. At the microlevel, we are in precisely the same position. It's much easier to work with the symbolic form of microinstructions, but the CPU requires the binary form, so we will write microcode in symbolic form, and use a program to translate the symbolic form to the binary form. We call the program that translates symbolic microcode to binary a *microlevel assembler.* The H1 software package includes a microlevel assembler called **has** (horizontal microlevel assembler). **has** translates horizontal microcode (the type of microcode that we have been discussing) from symbolic to binary form.

Let's use **has** to translate the symbolic microcode in Figure 6.14. First create a file named **b.has** containing this microcode (or you can use the **b.has** file in the H1 software package). To translate this file with **has**, enter

```
C:\H1>has b
```

has then produces a file named **b.hor** containing the binary form of the microcode. The output file name is formed from the base name of the input file ("b" in this example) and the extension ".hor". **has** also produces a list file **b.hst** similarly named but with the ".hst" extension.

When we invoke **has**, it automatically accesses the configuration file for the microcode that it is translating (i.e., the configuration file with the same base name). For example, when **has** translates **b.has**, it accesses **b.cfg**.

6.3.4   Assembling with a New Instruction Set

Once we have microcode implementing a new instruction set and its configuration file, we can write and assemble programs using the new instruction set. For example, consider the test program for the basic instruction set in Figure 6.17. Note that

FIGURE 6.17

```
 1              !b                  bprog.mas
 2 start:       ld        x        ; load from x
 3              flip               ; flip bits in ac
 4              addc      3        ; add the constant 3
 5              mult      y        ; multiply ac by y
 6              st        z        ; store product in z
 7              shll      2        ; shift left logical 2
 8              shrl      2        ; shift right logical 2
 9              jn        start    ; jump if ac is negative
10              dout               ; output ac in decimal
11              halt
12 x:           dw        -1
13 y:           dw        2
14 z:           dw        0
```

line 1 contains the !-directive `!b` that indicates to `mas` it should assemble it according to the information in `b.cfg`. Notice that we are using the `dout` and `halt` instructions in our test program even though we did not implement them in microcode. `dout`, `halt`, and the other pseudoinstructions are implemented by `sim`, and are, therefore, available regardless of the microcode. All the pseudoinstructions—the `bkpt`, `halt`, and I/O instructions—can be used with any microcode. Assuming the program in Figure 6.17 is in the file `bprog.mas`, we can assemble it with

```
C:\H1>mas bprog
```

`mas` then translates `bprog.mas` using the configuration file specified in the !-directive, and generates an output file `bprog.mac`, containing the machine code, and the list file `bprog.lst`.

6.3.5 Tracing at the Microlevel

We have been using `sim` to examine and trace the operations at the machine level of H1. We can similarly use `sim` at the microlevel. `sim` normally runs with its microlevel capabilities *disabled* (i.e., hidden from the user). To *enable* `sim`'s microlevel capabilities (i.e., to make microlevel activity visible to the user), enter

```
enable
```

at the debugger's prompt. To disable it, enter

```
disable
```

at the debugger's prompt. Regardless of `sim`'s default setting, we can always switch back and forth between enabled and disabled during a run by entering the `enable` and `disable` commands.

When `sim` runs enabled, `sim`'s debugger will respond to both machine and microlevel commands. Because the two levels have similar commands, uppercase letters are used for the machine-level commands and lowercase letters are used for microlevel commands. As usual, an asterisk following a command means "all"; a number following a command means "from the location specified by the number." For example, to display contents of all of *machine-level* store (i.e., main memory) in use when `sim` is enabled, enter

```
D*
```

in uppercase. To display all *micro*store, enter

```
d*
```

in lowercase.

Let's now use `sim` to trace the microcode for the basic instruction set. We will need the files `b.hor` (the microcode in binary), `b.cfg` (the configuration file), and `bprog.mac` (the machine language program). These files are in the H1 software package so you don't have to create them. We start by running `sim` with the `bprog` program:

```
C:\H1>sim bprog
```

`sim` will then automatically access `b.cfg`, load `b.hor` into microstore, and load `bprog.mac` into the main memory. You should see the messages "Reading configuration file b.cfg" and "Reading microcode file b.hor" that confirm that this process is taking place. The debugger in **sim** then generates a prompt showing the first machine instruction to be executed:

```
Starting session.  Enter h or ? for help.
---- [T7] 0: ld   /0 00A/
```

Let's run the program to completion by entering **g** (to go) to see if it works correctly. **sim** displays

```
    0: ld   /0 00A/ ac=0000/FFFF
    1: flip /A 000/ ac=FFFF/0000
    2: addc /8 003/ ac=0000/0003
    3: mult /C 00B/ ac=0003/0006
    4: st   /2 00C/ m[00C]=0000/0006
    5: shll /4 002/ ac=0006/0018
    6: shrl /6 002/ ac=0018/0006
    7: jn   /E 000/
    8: dout /FFFD / 6
    9: halt /FFFF /
Machine inst count =    A (hex) =     10 (dec)
```

From the trace, we can see the effect of the various instructions so that we can confirm that our microcode is working correctly.

One useful capability of **sim** is the display of microinstruction counts for each machine instruction it traces. A microinstruction count is the total number of microinstructions that are executed to fetch, decode, and execute a machine instruction. Microinstruction counts are a measure of the execution time of a machine instruction. Let's display microinstruction counts for the instructions in our program. Enter **o** (to do over), **mc** (to initiate the machine-level display mode plus counts), and then **g** (to go). We get

```
---- [T7] o
Starting session.  Enter h or ? for help.
---- [T7] 0: ld   /0 00A/ mc
Machine-level display mode + counts
---- [T7] 0: ld   /0 00A/ g
    0: ld   /0 00A/ ac=0000/FFFF    10t
    1: flip /A 000/ ac=FFFF/0000    7t
    2: addc /8 002/ ac=0000/0003    9t
    3: mult /C 00B/ ac=0003/0003    10t
    4: st   /2 00C/ m[00C]=0000/0003   8t
    5: shll /4 002/ ac=0004/0018    13t
    6: shrl /6 002/ ac=0010/0006    12t
    7: jn   /E 000/   8t
    8: dout /FFFD / 6 2t
    9: halt /FFFF /    2t
Machine inst count =    A (hex) =     10 (dec)
---- [T7]
```

The numbers at the right of each trace line are microinstruction counts. The suffix "t" at the end of each count indicates that the count is a decimal number ("t" stands for base 10).

The total microinstruction count for a program can be obtained with the **s** (status) debugger command. This command displays a variety of status information including the total microinstruction count. This count is also displayed whenever a program halts if `sim` is running enabled. A total microinstruction count for a program is useful because it is a precise measure of that program's execution time.

Now let's rerun the program and trace the microcode that corresponds to the execution of the `addc` instruction. To do this, enter **o** (to do over) and **enable**:

```
---- [T7] o
Starting session.  Enter h or ? for help.
---- [T7] 0: ld    /0 00A/ enable
Microlevel enabled
```

Next enter **T2** to execute the `ld` and `flip` instructions, making `addc` the next instruction to be executed. `sim` is now enabled so it is case sensitive. Be sure to enter **T2** with a capital "T":

```
---- [T7] 0: ld    /0 00A/ T2
  0: ld    /0 00A/ ac=0000/FFFF 10t
  1: flip /A 000/ ac=FFFF/0000 7t
---- [T2] 2: addc /8 002/
```

Then enter **m** (in lowercase) to change the *display mode* from machine-level to microlevel:

```
---- [T2] 2: addc /8 002/ m

Microlevel display mode

---- [T1] 0: pc = 1 + pc; mar = pc; /
```

In *machine-level display mode*, `sim` traces *machine-level* activity; in *microlevel display mode*, `sim` traces *microlevel* activity. Notice that the prompt that `sim` generates now contains the microinstruction to be executed next. Hit ENTER to execute the default command **T1**. **T1** (with a capital "T") causes the execution of one machine instruction. But because `sim` is in microlevel display mode, it displays all microlevel activity that occurs during the execution of this one machine instruction:

```
---- [T1] 0: pc = 1 + pc; mar = pc; / ←hit ENTER
  0: pc = 1 + pc; mar = pc;
     mar=001/002  pc=0002/0003
  1: rd;
     Rd from m[002] mdr=A000/8003  2: addc /8 003/
  2: ir = mdr;
     ir=A000/8003
  3: dc = ir; if (s) goto 7;
     dc=8000/8003
  7: dc = left(dc); if (s) goto C;
     dc=8003/0006
  8: dc = left(dc); if (s) goto 1D;
     dc=0006/000C
  9: goto 1B;
 1B: f = ir & xmask;
     f=0000/0003
 1C: ac = ac + f; goto 0;
     ac=0000/0003
---- [T1] 0: pc = 1 + pc; mar = pc; /
```

Each entry in the trace contains the address of the microinstruction, the microinstruction in symbolic form, and, below it, its effect. Observe that the microinstruction at location 1 reads an `addc` instruction into the **mdr**. The microinstructions at locations 3, 7, and 8 then decode its opcode. Finally the microinstructions at locations 1B and 1C perform the action required by the `addc` instruction. The **T1** command is quite handy in microlevel display mode precisely because it shows all the microlevel activity that occurs for *one* machine instruction.

In the previous trace, we see the following for the microinstruction at location 1 (this is the microinstruction that fetches the machine instruction to be executed next):

1: rd;

    Rd from m[002] mdr=A000/8003   2: addc /8 003/

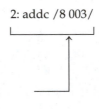

machine instruction
to be
executed next

Notice that the trace shows the machine instruction just fetched in assembly and hex forms.

To execute the first three microinstructions for the next machine instruction, enter **t3**:

```
---- [T1] 0: pc = 1 + pc; mar = pc; / t3
  0: pc = 1 + pc; mar = pc;
     mar=002/003   pc=0003/0004
  1: rd;
     Rd from m[003] mdr=8003/C00B  3: mult /C 00B/
  2: ir = mdr;
     ir=8003/C00B
---- [t3] 3: dc = ir; if (s) goto 7; /
```

From the trace of the microinstruction at location 1, we can see that the next machine instruction is the `mult` instruction at location 3 in main memory. **t3** is now the default command at the microlevel.

Now let's experiment with some of the other microlevel debugger commands. To unassemble the microcode starting at location 0, enter the **u0** command:

```
---- [t3] 3: dc = ir; if (s) goto 7; / u0
          C          A          B       ALU    MAR   RD    WR   COND   ADDR
/  0: pc          1          pc        +       1    0     0    0      0
   0:     pc = 1 + pc; mar = pc;

/  1: 0          0          0         0        0    1     0    0      0
   1:     rd;

/  2: ir         mdr        0         0        0    0     0    0      0
   2:     ir = mdr;
```

```
/  3: dc       ir        0       0       0   0   0   1     7
   3:       dc = ir; if (s) goto 7;
```

```
---- [t3] 3: dc = ir; if (s) goto 7; /
```

For each microinstruction, **sim** displays the values of its component fields on one line followed on the next line by its symbolic form. Notice that **sim** uses register names instead of numbers for the C, A, and B fields. It also uses symbols (+, -, &, etc.) to represent the ALU operation, except for the "straight-through" operation, for which it uses **0**.

If you want to see all the machine code in assembly and hex form, enter **U***:

```
---- [t3] 3: dc = ir; if (s) goto 7; / U*
   0: ld    /0 00A/ flip /A 000/ addc /8 003/ mult /C 00B/
   4: st    /2 00C/ shll /4 002/ shrl /6 002/ jn   /E 000/
   8: dout /FFFD / halt /FFFF / halt /FFFF / ld   /0 002/
   C: ld    /0 000/
---- [t3] 3: dc = ir; if (s) goto 7; /
```

Observe that the data word at location A is unassembled as a `halt` instruction because its value matches the opcode for a `halt` instruction. Similarly, the data items at locations B and C are unassembled as `ld` instructions.

To dump all microcode in hex, enter **d***:

```
---- [t3] 3: dc = ir; if (s) goto 7; / d*
   0: 304D2000    00001000    49400000    52400207
   4: 5281820A    52818211    0000060E    5281820C
   8: 5281821D    0000061B    52818217    00000613
   C: 52818221    0000061E    00122000    00001000
  10: 41400600    2A122000    00000E00    7A488400
  14: 42018000    7BC34400    00000614    7A488400
  18: 4201C000    7BC34400    00000618    7A448000
  1C: 421F0600    42004600    00122000    00001000
  20: 420AC600    02000223    00000600    32448600
---- [t3] 3: dc = ir; if (s) goto 7; /
```

And to dump all machine code, enter **D***:

```
---- [t3] 3: dc = ir; if (s) goto 7; / D*
   0: 000A A000 8003 C00B 200C 4002 6002 E000    ........
   8: FFFD FFFF FFFF 0002 0000                    .....
---- [t3] 3: dc = ir; if (s) goto 7; /
```

To show the contents of all registers, enter **r***:

```
---- [t3] 3: dc = ir; if (s) goto 7; / r*
    mpc   = 003     mar   = 003
    0     = 0000    1     = 0001    xmask = 0FFF    ymask = 00FF
    zmask = 000F    mdr   = C00B    pc    = 0004    ?     = 0000
    ac    = 0003    ir    = C00B    dc    = 000C    b     = 0000
    c     = 0000    d     = 0000    e     = 0000    f     = 0003
    10    = 0000    11    = 0000    12    = 0000    13    = 0000
    14    = 0000    15    = 0000    16    = 0000    17    = 0000
    18    = 0000    19    = 0000    1a    = 0000    1b    = 0000
    1c    = 0000    1d    = 0000    1e    = 0000    1f    = 0000
---- [t3] 3: dc = ir; if (s) goto 7; /
```

And to show the contents of only the machine-level registers (i.e., registers visible at the machine level), enter `R*`:

```
---- [t3] 3: dc = ir; if (s) goto 7; / R*
     pc   = 0004      ac   = 0003
---- [t3] 3: dc = ir; if (s) goto 7; /
```

Which registers are visible at the machine level depends on the microcode. For our basic microcode, only the `pc` and `ac` registers are at the machine level. In the standard instruction set, the `sp` register is also visible. Recall that the configuration file specifies which registers are at the machine level. This is how **sim** knows which registers to display for the `R*` command.

Now let's switch back to the machine-level display mode by entering `M`:

```
---- [t3] 3: dc = ir; if (s) goto 7; / M
Machine-level display mode + counts
---- [T2] 3: mult /C 00B/
```

Notice that the "plus counts" display mode is still active (it can be canceled with the MC- command). The prompt shows the machine instruction that is currently executing. Recall that we can enter **n** (either upper- or lowercase), in which case **sim** does not produce trace output. This mode is handy if you are interested in seeing what the program itself produces with the output instructions (`uout`, `sout`, `aout`, `hout`, and `dout`). Otherwise, this output tends to be buried in the trace output and is hard to find. Let's enter **n** to switch to no-display mode:

```
---- [T2] 3: mult /C 00B/ n
No display mode
---- [T1]
```

Finally, let's complete the execution of the program by entering **g**:

```
---- [T1] g
6
Machine inst count =     A (hex) =     10 (dec)
Micro   inst count =    51 (hex) =     81 (dec)
---- [T1]
```

sim then runs the program until it halts. We see the output that the `dout` instruction displays (even though **sim** is in its no-display mode), and the final instruction counts.

In addition to the display modes we have been using, **sim** has a "plus source" and a "source only" display mode at both the machine and microlevels. These modes display the original source code, including labels and comments, from which the executing instruction was translated. To activate machine-level display plus source when **sim** is disabled, enter **ms** in upper or lowercase. Use uppercase if **sim** is enabled. To activate microlevel display mode plus source, enter **ms** in lowercase when **sim** is enabled. The "source only" mode, is similarly activated with the **mso** command.

The debugger in **sim** is quite useful. You can easily trace any machine or microinstruction. If there are any bugs in your machine or microlevel programs, you should be able to find them quickly with the debugger. Two features of the debugger that are not illustrated by the sample session are the **B** and **b** commands (set breakpoint) and the **L** command (create log file). You will find these commands quite useful for debugging. The **B** and **b** commands set breakpoints at the machine and microlevels, respectively, both of which may coexist. The **L** (upper- or lowercase) command causes **sim** to create a log file that contains all tracing activity. You can print out this log file and then study it offline. This is the surest way to locate hard-to-find bugs. If you forget any of the commands, you can display a help screen by entering **h** or **?** at the debugger's prompt.

6.3.6 Encrypting Microcode

Now that we have our microcode file **b.hor**, we can distribute it to users of **sim**. If we distribute it "as is," users of **sim** will be able to examine the microcode it contains using the **u** (unassemble) or **d** (dump) commands. If we want to allow users to use our microcode but *not* examine it, we can do so by encrypting the microcode with the **enc** (microcode Encrypt) program. To do this, enter

```
C:\H1\enc b.hor
```

enc will then read the microcode in **b.hor**, encrypt it, and write it back (with the user's permission) to **b.hor**, overlaying its original contents. We can now distribute **b.hor** along with the configuration file **b.cfg**. Although **b.hor** is now encrypted, **sim** will still be able to use it. **sim**, however, will refuse to run in the enabled mode. Thus, users will be able to run machine-level programs, but will not be able to examine the controlling microcode. The microcode files in the software package for the optimal and stack instruction sets that we will discuss in Chapters 12 and 13 were encrypted in just this way.

6.3.7 Writing and Optimizing Complicated Microcode

A good starting point for writing microcode that implements a complicated instruction set is to study the microcode for the standard instruction set. The microcode for this instruction set is contained in the file **s.has** in the H1 software package and is also listed in Appendix C. This microcode, like the microcode for the basic instruction set, consists of three parts: instruction fetch, opcode decode, and instruction execution. The standard instruction set contains more instructions than the basic instruction set. Thus, its microcode contains more microinstructions in its opcode decode and execution parts. Moreover, unlike the microcode in **b.has**, it decodes every possible opcode.

We use labels in the file **s.has** that reflect the opcode decoded up to the point of each label. For example, control reaches the label **LF_F_0001** when the bits 1111 1111 0001 have been decoded. In these labels, 0 and 1 always represent the bits 0 and 1. Hex numbers greater than 1 represent their corresponding group of 4 bits.

All possible opcodes (0–E, F0–FE, FF0–FFE, FFF0–FFF4) are decoded in **s.has** even though some (F8–FFF4) have no corresponding instructions. If an opcode is fetched that has no corresponding instruction, control goes to its corresponding label at the end of **s.has**, where an unconditional branch to the beginning of the fetch microcode occurs. Thus, every unsupported opcode is effectively a *no-op* (i.e., an instruction that causes nothing to occur other than its fetch, the incrementation of the **pc**, and its decoding).

Because **s.has** already decodes all possible opcodes, adding support for a new instruction requires only the insertion of its execution microcode at its corresponding label. For example, to add support for opcode F8, we simply place the microcode for the new instruction at the label **LF_8**.

For clarity's sake, we structured the microcode in **s.has** into three distinct parts:

1. The code that fetches the machine instruction and increments the **pc**
2. The decoding microcode
3. The execution sequences for each machine instruction

We structured **b.has** in the same way. If we are willing to intermingle decoding microcode and execution sequences, we can produce microcode that is both

FIGURE 6.18   a)

```
            .
            .
            .

L000:       dc = left(dc); if (s) goto L0001;
            goto L0000;
            .

            .

            .

L0000:      /------------- LD -------------
            mar = ir;
            rd;
            ac = mdr; goto fetch;

L0001:      /------------- ST -------------
            mar = ir; mdr = ac;
            wr; goto fetch;
```
b)
```
            .

            .

            .

L000:       dc = left(dc); if (s) goto L0001;

L0000:      /------------- LD -------------
            mar = ir;
            rd;
            ac = mdr; goto fetch;
            .

            .

            .

L0001:      /------------- ST -------------
            mar = ir; mdr = ac;
            wr; goto fetch;
```

smaller and faster. Let's consider an example. Figure 6.18a shows the microcode in **s.has** that branches to **L0000** (the execution code for **ld**) and to **L0001** (the execution code for **st**). If we move the execution code at **L0000** (i.e., the code for **ld**) to where the unconditional branch to **L0000** is located, then we don't need the unconditional branch instruction anymore. Figure 6.18b shows the result. We save both space (we need one fewer microinstruction in microstore) and time (every time the **ld** instruction is decoded, one fewer microinstruction is executed). If we fully apply this optimization to the microcode in **s.has**, we will realize a considerable improvement in the average execution time of machine instructions. Because H1 and V1 are "teaching" computers, we opted for microcode with optimal clarity rather than optimal efficiency.

6.4 INTERPRETING MACHINE LANGUAGE INSTRUCTIONS

Programming language processors come in two basic types: compilers and interpreters. A *compiler* translates the source program, after which the translated program can be executed. Translation precedes execution. An *interpreter*, on the other hand, does not translate the program. Instead, it performs a sequence of operations for each source statement that simulates the effect of that statement. For example, for the statement

```
x = y + z;
```

an interpreter would access the values of **y** and **z**, add them, and place the result in **x**. To *interpret* an instruction is to "execute" that instruction by performing a sequence of operations that simulates its effect. In a sense, an interpreter translates each source statement (to the sequence of operations that simulates its effect). However, this translation differs from that of a compiler in two important ways: Translation and execution are intermingled, and a source statement is translated each time it is executed (rather than only once).

C++ programs are compiled to the machine language of the computer on which the programs are to run. Java programs, on the other hand, are compiled to *bytecode*—machine code for a particular machine (the Java Virtual Machine), regardless of the computer on which the program is to run. Thus, to run bytecode on, let's say, a personal computer, we have to run a program that interprets this bytecode.

sim executes a program by interpreting the machine language instructions in that program. For example, for a **ja** instruction, **sim** loads the variable that represents the **pc** register with the jump-to address. **sim** executes machine code for H1 in the same way the Java interpreter executes Java bytecode—by interpreting each instruction.

Now that you understand the difference between compilation and interpretation, we can make an interesting observation about H1 (the actual hardware if it existed—not the machine simulated by **sim**): H1 executes machine language code by *interpreting* each machine instruction. Each machine language instruction is, in effect, a subroutine call of a sequence of microinstructions whose execution performs the operations specified by the machine instruction.

6.5   HARDWIRED CONTROL

• •

The control section of H1 executes machine instructions by interpreting each instruction with a sequence of microinstructions. An alternate approach is to use a *hardwired* (or *random logic*) control section. In this approach, the control section generates control signals using combinational and sequential logic that support a specific instruction set. The instruction set is fixed by the "wiring" of control section logic—hence, the name "hardwired" control section.

Figure 6.19 shows the basic organization of a hardwired control section. The sequencer generates clock subcycles T1 to Tn. The *control-signal generator* is a combinational circuit that outputs control signals based on its inputs. For the first few clock subcycles, the control-signal generator outputs the sequence of control signals that fetch and load the next machine instruction into the **ir** (instruction register), and increments the **pc**. Once a machine instruction is in the **ir**, its bits drive a decoder (the *instruction decoder*) whose outputs provide additional inputs to the control-signal generator. On the subsequent clock subcycles, the control-signal generator outputs the control signals that execute the instruction specified by the instruction decoder's outputs. Not all machine instructions require the same number of clock subcycles to execute. Only the longest will require the subcycles through Tn. Thus, the control-signal generator resets the sequencer (via the sequencer's reset input) at the end of each machine instruction's execution.

The control-signal generator may require other inputs in addition to those provided by the decoder and sequencer. For example, on a conditional jump instruction, it will need to know the current state of the S, C, V, and Z flags.

Because H1 has a microprogrammed control section, its cost does not depend on the instruction set, assuming it can be implemented with H1's current organization. For example, H1 with the standard instruction set would cost the same as H1 with the basic instruction set; the only difference between the two versions of H1 is the contents of microstore. If, however, H1 had a hardwired control section, the size, complexity, and cost of its circuitry would depend on the instruction set—on both its size and complexity. For example, the control-signal generator in

FIGURE 6.19

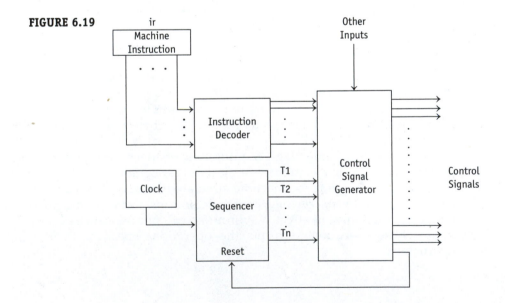

Figure 6.19 would have to be more complex for the standard instruction set than for the basic instruction set. Thus, for large and/or complex instruction sets, the hardwired approach is generally more costly than the microprogrammed approach. It also does not have the flexibility of the microprogrammed approach. The instruction set it implements is fixed. It, however, is faster, principally because it does not have the overhead associated with fetching microinstructions.

At one point, most computers had complex instruction sets, and were therefore microprogrammed because of cost-performance considerations. The few computers at that time with hardwired control sections were super-fast (and expensive) "number crunchers." Today, however, many computers have instruction sets sufficiently small and simple that the hardwired approach is better from a cost-performance point of view. Some computers even use both approaches: hardwired control for simple instructions and microprogrammed control for complex instructions.

6.6 VERTICAL MICROPROGRAMMING

H1 uses 32-bit microinstructions. H1's cousin, V1, uses 19-bit microinstructions. As one would expect, a 19-bit microinstruction is not as powerful as a 32-bit microinstruction. Thus, to do a given amount of work, we need to execute more of the shorter microinstructions. For example, consider the microcode in Figure 6.14 that implements our basic instruction set on H1. If we were to implement the same instruction set using the 19-bit microinstructions on V1, we would need more microinstructions. The microcode in Figure 6.14 contains 36 microinstructions. With the shorter microinstructions on V1, we would need 56 microinstructions. Figure 6.20 shows a pictorial representation of the two microcode sequences. The 32-bit version is horizontally wide, but not too tall. The 19-bit version is narrow horizontally, but tall vertically. Accordingly, we call the 32-bit microcode *horizontal microcode* and the 19-bit version *vertical microcode*.

A vertical microinstruction has fewer bits than a horizontal microinstruction. Thus, although vertical microcode may contain more microinstructions than horizontal microcode that performs the same function, the total number of bits required may be less. In fact, because of the inherent inefficiency of horizontal microcode that results from the unused bits in a typical microinstruction, the bit count of vertical microcode is usually considerably less than that of horizontal microcode. Fewer bits means less chip space occupied by microstore. Because of this advantage of the vertical approach, it is often preferred over the horizontal approach. By sacrificing some performance, vertical microcode saves chip space. It is one of many instances of a space-time tradeoff that faces computer designers.

The discussion of V1 that follows is not a prerequisite for any other part of the book. Thus, if you wish to get back to the software side of H1 as soon as possible, you may jump (or should I say branch) to the next chapter.

FIGURE 6.20

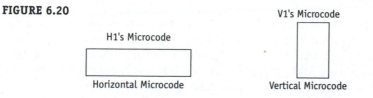

H1's Microcode

Horizontal Microcode

V1's Microcode

Vertical Microcode

6.6.1 Using V1

sim can simulate both H1 and V1. If sim is provided with horizontal microcode, it simulates H1; if it is provided with vertical microcode, it simulates V1. If sim is not provided with microcode, it uses the default horizontal microcode for the standard instruction set, and, therefore, simulates H1. We can, however, force sim to use the default vertical microcode for the standard instruction set by specifying the /ver argument when we invoke sim. For example, to execute a.mac on V1, enter

```
C:\H1>sim a /ver
```

sim responds with

```
---- [T7] 0: ld    /0 018/
```

Now enter enable. sim responds with

```
Microlevel enabled
---- [T7] 0: ld    /0 018/
```

Next, set the microlevel display mode by entering m. sim responds with

```
Microlevel display mode
---- [T1] 0: mar pc/
```

Observe that the debugger's prompt includes mar pc—the first vertical microinstruction in the standard vertical microcode. To see more vertical instructions, enter u0 to unassemble from location 0. sim responds with

```
0: mar     pc                     / 40006
1: rd                             / 68000
2: move    ir     mdr             / 2A4A0
3: add     pc     pc      1       / 018C1
---- [T1] 0: mar pc/
```

sim shows the address, the symbolic microinstruction, and its hex representation on each line of the unassembly. For example, the mar pc microinstruction is 40006 in hex. If you now enter u*, you will unassemble the complete vertical microcode for the standard instruction set. Try this to see how many vertical microinstructions there are. Now quit sim and reinvoke it, but without the /ver argument. Again enter enable, m, and u*. You will see all the horizontal microcode for the standard instruction set. How many microinstructions are in the horizontal microcode?

6.6.2 Making Shorter Microinstructions

The structure of V1 is quite similar to the structure of H1. Only a few changes are needed to reduce the size of the microinstructions from 32 bits to 19 bits. Let's examine these changes.

One glaring inefficiency of the 32-bit microinstruction is that every microinstruction has a branch-to address, although most microinstructions do not branch. Let's remedy this situation by using the A and B register fields to hold the 9-bit branch-to address for branching instructions (see Figure 6.21). Thus, in V1, the A and B fields drive the EA and EB decoders, *as well as the mpc*.

FIGURE 6.21   Address Field in Vertical Microinstruction

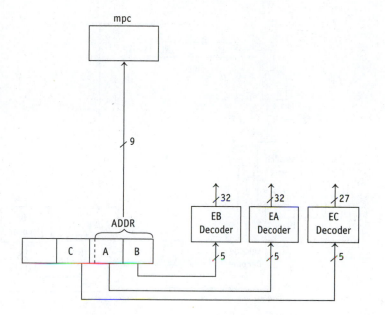

Using the register fields to hold the branch-to address means that a microinstruction cannot hold both register numbers and a branch-to address. Thus, *a microinstruction that specifies registers cannot also branch.* How, then, can a microinstruction do the following:

```
dc = left(dc); if (s) goto L01;
```

In this instruction, we specify a register (**dc**) and a branch-to address. Obviously, we cannot do both in a single microinstruction if we combine the branch-to address field with the register fields. Such an operation, however, can be accomplished with two consecutive microinstructions, the first to do the shift and the second to do the branch:

```
dc = left(dc);
if (s) goto L01;
```

But now we run into a problem that requires new circuitry. When the second microinstruction is executing, its address field is driving the address inputs of the **mpc** (as it should). However, it is also driving the register decoders, causing the contents of some registers to flow down the A and B buses into the ALU. Thus, the second microinstruction tests the ALU output for this garbage, and not the ALU output as it was for the preceding microinstruction. For the second microinstruction to test the ALU output produced by the first microinstruction requires that the first instruction save its ALU output. Actually, it has to save only the S and Z output. Then the second instruction (the branch) can test this saved output. To save the S and Z of the ALU, we have to add a new register that saves the S and Z output of the ALU whenever it may be needed by a subsequent instruction. We call this register the *sz register* (see Figure 6.22).

If we examine typical 32-bit microcode, we find that there are only 15 distinct operations that are ever performed. Figure 6.23 lists these 15 operations along with a mnemonic and C++ description of each (we will explain later why each operation also has an opcode).

FIGURE 6.22

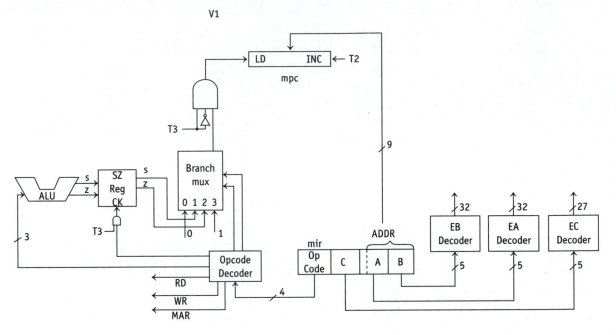

FIGURE 6.23

Opcode	(hex)	Assembly form	Name	Description
0	add	rc ra rb	Add	rc = ra + rb; set sz;
1	sub	rc ra rb	Subtract	rc = ra - rb; set sz;
2	mult	rc ra rb	Multiply	rc = ra * rb; set sz;
3	and	rc ra rb	Bitwise AND	rc = ra & rb; set sz;
4	flip	rc ra	Flip bits	rc = ~ra; set sz;
5	move	rc ra	Move register	rc = ra; set sz;
6	left	rc ra	Left shift	rc = left(ra); set sz;
7	right	rc ra	Right shift	rc = right(ra); set sz;
8	mar	rb	Load mar	mar = rb;
9	sz	ra	Set sz	set sz (with ra);
A	ba	addr	Branch always	mpc = addr;
B	bn	addr	Branch if neg	if (s) mpc = addr;
C	bz	addr	Branch if zero	if (z) mpc = addr;
D	rd	Read		mdr = mem[mar];
E	wr	Write		mem[mar] = mdr;

Every 32-bit microinstruction corresponds to one or more operations from Figure 6.23. For example, the 32-bit microinstruction

```
pc = pc + 1; rd;
```

corresponds to the two-operation sequence consisting of an add and a rd. Thus, if we restrict ourselves to these 15 operations, *we can still do anything that we can do with any sequence of 32-bit microinstructions.*

Observe that no operation listed in Figure 6.23 specifies registers and a branch-to address. Thus, each operation can be specified by a shortened microinstruction in which the A and B register fields hold either the A and B register numbers or the branch-to address, depending on the instruction. Moreover, we can specify any one of the 15 operations in Figure 6.23 with only 4 bits. Thus, our shortened microinstruction needs only $4 + 15 = 19$ bits: 4 to specify the operation plus 15 more to specify either three registers or a single branch-to address. But how can an operation field containing only 4 bits drive all the required control inputs (ALU, MAR, RD, WR, and COND)? We simply add an *opcode decoder*—a combinational circuit to the CPU that inputs the 4-bit operation field of the shortened microinstruction. Its outputs then drive the various control inputs in the datapath (see Figure 6.22). For example, suppose the microinstruction 1000000000000000110 (40006 hex) is loaded into the mir. Its B field (the rightmost 5 bits 00110) specifies the pc register. The leftmost 4 bits (1000) are applied to the control signal encoder, which in turn places a 1 on the line that drives the MAR control input of the mar. The effect of this microinstruction, therefore, is to load the mar with the contents of the pc register. Figure 6.23 shows in hex the 4-bit code for each operation. Each code represents an operation. Thus, we can appropriately call these codes *microlevel opcodes*. Each code when applied to the opcode decoder causes it to generate the control inputs required for that operation. Thus, the mar opcode causes the opcode decoder to place a 1 on the MAR control input of the mar. The add opcode (0000) causes the opcode decoder to place 100 on the ALU's control inputs, causing the ALU to add.

Let's summarize how V1 works. Successive microinstructions are placed in the mir (which is now a 19-bit register). The opcode bits drive the opcode decoder, which, in turn, drives various control inputs in the machine. The combined register/address field drives the register decoders and the address input of the mpc. The S and Z outputs of the ALU drive the inputs of the sz register. Some opcodes, but not all, cause the sz register to be loaded from the S and Z outputs of the ALU. For example, the add opcode does (because the result of the add may need to be tested by a subsequent branch instruction), but the rd opcode does not (because it does not make use of the ALU). Thus, when an add microinstruction is executed, the S and Z bits corresponding to its result are loaded into the sz register, where they can be tested by a subsequent branch instruction. The outputs of the sz register drive the branch multiplexer. Thus, when a branch instruction is executed, it tests the bits in the sz register, and not the S and Z outputs of the ALU (which carry garbage during the execution of the branch instruction).

6.6.3 Assembling Vertical Microcode

As with horizontal microcode, we want to be able to write vertical microcode in symbolic form, and then assemble it using an assembler program. The H1 software package includes a program called **vas** (vertical microcode assembler), which assembles vertical microcode.

The form of symbolic microcode that **vas** requires reflects the format of the vertical microinstruction: Each instruction has a mnemonic field and one, two, or three register fields; or a mnemonic field and one address field; or simply a mnemonic field. Note that the symbolic form for vertical microcode does *not* use the C++ form we use for horizontal microcode. Figure 6.23 shows the form of the vertical symbolic microinstructions for every opcode. ra, rb, and rc designate the three register fields, and `addr` designates the address field in branch instructions. Some instructions specify only one register (for example, the `mar` and `sz` instructions), which, depending on the instruction, goes in either the `ra` field or the `rb` field. For example, in

```
mar   pc
```

the number of the **pc** register appears in the B field, but in

```
sz    dc
```

the number of the **dc** register appears in the A field.

Let's write the vertical microcode that fetches into the `ir` the machine instruction pointed to by the **pc** register, and then increments the **pc** register. First, we have to load the **mar** register from the **pc** register. This operation is performed by the vertical microinstruction

```
mar pc
```

Next, we trigger a read with

```
rd
```

At the end of the read, the machine instruction is sitting in the **mdr**. Thus, the next step is to move the instruction from the **mdr** to the **ir** using

```
move ir mdr
```

To add 1 to the `pc` register, we use

```
add   pc pc 1
```

In this instruction we specify three registers (`pc`, `pc`, and `1`). The `add` is applied to the second and third registers, and the result goes into the first. Thus, the contents of **pc** and the 1 in register **1** are added, and the result goes into **pc**.

To decode the machine instruction in the `ir`, we move it into the **dc** register and then test its leftmost bit with `bn`:

```
move dc ir
bn    L1
```

As the contents of `ir` pass through the ALU as a result of the `move` microinstruction, the ALU sets its S and Z outputs. These outputs are loaded into the **sz** register. The `bn` instruction can then test the **sz** register, and, if negative, branch to the **L1** label. We can then repeatedly left shift the **dc** register to determine the rest of the opcode bits.

Figure 6.24 shows the complete sequence of vertical microcode that implements the basic instruction set.

To assemble the vertical microcode in Figure 6.24, we first create a file named **b.vas** containing this microcode (you can use the **b.vas** file in the H1 software package). To assemble our microcode in **b.vas**, enter

```
C:\H1>vas b
```

FIGURE 6.24

```
 1  / Basic Instruction Set Vertical Microcode        b.vas
 2
 3  / The label indicates the opcode decoded up to that point.
 4  / For example, control reaches the label L011 when opcode
 5  / bits 011 have been decoded.
 6
 7  /*********************************************************/
 8  /        Fetch instruction and increment pc register    /
 9  /*********************************************************/
10  fetch:        mar  pc
11                rd                    / fetch mach inst
12                move ir mdr           / move inst to ir
13                add  pc pc 1          / increment pc
14  /*********************************************************/
15  /            Decode opcode                              /
16  /*********************************************************/
17                move    dc ir
18                bn      L1            / test 1st bit
19  L0:           left    dc dc
20                bn      L01           / test 2nd bit
21  L00:          left    dc dc
22                bn      L001          / test 3rd bit
23                ba      L000
24  L1:           left    dc dc
25                bn      L11           / test 2nd bit
26  L10:          left    dc dc
27                bn      L101          / test 3rd bit
28                ba      L100
29  L01:          left    dc dc
30                bn      L011          / test 3rd bit
31                ba      L010
32  L11:          left    dc dc
33                bn      L111          / test 3rd bit
34                ba      L110
35  /*********************************************************/
36  /            Microcode for each instruction             /
37  /*********************************************************/
38  L000:         /-------------------- LD ------------------
39                mar    ir             / get address
40                rd                    / fetch operand
41                move   ac mdr         / move operand to ac
42                ba     fetch
```

(continued)

FIGURE 6.24
(continued)

```
43 L001:     /------------------ ST  ------------------
44           move    mdr ac        / prepare for write
45           mar     ir
46           wr                    / write
47           ba      fetch         / branch
48 L010:     /------------------ SHLL ------------------
49           and     f ir zmask    / get z-field
50           bz      fetch         / branch if 0
51 lloop:    left    ac ac         / shift ac left
52           sub     f f 1         / decrement count
53           bz      fetch         / branch if 0
54           ba      lloop         / branch
55 L011:     /------------------ SHRL ------------------
56           and     f ir zmask    / get z-field
57           bz      fetch         / branch if 0
58 rloop:    right   ac ac         / shift ac right
59           sub     f f 1         / decrement count
60           bz      fetch         / branch if 0
61           ba      rloop         / branch
62 L100:     /------------------ ADDC ------------------
63           and     f ir xmask    / get x-field
64           add     ac ac f       / add to ac
65           ba      fetch         / branch
66 L101:     /------------------ FLIP ------------------
67           flip    ac ac         / bitwise compl ac
68           ba      fetch         / branch
69 L110:     /------------------ MULT ------------------
70           mar     ir            / get address
71           rd                    / fetch operand
72           mult    ac ac mdr     / multiply ac by operand
73           ba      fetch         / branch
74 L111:     /------------------ JN  ------------------
75           move    0 ac          / get ac
76           bn      dojn          / branch is negative
77           ba      fetch         / branch
78 dojn:     and     pc ir xmask   / put x-field in pc
79           ba      fetch         / branch
```

vas then creates the file **b.ver**, containing the translated vertical microcode, and the list file **b.vst** (**has** uses the extension ".hst" for its list files; **vas** uses ".vst"). If a configuration file with the same base name as the microcode file exists, **vas** will automatically use it. If, for example, the file **b.cfg** exists, then the invocation of **vas** would automatically use it.

To run the machine-level program in `bprog.mac` on `sim` using the `b.cfg` and `b.ver`, enter

```
C:\H1>sim /mb.ver bprog
```

`sim` will respond with the messages "Reading configuration file b.cfg" and "Reading microcode file b.ver", and then start a debugging session. The `/m` argument tells `sim` which microcode file to use (in this case, `b.ver`). If we omitted it, `sim` would use the horizontal microcode in `b.hor`.

Figure 6.25 shows a sample session in which we demonstrate a few commands. We can use the same commands that we have been using for horizontal simulations.

FIGURE 6.25

```
Starting session. Enter h or ? for help.
---- [T7] 0: ld   /0 00A/ t2
  0: ld   /0 00A/ ac=0000/FFFF
  1: flip /A 000/ ac-FFFF/0000
---- [T2] 2: addc /8 003/ enable
Microlevel enabled
---- [T2] 2: addc /8 003/ m
Microlevel display mode
---- [T1] 0: mar pc/ t2
  0: mar pc
     mar=001/002
  1: rd
     Rd from m[002] mdr=A000/8003  2: addc /8 003/
---- [t2] 2: move ir mdr/ u0
  0: mar      pc                    / 40006
  1: rd                             / 68000
  2: move     ir       mdr          / 2A4A0
  3: add      pc       pc      1     / 018C1
---- [t2] 2: move ir mdr/ d0
  0: 40006  68000  2A4A0  018C1  2A920  5800B  32940  58010
  8: 32940  5801A  50016  32940  58013  32940  5802D  5002A
 10: 32940  58024  5001E  32940  58033  5002F  40009  68000
 18: 2A0A0  50000  29500  40009  70000  50000  1BD24  60000
---- [t2] 2: move ir mdr/ R*
      pc   = 0002     ac   = 0000
---- [t2] 2: move ir mdr/ n
No display mode
---- [T7] g
6
Machine inst count =     A (hex) =     10 (dec)
Micro   inst count =    7E (hex) =    126 (dec)
---- [T7] q
```

If we compare the performances of H1 and V1, H1 is the clear winner on speed. H1 uses substantially fewer microinstructions on both the decoding and execution of each machine instruction. We can easily see the difference between the two machines by executing the `bprog` program on both H1 and V1, and comparing total microinstruction counts. Both machines, of course, execute the same number of instructions at the machine level. However, at the microlevel, H1 executes 81 microinstructions versus 126 for V1. V1 executes 56 percent more microinstructions, and, therefore, requires 56 percent more time.

V1 has to execute more microinstructions because its 19-bit microinstructions do less than the 32-bit microinstructions on H1. Microinstruction size affects how much a single instruction can do. But it does not affect execution time per microinstruction—a short microinstruction takes as long as a long microinstruction. In fact, a short instruction might even take a little longer to execute because of the additional decoding it requires. Thus, V1's clock might have to run slower than H1's clock to provide time for this decoding.

V1, however, is better than H1 in one respect: the total number of bits in its microcode is less than in H1. As an example, let's consider the microcode that implements our basic instruction set. H1 requires 36 microinstructions; V1 requires 56. Thus, the total microcode bits for H1 is

$$36 \times 32 \text{ bits} = 1152 \text{ bits}$$

But the total microcode bits for V1 is

$$56 \times 19 \text{ bits} = 1064 \text{ bits}$$

The difference between the two machines is not substantial. For a savings of only 88 bits, we paid a major penalty in execution speed. However, on computers that use long horizontal microinstructions in which many fields are often unused, the vertical approach could yield considerably more savings in microstore (perhaps as much as 50 percent). For such a computer, the vertical approach could use a significantly smaller chip. You may think that chip size is not an important consideration, but, in fact, it is very important. The ratio of good to bad chips drops as chip size increases. Chip size can be only so big—any bigger than some particular size (depending on the technology), and the yield of good chips becomes unacceptably low. Thus, we might have a horizontally microprogrammed computer that requires more space than is available on a chip. But if we vertically microprogram it, it might fit.

PROStLEMS

6.1. Each device connected to the address, data, and control buses in Figure 6.1 must respond only to its own addresses. Figure 6.1 does not show how this requirement is enforced. Add logic to Figure 6.1 that does this. Assume main memory, the keyboard, and the monitor have CS (chip select) inputs. CS determines if a circuit is active (1 = active; 0 = inactive). Show how to add a CS input to the circuit in Figure 5.45 (in Chapter 5).

6.2. Would the implementation of memory-mapped I/O as descibed in Section 4.15 (in Chapter 4) be simpler if H1 had only 2048 words of memory (and still a 12-wire address bus)? Explain.

6.3. Can we do without the read-only registers `0`, and `1`? Hint: Can we obtain the constants 0, and 1 by some other means?

6.4. Why is the `mdr` in the register bank, but not the `mar`.

6.5. What happens when the following microinstructions are executed by `sim`:

```
mar = ir; mdr = ac; wr;
mar = pc; rd;
```

6.6. How can the contents of a register be tested at the microlevel without assigning them to a read-only register and without corrupting any register?

6.7. Rewrite the microcode in `b.has` so that it has as few microinstructions as possible.

6.8. Rewrite the microcode in `s.has` so that it has as few microinstructions as possible.

6.9. Suppose every horizontal microinstruction branched. How then could microinstructions be executed in memory order? Is there a flaw in this approach?

6.10. How do H1 and V1 compare with respect to the number of microinstructions executed during the execution of the `a.mac` file?

6.11. Is the "straight-through" function of the ALU needed? Can we get the same effect by using the add function of the ALU? Are there any tradeoffs if the add function is used?

6.12. Which vertical microinstructions set `sz`?

6.13. Propose a way to speed up the opcode decode process. Are there any tradeoffs with your proposal?

6.14. Design and implement the opcode decoder for V1.

6.15. What happens when a machine instruction with an invalid opcode is executed when H1 is using the microcode in `b.hor`?

6.16. Rewrite the microcode in `s.has` so that the opcodes for `ld` and `st` are interchanged. Do the same for `s.vas`.

6.17. Extend the microcode in `b.has` so that it also supports

```
add x        ac = ac + mem[x];
sub x        ac = ac - mem[x];
div x        ac = ac / mem[x];
```

Test your microcode with the following program:

```
        ld    w
        add   x
        dout
        sub   y
        dout
        div   y
        dout
        div   z
        dout
        halt
w:      dw    100
x:      dw    7
y:      dw    3
z:      dw    -2
```

6.18. The horizontal microcode for the `ja` machine instruction contains the microinstruction,

```
pc = ir & xmask; goto fetch;
```

In what way would H1 *at the machine level* behave differently if we changed this microinstruction to

```
pc = ir; goto fetch;
```

6.19. Replace the microcode for the `jzop` instruction in **s.has** with microcode for the add and increment instruction (mnemonic: `addi`). The `addi` instruction should add to the **ac** register just like the `add` instruction. But it should also add 1 to its 12-bit address field. Using the `addi` instruction, write and run an assembly language program that sums the following numbers and displays the result:

$$-2, 55, 22, 77, 999, -1, 55, 934, -1$$

6.20. All the 4-bit opcodes in the standard instruction set are in use. The 4-bit opcodes are important because they allow a 12-bit address to fit into the instruction. There is, however, a simple approach that will allow more instructions with 12-bit address fields: simply use two words for an instruction. The first word would contain a 4, 8, 12, or 16-bit opcode; the second word would contain an address.

Using this approach, add a multiply instruction (mnemonic: `mult`) with a 12-bit address in its second word to **s.has** that works as follows:

```
ac = ac * mem[x];
```

Do not replace any existing instruction. Use the opcode F8 hex for your multiply instruction. In your configuration file, specify " 1 2" (without the quotes) following the mnemonic `mult` to indicate that it corresponds to a one-operand two-word instruction.

Using your multiply instruction, write an assembly language program that multiplies the following pairs of numbers and displays the results:

$$\begin{array}{rr} 2, & 3 \\ -4, & 5 \\ 6, & -7 \\ -8, & -9 \end{array}$$

6.21. Replace the microcode for `jzop` in **s.has** with a load indexed instruction (mnemonic: `ldi`) that works as follows:

```
ac = mem[x + i++];
```

where **i** is a new index register.

Also add a swap i instruction (mnemonic: `swai`) that swaps the contents of **ac** and **i**.

Using `ldi` and `swai`, write an assembly language program that sums the following numbers and displays the result:

$$33, -4, 76, 123, 876, -200, 76, 88$$

6.22. A new machine is to have *only* the following five machine instructions:

```
st x      mem[x] = ac;                store accumulator register

ld x      ac = mem[x];                load accumulator register

ldct x    ct = mem[x];                load count register

decj x    if (--ct != 0) pc = x;   decrement and jump

addi x    ac = ac + mem[x+ct-1];      add indexed
```

Write the microcode for this new machine. Run the following program on **sim** using your new microcode.

```
            ld      zero
            ldct    ten
loop:       addi    array
            decj    loop
            st      sum
            dout
            halt
sum:        dw      0
zero:       dw      0
ten:        dw      10
array:      dw      1
            dw      1
            dw      2
            dw      3
            dw      5
            dw      8
            dw      13
            dw      21
            dw      34
            dw      55
```

6.23. Extend the **s.has** file to support

```
rotl   (rotate ac register left)
rotr   (rotate ac register right)
```

These instructions circularly shift the contents of the **ac** register one position. Test your new instructions with the following program:

```
            ld      xl
            rotl
            hout
            ldc     '\n'
            aout
            ld      xr
            rotr
            hout
            ldc     '\n'
            aout
            halt
xl:         dw      8110h
xr:         dw      0221h
```

6.24. What are the time percentages required for fetching, decoding, and executing the `dloc` instruction? The `ld` instruction?

6.25. Extend **s.has** to support a subtract one instruction (mnemonic: `sub1`) that works as follows:

```
ac=ac -1;
```

Create a new file `anew.mas` from `a.mas` by replacing the sub instruction with the new sub1 instruction (`a.mas` is in the H1 software package). Run `anew.mas` with your new microcode. How does the total number of microinstructions executed compare with the total number executed when the original `a.mas` is run with the standard microcode? Explain any significant differences.

6.26. Write an assembly language program that adds up a list of numbers contiguous in main memory. The tail end of your program should have the following statements:

```
xxx:    dw      0           / place final sum here
asum:   dw      xxx         / address of final sum
n:      dw      4           / list size
        dw      -2          / list starts here
        dw      26
        dw      -5
        dw      12
```

`asum` holds the address of the main memory location into which the final sum is to be placed. Access the **xxx** variable only indirectly—though the address in **asum**. **n** holds the number of numbers in the list. Use 4 for **n**. Your program, however, should work with any valid value in **n**. Your program should use a loop to add up the numbers in the list. Use the following looping statements exactly as shown:

```
loop:   ld      n
        sub     @1
        st      n
        jn      done

        ;LOOP BODY

        ja      loop
done:
```

After the sum is computed and placed in **xxx** (indirectly through **asum**), display the value in **xxx**, appropriately labeled.

Make your program as time-efficient as possible. Do not use the `jzop` instruction anywhere in your program. Determine the total number of machine instructions and the total number of microinstructions executed when your program is run.

Now modify your assembly language program as follows: Replace the three-instruction sequence that starts the loop with the following single instruction:

```
loop:   decm  n
```

The decrement memory instruction (mnemonic: `decm`) should do precisely what the `ld-sub-st` instruction sequence does. Substitute the `decm` instruction for the `jzop` instruction in the `s.has`. Run the new program with the new microcode. Determine the total number of machine instructions and the total number of microinstructions executed. Compare with the original version.

6.27. Is it difficult to add a carry flag to H1? Explain.

6.28. Redesign H1 so that its ALU has a carry/borrow flag and a zero flag.

6.29. What happens when the following sequence is executed?

```
mar = pc; mdr = 1;
rd; ac = mdr;
```

6.30. Under what circumstances would it make sense to use the **mdr** as a work register?

6.31. Is this a legal microinstruction:

```
mar = f; f = mdr;
```

6.32. Is this a legal microinstruction:

```
rd; f = mdr; if (s) goto xxx;
```

What goes into **f**?

6.33. Suppose the output of the ALU under some conditions needs to be equal to its right input. How could this be accomplished?

6.34. What determines the upper limit on the size of a computer's microprogram?

6.35. Describe how variable length instructions can be used to circumvent the lack of 4-bit opcodes.

6.36. Using **sim**, display all the microinstructions in the standard instruction set in symbolic form.

6.37. The 4-bit opcodes run from 0 hex to E hex. Why don't they run from 0 hex to F hex?

6.38. What is your "wish list" for H1? Specifically, what three instructions would you most like to see added to the standard instruction set? Justify your choices.

6.39. Why are the microinstruction counts for the `bkpt`, `halt`, and I/O instructions so low?

6.40. Assemble the program in **sprog.mas** and run on **sim** using the microcode in **buggy.hor** (specify /mbuggy.hor on the command line when you invoke **sim**). Determine which machine instructions are implemented incorrectly by **buggy.hor**.

6.41. H1 does not have a sign flag. What, then, do the `jzop` and `jn` instructions test? Would there be any advantage in having a sign flag?

6.42. Suppose H1 had an instruction whose effect was

```
sp = sp + ac;
```

and another instruction whose effect was

```
sp = sp - ac;
```

Explain how these instructions might be used.

6.43. Can the x-field of a relative instruction be viewed as a signed number? Explain.

6.44. Rewrite **s.has** so it will work with *both* the one-position and barrel shifter.

6.45. Rewrite **b.has** to work with a barrel shifter. Compare the total microinstruction counts for the two versions when **bprog.mas** is executed.

6.46. Add two instructions—`good` and `ugly`—to **s.has**. Both perform the operation

```
ac = ac * mem[sp++];
```

The two instructions differ in how they perform multiplication:

> `good`: Uses the multiplication circuit in the ALU.
> `ugly`: Uses repetitive addition in microcode. For example, to multiply 3 by 10, add ten 3's.

Determine the number of microinstructions executed for each instruction when 3 is multiplied by 10 (10 should be the stack operand).

For extra credit, also include the instruction

bad: Uses the shift-add algorithm in microcode (see Figure 13.4 in Chapter 13).

6.47.   Design a circuit that sets mpc to 0 and initializes the clock/sequencer to the beginning of the T1 subcycle. What might this circuit be used for?

6.48.   Compare s.hor and s.ver in size (i.e., total number of bits) and speed (use microinstruction counts for sprog.mas).

6.49.   Suppose microstore contained pointers to microinstructions stored in a *nanostore*. A microinstruction could then be specified a multiple number of times by having multiple pointers in microstore to a single instance of that microinstruction in nanostore. Assuming microstore has 512 slots and nanostore is as small as possible, how much savings (in bits) is possible using this dual-level control store approach for the microcode in s.has?

Chapter Seven

EVALUATING THE INSTRUCTION SET ARCHITECTURE OF H1: PART 1

7.1 INTRODUCTION

We are about to start a two-chapter sequence in which we will examine assembly code for H1 generated by a C++ compiler. Our examination of compiler-generated code will allow us to develop a sense of what features an instruction set should have to properly support C++ and similar languages. You should find our C++ examples easy to follow, even if you do not know C++. If, however, you need some extra help, try reading the C++ summary in Appendix H.

The earliest computers were very simple in organization. They had to be—vacuum tubes, the technology of the time, could support only the simplest of organizations. However, with the advent of the transistor and then of the integrated circuit, more complex organizations became possible. Instruction sets became larger, more powerful, and more complex. However, an examination of assembly code generated by compilers for these more complex computers revealed something very interesting: Compiler-generated code frequently did not take advantage of the more complex instructions in the instruction set. This observation suggested that one could build a less expensive computer with a smaller and simpler instruction set without sacrificing performance. Not surprisingly, a new type of architecture appeared in the 1980s called *RISC (reduced instruction set computer)* that reflected this new thinking on instruction sets—namely, bigger and more complex was not necessarily better. A RISC is characterized by an instruction set minimized in size and complexity but optimized for speed. In contrast, a computer whose instruction set is designed with power and versatility foremost in mind is called a *CISC (complex instruction set computer)*.

Computer designers have profited from examining compiler-generated code—it provides a sense of what constitutes a good architecture. For the same reason, we too will profit from examining compiler-generated code. By doing so, we will not only understand computer architecture better, but also develop a much better understanding of high-level languages like C++ and Java.

The characteristics of a computer's instruction set—the registers it uses, the types of instructions, and the operations each instruction performs—are called its *instruction set architecture (ISA)*. The ISA is what the assembly language programmer "sees" of the computer hardware. Although we will learn a great deal about programming languages in this chapter, our principal goal is the evaluation of the ISA of H1. We will discover firsthand that H1 has, in fact, a terrible ISA. However, H1 is not a hopeless case. In Chapter 12, we will explore changes to H1 that will substantially improve its ISA.

7.2 DUMB COMPILER

• •

We will examine code that is generated by a dumb C++ compiler. A *dumb compiler* produces correct code but not necessarily efficient code. In particular, it generates code for a statement in isolation from the surrounding statements. In other words, when translating a line of code, a dumb compiler neither remembers what it did on preceding lines nor looks ahead at what it will do on subsequent lines. For example, consider the C++ statements

```
x = 2;    // first assignment statement
y = x;    // second assignment statement
```

where **x** and **y** are global variables. A dumb compiler would generate

```
ldc  2   ; load 2 into the ac register
st   x   ; store in x
```

for the first assignment statement, and

```
ld   x   ; load value of x into the ac register
st   y   ; store in y
```

for the second assignment statement. If, however, the compiler were smart, it would remember what it did for the first assignment statement. It could then determine that an `ld` instruction is unnecessary for the second assignment statement (because the value of **x** is already in the **ac** register by virtue of the first assignment statement). Thus, a smart compiler would generate

```
ldc  2   ; load 2 into the ac register
st   x   ; store in x
```

for the first assignment statement, and

```
st   y   ; store in y
```

for the second assignment statement.

Our dumb compiler scans expressions in the C++ source program from left to right, and the code it generates generally reflects this order. For example, the statement

```
d = a + b + c;
```

where **a**, **b**, **c**, and **d** are global variables, is translated to

```
ld   a              ; access a first
add  b              ; access b next
add  c              ; access c last
st   d
```

The variables **a**, **b**, and **c** are accessed in the order in which they appear in the source statement. There are, however, three exceptions to this left-to-right order:

1. Our dumb compiler generates code in an order required by operator precedence and associativity. For example, for the statement
   ```
   d = a + b*c;
   ```
   our compiler must generate code to first evaluate **b*c** because multiplication has higher precedence than addition, and then add **a** to the result. In the statement
   ```
   a = b = c = 5;
   ```

our compiler must generate code to assign 5 to **c** first, then to **b**, and finally to **a**. This right-to-left order is required because the assignment operator is *right associative* (which simply means multiple operations must be evaluated right to left, unless parentheses force a different order). Most of the operators in C++ are *left associative*—that is, multiple operations must be evaluated left to right, unless parentheses force a different order.

2. Whenever our dumb compiler is generating code corresponding to a *binary operator* (i.e., an operator that takes two operands), it will access the operands in the order that results in the better code. For example, for the statement

```
a = b + 1;
```

our compiler can generate an `ldc` instruction to get the constant 1, but only if it generates this code before it generates code to access **b**:

```
ldc   1
add   b
st    a
```

If **b** were accessed first, then the `ldc` instruction could not be used to load 1 (it would destroy the value of **b** in the **ac** register). Thus, the compiler would have to generate

```
ld    b
add   @1
st    a
```

where **@1** is a compiler-generated label defined as

```
@1:   dw    1
```

Both sequences require three instructions; however, the second sequence is inferior. It requires a **dw**, which consumes an additional word of memory. Moreover, the execution of the `ld` instruction takes more time (it has to fetch its operand from memory) than the `ldc` in the first sequence. Our compiler performs this optimization only locally (i.e., it looks at only the two operands of the current operator). For example, for the statement

```
c = a + b + 1;
```

our compiler does not first scan the entire statement looking for constant operands. Instead, it scans left-to-right, sees **a** and **b** first, and generates code to add **a** and **b**. But then it cannot use an `ldc` instruction to subsequently get the constant 1 (because the **ac** register is in use holding the sum of **a** and **b**). Thus, the code is:

```
ld    a
add   b
add   @1
st    d
```

Our compiler does not use an `ldc` instruction in another situation: if accessing the nonconstant operand requires the use of the **ac** register. For example, in the statement

```
c = f(x) + 7;
```

the function **f** uses the **ac** register to return a value to the caller. Thus, our compiler cannot use an initial `ldc` instruction to load 7 because the subsequent call of **f** would overlay it in the **ac** register.

3. Our compiler always follows any order imposed by parentheses, even when such an order is not mathematically required. For example, our compiler would translate the C++ statement

```
v = (w + x) + (y + z);
```

to an assembly code sequence that would evaluate **w + x** first, then **y + z,** then add these two intermediate results, and finally assign the result to **v.** A smart compiler might, instead, ignore the parentheses in this statement, and generate code to first compute **w + x**, then to add **y**, then to add **z**, and finally to assign the result to **v.** This alternate sequence might consist of fewer instructions, and, therefore, be more desirable.

A *constant expression* is an expression, such as **2 + 3**, whose operands are constants. When a compiler translates a constant expression, it can either generate code that evaluates the expression at *run time* (i.e., when the translated program is executed) or it can evaluate the expression at *compile time* and then generate code that uses the computed result. For example, for the statement,

```
x = 2 + 3;
```

a compiler can generate

```
ldc   2
add   @3
st    x
```

where **@3** is defined as

```
@3:   dw     3
```

Thus, at run time the add instruction computes the value of 2 + 3. Alternatively, a compiler can add 2 and 3 at compile time to get 5, and then generate code to load and store 5:

```
ldc   5
st    x
```

The resulting machine code takes both less time and less space. The compile-time evaluation of constant expressions is called *constant folding.* Our dumb compiler performs this optimization as long as the constant operands precede any variables. For example, our dumb compiler would perform constant folding in the statement

```
x = 2 + 3 + y;
```

but not in

```
x = 2 + y + 3;
```

nor in

```
x = y + 2 + 3;
```

In the latter two expressions, the compiler scans the 2 and **y,** and generates code to compute their sum. But then it cannot perform constant folding when it scans the 3.

Because the standard instruction set does not include a multiplication or division instruction, our dumb compiler does not support any statement that requires these two operations. This shortcoming obviously excludes all arithmetic expressions that use multiplication or division. It also excludes arrays of two or more dimensions because the indexing of such arrays requires multiplication. However, in Chapter 12, we will add multiplication and division instructions to our instruction set, at which time we will upgrade our compiler to support multi-dimensional arrays.

Our dumb compiler is the compiler that you would design if you had to write one as quickly as possible—whose structure, therefore, would be as simple as possible. Our dumb compiler lacks all nonessential capabilities, except for a few whose implementation would *minimally* add to its complexity.

Our dumb compiler translates C++ programs into assembly language and then internally assembles the assembly language into machine language. It has the capability of outputting the assembly language program as well as the machine language program. This is a useful feature because it provides us with assembly code that we can easily study. If only the machine language program were available, it would be difficult to study the code the compiler generates.

7.3 GLOBAL VARIABLES

· ·

A *global variable* in C++ is a variable that is declared outside of a function definition. The *scope* (i.e., the range of the program over which an item can be referenced by name) of a global variable extends from its point of declaration to the end of the file containing its declaration excluding those functions in which an identically named local variable or parameter is declared. For example, consider the C++ program in Figure 7.1. **x** (line 4) and **y** (line 9) are both global variables because they

FIGURE 7.1

```
 1 #include <iostream>
 2 using namespace std;
 3
 4 int x;          // global variable with no initial value specified
 5 void fa()
 6 {               // cannot reference y from within fa
 7     x = x + x + 2;
 8 }
 9 int y = 3;      // global variable with initial value specified
10 void fb()
11 {
12     x = 5;
13     y = -2;
14     fa();
15 }
16 void main()
17 {
18     fb();
19     cout << "x = " << x << endl;      // displays "x = 12"
20     cout << "y = " << y << endl;      // displays "y = -2"
21 }
```

are declared outside the **fa, fb,** and **main** functions. The scope of **x** includes everything below its declaration on line 4 (i.e., the **fa, fb,** and **main** functions); the scope of **y** includes everything below its declaration on line 9 (i.e., just the **fb** and **main** functions). Both **x** and **y** can be referenced in **fb** and **main**. However, **x**, but not **y**, can be referenced in **fa**.

In C++, if an initial value is not specified for a global variable in its declaration, its initial value is guaranteed to be zero. Thus, at the start of the program in Figure 7.1, **x** (which has no initial value specified in its declaration on line 4) has the value 0; **y**, on the other hand, has the value 3, the initial value specified in its declaration on line 9.

Global variables are translated to **dw** directives at the assembly level. For example, the **x** and **y** variables in Figure 7.1 are translated to

```
x:      dw     0
y:      dw     3
```

Notice that the initial value of **x** is 0, although the C++ program does not specify an initial value for it.

Global variables are accessed using the direct instructions on H1. For example, the C++ statement

```
x = 5;
```

in Figure 7.1 is translated to

```
ldc   5
st    x      ; use a direct instruction
```

The **dw** directives that correspond to global variables create words for those variables in the machine language program. For example, the **dw** directives for the global variables **x** and **y** in Figure 7.1 each create a word in the machine language program (see Figure 7.2). These words are part of the machine language program. Thus, they exist before, during, and at the end of the execution of the machine language program. They are *not* created during the execution of the program. We call such variables *static variables*. Variables that are not static—that is, variables that are created during the execution of the program—are called *automatic* or *dynamic* variables.

The complete assembly language program for the C++ program in Figure 7.1 is given in Figure 7.3. Notice that we have commented each code sequence that corresponds to a C++ statement with that C++ statement. As we have already

FIGURE 7.2

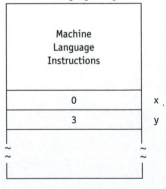

Machine Language Program

FIGURE 7.3

```
 1 fa:        ld      x          ; x = x + x + 2;
 2            add     x
 3            add     @2
 4            st      x
 5
 6            ret
 7 ;============================================================
 8 fb:        ldc     5          ; x = 5;
 9            st      x
10
11            ld      @_2        ; y = -2;
12            st      y
13
14            call    fa         ; fa()
15
16            ret
17 ;============================================================
18 main:      call    fb         ; fb()
19
20            ldc     @m0        ; cout << "x = " << x  << endl;
21            sout
22            ld      x
23            dout
24            ldc     '\n'
25            aout
26
27            ldc     @m1        ; cout << "y = " << y  << endl;
28            sout
29            ld      y
30            dout
31            ldc     '\n'
32            aout
33
34            halt
35 x:         dw      0          ; global variable
36 y:         dw      3          ; global variable
37 @2:        dw      2          ; @2 is a compiler-generated name
38 @_2:       dw      -2         ; @_2 is a compiler-generated name
39 @m0:       dw      "x = "     ; @m0 is a compiler-generated name
40 @m1:       dw      "y = "     ; @m1 is a compiler-generated name
41            end main
```

pointed out, the global variables are accessed using direct instructions. Function calls and returns are implemented, naturally enough, with the `call` and `ret` instructions. For example, the function call

```
fa();
```

is translated to

```
call fa
```

where the target of the call, **fa**, is the label on the first assembly instruction for the **fa** function. For the statement

```
x = x + x + 2;
```

the compiler generates an `ld` instruction and two `add` instructions. Because the second `add` instruction needs the constant 2 in memory, the compiler also generates the **dw**

```
@2:      dw     2
```

that defines 2. The label **@2** is a *compiler-generated name* (i.e., a name the compiler makes up). The compiler gives each integer constant it creates a unique name consisting of "@" (for a positive constant) or "@_" (for a negative constant) followed by the absolute value in decimal of the constant. For example, the constants 2 and −2 are declared with

```
@2:      dw        2
@_2:     dw       -2
```

String constants are also labeled with compiler-generated names, each consisting of "@m" followed by a sequence number ("m" stands for "message"). Thus, the two string constants in Figure 7.3 are labeled with **@m0** and **@m1**. Compiler-generated names usually have some special first character that identifies them as such. Our compiler uses the at sign (@).

Returning to the program in Figure 7.3, we can see that for the statement

```
x = x + x + 2;
```

the compiler generates the sequence

```
ld    x
add   x
add   @2
st    x
```

and, in addition, generates the **dw** for **@2** at the bottom of the program. An equivalent but slightly more efficient sequence is to load 2 first (with an `ldc` instruction) and then add **x** twice:

```
ldc   2
add   x
add   x
st    x
```

This sequence is both faster (because `ldc` takes less time than `ld`) and requires less memory (because the constant **@2** is not needed). However, our dumb compiler never globally examines expressions looking for constants before generating code for them. Thus, it generates the former, less efficient sequence.

The `cout` statements in Figure 7.1 output to the standard output device (i.e., the display). They are translated by our dumb compiler to a `sout-dout-aout` sequence of instructions (see lines 20 through 25 and 27 through 32 in Figure 7.3). `sout` outputs a label, `dout` outputs a value, and `aout` outputs the newline character (for the end-of-line symbol `endl`). We refer to this code as *inline* because it appears in the translated module and not in a separate routine. The typical C++ compiler, however, would not generate inline code for the `cout` statement. Instead, it would generate a `call` instruction that calls a separate function.

Notice that the code for

```
x = 5;
```

on lines 8 and 9 uses an `ldc-st` sequence,

```
ldc   5
st    x
```

But the code for

```
y = -2
```

on lines 11 and 12 uses a less efficient `ld-st` sequence,

```
ld    @_2
st    y
```

because an `ldc` instruction cannot load -2 (or any other negative number).

One important observation to make regarding Figure 7.3 is that the scope of `y` is not restricted at the assembly level. `y` is a label that can be referenced from anywhere in the assembly program, including from the `fa` function. At the C++ level, however, the scope of `y` excludes the `fa` function. The compiler enforces `y`'s restricted scope at the C++ level simply by refusing to generate any references to `y` from `fa` at the assembly level.

7.4   LOCAL VARIABLES

A *local variable* is a variable that can be referenced by name in only the function (or sub-block within a function) in which it is defined. Local variables can be either static or dynamic depending on how they are defined. Global variables, on the other hand, are always static. In Figure 7.4, `d1a` and `d1b` are dynamic local variables; `s1a` and `s1b` are static local variables. As you examine Figure 7.4, keep in mind that it, like most of the programs in this chapter, is an illustrative program—a program whose sole purpose is to illustrate some concept. Other than that, it is a "do-nothing" program, intentionally kept as simple as possible.

Static local variables have the following characteristics in common with global variables:

- Static local variables are defined at the assembly level with `dw` directives. They are part of the machine language program, and exist before and during the entire execution of the program.
- Static local variables for which no initial value is specified are guaranteed to be initialized to zero. For example, in Figure 7.4, `s1a` has the initial value 0 (see line 9).
- Static local variables are accessed with direct instructions.

FIGURE 7.4

```
 1 #include <iostream>
 2 using namespace std;
 3
 4 void fc()
 5 {
 6     int dla ;               // dynamic local variable
 7     int dlb = 7;            // dynamic local variable
 8
 9     static int sla;         // static local variable
10     static int slb = 5;     // static local variable
11
12     cout << sla << endl;
13     cout << slb << endl;
14     dla = 25;
15     dlb = 26;
16     sla = 27;
17     slb = 28;
18
19 }
20 void main()
21 {
22     fc();
23     // sla and slb retain values 27 and 28 between calls
24     fc();
25 }
```

Static local and global variables differ in scope: The scope of a static local variable is restricted to the function (or sub-block within a function) in which it is defined. The restricted scope of static locals is enforced by the compiler. The compiler will refuse to generate code that references a static local from outside the block in which it is declared. At the assembly level, however, both globals and static locals have global scope because both types are defined with **dw** directives.

A static local variable is initialized only once. Its initialization does *not* occur every time the function that contains it is called. Instead, it is initialized at *assembly time* when the assembler translates its defining **dw** directive (there is one exception to the assembly-time initialization of static local variables—see Problem 7.54). On the first call of a function that contains a static local variable, its initial value will be equal to whatever value appears in the **dw** directive that defines it. On subsequent calls, the value of a static local variable is whatever was left in the variable on the previous call. For example, in Figure 7.4, **sla** and **slb** are equal to 27 and 28, respectively, on exit from the **fc** function. On the next call of **fc**, **sla** and **slb** will still have these values. **sla** and **slb** are *not* reinitialized to 0 and 5 on each call. This behavior is precisely what we expect because static local variables are initialized via a **dw** directive, and are, therefore, initialized exactly once (at assembly time) before the program starts executing. If, on the other hand, **sla** and **slb** were initialized at the beginning of every call of **fc** with *machine language instructions,* then **sla** and **slb** would be reinitialized each time **fc** is called. But this is not the case—static local variables are *not* initialized with machine instructions.

The program in Figure 7.4 outputs

```
0        (initial value of sla on first call of fc)
5        (initial value of slb on first call of fc)
27       (initial value of sla on second call of fc)
28       (initial value of slb on second call of fc)
```

The C++ compiler does something very strange with static local variables. Instead of carrying over the variable name that appears in the C++ program to the **dw** directive in the assembly language program, the compiler uses a compiler-generated name. Each static local variable is given a name consisting of a unique prefix selected from the sequence **@s0**, **@s1**, **@s2**, ..., followed by an underscore and the C++-level name. For example, the static local variables **sla** and **slb** in Figure 7.4 are named **@s0_sla** and **@s1_slb.** That is, the compiler defines **sla** and **slb** with

```
@s0_sla:    dw    0
@s1_slb:    dw    5
```

Thus, the C++ statements

```
sla = 27;
slb = 28;
```

are translated to

```
ldc  27
st   @s0_sla
ldc  28
st   @s1_slb
```

The compiler gives the name of every static local variable a unique prefix. For example, suppose a C++ program has two functions, each containing two static local variables. Then the compiler would prefix the names of the first two with **@s0_** and **@s1_**, and the second two with **@s2_** and **@s3_**.

You can probably guess why the compiler renames static local variables. Consider a C++ program that is structured like the one in Figure 7.5. The C++ program contains a global variable **x** and two functions, each containing a static local variable named **x**. At the C++ level, the global variable and the identically named static variables do not clash because they have nonoverlapping scopes. However, if the compiler does not rename the static local variables, then it would generate three **dw** statements (one for the global **x** and one for each static local), each labeled with **x**. Thus, when the program is assembled, the assembler would generate the error message, "Duplicate label." To avoid such name conflicts, the compiler gives each static local variable a unique name at the assembly language level. Global variables do not have a similar problem. Because their scope at the C++ level is global, their C++ names must already be unique. Thus, the compiler can carry over their names to the assembly level without risking a name clash among them.

FIGURE 7.5

```
 1        C++ Program                      Assembler Program
 2
 3        int x;
 4        void f1()                        f1:
 5        {                                        .
 6               static int x;                     .
 7               .                                 .
 8               .
 9               .                                 ret
10        }
11        void f2()                        f2:
12        {                                        .
13               static int x;                     .
14               .                                 .
15               .
16               .                                 ret
17        }
18        void main()                      main:
19        {                                        .
20               .                                 .
21               .                                 .
22               .                                 halt
23        }                                        .
24                                                 .
25                                        x:        dw      0    ; global
26                                        x:        dw      0    ; static local in f1
27                                        x:        dw      0    ; static local in f2
```

Error: Duplicate labels

Dynamic local variables are handled completely differently from static local variables. Dynamic local variables are created by the execution of machine language instructions on entry into the function in which they are defined. They are destroyed on exit from the function. A dynamic local variable exists only when the function in which it is defined is executing. Unlike static local variables, dynamic local variables do not retain their values between successive calls of the function in which they are defined. How could they— they are *destroyed on exit* from the function.

Dynamic local variables are created on the stack. They remain on the stack until the function exits, at which time they are removed from the stack. It is very easy to create and remove dynamic variables. To create an *uninitialized* dynamic variable (like **dla** on line 6 in Figure 7.4), the instruction

```
aloc 1
```

is executed. This instruction moves the pointer in the **sp** register down one slot in memory, effectively reserving (but not initializing) a slot on the stack for the variable. To remove the variable on exit from the function (and to restore the **sp** register to its value just prior to the execution of the `aloc` instruction), the instruction

```
dloc 1
```

is executed. To create multiple uninitialized dynamic variables, our dumb compiler generates multiple `aloc` instructions, one for each variable. But to deallocate dynamic local variables on exit from a function, our compiler generates a single `dloc` that deallocates all of them. A single deallocation is not difficult for our dumb compiler to generate. It simply keeps track of the total number of words allocated by the `aloc` instructions it generates. Then, at the end of function, it generates a single `dloc` to deallocate this total amount. For example, our compiler translates a function with three uninitialized dynamic local variables to

```
aloc 1   ; create uninitialized dynamic local variable
aloc 1   ; create uninitialized dynamic local variable
aloc 1   ; create uninitialized dynamic local variable
    .
    .
    .

dloc 3   ; remove all three variables
```

A smart compiler would generate a single `aloc` to allocate all three variables.

The `aloc` and `dloc` instructions are like the `push` and `pop` instructions, except that no data transfer occurs between the **ac** register and the stack. Unlike the `push` instruction, the `aloc` instruction does not initialize the slot on the stack it reserves.

If a dynamic local variable is *initialized* in its C++ declaration (like **dlb** on line 7 in Figure 7.4), then it is created with a `push` instruction instead of an `aloc` instruction. The `push` instruction both creates and initializes the variable on the stack. For example, the initialized dynamic local variable, **dlb**, in Figure 7.4 is created with the sequence

```
ldc   7    ; get 7
push       ; create variable and initialize with 7
```

The `push` instruction pushes a 7 onto the stack, thereby both creating and initializing (to 7) a slot for the **dlb** variable. An alternative sequence to create and initialize a local variable is

```
aloc 1     ; create variable
ldc   7    ;
str   0    ; store 7 in variable (its relative address is 0)
```

The latter sequence is inferior (it uses three instructions instead of two), and is no less difficult for our compiler to generate. Thus, our compiler always generates the more efficient two-instruction sequence.

Our compiler generates code for each dynamic local variable as soon as it scans its declaration. For example, suppose a function had the following local declarations:

```
int w, x = 3;
int y, z = 5;
```

Then the compiler would generate

```
aloc 1   ; allocate w
ldc  3   ; allocate and initialize x
push
aloc 1   ; allocate y
ldc  5   ; allocate and initialize z
push
    .
    .
    .
dloc 4  ; deallocate all four variables
```

Initialized local variables are removed from the stack with the same `dloc` instruction that removes the uninitialized local variables.

Because initialized dynamic local variables are initialized by machine instructions during run time at the beginning of the function in which they are defined, they are initialized *every time* the function is called. Dynamic local variables for which an initial value is not specified are *not initialized.* Their initial values will be *whatever garbage happens to be in the stack slots* reserved for them by the `aloc` instruction.

Figure 7.6 shows the stack at various points in the execution of the **fc** function in Figure 7.4. On entry into the function, the **sp** register points to the return address on the stack (see Figure 7.6a). Next, the slot for **dla** is created with an `aloc` instruction (see Figure 7.6b). Finally, the slot for **dlb** is created and initialized with a `push` instruction (see Figure 7.6c).

Figure 7.7 shows the basic form of the assembly language version of the C++ program in Figure 7.4. For the function **fc**, we have shown only the entry and exit instruction sequences. Note that the `dloc` instruction at the end of **fc** removes both **dla** and **dlb** from the stack. The **end** directive specifies **main** as the entry point.

Now let's see how dynamic local variables are accessed. Global and static local variables are easy to access because they are created by **dw** directives. The label on the **dw** directive is the symbolic address of the variable. To access the variable, we simply use the label in a direct instruction. For example, if **x** is an uninitialized global variable, then it is defined by

```
x:    dw    0
```

To store into **x**, we simply use the direct instruction

```
st    x
```

Dynamic local variables, on the other hand, are accessed quite differently from global and static local variables. Dynamic local variables have names at the C++ level (e.g., **dla**, **dlb** in Figure 7.4), but they do *not* have names at the assembly level. Names of variables at the assembly level come from **dw** directives. Because dynamic local variables are not created with **dw** directives, they do not have assembly-level names. In Figure 7.8, we have the complete assembly program that corresponds to the C++ program in Figure 7.4. You will not see the labels **dla** or **dlb** because the corresponding variables are not created with **dw** directives. There are, however, labels (**@s0_sla** and **@s1_slb**) for the static local variables because they are created with **dw** directives.

FIGURE 7.6   a) On entry into the function `fc`

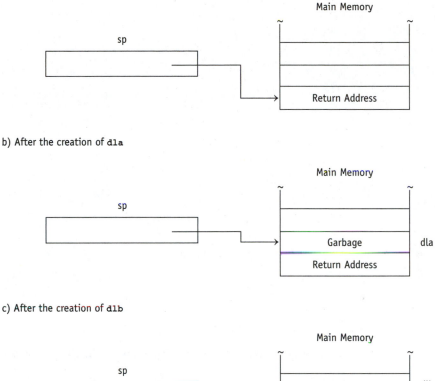

b) After the creation of `dla`

c) After the creation of `dlb`

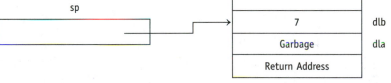

Because labels for **dla** or **dlb** do not exist, we obviously cannot use the instructions

```
ld    dla
```

or

```
ld    dlb
```

to load from these variables. The assembler would flag these instructions by generating the error message, "Undefined symbol."

To access dynamic local variables, we use relative instructions. Look at Figure 7.6c. The **sp** register is pointing to the last dynamic local variable created (**dlb**). We can easily access this variable with a relative instruction that specifies the relative address 0. For example, the C++ statement

```
dlb = 26;
```

is translated to

```
ldc   26
str   0
```

FIGURE 7.7

```
 1      fc:        aloc 1      ; int dla;

 2

 3                 ldc  7      ; int dlb = 7;

 4                 push

 5                            .

 6                            .

 7                            .

 8                 dloc 2      ; deallocate dla and dlb

 9                 ret

10      ;==================================================

11

12      main:      call fc     ; fc();

13

14                 call fc     ; fc();

15

16                 halt

17      @s0_sla:   dw   0      ; static local variable sla

18      @s1_slb:   dw   5      ; static local variable slb

19                 end  main
```

We similarly access **dla** using the relative address 1. For example, the C++ statement

```
dla = 25;
```

is translated to

```
ldc  25
str  1
```

A global or static local variable for which an initial value is not specified in its C++ declaration is initialized to zero. We call this initialization the *default initialization.* Default initialization, however, is not done for dynamic local variables. For example, in the program shell in Figure 7.9, the initial values of **x** (global) and **y** (static local) are guaranteed to be 0, but the initial value of **z** (dynamic local) could be anything—a specific initial value is not guaranteed.

We now can understand how this inconsistency in default initialization comes about: **x** and **y** are created and initialized with the following **dw** directives:

```
x:         dw   0
@s0_sla:   dw   0
```

z, on the other hand, is created on the stack (but not initialized) with the instruction

```
aloc 1
```

Here is an important question: Why did the designers of C++ (and its predecessor C) not require default initialization for dynamic locals? If they had, then the variable **z** in Figure 7.9 would have to be both created and initialized. Is there some problem in doing this? Not at all. Here is the required code:

```
ldc  0
push       ;  create slot containing 0 on stack for z
```

FIGURE 7.8

```
 1 fc:          aloc 1          ; int dla;
 2
 3               ldc 7           ; int dlb = 7;
 4               push
 5
 6               ld @s0_sla      ; cout << sla << endl;
 7               dout
 8               ldc '\n'
 9               aout
10
11               ld @s1_slb      ; cout << slb << endl:
12               dout
13               ldc '\n'
14               aout
15
16               ldc  25         ; dla = 25;
17               str  1
18
19               ldc  26         ; dlb = 26;
20               str  0
21
22               ldc  27         ; sla = 27;
23               st   @s0_sla
24
25               ldc  28         ; sla = 28;
26               st   @s1_slb
27
28               dloc 2          ; remove dla and dlb
29               ret
30 ;============================================================
31 main:    call fc         ; fc();
32
33               call fc         ; fc();
34
35               halt
36 @s0_sla: dw              0     ; static local variable sla
37 @s1_slb: dw              5     ; static local variable slb
38               end  main
```

Can we then conclude that this inconsistency in C++ is an oversight on the part of its designers? On the contrary, the designers of C++ knew exactly what they were doing. The default initialization of global and static local variables involves no penalty. The **dw** directive creates a word for a global or static local variable in the machine language program. This word has to contain some

FIGURE 7.9

```
1 int x;                    // global, initial value = 0
2 void fd()
3 {
4     static int y;     // static local, initial value = 0
5     int z;            // dynamic local, initial value undefined
6        .
7        .
8        .
9 }
10 void main()
11 {
12     fd();
13 }
```

FIGURE 7.10

```
void fe() {
    int z;

      .

      .

    z = x + y;

      .

      .

}
```

value—it might as well be 0. Extra instructions are not required for its initialization. Thus, there is neither a *time* penalty nor a *space penalty* for its initialization (i.e., the program neither runs longer nor is bigger). There is, however, a time and space penalty for the default initialization of a dynamic local variable: Two instructions are needed (`ldc` and `push`) instead of one (`aloc`). This default initialization is of no value if the default value is not subsequently used (which would often be the case). For example, if a variable **z** is declared and then later assigned a value (see Figure 7.10), the default initialization (with its extra instruction) would be unnecessary. It would be a waste of one instruction—both the time it takes to execute it and the space it occupies. Thus, the designers of C++ wisely allowed a dynamic local variable to be uninitialized. Of course, a C++ programmer can always specify an initial value in a variable's declaration (as with **dlb** in Figure 7.4). Then the compiler would generate the necessary initialization code.

7.5   CHANGING RELATIVE ADDRESSES

In C++, it is legal for local variable declarations to appear in a function *after* executable statements. For example, consider the C++ program and its corresponding assembly code in Figure 7.11.

FIGURE 7.11

```
          C++                  |  Assembly Language
                               |
 1  void legal()               |  legal:
 2  {                          |
 3      int x;                 |    aloc 1 ; allocate x
 4                             |
 5      x = 3;                 |    ldc  3
 6                             |    str  0   ; relative address of x is 0
 7                             |
 8      int y;                 |    aloc 1   ; allocate y--changes rel add of x
 9                             |
10      x = 5;                 |    ldc  5
11                             |    str  1   ; relative address of x is 1
12                             |
13                             |    dloc 2
14  }                          |    ret
```

The declaration of **y** in the C+ function on line 8 appears *after* the executable statement on line 5. This program illustrates a problem with H1: Relative addresses for a local variable can change during the execution of a function. The relative address of **x** on line 5 is 0; however, on line 10, the relative address of **x** is 1 because of the intervening declaration of **y**.

A compiler must know the relative address of a local variable to generate code referencing it. But because relative addresses on H1 can change, the compiler is burdened with the task of keeping track of such changes. So, too, must an assembly language programmer keep track of changes in relative addresses. This is a task many programmers might forget to do or do incorrectly, resulting in incorrect code. In fact, one of the two most common errors in assembly code is to use an incorrect relative address (the other is to forget to deallocate local variables at the end of a function).

The problem of changing relative addresses stems from the dual use of the **sp** register. We use it both as the base register for relative instructions and as the top-of-stack pointer. Whenever we perform a push or pop—common occurrences during the execution of a function—the **sp** register changes, and, therefore, so do relative addresses. We are stuck with this problem for now. However, in Chapter 12, we will introduce a modification to H1 that fixes this problem.

7.6 PARAMETERS AND CALL BY VALUE

Before we study how the parameter mechanism in C++ is implemented at the assembly level, let's review some basic concepts. Consider the program in Figure 7.12. The definition of the function **fg** starts with the line

```
void fg(int x)
```

FIGURE 7.12

```
1 int m = 5;           // m is a global variable
2 void fg(int x)        // x is the parameter
3 {
4      int y;           // y is a dynamic local variable
5      y = 7;
6      x = y + 2;
7 }
8 void main()
9 {
10     fg(m);           // m is the argument
11 }
```

The item inside parentheses (**x** in this case) is called a *parameter*. **fg** is called from **main** by the statement

```
fg(m);
```

In a function call, the item inside parentheses (**m** in this case) is referred to as the *argument*. The function that contains the call is referred to as the *calling function*; the function that is invoked is referred to as the *called function*. In Figure 7.12, **main** is the calling function; **fg** is the called function.

When a function is called, the value of the argument in the function call is *passed* to the parameter. Specifically, the value of the argument is automatically assigned to the parameter. This parameter-passing mechanism is referred to as *call by value*. Because the parameters in the call-by-value mechanism receive the value of their corresponding arguments, they are called *value parameters*.

We have seen in the previous section that the creation and removal of local variables are handled by the *called* function. Parameters, in contrast, are handled by the *calling* function. They are created, initialized, and removed by the *calling* function. During a function call, the *calling* function must

1. Create and initialize the parameters, if any (with push instructions).
2. Call the function (with the call instruction).
3. On return from the called function, remove the parameters, if any (with the dloc instruction).

The *called* function must

1. Create dynamic local variables, if any, on entry (with the aloc or push instructions).
2. Perform its function.
3. Remove dynamic local variables, if any, on exit (with the dloc instruction).
4. Return to the calling function (with the ret instruction).

Parameters are created on the stack by the calling function with push instructions.

Let's look at the details of the parameter mechanism by examining what happens when the function **fg** in Figure 7.12 is called. Assume that the **sp** register is initialized with 0 (thus, the first push stores into location FFF hex). The step-by-step sequence of events is as follows:

1. Before the call of **fg**, the parameter **x** does not exist. **m** is global, so it is part of the machine language program that is sitting in low main memory.

FIGURE 7.12A

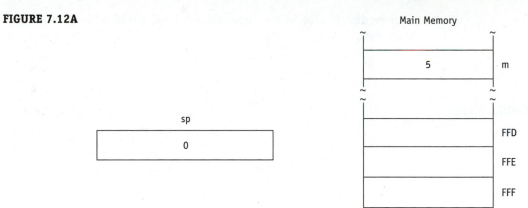

2. Before passing control to **fg**, **main** both creates and initializes the parameter **x** on the stack by pushing the *value* of the argument **m** onto the stack with the instructions

```
ld    m    ; get value of argument m
push
```

The push instruction decrements the value in **sp** to FFFF. Because only the right-most 12 bits are used for addressing purposes, the value of **m** goes into location FFF.

FIGURE 7.12B

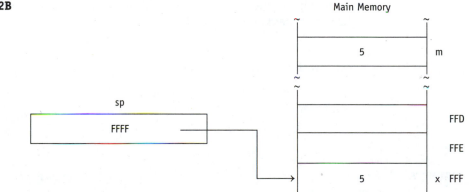

3. **main** then executes the call instruction, which pushes the return address onto the stack and passes control to **fg**.

FIGURE 7.12C

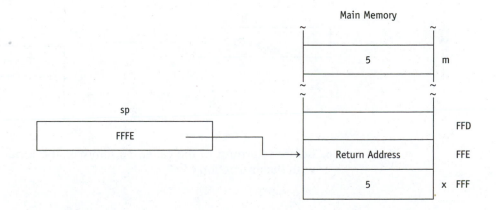

4. fg immediately creates the uninitialized local variable **y** on the stack with the instruction

```
aloc 1
```

FIGURE 7.12D

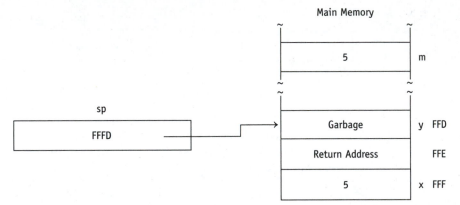

5. The body of **fg** then executes. 7 is stored in **y**; 9 in **x**. The assignment to **x** does *not* affect the value in its corresponding argument **m**. **x** and **y** are accessed with relative instructions with relative addresses 2 and 0, respectively. For example, the assignment statement

```
x = y + 2;
```

appears at the assembly level as

```
ldc  2     ; get the constant 2
addr 0     ; add y
str  2     ; store sum in x
```

FIGURE 7.12E

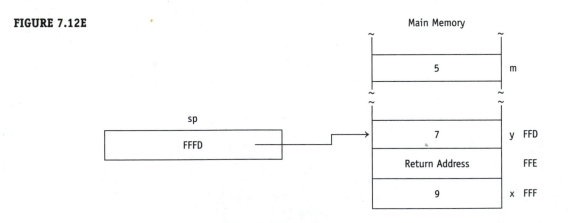

6. Before returning to the caller, **fg** removes the local variable **y** from the stack with the instruction

```
dloc 1
```

FIGURE 7.12F

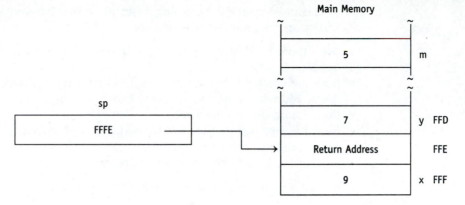

7. **fg** then returns to the calling function (**main**) by executing

```
ret
```

which pops the return address into the **pc** register.

FIGURE 7.12G

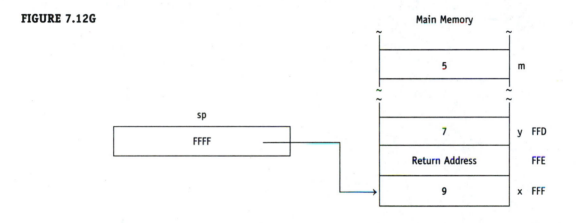

8. Finally, **main** removes the parameter **x** from the stack with the instruction

```
dloc 1
```

FIGURE 7.12H

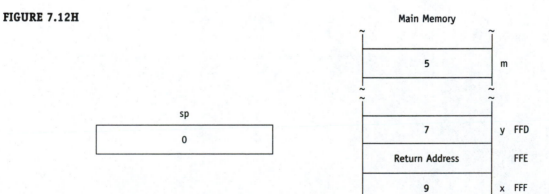

We can see from the foregoing description that parameters and dynamic local variables are very similar. In particular,

- Both have local scope—access is limited to the function in which they are defined.
- Both are created when a function in which they are defined is called, and are destroyed when the function completes.
- Both are created on the stack.
- Both have names that are *not* carried over to the assembly level because they are not defined with **dw** directives.
- Both are accessed using relative instructions.

There are two major differences between parameters and dynamic local variables:

- Parameters are always initialized (by pushing the values of their corresponding arguments onto the stack). Dynamic local variables, on the other hand, are initialized only if initial values are specified in their C++ declarations.
- Parameters are created and destroyed by the *calling* function. Dynamic local variables, on the other hand, are created and destroyed by the *called* function.

The complete assembly language program for the program in Figure 7.12 is given in Figure 7.13. We can see at lines 13 through 16 the following instructions, which implement the call of **fg**:

```
ld    m       ; fg(m);
push          ; create parameter x on stack
call fg
dloc 1        ; remove parameter x from stack
```

FIGURE 7.13

```
 1 fg:        aloc 1            ; int y;
 2
 3            ldc 7             ; y = 7;
 4            str 0
 5
 6            ldc 2             ; x = y + 2;
 7            addr 0
 8            str 2
 9
10            dloc 1            ; deallocate y
11            ret
12 ;================================================
13 main:      ld m              ; fg(m);
14            push
15            call fg
16            dloc 1
17
18            halt
19 m:         dw 5
26            end  main
```

The push before the call instruction creates the parameter **x** by pushing the value of **m**; the dloc after the call removes **x**. At line 1 (the beginning of **fg**), we find the instruction that creates the dynamic local variable **y**:

```
aloc 1
```

and at line 10, we find the instruction that removes **y**:

```
dloc 1
```

The call-by-value mechanism in Figure 7.13 has a very important property: Changes to the parameter do not affect the corresponding argument. The reason for this argument-parameter independence is simple: The argument and the parameter reside in separate memory slots.

The argument-parameter independence in call by value is both a strength (it prevents an unintended change of an argument by the called function) and a weakness (it prevents such a change even when it is desired). When we want the argument to reflect changes to the parameter, we should use the *call-by-reference* parameter passing mechanism (see Section 8.2). In call by reference, the argument and parameter are *not* independent.

A function call, of course, can specify multiple arguments. Then the called function must have multiple parameters, with one parameter for each argument. In C++, multiple arguments are handled in right-to-left order by the calling function. For example, suppose the function **fh** has three parameters, **x, y, z**:

```
void fh(int x, int y, int z)

{

    . . .

}
```

If **a, b**, and **c** are global variables, then the call,

```
fh(a, b, c);
```

is translated to

```
ld   c
push      ; create z
ld   b
push      ; create y
ld   a
push      ; create x
call fh
dloc 3    ; remove all three parameters
```

Notice that the value of the rightmost argument (**c**) is pushed first in the calling sequence (creating **z**), then **b** (creating **y**), and then **a** (creating **x**). The compiler processes arguments in right-to-left order, thereby creating the parameters in right-to-left order. The value of the leftmost argument (**a**) is pushed last (by the push instruction immediately preceding the call instruction). Thus, its corresponding parameter (**x**) sits on the stack immediately above the return address when the called function is executing (see Figure 7.14).

Suppose the function **fh** above has no local variables. Then the parameters **x, y**, and **z** would be accessed using relative instructions containing the addresses 1, 2, and 3, respectively.

FIGURE 7.14   Main Memory

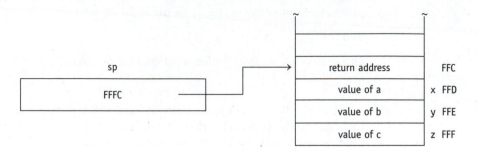

7.7   RETURNING VALUES

• •

One way in C++ for the called function to pass values back to the calling function is to use the *return* statement. Consider the program in Figure 7.15. In the statement

```
y = add_one(x);
```

the **add_one** function is called and passed the value of **x**. The **add_one** function, on completion, returns a value to the calling function using the **return** statement. It is this value that is used in the previous assignment statement—it is assigned to **y**.

The **return** statement uses the **ac** register to carry a value back to the calling function. For example, when executing the statement

```
return z + 1;
```

the called function first computes the value of **z + 1**. It then places this value into the **ac** register, if it is not already there. Finally, the called function executes the **ret** machine instruction, passing control back to the caller. The assembly code is

```
ldc  1          ; load ac with 1
addr 1          ; add z
ret             ; return to the caller with value in ac
```

FIGURE 7.15

```
 1 #include <iostream>
 2 using namespace std;
 3
 4 int x, y;
 5 int add_one(int z)
 6 {
 7    return z + 1;
 8 }
 9 void main()
10 {
11    x = 1;
12    y = add_one(x);     // value returned is assigned to y
13    cout << "y = " << y << endl;
14 }
```

When the called function receives control back from the called function, the value returned is sitting in the **ac** register. Before using this value, the calling function first completes the function call. In particular, it removes the parameters, if any, from the stack. It then takes the appropriate action with the returned value in the **ac** register. Thus, the code for

```
y = add_one(x);
```

is

```
ld   x          ; get value of x
push            ; create parameter on the stack
call add_one
dloc 1          ; remove parameter
st   y          ; use value returned in ac
```

The complete assembly language program for the C++ program in Figure 7.15 appears in Figure 7.16.

FIGURE 7.16

```
 1 add_one:    ldc  1              ;return z + 1;
 2             addr 1
 3             ret
 4 ;==========================================================
 5 main:       ldc  1             ; x = 1;
 9             st   x
10
11             ld   x             ; y = add_one(x);
12             push
13             call add_one
14             dloc 1
15             st   y
16
17             ldc  @m0           ; cout << "y = " << y << endl;
18             sout
19             ld   y
20             dout
21             ldc  '\n'
22             aout
23
24             halt
25 x:          dw   0
26 y:          dw   0
27 @m0:        dw   "y = "
28             end  main
```

7.8 WHY RELATIVE INSTRUCTIONS ARE NEEDED

• •

Let's see if relative instructions are really necessary. Can we replace them with direct instructions? Consider the program in Figure 7.17. When **main** calls **sum**, it pushes the arguments 10 and 5 (in that order), creating the parameters **y** and **x** on the stack. The **call** instruction then pushes a return address on the stack. On entry, **sum** immediately reserves a slot on the stack for the local variable **z**. Thus, when **sum** executes, the stack looks like that shown in Figure 7.18. **x, y**, are **z** are accessed using relative instructions with relative addresses 2, 3, and 0, respectively.

We call the collection of slots created on the stack associated with a function call—the parameters, the return address, and the local variables—a *stack frame* or *activation record*. Because the **sp** register is initialized to 0 (which causes the stack to start at the top of memory), the stack frame for the call of **sum** is in locations FFC through FFF. Are relative instructions necessary to access **x, y**, and **z** in Figure 7.17? Could we not replace them with direct instructions? **x, y**, and **z** can indeed be accessed with direct instructions containing the addresses FFE, FFF, and FFC, respectively. For example, we could replace the relative instruction that loads **x**,

```
ldr   2         ; load x
```

with the direct instruction

```
ld    FFEh      ; load x
```

because **x** is at location FFE. With this replacement, the program will work perfectly.

FIGURE 7.17

```
1 void sum(int x, int y)
2 {
3    int z;
4
5    z = x + y;
6 }
7 void main()
8 {
9    sum(5, 10);
10 }
```

FIGURE 7.18

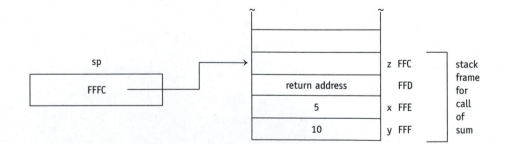

FIGURE 7.19

```
 1  sum:      aloc 1
 2
 3            ldr  2       ; replace with ld  FFEh
 4            addr 3       ; replace with add FFFh
 5            str  0       ; replace with st  FFCh
 6
 7            dloc 1
 8            ret
 9  ;==========================================
10  main:     ldc  10      ; sum(5,10);
14            push
15            ldc  5
16            push
17            call sum
18            dloc 2
19
20            halt
21            end  main
```

Figure 7.19 shows the assembly version of the program that uses relative instructions. The comments show the direct instructions that can replace the relative instructions without affecting the proper operation of the program.

It appears that relative instructions are not necessary. We can replace them with direct instructions. However, now consider the program in Figure 7.20. In this program, the **sum** function from Figure 7.18 appears again. It is called twice: once from **main** and once from **fk**. When **sum** is called from **main**, its stack frame is exactly like that shown in Figure 7.18. **x**, **y**, and **z** are in locations FFE, FFF, and FFC, respectively. The stack frame occupies locations FFC through FFF. However, when **sum** is called from **fk**, its stack frame occupies a different set of locations—FFB through FFE—because the stack frame for **fk** is above it. Because **fk** has neither parameters nor local variables, its stack frame consists of just one slot for the return address (see Figure 7.21). Thus, for the call of **sum** from within the **fk** function, **x**, **y**, and **z** are now in locations FFD, FFE, and FFB.

Now consider the relative instruction in **sum** that loads **x**:

```
ldr  2
```

Let's try to replace it with

```
ld   FFEh
```

This instruction would work for the first call of **sum** (when **x** is at location FFE) but not for the second (when **x** is at location FFD). Nor can we use

```
ld   FFDh
```

because this instruction would work for the second call of **sum** (when **x** is at location FFD) but not for the first (when **x** is at location FFE). Because the local variable **x** occupies different locations for the two calls of **sum**, there is no direct instruction replacement for the relative instruction that will work in both cases.

FIGURE 7.20

```
 1 void sum(int x, int y)
 2 {
 3     int z;
 4
 5     z = x + y;
 6 }
 7 void fk()
 8 {
 9     sum(5, 10);
10 }
11 void main()
12 {
13     sum(5, 10);
14     fk();
15 }
```

FIGURE 7.21

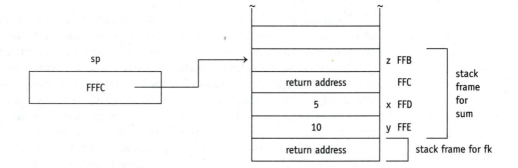

However, in both cases the relative address of **x** is the same. Thus, the relative instruction works correctly in both cases. We conclude that relative instructions are, indeed, necessary.

7.9 DETERMINING THE ADDRESS OF DYNAMIC LOCALS AND PARAMETERS

Suppose **x** and **y** are global variables. Because **x** and **y** are defined with **dw** directives, the C++ statement

```
y = &x;     // "&" means "address of"
```

is translated to the assembly code

```
ldc  x    ; load address of x
st   y    ; store in y
```

When this sequence is assembled, the assembler determines the addresses of **x** and **y** and places them into the `ldc` and `st` machine instructions. This example illustrates an important point: *Addresses of global variables are determined at assembly time.* Now suppose **x** and **y** are static local variables. Then

```
y = &x;
```

would be translated to

```
ldc   @s0_x
st    @s1_y
```

assuming **@s0** and **@s1** are the compiler-generated prefixes for **x** and **y**, respectively. Here, too, the assembler determines the addresses of **x** and **y**. For both global and static local variables, addresses are determined at assembly time. If an item is created with a **dw** directive, then its address can be determined at assembly time by the assembler.

The situation for dynamic local variables and parameters, however, is more complex. Their addresses cannot be determined at assembly time because they are not created until run time. Even more important, their *addresses* can vary during the course of one run. To see this, consider the program in Figure 7.22. The function **fm** is called twice: once directly from **main**, and once from the function **fn**.

On the first call of **fm**, **x** will appear at location FFE (see Figure 7.23a). The execution of

```
p = &x;
```

should put 0FFE into **p**. On the second call of **fm**, **x** will appear lower in memory. The call of **fn** pushes a return address onto the stack. Thus, the stack frame for **fm** will appear one location lower in memory. On the call of **fm** from within **fn**, the statement

```
p = &x;
```

FIGURE 7.22

```
 1 void fm()
 2 {
 3     int x;
 4     int *p;
 5
 6     p = &x;        // assigning address of local variable
 7 }
 8 void fn()
 9 {
10     fm();
11 }
12 void main()
13 {
14     fm();
15     fn();
16 }
```

FIGURE 7.23   a)

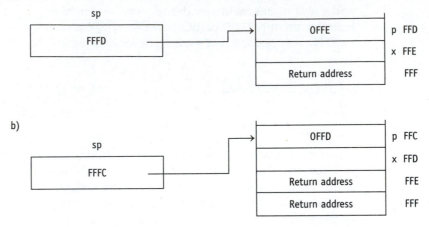

should put 0FFD into **p** (see Figure 7.23b). The address of **x** varies between calls of **m**, so its address must be determined each time the statement

```
p = &x;
```

is *executed*. Clearly, addresses of dynamic local variables must be determined at *run time*. The addresses of parameters, for exactly the same reason, must also be determined at run time. Unfortunately, there is no single instruction in the standard instruction set that can directly provide the absolute address of a dynamic local variable or a parameter, given its relative address. Thus, to determine the address of the variable **x** in the program in Figure 7.22, we have to use a sequence of instructions that adds the value in the **sp** register and the relative address of **x**. Lines 6 to 11 in Figure 7.24, the assembly form of the C++ program in Figure 7.22, shows this technique. First, we swap and save to memory the contents of the **sp** register with

```
swap
st    @spsave
```

@spsave is the label on a **dw** directive at the bottom of the program. We then restore the **sp** register with another swap:

```
swap
```

We then load the **ac** register with the relative address of **x**:

```
ldc   1
```

Finally, we add the saved contents of the **sp** register:

```
add   @spsave
```

Although we can determine the address of a dynamic local variable or a parameter with the standard instruction set, it requires an awkward, inefficient sequence of instructions. Moreover, this sequence briefly corrupts the contents of the **sp** register (when between the two swaps). On most computers (but not on H1), corrupting the pointer to the top of the stack—even when the program currently executing is not performing any stack operations—can result in a system failure. We will learn the reason for this when we study interrupts in Chapter 14. Ideally,

FIGURE 7.24

```
 1 fm:          aloc 1           ; int x;
 2
 3              aloc 1           ; int *p;
 4
 5                               ; p = &x;
 6              swap                ; get sp
 7              st   @spsave        ; save it
 8              swap                ; restore sp
 9              ldc  1              ; get relative address of x (1)
10              add  @spsave        ; convert to an absolute address
11              str  0              ; store absolute address in p
12
13              dloc 2              ; deallocate x and p
14              ret
15 ;            ==================================================
16 fn:          call fm           ; fm();
17              ret
18 ;            ==================================================
19 main:        call fm           ; fm();
20              call fn           ; fn();
21              halt
22 @spsave:     dw   0
23              end  main
```

H1 would have an instruction that could determine the address of a stack item quickly and without corrupting the **sp** register. Suppose, for example, that H1 had a *convert relative address* (mnemonic: cora) instruction that replaces the relative address in the **ac** register with the absolute address to which it corresponds, without affecting the contents of the **sp** register. For example, in the sequence

```
ldc  1        ; load relative address
cora          ; convert relative address to an absolute address
```

the ldc instruction would first place the relative address 1 in the **ac** register, then the cora instruction would replace this address with the corresponding absolute address. With this sequence, the statement

```
p = &x;
```

in Figure 7.22 could be translated to a sequence that does not corrupt the **sp** register and is more efficient:

```
ldc  1        ; get relative address of x
cora          ; convert to absolute address
str  0        ; store in p
```

In Chapter 12, we will again consider the cora instruction. There, we will see if we can somehow incorporate it into the instruction set.

7.10 DEREFERENCING POINTERS

• •

Whenever we declare a pointer in C++, we must specify the type of the item to which the pointer will point. For example, the declaration

```
int *p;
```

declares **p** as a pointer to an item of type `int`. Similarly,

```
long *q;
```

declares **q** as a pointer to an item of type `long`. An `int` and a `long` can have different sizes. For example, on H1, an `int` variable is one word; a `long` variable is two words. However, there is no reason why a *pointer* to an `int` and a *pointer* to a `long` should have different sizes. Both have to contain an address, and the address of an `int` and a `long` on H1 both require one word (actually only 12 bits of one word). Thus, **p** and **q** are essentially identical in size (i.e., both hold one word) and in function (i.e., both hold an address). You may wonder, therefore, why we have to specify the type of the item pointed to in their declarations. The reason is that the specifics of pointer operations usually depend on this type. For example, the statement

```
*p = 0;
```

zeros one word, the `int` item pointed to by **p**. But

```
*q = 0;
```

zeros two words, the `long` item pointed to by **q**. For the former statement the compiler generates

```
ldc   0
push
ld    p        ; get address in p
sti
```

But for the latter statement the compiler has to generate a completely different sequence:

```
ldc   0        ; prepare for sti
push
ld    q        ; get address in q
sti            ; put zero in first word
ldc   0
push           ; prepare for sti
ldc   1        ; get 1
add   q        ; get (address in q) + 1
sti            ; put zero in second word
```

Clearly, the compiler must know the type of a pointer to generate code dereferencing that pointer.

Suppose **p**, **x**, and **y** are declared as follows:

```
int *p;
int x;
long y;
```

Then the statement,

```
p = &x;        // assign the address of x to p
```

makes sense because both sides have the same type (both sides are `int` pointers). But

```
p = &y;
```

does *not* make sense because the address of **y** is a `long` pointer (because **y** is of type `long`). If, for some reason, we really need to assign **p** the address of **y**, we should use a cast:

```
p = (int *)&y;
```

But, now if we dereference **p**, we access only the first word of **y**. For example,

```
*p = 0;
```

sets only the first half of **y** to 0.

PROGRAMS

7.1. Suppose each instruction that referenced memory had an extra bit that specified the type of addressing (direct or relative). Then we would not need two sets of instructions (one for direct, one for relative). Which is the better approach—using an addressing bit or using two sets of instructions?

7.2. If main memory were expensive, would it make sense to have an instruction set with complex instructions? Explain.

7.3. Suppose a computer has a large number of registers. Could registers rather than the stack be used to pass arguments? What are the advantages of this approach? Disadvantages?

7.4. If an ISA had many general-purpose registers, would it make sense to keep local variables in registers? Global variables?

7.5. What parameter-passing mechanism does Java use?

7.6. Explain how the difficulty of designing and implementing a compiler depends on the ISA. Be specific.

7.7. What impact would removing the `sp` register and associated instructions have on H1's appropriateness for C++? Could we still use it for the programs in this chapter?

7.8. How important is an efficient mechanism for calling and returning from functions?

7.9. Suppose in addition to the `ld` and `st` instructions, we had an `li` (load indirect) and an `si` (store indirect) instruction that functioned as follows:

```
li x      ac = mem[mem[x]];
si x      mem[mem[x]] = ac;
```

How useful would these instructions be?

7.10. Suppose **p** is a global variable that contains the address of a function that takes no parameters. Write the assembler code to call this function.

7.11. On a computer with a byte-addressable memory, by how much would the `sp` register change on each `push`, `pop`, `call`, or `ret` instruction?

7.12. The `cora` instruction could be designed to hold the relative address to convert in its **x** field. For example,

```
cora 1
```

would convert the relative address 1 to an absolute address. Why was the `cora` instruction in Section 7.9 not designed in this way?

7.13. Why does the code for a function call that returns a value remove the parameters from the stack before using the value returned? Why not the opposite order?

7.14. Translate to assembly language as a dumb compiler would:

```
v = w + x + y + z;
v = (w + x) + (y + z);
v = w + ( x + (y + z));
```

Assume v, w, x, y, and z are global variables.

7.15. Should the assembly language programs to which C++ programs are translated be assembled by a case-sensitive or case-insensitive assembler? Why?

7.16. If an assembly language program has more lines of code than a functionally identical C++ program, is its machine language program necessarily bigger than the machine language program for the C++ program? Why?

7.17. Why are compiler-generated names used for static local variables at the assembly level?

7.18. Write the assembly language program for Problem 7.33, using the st instruction in place of the str instruction.

7.19. Show the contents of the stack at its greatest depth when the program in Problem 7.33 is executed. Also show the stack when execution is in the **f** function for the first time.

7.20. Improve upon the assembly code at line 1 in Figure 7.3 that corresponds to the statement

```
x = x + x + 2;
```

Would it be difficult for a compiler to generate the more efficient code?

7.21. Because most assemblers allow "@" in label names, you might expect C++ to allow "@" in identifier names. Does it?

7.22. Explain the following statement: Static local variables have global scope at the assembly level.

7.23. Show the contents of the stack at its greatest depth when the following program is executed:

```
void f()
{
    return;
}
void g()
{
    f();
}
void h()
{
    g();
}
void i()
{
    h();
}
void j()
{
    i();
}
void main()
```

```
    {
        j();
    }
```

7.24. For a direct instruction that references a global variable, the assembler determines the address of the variable at assembly time. However, at run time, the actual address of the variable might be different from the address that the assembler determines. How can this be?

7.25. The scope of **sla** in the assembly version of Figure 7.4 is global. How, then, is its scope restricted to just **fc**?

7.26. Suppose **p** and **q** are integer and long pointers, respectively. Does

```
p++;
```

have the same effect on **p** that

```
q++;
```

has on **q**?

7.27. Will the following program compile correctly? Compile it using a C++ compiler and see what happens.

```
int f()
{
    return 5;
}
void main()
{
    f();
}
```

7.28. Are there any potential problems with naming global variables at the assembly level with their C++-level names?

7.29. How many machine language instructions will a dumb compiler generate for

```
v = (w + x) + (y + z);
```

and for

```
v = (( w + x ) + y) + z;
```

Assume all variables are global.

7.30. Formulate rules that would specify when parentheses in an arithmetic expression can be ignored without changing the expression's value.

7.31. When should the addition in

```
x = 2 + 3?
```

be performed? At compile time, assembly time, or run time? Explain.

For the following problems, translate the given program to assembly language, assemble, and run on **sim**.

7.32.
```
#include <iostream>
using namespace std;
void f()
{
    static int x = 2;
    int y = 3;
```

```
        int z = 5;
        cout << x << " " << y << " " << z << endl;
        x = 1;
        y = 2;
        z = 3;
    }
    void g()
    {
        static int x = 44;
        int y = 50;
        cout << x << " " << y << endl;
        y = 22;
        x = y;
    }
    void main()
    {
      f();
      f();
      g();
      g();
    }
```

7.33.
```
    #include <iostream>
    using namespace std;
    void f()
    {
        int x;
        x = 1;
        cout << x << endl;
    }
    void g() {
        f();
    }
    void main()
    {
        f();
        g();
    }
```

7.34.
```
    #include <iostream>
    using namespace std;
    int x = 1, y = 2;
    void f(int x)
    {
        int y = 7;
        x = y;
        cout << x << " " << y << endl;
    }
    void main() {
        f(x);
        f(y);
        cout << x << " " << y << endl;
    }
```

7.35.
```cpp
#include <iostream>
using namespace std;
int x = 1, y = 2, z = 3;
void f(int x)
{
    int y = 7;
    x = y;
    cout << x << " " << y << endl;
    int z = 8;
    x = z;
    cout << x << " " << z << endl;
}
void main()
{
    f(x);
    cout << x << " " << y << " " << z << endl;
}
```

7.36.
```cpp
#include <iostream>
using namespace std;
int x = 99;
void f(int x)
{
    ++x;
}
void main()
{
    f(++x);
    cout << x << endl;
    f(x++);
    cout << x << endl;
}
```

7.37.
```cpp
#include <iostream>
using namespace std;
int x, y, z = 6;
void f(int a, int b, int c)
{
    static int h, i, j;
    b = c = h = i = ++j;
    cout << a << " " << b << endl;
}
void main()
{
    x = 1;
    y = 2;
    f(x, y, z);
    f(z, y, z);
}
```

7.38.
```cpp
#include <iostream>
using namespace std;
int x, y = 5;
```

```cpp
void f(int x)
{
    int y;
    y = x + 3;
    cout << x << " " << y << endl;
}
void main()
{
    cout << x << " " << y << endl;
    cin >> y;
    f(y);
    cout << x << " " << y << endl;
}
```

7.39.
```cpp
#include <iostream>
using namespace std;
void f(int x, int y, int z)
{
    static int q;
    q = x + y + y + z + z + z;
    cout << "q = " << q << endl;
}
void main()
{
    f(1, 2, 3);
}
```

7.40.
```cpp
#include <iostream>
using namespace std;
int x, y = 5;
void f(int x, int y)
{
    int p, q = 8;
    static int s, t = 17;
    p = q++;
    s = t++;
    x = ++y;
    cout << p << " " << q << " " << s << " " << t <<endl;
}
int z;
void main()
{
    z = 5;
    f(x, y);
    cout << x << " " << y << " " << z << endl;
    f(y, x);
    cout << x << " " << y << " " << z << endl;
}
```

7.41.
```cpp
#include <iostream>
using namespace std;
void main()
```

```
        {
            int x;
            int y = 3;
            x = y + 5;
            cout << "x = " << x << endl;
            cout << "y = " << y << endl;
        }
```

7.42.
```
    #include <iostream>
    using namespace std;
    int g = 20;
    void f1(int x)
    {
        x = x + 5;
        cout << "x = " << x << endl;
    }
    void f2(int *p)
    {
        *p = 3;
    }
    void f3(int *p, int x)
    {
        *p = x;
    }
    void main()
    {
        cout << "g = " << g << endl;
        f1(g);
        cout << "g = " << g << endl;
        f2(&g);
        cout << "g = " << g << endl;
        f3(&g, 20);
        cout << "g = " << g << endl;
    }
```

7.43.
```
    #include <iostream>
    using namespace std;
    char gc;
    int  gi;
    void f(char c, int i, char *cp, int *ip)
    {
        c = 'A';
        i = 2;
        *cp = 'B';
        *ip = 3;
    } void main() {
        f('X', 5, &gc, &gi);
        cout << "gc = " << gc << "  gi = " << gi << endl; }
```

7.44.
```
    #include <iostream>
    using namespace std;
    void f1(int x, unsigned y, short z)
    {
```

```
        x = 1;
        y = 2;
        z = 3;
        cout << x << " " << y << " " << z << endl;
}
void f2(int x, int y, int z)
{
        x = 4;
        y = 5;
        z = 6;
        cout << x << " " << y << " " << z << endl;
}
void main()
{
        f1(10, 11, 12);
        f2(20, 21, 22);
}
```

7.45.   ```
#include <iostream>
using namespace std;
void f()
{
        int x, y = 2;
        x = 10;
        {
            int x, y = 4;
            x = 5;
            cout << "x = " << x << " y = " << y << endl;
        }
        cout << "x = " << x << " y = " << y << endl;
}
void main()
{
        f();
}
```

7.46.    ```
#include <iostream>
using namespace std;
long x, *p; int *q, *r;
void main()
{
        p = &x;
        *p = 2;
        q = (int *)p;
        r = q + 1;
        cout << *q << endl;
        cout << *r << endl;
}
```

7.47.   ```
#include <iostream>
using namespace std;
int a, b;
```
```

```
void f(int x, int *p)
{
    x = 44;
    *p = 55;
}
void main()
{
    f(a, &b);
    cout << a << " " << b << endl;
}
```

7.48.
```
#include <iostream>
using namespace std;
int x = 1;
void f(int *p)
{
    *p++;
    cout << x << endl;
    *(p++);
    cout << x << endl;
    (*p)++;
}
void main()
{
    f(&x);
    cout << x << endl;
}
```

7.49.
```
#include <iostream>
using namespace std;
int x = 3;
void f(int *p)
{
    cout << *p << endl;
}
void g(int *p)
{
    f(p);
}
void main()
{
    g(&x);
}
```

7.50.
```
#include <iostream>
using namespace std;
int x = 1, y = 2;
void f(int x)
{
    x++;
    cout << x << endl;
}
```

```
      void main()
      {
          f(x + y + 5);
          cout << x << " " << y << endl;
      }
```

7.51.
```
#include <iostream>
using namespace std;
int x = 20;
int f()
{
    return x + 10;
}
void main()
{
    x = f();
    cout << x << endl;
}
```

7.52.
```
#include <iostream>
using namespace std;
int a = 5;
void f(int x)
{
    cout << "x = " << x << endl;
    cout << "a = " << a << endl;
}
void main()
{
    f(a++);     // is a incremented before f is executed?
}
```

7.53.
```
#include <iostream>
using namespace std;
int f(int x, int y, int z)
{
    cout << x << " " << y << " " << z << endl;
    return 1;
}
int g(int a, int b, int c)
{
    return f(c, b, a) + 10;
}
void main()
{
    cout << g(1, 2, 3) << endl;
}
```

7.54.
```
#include <iostream>
using namespace std;
void f()
{
    int x;
```

```
        // enter 5 first time, enter 6 second time
        cin >> x;
        static int y = x;    // y initialized only once
        cout << y << endl;   // outputs 5 both times
    }
    void main()
    {
        f();
        f();
    }
```

7.55.
```
#include <iostream>
using namespace std;
void f()
{
    static int y = 3;
    int x = y;
    cout << x << endl;
}
void main()
{
    f();
}
```

7.56.
```
#include <iostream>
using namespace std;
void f()
{
    int x, y, z;
    cout << "Enter 3 integers\n";
    cin >> x >> y >> z;
    cout << x << y << z << endl;
}
void main()
{
    f();
}
```

Chapter Eight

EVALUATING THE INSTRUCTION SET ARCHITECTURE OF H1: PART 2

8.1   INTRODUCTION

In this chapter, we will continue our examination of compiler-generated code. By examining various features of C++ at the assembly level, we will uncover additional weaknesses of the standard instruction set that make it painfully inadequate for C++. We will consider

- Call by reference (one of the two parameter-passing mechanisms in C++)
- Function overloading
- Structs
- Arrays
- Pointers to functions
- Multiword addition (which occurs when performing computation on variables of type **long** on H1)
- Bit-level operations
- Recursion

8.2   CALL BY REFERENCE

C++ has two parameter-passing mechanisms: call by value and call by reference. In call by value, the *value* (i.e., contents) of a variable is passed; in call by reference, the *address* of a variable is passed.

8.2.1   Implementation of Call by Reference

The program in Figure 8.1 has three functions, **fv**, **fr**, and **fvr**. **fv** uses the call-by-value mechanism. Specifically, the *value* of the argument **y** is automatically assigned to the parameter **x**. **x** and **y** have separate slots in memory. Thus, when the statement

```
x = x + 5;
```

is executed, only **x** is affected; **y** remains equal to 1, and the first **cout** statement displays

```
y = 1
```

In both the call of **fv** (line 19) and the call of **fr** (line 21), the value of the argument is assigned to its corresponding parameter. However, in the call of **fr**, the value of

FIGURE 8.1

```
1 #include <iostream>
2 using namespace std;
3
4 int y = 1;
5 void fv(int x)
6 {
7     x = x + 5;
8 }
9 void fr(int *p)
10 {
11     *p = *p + 5;       // dereference pointer to access y
12 }
13 void fvr(int x, int *p)
14 {
15     *p = x;
16 }
17 void main()
18 {
19     fv(y);              // call by value—pass value
20     cout << "y = " << y << endl;
21     fr(&y);             // call by reference—pass address
22     cout << "y = " << y << endl;
23     fvr(20, &y);        // call by value and reference
24     cout << "y = " << y << endl;
25 }
```

its argument, &**y**, is the *address* of **y**. In the call of **fv**, the value of its argument, **y**, is the *contents* of **y**. We will designate the special case of a call in which the value of the argument is an address as a *call by address* or *call by reference*, although the underlying mechanism is still the usual call by value. To avoid confusion, we will use the term *call by value* only for calls that do *not* pass an address, and the term *call by reference* for calls that do pass an address. Accordingly, **fv** in Figure 8.1 uses call by value; **fr** uses call by reference; and **fvr** uses both call by value (for the first argument) and call by reference (for the second argument).

When **fr** is called, the value of the argument (the address of **y**) is assigned to the parameter **p**. Thus, when **fr** is executing, **p** points to **y** (see Figure 8.2). **fr** then dereferences **p** to access **y**. The assignment statement

```
*p = *p + 5;
```

accesses the value pointed to by **p** (which is **y**), adds 5, and then assigns the sum to the location to which **p** points (which is **y**). The effect, of course, is to increase the value in **y** by 5. Thus, the second **cout** statement displays

```
y = 6
```

In the call of **fvr**, **p** again points to **y**. Thus, the statement

```
*p = x;
```

FIGURE 8.2

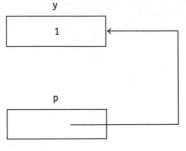

assigns to **y** the value of **x** (20), and the third **cout** statement displays

```
y = 20
```

The significant difference between call by value and call by reference is illustrated by the **fv** and **fr** functions in Figure 8.1. **fv** is passed the *value* of **y**, whereas **fr** is passed the *address* of **y**. Because **fr** gets the address of **y**, it can dereference that address to access or change **y**. The **fv** function, on the other hand, gets only the contents of **y**. **fv** does not know where **y** is. Thus, it *cannot change* **y**.

Let's examine the assembly language needed for the **fv** and **fr** functions. To call **fv** from **main**, we need

```
ld y        ; get value of y
push        ; create and initialize parameter x
call fv
dloc 1      ; remove x
```

To call **fr**, we need

```
ldc y       ; get the address of y
push        ; create and initialize parameter p
call fr
dloc 1      ; remove p
```

The only difference between the two calls is the `ld` instruction (which loads a value) in the **fv** calling sequence versus an `ldc` instruction (which loads an address) in the **fr** calling sequence. Figure 8.3 shows the state of the stack on entry into the **fv** and **fr** functions. The stack contains the parameter **x** (when **fv** is called) or **p** (when **fr** is called), below which is the return address (pushed there by the `call` instruction). For both functions, the parameter (**x** for function **fv**, **p** for function **fr**) can be accessed with a relative instruction using the relative address 1.

The assembly language for the statement

```
x = x + 5;
```

within the **fv** function is a straightforward access of **x** with relative instructions:

```
ldc 5      ; get 5
addr 1     ; add x
str 1      ; store sum in x
```

When **fv** executes, the **sp** register points to the return address. **x** is on the stack, one location above the return address. Thus, the relative instructions use relative address 1 to access **x**.

FIGURE 8.3   a) On entry into fv

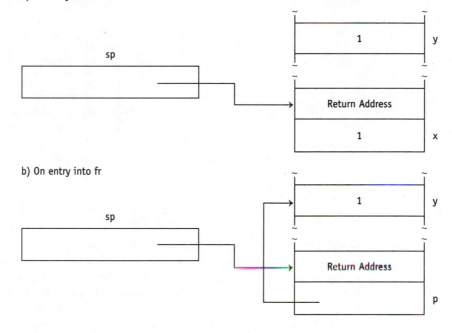

b) On entry into fr

The assembly language for the statement

```
*p = *p + 5;
```

within the **fr** function, unfortunately, is more complicated. Its complexity stems from the two dereferencing operations that it requires. Moreover, we have to contend with the problem of a changing relative address. We first must load the **ac** register from **p**:

```
ldr 1    ; load address in p into ac
```

We then use an `ldi` instruction to load the value that is pointed to by the **ac** register (and **p**) into the **ac** register:

```
ldi      ; load what ac (and p) point to
```

We then use a direct instruction to add 5:

```
add @5
```

Finally, we use a `push-ldr-sti` sequence to store the sum into the location pointed to by p:

```
push     ; push sum onto stack
ldr 2    ; load address in p into ac
sti      ; store top-of-stack into loc pointed to by ac
```

The push in this sequence saves the sum on the stack. The `ldr` instruction then loads the **ac** register with the pointer in **p**. The first time we accessed **p**, we used

```
ldr 1
```

However, the second time we must use the relative address 2 because we have pushed an additional word (the sum) onto the stack, causing the **sp** register to

FIGURE 8.4

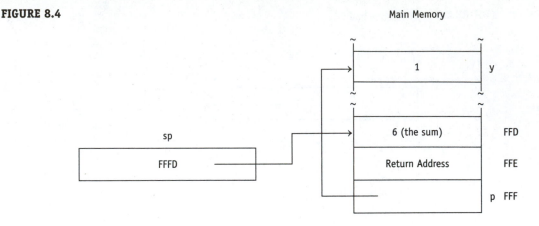

Main Memory

point one word farther away from **p** (see Figure 8.4). This inconstancy of relative addresses is an annoying feature of the standard instruction set. It requires the compiler (or assembly language programmer) to anticipate at compile time what happens to the **sp** register at run time in order to determine relative addresses. For the **fr** function, figuring out the correct relative address is not hard to do, but this is not always the case. In Chapter 12, we will modify H1 so that relative addresses never change during the execution of a function.

The complete assembly language program for the program in Figure 8.1 is given in Figure 8.5. Notice that the same string constant "y =" appears in three separate **dw** statements (lines 67, 68, and 69). In Section 9.5, we will learn why even a smart compiler should do this.

In the call by reference mechanism, a pointer (i.e., an address) is passed to the called function. The called function dereferences this pointer to access the item to which the pointer points. For example, in Figure 8.1, a pointer to **y** is passed to the **fr** function. The **fr** function then dereferences this pointer to access **y**. In the C programming language (the predecessor of C++), the programmer *must* explicitly specify the address and dereferencing operations required by the call-by-reference mechanism. This is precisely what we did in the C++ program in Figure 8.1—we used the address operator & (in the call of the function **fr**) and the dereferencing operator * (within the **fr** function). However, C++, has an alternate approach in which the programmer specifies only that call by reference is to be used. Then the compiler automatically generates the required address and dereferencing operations. For example, consider the program in Figure 8.6. This program is the alternate version of the program in Figure 8.1. The definition of the **fr** function starts with

```
void fr(int &z)
```

The "&" that appears before the parameter name **z** signals to the C++ compiler that it should use call by reference for this parameter. Such parameters are called *reference parameters*. The ordinary type of parameter (those without the "&") are called *value parameters*. Reference parameters receive the address—not the value—of their corresponding arguments. Moreover, the compiler automatically generates dereferencing code wherever a reference parameter is used within a function. Thus, wherever **z** is used in the **fr** function, the compiler generates code that dereferences the address it contains, thereby accessing whatever **z** points to.

FIGURE 8.5

```
 1                              ; x = x + 5;
 2 fv:        ldc  5           ; get 5
 3            addr 1           ; add x
 4            str  1           ; store in x
 5
 6            ret
 7 ;======================================================
 8                              ; *p = *p + 5;
 9 fr:        ldr  1           ; get p
10            ldi              ; get *p
11            add  @5          ; add 5
12            push             ; prepare for sti
13            ldr  2           ; get p
14            sti              ; store into *p
15
16            ret
17 ;======================================================
18                              ; *p = x;
19 fvr:       ldr  1           ; get x
20            push             ; prepare for sti
21            ldr  3           ; get p
22            sti              ; store into *p
23
24            ret
25 ;======================================================
26 main:      ld   y           ; fv(y);
27            push
28            call fv
29            dloc 1
30
31            ldc  @m0         ; cout << "y = " << y << endl;
32            sout
33            ld   y
34            dout
35            ldc  '\n'
36            aout
37
38            ldc  y           ; fr(&y);
39            push
40            call fr
41            dloc 1
42
43            ldc  @m1         ; cout << "y = " << y << endl;   (continued)
```

FIGURE 8.5
(continued)

```
44              sout
45              ld    y
46              dout
47              ldc   '\n'
48              aout
49
50              ldc   y          ; fvr(20, &y);
51              push
52              ldc   20
53              push
54              call  fvr
55              dloc  2
56
57              ldc   @m2        ; cout << "y = " << endl;
58              sout
59              ld    y
60              dout
61              ldc   '\n'
62              aout
63
64              halt
65 @5:          dw    5
66 y:           dw    1
67 @m0:         dw    "y = "
68 @m1:         dw    "y = "
69 @m2:         dw    "y = "
70              end   main
```

Because **y** is the argument that corresponds to the parameter **z**, **z** contains the address of **y**. Thus, **y** is accessed wherever **z** appears. When the statement

```
z = z + 5;
```

within the **fr** function is executed, the variable **y** is accessed wherever **z** appears. It is as if the statement were temporarily transformed into

```
y = y + 5;
```

by the call by reference mechanism. The assignment to **z** is, in effect, an assignment to **y**. Thus, the assignment to **z** causes a *side effect* (i.e., a change to a nonlocal item)—namely, the change in the value of the nonlocal variable **y**.

The **main** function in Figure 8.6 contains three function calls. In the first call,

```
fv(y);
```

the argument **y** is passed using the call-by-value mechanism because its corresponding parameter **x** is a value parameter. Thus, the C++ compiler generates code that passes the value of **y**:

FIGURE 8.6

```
1 #include <iostream>
2 using namespace std;
3
4 int y = 1;
5 void fv(int x)                      // x is a value parameter
6 {
7     x = x + 5;
8 }
9 void fr(int &z)                     // z is a reference parameter
10 {
11     z = z + 5;
12 }
13 void fvr(int x, int &z)            // x is value, z is ref parameter
14 {
15     z = x;
16 }
17 void main()
18 {
19     fv(y);                         // call by value
20     cout << "y = " << y << endl;   // y is still 1
21     fr(y);                         // call by reference
22     cout << "y = " << y << endl;   // y is now 6
23     fvr(20, y);
24     cout << "y = " << y << endl;   // y is now 20
25 }
```

```
ld y      ; get value of y
push
call fv
dloc 1
```

However, in the second function call,

```
fr(y);
```

y corresponds to the reference parameter **z** in the function **fr**. Thus, the C++ compiler generates code that *passes the address* of **y**, even though the address operator & is not explicitly specified (nor should it be) in the call of **fr**. The corresponding code is

```
ldc y     ; get address of y
push
call fr
dloc 1
```

In addition, because **z** is a reference parameter, the C++ compiler automatically generates dereferencing code for each appearance of **z** in the statement

```
z = z + 5;
```

within the `fr` function. Thus, the instructions that the C++ compiler produces for this assignment statement are

```
ldr 1    ; load address in z into ac
ldi      ; get what ac (and z) point to
add @5   ; add 5
push     ; push sum
ldr 2    ; load address in z into ac
sti      ; store top-of-stack into loc pointed to by ac
```

These instructions are exactly the same as those produced by the C++ compiler when it translates the statement

```
*p = *p + 5;
```

in the program in Figure 8.1. In fact, both programs result in the same assembly language code (the code given in Figure 8.5). The only difference between the two programs is at the C++ level. Both programs pass and dereference addresses. One program specifies these operations explicitly; the other, implicitly.

To use call by reference in C++, the programmer must either write code that explicitly passes and dereferences pointers (as we did in Figure 8.1) or, alternatively, simply use reference parameters (as we did in Figure 8.6). Reference parameters "hide" the details of the call-by-reference mechanism, and, in so doing, make programs easier to write and understand.

8.2.2   Conceptual View of C++ Reference Parameters

We can view the C++ reference parameter mechanism as a replacement mechanism: It replaces the reference parameter within the called function with the argument from the calling function. For example, in the C++ program in Figure 8.7, **z** is a reference parameter in the **fr** function. As you know from our discussion in the previous section, the compiler automatically generates dereferencing code for each appearance of **z**. Thus, each appearance of **z** is, in effect, a reference to its corresponding argument (**x** on the first call, **y** on the second call).

It is as if the statement

```
z = z + 5;
```

FIGURE 8.7

```
 1 #include <iostream>
 2 using namespace std;
 3
 4 int x = 5, y = 6;
 5 void fr(int &z)   // z is a reference parameter
 6 {
 7      z = z + 5;
 8 }
 9 void main()
10 {
11      fr(x);                          // x is the argument
12      fr(y);                          // y is the argument
13 }
```

FIGURE 8.8

```
 1 #include <iostream>
 2 using namespace std;
 3
 4 int x = 100;
 5 void fr(int &z)
 6 {
 7     z = z + 5;       // adds 5 to x
 8 }
 9 void ft(int &y)
10 {
11     y = y + 1;       // adds 1 to x
12     fr(y);           // reference parameter now is argument
13 }
14 void main()
15 {
16     ft(x);
17     cout << "x = " << x << endl;
18 }
```

in **fr** were temporarily changed to

```
x = x + 5;
```

on the first call (when **x** is the argument), and to

```
y = y + 5;
```

on the second call (when **y** is the argument). Thus, the call

```
fr(x);
```

in effect *passes the variable* **x** (not its value) to **fr**, where it *replaces* all occurrences of the reference parameter **z**. This is a convenient way to conceptualize the call-by-reference mechanism. It is the way one typically describes the mechanism to beginners who know nothing about addresses, pointers, and dereferencing. But be sure to keep in mind how it actually works: The function call passes the address of the argument, and the called function automatically dereferences this address.

The conceptual view of the reference parameter mechanism is sometimes an aid in understanding how more complicated parameter-passing scenarios work. For example, consider the program in Figure 8.8.

In the function **ft**, **y** is a reference parameter. **y** also is the argument in the call of the function **fr**. **z**, the parameter in **fr** corresponding to **y**, *is also a reference parameter*. This double use of **y** in t—as both a reference parameter and an argument corresponding to another reference parameter—is confusing at first. However, if we use our conceptual view of the reference mechanism (as a variable-passing/replacement mechanism), then the operation of the program becomes clear. First, let's consider what happens when **ft** is called. The argument **x** replaces the reference parameter **y**. Thus, the body of **ft** becomes

```
x = x + 1;
fr(x);
```

x, in effect, is the argument in the call of **fr**. Thus, **x** replaces the reference parameter **z** in **fr**. The body of **fr** becomes

```
x = x + 5;
```

Both **ft** and **fr** access **x**. **ft** increases **x** by 1; **fr** increases **x** by 5. Thus, on return to **main**, **x** contains 106 and **main** displays

```
x = 106
```

8.2.3 When a C++ Reference Parameter Is Not Dereferenced

In Section 8.2.1, we saw that a C++ reference parameter is dereferenced automatically wherever it is used. There is one case, however, in which a reference parameter is *not* dereferenced. Consider the body of the **ft** function in Figure 8.8. In the first statement,

```
y = y + 1;
```

the reference parameter appears twice and is dereferenced twice. The corresponding assembly code is

```
ldr 1    ; get y parameter (an address)
ldi      ; dereference y
add @1
push
ldr 2    ; get y parameter (an address)
sti      ; dereference y
```

However, the second statement in **ft**,

```
fr(y);
```

illustrates the one case in which a reference parameter is not dereferenced: when the reference parameter is an argument that corresponds to another reference parameter. The corresponding assembly code is

```
ldr 1    ; get y--do NOT dereference
push     ; create z by pushing y
call fr
dloc 1   ; remove z
```

It is not hard to understand why **y** is not dereferenced here. When **main** calls **ft**, it, in our conceptual view, passes the variable **x** to **ft** (by passing the address of **x**). **ft** then, in turn, passes the variable **x** to **fr**. For **ft** to pass the variable **x** (as opposed to the value of **x**) to **fr**, it too must pass the *address* of **x**. But if the calling sequence dereferences **y**, it would pass the value of **x**, not its address.

8.2.4 Comparing Call by Value and Call by Reference

Call by value is like a one-way street. The calling function passes a value to the called function via a parameter, but the called function cannot similarly pass a value back to the caller via the parameter mechanism. Call by reference, on the other hand, is like a two-way street. The calling function passes a pointer to the called function, which can then use this pointer to both obtain from and return to the calling function a value. For example, in Figure 8.1, the function **fv** receives the value 1 but does not return anything because the assignment to the parameter **x** does not affect its corresponding argument **y**. In contrast, the function **fr** both *receives* the value 1 from **y** (via dereferencing) and *returns* 6 in **y** (again via dereferencing).

The ability to return values to the calling function is an important advantage of call by reference. Its disadvantage is the time and space penalty associated with the dereferencing operations it requires. For example, suppose **x** is a value parameter with a relative address 3. Then the statement

```
x = 20;
```

corresponds to the two assembly statements:

```
ldc 20
str 3
```

Suppose instead that **x** is a reference parameter with a relative address of 3. Then the same C++ statement requires four instructions:

```
ldc 20     ; load 20 into ac
push       ; push it
ldr 4      ; load address in x into ac
sti        ; pop 20 into location pointed to by ac (and x)
```

The same C++ statement requires four instead of two instructions because of the dereferencing operations. Note that the push instruction has the effect of decreasing the value in the **sp** register, thereby increasing the relative address of the parameter **x**. Thus, we must use the relative address 4 instead of 3 in the ldr instruction.

When a "two-way street" via a parameter is needed, a programmer cannot use call by value. If, on the other hand, only a "one-way street" is needed, a programmer can use either call by value or call by reference. In the latter case, is it always better to use call by value? Not necessarily. The correct choice depends on the size of the argument. Recall that call by value makes a copy of an argument on the stack, thereby creating its corresponding parameter. For a large argument, this copy operation requires a large amount of stack space and a large amount of time to perform the copy operation. But with call by reference, *only the address* of the argument (a single word) is created on the stack, regardless of the argument's size. The overhead associated with copying a large argument in call by value may be more (and usually is) than the dereferencing overhead associated with call by reference. Thus, in most cases, it is better to use call by reference when passing large arguments, such as arrays, even if a "two-way street" is not needed. This efficiency consideration is the reason why arrays in C++ are automatically passed using call by reference (we will examine passing arrays in Section 8.7).

8.2.5 Constants and Expressions as Arguments

When we use the call-by-value mechanism, the argument can be a constant, a variable, or an expression. If the argument is a constant or a variable, the calling sequence accesses its value and pushes it on the stack. For example, in Figure 8.9, the function call

```
fv2(100);
```

FIGURE 8.9

```
1 #include <iostream>
2 using namespace std;
3
4 int x = 1, y = 2;
5 void fv2(int z)        // uses call by value
6 {
7      cout << "z = " << z << endl;
8      z = 5;
9 }
10 void fr2(int &z)      // uses call by reference
11 {
12      cout << "z = " << z << endl;
13      z = 5;
14 }
15 void main()
16 {
17      fv2(x);              // z = 1    is displayed
18      fv2(100);            // z = 100 is displayed
19      fv2(x + y);          // z = 3    is displayed
20      fr2(x);              // z = 1    is displayed, x is assigned 5
21      fr2(100);            // z = 100 is displayed
22      fr2(x + y);          // z = 7    is displayed
23 }
```

is translated to

```
ldc 100
push
call fv2
dloc 1
```

The function call

```
fv2(x);
```

where x is a global variable is translated to

```
ld x
push
call fv2
dloc 1
```

However, if the argument is an expression, then the calling function must *compute* its value. For example, the function call

```
fv2(x + y);
```

where **x** and **y** are global variables is translated to

```
ld x     ; compute value of argument
add y
```

```
push    ; push value of argument
call fv2
dloc 1
```

The first two instructions in this calling sequence—`ld` and `add`—compute the value of the argument. This value is then passed to the called function via the stack.

In call by reference, the address of the argument is passed by the calling function. This makes sense when the argument is a single variable, but what if the argument is a constant or an expression? Let's consider the calls of the function **fr2** in Figure 8.9.

In the first call of **fr2** (line 20), the argument is **x**. Because the corresponding parameter, **z**, is a reference parameter, the calling function passes the address of **x** to **fr2**. This address is dereferenced in **fr2** wherever the parameter **z** is used. Thus, every occurrence of **z** is, in effect, replaced by its corresponding argument **x**. The statement

```
z = 5;
```

on line 8 becomes

```
x = 5;
```

However, in the second and third calls of **fr2** (lines 21 and 22), the arguments are 100 and **x + y**. Thus, the assignment statement

```
z = 5;
```

becomes

```
100 = 5;
```

for the second call, and

```
x + y = 5;
```

for the third call, neither of which makes sense.

Most compilers will flag the second and third calls of **fr2** in Figure 8.9 as syntax errors. There is, however, one way to make these calls legal: Use the keyword **const** in the declaration of the parameter **z** on line 10 like so:

```
void fr2(const int &z)
```

Here, **const** indicates that **z** cannot be given a new value (for example, it cannot appear on the left side of an assignment statement). Thus, its use within the function will never give rise to the nonsensical statements that we saw above. Of course, the assignment statement on line 13 in Figure 8.9 would then be illegal, and would have to be deleted for a compile to succeed.

Some compilers will allow the second and third calls in Figure 8.9 exactly as they appear, even without the **const** keyword in the declaration of **z**. Let's examine how these compilers treat these nonsensical calls. For the call of **fr2** with the argument 100 (line 21), the calling sequence

1. Creates a temporary local variable on the stack containing 100 by pushing 100.
2. Obtains the address of this temporary variable (using a `swap-st-swap-ld` sequence).
3. Pushes this address, thereby creating the parameter **z**.

4. Calls **fr2**.

5. Deallocates both the parameter and the temporary local variable with a single `dloc` instruction.

The assignment to **z** in **fr2** is, in effect, an assignment to the temporary variable on the stack. Here is the assembly code for this call of **fr2**:

```
ldc   100
push                 ; create temporary variable on stack
swap                 ; get address of temporary variable
st    @spsave
swap
ld    @spsave
push                 ; pass this address to fr2
call  fr2
dloc  2              ; deallocate parameter and temp variable
```

The calling sequence for the call of **fr2** with **x + y** as the argument (line 22) is almost the same. Instead of pushing 100 to create the temporary local variable, it pushes the value of **x + y**. We call the temporary local variables that the compiler creates for these calls *implicit* local variables because they are not declared at the C++ level ("implicit" means "implied").

The complete assembly language program for the C++ program in Figure 8.9 is given in Figure 8.10.

FIGURE 8.10

```
 1 fv2:      ldc   @m0      ; cout << "z = " << z << endl;
 2           sout
 3           ldr   1
 4           dout
 5           ldc   '\n'
 6           aout
 7
 8           ldc   5              ; z = 5;
 9           str   1
10
11           ret
12 ;==========================================================================
13                            ; cout << "z = " << z << endl;
14 fr2:      ldc   @m1      ; get address of @m1
15           sout           ; display "z ="
16           ldr   1        ; get z
17           ldi            ; dereference z
18           dout           ; display it
19           ldc   '\n'     ; newline
20           aout
21
```

(continued)

FIGURE 8.10 (continued)

```
22              ldc   5          ; z = 5;
23              push
24              ldr   2
25              sti
26
27              ret
28  ;==========================================================================
29  main:       ld    x          ; fv2(x);
30              push
31              call fv2
32              dloc 1
33
34              ldc   100        ; fv2(100);
35              push
36              call fv2
37              dloc 1
38
39              ld    x          ; fv2(x+y);
40              add   y
41              push
42              call fv2
43              dloc 1
44
45              ldc   x          ; fr2(x);
46              push
47              call fr2
48              dloc 1
49
50                               ; fr2(100);
51              ldc   100           ; get 100
52              push                ; create and init implicit var on stack
53              swap                ; get sp
54              st    @spsave       ; save it
55              swap                ; restore sp
56              ld    @spsave       ; get address of implicit var on tos
57              push                ; pass this address to fr2
58              call fr2
59              dloc 2              ; deallocate parameter and implicit variable
60
61                               ; fr2(x+y);
62              ld    x             ; get x
63              add   y             ; add y
```

(continued)

FIGURE 8.10 (continued)

```
64              push                 ; create and init implicit var on stack
65              swap                 ; get sp
66              st   @spsave         ; save it
67              swap                 ; restore sp
68              ld   @spsave         ; get address of implicit var on tos
69              push                 ; pass this address to fr2
70              call fr2
71              dloc 2               ; deallocate parameter and implicit variable
72
73              halt
74 x:           dw   1
75 y:           dw   2
76 @m0:         dw   "z = "
77 @m1:         dw   "z = "
78 @spsave:     dw   0
79              end  main
```

Although some compilers allow the use of arguments that are constants or expressions in call by reference, such a use does not provide any advantages for the following reason. When an argument is a constant or an expression, the side effect that call by reference can produce affects only the implicit local variable that holds the argument's value. The value in this variable cannot be accessed at the C++ level in the calling function. Thus, with such arguments, call by reference is essentially a "one-way street," just like call by value. But unlike call by value, call by reference has dereferencing overhead. Thus, when an argument is a constant or an expression that is a single value, it is always better to use call by value.

8.3   FUNCTION OVERLOADING AND NAME MANGLING

C++ allows function *overloading*—that is, the use of the same name for more than one function. For example, the program in Figure 8.11 has three functions named `fo1`.

These three functions, however, differ in their parameters: the first `fo1` function has no parameters; the second `fo1` function has one `int` parameter; and the third `fo1` function has two `int` parameters. Wherever a call to an overloaded function occurs, we can (and so can a compiler) determine which function is to be invoked by comparing the arguments in the call with the parameters in overloaded functions. For example, the first call of `fo1` on line 19 in Figure 8.11 contains one `int` argument. Thus, it must be a call of the second `fo1` function (the one with one `int` parameter). Similarly, the second call of `fo1` (the one with no arguments) must be a call of the first `fo1` function (the one with no parameters). The third call of `fo1` (the one with two `int` arguments) must be a call of the third `fo1` function (the one with two `int` parameters). As long as overloaded functions differ in the number, order, and/or type of parameters, the compiler can determine the appropriate function to be called by inspecting the argument list in the call.

FIGURE 8.11

```
 1 #include <iostream>
 2 using namespace std;
 3
 4 int x = 1;
 5 void fol()                 // fol with no parameters
 6 {
 7     x = x + 1;
 8 }
 9 void fol(int n)            // fol with one int parameter
10 {
11     x = x + n;
12 }
13 void fol(int n, int m)     // fol with two int parameters
14 {
15     x = x + n + m;
16 }
17 void main()
18 {
19     fol(10);               // calls 2nd fol function
20     cout << x << endl;
21     fol();                 // calls 1st fol function
22     cout << x << endl;
23     fol(2, 3);             // calls 3rd fol function
24     cout << x << endl;
25 }
```

A function's *signature* is its name and parameter list. Restating our earlier observations, we can say that multiple functions with the same name can be defined in a program as long as they have different signatures.

A compiler implements function overloading by renaming each function so that its name encodes its parameter list. Such renaming gives each function a unique name. For example, the first `fol` function in Figure 8.11 might be renamed "@fol$v". Between the "@" and the "$" is the function's name at the C++ level. Following the "$" is the encoding of the parameter list. We use "v" to represent a void parameter list. The second `fol` function could be renamed "@fol$i". In this name, the parameter list encoding, "i", represents a single **int** parameter. The third `fol` function could be renamed "@fol$ii". Here, "ii" represents two **int** parameters. The compiler would then generate assembly code using these new and unique names. Thus, overloaded functions at the C++ level are *not* overloaded at the assembly level.

If two functions with the same name had parameter lists that were identical with respect to number, order, and type, then this renaming scheme would result in identical labels for the two functions at the assembly level. The two identical labels would then produce an assembly-time error. This is the reason why overloaded functions *must* have parameter lists that differ in number, order, and/or type.

Here are some additional suggested encodings of parameters. For pointers, we can prefix "p" to the underlying type; for example, we can use "pi" for an **int** pointer. For reference parameters, we can prefix "r" to the underlying type; for

FIGURE 8.12

Type	Encoding
void	v
boolean	b
signed char	zc
unsigned char	uc
char	compiler dependent: zc or uc depending on how compiler treats **char** (see Section 1.9)
int	i
signed int	i
unsigned int	ui
short int	s
signed short	s
signed short int	s
unsigned short	us
unsigned short int	us
long	l
long int	l
signed long int	l
unsigned long	ul
unsigned long int	ul
float	f
double	d
long double	g
pointer	prefix p
reference	prefix r

example, we can use "ri" for an **int** reference parameter. Figure 8.12 gives a complete list of primitive C++ types and their respective encodings (these are the encodings that the Borland C++ compiler uses).

When the compiler translates a function call, it does not necessarily use the name derived from its arguments in the call. To see how this can occur, consider a program containing a single function **f** of the following form:

```
void f(int x)
{
    .
    .
    .

}
```

Its mangled name, therefore, is **@f$i**. Now consider the call

```
f(a);
```

where **a** is type **short**. The mangled name of this call, **@f$s**, does not match the mangled name of the defined function. Nevertheless, it is a legal call because its argument **a** is compatible with its corresponding parameter **x**. Thus, in this case, the compiler should use the mangled name of the defined function, and not the mangled name of the call. Whenever the compiler translates a call, it should use the mangled name of the call *only* if there is a defined function with the same mangled name. Otherwise, it should use the mangled name of a defined function that is the closest compatible match.

The return type of a function is not used in the renaming scheme for overloaded functions. Thus, like-named functions with different return types but with identical parameter lists have identical mangled names, and *cannot* be overloaded.

Figure 8.13 shows the assembly language program for the C++ program in Figure 8.11.

Because there must be exactly one **main** function in every C++ program, the name **main** is never mangled. Global variable names are also not mangled. We can see this in Figure 8.13—**main** and the global variable **x** are carried over unchanged

FIGURE 8.13

```
 1 @fol$v:    ldc  1              ; x = x + 1;
 2            add  x
 3            st   x
 4
 5            ret
 6 ;================================================
 7 @fol$i:    ld   x              ; x = x + n;
 8            addr 1
 9            st   x
10
11            ret
12 ;================================================
13 @fol$ii:   ld   x              ; x = x + n + m;
14            addr 1
15            addr 2
16            st   x
17
18            ret
19 ;================================================
20 main:      ldc  10             ; fol(10);
21            push
22            call @fol$i
23            dloc 1
24
25            ld   x              ; cout << x << endl;
26            dout
27            ldc  '\n'
28            aout
```

(continued)

FIGURE 8.13
(continued)

```
29
30              call @fol$v        ; fol();
31
32              ld    x            ; cout << x << endl;
33              dout
34              ldc   '\n'
35              aout
36
37              ldc   3            ; fol(2, 3);
38              push
39              ldc   2
40              push
41              call @fol$ii
42              dloc 2
43
44              ld    x            ; cout << x << endl;
45              dout
46              ldc   '\n'
47              aout
48
49              halt
50 x:           dw    1
51              end   main
```

from the C++ program in Figure 8.11. Not changing these names, however, can cause problems for some assemblers. For example, suppose **org** were a reserved word at the assembly level that could be used only as a directive (in which case, using **org** as a label would be illegal). If a C++ program contained a global variable named **org**, then **org** would illegally appear as a label at the assembly level.

To avoid clashes with reserved words at the assembly level, compilers typically prefix a special symbol, such as the underscore character, to all global variable names and the function name **main** at the assembly level. Thus, the global variable names **x** and **org**, and the function name **main** in a C++ program would appear as **_x**, **_org**, and **_main** at the assembly level. Because the **mas** assembly language has no reserved words, our compiler does not perform these name modifications. However, it does mangle function names, except for **main**. For simplicity's sake, we have not shown mangled function names up to now. However, from this point on, all our listings will correctly show mangled function names.

8.4   STRUCTS

· ·

In C++, a **struct** is a user-defined type that can contain both functions and data fields. However, in this book, all our structs will contain data fields only. To create a type that contains functions as well as data fields, we will use a **class**. We consider **class**es in Chapter 13.

FIGURE 8.14

```
1 struct Coordinates {
2       int x;
3       int y;
4 };
5 Coordinates gs;                // global struct
6 void tests(Coordinates *ps)
7 {
8       Coordinates ls;          // local struct
9       int li = 5;              // local int
10      ls.y = 4;
11      ps -> y = li;
12 }
13 void main()
14 {
15      tests(&gs);
16      gs.y = 3;
17 }
```

When implementing a **struct**, we must consider three cases:

- Global structs
- Structs on the stack (i.e., local or parameter structs)
- Structs accessed via a pointer

Let's examine the C++ program in Figure 8.14. This program includes all three cases.

The global **struct**, **gs**, is created with a **dw**:

```
gs:     dw     2 dup 0
```

The compiler maps the successive fields of a **struct** to successively higher locations in memory. Thus, the word at **gs** is the **x** member of the **struct**; the word at **gs** + 1 is the **y** member. We access the members of **gs** with direct instructions. For example,

```
gs.y = 3;
```

is translated to

```
ldc     3
st      gs + 1     ; store in gs.y
```

The compiler knows that the displacement of the **y** field from the beginning of the **struct** is 1, and, accordingly, generates the + 1 offset in the st instruction above. Then, at assembly time, the assembler determines the address corresponding to **gs** + 1, and places it in the st instruction.

The compiler maps successive fields of a **struct** to successively higher memory locations. It could also do the reverse (i.e., map successive fields to successively lower memory locations). Either approach will work fine; however, the compiler should be consistent, and use the same approach for all types of structs: globals, locals, and parameters. Suppose, to the contrary, it used different approaches for global and local variables. Then, to copy a local **struct** to a global

struct, or vice versa, we could not do a *block copy* (i.e., a move of a multiple-word block of memory from one location to another). We would have to copy field by field because of the different mappings.

The local variables in **tests** (**ls** and **li**) are created with

```
aloc 2    ; allocate ls
ldc 5     ; allocate and initialize li
push
```

ls is mapped to memory in the same way **gs** is—namely, the **y** field is higher in memory than the **x** field.

The members of **ls** can be accessed with relative instructions. For example,

```
ls.y = 4;
```

is translated to

```
ldc 4
str 2     ; 2 is the relative address of ls.y
```

To determine the relative address of **ls.y**, the compiler adds the relative address of the beginning of the **struct** (which is 1) with the *offset* of the **y** field from the beginning of the **struct** (which is also 1). This computation is performed by the compiler at compile time. However, it is not until run time (when the str instruction is executed) that the absolute address of **ls.y** is computed.

A **struct** is accessed via a pointer by dereferencing the pointer after it has been adjusted for the required field. For example,

```
ps -> y = li;
```

is translated to

```
ldr 0;    ; get li
push      ; push value to be assigned
ldc 1     ; get displacement of y field
addr 5    ; add ps (the relative address of ps is 5)
sti       ; store 5 into the y field
```

Here the compiler generates code to add the offset of the **y** field and the address in **ps** to get the absolute address of the **y** field. Then it generates an sti instruction to store at this address.

The complete assembly language for the C++ program in Figure 8.14 is given in Figure 8.15.

Notice on line 1 how the compiler mangles the function name **tests** to **@tests$p11Coordinates**. The "p" in the mangled name indicates that the parameter is a pointer, and "11Coordinates" is the encoding of the type **Coordinates**. The "11" here is the length of the name **"Coordinates"**. We need this length field to avoid ambiguity in the names of user-defined types. Suppose, for example, we encoded the parameter without this length field to get "pCoordinates". Then this encoding could be interpreted either as a single encoding ("pCoordinates") or as two encodings ("pCoordinate" and "s") corresponding to two parameters (a pointer to type **Coordinate**, and a **short**). With the length field 11, however, the type name is unambiguous: It must be the 11 characters that follow the length field—namely **Coordinates**.

We learned in Section 7.7 that the C++ **return** statement uses the **ac** register to return a value to the calling function. What if the value to be returned by the

FIGURE 8.15

```
1  @tests$p11Coordinates:
2            aloc  2       ; Coordinates ls
3
4            ldc   5       ; int li = 5;
5            push
6
7                          ; ls.y = 4;
8            ldc   4         ; get relative address of ls.y
9            str   2         ; store into ls.y
10
11                         ; ps -> y = li;
12           ldr   0         ; get li
13           push            ; push it
14           ldc   1         ; get offset of y field
15           addr  5         ; add ps
16           sti             ; assign li to ps -> y
17
18           dloc  3        ; deallocate locals
19           ret
20 ;=================================================
21 main:    ldc   gs      ; tests(&gs);
22           push
23           call  @tests$p11Coordinates
24           dloc  1
25
26           ldc   3        ; gs.y = 3
27           st    gs + 1
28
29           halt
20 gs:      dw    2 dup 0
31           end   main
```

return statement is too big to fit into the **ac** register? For example, suppose the **return** statement returns **s**, where **s** is a two-word **struct**. To handle this case, the *calling* function passes the address of a return area to the called function via the stack. The called function returns a **struct** by copying the **struct** to this return area. For example, consider the program in Figure 8.16.

The function **ret_struct** creates the **struct s**, initializes it, and then returns it to **main** via the **return** statement. Figure 8.17 shows the corresponding assembly code.

The calling sequence (lines 25—28) in **main** passes the address of **t** to **ret_struct** as an implicit parameter. Before **ret_struct** returns to **main**, it copies **s** word by word to this address (lines 11—18), thereby returning it to **main**.

The word-by-word copy that **ret_struct** performs would be inefficient for a large **struct**. A much better approach in this case would be to use a *block copy instruction*. A single block copy instruction can copy a multiple-word block of

FIGURE 8.16

```
1 struct S {
2     int x;
3     int y;
4 };
5 S t;
6 S ret_struct() {
7     S s;
8     s.x = 1;
9     s.y = 2;
10     return s;     // return a struct
11 }
12 void main()
13 {
15     t = ret_struct();
16 }
```

memory from one location to another. Thus, it is well-suited for copying large structs. Before we can copy a **struct** with a block copy instruction, we have to provide the instruction with three items: the source address, the destination address, and the number of words to copy. Its execution would then copy the entire **struct**. The standard instruction set on H1, unfortunately, does not have a block copy instruction. For now, we will have to copy structs word by word. However, in Chapter 12, we will add a block copy to our instruction set, at which time we can upgrade our compiler to use it when large structs have to be copied.

8.5   ARE THERE POINTERS IN JAVA?

Which statement is correct: "Java *has* pointers" or "Java *does not have* pointers"? Actually, both are correct. Java, indeed, has pointers, but they are hidden. Thus, in some sense, Java does not have pointers. We have an analogous situation with reference parameters in C++. A reference parameter is really a pointer. But its true nature is hidden at the C++ level.

Let's examine the C++ program and its parallel Java program in Figure 8.18. Both use pointers.

On line 9 in the C++ program, an **s** object is created, and its address is assigned to **p**. Then on lines 10 and 11, **p** is dereferenced to access the **x** and **y** fields of that object. The Java program proceeds in exactly the same way. On line 9, an **s** object is created, and its address is assigned to the pointer **p**. However, in Java, we do not call **p** a pointer; we call it a *reference*. Then on lines 10 and 11, **p** is dereferenced to access the fields of the object to which **p** points. The expression **p.x** in the Java program dereferences **p** in essentially the same way that **p -> x** dereferences **p** in the C++ program.

Java programmers sometimes think of a reference as the object itself. But it is not—it is a pointer to an object. This misunderstanding is a frequent source of error. For example, suppose **p** and **q** are references that point to different objects of the same type (See Figure 8.19a).

FIGURE 8.17

```
 1 @ret_struct$v:
 2              aloc 2      ; S s
 3
 4              ldc  1      ; s.x = 1;
 5              str  0
 6
 7              ldc  2      ; s.y = 2;
 8              str  1
 9
10                          ; return s;
11              ldr  1       ; get s.y
12              push         ; push s.y
13              ldr  1       ; get s.x
14              push         ; push s.x
15              ldr  5       ; get address of return area
16              sti          ; pop value of s.x into return area
17              add  @1      ; get address of next word in return area
18              sti          ; pop value of s.y into return area
19              dloc 2       ; deallocate s
20              ret
21 ;=================================================================
22 main:
23
24                          ; t = ret_struct();
25              ldc  t       ; get address of t
26              push         ; create implicit parameter
27              call @ret_struct$v
28              dloc 1       ; deallocate parameter
29
30              halt
31 t:           dw        2 dup 0
32 @1:          dw        1
33 @spsave: dw           0
34              end       main
```

If we then execute the statement

q = p;

the contents of the **p** object are *not* assigned to the **q** object, creating two identical objects. Instead, the address in **p** is assigned to **q**, causing **p** and **q** to point to the *same* object (see Figure 8.19b). If we then execute

p.x = 5;

the value of **q.x** would become 5 because **p.x** and **q.x** both reference the same field of the same object. The object to which **q** was pointing originally is still there (at least until its storage is reclaimed)—**q** is simply not pointing to it anymore.

FIGURE 8.18   a) C+ program with pointer p.

```
1 class S {
2   public:
3   int x;
4   int y;
5 };
6 void main()
7 {
8   S *p;            // declare a pointer p
9   p = new S();     // create object and assign its address to p
10   p -> x = 3;      // (*p).x = 3;
11   p -> y = 4;      // (*p).y = 4;
12 }
```

b) Java program with reference p

```
1 class S {
2   int x;
3   int y;
4 }
5
6 class Pex {
7    public static void main(String arg[]) {
8       S p;                // create reference p
9       p = new S();        // assign p an instance of S
10       p.x = 3;            // access x via p
11       p.x = 4;            // access y via p
12    }
13 }
```

Although there are pointers in Java, they are hidden, and their use is so constrained that one can reasonably say that Java does not have pointers. Their exact nature depends on the implementation of the Java Virtual Machine on which the Java program runs. They can be actual memory addresses (just like in C++), or they can be indices into a table containing memory addresses. Either way, they contain location information of objects and arrays, and therefore can be appropriately called "pointers."

In Java, pointers (i.e., references) can only be created, assigned, passed, and destroyed. Pointer arithmetic and unrestrained casting that are permitted in C++ are not allowed in Java. These restrictions make good sense from a reliability point of view (pointer bugs in C++ are both common and hard to detect), although they reduce the flexibility of the language.

8.6   POINTERS TO FUNCTIONS

The program in Figure 8.20 uses **p** as a pointer to the function **fp**. We can call **fp** using its name (line 13), but we can also call it using the pointer in **p** (line 15).

FIGURE 8.19   a)

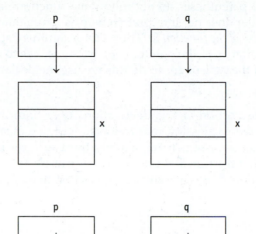

b)

FIGURE 8.20

```
 1 #include <iostream>
 2 using namespace std;
 3
 4 int y;
 5 int (*p)(int);
 6 int fp(int x)
 7 {
 8     cout << x << endl;
 9     return x;
10 }
11 void main()
12 {
13     y = fp(3);      // call fp
14     p = fp;
15     y = p(3);       // call fp via p pointer
16 }
```

The statement on line 13,

```
y = fp(3);
```

calls **fp**, passing it the value of 3. **fp** then displays and returns this value to the caller, where it is assigned to **y**. Now examine the statement of line 14:

```
p = fp;
```

Notice that parentheses do not follow the function name `fp`. For this reason, the C++ compiler does not interpret `fp` here as a function call. Instead, it interprets it as the *address of the function fp*. Thus, this assignment statement assigns the address of the function `fp` to the pointer `p`. `p`, of course, has to be declared as a pointer to a function of the type of `fp`. To do this we use the declaration

```
int (*p)(int);
```

The middle portion of this declaration, `(*p)`, indicates that `p` is a pointer. The parenthesized expression that follows, `(int)`, indicates that `p` is a pointer to a function that is passed an `int`. Finally, the `int` at the beginning of the declaration indicates that the function pointed to returns an `int`. Thus, the entire declaration reads as follows: "`p` is a pointer to a function that is passed an `int` and returns an `int`."

Once the assignment statement

```
p = fp;
```

is executed, `fp` (without parentheses) and `p` are essentially the same: They have the same value (the address of the function `fp`) and the same type. The only difference is that `p` is a variable pointer (its value can change) and `fp` is a constant pointer (its value is fixed). Because `p` and `fp` are essentially the same, we should be able to use them interchangeably (except for assigning `fp` a new value). And indeed we can. Lines 13 and 15 in Figure 8.20 have exactly the same effect: both call `fp` and pass it 3.

The code corresponding to lines 13 and 14 in Figure 8.20 is straightforward:

```
ldc   3          ; y = fp(3);
push
call @fp$i
dloc 1
st    y

ldc   fp         ; p = fp;
st    p
```

The function call on line 13 is simple because its calling sequence invokes the function *via its name*. However, the function call on line 15 requires a calling sequence that invokes the function *via the pointer in* `p`. Can we do this on H1? We can, but it requires a very awkward sequence of code. We have to "manufacture" the appropriate `call` instruction. First, we load the `ac` register with a `call` instruction that has zero in its `x` field:

```
ld    @call
```

where `@call` is defined with

```
@call:    call 0
```

Next we add the address in `p` to the `ac` register. This addition changes the address in the `call` instruction from 0 to that in `p`. Finally, we execute

```
st    * + 3      ; store call into dw below
ld    3          ; create x parameter containing 3
push
dw    0          ; execute manufactured call
dloc 1           ; remove parameter
st    y          ; store returned value in y
```

which stores the manufactured `call` instruction into the `dw` that follows the `push` instruction (recall that *** + 3** is the current address plus 3). The `ld` and `push` instructions create the parameter **x**. Finally, the **dw** (now a `call` instruction) calls the function and, on return, the `dloc` instruction removes the parameter.

This code that invokes a function via a pointer is, to say the least, an awkward sequence that reflects a shortcoming in H1's design. We should be able to call a function given its address with a single instruction. In Chapter 12, we will introduce a modification to H1 that fixes this problem.

8.7　ARRAYS

An array is a multiple-slot variable in which each slot has the same type. Each slot of an array has an *index*, a number that identifies that slot.

The process of determining the address of an array slot given its index is called *indexing*. Indexing can occur at a variety of times: at compile time, at assembly time, or at run time.

It is more efficient to pass arrays using call by reference than call by value. Call by reference passes only the address of the array (by creating a slot on the stack with this address); call by value, however, passes the entire array (by creating a copy of the array on the stack). Thus, for large arrays, call by value can take much more time and space than call by reference. It is for this reason that C++ automatically passes arrays using call by reference.

8.7.1　Defining and Accessing Arrays

Defining arrays at the assembly level is easy. For example, suppose **table** is an array defined in C++ with

```
int table[3];
```

If **table** is a global, it would be defined at the assembly level with

```
table:      dw    3 dup 0
```

If **table** is a static local, it would be defined with

```
@s0_table:      dw    3 dup 0
```

assuming **@s0** is the compiler-generated prefix for **table**. If **table** is a dynamic local, it would *not* be defined with a **dw** directive. Instead, it would be created by the execution of the instruction

```
aloc 3
```

at the beginning of the function containing **table**. This `aloc` instruction reserves three slots on the stack for **table**. Immediately after the execution of the `aloc` instruction, the **sp** register would point to the array on the stack. Thus, local instructions with relative addresses 0, 1, and 2 would access the array slots **table[0]**, **table[1]**, and **table[2]**, respectively (see Figure 8.21). Of course, the relative addresses needed to access **table** would change if any additional `aloc` or `push` instructions are executed after **table** is created.

Because there are only 8 bits in the `aloc` instruction for the constant it holds (the opcode takes up the other 8 bits), its maximum value is 11111111 binary = 255

FIGURE 8.21

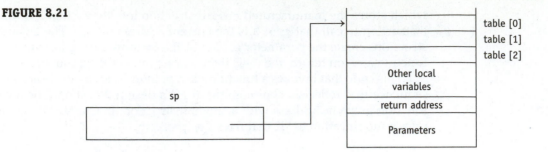

decimal. That is, a single `aloc` instruction can subtract at most 255 from the **sp** register. Thus, if the size of a dynamic local array is greater than 255 words, more than one `aloc` instruction has to be executed to create it on the stack. The `dloc` instruction has a similar limitation—a single `dloc` instruction can remove at most 255 words from the stack. The limitations of the `aloc` and `dloc` instructions is a shortcoming that we will fix in Chapter 13.

Accessing the contents of a particular slot of an array is easy if the index specified is a constant. For example, consider the assignment statement

```
table[2] = 33;
```

If **table** is global, this statement is translated to

```
ldc 33
st table + 2
```

When the assembler translates the instruction

```
st table + 2
```

it determines the address of **table** (from the symbol table), adds 2, and places the resulting address in the `st` machine instruction. Thus, the assembler determines the address of **table[2]** at *assembly time*.

If **table** is a static local, the assignment statement is translated to

```
ldc 33
st @s0_table + 2
```

assuming **@s0** is the compiler-generated prefix for **table**. Here, again, the assembler determines the address of **table[2]** at assembly time.

If **table** is a dynamic local, the assignment statement is translated to

```
ldc 33
str 2
```

assuming the **sp** register is as shown in Figure 8.21. In this case, it is the compiler at compile time that determines the address (i.e., the relative address) of **table[2]**. The compiler knows the relative address of the beginning of **table** (0 in this example). It adds the given index (2 in this example) to this relative address to get the relative address of **table[2]**, and then generates the `str` instruction with this relative address.

Now consider the statement

```
table[x] = 33;
```

where **x** is a variable. Let's consider the case when **table** is a global. Because the statement

```
table[2] = 33;
```

is translated to

```
ldc 33
st table + 2
```

we might reason analogously that

```
table[x] = 33;
```

should be translated to

```
ldc 33
st table + x
```

This `st` instruction, however, will not work (in fact, it won't even assemble). To assemble an `st` instruction with the correct address (the address of **table[x]**), the assembler would have to know at *assembly time* the value of **x** at *run time*. But this is impossible. Moreover, what if the assignment statement were executed several times, each time with a different value in **x**? Then even if the assembler could determine the run time values of **x** in advance, there would be no single correct address to put into the `st` instruction. We conclude that our assignment statement cannot be translated to a simple `ldc-st` sequence. Instead it must be translated to a sequence of instructions that determines at *run time* the address of **table[x]** using the current value in **x**, and then stores 33 at this address. The required sequence is fairly simple. First, we push 33 onto the stack:

```
ldc 33
push
```

Next, we get the address of **table[x]** into the **ac** register. To do this, we first load the address of the beginning of **table**, and then add the value in **x**:

```
ldc table
add x       ; ac now has address of table[x]
```

Finally, we pop the 33 off the stack into the location that the **ac** register is pointing to with

```
sti
```

If **table** is a static local, the code needed is exactly the same. However, if **table** is dynamic local, the code is a little more complicated. All these variations are illustrated in the C++ program in Figure 8.22.

The assembly language program corresponding to Figure 8.22 is given in Figure 8.23. Study carefully lines 31 to 40 in Figure 8.23 to see how the assignment to the dynamic local array **dla** using a variable **x** as an index is handled. Determining the beginning address of **dla** requires the awkward sequence using **@spsave** (see Section 7.9). In Chapter 12 we will modify our instruction set so we can avoid this awkward sequence.

8.7.2 Arrays as Arguments

Suppose **table** and **p** are global variables that are declared as follows:

```
int table[10];
int *p;
```

FIGURE 8.22

```
1 #include <iostream>
2 using namespace std;
3
4 int ga[3], x;                   // ga is global array
5 void arrays()
6 {
7        static int sla[3];       // sla is a static local array
8        int dla[3];              // dla is a dyn local array
9
10       cout << "enter index\n";
11       cin >> x;
12
13       ga[2] = 99;
14       ga[x] = 99;
15
16       sla[2] = 99;
17       sla[x] = 99;
18
19       dla[2] = 99;
20       dla[x] = 99;
21
22 }
23 void main ()
24 {
25   arrays();
26 }
```

FIGURE 8.23

```
1 @arrays$v:
2            aloc 3              ; int dl[3];
3
4            ldc   @m0            ; cout << "enter index\n";
5            sout
6
7            din                 ; cin >> x;
8            st    x
9
10           ldc   99            ; ga[2] = 99;
11           st    ga + 2
12
13           ldc   99            ; ga[x] = 99;
14           push
15           ldc   ga
16           add   x
```

(continued)

FIGURE 8.23
(continued)

```
17              sti
18
19              ldc   99            ; sla[2] = 99;
20              st    @s0_sla + 2
21
22              ldc   99            ; sla[x] = 99;
23              push
24              ldc   @s0_sla
25              add   x
26              sti
27
28              ldc   99            ; dla[2] = 99;
29              str   2
30
31                                  ; dla[x] = 99;
32              ldc   99              ; get 99
33              push                 ; prepare for sti
34              swap                 ; get sp
35              st    @spsave        ; save it
36              swap                 ; restore sp
37              ldc   1              ; get rel address of dla[0]
38              add   @spsave        ; get abs address of dla[0]
39              add   x              ; get abs address of dla[x]
40              sti                  ; store 99 into dla[x]
41
42              dloc 3
43              ret
44 ;===============================================================
45 main:        call @arrays$v   ; arrays();
46
47              halt
48 ga:          dw    3 dup 0     ; global array
49 @s0_table:dw    3 dup 0        ; static local array
50 x:           dw    0
51 @m0:         dw    "enter index\n"
52 @spsave:     dw    0
53              end   main
```

table is an **int** array whose first slot, **table**[0], is of type **int**. Thus, &**table[0]** (the address of **table[0]**) is an **int** pointer. Now here is a feature of C++ that is vitally important for you to understand: *the value of the name of an array without square brackets is the address of its first slot*. In other words, wherever the name of an array is specified without square brackets, it is interpreted by the compiler as the address of the first slot of the array. For example, **table** (without square brackets) is interpreted as &**table**[0]. Thus, **table** (without square brackets) is an *int pointer—*

specifically, a pointer to the first `int` slot of the `table` array. Accordingly, when the statement,

```
p = table;
```

is executed, `p` is assigned the address of the first slot of the `table` array. Once this statement is executed, `p` and `table` (without square brackets) become essentially identical—both are `int` pointers and both point to `table[0]`. Because they have the same type and value, *we should be able to use them interchangeably*. And, indeed, we can in almost all cases. For example, we can use `table` as an array:

```
table[2] = 5;
```

But we can also use `p` as if it were an array:

```
p[2] = 5;
```

We can use `p` as a pointer:

```
*(p + 2) = 5;
```

But we can also use `table` as a pointer:

```
*(table + 2) = 5;
```

The code the compiler generates for these statements does not depend on which form—array or pointer—we use. For example, for both

```
table[2] = 5;
```

and

```
*(table + 2) = 5;
```

the compiler generates the assembly code

```
ldc 5
st   table + 2
```

Similarly, for both

```
*(p + 2) = 5;
```

and

```
p[2] = 5;
```

the compiler generates the assembly code

```
ldc 5
push
ldc 2
add p
sti
```

As we have pointed out, once the statement

```
p = table;
```

is executed, `p` and `table` are essentially the same (i.e., they have the same type and value) and, therefore, can be used interchangeably. The only difference between `p` and `table` is that `p` is a variable pointer (i.e., we can change its value), and `table` (without square brackets) is a constant pointer (i.e., its value cannot be changed—`table` always points to `table[0]`). Thus, `p` and `table` are not completely interchangeable. For example, the statement

```
p = &x;        // okay to assign new value to p
```

FIGURE 8.24
```
1 int table[3];
2 void tabfun(int t[])    // t is parameter
3 {
4     t[2] = 5;
5 }
6 void main()
7 {
8     tabfun(table);      // array table is an argument
9 }
```

where **x** is an **int** variable is legal. But

```
table = &x;    // cannot assign new address to table
```

is not. We, of course, can assign new values to the slots that make up the **table** array with a statement such as

```
table[2] = 5;
```

But we cannot associate a new address, such as the address of **x**, with the identifier **table** because **table** (without square brackets) always points to **table[0]**.

Now consider the program in Figure 8.24, in which the array **table** appears as an argument in a function call on line 8.

Because the argument **table** appears on line 8 without square brackets, it is treated as the address of **table[0]**. Thus, in the call of **tabfun**, *only the address of table[0] is passed*. Although the declaration of the parameter **t** in **tabfun** has the form of an array declaration, **t** is actually just a *single* **int** pointer that receives the address passed to **tabfun** by the function call. In fact, the compiler treats the array-like declaration of the parameter **t** in

```
void tabfun(int t[])
```

exactly as if it were declared as an **int** pointer:

```
void tabfun(int *t)
```

Because **t** is really an **int** pointer, it does not make sense to specify an array size in its declaration. For example, if you were to declare **t** with

```
void tabfun(int t[3])  // specifying 3 does not make sense
```

the compiler would simply ignore the array size 3.

When **tabfun** in Figure 8.24 is called, **t** is assigned the address of the array **table** (see Figure 8.25).

t points to an array, so we can use **t** as if it were an array name, or we can use it as an ordinary **int** pointer. Thus, inside **tabfun**, we can assign 5 to the slot with index 2 with either

```
t[2] = 5;        // use t as array name
```

or

```
*(t + 2) = 5;   // use t as int pointer
```

The two assignment statements are equivalent and result in the same assembly code. This assembly code, when executed, assigns 5 to **table[2]** because **t** points to **table** when **tabfun** is called.

FIGURE 8.25

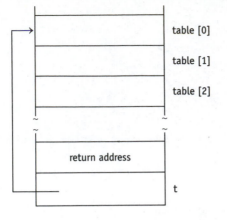

In a function call with an array argument (like line 8 in Figure 8.24), the *address* of the array—not its contents—is passed to the called function. Thus, the parameter-passing mechanism that C++ uses for arrays is call by reference. References to an array parameter (like t in Figure 8.24) are actually references to the corresponding array argument (like `table` in Figure 8.24). Call by value is *not* used for array passing for a good reason. In call by value, a copy of the argument is created on the stack (this copy becomes the parameter). Thus, for an argument that is a large array, making a copy would necessarily require a large amount of time and memory space.

Figure 8.26 shows three more forms that the `tabfun` function can take. In Figure 8.26a, t is declared and used as a pointer. In Figure 8.26b, t is declared as a pointer but used as an array. In Figure 8.26c, t is declared as an array but used as a pointer. For all of these forms, including the form in Figure 8.24, the compiler treats t as an `int` pointer and generates code accordingly (see Figure 8.27).

Notice that the compiler mangles the name of `tabfun` to `@tabfun$pi`. The parameter encoding, "pi", in this mangled name is an indication that the compiler is treating the parameter as a pointer to an `int`, even though the parameter was not explicitly declared as such.

FIGURE 8.26

a)
```
void tabfun(int *t)
{
    *(t+2) = 5;          // use t as an int pointer
}
```

b)
```
void tabfun(int *t)
{
    t[2] = 5;            // use t as an array name
}
```

c)
```
void tabfun(int t[])
{
    *(t + 2) = 5;        // use t as an int pointer
}
```

FIGURE 8.27

```
 1  @tabfun$pi:
 2                          ;t[2] = 5;
 3          ldc   5         ; get 5
 4          push            ; prepare for sti
 5          ldc   2         ; get index 2
 6          addr  2         ; get address of t[2]
 7          sti             ; store 5 in t[2]
 8
 9          ret
10  ;================================================
11
12  main:   ldc   table     ; call tabfun(table);
13          push
14          call  @tabfun$pi
15          dloc  1
16
17          halt
18  table:  dw    3 dup 0
19          end   main
```

Because of the interchangeability of a pointer to an array and the name of an array, we can treat dynamically allocated memory as an array. For example, if we allocate memory with

```
p = new int[100];    // allocate 100 int slots
```

where **p** is an **int** pointer, we can then use **p** as if it were the name of the array consisting of the allocated memory. For example, if we want to zero out each slot of the allocated memory, we can simply zero out each slot of the "**p**" array with

```
for (int i = 0; i < 100; i++)
   p[i] = 0;   // equivalent to *(p + i) = 0;
```

Alternatively, we can assign **p** to **q** and then dereference and increment **q** in a loop:

```
for (int *q = p, int *stop = &p[99]; q <= stop; q++)
   *q = 0;
```

The latter approach does not have the overhead associated with indexing an array. Thus, it probably results in more efficient code on most compilers.

8.7.3 Arrays in Java

In Java, when we define an array variable, we specify its type and the number of dimensions, but not its size. For example, we know from the declaration

```
int ja[];
```

that **ja** is one dimensional (indicated by the single set of square brackets) and of type **int**. You can probably guess why the size is missing: because **ja**, in fact, is *not* an array; rather, it is a reference (i.e., a pointer) to the array. To actually create an array, we use the `new` operator. For example, to create a 10-element array and assign its address to `ja`, we use

```
ja = new int[10];
```

Although `ja` is really a pointer, we use it as if it were an array (in precisely the same way we use `t` in Figure 8.26b). For example, to assign 99 to the element with index 5, we use

```
ja[5] = 99;
```

8.8   CONTROL STATEMENTS

When translating the various control statements in C++, we sometimes need a "jump on true" or a "jump on false." For example, suppose we wish to translate a `while` loop of the form

```
while (expression)
    s;
```

Figure 8.28 shows the structure of the corresponding assembly code. First the expression is evaluated. If it is false, a jump out of the loop occurs. Next the code for `s`, the body of the loop, appears. At the bottom of loop, we need an unconditional jump back to the code that evaluates the expression. We see that the `while` loop requires a "jump on false" and an unconditional jump. A `do-while` loop, on the other hand, requires a "jump on true."

For example, the assembly code for

```
while (x) {    // assume x is a global int
    cout << x << endl;
    x++;
}
```

where `x` is a global variable is

```
@L0: ld x
     jz @L1        ; jump on false

     ld x          ; cout << x << endl;
     dout
     ldc '\n'
     aout

     ldc 1         ; x++
     add x
     st  x

     ja @L0        ; jump always
@L1:
```

The labels `@L0` and `@L1` are compiler-generated. Whenever the compiler needs a label for the target of a jump, it generates the next available one from the sequence `@L0, @L1, . . . .`

Figure 8.28 shows the assembly forms that our dumb compiler generates for the various control statements in C++. There are, however, more efficient forms

FIGURE 8.28   C++ form   Assembly form

```
while (expression)                  Evaluate expression
    s;
                                    Jump on false to

                                    Code for s

                                    Jump always to
```

```
do {                                Code for s
    s;
} while (expression);               Evaluate expression

                                    Jump on true to
```

```
for (s1; expression; s2)            Code for s1
    s3;
                                    Evaluate expression

                                    Jump on false to

                                    Code for s3

                                    Code for s2

                                    Jump always to
```

```
if (expression)                     Evaluate expression
    s;                              Jump on false to

                                    Code for s
```

```
if (expression)                     Evaluate expression
    s1;
else                                Jump on false to
    s2;
                                    Code for s1

                                    Jump always to

                                    Code for s2
```

for the loops with a leading exit test (the `while` and `for` loops). The superior form for the `while` is

```
Jump always to
Code for s
Evaluate expression
Jump on true to
```

This form has the same size as the form in Figure 8.28; however, each iteration of the loop now requires the execution of only one jump instruction (the jump on true) instead of two. Thus, this form runs faster. Rewriting the previous `while` loop in this form, we get

```
      ja   @L2        ; jump always

@L3:  ld   x          ; cout << x << endl;
      dout
      ldc  '\n'
      aout

      ldc  1          ; x++
      add  x
      st   x
@L2:  ld   x
      jnz  @L3        ; jump on true
```

8.9 SIGNED AND UNSIGNED COMPARISONS

Because H1 was designed to be as simple as possible, it does not have a carry, sign, or overflow flag. Thus, we cannot compare two numbers on H1 as we described in Sections 1.15 and 1.16. To compare two numbers, we have to subtract one from the other and examine the result. Let's consider the example in Figure 8.29 that shows C++ code and its corresponding assembly code. In this example, **x** and **y** are signed (i.e., their type is `int`).

FIGURE 8.29

C++	Assembly Language
if (x>=y) {	ld x
	sub y
	jn @L0
.	.
.	.
.	
}	@L0:

The assembly code in Figure 8.29 evaluates the relational expression, **x >= y**, by subtracting **y** from **x**. A negative result implies **x** is less than **y**, which, in turn implies that **x >= y** is false. Accordingly, on a negative result, the `jn` instruction jumps over the body of the **if** statement. Unfortunately, there is a serious bug in this code: It does not work if overflow occurs during the subtraction. For example, suppose **x** is 7FFF (32,767 decimal) and **y** is FFFF (−1 decimal). To subtract, H1 adds the complement of **y** to **x**:

$$7FFF \quad x$$
$$\underline{+0001} \quad \text{complement of } y$$
$$8000$$

Because of overflow, the result (8000) is a negative number, and incorrectly implies that **x** is less than **y**. Thus, the `jn` instruction for this case incorrectly jumps over the body of the **if** statement.

We have an even more serious problem comparing unsigned numbers. As you learned in Section 1.16, to compare unsigned numbers, we subtract and then examine the carry/borrow flag. But H1 does not have a carry/borrow flag. Moreover, it does not makes sense to examine the result of the subtraction. The result by itself *does not tell us anything*. For example, if we subtract 1 from FFFF, we get FFFE. But if we subtract 3 from 1, we also get FFFE. In the former case the top number is the larger number; in the latter case, the bottom number is larger.

For now, we will compare signed numbers assuming (incorrectly) that overflow never occurs, and we will avoid unsigned numbers altogether. In Chapter 12, we will fix H1 so that it can correctly compare (albeit somewhat inefficiently) both signed and unsigned numbers.

8.10 MULTI-WORD ADDITION

• •

On H1, an **int** variable corresponds to one word, a **long** to two words. Because H1 can add only two one-word numbers at a time, a single addition of **long** variables necessarily requires H1 to perform two additions. For example, suppose **x**, **y**, and **z** are **long** globals. Then the statement

```
z = x + y;
```

corresponds to the assembly code

```
ld x + 1
add y + 1     ; add lower halves
st z + 1
ld x
add y         ; add upper halves
st z
```

The first `add` instruction adds the lower halves of **x** and **y**; the second `add` instruction adds the upper halves. However, there is a serious bug in this code. When adding the lower halves, a carry out of the leftmost position might occur. If it does, this carry must be included in the sum of the upper halves to get the correct result. Unfortunately, H1 has no way of remembering if a carry out occurs in one addition, and including it in the next. Although it is possible to write assembly code using the standard instruction set that correctly adds two `long` variables, the code is complex and inefficient. Thus, H1 at present is extremely ill-suited for multi-word arithmetic. We will fix this problem in Chapter 12.

8.11 BIT-LEVEL OPERATIONS

One of the features of C++ is that it permits a variety of bit-level operations. For example, in the program in Figure 8.30 we are using two bit-level operations: the bitwise AND operation and the left shift operation. This program inputs a decimal number and then displays its binary equivalent. It does this by examining each bit of the internal representation of the input number one bit at a time, from left to right. For each 1 bit it finds, it outputs a "1"; for each 0 bit it finds, it outputs a "0".

During each iteration of the `for` loop, the program determines the value of the leftmost bit in `x` by evaluating

```
x & mask
```

The single ampersand (`&`) in this expression specifies the bitwise AND operation. In this operation, corresponding pairs of bits from `x` and `mask` are ANDed together—the leftmost from `x` with the leftmost from `mask`, the next bit from `x` with the next bit from `mask`, and so on. If `x` and `mask` each have 16 bits, then 16 ANDs occur. The results of these 16 ANDs make up the 16 bits of the result. Only the leftmost bit of mask equals 1, so the result is equal to the number `x` with all its bits, except its leftmost, set to 0. Thus, this expression is true (i.e., nonzero) if and only if the leftmost

FIGURE 8.30

```
1 #include <iostream>
2 using namespace std;
3
4 void main()
5 {
6    int x;
7    int  count = 16;              // count = number bits in int
8    int mask = 0x8000;            // mask has only leftmost bit= 1
9    cout << "Enter a decimal number: ";
10   cin >> x;
11   cout << "Binary equivalent = ";
12   for (int i = 1; i <= count; i++) {
13     if (x & mask)               // bitwise AND; leftmost bit == 1?
14        cout << 1;
15     else
16        cout << 0;
17     x = x << 1;                 // left shift x one position
18   }
19   cout << endl;
20 }
```

bit of **x** is 1, in which case "1" is displayed; otherwise, "0" is displayed. Before the next iteration of the loop, **x** is shifted left one position with

```
x = x << 1;
```

Here << is not the stream insertion operator but the left shift operator. This shift makes the next bit in **x** leftmost so that the **if** statement tests it on the next iteration of the loop.

Most computers have a variety of bit-level machine instructions. Unfortunately, the standard instruction set of H1 does not (it has only the jzop and jn instructions, which test the leftmost bit in the **ac** register). Thus, on H1, bit-level operations have to be translated to awkward code sequences at the assembly level. Left shifting is easy on H1 (just add a number to itself to shift left one position). The bitwise NOT operation (i.e., flip all bits) is also easy (just subtract it from 0 and subtract 1). But we have no easy way to right shift, nor do we have an easy way to do the bitwise AND or OR operations. The bitwise AND, for example, of two 16-bit numbers would require a loop to individually AND 16 pairs of bits.

Sometimes bitwise operations can be avoided, and for a machine like H1 it would be prudent to do so. For example, in the program in Figure 8.30, we can simply have the **if** statement test if **x** is less than zero (which implies its leftmost bit is 1). The statement then becomes

```
if (x < 0)      // test leftmost bit
   cout << "1";
else
   cout << "0";
```

With this **if** statement, a C++ compiler for H1 could then translate the program to efficient assembly code.

The lack of bit-level instructions on H1 is a serious shortcoming that we will fix in Chapter 12.

8.12 RECURSION

• •

Recursion is a programming technique in which a function calls itself—that is, within a function definition, there is a call of the same function. Functions that contain recursive calls are referred to as *recursive functions*. For example, **frec** in Figure 8.31 is a recursive function. Line 10 contains a *recursive call*—that is, a call of **frec** from within **frec**.

A recursive function call acts just like a nonrecursive function call. Specifically,

- It pushes the values of the arguments onto the stack, thereby creating the parameters.
- It calls a function.
- On return, it removes the parameters from the stack.
- If the function returns a value in the **ac** register, it uses that value as specified by the statement in which the function call appears.

In a very real sense, there is nothing new for you to learn in order to understand recursion. If you understand the regular function call mechanism, then you theoretically understand recursion.

Let's step through the execution of the program in Figure 8.31. As we describe the sequence of events, we will refer to the arrows labeled with a to i in Figure 8.32.

FIGURE 8.31

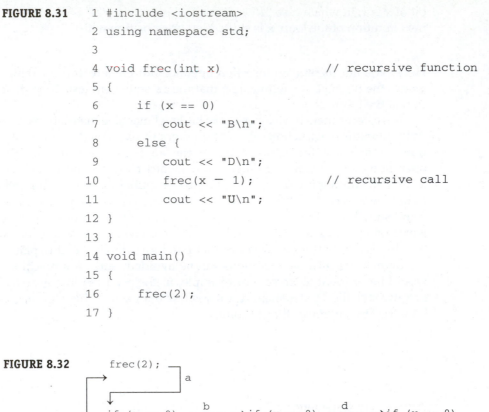

```
1 #include <iostream>
2 using namespace std;
3
4 void frec(int x)                    // recursive function
5 {
6     if (x == 0)
7         cout << "B\n";
8     else {
9         cout << "D\n";
10        frec(x - 1);                // recursive call
11        cout << "U\n";
12    }
13 }
14 void main()
15 {
16     frec(2);
17 }
```

FIGURE 8.32

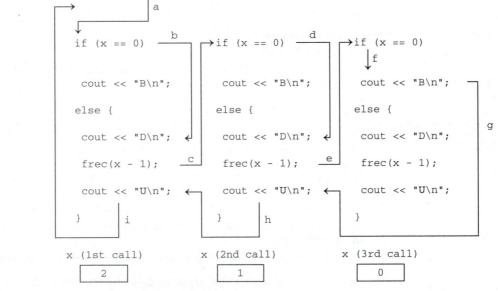

When the call of **frec** from the **main** function is executed, the calling sequence creates the parameter **x** by pushing 2 onto the stack. This **x** is the leftmost **x** box in Figure 8.32. It then transfers control to the beginning of the **frec** function (arrow a). Because **x** is 2, control jumps to the **else** part of the **if** statement (arrow b), where "D" (for "down") is displayed and **frec** is called recursively. The calling sequence here pushes the value of **x** − 1 (which is 1) onto the stack, creating another **x** (the middle **x** box in Figure 8.32). It then passes control to the beginning of the **frec** function (arrow c). For this second call of **frec**, the same sequence of events occurs: Control jumps to the **else** part (arrow d), "D" is displayed, and **frec** is called recursively (arrow e). The only difference is that the value of **x** for this call is 1 instead of 2. Thus, when the calling sequence pushes the value of **x** − 1, it pushes 0, creating a third **x** box that contains 0. On this third call, **x == 0** is true. Thus, control passes to the first part of the **if** statement (arrow f), and "B" (for "bottom") is displayed. Next, control returns to the caller (arrow g) where the third **x** is removed from the stack. "U" (for "up") is then displayed, after which control returns to the caller (arrow h). Here, the second **x** is removed and "U" is again displayed. Finally control returns to the call in **main** (arrow i) where the first **x** is removed.

In Figure 8.32, we show three copies of **frec**, one for each call. However, in reality, there is only one copy of the machine code for **frec** in memory during its execution. Thus, arrows a, c, and e all represent a transfer of control to the start of this one copy.

We can view each call of a recursive function as "going down one level." For example, in the program in Figure 8.31, the top level is the **main** function. Each call of **frec** creates a new level below the previous one. As a recursive function is executed, we go "down" on every call until we hit "bottom." Then as the various function calls complete, we return to the caller, "going up" one level on each return.

The statements that precede a recursive function call are executed "on the way down." The statements that follow a recursive function call are executed "on the way up." For the program in Figure 8.31,

```
cout << "D\n"
```

precedes the recursive call, and is, therefore, executed on the way "down."

```
cout << "U\n";
```

follows the recursive call and is executed on the way "up."

```
cout << "B\n;
```

is executed when we "hit bottom." Thus, the program produces the output

```
D
D
B
U
U
```

When the compiler translates a recursive function to assembly language, it does not treat a recursive function call in any special way. For example, the recursive call within the **frec** function

```
frec(x − 1);
```

is translated in the usual way:

```
ldr 1          ; get value of x
sub @1         ; compute value of x − 1
push           ; create parameter on stack (the next x)
call @frec$i
dloc 1         ; remove the parameter from the stack
```

FIGURE 8.33

```
 1 @frec$i: ldr  1           ; if (x == 0)
 2          jnz  @L0
 3
 4          ldc  @m0         ; cout << "b\n";
 5          sout
 6
 7          ja   @L1
 8
 9 @L0:     ldc  @m1         ; cout << "D\n";
10          sout
11
12          ldr  1           ; frec(x - 1);
13          sub  @1
14          push
15          call @frec$i
16          dloc 1
17
18          ldc  @m2         ; cout << "U\n";
19          sout
20
21 @L1:     ret
22 ;=============================================
23 main:    ldc  2           ; frec(2);
24          push
25          call @frec$i
26          dloc 1
27
28          halt
29 @m0:     dw   "B\n"
30 @m1:     dw   "D\n"
31 @m2:     dw   "U\n"
32 @1:      dw   1
33          end  main
```

The assembly form for the entire program is given in Figure 8.33.

Figure 8.34 shows the log generated by **sim** for the recursive program in Figure 8.33. In this run, we set a breakpoint at location 0 (the beginning of the **frec** function) with the **b0** command. We also turn off trace output with the **n** command. We then run the program with the **g** command, and view the stack (with the **d$** command) at each breakpoint.

At the first breakpoint (on entry into **frec** from **main**), the display of the stack shows several hexadecimal numbers:

```
FFE: 0012 0002
```

FIGURE 8.34

```
Starting session.  Enter h or ? for help.
---- [T7] F: ldc  /8 000/ b0
Machine-level breakpoint set at 0
---- [T7] F: ldc  /8 000/ n
No display mode
---- [T1] g
Machine-level breakpoint at 0
---- [T1] d$
FFE:  0012  0002 ←————————————————— first x
---- [T1] g
D
Machine-level breakpoint at 0
---- [T1] d$
FFC:  000B  0001  0012  0002 ←————————first x
---- [T1] g     ↑
D               |
                |———————————————————————second x
Machine-level breakpoint at 0000
---- [T1] d$
FFA:  000B  0000  000B  0001  0012  0002 ←————first x
---- [T1] g     ↑                ↑
B               |                |
U               |                |————————second x
U               |————— third x
Machine inst count =     23 (hex) =     35 (dec)
---- [T1] q
```

FFE is the address in the **sp** register. 0012 on top of the stack is the return address that the `call` instruction in **main** pushed. Above it is 0002, the parameter that **main** pushed. In picture form, the stack looks like the following:

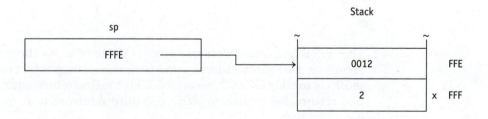

The first instruction in the **frec** function

```
ldr 1
```

is supposed to load the value of the parameter **x**. Indeed, it does.

At the second breakpoint (right after the first recursive call), the stack display shows

```
FFC: 000B 0001 0012 0002
```

which in picture form is

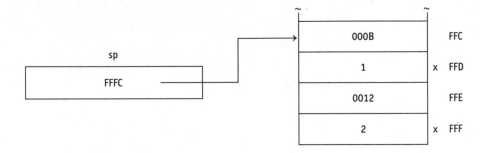

On this call of the **frec** function, the *same* first instruction

```
ldr 1
```

*now accesses the second parameter **x*** because **sp** is now pointing to the stack frame for the second call of **frec**. The return address for this call (000B) is the address of the instruction in **frec** following the recursive call. At the third breakpoint, the stack display is

```
FFA: 000B 0000 000B 0001 0012 0002
```

which in picture form is

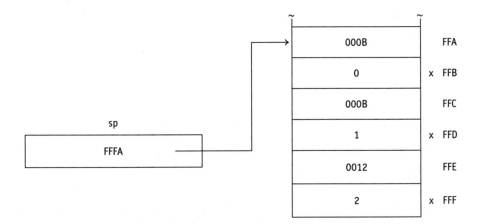

The initial `ldr` instruction *now accesses the third **x***. As the various function calls complete, the return addresses and parameters are popped off the stack. The first return is to address 000B, because 000B is the first return address popped. The second return also returns to 000B. The third return returns to address 0012 in the **main** function.

At its greatest depth, the stack contains three stack frames: one for the call of **frec** from **main**, and two more for the recursive calls of **frec** from inside **frec**. Each frame consists of the parameter **x** and a return address. As the function calls complete, the frames are popped off the stack.

Try tracing through the execution of each instruction in the program in Figure 8.34, keeping track of the stack contents as you go. You may need to do this several times before you really understand the recursion mechanism. Once you do understand it, you will find that recursion is not at all complicated. Recursion is very easy to understand once you understand it!

Recursion is a very significant feature of a programming language from an architectural point of view for the following reason: *Recursion requires a stack*. Before programming languages supported recursion (i.e., in the days when FORTRAN and COBOL were the most popular languages), computers had no architectural support for a stack because there was no need for one. However, recursion requires a stack. So as languages supporting recursion became popular, computer architects started designing computers with architectural support for stacks. H1 is reminiscent of the computers of the 1950s because of its simple structure. However, in one way it is modern: It has features that support a stack. For example, it has a stack-pointing register (`sp`) and a variety of instructions that use the stack (`push`, `pop`, `ldi`, `sti`, `aloc`, `dloc`, `call`, `ret`, `swap`, and the relative instructions).

When a function calls itself, new copies of its parameters and dynamic local variables must be created. Thus, parameters and local variables cannot be implemented with `dw` statements. `dw` statements create only a single instance of a variable. A stack, on the other hand, is perfect for a function that calls itself because of the simplicity of creating and destroying parameters and local variables on a stack.

Suppose a programming language did *not* support recursion. Then local variables and parameters could all be defined with `dw` statements (just like `static` local variables in C++). Temporary variables could also be replaced by `dw` statements. The call/return mechanism could use registers and memory defined by `dw` statements in place of the stack to hold the return address. Thus, our recursionless programming language would not need a stack.

This connection between recursion and a stack illustrates an important point on computer architecture: The design of a computer's architecture is highly dependent on the programming languages the computer has to support. There is no one architecture that is best for all languages.

PROSLEMS

· ·

8.1. Suppose there is one programming language that is used more than any other. Would it be wise to design an architecture that is optimized for this architecture? Explain.

8.2. In how many ways can a new type be created in C++? In Java?

8.3. Describe how a computer without a stack could handle a chain of function calls. Specifically, how would it save multiple return addresses?

8.4. Propose a new instruction for H1 that would simplify calling a function given its address.

8.5. What is a minimum set of bitwise instructions from which all the bitwise operations can be implemented?

8.6. What would be the best way to implement parameter passing and local variables if programming languages did not support recursion?

8.7. Show that flipping the bits in a number is accomplished by negating it and subtracting 1.

8.8. How can flipping the bits in a number be accomplished if sign-magnitude representation is used?

8.9. If you were designing a high-level language, would you include machine-level capabilities like shifting and the bitwise operations? Explain.

8.10. True or false: Static local variables' names are, in a sense, mangled at the assembly level. Explain.

8.11. In C++, arrays are passed using call by reference. However, it is possible to write a C++ program in which call by value is used instead (by writing explicit instructions that pass an array by value). Write such a C++ program.

8.12. Show what the stack looks like at its greatest depth during the execution of the program in Problem 8.68.

8.13. Give an algorithm for comparing unsigned numbers that does not make use of a carry flag.

8.14. Give an algorithm for comparing signed numbers that does not make use of an overflow flag.

8.15. Rewrite the program in Figure 8.30 so that it will work correctly regardless of the length of an `int`.

8.16. The following program is not valid C++ code but its intention is clear. Translate it to assembly language as a dumb compiler would. Assume $0 \le x \le 255$. Assemble and run on **sim**.

```
#include <iostream>
using namespace std;
int x;
void f()
{
    int a[x], b;

    a[1] = 55;
    b = 33;
}
void main()
{
    cout << "enter number\n";
    cin >> x;
    f();
}
```

8.17. Same as Problem 8.16, except assume that $x \ge 0$.

8.18. Why does C++ not allow code like that in Problem 8.16?

8.19. Why do C++ compilers rename function names, even when they are not overloaded?

8.20. Why is the function name **main** never mangled like other function names?

8.21. Compile a C++ program in which you have two functions with the same name, one with an integer pointer parameter and the other with an integer array parameter. What happens?

8.22. Will the following program compile correctly? Justify your answer.

```
int x = 10, y;
void f()
{
    x = x + 1;
}
int f()
```

```
{
    return x + 1;
}
void main()
{
    f();
    y = f();
}
```

8.23   Will the following program compile correctly? Justify your answer.

```
int x = 10, y;
void f(int n)
{
    x = x + n;
}
int f(int zebra)
{
    return x + zebra;
}
void main()
{
    f(2);
    y = f(3);
}
```

8.24.   Why is a function's return type not used in the function renaming scheme for overloaded functions?

8.25.   Does it matter in what order the fields of a **struct** are laid out in memory?

8.26.   Write, assemble, and run on **sim** an assembly language program that
  a. Prompts for and reads in two hex numbers, each containing four hex digits that represent a signed number
  b. Adds the two numbers
  c. Outputs "OVERFLOW" if signed overflow occurs; otherwise, outputs "NO OVERFLOW"

8.27.   Same as Problem 8.26, except use unsigned numbers.

8.28.   Same as Problem 8.26, except subtract instead of add.

8.29.   Write the sequence of instructions needed to test the rightmost bit in the **ac** register. If the rightmost bit is 1, your code should jump to the label **is1**; otherwise, your code should jump to the label **is0**.

8.30.   Using instructions from the standard instruction set, write the sequence of instructions needed to bitwise complement the number in the **ac** register.

8.31.   Suppose **p** is a global variable that points to a function that has no parameters. Does the following sequence correctly call the function? Explain.

```
ld p
add * + 2
st * + 1
call 0
```

8.32.   Does the evaluation of **x** < **y** on H1 depend on whether **x** and **y** are signed or unsigned? Explain.

8.33. Suppose **x** and **y** are global variables of type `int` and the following code is executed:

```
ld x
sub y
jzop dog
```

Will the jump to **dog** always occur if $x >= y$? Explain.

8.34. Write and run an assembly langauge program that displays "TRUE" or "FALSE" depending of the value of $x >= y$, where **x** and **y** are signed integers. Test your code with the following (**x**, **y**) hex pairs: (7FFF, FFFF), (8000, 0001), (7FFF, 0001), and (8000, FFFF).

8.35. Same as Problem 8.34, but assume **x** and **y** are unsigned.

8.36. When the following statements are executed, is it possible that the value assigned by the first statement might differ from the value assigned by the second? Explain.

```
v = w + x + y + z;
v = (w + x) + (y + z);
```

8.37. Ackermann's function is a famous function from computability theory that uses double recursion. It is defined as follows:

```
A(x,y) = y + 1                    if x == 0
A(x,y) = A(x - 1,1)               if x > 0 and y == 0
A(x,y) = A(x - 1, A(x,(y - 1)))   if x > 0 and y > 0
```

Write a C++ program in which you define Ackermann's function. Your program should call Ackermann's function three times to determine the values of A(0, 0), A(1, 1), and A(2, 2). Display these values, appropriately labeled. Translate your C++ program to assembly language, assemble, and run on **sim**.

8.38. Section 8.8 shows two assembly-level forms for the **while** loop. Is the first form (the less efficient one) always better than the second? Explain.

8.39. Declare a pointer variable **p** that can point to a function whose prototype is

```
int *f(int *q, int x);
```

8.40. Is it possible that a clash with a reserved word at the assembly level could occur even after globals are prefixed with the underscore character?

For the following problems, translate the given program to assembly language, assemble, and run on **sim**. Use mangled function names.

8.41.
```
#include <iostream>
using namespace std;
int x = 1, y = 2;
void f(int &x)
{
    x++;
    cout << x << endl;
}
void main()
{
    f(x + y + 5);
    cout << x << " " << y << endl;
}
```

8.42.
```
#include <iostream>
using namespace std;
int x;
void f(int &x)
{
    x = 5;
}
void main()
{
    f(x);
    cout << x << endl;
}
```

8.43.
```
#include <iostream>
using namespace std;
struct S {
    int x, y, z;
};
S b;
S f()
{
    S a;
    a.x = a.y = a.z = 5;
    return a;
}
void main()
{
    b = f();
    cout << b.x << " " << b.y << endl;
}
```

8.44.
```
#include <iostream>
using namespace std;
int x = 1, y = 2;
void f(int &x)
{
    x--;
}
void main()
{
    f(x - y);
    cout << x << " " << y << endl;
}
```

8.45.
```
#include <iostream>
using namespace std;
int y = 3;
void f(int &x)
{
    if (x) {
        cout << "hello\n";
        x = x - 1;
```

```
            f(x);
        }
    }
    void main()
    {
        f(y);
        cout << y << endl;
    }
```

8.46.
```
#include <iostream>
using namespace std;
int a = 3;
void g(int &y)
{
    y = 4;
}
void f(int &x)
{
    g(x);
}
void main()
{
    f(a);
    cout << a << endl;
}
```

8.47.
```
#include <iostream>
using namespace std;
int z = 100;
void f(int x)
{
    cout << x << endl;
}
void f(int a[])
{
    a[0] = 5;
}
void main()
{
    f(3);
    f(&z);
    cout << z << endl;
}
```

8.48.
```
#include <iostream>
using namespace std;
int n = 20, int z[] = { 100, 101, 102 };
void f(int a[])
{
    a[1] = a[1] + 5;
    cout << a[1] << endl;
}
void f(int x)
```

```
    {
        x = x + 3;
        cout << x << endl;
    }
    void main()
    {
        f(n);
        f(z);
    }
```

8.49.
```
    #include <iostream>
    using namespace std;
    int x, a[10], b[10] = { 2, 3, 4 };
    void f()
    {
        int c[10];

        a[x] = 1;
        b[x+1] = 2;
        c[x+2] = 3;
        cout << c[2] << endl;
    }
    void main()
    {
        f();
        cout << a[0] << " " << b[1] << " " << c[2] << endl;
    }
```

8.50.
```
    #include <iostream>
    using namespace std;
    int a[5];
    void f()
    {
        int b[5];
        static int c[5];
        a[0] = 1;
        b[1] = 3;
        c[3] = 22;
        c[b[a[0]]] = 12;
        cout << c[3] << endl;
    }
    void main()
    {
        f();
    }
```

8.51.
```
    #include <iostream>
    using namespace std;
    int a[10];
    void f()
    {
        int b[10];
        static int c[10];
```

```
        int *p, *q, *r *s, *t *u;

        p = a;
        q = b;
        r = c;

        *p = 10;
        *q = 11;
        *r = 12;
        s = &a[3];
        t = &b[3];
        u = &c[3];
        *s = 1;
        *t = 2;
        *u = 3;
        cout << a[0] << " " << a[3] << endl;
        cout << b[0] << " " << b[3] << endl;
        cout << c[0] << " " << c[3] << endl;
    }
    void main()
    {
        f();
    }
```

8.52.
```
#include <iostream>
using namespace std;
void f()
{
    int a[500];

    a[499] = 56;
    cout << a[499] << endl;
}
void main()
{
    f();
}
```

8.53.
```
#include <iostream>
using namespace std;
struct A {
    int x,y;
};
A s;
void f()
{
    A *p;
    p = &s;
    p -> x = 1;
    p -> y = 2;
    cout << s.x << endl;
    cout << s.y << endl;
}
```

```
void main()
{
    f();
}
```

8.54.
```
#include <iostream>
using namespace std;
int table[] = { 5, 6, 7 };
int *p;
void main()
{
    p = &table[1];
    cout << p[1] << endl;
}
```

8.55.
```
#include <iostream>
using namespace std;
int g = 20;
void f(int x)
{
    x = x + 5;
    cout << "x = " << x << endl;
}
void f(int *p)
{
    *p = 3;
}
void f(int *p, int x)
{
    *p = x;
}
void main()
{
    cout << "g = " << g << endl;
    f(g);
    cout << "g = " << g << endl;
    f(&g);
    cout << "g = " << g << endl;
    f(&g, 20);
    cout << "g = " << g << endl;
}
```

8.56.
```
#include <iostream>
using namespace std;
void f(int x, unsigned y, short z)
{
    x = 1;
    y = 2;
    z = 3;
    cout << x << " " << y << " " << z << endl;
}
void f(int x, int y, int z)
```

```
        {
            x = 4;
            y = 5;
            z = 6;
            cout << x << " " << y << " " << z << endl;
        }
        void main()
        {
            f(10, -11, 12);
            f(10, 11, 12);
            f(10, 40000, 12);
        }
```

8.57.   ```
        #include <iostream>
         using namespace std;
         int x;
         void main()
         {
            for (x = 0; x <= 10; x++)
               cout << "hello\n";
         }
        ```

8.58.   ```
        #include <iostream>
         using namespace std;
         int x = 1;
         void main()
         {
            while (++x + 2 < 20)
            cout << "hello\n";
         }
        ```

8.59.   ```
        #include <iostream>
         using namespace std;
         int x = 1;
         void main()
         {
            do {
               cout << "hello\n";
            } while (x++ != 10);
         }
        ```

8.60.   ```
        #include <iostream>
        using namespace std;
        int x;
        void main()
        {
            cout << "enter\n";
            cin >> x;
            if (x + 5)
               cout << "hello\n";
            if (x > 44)
               cout << "big\n";
            else {
               cout << "small\n");
        ```

```
            if (x < 30)
                cout << "really small\n";
            }
        }

8.61.   #include <iostream>
         using namespace std;
         int x;
         void main()
         {
            cout << "enter\n";
            cin >> x;
            if (x >= 5)
                cout << "hello\n";
            if (x <= -6)
                cout << "small\n";
            else {
                cout << "big\n");
            if (x > 30)
                cout << "really big\n";
            }
          }

8.62.   #include <iostream>
        using namespace std;
        int x, y;
        void main()
        {
            cout << "enter\n";
            cin >> x;
            cout << "enter\n";
            cin >> y;
            if (x >= y)
                cout << "hello\n";
            else
                cout << "bye\n";
            }
        }

8.63.   #include <iostream>
        using namespace std;
        int x, y;
        void main()
        {
            cout << "enter\n";
            cin >> x;
            cout << "enter\n";
            cin >> y;
            if (x >= y)
                cout << "hello\n";
                cout << "bye\n";
            }
        }
```

8.64.
```
#include <iostream>
using namespace std;
int x = 1, y = 10, z;
void main()
{
    z = x < y;
    cout << z << endl;
    if (x < y)
        cout << "good\n";
    else
        cout << "bad\n");
}
```

8.65.
```
#include <iostream>
using namespace std;
void (*p)(int, int);
void f(int x, int y)
{
    cout << x + y << endl;
}
void main()
{
    p = f;
    f(1, 2);
    p(3, 4);
}
```

8.66.
```
#include <iostream>
using namespace std;
void f()
{
    cout << 'A';
    f();
}
void main()
{
    f();
}
```

8.67.
```
#include <iostream>
using namespace std;
int mult(int x, int y)
{
    if (y == 0)
        return 0;
    return mult(x, y - 1) + x;
}
int exp(int x, int y)
{
    if (y == 0)
        return 1;
```

```
        return mult(exp(x, y - 1), x);
    }
    void main()
    {
        cout << exp(2,3) << endl;
    }
```

8.68.
```
    #include <iostream>
    using namespace std;
    void f(int x)
    {
        if (x == 0) {
            cout << "hello\n";
            return;
        }
        cout << "good\n";
        f(x - 1);
        cout << "bad\n";
        f (x - 1);
        cout << "so so\n";
    }
    void main()
    {
        f(3);
    }
```

8.69.
```
    #include <iostream>
    using namespace std;
    int s,t;
    int tough(int x, int *p)
    {
        int a,b;
        a = x;
        b = *p;
        if (a == 0) return *p;
        return tough(x - 1, &b);
    }
    void main()
    {
        s = 5;
        t = tough(3, &s);
        cout << "s = " << s << endl;
        cout << "t = " << t << endl;
    }
```

Chapter Nine

ADVANCED ASSEMBLY LANGUAGE PROGRAMMING

9.1 INTRODUCTION

In this chapter, we will learn how to implement the following at the assembly level:

- Pointers to pointers
- Relational and Boolean expressions
- Strings
- Variable-length argument lists

In Chapter 8, we learned how the compiler generates code for call by reference. In this chapter we learn how *not* to write assembly code for call by reference. In particular, we will study an approach to call by reference that has a subtle bug. This bug can appear in a variety of contexts—not just call by reference. Thus, it is important to study this bug so we know how to avoid it.

We also will investigate call by value-result, another parameter-passing mechanism. Although it is not supported by C++, we include it in our discussion to provide a better overall picture of parameter-passing mechanisms.

This chapter is a "must-read" if your principal goal is to develop expertise in assembly language and programming languages. However, it is not a prerequisite for any other chapters. Thus, if you wish to explore new areas of H1 as soon as possible, you may jump to the next chapter, or, alternatively, cover only those topics in this chapter that interest you the most.

We should mention one programming construct that we will *not* study in this chapter: the object. We will wait to discuss objects until Chapter 13 so that we can take advantage of the improvements to H1 that are described in Chapter 12.

9.2 POINTERS TO POINTERS

Before we examine pointers to pointers, let's review the basics of parameter passing. Suppose **x** is a *local* variable in the function **main**, and **f** is a function that needs to place a value in **x**. **f** cannot reference **x** by its name because **x** is local to **main**. **f** can, however, access **x** if it is provided with the *address* of **x**. **f** can then dereference this address to access **x**, either to retrieve its current value or to assign it a new value. If **f**, on the other hand, were provided with the *contents* of **x** instead of the *address* of **x**, it would *not* be able to access **x** because it would not know its location. Figure 9.1 shows a program in which **main** passes the address of **x** to the function **f**. **f** then assigns 3 to **x** by dereferencing the address it is passed

FIGURE 9.1

```
1 #include <iostream>
2 using namespace std;
3
4 void f(int *p)                      // p receives the address of x
5 {
6     *p = 3;                         // x is assigned 3
7 }
8 void main()
9 {
10    int x;
11    f(&x);                          // &x is an int *
12    cout << "x = " << x << endl;    // outputs 3
13 }
```

FIGURE 9.2

```
1 #include <iostream>
2 using namespace std;
3
4 void f(int &z)                      // z is a reference parameter
5 {
6     z = 3;                          // x is assigned 3
7 }
8 void main()
9 {
10    int x;
11    f(x);                           // x itself is passed to f
12    cout << "x = " << x << endl;    // outputs 3
13 }
```

(which is in the parameter **p**). Note that we declare **p** as an **int** pointer because its corresponding argument, &**x**, is an **int** pointer. The **cout** statement in **main** outputs

x = 3

confirming that **f** assigns 3 to **x**.

Rather than explicitly passing the address of **x** to **f**, we can use the reference parameter mechanism that we discussed in Section 8.2. Figure 9.2 shows the program in Figure 9.1 rewritten with a reference parameter. Because **z** is a reference parameter in the function **f**, its corresponding argument (the variable **x** itself—not its contents) is passed to **f**, replacing every occurrence of **z**. Thus, the statement on line 6 in **f**

z = 3;

becomes an assignment to **x**.

FIGURE 9.3

```
 1 #include <iostream>
 2 using namespace std;
 3
 4 int gv = 5;
 5 void f(int **pp)                    // pp receives address of x
 6 {
 7     *pp = &gv;                      // assigns x address of gv
 8     cout << **pp << endl;          // outputs contents of gv
 9 }
10 void main()
11 {
12     int *x;
13     f(&x);                         // &x is an int **
14     cout << *x << endl;            // outputs contents of gv
15 }
```

As we noted in Section 8.2, the reference mechanism hides the address-passing and dereferencing that take place at the assembly level. Although the call of **f** on line 11 in Figure 9.2 does not specify the address of **x**, the compiler, nonetheless, generates code to pass the address of **x**. For the assignment statement

```
z = 3;
```

on line 6 in **f**, the compiler generates code that dereferences this address (which is in the parameter **z**). The result is that at the assembly level, the program in Figure 9.2 is identical, except for name mangling, to the program in Figure 9.1. In both programs, we are allowing **f** to *change* the value of **x** by passing it the *address of x*.

Let's now examine the program in Figure 9.3, which is similar to the program in Figure 9.1. In both programs, **main** passes the address of **x** to a function **f**. **f** then stores something in **x** by dereferencing the address it is passed. The significant difference between the two programs is that in Figure 9.1, **x** is an integer and, therefore, the argument that **main** passes (the address of **x**) is a *pointer to an int*. But in Figure 9.3, **x** is an integer pointer, and, therefore, the argument that **main** passes (the address of **x**) is a *pointer to an int pointer*. Accordingly, in Figure 9.1, the parameter **p** has type **int *** to match its argument; similarly, the parameter **pp** in Figure 9.3 has the type **int **** (which means a pointer to an **int** pointer) to match its argument. Although the double asterisk in the declaration **int **pp** looks confusing at first, its meaning is clear if we break the declaration up into two parts: We interpret the second part (***pp**) as indicating "**pp** is a pointer." The first part (**int ***) indicates the type of the item to which **pp** is pointing. Thus, the declaration reads as follows: "**pp** is a pointer to an **int** pointer."

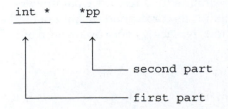

FIGURE 9.4   a)

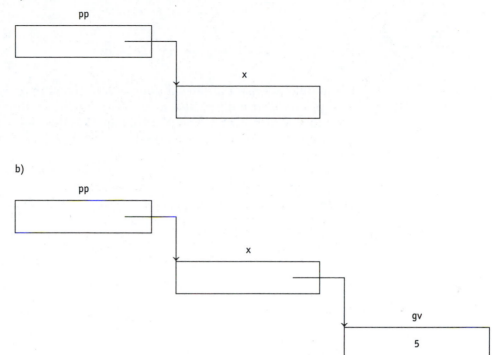

b)

When **main** calls **f**, the address of **x** is assigned to **pp**. Thus, on entry into **f**, **pp** points to **x** (see Figure 9.4a). **f** then executes

```
*pp = &gv;
```

which assigns the address of **gv** to the location **pp** is pointing to (i.e., to **x**), creating the pointer structure in Figure 9.4b. **pp** points to **x** which, in turn, points to **gv**. We call **pp** a *pointer to a pointer*.

Going back to Figure 9.1, notice that the asterisk has two distinct uses. One use is in the declaration

```
int *p
```

in which the asterisk indicates that **p** is a pointer. The other use is in the assignment statement

```
*p = 3;
```

in which the asterisk specifies a dereferencing operation. Similarly, in Figure 9.3, the double asterisk has two uses. In the declaration

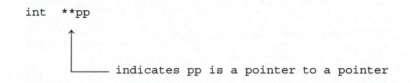

the double asterisk indicates that **pp** is a pointer to a pointer. In

```
cout  <<  **pp  <<  endl;
```

double dereference

the double asterisk indicates a double dereferencing of **pp**. To double dereference **pp**, we start with **pp** and follow its pointer (the first dereferencing operation) to **x**, which contains another pointer. We then follow this second pointer
(the second dereferencing operation) to **gv**. Thus, the **cout** statement outputs the
value in **gv**.

   If we rewrite the program in Figure 9.3 to use a reference parameter, we get the
program in Figure 9.5. The program we get does not have the *explicitly specified* single and double dereferencing operations that are in Figure 9.3, but they still occur.

   In the statement

```
z = &gv;
```

one dereferencing operation occurs here

one dereferencing operation occurs because **z** is a reference parameter. Thus, the
address of **gv** is assigned to what **z** is pointing to (which is **x**), and not to **z** itself. In
the statement

```
cout  <<  *z  <<  endl;
```

two dereferencing operations occur here

FIGURE 9.5

```
 1 #include <iostream>
 2 using namespace std;
 3
 4 int gv = 5;
 5 void f(int *&z)                    // z is a reference parameter
 6 {
 7     z = &gv;                       // x assigned address of gv
 8     cout << *z << endl;            // display *x
 9 }
10 void main()
11 {
12     int *x;
13     f(x);                          // call by reference
14     cout << *x << endl;            // display *x
15 }
```

FIGURE 9.6

```
 1 @f$rpi:                        ; *pp = &gv;
 2          ldc   gv              ; get address of gv
 3          push
 4          ldr   2               ; get pp
 5          sti                   ; pop address of gv into *pp
 6
 7                                ; cout << **pp << endl;
 8          ldr   1               ; get pp
 9          ldi                   ; load *pp
10          ldi                   ; load **p
11          dout                  ; display it
12          ldc   '\n'            ; newline
13          aout
14
15          ret
16 ;=================================================================
17 main:    aloc  1               ; int *x;
18
19                                ; f(&x);
20          swap
21          st    @spsave
22          swap                  ; restore sp
23          ld    @spsave         ; get absolute address of x
24          push                  ; create parameter
25          call  @f$rpi
26          dloc  1               ; deallocate parameter
27
28                                ; cout << *x << endl;
29          ldr   0               ; get x
30          ldi                   ; get *x
31          dout                  ; display it
32          ldc   '\n'            ; newline
33          aout
34
35          dloc  1               ; deallocate x
36          halt
37 gv:      dw    5
38 @spsave: dw
39          end   main
```

two dereferencing operations occur. The first—implicitly required because **z** is a reference parameter—gets what **z** is pointing to (the pointer in **x**). The second—explicitly specified by the asterisk—gets what **x** is pointing to.

As with the pair of programs in Figures 9.1 and 9.2, at the assembly level, the programs in Figures 9.3 and 9.5 are identical, except for name mangling. Figure 9.6

shows the assembly version corresponding to Figure 9.5. The double dereferencing operation in the `cout` statement is handled with an `ldr-ldi-ldi` sequence at the assembly level (see lines 8–10). The initial `ldr` and `ldi` (the first dereferencing operation) get the pointer in `x` into the `ac` register. Then the second `ldi` (the second dereferencing operation) loads what the `ac` register is pointing to (which is `gv`) into the `ac` register so that the `dout` instruction can output it.

The call of `f` starting on line 20 passes the address of `x`. Because `x` is a local variable, its address has to be computed using the awkward sequence involving `@spsave` (see Section 7.9).

The purpose of these programs is to illustrate pointers to pointers—they are not "real" programs that perform a useful computation. However, pointers to pointers do, in fact, appear frequently in real programs, particularly those involving linked lists. For example, suppose we want to add a new node containing the value of `x` to the beginning of a linked list pointed to by the pointer `head` (see Figure 9.7a). To do this, we can call a function `add_node` to perform the required operation. The `add_node` function has to put a new pointer in `head` (so that `head` points to the new node that `add_node` is inserting at the beginning of the linked list). Thus, in a call of `add_node`, we have to pass both

- The *address* of `head` (to allow `add_node` to change `head`)
- The value of `x`

Accordingly, a call of `add_node` should look like this:

```
add_node(&head, x);
```

The first argument in this call is the address of `head`, which is a pointer to a pointer. Assuming the type `NODE` is defined with

```
struct NODE {
  int data;
  NODE *link;
};
```

we can define `add_node` with

```
void add_node(NODE **headp, int x)
{
    NODE *q;

    q = new NODE;      // create new node
    q -> data = x;     // add data to new node
    q -> link = *headp;   // head to link of new node
    *headp = q;           // get head to point to new node
}
```

The parameter `headp` is declared as a `NODE` ** because it receives from the caller the address of `head`, which is, of course, a pointer to a `NODE` pointer.

On entry into `add_node`, `headp` points to `head` (see Figure 9.7b). Thus, the statement

```
q -> link = *headp;
```

assigns the contents of `head` to the link field of the new node (see Figure 9.7c). Then the statement

```
*headp = q;
```

FIGURE 9.7

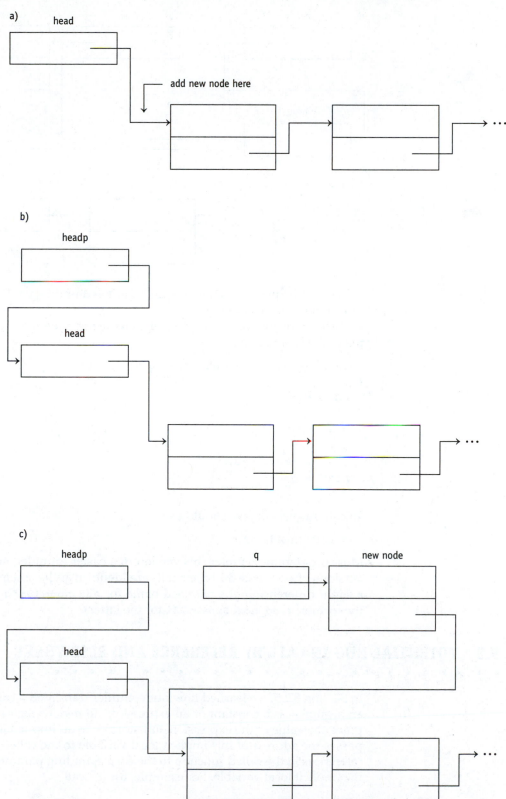

FIGURE 9.7   d)

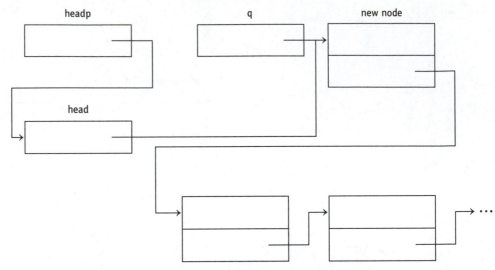

assigns **q** (the pointer to the new node) to **head** (see Figure 9.7d), completing the insertion of the new node.

Alternatively, we can define **add_node** using a reference parameter to receive the address of **head**:

```
void add_node(NODE *&head, int x)
{
  NODE * q;

  q = new NODE;
  q -> data = x;
  q -> link = head;
  head = q;
}
```

To call this version, we should use

```
add_node(head, x);
```

Most programmers prefer this version (it's easier to understand). However, both versions of **add_node** and their calls are identical at the assembly level, except for a slight difference in the mangled name for **add_node** (**@add_node$pp4NODEi** for the former; **@add_node$rp4NODEi** for the latter).

9.3   POTENTIAL BUG IN CALL BY REFERENCE AND ELSEWHERE

In Section 8.2.5, we learned how our compiler translated a call by reference when an argument is a constant or an expression. To review, the calling sequence computes the value of the expression and stores it in an implicit local variable. It then passes the address of this implicit local variable to the called function. Thus, any references in the called function to the corresponding parameter are references to the implicit local variable. For example, for the call

```
r(x + y);
```

where **x** and **y** are global variables, the calling sequence is

```
ld  x           ; get x
add y           ; compute x + y (assuming y is a global variable)
push            ; store result in implicit variable
swap            ; get address of this variable
st    @spsave
swap
ld    @spsave
push            ; push address of implicit local variable
call r
dloc 2          ; deallocate parameter and implicit variable
```

An alternative approach—one that does not require the awkward swap-st-swap sequence—is to use a temporary variable created by a **dw** statement instead of an implicit local variable. Then the calling sequence becomes

```
ld  x
add y
st    @temp
ldc   @temp
push
call r
dloc 1
```

where **@temp** is defined with

```
@temp:    dw    0
```

Our use of the **@temp** variable in this calling sequence looks straightforward enough. Unfortunately, this code has a subtle bug. The bug appears when the calling sequence is a recursive call. Then, as each recursive call uses **@temp**, it corrupts the value in **@temp** placed there by the preceding call. Consider, for example, the program in Figure 9.8.

FIGURE 9.8

```
 1 #include <iostream>
 2 using namespace std;
 3
 4 int x = 3;
 5 void bug(const int &m)
 6 {
 7     if (m != 0)
 8         bug(m - 1);
 9     cout << m << endl;
10 }
11 void main()
12 {
13     bug(x);
14 }
```

FIGURE 9.9

```
1                     ; compute value of m - 1
2            ldr    1          ; get the address in m
3            ldi               ; dereference this address
4            sub    @1         ; compute value of argument
5
6                     ; store this value in @temp
7            st     @temp
8
9                     ; pass the address of @temp
10           ldc    @temp      ; get address of @temp
11           push              ; create parameter (the next m)
12           call @bug$rxi
13           dloc   1          ; deallocate parameter
```

If we translate this program using the implicit variable approach, and run it, it displays

```
0
1
2
3
```

This is the correct output. If, however, we translate the same program using the **@temp** approach, we get something different:

```
0
0
0
3
```

Let's analyze this version to see exactly where the problem occurs.

We can view the **@temp** version of the program as having two kinds of the parameter **m**. On the first call of **bug**, **m** references its corresponding argument, the global variable **x**. This is the first kind of **m**. For all the calls of **bug** from within **bug**, the calling sequence passes the address of **@temp**. Thus, for all these calls the parameter **m** references **@temp**. This is the second kind of **m**. Now examine the code in Figure 9.9 for the calling sequence for the recursive call within **bug**. Notice it first computes the value of the argument **m** - **1** (lines 2 to 4). It then *stores this value in @temp* (line 7). On the fourth (and last) call of **bug**, the value of the argument is 0. Thus, the calling sequence *stores 0 into @temp*. But then all the **m** parameters of the second kind (i.e., those that reference **@temp**) assume the value 0. The program, therefore, displays three 0's and one 3. Because the **cout** statement follows the recursive call within **bug**, all the recursive calls finish before the **cout** for the first call is executed. Thus, the program displays 3 last.

You may think that this bug is not significant because the context in which it occurs is so unlikely. However, it can occur in other contexts that are more common. For example, consider the program in Figure 9.10. Note that in this program, we are not using call by reference. For line 8, the compiler generates code that computes the value of the initial subexpression **a** + **1**. When executed, this code leaves the value of **a** + **1** in the **ac** register. The compiler also generates code to call **f**. But, because **f** needs the **ac** register (to return a value, and

FIGURE 9.10

```
 1 #include <iostream>
 2 using namespace std;
 3
 4 int f(int a)
 5 {
 6     int y;
 7     if (a != 0) {
 8         y = (a + 1) + f(a - 1);        // bug if @temp used
 9         return y;
10     }
11     return 10;
12
13 }
14 void main()
15 {
16     cout << f(2) << endl;
17 }
```

perhaps for its internal computations), the compiler must generate code to save **ac** in a temporary location before it generates the call of **f**. If the compiler generates code that stores **ac** using the **@temp** approach instead of on the stack, we have the same bug that we had in call by reference: Each invocation, except for the first, uses (and corrupts) **@temp** before the previous invocation is finished with it. Correctly translated, the program in Figure 9.10 will display 15. What do you think it displays if it is translated with the **@temp** approach?

The program in Figure 9.10 is another example of changing relative addresses. Consider the code (the correct code that uses an implicit variable on the stack) for the assignment statement on line 8:

```
ldc 1       ; get 1
addr 2      ; add a
push        ; save value of subexpr by pushing
ldr 3       ; get a
sub @1      ; subtract 1
push        ; create parameter for f
call @f$i   ; call f
dloc 1      ; remove parameter
addr 0      ; add saved value of first subexpression
dloc 1      ; remove saved value from stack
str 0       ; store in y
```

We use the relative address 2 for **a** in the first subexpression. But we use the 3 in the second subexpression because the intervening push increases relative addresses. Alternatively, at the very beginning of the sequence, we can allocate a slot on the stack in which to save the value of the first subexpression. Then the relative address of **a** would be 3 for both cases. Our compiler does not do this, however, because it requires a "look ahead" during the scanning of the expression to determine if a such a stack slot is needed.

9.4 RELATIONAL AND BOOLEAN EXPRESSIONS

• •

When a relational expression is used in an assignment statement, the compiler must generate code that produces and assigns the expression's value. For example, in the statement,

```
z = x == y;
```

we are assigning the value of the relational expression **x == y** to **z**. For this statement, a compiler must produce code that provides a value for the relational expression, which can then be assigned to **z**. Our compiler will generate code that produces either 1 (for true) or 0 (for false). The assembly code for this statement is

```
        ld    x
        sub   y
        jnz   @L4    ; jump if relational expression is false
        ldc   1      ; load true
        ja    @L5
@L4:    ldc   0      ; load false
@L5:    st    z      ; assign value to z
```

We would have similar code for a function call in which the relational expression appeared as an argument. For example,

```
f(x == y);
```

is translated to

```
        ld x
        sub y
        jnz @L6      ; jump if relational expression is false
        ldc 1        ; load true
        ja @L7
@L6:    ldc 0        ; load false
@L7:    push
        call @f$i
        dloc 1
```

However, if we do not need to assign the value of a relational expression, then we can use a simplified sequence that does not provide a 1 or 0 value. For example, the **if** statement

```
if (x == y)
   z = 10;
```

can be translated to

```
        ld x
        sub y
        jnz   @L8  ; jump if false
        ldc   10   ; assign 10 to z
        st    z
@L8:
```

Thus, the context in which a relational expression appears affects the code that a compiler generates for it. Although our compiler has limited capabilities, it is smart enough to use context when generating code for relational expressions.

Consider the following Boolean expression:

```
a == b || c == d
```

evaluate this subexpression first

In C++, the subexpression to the left of || (the Boolean OR operator) is evaluated first. If it is true, then the whole expression is necessarily true, and the subexpression to the right of || does not have to be evaluated. Similarly, in the expression

```
a == b && c == d
```

if the left subexpression is false, then the whole expression is necessarily false. Thus, here too, the right subexpression does not have to be evaluated.

In C++, the evaluation of boolean expressions is short-circuited (i.e., terminated early) as soon as the value of the whole expression can be determined. Thus, the code for

```
if (x == y || x == z)
    z = 10;
```

is

```
        ld x     ; evaluate left subexpression
        sub y
        jz @L0   ; jump immediately to assignment stmt if true
        ld x     ; evaluate right subexpression
        sub z
        jnz @L1
@L0:    ldc  10
        st  z
@L1:
```

Notice that if the left subexpression is true, a jump immediately occurs to the code for the assignment statement, in which case the right subexpression is not evaluated.

The short-circuited evaluation of Boolean expressions saves execution time (by evaluating subexpressions only when necessary). Furthermore, it is a feature that has an important use in preventing illegal dereferencing and indexing operations. For example, in C++, dereferencing a null pointer is an illegal operation (a null pointer is not pointing anywhere so it cannot be dereferenced). In the following statement, when **p** is null, dereferencing of **p** is prevented by the short-circuited evaluation of the Boolean expression:

```
if (p != NULL && *p == 5) {
    .
    .
    .
}
```

The right subexpression in which **p** is dereferenced is evaluated only when the left expression is true—that is, only when **p** is non-null. In the following statement, we are again taking advantage of the short-circuited evaluation of Boolean expressions to prevent an illegal operation:

```
if (i >= 0 && i  < SIZE && a[i] == 5) {
   .
   .
   .
}
```

Here, the array **a** is indexed by **i** only if the value of **i** is within the bounds of the array (assume **SIZE** is the size of the array **a**).

If the evaluation of Boolean expressions were not short-circuited (as is the case for some programming languages), then we would need more complex statements to prevent illegal dereferencing and indexing. For example, the construct

```
if (p != NULL && *p == 5) {
   .
   .
   .
}
```

would have to be written with nested **if** statements:

```
if (p != NULL)
   if (*p == 5) {
      .
      .
      .
   }
```

The latter statement is not much more complicated than the former. But now consider the construct

```
while (p != NULL && *p == 5) {
   .
   .
   .
}
```

Without short-circuited evaluation, we need the following more complicated and less efficient structure:

```
more = true;
while (p != NULL && more)
   if(*p == 5) {
      .
      .
      .
   }
   else
      more = false;
```

We have seen that the manner in which Boolean expressions are evaluated—short-circuited or not—affects execution time and program complexity. However, it can also affect the computation performed by a program. For example, in the C++ expression

```
( x == y || y == f() )
```

if the left subexpression is true then the right subexpression is not evaluated, and, thus, the function **f** is not called. Because **f** could have side effects (such as changing global variables or outputting to a file), a program containing this expression might behave completely differently if its evaluation were not short-circuited.

Java, like C++, uses the short-circuited evaluation of Boolean expressions. Java, however, has a second set of Boolean operators that perform full evaluations. For example, in Java, both **b1 && b2** and **b1 & b2** (assuming **b1** and **b2** are Boolean) specify the Boolean AND operation. In the former case, the evaluation is short-circuited; in the latter, it is not. In C++, the operator **&** is only the bitwise AND operator. In Java, however, it is the Boolean AND (if its operands are Boolean) or the bitwise AND (if its operands are an integer type).

As with relational expressions, the code generated for a Boolean expressions depends on context. For example, for the statement

```
b = b1 && b2;
```

the compiler has to generate code to produce 1 (true) or 0 (false), which can then be assigned to b. However, in the statement

```
if (b1 && b2) {
.
.
.
}
```

the compiler does not have to generate code that produces the 1 and 0 values because the value of the Boolean expression is not assigned to anything.

9.5 STRINGS

As we learned in Section 8.7, the value of an array name without square brackets is the address of the first slot of that array. This means that whenever the name of an array appears without square brackets in a C++ program, the compiler generates code that uses the address of the array's first slot. For example, in the statement,

```
p = ctab;
```

where **ctab** is an array, the *address* of **ctab** is assigned to **p**. The corresponding assembly code is

```
ldc    ctab
st     p
```

assuming **ctab** and **p** are global variables. The compiler behaves similarly with string constants. Whenever a string constant appears in a program, the compiler generates code that uses the address of the first character in that string. This similarity to arrays is not unexpected because a string constant is really a constant character array. Thus, in the statement

```
p = "hello";
```

where **p** is a **char** pointer, the *address* of "hello" is assigned to **p**. Its corresponding code is

```
ldc     @m0
st      p
```

where **@m0** is defined as

```
@m0:    dw "hello"
```

Now consider the following (illegal!) statement,

```
ctab = "hello";
```

where **ctab** is a **char** array. This type of statement is often used by novice programmers who do not understand what **ctab** and "hello" really mean in C++. This statement is supposed to load the string "hello" into the array **ctab**. It, of course, does *not* do this because its right-hand side is treated as the address of the string "hello". Thus, this statement is, in fact, attempting to assign the address—not the string itself—to **ctab**. Moreover, **ctab** on the left-hand side is a *constant pointer*. **ctab** without square brackets always points to the first slot of the **ctab** array. It is illegal to assign it a new address. In contrast, the statement

```
p = "hello";
```

is legal because **p** is a pointer that is a *variable*. **ctab** without square brackets, however, is a pointer that is a *constant*. The compiler, therefore, would flag any assignment to **ctab** without square brackets as a syntax error. The correct way to load **ctab** with the string "hello" is to use the **strcpy** function:

```
strcpy(ctab, "hello");
```

In this call, we are passing **strcpy** two addresses: the address of **ctab** (because the compiler uses the address of an array wherever the array appears without square brackets) and the address of "hello" (because the compiler uses the address of a string constant wherever the string constant appears). Thus, the code for this call is

```
ldc @m1     ; get address of the string constant "hello"
push
ldc ctab    ; get address of the array ctab
push
call strcpy
dloc 2
```

where @m1 is defined as

```
@m1:    dw      "hello"
```

The name of an array without square brackets has an associated type. Because its value is the address of the first slot, its type is a pointer to that kind of slot. For example, if **ctab** is a **char** array, **ctab** without the square brackets is a **char** pointer. If, on the other hand, **ctab** is an **int** array, then **ctab** without square brackets is

FIGURE 9.11

```
1 #include <iostream>
2 using namespace std;
3
4 char *gp;
5 void mod_string(char *p)
6 {
7     *p = 'X';
8 }
9 void main()
10 {
11     mod_string("abc");
12     gp = "abc";
13     cout << gp << endl;      // would output Xbc if only one dw for "abc"
14 }
```

an **int** pointer. A string constant also has an associated type. Its value is the address of the first character, so it is a **char** pointer. Accordingly, in the statements

```
p = ctab;     // assigns p a char pointer
q = "bye";    // assigns q a char pointer
```

where **ctab** is a **char** array, both **p** and **q** should be of type **char ***.

If the same string constant appears more than once in a C++ program, the compiler should generate a separate **dw** for each occurrence. It should do this because string constants can be corrupted by functions that are passed their addresses. For example, consider the program in Figure 9.11. The function **mod_string** is passed the address of the string constant "abc". **mod_string** then corrupts this string constant by overlaying 'a' with 'x'. Thus, if only one **dw** were used for both occurrences of "abc", **gp** would be assigned the address of "Xbc" instead of "abc".

9.6 CALL BY VALUE-RESULT

• •

Call by value-result is a parameter-passing mechanism that combines the advantages of call by value and call by reference. In particular, it has the efficiency of call by value (it does not have the dereferencing overhead associated with call by reference) but it still permits side effects.

C++ does not support call by value-result. Let's see how we can add support for call by value-result to C++. We will use the symbol $ to designate a value-result parameter in the same way C++ uses & to designate a reference parameter. For example, consider the program in Figure 9.12. The definition of the function **ref** starts with

```
void ref(int &x)
```

The & before the parameter name **x** signals that **x** is a reference parameter in this function. Similarly, the $ before the parameter **x** at the beginning of the **vr** function

```
void vr(int $x)
```

FIGURE 9.12

```
1 #include <iostream>
2 using namespace std;
3
4 int y;
5 void ref(int &x)               // & signals the reference mechanism
6 {
7     x = x + 5;
8 }
9
10 void vr(int $x)                // $ signals the value-result mechanism
11 {
12    x = x + 5;
13 }
14
15 void v(int x)                  // just x signals the value mechanism
16 {
17    x = x + 5;
18 }
19
20 void main()
21 {
22    y = 1;
23    ref(y);
24    cout << "y = " << y << endl;
25    y = 1;
26    vr(y);
27    cout << "y = " << y << endl;
28    y = 1;
29    v(y);
30    cout << "y = " << y << endl;
31 }
```

signals that **x** is a value-result parameter in the **vr** function. The definition of the **v** function starts with

```
void v(int x)
```

The absence of & and $ indicates that **x** is a value parameter in this function.

When the function **vr** is executed, it causes a side effect: **y** has its value increased by 5 as a result of the assignment statement

```
x = x + 5;
```

within the **vr** function. The effect of using the value-result mechanism is like that produced by the reference mechanism. Both **ref** (which uses the reference mechanism) and **vr** (which uses the value-result mechanism) increase the value in **y** by 5.

The **v** function, of course, has no side effect because it uses the value mechanism. Thus, the program in Figure 9.12 outputs

```
y = 6
y = 6
y = 1
```

The value of **y** is changed by both **ref** and **vr**, but not by **v**.

The beauty of call by value-result is that it does not use any dereferencing operations. In fact, the assembly language form of the **vr** function (which uses the value-result mechanism) in Figure 9.12 is the same as the assembly language form of the **v** function (which uses the value mechanism). Both are translated to

```
ldc  5     ; get 5
addr 1     ; add x
str  1     ; store result back into x
ret
```

The difference between the value and value-result mechanisms occurs in the calling sequence. In the calling sequence for call by value, the parameters are removed from the stack immediately on return to the calling function. For example, the calling sequence for

```
v(y);
```

is

```
ld    y
push       ; create parameter x
call @v$i
dloc 1     ; remove parameter x
```

In the sequence for call by value-result, something different occurs on return: The value-result parameters on top of the stack are both popped from the stack and assigned to their corresponding arguments. These assignments cause the desired side effects. For example, the calling sequence for

```
vr(y);
```

is

```
ld    y
push        ; create parameter x
call @vr$mi
pop         ; remove parameter x by popping into ac reg
st    y     ; store value of parameter x in argument y
```

The `pop-st` sequence following the call produces the desired side effect: The final value of the parameter **x** is assigned to the argument **y**. At the same time, it removes the parameter **x** from the stack. Notice that in the mangled name of **vr**, we have encoded its integer parameter with "mi". The prefix "m" indicates that the parameter is a value-result parameter; the "i" indicates that the parameter is of type **int**. We similarly encode the parameter for the **ref** function, except we use "r" (for "reference") instead of "m". The complete assembly form for the program in Figure 9.12 is given in Figure 9.13.

Let's compare the **vr** and **ref** functions in Figure 9.12. Both produce the same side effect, except that in the **ref** function

FIGURE 9.13

```
 1 @ref$ri:   ldr    1              ; x = x + 5;
 2            ldi
 3            add    @5
 4            push
 5            ldr    2
 6            sti
 7
 8            ret
 9 ;================================================================
10 @vr$mi:    ldc    5              ; x = x + 5;
11            addr   1
12            str    1
13
14            ret
15 ;================================================================
16 @v$i:      ldc    5              ; x = x + 5;
17            addr   1
18            str    1
19
20            ret
21 ;================================================================
22 cout:      ldc    @m0
23            sout
24            ld     y
25            dout
26            ldc    '\n'
27            aout
28            ret
29 ;================================================================
30 main:      ldc    1              ; y = 1;
31            st     y
32
33            ldc    y              ; ref(y);
34            push
35            call @ref$ri
36            dloc 1
37
38            call cout             ; cout << "y = " << y << endl;
39
40            ldc    1              ; y = 1;
41            st     y
42
43            ld     y              ; vr(y);
```

(continued)

FIGURE 9.13
(continued)

```
44                  push
45                  call @vr$mi
46                  pop
47                  st    y
48
49                  call cout         ; cout << "y = " << y << endl;
50
51                  ldc   1           ; y = 1
52                  st    y
53
54                  ld    y           ; v(y);
55                  push
56                  call @v$i
57                  dloc 1
58
59                  call cout         ; cout << "y = " << y << endl;
60
61                  halt
62  y:              dw    0
63  @5:             dw    5
64  @m0:            dw    "y = "
65                  end   main
```

- The side effect occurs inside the called function and not in the calling function.
- The side effect occurs immediately (i.e., as soon as the assignment to **x** in the function occurs).
- The side effect involves two dereferencing operations (one for each occurrence of **x** in the assignment statement).
- Three more instructions are executed than within the **vr** function (because of the overload of dereferencing).

The advantage of call by value-result over call by reference becomes significant if the parameters appear inside a loop. For example, suppose the bodies of the **ref** and **vr** functions were changed to

```
for (int i = 0; i < 30000; i++)
    x = x + 5;
```

Each execution of the assignment statement in **ref** requires the execution of three more instructions (for dereferencing) than in the **vr** function. Because the assignment statement is executed 30,000 times, $3 \times 30,000 = 90,000$ additional instructions are executed. However, the calling sequence for **ref** has one fewer instruction than that for **vr**. Thus, the call and execution of **ref** requires $90,000 - 1 = 89,999$ more instructions than **vr**.

Given the efficiency of call by value-result over call by reference, you may wonder why the designers of C and C++ did not include support for call by value-result. Is the lack of support for call by value-result a design flaw of C

FIGURE 9.14

```
1   void simvr(int *p)
2   {
3       int x;
4       x = *p;
5
6       // body of function-use x instead of *p
7
8       *p = x;
9   }
```

and C++? Not at all. The efficiency of call by value-result can be achieved easily in C and C++. Figure 9.14 shows how it is done. At the beginning of a function, the value of the argument is assigned to a local variable (this requires one dereferencing operation). The local variable—not the parameter—is then used within the body of the function, thereby avoiding dereferencing operations. Just before the end of the function, the value in the local variable is assigned to the argument (this requires one dereferencing operation) to produce the side effect. With this technique, we never need more than two dereferencing operations per parameter.

Although call by value-result and call by reference both produce side effects, the two mechanisms are not completely interchangeable. The C++ program in Figure 9.15 illustrates how the two mechanisms can produce different results.

FIGURE 9.15

```
1  #include <iostream>
2  using namespace std;
3
4  int y;
5  void putoff(int $x)
6  {
7      x = x + 5;                      // side effect is delayed
8      cout << "y = " << y << endl;
9  }
10 void rightnow(int &x)
11 {
12     x = x + 5;                      // side effect is immediate
13     cout << "y =" << y << endl;
14 }
15 void main()
16 {
17     y = 1;
18     putoff(y);
19     y = 1;
20     rightnow(y);
21 }
```

FIGURE 9.16

```
 1 #include <iostream>
 2 using namespace std;
 3
 4 int x, y;
 5 int add_one(int $z)
 6 {
 7     return z + 1;
 8 }
 9 void main()
10 {
11     x = 1;
12     y = add_one(x);     // value returned is assigned to y
13     cout << "y = " << y << endl;
14 }
```

In the **putoff** function (which uses call by value-result), the side effect of the assignment statement is delayed. In particular, the value of the argument **y** does not change until the function returns to its caller. Thus, the **cout** statement in the **putoff** functions outputs 1, the initial value of **y**. In the **rightnow** function, on the other hand, the side effect is immediate. Thus, the **cout** statement outputs 6, the new value in **y**. The two mechanisms both produce side effects but at different times and, therefore, produce different results.

A problem occurs when a function that returns a value with the **return** statement also has value-result parameters. Consider the program in Figure 9.16. Because **z** is a value-result parameter, the calling sequence for **add_one** must pop the stack to obtain the final value of the parameter **z**, and then store this value in its corresponding argument **x**. Here is the necessary code:

```
ld x
push
call @add_one$mi
pop             ; get value of z--clobbers ac register
st   x          ; store value of z in x
```

But, by doing so, it destroys the value in the **ac register** that the **add_one** function is returning. We, of course, need this return value (it has to be assigned to **y**). The fix for this problem in this case is simple: On return from **add_one**, we first use the return value in the **ac** register. We can then pop the stack to obtain the value of **z**:

```
ld   x
push
call @add_one$mi
st   y          ; use value returned in ac register
pop             ; get value of z
st   x          ; store value of z in x
```

Unfortunately, this simple fix—using the return value first—does not always work. Suppose, for example, the call of **add_one** appears as an argument in another function call:

```
f(add_one(x), 3);
```

Here, "using the return value" means the calling sequence pushes it onto the stack after it pushes 3 (remember, arguments are pushed right to left). Before performing these push operations, the calling sequence of **f** must first finish the call of **add_one**. In particular, it must remove **add_one**'s parameter from the stack. Thus, in this case, it cannot first use the return value. But neither can it finish the call of **add_one**, because it would then destroy the return value. For this example, one approach that works is to

1. Save the return value in an implicit local variable when **add_one** returns.
2. Finish the call of **add_one** (i.e., pop the parameter and store in **x**).
3. Use the saved return value.

Here is the required code:

```
                    ; start call of f
ldc   3             ; push arg 3 for call of f
push

                    ; start call of add_one
aloc 1              ; create an implicit local variable
ld x
push
call @add_one$mi
str 1               ; save return value in implicit local variable
pop                 ; finish call of add_one
st    x
                    ; now continue the call of f
                    ; we don't have to push returned value
                    ; because it is already on the stack
call f
dloc 2
```

This complication with call by value-result is a good reason why C++ does not support it.

Let's assume that our compiler always uses an implicit local variable to save the return value when a function has a value-result parameter. Then our compiler would translate the calling sequence for the **add_one** function in Figure 9.16 to

```
aloc 1
ld    x
push
call @add_one$mi
str 1               ; save return value
pop                 ; now can pop parameter into ac
st    x             ; store value of parameter in x
pop                 ; now use saved return value
st    y
```

9.7 VARIABLE-LENGTH ARGUMENT LISTS
• •

As you learned in Section 7.6, C++ compilers process the arguments in a function call in right-to-left order. However, it would be easier to process the arguments in a left-to-right order, because that is the order in which the compiler

FIGURE 9.17

```
1 #include <iostream>
2 using namespace std;
3
4 int add(int count, ...)        // ... means variable number of parameters
5 {
6     int i, sum = 0;
7     int *p;
8
9     p = &count + 1;            // p now points to first param to be added
10
11    for (i = 1; i <= count; i++)
12    sum = sum + *p++;
13
14    return sum;
15 }
16 //   ;================================================================
17 void main()
18 {
19    // arguments are pushed in right-to-left order
20    cout << add(3, 4, 5, 6) << endl;       // outputs 15
21    cout << add(2, -10, 20) << endl;       // outputs 10
22    cout << add(1, 7) << endl;             // outputs 7
23 }
```

scans the arguments. With the left-to-right order, the compiler would simply generate the code for each argument as each one is scanned. The right-to-left order, however, requires the compiler to remember all the arguments as it scans them left-to-right. Then, when it finally reaches the last argument, it generates the code for each argument in right-to-left order using the list of arguments it has remembered.

If the left-to-right order is easier, why do it in right-to-left order? The reason has to do with function calls that can have a variable number of arguments. Let's examine the C++ program in Figure 9.17, in which the function **add** takes a variable number of arguments. **main** has three calls to **add**, each with a different number of arguments. For all the calls, the first argument indicates how many arguments follow it. Accordingly, in the first call to **add**, the first argument is 3, indicating three more arguments follow. For this call, **add** sums the values of the three arguments that follow the first, and returns their sum. In the definition of **add**, an ellipsis (...) is used in the parameter list to indicate to the compiler that the function can be called with a variable number of arguments.

During the first call of **add**, **main** pushes the values of the arguments—3, 4, 5, and 6—onto the stack in right-to-left order. It then calls **add**, pushing a return address onto the stack. **add** then allocates **i**, **sum**, and **p** on the stack. Figure 9.18a shows the stack at this point. Next, **add** executes the statement on line 9

```
p = &count + 1;
```

FIGURE 9.18   a)

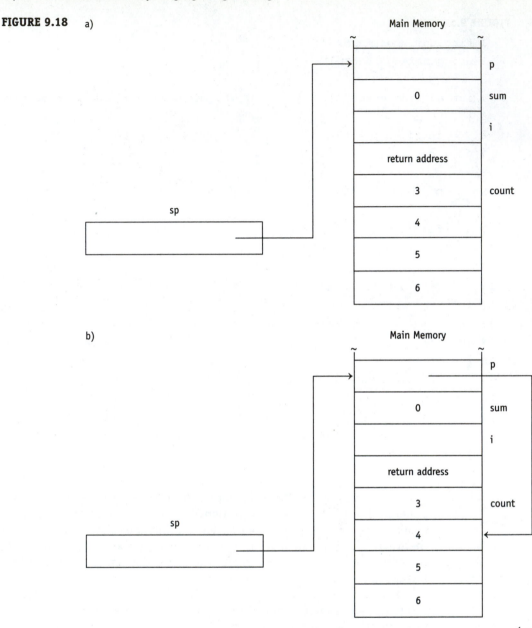

(continued)

which assigns to **p** the address of the word in the stack right above **count** (see Figure 9.18b). Thus, **p** points to the first parameter to be added. The statement in the body of the **for** loop (line 12) then repeatedly adds to **sum** the integer pointed to by **p**, and then post-increments **p**. Thus, **p** moves up in memory on each iteration of the loop, pointing to the parameters to be added, one after the other.

The compiler is able to translate the statements in Figure 9.17 that directly reference **count** (lines 9 and 11) because the compiler knows where **count** will be located on the stack (it will be right above the return address) during run time. Because **count** is pushed last in the calling sequence, its location does *not* depend on the number of parameters.

Now suppose that the C++ compiler processed the arguments in the function calls in Figure 9.17 left to right instead of right to left. Then the location of

FIGURE 9.18
(continued)

c)

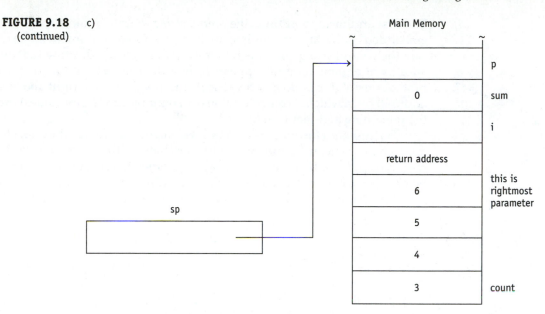

the parameter **count** would *depend on the number of parameters*. For example, in the first call of **add**, four parameters are pushed, placing **count** four words above the return address (see Figure 9.18c). If the call had 10 arguments instead, then **count** would be 10 words above the return address. This situation presents a predicament for the compiler: To directly reference **count** requires knowledge of the number of parameters, but the only way to determine the number of parameters is to first access **count**. The result is that the compiler will not be able to generate code for lines 9 and 11 in Figure 9.17 because they reference **count**.

The parameter that is pushed *last* in a function calling sequence appears on the stack right above the return address. Because its location does not depend on the number of arguments, the compiler can generate code that can reference it. For right-to-left processing of arguments (as in C++), the last parameter pushed is the leftmost. Thus, the count in a call with a variable number of arguments must be the leftmost parameter. But for left-to-right processing, the last parameter pushed is the rightmost. Thus, the count must be *rightmost*.

We are now finally in a position to understand why compilers for C++ and its predecessor, C, process arguments right to left. The designers of C felt that in function calls with a variable number of arguments, the count should appear first in the argument list. This decision meant, as we observed earlier, that arguments have to be processed in right-to-left order so that the count is pushed last. Had the designers of C felt that the count should appear last, then argument processing would have necessarily been left to right.

Some functions in C and C++ that take a variable number of arguments have the argument count specified indirectly by the first argument. For example, consider the following function call:

```
printf ("x  =  %d    y  =  %d\n",  x,  y);
```

conversion codes

The first argument to **printf**, the *control string*, must contain a *conversion code* (an embedded code that starts with **%**) for every additional argument in the call. In this call, the control string contains two conversion codes, indicating that exactly two additional arguments must appear in the call. The **printf** function accesses its first argument (it can do this because its location is always right above the return address) from which it can determine (by counting conversion codes) the count of the remaining arguments in the call.

C++ provides the macros **va_list**, **va_start**, **va_arg**, and **va_end** to simplify accessing parameters in functions with variable-length argument lists. A *macro* is a mechanism that substitutes one string for another. In C++, this substitution occurs before compile time. Thus, its effect is to modify the source input to the compiler. A *macro call* initiates this string substitution mechanism. For example, in the macro call

```
va_list (p);
```
              ↑
              └───── argument of macro call

va_list is the name of the macro; **p** is the argument of the macro call. In a C++ program, this macro call is replaced with the string

```
void *p;
```
        ↑
        └───── argument of macro call inserted here

Arguments in a macro call (the items within parentheses) are used in the string that replaces the macro call. In this example, the argument **p** is inserted immediately following void * in the output string. If we were to use a different argument, we would get a different output string. For example, the macro call

```
va_list (hello);
```

is replaced with the string

```
void *hello;
```

The **va_start** macro call

```
va_start (p, count);
```

is replaced with the string

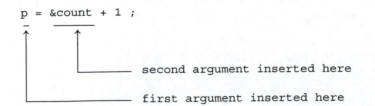

```
p = &count + 1 ;
```
    ↑   ↑
    │   └───────── second argument inserted here
    │
    └───────────────── first argument inserted here

For this macro, we use two arguments, both of which appear in the output string. The **va_arg** macro call

```
va_arg(p, int);
```

is replaced with the string

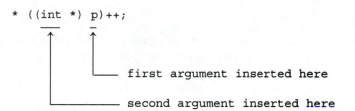

The program in Figure 9.17, rewritten using the **va** macros, is given in Figure 9.19. The comments show the substitutions for the various **va** macros. Keep in mind that these substitutions occur before the program is compiled. After the macro substitutions, the resulting program is almost identical to the program in Figure 9.17. The only difference is that **p** is a void pointer, and, therefore, has to be cast to an **int** pointer before it is dereferenced. Of course, if the arguments were of some other type, **p** would have to be cast to that type. That is why the **va_arg**

FIGURE 9.19

```
1 #include <cstdarg>
2 #include <iostream>
3 using namespace std;
4
5 int add(int count, ...)
6 {
7     int i, sum = 0;
8     va_list(p);                    // void *p;
9
10    va_start(p, count);            // p = &count + 1;
11
12    for (i = 1; i <= count; i++)
13        sum = sum + va_arg(p, int);    // sum = sum + *((int*)p)++;
14
15    va_end(p);                     // does nothing
16    return sum;
17 }
18 void main()
19 {
20    cout << add(3, 4, 5, 6) << endl;    // outputs 15
21    cout << add(2, -10, 20) << endl;    // outputs 10
22    cout << add(1, 7) << endl;          // outputs 7
23 }
```

macro requires the type of the parameter. Given this type, **va_arg** replaces itself with a string with the appropriate cast. For example, to access parameters of type **long**, we should use

```
va_arg(p, long)
```

which would be replaced with

```
*((long*)p)++
```

Because of the **long** cast, this expression would access the **long** item pointed to by **p**, and then increment **p** by the length of the **long** item.

    va_end is for cleanup. However, because no cleanup is needed in this program, **va_end** is replaced with the null string.

    To use the **va** macros, you must include the header file **cstdarg** in your program. This header file contains the definitions of the **va** macros.

PROGRAMS

PROBLEMS

9.1. In call by value-result, the called function behaves exactly as it would in call by value. Another implementation of call by value-result is to have the calling sequence behave exactly as it would in call by reference. Then the called function must take the appropriate steps to access the parameter's value, use it locally, and, on exit, cause a side effect. Translate the program in Figure 9.12 using this alternative approach to call by value-result. Is this new approach in any way better than the standard approach?

9.2. Give an arithmetic expression that requires five distinct implicit local variables during its evaluation.

9.3. What happens when the program in Problem 9.21 is executed? Show what the stack looks like as execution progresses.

9.4. Why is the **va_end** macro needed if it does nothing?

9.5. Write a C++ function named **last** that is passed a variable number of arguments, all of type **int**. Your function should display the value of the last, and only the last, argument. Write your function so that it is as efficient as possible. The first argument is always the count of the number of arguments that follow the first. Incorporate your function in a C++ program that calls **last** as follows:

```
last(3, -3, 5, 8);          // displays 8
last(1, 4);                 // displays 4
last(5, 1, 2, 3, 4, 50);    // displays 50
last (0);                   // displays nothing
```

Translate your C++ program to assembly language, assemble, link, and run on **sim**.

9.6. Multiple occurrences of the same string constant in a C++ program should not be represented by a single **dw** at the assembly level. What about other types of constants?

9.7. Write your own version of the **strcpy** function in C++.

9.8. Can a compiler easily determine if a function is recursive? Why might this be useful?

9.9. Translate the following statement to assembly language. Save intermediate values on the stack. Assume all variables are global.

```
x = a + (b + c) + ((d + e) + (f + g));
```

Redo this statement, but use "temps" defined with **dw** directives to hold intermediate values. Which way is faster? Which way uses less memory? Is there a potential bug in the "temp" approach?

9.10. Is there an upper limit to the number of intermediate values needed during the evaluation of an arithmetic expression? Hint: See Problem 9.9.

9.11. What is displayed when the program in Figure 9.10 is executed, assuming it has been translated to assembly language using the **@temp** approach.

9.12. How should call by result be implemented? Call by result is like call by value-result except that initial values are not passed to the called function. Give an example of a simple C++-like function that uses call by result and its corresponding assembly code.

For the following problems, translate the given program to assembly language. Use mangled function names. Assemble, link with start-up code, and run on **sim**.

9.13.
```
#include <iostream>
using namespace std;
int x, y;
int f()
{
  cout << "hello\n"
  return 1;
}
void main()
{
  while (x < 5 && y < 12 && f()) {
    x = x + 1;
    y = y + 2;
    cout << "bye\n";
  }
}
```

9.14.
```
#include <iostream>
using namespace std;
int x = 1, y = 10, z;
void main()

{
  z = x < y;
  cout << z << endl;
  if (x < y)
    cout < "good\n";
  else
    cout << "bad\n");
}
```

9.15.
```
#include <iostream>
using namespace std;
int x = 1, *p, **q;
void main()
{
  p = &x;
```

```
            q = &p;
            cout << *p << " " << **q << endl;
        }
```

9.16.
```
        #include <iostream>
        using namespace std;
        int *q, x;
        void f(int **p)
        {
            *p = &x;
        }
        void main()
        {
            f(&q);
            *q = 55;
            cout << x << endl;
        }
```

9.17.
```
        #include <iostream>
        using namespace std;
        struct A {
            int x,y;
        };
        A s;
        A *p;
        void f(A **p)
        {
            (*p) -> x = 1;
            (*p) -> y = 2;
            cout << s.x << endl;
            cout << s.y << endl;
        }
        void main()
        {
            p = &s;
            f(&p);
            cout << s.x << endl;
            cout << s.y << endl;
        }
```

9.18.
```
        #include <iostream>
        using namespace std;
        int y = 2;
        void f(int $x)
        {
            x--;
        }
        void main()
        {
            f(xy);
            cout << y << endl;
        }
```

9.19.
```
#include <iostream>
using namespace std;
int x;
void f(int $x)
{
    x = 5;
}
void main()
{
    f(x);
    cout << x << endl;
}
```

9.20.
```
#include <iostream>
using namespace std;
int s, a = 1, b = 2, c = 3;
int f(int x, int $y, int &z)
{
    x++:
    y++;
    z++;
    return x + y + z;
}
void main()
{
    s = f(a, b, c);
    cout << s << endl;
    cout << a << endl;
    cout << b << endl;
    cout << c << endl;
}
```

9.21.
```
#include <iostream>
using namespace std;
int x, y;
void f(int &m) {
    cout << "enter\n";
    cin >> x >> y;
    m = x;
    if (x != y) {
        f(x + y);
    }
    cout << m << endl;
}
void main() {
    f(3);
}
```

9.22.
```
#include <iostream>
using namespace std;
int x = 5;
void f(const int &m)
```

```
{
  if (m != 0)
     f(m - 1);
  cout << m << endl;
}
void main()
{
  f(x);
}
```

Chapter Ten

LINKING AND LOADING

10.1 INTRODUCTION

Suppose we want to write a large assembly language program. One approach we might take is to create a single large file containing the entire program. Another approach—and as you shall see, a better approach—is to create many files, each holding the source code for only a single function, or for, at most, a few closely related functions. In this approach, we call each of these files a *source module*. Once we have created all of our source modules, we can then create an executable program by performing two steps. First, we assemble each source module. Each assembly produces an output file called an *object module* (see Figure 10.1). Second, we combine all the separate object modules into a single executable program. The process of combining object modules into an executable program is called *linking* or *link editing*. A program that performs linking is called a *linker* or a *link editor* (see Figure 10.2). The executable program that the linker produces is sometimes called a *load module* because it can be loaded into memory and executed.

In our H1 system, we use the extensions ".mas", ".mob", and ".mac", respectively, for assembly source, object, and executable files. Different systems use different

FIGURE 10.1   Step 1

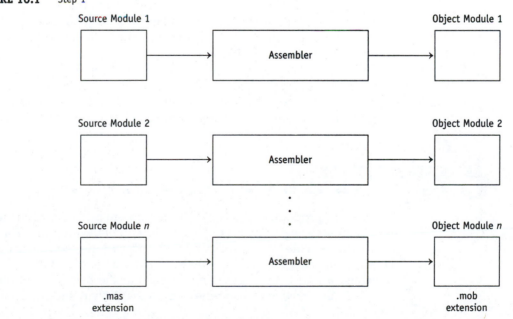

FIGURE 10.2   Step 2

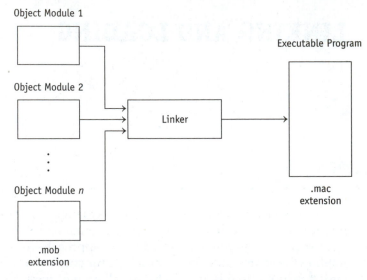

extensions. For example, Microsoft Windows uses the extensions ".asm", ".obj", and ".exe".

The **mas** assembler automatically outputs a ".mac" (i.e., executable) file if its input is a *complete* program. It is for this reason that we did not have to link any of the programs in the preceding chapters. However, if the input to **mas** is not a complete program, then **mas** outputs a ".mob" file.

There must be some significant advantages in creating executable programs using the separate assembly and linking approach. Otherwise, programmers would never use this multi-step approach. In this chapter, we will learn what these advantages are.

The principal activity of a linker is adjusting the addresses in the modules that it is linking. A *loader* (the part of an operating system that loads an executable program into memory for execution) similarly adjusts addresses (in the executable program it is loading). It is no surprise then that a linker and a loader have some similar features at the internal level.

In this chapter, we examine the linking and loading processes in detail. We start with the loading process because it is considerably less complex than the linking process. We also cover some topics related to linking—namely, libraries, start-up code, and the form of separately compiled C++ modules at the assembly level.

10.2   RELOCATABLE FIELDS

• •

Consider the program in Figure 10.3. This program is structured in an unusual way: Its data is at the beginning rather than at the end of the program. The CPU does not attempt to "execute" the data, however, because a ja instruction at the beginning of the program causes the CPU to jump over the data. Alternatively, we could have prevented the CPU from executing the data at the beginning of this program by using an **end** directive that specifies **add** as the entry point (see Section 3.13). Then

FIGURE 10.3

```
          LOC      OBJ              SOURCE
          hex*dec
          0  *0    9004         ja    add
          1  *1    0001    x:   dw    1
          2  *2    0008    y:   dw    8
          3  *3    0000    z:   dw    0
          4  *4    0001    add: ld    x
          5  *5    2002         add   y
          6  *6    1003         st    z
          7  *7    FFFF         halt
          8  *8 ==================== end of program =====================
```

the initial ja instruction would not be necessary. However, for our present discussion, let's use the program in Figure 10.3, which uses the initial ja instruction rather than the **end** directive.

When we run this program on **sim**, it adds the value in **x** (1) and the value in **y** (8) and stores the sum (9) at **z**.

sim normally loads programs into memory starting at location 0. On most computers, however, low main memory is occupied by the operating system. On such computers, programs are never loaded at location 0, but higher up, above the operating system. We call the starting address at which a program is loaded its *load point*.

Suppose the program in Figure 10.3 were loaded at location 500 hex. Would it work correctly? To answer this important question, observe that the location of **x** is 1 when the load point is 0. If we now increase the load point to 500 hex, we, of course, increase the location of **x** by 500—from 1 to 501. Note that the machine code for the ld instruction in Figure 10.3 is 0001. This instruction is supposed to load from **x**; however, the address it contains, 001, is the address of **x** *only* if the program's load point is 0. If, instead, the load point were 500, then the address of **x** would be 501. For this load point, the ld instruction in Figure 10.3 contains the *wrong* address—it should contain 501 instead of 001. Similarly, the addresses in the ja, add, and st instructions are also incorrect. For example, the ja instruction should be 9504 instead of 9004 if the load point is 500.

Figure 10.4 shows two machine versions of our program. In both versions, we show the addresses in boldface. Version 1 is produced by the assembler and is contained in the ".mac" file that it creates. Version 1 works when the load point is 0. Version 2 works when the load point is 500. We obtained version 2 from version 1 by adjusting its addresses. In particular, we increased all the addresses in version 1 by the load point 500.

We call the process of adjusting addresses in a machine language program to accommodate a different starting address *relocation*. The fields that have to be relocated are called *relocatable fields*. To relocate a field means to *adjust the address it contains*. It does *not* mean to move it to a new location.

Not every word in a machine language program contains a relocatable field. For example, in Figure 10.4, the three data words and the halt instruction do not contain addresses, and, therefore, do not contain relocatable fields.

sim normally loads programs starting at location 0, but it can also load programs at nonzero load points. To make **sim** do this, we invoke **sim** with the /p

FIGURE 10.4

Version 1 load point = 0		Version 2 load point = 500 hex		Assembly Code		
Loc		Loc				
0	9004	500	9504		ja	start
1	0001	501	0001	x:	dw	1
2	0008	502	0008	y:	dw	8
3	0000	503	0000	z:	dw	·0
4	0001	504	0501	start:	ld	x
5	2002	505	2502		add	y
6	1003	506	1503		st	z
7	FFFF	507	FFFF		halt	

command line argument. For example, to make **sim** load a program at 500 hex, we invoke **sim** with

sim /p500

Let's try running the program in Figure 10.3 on **sim**. Because the ".mac" file produced by the assembler contains version 1 of the machine program, we expect the program to work correctly when the load point is 0, but not when the load point is 500. Assuming **fig1003.mas** is the name of the file containing the source code for the program in Figure 10.3, we first assemble it with

mas fig1003

mas will then create an executable file named **fig1003.mac**. This file corresponds to version 1 in Figure 10.4. We then invoke **sim** without the **/p** parameter, thereby causing the load point to default to 0. Finally, we use the **d***, **g**, and **q** commands, respectively, to display the machine code that makes up the program, to run the program, and to quit (see Figure 10.5).

FIGURE 10.5

```
C:\sim>sim fig1003   ←——— load point defaults to 0
Simulator Version x.x

Starting session.  Enter h or ? for help.
---- [T7] 0: ja   /9 004/ d*
  0:  9004  0001  0008  0000  0001  2002  1003  FFFF        ........
---- [T7] 0: ja   /9 004/ g
  0: ja    /9 004/ pc=0001/0004
  4: ld    /0 001/ ac=0000/0001
  5: add   /2 002/ ac=0001/0009
  6: st    /1 003/ m[003]=0000/0009
  7: halt /FFFF /

Machine inst count =       5 (hex) =    5 (dec)
---- [T7] q
```

If we examine the output in Figure 10.5 produced by the d* command, we see the following machine code (we have added boldfacing to the addresses):

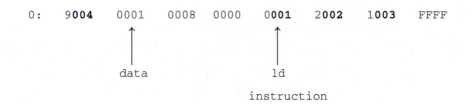

```
0:     9004    0001   0008   0000   0001   2002   1003    FFFF

                                      |
                data                  ld
                             instruction
```

As we expect, we see that memory contains the version of the machine program that the assembler creates (version 1 in Figure 10.4). Note that the second and fifth words look exactly alike (both are 0001) although the second word is data and the fifth word is an instruction. The trace for the st instruction is

```
6: st    /1 003/ m[003]=0000/0009
```

which indicates that the st instruction stored the sum (0009) into location 3 (i.e., into z), as it should.

Now let's see what happens when the load point is 500 (see Figure 10.6). This time we invoke sim with

sim fig1003 /p500

Again we use the d*, g, and q commands. Surprisingly, the d* command shows that the machine program in memory has addresses that are correct for a load point of 500:

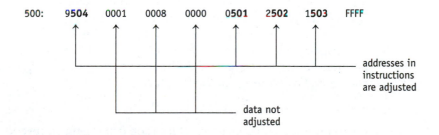

```
500:   9504   0001   0008   0000   0501   2502   1503   FFFF
```

addresses in instructions are adjusted

data not adjusted

Somehow sim adjusted the addresses in the machine program when it loaded the program into memory. Moreover, we can see from the trace that the program works correctly: The trace for the st instruction shows that the sum is stored into z (now at location 503):

```
506: st    /1 503/ m[503]=0000/0009
```

Apparently, when sim loads a program, it adjusts the addresses in the program according to the load point. If the load point is 500, then sim adds 500 to each address. But *how does sim know where the addresses are in the machine program?* Look at the data word corresponding to x (the second word in the program) in the memory display in Figure 10.6. It is still 0001—it correctly was not adjusted because it does not contain an address. But the ld instruction, originally 0001, correctly was adjusted to 0501. How did sim know to adjust the second occurrence of 0001 (the ld instruction) but not its first occurrence (the data word)? We, of course, know

FIGURE 10.6　C:\H1>**sim /p500**　◄──────── load point is 500 hex

```
Simulator Version x.x

Starting session.   Enter h or ? for help.
---- [T7] 500: ja    /9 504/ d*

500:  9504   0001   0008   0000   0501   2502   1503   FFFF   ........
---- [T7] 500: ja    /9 504/ g

500: ja    /9 504/ pc=0501/0504
504: ld    /0 501/ ac=0000/0001
505: add   /2 502/ ac=0001/0009
506: st    /1 503/ m[503]=0000/0009
507: halt /FFFF /

Machine inst count =    5 (hex) =     5 (dec)
---- [T7] q
```

that the first occurrence of 0001 does not contain an address because we have seen the assembly language program in Figure 10.3. But when **sim** is loading in a ".mac" file, it has no access to the assembly language version of the program.

The explanation for **sim**'s ability to correctly identify and adjust only addresses when loading a program is this: The ".mac" file contains information that tells **sim** where the addresses are. Let's examine the inside of the ".mac" file for the program in Figure 10.3. The ".mac" file in Figure 10.7, like all ".mac" files, consists of two parts: the *header* (the part that contains information on the addresses) and the machine code. The last entry in the header contains the letter T (and is, therefore, called a *T entry*). The letter T stands for the word "text". It signals that the machine code *text* (i.e., binary machine code) follows immediately.

Preceding the T entry in the header are four R entries. Each *R entry* contains the letter R followed by a pointer to a relocatable field in the machine code. The pointers in the R entries are addresses relative to the beginning of the machine code text. For example, in the first R entry,

R 0000

the pointer 0000 indicates that at location 0 in the machine code there is an address that needs to be adjusted.

Our picture in Figure 10.7 of a ".mac" file is a little misleading. For example, the header entries are not all the same size, although they appear to be in Figure 10.7. In reality, the T entry occupies only one word, and each R entry occupies two words (one for R and one for the pointer). Furthermore, the header, of course, contains only binary numbers. In Figure 10.7 we are displaying these binary numbers in two different ways: For ASCII codes, we are displaying their corresponding characters (e.g., R and T); for pointers, we are displaying their hex equivalents. For now, let's not focus on the bit-level details of ".mac" files—we will do that a little later. Because of its imprecise nature, we call the picture in Figure 10.7 a *conceptual picture*.

When **sim** loads a ".mac" file, it reads in, strips off, and saves the header, and then loads the machine code, as is, into memory, starting at the load point. Next, **sim** must determine where the relocatable fields are in the machine code as it sits in memory. These relocatable fields, of course, must be adjusted before the program can run. It's easy for **sim** to determine the location of each relocatable field. Each

FIGURE 10.7

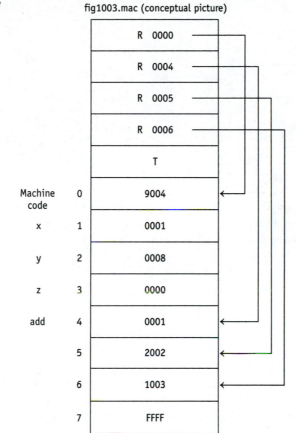

fig1003.mac (conceptual picture)

pointer in an R entry is the location of a relocatable field **relative** to the beginning of the machine code. Thus, the location of the relocatable field in memory is

```
the location of the beginning of the machine
code text in memory (i.e., the load point)
              +
the pointer value in the R entry
```

For example, if the program in Figure 10.7 is loaded starting at location 500, then the locations of relocatable fields in the machine code sitting in memory are computed from the R entries as follows:

```
Load Pt     Pointer value in
            R entries



    500   +    0   =   500

    500   +    4   =   504
                                 locations of relocatable fields
    500   +    5   =   505

    500   +    5   =   506
```

FIGURE 10.8

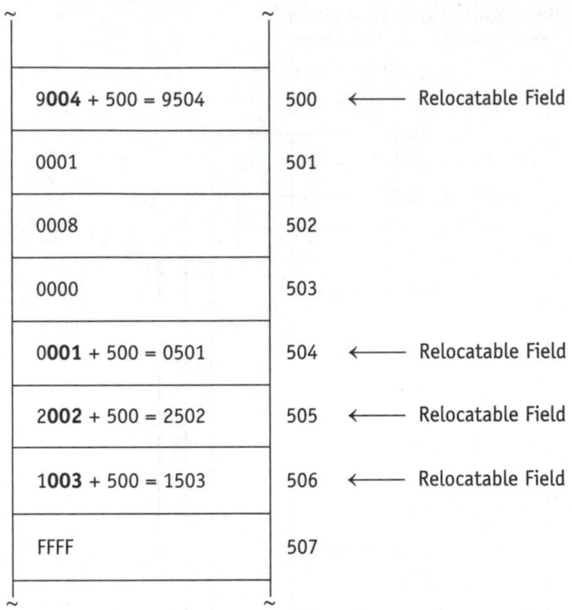

Value	Address	
9004 + 500 = 9504	500	⟵ Relocatable Field
0001	501	
0008	502	
0000	503	
0001 + 500 = 0501	504	⟵ Relocatable Field
2002 + 500 = 2502	505	⟵ Relocatable Field
1003 + 500 = 1503	506	⟵ Relocatable Field
FFFF	507	

As **sim** determines the addresses of the relocatable fields, it adjusts them by adding the load point to the words at these addresses (see Figure 10.8).

In a real computer system, the loading of executable programs is handled by the operating system. Like **sim**, operating systems must adjust addresses in executable programs if the load point is not 0. They do so using the information provided in the executable file, in the same way that **sim** does.

10.3 PROGRAMS THAT DISPLAY THE HEADER AND THE MACHINE CODE TEXT

We can use the programs **pic** and **mex** in the H1 software package to display the contents of a ".mac" file. **pic** (display conceptual *pic*ture) produces a formatted display similar to the conceptual picture in Figure 10.7. **mex** (*m*odule *ex*aminer) produces a hex/ASCII display. The **mex** program is useful when you want to examine a program at the bit level.

Suppose the ".mac" file corresponding to the program in Figure 10.3 is named **fig1003.mac**. To produce a formatted display, we invoke the **pic** program with

```
pic fig1003.mac
```

pic then produces the display in Figure 10.9. R entries do not use the symbol column that appears on the right of the header display. This column is used for the P and E header entries, which we will discuss later in this chapter. Similarly, the symbol column for the machine code text is blank. Although there are symbols associated with some of these locations (the labels **x**, **y**, **z**, and **add** correspond to locations 1, 2, 3, and 4, respectively), **pic** has no way of knowing what these labels are, and, therefore, cannot include them in its display. In our conceptual picture in Figure 10.7 we were able to include these symbols by examining the original assembly language program.

The output **pic** produces is directed to both the display monitor and a list file whose name consists of the base name of the input file plus the extension ".pic".

FIGURE 10.9   `Conceptual Picture Version x.x`

```
            Header:

                Type      Address     Symbol
                 R          0000
                 R          0004
                 R          0005
                 R          0006
                 T


            Text:

                Loc        Text        Symbol
                 0          9004
                 1          0001
                 2          0008
                 3          0000
                 4          0001
                 5          2002
                 6          1003
                 7          FFFF

        Input file   = fig1003.mac
        List file    = fig1003.pic
```

FIGURE 10.10

```
Module Examiner Version x.x
Header:
    0:    0052   0000   0052   0004   0052   0005   0052   0006   R.R.R.R.
    8:    0054                                                     T

Text:
    0:    9004   0001   0008   0000   0001   2002   1003   FFFF   ........

Input file = fig1003.mac
List file  = fig1003.mex
```

For example, if we use `pic` to display the file `fig1003.mac`, its output goes to a file named `fig1003.pic` in addition to the display monitor.

The `mex` program displays a ".mac" file in hex and ASCII. To display the contents of `fig1003.mac` with `mex`, we invoke the `mex` program with

mex fig1003.mac

`mex` then produces the display in Figure 10.10. Each line in the display that `mex` produces starts with the address of the first word on that line. For the header, this address is relative to the beginning of the header; for the machine code text, this address is relative to the beginning of the machine code text. Each line in the display contains both a *hex display* (on the left) and a corresponding *ASCII display* (on the right). The ASCII display shows the characters corresponding to the codes that appear in the hex display; for example, in the display in Figure 10.10, the first word in the header contains 0052 hex. Now look at the beginning of the ASCII display on the same line. We see R displayed, the character that corresponds to 0052 in ASCII. If the hex display contains a code for which there is no corresponding character in ASCII, then `mex` displays a period in the ASCII display. For example, the second word in the header in Figure 10.10 contains 0000 hex. There is no corresponding ASCII character, so `mex` displays a period in the second position of the ASCII display.

The ASCII display is very useful for identifying the header entries in the header. For example, in Figure 10.10, each R entry in the header is clearly identified by an R that appears in the ASCII display.

Like `pic`, `mex` also produces a list file. Its name consists of the base name of the input file name plus the extension ".mex".

10.4   SMALL-S ENTRY

• •

In Figure 10.3 we saw a program in which a jump instruction jumps over the data at the beginning of the program. We can eliminate the jump instruction yet still have the data at the beginning of the program if we use an **end** directive to specify the correct entry point. If we do so, we get the program in Figure 10.11. If **sim** loads this program starting at location 0, the program will start executing at the `ld` instruction (i.e., location 3). If **sim** loads the program starting at location 500, then the program will also start at the `ld` instruction (now at location 503). How does **sim** know to start at the `ld` instruction instead of the physical beginning of the program? The very first word of the program is 0001, which we know to be a data item. But 0001 could also be an `ld` instruction. Similarly, the next two words, 0008 and 0000, are data but could also be `ld` instructions. There is nothing in the machine code itself that specifies the entry point. What about the **end** directive? The **end** directive appears in the assembly program but *not* in the machine code.

You can probably guess how **sim** knows the right start address when there is an **end** directive at the assembly level: There must be something in the header of

FIGURE 10.11

```
         LOC      OBJ    SOURCE
         hex*dec


         0  *0     0001   x:     dw     1

         1  *1     0008   y:     dw     8

         2  *2     0000   z:     dw     0

         3  *3     0000   add:   ld     x

         4  *4     2001          add    y

         5  *5     1002          st     z

         6  *6     FFFF          halt

                                 end    add

         7  *7  ================= end of program ==============
```

FIGURE 10.12

```
Type      Address     Symbol

  R        0003
  R        0004
  R        0005
  S        0003      ←——————  small-s entry
  T
```

the ".mac" file that indicates the correct entry point. When **sim** loads a program, it uses the entry point information in the header to determine the correct entry point. It then starts the CPU executing at this entry point.

Figure 10.12 shows the header for the program in Figure 10.11. We can see a new type of entry, the *small-s entry* ("s" stands for "starting address"):

```
s      0003
```

The address that appears in a small-s entry is the address of the entry point *relative to the beginning of the machine code*. For example, if the load point is 0 and the small-s address is 3, then the entry point is 0 + 3 = 3. If, on the other hand, the load point is 500, then the entry point is 500 + 3 = 503. The **end** directive does not cause any machine code to be generated. Its *only* effect is to cause the assembler to insert a small-s entry into the header of the ".mac" file. This s entry then causes **sim** to start execution of the program at the correct entry point. When **sim** (or an operating system) loads a program, it adds the starting address obtained from the small-s entry with the load point to obtain the correct starting address for the program in memory.

We refer to the small-s entry as "small" to distinguish it from a big-S entry (which we will discuss in the next section).

10.5 INHIBITING RELOCATION

The program in Figure 10.13 is exactly the same as the program in Figure 10.11 except that absolute addresses are used instead of labels. Notice the machine code is identical to that in Figure 10.11. Obviously, the two programs are completely

FIGURE 10.13

```
LOC       OBJ    SOURCE
hex*dec

0   *0    0001   x:     dw    1
1   *1    0008   y:     dw    8
2   *2    0000   z:     dw    0
3   *3    0000   add:   ld    0
4   *4    2001          add   1
5   *5    1002          st    2
6   *6    FFFF          halt
                        end   3
7   *7 ===================== end of program ===============
```

FIGURE 10.14
```
Type    Address    Symbol
 S       0003
 T
```

equivalent. Right? Absolutely not. Whenever an absolute address is specified, the assembler assumes that the address is the address you want when the program is executed, *regardless of its load point*. For example, the instruction,

```
st     2
```

in Figure 10.13 stores at location 2 even if the program's load point is 500. The address in this instruction, therefore, should *not* be relocated (i.e., adjusted) according to the program's load point. The assembler inhibits relocation by simply not generating any R entries for absolute addresses (the R entry is what flags an address as relocatable). Thus, absolute addresses are not adjusted when the program is loaded into memory.

The **end** directive also works differently if it specifies an absolute address instead of a label for an entry point. The assembler assumes that the absolute address specified is where you want execution to start, regardless of the load point. Thus, if the program in Figure 10.13 is loaded at location 500, execution still starts at location 3. Of course, this program will fail if its load point is anything other than 0 because then both its addresses and its entry point will not be correct.

Figure 10.14 shows the header for the program. Note that the assembler did not generate R entries for the absolute addresses. Thus, the absolute addresses are not adjusted when the program is loaded into memory. The header, however, must still contain information on the entry point. Accordingly, the assembler generates a *big-S entry* to hold the entry point. The big-S (as opposed to a small-s) indicates that 3 (the entry point address) should not be adjusted according to the load point. Thus, after **sim** loads this program, it obtains 3 from the big-S entry, and starts the execution from that location, regardless of the program's load point.

If an assembly language program does not include an **end** directive, then its corresponding ".mac" file contains neither a small-s nor a big-S entry. When **sim** executes such a program, it assumes that the load point is its entry point. For example, if the program is loaded starting at location 500, then its execution would also start at location 500.

There are some types of programs (e.g., operating systems) that need to access specific memory locations. For example, most computers have special words at specific locations in memory (usually low memory) that are controlled by the operating system. These special words contain system information such as the current time, the status of the keyboard, or the addresses of some special routines. In these situations, using absolute addresses in an assembly program allows these specific locations to be accessed.

10.6   SEPARATE ASSEMBLY

• •

When we write a program as a collection of functions, the functions—whether separately assembled or not—need to communicate (i.e., call each other, share data, and pass data). If the entire program is in one file, then communication between functions is easy. All of the labels in the program are accessible by every function. For example, if one function has a variable defined as

```
x:      dw      17
```

then any other function can directly reference **x** with, for example, the instruction

```
ld    x
```

Similarly, one function can easily call another. For example, the **main** function can call the **sub** function with the instruction

```
call sub
```

Figure 10.15 shows an assembly program consisting of two functions, **main** and **sub**. Communication between **main** and **sub** is easy because the two functions are assembled together in the same file. The assembler scans the entire program in pass 1 to determine the locations of every label. Thus, in pass 2, wherever a label appears, the assembler can translate it to the correct address.

Although communication between functions assembled together is easy, this is not the case for separately assembled functions. Let's consider the simple program in Figure 10.16. This program consists of two separately assembled modules that are exactly like the two functions in Figure 10.15, except that the label **done** now appears in both modules. Both occurrences of **done** are unnecessary; we have included them so that we can illustrate a point later on. Each module contains one

FIGURE 10.15

```
LOC     OBJ    SOURCE
hex*dec

0   *0   E004   main:    call   sub       ; call other module sub
1   *1   1008            st     total     ; total is in sub
2   *2   FFFF            halt
3   *3   0011   x:       dw     17
                         end    main
              ;==================================================
4   *4   0003   sub:     ld     x         ; x is in main
5   *5   2007            add    y
6   *6   F000            ret
7   *7   0022   y:       dw     34
8   *8   0000   total:   dw     0
9   *9          ========== end of fig1015.mas ==========================
```

FIGURE 10.16

```
          m1.mas                        m2.mas

┌─────────────────────────┐   ┌─────────────────────────┐
│ main:   call    sub     │   │ sub:    ld      x       │
│         st      total   │   │         add     y       │
│ done:   halt            │   │ done:   ret             │
│ x:      dw      17      │   │ y:      dw      34      │
│         end     main    │   │ total:  dw      0       │
└─────────────────────────┘   └─────────────────────────┘
        Module 1                      Module 2
```

function and is a separate file. Module 1 (which contains the `main` function) is in the file `m1.mas`; module 2 (which contains the `sub` function) is in the file `m2.mas`. Module 1 references `sub` and `total`, both labels that appear in module 2. Because the labels `sub` and `total` are external to module 1, we call them *external symbols* with respect to module 1. Each use of an external symbol is an *external reference*. For example, the instructions

```
call sub
st   total
```

in module 1 contain external references to the external symbols `sub` and `total`. Similarly, the instruction

```
ld   x
```

in module 2 contains an external reference to `x` in module 1.

When the assembler is assembling module 1 in Figure 10.16, it does not know that `sub` and `total` are external symbols. Thus, it will look for `sub` and `total` within `m1.mas`, not find them, generate an error message, and terminate the assembly. The assembly of module 2 will similarly fail because of the external reference to `x`. The use of the label `done` in both modules, on the other hand, does not cause a problem. When the assembler assembles each of these modules, it is not aware of the occurrence of `done` in the other module. However, if both modules were in one file and assembled together, then the duplicate use of `done` would cause an error.

In Figure 10.16, the *scope* of `x`—the range of the program over which it is accessible—is limited to module 1, the module in which it is defined. Similarly, the scope of `sub` and `total` is limited to module 2.

To fix the problem with the program in Figure 10.16, we need to tell the assembler that

- The symbols `sub` and `total` in module 1 and `x` in module 2 are external symbols (then the assembler will not flag these symbols as errors).
- The symbol `x` in module 1 and `sub` and `total` in module 2 are public. A *public* symbol is global—that is, its scope extends to any file that makes up the program, not just the file in which it is defined. If we make `x` public, it becomes accessible from module 2; if we make `sub` and `total` public in module 2, they become accessible from module 1.

Figure 10.17 shows the corrected version of the program. We use two new assembler directives. The `extern` directive tells the assembler that the indicated symbol

FIGURE 10.17

m1.mas

```
main:   call     sub
        st       total
done:   halt
x:      dw       17
        public   x
        extern   sub
        extern   total
        end      main
```

Module 1

m2.mas

```
sub:    ld       x
        add      y
done:   ret
y:      dw       34
total:  dw       0
        public   sub
        public   total
        extern   x
```

Module 2

is external—that is, defined in a separately assembled module. The `public` directive tells the assembler that the indicated symbol should be public (i.e., have global scope). The `public` directive should be used in the module in which the indicated symbol is defined. The `extern` directive should be used in every other module that references this symbol. Both directives can appear on any line within a module, although we typically place them at either the beginning or the end.

In module 1, `sub` and `total` appear on `extern` directives to indicate to the assembler that they are external symbols. `x` appears on a `public` directive to indicate that `x` should have global scope (thereby making it accessible from module 2). In module 2, `sub` and `total` appear on `public` directives to indicate that they should have global scope (thereby making them accessible from module 1). `x` appears on an `extern` directive to indicate that it is an external symbol. As we mentioned earlier, the appearance of `done` in both modules does not cause problems. If, however, both modules contained a `public` directive for `done`, then the two would conflict because their scopes would overlap. The linker at link time would detect this multiple definition and generate an error message. The use of `sub` in both modules does *not* cause a similar problem because `sub` is made public in module 2 only. Thus, there is only one `sub` whose scope extends over modules 1 and 2.

Figure 10.18 shows the assembly listings for module 1 and module 2. Because the assembler does not know the addresses of `sub` and `total` when it assembles module 1, or the address of `x` when it assembles module 2, it uses 0 for their addresses. Thus, the instructions in module 1

```
call sub
st   total
```

are translated to

```
E000
1000
```

and the instruction in module 2

```
ld   x
```

FIGURE 10.18

	Module 1			
LOC hex*dec	OBJ	SOURCE		
0 *0	E000	main:	call	sub
1 *1	1000		st	total
2 *2	FFFF	done:	halt	
3 *3	0011	x:	dw	17
			public x	
			extern sub	
			extern total	
			end	main

Input file   = m1.mas
Output file = m1.mob

	Module 2			
LOC hex*dec	OBJ	SOURCE		
0 *0	0000	sub:	ld	x
1 *1	2003		add	y
2 *2	F000	done:	ret	
3 *3	0000	y:	dw	34
4 *4	0022	total:	dw	0
			public sub	
			public total	
			extern x	

Input file   = m2.mas
Output file = m2.mob

is translated to

`0000`

These addresses will be modified *at link time* when the linker determines the actual addresses of **sub**, **total**, and **x** as it combines module 1 and module 2. For example, the linker will change the address field of the st instruction in module 1 to the actual address of **total** in the combined program. Suppose that the linker places module 2 after module 1 in the combined program. Because module 1 is first, it occupies locations 0 through 3. Thus, module 2 starts at address 4. The actual address of **total** in the combined program is given by

$$
\begin{array}{rl}
4 & \text{(the starting address of module 2 in the combined program)} \\
+\ \ 4 & \text{(the address of } \textbf{total} \text{ relative to the beginning of module 2)} \\
\hline
8 & \text{(the address of } \textbf{total} \text{ in the combined program)}
\end{array}
$$

Thus, the linker changes the st instruction in module 1 from 1000 to 1008. This process of adjusting the address fields corresponding to external references is called *resolving external references*. The ".mac" file produced by the linker contains these adjusted addresses. At load time, these addresses will again be adjusted by the loader if the load point is not 0.

The add instruction in module 2 contains a reference to **y**. This reference is not an external reference. Instead, it is an internal (i.e., local) reference because **y** and the add instruction are in the same module. Nevertheless, the address in this instruction must also be adjusted by the linker to reflect its address in the combined program. The address of **y** in the add machine instruction that is produced by the assembler (3) is the address of **y** *relative to the beginning of module* 2. Thus, to adjust this address, the linker must *add* to it the address at which module 2 starts in the combined program:

$$
\begin{array}{rl}
3 & \text{(address in add instruction put there by the assembler)} \\
+\ \ 4 & \text{(address at which module 2 starts in the combined program)} \\
\hline
7 & \text{(new address in the add instruction—the address of } \textbf{y} \\
& \text{in the combined program)}
\end{array}
$$

When the linker adjusts addresses corresponding to internal references, it uses the same mechanism that **sim** uses when it loads a program into memory at a non-zero load point. Recall from Section 10.2 that this mechanism involves two actions:

- The R entries are used to identify the relocatable fields.
- The address at which the module is loaded (i.e., its new starting address) is added to these relocatable fields.

The header in the file **m2.mob** contains an R entry that points to the add instruction. This R entry tells the linker that the address in the add instruction has to be adjusted whenever the starting address of module 2 is changed. This same R entry is what causes **sim** to again adjust the address if the load point is not zero.

The assembler produces two ".mob" files, **m1.mob** and **m2.mob**, when it assembles the modules in Figure 10.18. Because of the inclusion of the **extern** and **public** directives, the assembler knows these modules individually are not complete programs. Accordingly, the assembler generates an object file (i.e., a ".mob" file) instead of an executable file (i.e., a ".mac" file). To link the two ".mob" files, we invoke the linker, **lin**, with

`lin m1 m2`

lin then links **m1.mob** and **m2.mob** (extensions default to ".mob" for the input files) to create an executable file **m1.mac** (the base name of the output file defaults to the base name of the first input file). The order in which **lin** places modules in the combined program is determined by the order in which we specify the input modules. For example, if we invoke **lin** with

```
lin m2 m1
```

then **m2.mob** will appear first in the combined program in the output file **m2.mac**. Because module 1 in **m1.mas** contains an **end** directive specifying the entry point, the order in which **m1.mob** and **m2.mob** are linked is not important. If, however, **m1.mas** did not contain an **end** directive, then the entry point defaults to the physical beginning of the code. In this case, **m1.mob** would have to be linked first if it is to get control first.

To better understand the linking mechanism, let's examine in detail the object modules **m1.mob** and **m2.mob** produced by the assembly of the modules in Figure 10.18, and the executable module **m1.mac** produced when they are linked. The **pic** program is quite useful in this endeavor. To display **m1.mob**, **m2.mob**, and **m1.mac**, we invoke **pic** three times:

```
pic m1.mob
pic m2.mob
pic m1.mac
```

Figure 10.19 shows the display that **pic** produces for both **m1.mob** and **m2.mob**. In the header for **m1.mob**, we see an E entry for the external reference to **sub**. An *E entry* indicates

- The address of the external reference, relative to the beginning of the module's machine text
- The external symbol

FIGURE 10.19

Header:

Type	Address	Symbol
E	0000	sub
E	0001	total
P	0003	x
S	0000	
T		

Text:

Address	Text	Symbol
0	E000	^sub
1	1000	^total
2	FFFF	
3	0011	x

Input file   = m1.mob
List file   = m1.pic

Header:

Type	Address	Symbol
E	0000	x
R	0001	
P	0000	sub
P	0004	total
T		

Text:

Address	Text	Symbol
0	0000	sub^x
1	2003	
2	F000	
3	0022	
4	0000	total

Input file   = m2.mob
List file   = m2.pic

FIGURE 10.20

```
Module Examiner Version x.x
Header:
         0:   0045  0000  0073  0075  0062  0000  0045  0001      E.sub.E.
         8:   0074  006F  0074  0061  006C  0000  0050  0003      total.P.
        10:   0078  0000  0073  0000  0054                        x.s.T
Text:
         0:   E000  1000  FFFF  0011                              ....
Input file = m1.mob
List file  = m1.mex
```

For example, the entry

```
E      0000     sub
```

in the header of **m1.mob** indicates that an external reference to **sub** occurs at location 0000 from the start of the machine text in **m1.mob**.

In the symbol column in Figure 10.19, we can see the public and external symbols associated with every location. For example, **^total** appears in the symbol column at location 1 in the machine text for **m1.mob**, indicating that this location makes an external reference to **total** (^ marks the external symbols). **sub^x** appears in location 1 of **m2.mob**, indicating that this location both defines **sub** and makes an external reference to **x**.

The **mex** program can also display object modules (we have already used it to display executable modules). Figure 10.20 shows the display of **m1.mob** that **mex** produces (we have added boldfacing to the first E entry it contains). The E entry within the header starts with 0045 (the ASCII code for E) and is followed by the address 0000 and the null-terminated string "sub" (0073, 0075, 0062, 0000).

In the header of an object module, there is one E entry for *every* external reference. Thus, it is possible for a module to contain only one **extern** directive but several E entries. For example, the following module produces three E entries, *one for each external reference to* **t** although it has only one **extern**:

```
extern t        ; only 1 extern directive
ld   t          ; first external reference to t
add  t          ; second external reference to t
st   t          ; third external reference to t
halt
```

The three E entries are

```
E      0000     t
E      0001     t
E      0002     t
```

which point, respectively, to the ld, add, and st instructions.

Returning to Figure 10.19, we can see the P entry for **x** in the header for module 1. A *P entry* contains the letter *P* plus

- The address of the public symbol, relative to the beginning of the module's machine text
- The public symbol

For example, the entry

```
P     0003    x
```

indicates that the address of **x** relative to the beginning of the machine text in **m1.mob** is 0003. This P entry is *what makes* **x** *a public* (i.e., global) *symbol*. In Figure 10.20, we can see that the hex form in **m1.mob** for this P entry consists of

```
0050 0003 0078 0000
```

0050 is the ASCII code for *P*. The next word, 0003, is the address. The last two words, 0078 and 0000, form the null-terminated string "x". Unlike the **extern** directive, every **public** directive generates exactly one header entry.

Notice in Figure 10.19 that there are no header entries for **done** because it is a local label in both modules. The lack of a P entry for **done** is *what makes* **done** *a local symbol*.

Now let's examine in detail what **lin** does when it is invoked with

```
lin m1 m2
```

First, it reads in **m1.mob** and **m2.mob**, stripping off their headers but saving them for future use. **lin** combines the text (i.e., machine code) parts of each module in memory in an area called a *text buffer*. In particular, **lin** appends the text part of each object module to the end of the text of the previous module. Thus, after **lin** processes every object module, the text buffer contains the text for the combined program. Locations in the text buffer are numbered starting with 0. Thus, location 0 in the text buffer contains the first word of machine text in the combined program.

As **lin** saves the header entries, it adjusts the addresses that the header entries contain; that is, **lin** adjusts the addresses to reflect locations in the combined program. For example, in the P entry in **m2.mob**

```
P   0000   sub
```

the address 0000 is the address of **sub** relative to the beginning of module 2. Because module 2 starts at location 4 in the combined program, **lin** must add 4 to the address in the P entry to get the address of **sub** in the combined program. Similarly, the addresses in the E and R entries in **m2.mob** are adjusted by adding 4. The addresses in the header entries for **m1.mob** do not need to be adjusted because module 1 appears first in the combined program

lin saves headers entries in internal tables. P, E, R, and s/S entries, respectively, are saved in the p, e, r, and s tables. Unlike the other tables, the S table consists of only a single slot because there can be at most one s/S entry for a program. Figure 10.21 shows the contents of these tables when linking **m1.mob** and **m2.mob**.

Because the P table holds only P entries, there is no need to store the P identifier that starts every P entry. Similarly, the E and R tables do not store the E and R identifiers. However, the S table must retain the s/S identifier so that a small-s entry can be distinguished from a big-S entry.

As **lin** saves R entries in the R table, it also saves the module address corresponding to each R entry. For example, the R table in Figure 10.21 contains an R entry from module 2. Thus, **lin** also saves in this table entry the address at which module 2 starts in the combined program. It will later use this address when it processes this R entry.

Next, **lin** processes every saved E entry. For each E entry, **lin**

FIGURE 10.21   Saved Header Entries

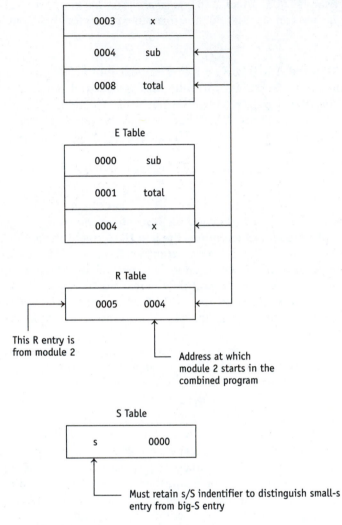

P Table

0003	x
0004	sub
0008	total

E Table

0000	sub
0001	total
0004	x

R Table

0005	0004

This R entry is from module 2

Address at which module 2 starts in the combined program

S Table

s	0000

Must retain s/S indentifier to distinguish small-s entry from big-S entry

Header entries from m2.mob with adjusted addresses

1. Obtains the address in the E entry. This address is the address in the combined program of the external reference.
2. Determines the address in the combined program of the external symbol that appears in the E entry. To do this, lin searches for a saved P entry that contains the same symbol as the E entry. The address in such a P entry is the address of the external symbol.
3. Adds the address of the symbol (obtained from the saved P entry) to the location of the external reference (obtained from the E entry). For example, when processing the E entry from module 1

```
E       0000      sub
```

lin adds 0004, the address of **sub** obtained from the saved P entry,

```
P       0004      sub
```

FIGURE 10.22

a) Before resolution of external references

Before relocation of addresses

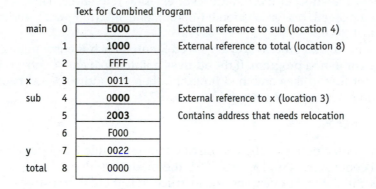

Text for Combined Program

main	0	**E**000	External reference to sub (location 4)
	1	**1**000	External reference to total (location 8)
	2	FFFF	
x	3	0011	
sub	4	**0**000	External reference to x (location 3)
	5	**2**003	Contains address that needs relocation
	6	F000	
y	7	0022	
total	8	0000	

b) After resolution of external references

Before relocation of addresses

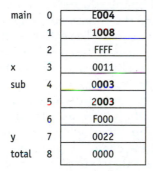

Text for Combined Program

main	0	**E**004	Resolved external reference to sub
	1	**1**008	Resolved external reference to total
	2	FFFF	
x	3	0011	
sub	4	**0**003	Resolved external reference to x
	5	**2**003	Contains address that needs relocation
	6	F000	
y	7	0022	
total	8	0000	

c) After resolution of external references

After relocation of addresses

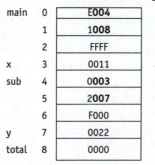

Text for Combined Program

main	0	**E**004	Resolved external reference to sub
	1	**1**008	Resolved external reference to total
	2	FFFF	
x	3	0011	
sub	4	**0**003	Resolved external reference to x
	5	**2**007	Contains adjusted address
	6	F000	
y	7	0022	
total	8	0000	

to location 0 (the location of the external reference to `sub` obtained from the E entry) in the text buffer.

For each E entry, `lin` performs steps 1, 2, and 3. Figures 10.22(a) and 10.22(b) show the effect of the resolution of external references. Three external references are resolved, one at location 0 (to `sub`), one at 1 (to `total`), and the third at location 4 (to `x`).

Next, `lin` processes every saved R entry. Each R entry points to an address in the combined program. If the address pointed to by an R entry is in a module that is not first in the combined program, then the address must be adjusted. For example, the saved R entry from module 2 is

```
R       0005    0004
```

This entry points to the `add` instruction in module 2 at location 0005. To process this entry, `lin` simply adds 0004, the module address in the R entry to location 0005 in the text buffer. The `add` instruction is thereby transformed from

```
2003
```

which contains 003, the address of `y` relative to the beginning of module 2, to

```
2007
```

which contains 007, the address of `y` in the combined program. Figures 10.22(b) and 10.22(c) show the effect of relocating the address in the `add` instruction.

Before `lin` can output the text for the combined program, it must create a header appropriate for the combined program. The external references in the individual modules become ordinary references in the combined program because the external symbols are not external in the combined program. Thus, the E entries for the individual modules turn into R entries in the combined program. The saved P, R, and s/S entries from the individual modules are carried over as is into the combined program. Recall that `lin` adjusts the addresses in the header entries from individual modules as it saves them. Thus, their addresses already correspond to locations relative to the beginning of the combined program. Thus, to create the header for the combined program, `lin` only has to output its saved entries, changing the E entries to R entries. After outputting the header for the combined program, `lin` outputs a T followed by the adjusted text for the combined program (which is sitting in the text buffer) and terminates.

Figure 10.23 shows the executable program in the `m1.mac` file produced by `lin` as displayed by `pic` and `mex`.

`lin` also creates a *table file* containing a display of the tables and text that it builds during the link process. `lin` gives this file the same base name that the executable file has, plus the extension ".tab". For example, if `lin` creates an executable file `m1.mac`, it also creates a table file `m1.tab`. Figure 10.24 shows the file `m1.tab` for the link we just performed. We can see the contents of the P, E, R, and s/S tables that `lin` builds to hold the saved header entries. Notice that the R table entry contains not only the address of the relocatable field (from the R entry in the header), but also the corresponding module address (4 is the address at which module 2 starts in the combined program). We can also see the machine text before E-entry processing, after E-entry/before R-entry processing, and after R-entry processing (compare with Figure 10.22). Each text display conveniently flags any word that has changed since the previous display with the label `change>`. The third file `lin` creates is the *cat file* used by `sim` for source-level tracing.

FIGURE 10.23

a) **pic** Display

Conceptual Picture Version x.x

Header:

Type	Address	Symbol
P	0003	x
P	0004	sub
P	0008	total
R	0005	
R	0000	
R	0001	
R	0004	
s	0000	
T		

Text:

Address	Text	Symbol
0	E004	
1	1008	
2	FFFF	
3	0011	x
4	0003	sub
5	2007	
6	F000	
7	0022	
8	0000	total

Input file = m1.mac
List file   = m1.pic

===

b) **mex** Display

Module Examiner Version x.x

Header:

0:	0050	0003	0078	0000	0050	0004	0073	0075	P.x.P.su
8:	0062	0000	0050	0008	0074	006F	0074	0061	b.P.tota
10:	006C	0000	0052	0005	0052	0000	0052	0001	l.R.R.R.
18:	0052	0004	0073	0000	0054				R.s.T

Text:

0:	E004	1008	FFFF	0011	0003	2007	F000	0022	........"
8:	0000								.

Input file = m1.mac
List file = m1.mex
===

FIGURE 10.24
The third file *lin* creates
the *cat file*—a file used by
sim for source-level tracing.

```
lin Version x.x Table Trace

Tables constructed from user-specified modules:

P Table       Address (hex*dec)        Symbol
              3*3                       x
              4*4                       sub
              8*8                       total

E Table       Address (hex*dec)        Symbol
              0*0                       sub
              1*1                       total
              4*4                       x

R Table       Address (hex*dec)        Module Address (hex*dec)
                   5*5                            4*4

S Table       Address (hex*dec)        Type
                   0*0                       s


================================================================

Text as transformed by E-entry and R-entry processing:

Address       Before E                After  E        After E
hex*dec       Before R                Before R        After R

0   *0             E000       change> E004             E004
1   *1             1000       change> 1008             1008
2   *2             FFFF               FFFF             FFFF
3   *3         x 0011                 0011             0011
4   *4       sub 0000       change> 0003             0003
5   *5             2003               2003   change> 2007
6   *6             F000               F000             F000
7   *7             0022               0022             0022
8   *8    total 0000                  0000             0000

Output file  = m1.mac
Table file   = m1.tab
Cat file     = m1.cat
Label status = case sensitive
```

10.7 SUBROUTINES THAT MULTIPLY

• •

The standard instruction set on H1 does not include a multiply instruction, so let's write a subroutine that multiplies using instructions that are available on H1. If we need to multiply in a program, we can always copy our multiply subroutine into the program and assemble it along with the rest of the program. However, instead of doing this, let's separately assemble our multiply routine and then link its object module as required. Using separate assembly, we do not have to reassemble the assembly code for the multiply subroutine every time we write a program that needs to multiply.

Let's write a special-purpose multiply subroutine that multiplies by 15 only (we will consider general-purpose multiply subroutines in Chapter 13). An obvious, but inefficient, implementation is to repeatedly add the number that is being multiplied. For example, $15 \times n$ can be computed by summing 15 n's. A subroutine to do this would use a loop, each iteration of which would add one n. There is, however, a much better way to compute $15 \times n$. We can start with n and double it four times. On the first doubling operation, we get $2 \times n$. We then double this value to get $4 \times n$. After four doubling operations, we have $16 \times n$. If we now subtract the original n, we get

$$16 \times n - n = 15 \times n$$

Each doubling operation requires only one addition. Thus, we need only four additions and one subtraction instead of the 14 additions required by the loop approach. Moreover, our doubling approach does not need a loop. Because it uses fewer additions and has no loop overhead, our doubling approach is far more efficient than the loop approach.

Figure 10.25 shows a multiply-by-15 subroutine, `mult15`, that uses the doubling approach. The subroutine uses a local variable on the stack (at relative address 0) to store the result of each doubling, which is then used in the next doubling operation. We pass the number to be multiplied to the subroutine on the stack (at relative address 2). The result of the multiplication is passed back to the caller in the `ac` register.

There are two names associated with the module in Figure 10.25. First, there is `mult15`, the *calling name* (i.e., the name used by the call instruction to invoke the module). Second, there is `fmult15.mas`, the *file name* (i.e., the name of the file that holds the assembly source for the module). The calling and file base name can be the same. For example, we could have used `mult15` for the calling name and `mult15.mas` for the file name. However, to keep things clear in the following discussion, we will use distinct names for the calling name and the file name. In particular, for the file name, we will use the calling name prefixed with the letter "f" and suffixed with ".mas". Accordingly, the name of the file containing the source code for the `mult15` module is `fmult15.mas`. Notice that the program in Figure 10.25 includes a `public` directive that makes the calling name `mult15` global.

FIGURE 10.25

```
1                              ; fmult15.mas
2 mult15:   aloc   1           ; allocate local variable temp
3           ldr    2           ; get parameter (n)
4           addr   2           ; get 2n
5           str    0           ; save 2n in temp
6           addr   0           ; get 4n
7           str    0           ; save 4n in temp
8           addr   0           ; get 8n
9           str    0           ; save 8n in temp
10          addr   0           ; get 16n
11          subr   2           ; get 16n - n = 15n
12          dloc   1           ; deallocate local variable temp
13          ret                ; product returned in ac reg
14          public mult15
```

FIGURE 10.26

```
 1                                      ; fsquare.mas
 2 square:    aloc    2                 ; create local variables sum, odd
 3            ldc     0
 4            str     1                 ; initialize sum to 0
 5            ldc     1                 ; initialize odd to 1
 6            str     0
 7 loop:      ldr     3                 ; get parameter (count)
 8            jz      done              ; all done if count = 0
 9            sub     @1                ; subtract 1 from count
10            str     3                 ; save count
11            ldr     1                 ; get sum
12            addr    0                 ; add odd to sum
13            str     1                 ; save sum
14            ldr     0                 ; get odd
15            add     @2                ; add 2 to odd
16            str     0                 ; save odd
17            ja      loop
18 done:      ldr     1                 ; get sum
19            dloc    2                 ; deallocate local variables
20            ret                       ; square returned in ac reg
21 @1:        dw      1
22 @2:        dw      2
23            public square
```

Another interesting subroutine is in Figure 10.26. This subroutine squares the number that is passed. It uses the equation n^2 = the sum of the first n odd integers. For example,

$$4^2 = 1 + 3 + 5 + 7 = 16$$

The **square** subroutine uses a loop that adds **odd** to **sum** on each iteration. **odd** assumes the values 1, 3, 5, . . . on successive iterations of the loop. Thus, **sum** accumulates the value of $1 + 3 + 5 + \ldots$. **square** uses the parameter that it is passed as the loop counter. Its initial value determines the number of times the loop executes. For example, if we pass 4 to **square**, then the loop executes four times, resulting in **sum** accumulating the sum of the first four odd numbers $(1 + 3 + 5 + 7)$, thereby computing 4^2.

Now that we have subroutines that square (**square**) and multiply by 15 (**mult15**), we can easily write a subroutine that computes $15 \times n^2$. The **poly** subroutine in Figure 10.27 performs this computation on the parameter it is passed (at relative address 1). It calls the **square** and **mult15** subroutines.

10.8   USING A LIBRARY

• •

Let's write a module called **main** that calls our **poly** subroutine, which, in turn, calls **square** and **mult15**. We show the **main** module in Figure 10.28. Assume that our **main** module is in the file **fmain.mas**, and the **mult15**, **square**, and **poly** sub-

FIGURE 10.27

```
1                                    ; fpoly.mas
2 poly:    ldr      1               ; get parameter to poly
3          push                     ; create parameter to square
4          call     square
5          dloc     1               ; remove parameter
6          push                     ; create parameter to mult15
7          call     mult15
8          dloc     1               ; remove parameter
9          ret                      ; return result
10         public poly
11         extern square
12         extern mult15
```

FIGURE 10.28

```
1                                   ; fmain.mas
2 main:    ldc      2               ; pass poly 2
3          push
4          call     poly
5          dloc     1
6          dout                     ; output is 15 x 2 squared = 60
7          ldc      '\n'
8          aout
9          halt
10         extern poly
```

routines, respectively, are in the files **fmult15.mas**, **fsquare.mas**, and **fpoly.mas**. To create an executable program, we first must assemble each module. If this were not the first use of our subroutines, then they would have been previously assembled, and there would, of course, be no need to reassemble them now. The commands to assemble our modules are

mas fmain
mas fmult15
mas fsquare
mas fpoly

The four assemblies produce the object modules **fmain.mob**, **fmult15.mob**, **fsquare.mob**, and **fpoly.mob**. Next we link all the object modules. In the command invoking **lin**, we must specify the **main** module first so that it appears first (and, therefore, gets control first) in the executable program. If we had used an **end** directive in the **main** module, then the order would not matter. The order in which we specify the subroutines **fmult15**, **fsquare**, and **fpoly** is not important. The command to link all the object modules and produce an executable file **fmain.mac** is

lin fmain fmult15 fsquare fpoly

must be first

The command invoking `lin` becomes increasingly complex as the number of subroutines needed by a program increases. Because of this increasing complexity, it is easy to make an error when invoking `lin`, such as neglecting to enter the names of some of the modules that are needed. For example, because the **main** module calls only the **poly** module (which is in the file `fpoly.mob`), we might incorrectly conclude that we need to specify only `fmain.mob` and `fpoly.mob` in the `lin` command. Thus, we might enter:

```
lin fmain fpoly
```

`lin` would respond with the error message

```
Unresolved external reference square
```

because the **poly** module in `fpoly.mob` needs a **square** module, and a **square** module is not among the input files given to `lin`. Another problem we may encounter when linking numerous modules is that we may forget which files contain the modules that a program needs. For example, suppose a module calls the **mult15** module. We might forget which file contains **mult15**, particularly if we are not using a file-naming convention that allows us to determine the file name from the calling name. Clearly, we need to simplify the process of specifying which modules need to be linked with a program. Ideally, `lin` would do everything for us. In particular, it would identify which modules need to be linked, find these modules, and then link these modules. This automated operation is precisely what `lin` can do; however, it requires that we first collect the object modules of all our subroutines (the entire collection—not just those needed by a particular program) into a single file called a *library*. For example, to create a library consisting of copies of `fmult15.mob`, `fsquare.mob`, and `fpoly.mob`, we invoke the library program, `lib`, with

```
lib fmult15 fsquare fpoly
```

`lib` then combines the listed modules (it assumes the extension ".mob" for input files) to create the library `fmult15.lib` (the base name of the library defaults to the base name of the first input file).

Figure 10.29 shows the structure of `fmult15.lib` file that `lib` creates. The library starts with the ASCII code for L. This code identifies `fmult15.lib` as a library. (`lin` will not use a file as a library unless it has this leading L.) Following the L are copies of the object modules `fmult15.mob`, `fsquare.mob`, and `fpoly.mob`. Immediately preceding each object module in the library is a length field containing the length of the object module it precedes. When searching `fmult15.lib`, the `lin` program uses the values in the length fields to jump from one object module to the next.

The **pic** and **mex** programs can display libraries as well as executable and object modules. Figure 10.30 shows the display of `fmult15.lib` that **mex** produces. We see that the library starts with 004C (the ASCII code for L), which is followed by a length field containing 0016 hex. This is the length of the first module (**mult15**). The header starts with 0050 (the ASCII code for P). This is the beginning of a P entry for **mult15**. Modules 2 and 3 in the display are the **square** and **poly** modules.

Now that we have constructed our library `fmult15.lib`, we can link the **main** module without having to specify the modules that it needs with

```
lin fmain /Lfmult15
```

FIGURE 10.29   `fmult15.lib`

L
Length
Object module for mult15
Length
Object module for square
Length
Object module for poly

The `/L` argument specifies the library (`lin` assumes the extension ".lib" for library names). `lin` then performs the following steps:

1. `lin` inputs the specified input files (only `fmain.mob` in this example), adjusting and saving the header entries, and appending the text to the text in its text buffer. (Initially, the text buffer is empty.)
2. For each saved E entry, `lin` performs the following operations:
   a. It gets the external symbol that is stored in the E entry.
   b. It searches among its saved P entries for an entry for this symbol.
   c. If it cannot find the required P entry among its saved entries, it then searches for it in the libraries specified on the command line (`fmult15.lib` in this example). If it finds a module with the required P entry in a library, it inputs this module, adjusting and saving its header entries and appending its text to the text in the text buffer. If, on the other hand, it cannot find the P entry in any library, it generates an "unresolved external reference" error message and terminates.
   d. Assuming `lin` finds the P entry it needs, it resolves the external reference that it is currently processing.
3. `lin` adjusts all the locations in the text that require it, which are those pointed to by the saved R entries. `lin` adjusts these locations by adding to them their corresponding module addresses that also appear in the R table entry (see Figure 10.21).
4. `lin` outputs a header that is appropriate for the final executable program to the output file (`fmain.mac` in this example). This header consists of all the saved header entries, with all the E entries converted to R entries.
5. It outputs the text in the text buffer (which is now resolved and adjusted) to the output file (`fmain.mac` in this example).

In our example (in which `lin` links `fmain.mob` using the `fmult15.lib` library), `lin` repeats step 2 three times. Initially there is only one saved E entry (for `poly`).

FIGURE 10.30

```
004C (L for Library)

===================== Module Number 1 ================================

Length = 0016 (hex) 22 (decimal)

Header:
        0:   0050 0000 006D 0075 006C 0074 0031 0035    P.mult15
        8:   0000 0054                                   .T

Text:
        0:   F501 4002 6002 5000 6000 5000 6000 5000    ........
        8:   6000 7002 F601 F000                         ....

===================== Module Number 2 ================================

Length = 0027 (hex) 39 (decimal)

Header:
        0:   0052 0006 0052 0007 0052 000D 0052 000F    R.R.R.R.
        8:   0050 0000 0073 0071 0075 0061 0072 0065    P.square
       10:   0000 0054                                   .T

Text:
        0:   F502 8000 5001 8001 5000 4003 C010 3013    ........
        8:   5003 4001 6000 5001 4000 2014 5000 9005    ........
       10:   4001 F602 F000 0001 0002                    .....

===================== Module Number 3 ================================

Length = 0022 (hex) 34 (decimal)

Header:
        0:   0045 0002 0073 0071 0075 0061 0072 0065    E.square
        8:   0000 0045 0005 006D 0075 006C 0074 0031    .E.mult1
       10:   0035 0000 0050 0000 0070 006F 006C 0079    5.P.poly
       18:   0000 0054                                   .T

Text:
        0:   4001 F300 E000 F601 F300 E000 F601 F000    ........

Input file = fmult15.lib
List file  = fmult15.mex
```

Thus, on the first execution of step 2, **lin** inputs the **poly** module from **fmult15.lib**, and resolves the external reference to it from **main**. The **poly** module brings with it two more E entries, one for **square** and one for **mult15** (see Figure 10.27). Thus, **lin** performs step 2 two more times. On the second execution of step 2, **lin** brings in the **square** module from **fmult15.lib**; on the third execution of step 2, **lin** brings in the **mult15** module.

FIGURE 10.31

```
             public f1
             public f2
             public f3
f1:      aloc 5.
         ...
         ret
;=================
f2:      ldc   5
         ...
         ret
;=================
f3:      aloc 1
         ...
         ret
```

When `lin` uses a library, it links only those modules in the library that are needed. In our previous example, `lin` linked all three modules in the library `fmult15.lib` only because all three are needed by the **main** module. Typically, however, a library contains many modules, only a small subset of which are needed during any one execution of `lin`.

When `lin` is invoked, more that one object module and more than one library can be specified. For example, if we invoke `lin` with

```
lin z1 z2 /Llib1 /Llib2 /Llib3
```

then `lin` links `z1.mob` and `z2.mob` with additional modules from the specified libraries as required by the external references. The order in which libraries are specified determines the order in which they are searched. Thus, if two versions of a module appear in two libraries, `lin` will use the version in the library that is specified earlier. `lin` searches a library sequentially—from top to bottom. Thus, if two versions of the same module are in a library, the version that appears first will be used.

It is legal to write an assembly module that contains multiple functions—just place one function after another in the source program. For example, in Figure 10.31, we show the skeleton of a single module that contains three functions, **f1**, **f2**, and **f3**. We can then assemble this multiple-function module and place its object module in a library. However, the module can be linked only as a unit. Thus, if only the **f2** function is needed, the entire module, including **f1** and **f3**, is linked.

It is very instructive to examine the table trace that `lin` can produce when linking with libraries. For example, if we invoke `lin` with

```
lin fmain /Lfmult15
```

`lin` will output the file `fmain.tab` containing the table trace shown in Figure 10.32. This trace shows several snapshots of the P, E, R, and S tables. In the first, we see an E entry for **poly**, but no corresponding P entry (because `lin` at this point has not yet input the **poly** module). Next, we see the message "Searching for poly in

FIGURE 10.32   lin Version x.x Table Trace

Tables constructed from user-specified modules:

P Table empty

E Table   Address (hex*dec)   Symbol
                     2*2   poly

R Table empty

S Table empty

==

***** Searching for poly in fmult15.lib library
***** Inputing poly module from fmult15.lib library

==

Tables updated with header information from poly module:

P Table   Address (hex*dec)   Symbol
                     8*8   poly

E Table   Address (hex*dec)   Symbol
                     2*2   poly
                    A*10   square
                    D*13   mult15

R Table empty

S Table empty

==

***** Searching for square in fmult15.lib library
***** Inputing square module from fmult15.lib library

==

Tables updated with header information from square module:

P Table   Address (hex*dec)   Symbol
                     8*8   poly
                    10*16   square

E Table   Address (hex*dec)   Symbol
                     2*2   poly
                    A*10   square
                    D*13   mult15

R Table   Address (hex*dec)   Module Address (hex*dec)
                    16*22   10*16

(continued)

438

FIGURE 10.32
(continued)

```
                              17*23                 10*16
                              1D*29                 10*16
                              1F*31                 10*16

S Table empty


============================================================

***** Searching for mult15 in fmult15.lib library
***** Inputing mult15 module from fmult15.lib library


============================================================

Tables updated with header information from mult15 module:

P Table          Address (hex*dec)      Symbol
                        8*8                poly
                        10*16              square
                        25*37              mult15

E Table          Address (hex*dec)      Symbol
                        2*2                poly
                        A*10               square
                        D*13               mult15

R Table          Address (hex*dec)      Module Address (hex*dec)
                        16*22                  10*16
                        17*23                  10*16
                        1D*29                  10*16
                        1F*31                  10*16

S Table empty


============================================================

Text as transformed by E-entry and R-entry processing:
```

Address hex*dec	Before E Before R	After E Before R	After E After R
0 *0	8002	8002	8002
1 *1	F300	F300	F300
2 *2	E000	change> E008	E008
3 *3	F601	F601	F601
4 *4	FFFD	FFFD	FFFD
5 *5	800A	800A	800A
6 *6	FFFB	FFFB	FFFB
7 *7	FFFF	FFFF	FFFF
8 *8	poly 0000	change> 4001	4001
9 *9	0000	change> F300	F300
A *10	0000	change> E010	E010

(continued)

FIGURE 10.32
(continued)

B	*11		0000	change> F601		F601
C	*12		0000	change> F300		F300
D	*13		0000	change> E025		E025
E	*14		0000	change> F601		F601
F	*15		0000	change> F000		F000
10	*16	square	0000	change> F502		F502
11	*17		0000	change> 8000		8000
12	*18		0000	change> 5001		5001
13	*19		0000	change> 8001		8001
14	*20		0000	change> 5000		5000
15	*21		0000	change> 4003		4003
16	*22		0000	change> C010	change> C020
17	*23		0000	change> 3013	change> 3023
18	*24		0000	change> 5003		5003
19	*25		0000	change> 4001		4001
1A	*26		0000	change> 6000		6000
1B	*27		0000	change> 5001		5001
1C	*28		0000	change> 4000		4000
1D	*29		0000	change> 2014	change> 2024
1E	*30		0000	change> 5000		5000
1F	*31		0000	change> 9005	change> 9015
20	*32		0000	change> 4001		4001
21	*33		0000	change> F602		F602
22	*34		0000	change> F000		F000
23	*35		0000	change> 0001		0001
24	*36		0000	change> 0002		0002
25	*37	mult15	0000	change> F501		F501
26	*38		0000	change> 4002		4002
27	*39		0000	change> 6002		6002
28	*40		0000	change> 5000		5000
29	*41		0000	change> 6000		6000
2A	*42		0000	change> 5000		5000
2B	*43		0000	change> 6000		6000
2C	*44		0000	change> 5000		5000
2D	*45		0000	change> 6000		6000
2E	*46		0000	change> 7002		7002
2F	*47		0000	change> F601		F601
30	*48		0000	change> F000		F000

```
Output file  = fmain.mac
Table file   = fmain.tab
Cat file     = fmain.cat
Label status = case sensitive
```

`fmult15.lib` library" that `lin` generates when it starts its library search for `poly`. On finding it, `lin` inputs the module that contains it and generates the message, "Inputing poly module from fmult15.lib library." The next snapshot shows that the symbol `poly` is now defined (i.e., it appears in a P entry). However, we now have two new E entries—`square` and `mult15`—for which there are no corresponding P entries. As the next two snapshots show, `lin` then searches for and inputs the modules in which `square` and `mult15` are defined. In the first text snapshot, all the words corresponding to the `poly`, `square`, and `mult15` modules are zero because this snapshot is taken before `lin` starts its library search.

10.9 ADVANTAGES OF SEPARATE ASSEMBLY

Let's consider the advantages of separate assembly—that is, implementing a program with a collection of separately assembled modules. Most of the advantages become significant only when program size is large.

One advantage of separate assembly is that it is a means of controlling the scope of labels. The scope of labels does not extend beyond the file in which they appear unless we use the `public` and `extern` directives. Thus, two separately assembled modules can use the same labels without creating conflicts. If a program were assembled in one big file, then every label would have to be unique. If the program consisted of 100 modules, each written by a different programmer, each programmer would have to check with 99 other programmers to make sure that no local label was duplicated. Some assemblers have special directives to control the scope of labels (`mas` does not). However, even with such assemblers, separate assembly—because of its simplicity—is the usual choice for controlling scope.

Suppose a program is implemented with a collection of separately assembled modules. Then if one module needs to be modified, only that module needs to be reassembled. For a small program, this is not much of a consideration. However, for a large program—let's say one with 100,000 lines of code—reassembling one 100-line module is clearly far better than reassembling all 100,000 lines. Of course, the separate assembly approach requires the link step. However, when the program is large, the overhead of linking is less than the overhead of reassembling an entire program.

Many assemblers have limitations that a large program might exceed, causing the assembly to fail. For example, assemblers typically have an upper limit on the size of the symbol table that it builds during pass 1. If a large program has so many labels that the symbol table overflows, the assembly is forced to fail. The simple solution here, of course, is separate assembly. Each separate assembly is small, allowing the assembler to complete without any danger of symbol table overflow.

All the aforementioned advantages of separate assembly are important. However, by far the most important advantage of separate assembly is that it allows the use of libraries. Once a large library of useful routines is constructed, a programmer's task is greatly simplified. Whenever a function is needed, the programmer need only call the prewritten function in the library and include the appropriate `extern` directive in the calling module.

The use of libraries is important for high-level languages as well as assembly language. For example, every C++ compiler comes with a standard library containing a large collection of useful functions. Additional libraries are readily available that provide special purpose capabilities (e.g., windowing). In contrast to

C++, standard Pascal allows no linking, and, therefore, does not support libraries. This aspect of standard Pascal contributed more to its short lifespan as a popular programming language than any other.

10.10 START-UP CODE

In the C++ programs that we have compiled up until now, we showed the **main** function as the function that gets control directly from the operating system (i.e., **sim**), and gives back control to the operating system when it executes a `halt` instruction. This sequence, however, does not take place when a real C++ program executes. Before a C++ program can start executing (i.e., before control is passed to the **main** function), a start-up initialization must be performed. The operating system does not perform this initialization; however, it has to be done *before* the **main** function gets control. Thus, there must be an initialization module that gets control before the **main** function starts executing. This initialization module is called *start-up code*. When a compiled C++ program is linked, it is always linked with the object module for start-up code as well as with any other modules it needs. Thus, start-up code is always part of the executable program. It gets control directly from the operating system, performs its initialization tasks, and then calls the **main** function.

Start-up code has to perform a variety of tasks. For example, some of the functions in the standard C++ library use data structures. These data structures need to be initialized by start-up code. Start-up code also constructs the **argc** and **argv** parameters that are passed to the **main** function. These two parameters contain information from the command line invoking the program. For example, suppose we invoke **test**, a compiled and linked C++ program, with

```
test a1 a2 a3
```

The operating system would then make this command line available to start-up code, which, in turn, would

1. Parse (i.e., break up) the command line into its component parts
2. Build the two arguments shown in Figure 10.33, commonly named **argc** and **argv**, containing information on the command line
3. Call the **main** function, passing it **argc** and **argv**.

argc contains the number of items on the command line; **argv** is a pointer to an array of pointers, which, in turn, point to the individual items on the command

FIGURE 10.33

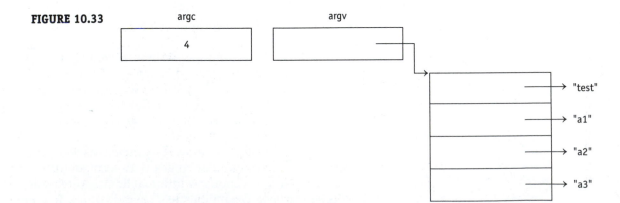

line. When the operating system reads in a command line, it places it *as is* (i.e., as one continuous string) in some area that is accessible to the start-up code in the program that is about to execute. Start-up code must parse this string into its component parts and place pointers to these parts into an array. It then pushes onto the stack the address of this array and the argument count, thereby creating the **argc** and **argv** parameters that **main** can access.

After start-up code has performed the required initialization, it calls the **main** function with the instruction

```
call main
```

This instruction within start-up code is what requires every C++ program to have a **main** function, and it is why the **main** function always gets control first, after start-up code. If we changed this instruction to

```
call ostrich
```

then every C++ program would have to have an **ostrich** function, which would get control first. When **main** completes, it returns to start-up code. Start-up code then does some final housekeeping and returns to the operating system.

Let's look at a more realistic compilation of a C++ program. Consider a program consisting of two files that has the structure shown in Figure 10.34. Note that **main** returns a return code. In the previous chapters, none of our **main** functions returned return codes, but this, as you shall soon see, is a bad practice. Thus, from now on, all of our **main** functions will return a return code (0 for a normal termination, nonzero for an abnormal termination).

Figure 10.35 shows the assembly form for the program in Figure 10.34. The **main** function is now like any other called function. In particular, it terminates by means of a `ret` instruction instead of a `halt` instruction. Moreover, because it is assembled separately from start-up code, it contains a **public** directive for **main**, making **main** accessible from start-up code. Start-up code contains an **end** directive that specifies the entry point of the program (the label **start_up**). Of course, only start-up code should contain an **end** directive.

To create a complete program from the modules in Figure 10.35, we first have to assemble **fmain.mas** and **fsub.mas** to create the object modules **fmain.mob** and **fsub.mob**. The H1 software package contains the object module for start-up code (in the file **sup.mob**), so we don't have to assemble start-up code. To perform the assemblies and link, we enter

```
mas fmain
mas fsub
lin fmain fsum sup
```

FIGURE 10.34

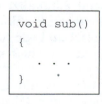

fmain.cpp

```
int main()
{
    . . .
    sub();
    . . .
    return 0;
}
```

fsub.cpp

```
void sub()
{
    . . .
}
```

FIGURE 10.35

sup.mas

```
; standard start-up code
start_up:
;       initialization code
        . . .
        call main
;       final housekeeping code
        . . .
        extern main
        end start_up
```

fmain.mas

```
; main function
main:     . . .
          call @sub$v
          . . .
          ldc  0
          ret
          public main
          extern @sub$v
```

fsub.mas

```
; sub function
@sub$v:  . . .
         . . .
         . . .
         ret
         public @sub$v
```

which creates an executable file **fmain.mac**. If we then invoke **sim** with

sim fmain a1 a2 a3 /L

sim passes that portion of the command line that follows "sim" to start-up code. Specifically, it passes the string "fmain a1 a2 a3". The argument **/L** (which requests a log file) is not included in this string because it is an argument for **sim** and not for the test program. Start-up code then builds and passes to **main** the **argc** and **argv** arguments exactly as we see in Figure 10.33.

C++ compilers typically output object modules, not assembly language modules. Thus, if we compile **fmain.cpp** and **fsub.cpp** in Figure 10.34 with a C++ compiler, we do not have to perform a separate assembly step to create object modules for the link step, as we did earlier. In fact, most modern compilers have a *project* or *make* facility that allows a user to trigger both the compilation and linking of multiple modules with a single command.

Let's examine the standard start-up code for H1 given in Figure 10.36.

Lines 6 and 7 initialize **sp**. Although machine code to initialize **sp** is not necessary (because **sim** initializes all the read/write registers to zero), it is one of the tasks start-up code has to do on most computers. We include it in our start-up code so that it better models what you will typically find on other computer systems.

Lines 10 to 64 constitute a loop, each iteration of which processes one argument from the command line. We will call this loop the "outer loop." Suppose we invoke **sim** with

sim test a1 a2 a3

FIGURE 10.36

```
 1 ; standard start-up code                            sup.mas
 2 ; ================================================================
 3 loc0:        dw    'Z'              ; to test for null pointer assignment
 4
 5 ;            initialize sp register
 6 start_up:    ldc   0
 7              swap
 8
 9 ;            test if clptr has reached the end of the command line
10 getarg:      ld    clptr            ; get next char in command line
11              ldi
12              jz    alldone          ; if null char, all done
13
14 ;            check if too many args—max = 20
15              ld    argc             ; get current count
16              sub   @20
17              jnz   * + 4
18              ldc   errmsg1          ; display error message
19              sout
20              ja    done             ; terminate execution if count at 20
21
22 ;            move contents of clptr into next avail slot in vector
23              ld    clptr            ; get address of next arg
24              push
25              ld    vectorptr
26              sti                    ; put address into vector
27
28 ;            move clptr to end of current argument
29              ld    clptr
30 getchar:     ldi                    ; get next char in command line
31              jz    endarg           ; ja   if null char
32              sub   blank
33              jz    endarg           ; ja   if space
34              ld    clptr            ; move command line ptr to next char
35              add   @1
36              st    clptr
37              ja    getchar
38
39 ;            terminate argument with null character
40 endarg:      ldc   0
41              push
42              ld    clptr            ; clptr points to where null char goes
```

(continued)

FIGURE 10.36 (continued)

```
43              sti
44
45 ;           increment count in argc
46              ld   argc
47              add  @1
48              st   argc
49
50 ;           prepare for next argument
51
52 ;           move vectorptr to next slot in vector
53              ld   vectorptr
54              add  @1
55              st   vectorptr
56
57 ;           move clptr to beginning of next arg
58 nextarg:     ld   clptr
59              add  @1
60              st   clptr
61              ldi
62              sub  blank
63              jz   nextarg         ; move over blanks
64              ja   getarg          ; now process next arg
65
66 ; ==========================================================================
67 ;           pass argv (the address of vector) and argc args to main
68 alldone:     ldc  vector          ; push address of vector
69              push
70              ld   argc            ; push number of args
71              push
72              call main
73              dloc 2               ; deallocate parameters
74              st   retcode         ; save return code from main
75 ; ==========================================================================
76 ;           final housekeeping code
77
78 ;           check if word at loc0 still has 'Z'
79 testloc0:    ld   loc0
80              sub  z
81              jz   done            ; if still there, ja to done
82              ld   testloc0        ; start-up code at loc 0?
83              jz   atloc0          ; if yes, display null ptr message
84              ldc  errmsg2         ; if not, display other message
```

(continued)

FIGURE 10.36 (continued)

```
85                  ja    outmsg
86 atloc0:          ldc   errmsg3
87 outmsg:          sout
88
89 done:            ld    retcode        ; restore ret code from main
90                  halt                 ; return to op sys (sim)
91 ; ————————————————————————————————————————————————————
92 ;                constants and variables
93 @1:              dw    1
94 @20:             dw    20
95 clptr:           dw    3900           ; address of command line
96 vectorptr:       dw    vector         ; array of char ptrs to the arguments
97 blank:           dw    ' '
98 argc:            dw    0              ; count of the number of arguments
99 vector:          dw    20 dup 0       ; space for 20 arg pointers
100 z:              dw    'Z'
101 retcode:        dw    0
102 errmsg1:        dw    "\nToo many command line arguments\n"
103 errmsg2:        dw    "\nStart-up code corrupted\n"
104 errmsg3:        dw    "\nNull pointer assignment\n"
105                 extern main
106                 end start_up
```

Then before the outer loop starts executing, we have the following data structures in effect (see Figure 10.37a):

- The command line, "test a1 a2 a3", appears in main memory as a null-terminated string starting at location 3900 decimal (placed there by **sim**).
- **clptr** (the "command line pointer") on line 95 points to the beginning of this string.
- **vectorptr** on line 96 points to the first slot in **vector**.
- **argc** (the argument counter) on line 98 contains 0.

On the first iteration of the outer loop, lines 23 to 26 place the initial contents of **clptr** into the slot of **vector** to which **vectorptr** initially points. On the first iteration, **vectorptr** points to **vector**'s first slot. Thus, the first slot of **vector** is assigned a pointer to the beginning of the command line in memory. The nested loop on lines 30 to 37 increment **clptr** until it points to the blank following "test." Lines 40 to 43 then store the null character over this blank, thereby creating a string consisting of only the first argument (i.e., "test"). Next, lines 46 to 48 increment the argument counter, **argc**. The remainder of the outer loop prepares for its next iteration. Specifically, lines 53 to 55 increment **vectorptr**, and lines 60 to 66 increment **clptr** until it points to the beginning of the next argument. Figure 10.37b shows the data structures in effect at the end of the first iteration of the outer loop.

The next three iterations of the outer loop similarly process the remaining three arguments. Figure 10.37c shows the data structures at the end of the fourth iteration.

FIGURE 10.37a   Initial Data Structures

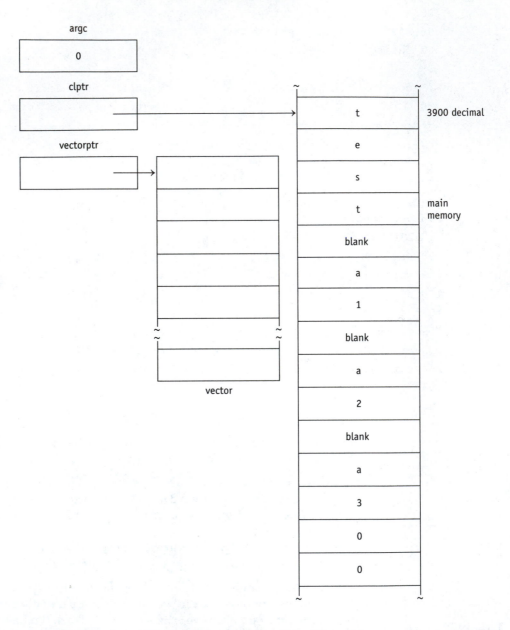

In the fourth iteration of the outer loop, lines 58 to 64 increment `clptr` until it points to a nonblank character. Because there are no more arguments, `clptr` ends up pointing to the null character following the fourth argument (see Figure 10.37c). The null character to which `clptr` points triggers an exit from the outer loop on line 12 at the beginning of the fifth iteration.

The code on lines 68 to 73 that calls `main` follows the outer loop. Line 69 pushes the address of **vector** (which creates the **argv** parameter that is passed to `main`). Line 71 pushes the value of **argc** (which creates the **argc** parameter that is passed to `main`). Next, line 72 calls `main`, and, when `main` returns, line 73 removes the **argc** and **argv** parameters from the stack. Line 74 then saves the return code from `main`. This return code will ultimately be returned to the operating system (i.e., `sim`) by start-up code.

FIGURE 10.37b

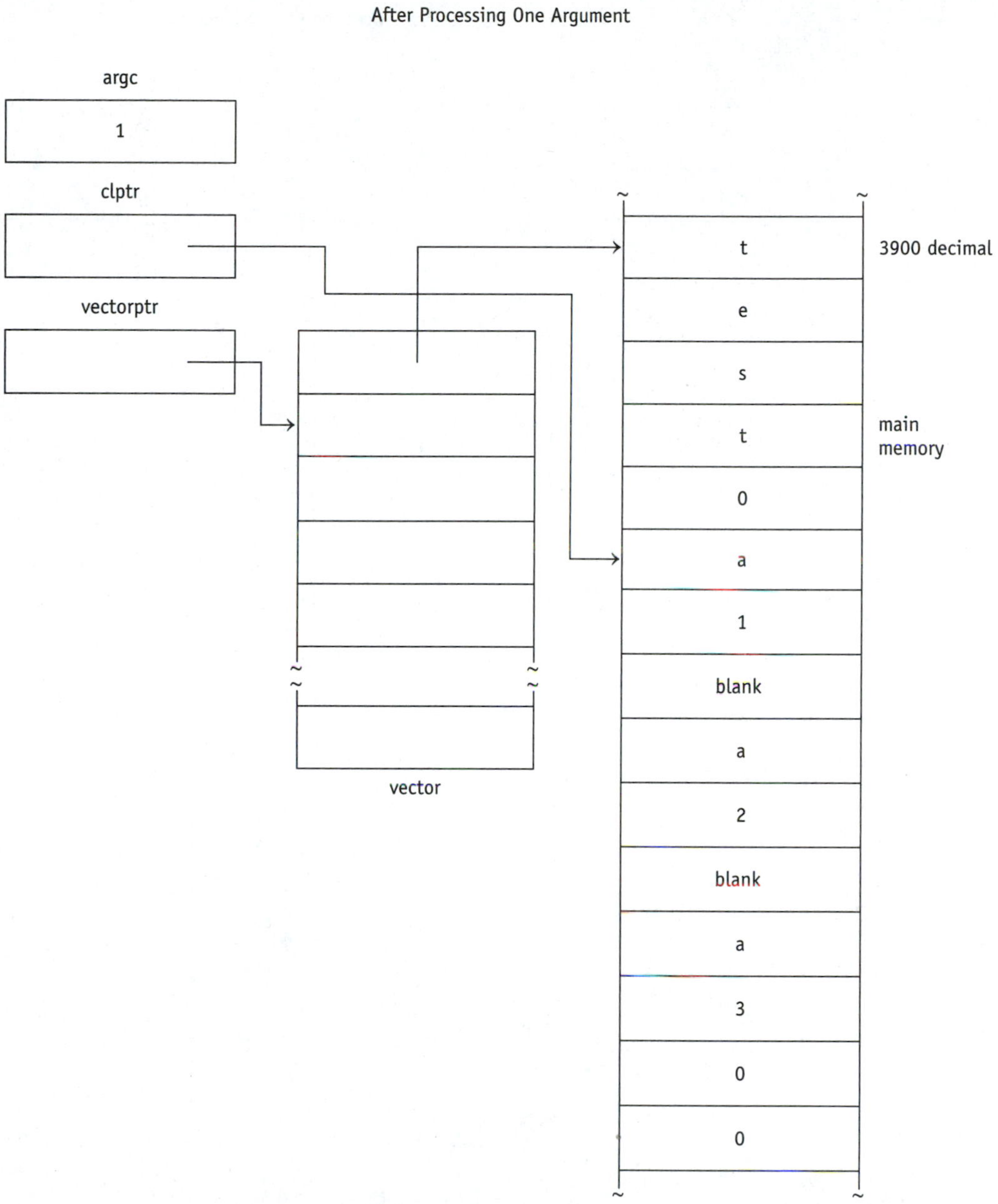

After Processing One Argument

After the calling sequence for **main** is complete, start-up code performs a test for null pointer assignments. A *null pointer assignment* is an assignment to a location accessed by dereferencing the null pointer. For example, suppose **p** is a pointer that contains the null pointer (i.e., it contains 0). Then the following statement

```
*p = 5;
```

is an error because it dereferences the null pointer. This assignment statement performs a null pointer assignment, and has the effect of assigning 5 to location 0.

Null pointer assignments cannot be detected at compile time because compilers do not know what will be in pointer variables like **p** at run time. However, the start-up code in Figure 10.36 performs a simple check that can, in fact, detect at

FIGURE 10.37C

After Processing Four Arguments

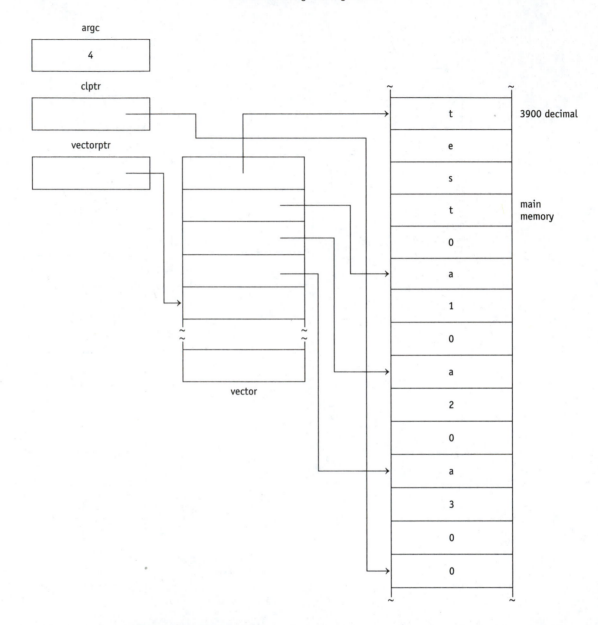

run time a null pointer assignment. Line 3, the first word in the start-up code, defines a word containing 'Z'. If start-up code occupies memory starting at location 0, then its first word (the word containing 'Z') is at location 0. Thus, a null pointer assignment would overlay this 'Z'. To determine if a null pointer assignment occurred, start-up code on lines 79 to 81 checks if this 'Z' is still there after the return from `main`. If the 'Z' is not there (indicating that a null pointer assignment overlaid it), lines 86 and 87 display the error message

`Null pointer assignment`

If the load point of the program is not 0, or if start-up code is not the first module linked, then start-up code does *not* reside at location 0. In this case, a null pointer assignment—which corrupts location 0—will not corrupt the first word of start-up code. Thus, the test of the first word of start-up code simply detects the corruption of this word. Accordingly, lines 84, 85, and 87 of start-up code display the error message

```
Start-up code corrupted
```

Lines 82 and 83 determine if start-up code starts at location 0 by checking the memory location corresponding to the label **testloc0**. The **ld** instruction at this location contains the address of the first word of start-up code. Thus, if this address is zero, start-up code starts at location 0.

Let's consider a simple C++ program in which we use the **argc** and **argv** parameters. From Figure 10.33, we can see that **argv** is a pointer that, in turn, points to a **char** pointer. Thus, we should declare it in **main** as

```
char **argv
```

We should read this declaration in two parts. We read the right part

```
*argv
```

as "**argv** is a pointer"; we then read the left part,

```
char *
```

as "to a **char** pointer." Thus, **argv** is a pointer to a **char** pointer. As you learned in Section 8.7, we can also declare **argv** as

```
char *argv[]
```

The empty pair of square brackets tells the compiler that **argv** is a pointer, and **char** * tells the compiler that this pointer points to a **char** pointer. Both declarations are equivalent—they both declare **argv** as a pointer to a **char** pointer. As you learned in Section 8.7, we can use **argv** either as a pointer or as the name of the array to which it points. For example, the following two statements are equivalent and produce *exactly* the same code at the assembly level:

```
cout << argv[1];      // using argv as an array
cout << *(argv + 1);  // using argv as a pointer
```

Figure 10.38 shows a C++ program that outputs the value in **argc** and the strings pointed to by **argv[0]** and **argv[1]**. Suppose the file that contains the program in Figure 10.38 is named **kangaroo.cpp**. If we compile and link it on a Microsoft system we get an executable file name **kangaroo.exe**. If we then invoke this program with

```
C:\>kangaroo hello
```

FIGURE 10.38

```
1   #include <iostream>
2   using namespace std;
3
4   int main(int argc, char *argv[])
5   {
6     cout << "argc    = " << argc << endl;
7     cout << "argv[0] = " << argv[0] << endl;
8     cout << "argv[1] = " << argv[1] << endl;
9   }
```

FIGURE 10.39

```
 1 main:      ldc   @m0        ; cout << "argc = << argc << endl;
 2            sout
 3            ldr   1
 4            dout
 5            ldc   '\n'
 6            aout
 7
 8            ldc   @m1        ; cout << "argv[0] = "<< argv[0] << endl;
 9            sout
10            ldr   2
11            ldi
12            sout
13            ldc   '\n'
14            aout
15
16            ldc   @m2        ; cout << "argv[1] = "<< argv[1] << endl;
17            sout
18            ldr   2
19            add   @1
20            ldi
21            sout
22            ldc   '\n'
23            aout
24
25            ldc   0
26            ret
27 @m0:       dw    "argc   = "
28 @m1:       dw    "argv[0] = "
29 @m2:       dw    "argv[1] = "
30 @1:        dw    1
31            public main
```

the program will respond with

```
argc =     2
argv[0] = C:\KANGAROO.EXE
argv[1] = hello
```

The form of the first argument, **argv[0]**, depends on the operating system. In this example, **argv[0]** is the complete path name of the executable program (C:\KANGAROO.EXE). Some operating systems, however, might provide only the file basename.

Figure 10.39 shows the assembly version of the C++ program in Figure 10.38. Line 10 accesses **argv**, and line 11 dereferences it to access the **argv[0]** pointer. Similarly, line 19 accesses **argv**, line 20 computes **argv** + 1, and line 21 dereferences `argv` + 1 to access the `argv[1]` pointer. Assume the program in Figure 10.39 is in the file `kangaroo.mas`. To run this program, we first assemble it with

`mas kangaroo`

Whenever an input file contains any `public` or `extern` directives, `mas` assumes it is not a complete program, and outputs a ".mob" file instead of a ".mac" file. Thus, when `mas` assembles `kangaroo.mas` it outputs a ".mob" file, `kangaroo.mob`. `mas` also outputs a list file, `kangaroo.1st`, which can be useful for debugging the program. Next, we link `kangaroo.mob` with start-up code, using

`lin kangaroo sup`

to create the executable file `kangaroo.mac`. By linking `kangaroo.mob` first, we make the run-time memory locations of the `kangaroo` program match the addresses that appear in the list file `kangaroo.1st` that `mas` produces. This correspondence simplifies debugging or tracing with `sim`'s debugger because it allows us to read the memory locations of the program directly from the list file. If, instead, we were to link `sup.mob` first, we would have to add the size of start-up code to the addresses in `kangaroo.1st` to determine the corresponding memory locations.

Let's now run the executable file `kangaroo.mac` with

`sim /z kangaroo hello`

The `/z` argument disables `sim`'s debugger. `sim`

1. Loads `kangaroo.mac`.
2. Places the command line (excluding `sim` itself and any argument that starts with '/' or '-') into main memory starting at location 3900 decimal
3. Passes control to start-up code within `kangaroo.mac` (because of the `end` statement in start-up code).

Start-up code creates and passes the `argc` and `argv` parameters to the `main` function in `kangaroo.mac`. The `main` function then outputs

```
argc    = 2
argv[0] = kangaroo
argv[1] = hello
```

On line 89 in Figure 10.36, start-up code loads the return code from `main` that it previously saved on line 74. It then returns to the "operating system" (i.e., `sim`). The operating system can then determine the completion status of the program: A zero in the `ac` register indicates a normal completion; a nonzero indicates an abnormal completion. Now consider what happens if `main` does not return a return code, as was the case for all our `main` functions in the previous chapters. Start-up code would treat whatever garbage happens to be in the `ac` register on return from `main` as the return code (see line 74). Start-up code would then return this garbage to the operating system (see lines 89 and 90). Thus, the operating system gets a return code from `main` *whether or not* `main` *explicitly returns one*. Thus, it is important for `main` to return the correct return code; otherwise, the operating system will get a garbage return code.

Let's look at an example in which we use return codes to the operating system. Figure 10.40 shows two UNIX shell scripts—named `s1` and `s2`—that contain UNIX commands. Suppose `p1` and `p2` are the names of two executable programs. If the user enters `s1` at the UNIX prompt, UNIX will execute the commands within the `s1`

FIGURE 10.40

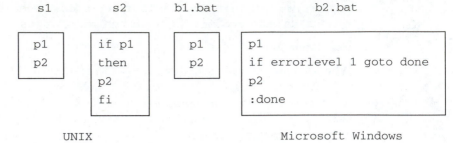

```
        s1              s2         b1.bat              b2.bat

      ┌─────┐        ┌───────┐    ┌─────┐    ┌──────────────────────────┐
      │ p1  │        │ if p1 │    │ p1  │    │ p1                       │
      │ p2  │        │ then  │    │ p2  │    │ if errorlevel 1 goto done│
      └─────┘        │ p2    │    └─────┘    │ p2                       │
                     │ fi    │               │ :done                    │
                     └───────┘               └──────────────────────────┘

            UNIX                              Microsoft Windows
```

file. That is, it will execute p1 and p2, in that order. Now suppose p2 uses a file that p1 creates. If p1 fails, it would not make sense to also execute p2. **s1**, however, executes both p1 and p2, regardless of the termination status of p1. **s2**, on the other hand, executes p2 only if p1 terminates normally (i.e., returns a return code of 0). The **if** statement causes the UNIX shell to test the return code from p1. If it is true (i.e., equal to 0), UNIX executes the statement within the **if** statement—that is, it executes p2; otherwise, it skips p2. **fi** is a keyword that marks the end of the **if** statement.

b1.bat and **b2.bat** in Figure 10.40 are batch files that function in a Microsoft system in a way comparable to **s1** and **s2**. The conditional "errorlevel 1" in **b2.bat** is true whenever the most recently executed program (p1 in this case) returns a return code greater than or equal to 1. Thus, on an abnormal termination of p1, the **goto** command is executed, causing the p2 command to be skipped.

Clearly, if **s2** or **b2.bat** are to work correctly, p1 must return the correct return code. But if we create p1 from a C++ program with a **void**-type **main** function, it would return garbage for a return code. Thus, we should always write **main** so that it returns a valid return code (and we will do so from now on).

10.11   SEPARATE COMPILATION OF C++ MODULES

In Section 10.9 we learned about the advantages of writing a large assembly language program as a collection of small, separately assembled modules. Writing a large C++ program as a collection of separately compiled modules has the same advantages.

Let's look at both a C++ program consisting of separately compiled modules and its corresponding assembly code. Consider the program in Figure 10.41. This C++ program is contained in two separate files. In module 2 in Figure 10.41 the keyword **static** appears in three places:

- In the definition of the global variable **sgv**
- In the definition of the function **f1**
- In the definition of the static local variable **slv**

Let's first consider **slv**. Recall from Section 7.4 that the **static** keyword on a *local* variable definition makes the variable appear as a **dw** directive at the assembly level. Because it appears as a **dw**, it retains its value between successive calls of the function in which it is defined. The variable's scope, however, remains local. Without the **static** keyword, a local variable defaults to **automatic** (i.e., dynamic).

Now consider the two other uses of **static** in Figure 10.41—in a global variable definition and a function definition. Surprisingly, the effect of the **static**

FIGURE 10.41

```
 1    // module 1
 2    void f1();
 3    void f2();
 4    extern int gv;
 5    extern int sgv;
 6    int main()
 7    {
 8       gv = 0;
 9       f2();
10       sgv = 1;   // link error
11       f1();      // link error
12       return 0;
13    }
14
15
16
17
18
```

```
// module 2
int gv;
static int sgv;
static void f1()
{
   int lv;
   static int slv;
   gv = 2;
   sgv = 3;
   lv = 4;
   slv = 5;
}
void f2()
{
   gv = 6;
   sgv = 7;
   f1();
}
```

keyword on a global variable or a function is *completely* different from its effect on a local variable: When the **static** keyword is used in the definition of a global variable or a function, its *only* effect is to restrict their scope to the *file* in which the definitions appear. Thus, in Figure 10.41, the global variable **sgv** and the function **f1** can be referenced only from within module 2. Module 1 can reference **gv** and **f2** (which are not **static**) but it cannot reference **sgv** and **f1**. Thus, lines 10 and 11 in module 1 will cause a link-time error.

Figure 10.42 shows the assembly code that corresponds to the two C++ modules in Figure 10.41. The effect of the various uses of the **static** keyword become easy to understand once we see their effect at the assembly level.

In module 2, the global variable **gv** and the static global variable **sgv** are both defined with **dw** directives. However, a **public** directive appears only for **gv**. The use of **static** in the definition for **sgv** causes the compiler to *not* generate a **public** directive for it. Thus, **sgv** cannot be referenced from outside module 2. Similarly, the use of **static** in the definition of **f1** causes the compiler to *not* generate a **public** directive for it. Thus, it, too, cannot be referenced from outside module 2. Both **gv** and the mangled name for **f2**, on the other hand, have **public** statements because **static** was *not* specified in their definitions. Thus, both **gv** and the mangled name for **f2** can be referenced from outside module 2.

In module 1, **@f2$v**, the mangled name for **f2**, is not locally defined. Thus, the compiler automatically generates an **extern** directive for it in the assembly language program it produces. Similarly, the compiler also generates an **extern** directive for **@f1$v**. However, at link time, the linker will not be able to find **@f1$v** because there is no **public** directive for **@f1$v** in module 2. The compiler also generates **extern** directives for **gv** and **sgv** because both are specified in **extern** declarations at the C++ level. If these **extern** declarations were not present at the C++ level, the compiler would treat **gv** and **sgv** as undefined symbols, and, accordingly, generate error messages. With the program as is, the linker will find **gv** but not **sgv** because there is no **public** directive for **sgv** in module 2.

FIGURE 10.42

```
 1 ;         module 1                      |  ;          module 2
 2 main:   ldc   0        ; gv = 0;        |  @f1$v:   aloc 1         ; allocate lv
 3         st    gv                        |
 4                                         |           ldc   2        ; gv = 2;
 5         call  @f2$v    ; f2();          |           st    gv
 6                                         |
 7         ldc   1        ; sgv = 1;       |           ldc   3        ; sgv = 2;
 8         st    sgv                       |           st    sgv
 9                                         |
10         call  @f1$v    ; f1();          |           ldc   4        ; lv = 4;
11                                         |           str   0
12         ldc            0                |
13         ret                             |           ldc   5        ; slv = 5;
14         public main                     |           st    @s0_slv
15         extern gv                       |
16         extern sgv                      |           dloc  1        ; dealloc lv
17         extern @f2$v                    |           ret
18         extern @f1$v                    |  gv:       dw    0
19                                         |  sgv:      dw    0
20                                         |  @s0_slv:  dw    0
21                                         |            public gv
22                                         |  ;
23                                         |  @f2$v:   ldc   6        ; gv = 6;
24                                         |           st    gv
25                                         |
26                                         |           ldc   7        ; sgv = 2;
27                                         |           st    sgv
28                                         |
29                                         |           call  @f1$v    ; f1();
30                                         |
31                                         |           ret
32                                         |           public @f2$v
```

Why does a C++ compiler flag a reference to a nonlocal variable that is not ac-companied by a C++-level **extern** declaration? Why doesn't a C++ compiler sim-ply treat such a reference as a legitimate external reference, and, accordingly, generate an **extern** directive (as it does with function calls to nonlocal functions)? Consider what would happen if the compiler did *not* flag such nonlocal references. The compiler would then incorrectly treat every misspelling of a local variable as a legitimate external reference. For example, for the program in Figure 10.43, the compiler would not detect the misspelling of the variable **temp** as **temmp**. Instead, it would assume **temmp** is a reference to an externally defined variable, and, accord-ingly, generate an **extern** directive for it. Thus, *the misspelling would go unflagged* until link time, and then only if there were no global variable named **temmp**. Clear-

FIGURE 10.43

```
1     void test()
2   {
3       .
4       .
5       .
6   }
7   int main()
8   {
9       int temp;
10      temmp = 22;     // misspelling of variable temp
11      tesst();        // misspelling of function test
12      .
13      .
14      .
15      return 0;
16  }
```

ly, not flagging references to nonlocal variables not accompanied by a C++-level **extern** declaration is a bad idea.

It certainly makes sense for the compiler to flag misspelled references to local variables. Similarly, it makes sense for the compiler to flag misspelled function calls. In C (the predecessor of C++), a call to a nonlocal function for which no prototype is provided is always treated as a legitimate external reference. Thus, a C compiler would not flag a misspelled call to a local function (which, because of the misspelling, looks like a call to a nonlocal function). For example, a C compiler would flag the reference to the variable **temmp** in Figure 10.43, but not the reference to the function **tesst**, both of which are misspellings. A C++ compiler, on the other hand, would flag both types of misspellings. In C++, every function call *must* be preceded by either the function definition or a prototype. Thus, in a C++ program, a *misspelled* function call would be preceded with a function definition or prototype—but, because of the misspelling, not one with a matching name. Thus, the C++ compiler would flag the misspelled function call as having no preceding definition or prototype.

We can see from Figure 10.43 that the *definition* of a function or a global variable in C++ always causes the generation of a corresponding **public** directive at the assembly level unless it is explicitly suppressed by the keyword **static**. The presence or absence of the **public** directive determines whether the scope of a global variable or function extends beyond the file in which it is compiled. A call to a nonlocal function always causes the generation of an **extern** directive. A reference to a nonlocal variable, on the other hand, also causes the generation of an **extern** directive, but only if a corresponding **extern** declaration appears at the C++ level. Without the **extern** declaration at the C++ level, the C++ compiler would flag the reference as an undefined symbol.

We should now correct an imprecision that appears in previous chapters. The assembly code for the global variables and functions should all have corresponding **public** directives because we did not use the **static** keyword in any of their definitions. Because all the programs in Chapters 7, 8, and 9 are single-file programs, the lack of proper **public** directives does not cause any problems. However, a C++ compiler would always generate the `public` directives, even for single-file programs. In addition, all the `main` functions should be in the form shown in Figure 10.35 (i.e., callable from start-up code). From now on, we'll update our dumb compiler so that it translates C++ programs the way a C++ compiler should. Specifically, it should translate `main` as a function called by start-up code. Thus, `main` should terminate by executing a `ret` instruction instead of a `halt` instruction. It should also include `public` directives for all nonstatic function names and nonstatic global variables, and `extern` directives for all externally defined functions and data. Finally, it should continue to use mangled function names.

PROBLEMS

· ·

10.1. Under precisely what conditions does `mas` output a ".mob" file instead of a ".mac" file.

10.2. Create a program that consists of three separately assembled modules: `main`, `b`, and `c`. `main` calls `b`, `b` calls `c`, and `c` displays "in c". Assemble, link, and run your program on `sim`.

10.3. Input to `lin` can be a ".mac" file. A ".mac" file is already a complete program, so why would a ".mac" file ever need to be linked by `lin`?

10.4. The following is the display of a ".mob" file produced by `mex`. Unassemble the file. If possible, use the same labels that were used in the original assembly program.

```
Header:
    0:  0050 0004 0078 0000 0050 0005 0079 0000
    8:  0052 0000 0052 0001 0045 0002 007A 0000
   10:  0054

Text:
    0:  0004 3005 1000 FFFF 0014 001E
```

10.5. The following is the header of a ".mob" file as displayed by the `pic` program. Show the same header in hex form.

```
Type   Address   Symbol


P      0005      aaa
R      0000
E      0001      bbb
E      0002      bbb
R      0003
T
```

10.6. Show the contents of the ".mob" file that correspond to the following program. Use the same format that `pic` uses.

```
       public x
       extern y
s:     call   y
       add    x
       add    y
       halt
x:     dw     -5
       end    s
```

10.7. Show the contents of the ".mob" file that correspond to the module in Problem 10.6. Use the same format that **mex** uses.

10.8. Suppose the file **p1.mas** contains

```
a:      dw      5
        public a
```

and the file **p2.mas** contains

```
x:      dw      10
        dw      a
        extern a
```

Suppose **p1.mas** and **p2.mas** are assembled and the following two commands are then entered:

```
lin p1 p2
lib p1 p2
```

Show the contents of **p1.mob**, **p2.mob**, **p1.mac**, and **p1.lib**. Use the same format that **pic** uses.

10.9. Does it ever make sense to have a module in a library that does not have any public symbols?

10.10. Does it ever make sense to have start-up code in a library?

10.11. Show the contents of the ".mob" file that correspond to the following program. Use the same format that **pic** uses.

```
        ld       x
        public x
        add      y
        extern y
        end      25
x:      st       6
        halt
```

10.12. Create the **fmult15.lib** library that is described in Section 10.8.

10.13. Create a library that contains everything in **fmult15.lib**, as well as a function that computes fourth powers. Write and run an assembly language program that computes and displays the value of $x^4 - x^2 + 6$ for $x = 0, 1, 2, 3, 4$. Use your new library.

10.14. Under what circumstances is it desirable to have an object module in a library contain several functions? Under what circumstances is it desirable to have an object module in a library contain only one function?

10.15. What happens when the following program, which consists of three separate modules, is assembled, linked, and run?

```
        extern x        |        public x        |        public y
        extern y        | x:     dw 5            | x:     dw      50
ok: ld      x + 1       | y:     dw 6            | y:     dw      60
        add      y - 1  |                        |
        dout            |                        |
        ldc      '\n'   |                        |
        aout            |                        |
        halt            |                        |
        end      ok     |                        |
```

10.16. Show the contents of the three ".mob" files and the executable ".mac" file that correspond to the program in Problem 10.15. Use the same format that `pic` uses.

10.17. When the linker resolves an external reference, it *adds* the address of the external symbol to the field that corresponds to the external reference. Why does it add? Why not simply *overlay* the external field with the address of the external symbol? Hint: See Problem 10.15.

10.18. Show the contents of the ".mob" file that correspond to the following program. Use the same format that `pic` uses.

```
extern x
ld   x
```

10.19. Show the contents of the ".mob" file that correspond to the following program. Use the same format that `pic` uses.

```
extern x
ld   x
ld   x + 2
ld   x - 2
```

10.20. What happens when the following program, which consists of two separate modules, is assembled, linked, and run? Does the order in which the two modules are linked affect the run-time behavior of the program?

```
        extern x              |         public x
        extern y              |         public y
start:  ld    x              |   y:    dw      0
        st    y - 1          |   x:    dw      -1
cat:    ja    cat            |
        end   start          |
```

10.21. Show the contents of the two ".mob" files and the executable ".mac" file that correspond to the program in Problem 10.20. Use the same format that `pic` uses.

10.22. Show the ".mob" file that corresponds to the following program. Use the same format that `pic` uses.

```
        extern sub
        ldc   0
        push
        ldc   msg
        call  sub
        call  sub
        halt
msg:    dw    "Programming is fun"
        end   0
```

10.23. How many header entries does a `public` directive generate? How many header entries does an `extern` directive generate?

10.24. Suppose the following two modules are assembled and linked in the order given. Show the contents of the ".mac" file that is produced. Use the same format that `pic` uses.

```
        extern a             |         extern b
        public b             |         public a
b:      dw    a             |   a:    dw    b
```

10.25. Create a library with `lib` that contains modules that are neither ".mob" nor ".mac" files. Does `lib` detect the invalid input? Try `lin` with your library. Does `lin` detect the invalid modules in the bogus library?

10.26. One function that start-up code performs after `main` completes is to determine if a null pointer assignment has occurred. How does start-up code do this?

10.27. Suppose the files `t1.mas` and `t2.mas` contain the following:

```
    ; t1.mas                    ; t2.mas
a:      dw      5           q:      dw      6
b:      dw      a+1         b:      dw      a+10
c:      dw      x+5         x:      dw      q
        extern  x                   public  x
        public  a                   extern  a
                                    end     q
```

Assume the files are assembled and linked as follows:

```
mas t1
mas t2
lin t1 t2
```

Show the contents of `t1.mob`, `t2.mob`, and `t1.mac`. Use the same format that `pic` uses.

10.28. The following is a display of a ".mac" file produced by `mex`. Unassemble the file. If possible, use the same labels that were used in the original assembly program.

```
Header:
        0:  0054
Text:
        0:  0000 0001 FFFF
```

10.29. The following is a display of a ".mob" file produced by `mex`. Unassemble the file. If possible, use the same labels that were used in the original assembly program.

```
Header:
        0:  0050 0000 0078 0000 0050 0001 0079 0000
        8:  0052 0000 0052 0001 0054
Text:
        0:  0000 0001 FFFF
```

10.30. Why are the addresses for the module that `lin` places first in the combined program not adjusted?

10.31. When `lin` links several modules, it saves their header entries. It then uses these saved entries to create the header for the combined program. Explain precisely how it does this. What does it do with its saved E entries?

10.32. Each length field in a library is one word. Is one word always sufficient to hold the length of a module?

10.33. The `see` program displays its input file in hex/ASCII. Display a ".mac" or ".mob" file with both `see` and `mex`. Compare the two displays. Do you see any discrepancies?

10.34. Display a library file with both `see` and `mex`. Examine the length fields in the library file. What do you conclude?

10.35. Translate the following program (including the `exit` function) to assembly language, assemble, and run on **sim**.

```
#include <iostream>
using namespace std;
void exit(int rc)
{
    // code to terminate execution and return 1 to
    // start-up code
}
void f() {
    cout << "in f\n";
    exit(1);
    cout << "bug\n";
}
void g()
{
    cout << "in g\n";
    f();
    cout << "bug\n";
}
int main()
{
    g();
    return 0;
}
```

10.36. If the assembler were to assume that every undefined symbol were an external symbol, then the `extern` directive would never be needed. Would it be desirable to have the assembler work this way? Can you think of any language that works this way?

10.37. If the assembler were to assume that every symbol that was not external was public, then the **public** directive would never be needed. Would it be desirable to have the assembler work this way?

10.38. Would it be easier for a C++ compiler to generate **public** and **extern** directives at the end rather than the beginning of the object module it produces?

10.39. Translate the following program as a C compiler would. What would happen if it were compiled by a C++ compiler?

```
void test()
{
    return;
}
int main()
{
    tesst();
    return 0;
}
```

10.40. Write and run an assembly language program that computes and outputs the sum of two positive integers, each a single digit, given on the command line when **sim** is invoked.

10.41. Same as Problem 10.40, but assume multiple-digit positive numbers.

10.42. Write and run an assembly language program that determines and outputs the length of a string (not including the null character) given on the command line when **sim** is invoked.

10.43. Write and run on **sim** an assembly language program that concatenates all the strings pointed to by the **argv** array with no intervening spaces, and displays the resulting string.

10.44. **sim** places command line arguments in main memory starting at location 3900 decimal (unless the **/w** argument is specified). What problems may result with this location?

10.45. When linking start-up code with a module, should start-up code always be linked first?

10.46. If **main** returns 0 (normal termination), the start-up code in Figure 10.36 will also **return** 0 even if a null pointer assignment is detected. Does this make sense? Determine if your own C++ compiler behaves similarly.

10.47. What happens if we invoke the program in Figure 10.39 with

```
sim /z kangaroo hello bye
```

10.48. Can a label appear as a local symbol in one module and as a global label in another module in the same program? Explain.

10.49. Does it ever make sense to declare **main** in a C++ program as a **static** function? Try it. What happens?

10.50. If **lin** inputs a single ".mac" file, is its output file identical to its input file?

For the following problems, translate the given program to assembly language. Include all assembly directives that would normally appear in compiler-generated assembly code, and use mangled function names. Assemble, link with start-up code, and run on **sim**.

10.51.
```cpp
#include <iostream>
using namespace std;
int main(int argc, char *argv[])
{
    cout << argc << endl;
    cout << argv[0] << endl;
    cout << argv[argc - 1] << endl;
    return 0;
}
```

10.52.
```cpp
#include <iostream>
using namespace std;
// run with program with the following command line args:
//    a1 a2 a3 a4
int main(int argc, char *argv[])
{
    while (--argc)
        cout << argv[argc] << endl;
    return 0;
}
```

10.53.
```cpp
#include <iostream>
using namespace std;
int x = 5;
```

```
        int y;
        static void f(int a, int b)
        {
          y = a + b + x;
        }
        int main()
        {
          int z = 10;
          f(z, z + 3);
          cout << "x = " << x << endl;
          cout << "y = " << y << endl;
          cout << "z = " << z << endl;
          return 0;
        }
```

10.54.
```
#include <iostream>
using namespace std;
int x = 5;
static int y;
static f(int *p)
{
  *p = 5;
}
int main()
{
  static int a = 1;
  int b = 2;
  f(&x);
  f(&y);
  f(&a);
  f(&b);
  cout << a << " " << b << " " << x << " " << y << endl;
  return 0;
}
```

10.55.
```
#include <iostream>
using namespace std;
int main()
{
  int a, b[5];
  cout << "enter number\n";
  cin >> a;
  b[a] = 5;
  cout << "a = " << a << endl;
  for (a = 0; a < 5; a++)
    cout << b[a] << endl;
  return 0;
}
```

10.56.   // Assume that the program is in two files

```
// first file:
#include <iostream>
```

```
using namespace std;
static void f(int x)
{
    cout << "x = " << x << endl;
}
int main()
{
    int a;
    int b = 1;
    f(b);
    g(&a);
    cout << "a = " << a << endl;
    return 0;
}
//=================================
// second file:
void g(int *p)
{
    *p = 100;
    f();
}
void f()
{
    cout << "hello\n";
}
```

Chapter Eleven

IMPLEMENTING AN ASSEMBLER AND A LINKER USING C++ OR JAVA

11.1 INTRODUCTION

. . . .

In this chapter, you will learn how to write an assembler and a linker. Writing these two programs is the best and, perhaps, only way to obtain a thorough understanding of the assembly and linking processes. Ideally, you should study this chapter carefully, and then implement both an assembler and a linker. If, however, time is at a premium, you may skip this chapter. This chapter is not a prerequisite for any of the chapters that follow.

If you compare our description of the assembly process (see Section 3.7) with our description of the linking process (see Section 10.6), you will probably conclude that writing a linker is more complex and, therefore, more difficult than writing an assembler. However, just the opposite is true. The difficulty in writing an assembler comes from the variety of jobs an assembler has to do. For example, consider all the different types of items that can occupy the operand field in an assembly language statement:

- Absolute address
- Signed numbers
- Unsigned numbers
- External label
- Internal (i.e., local) label
- Public label
- Null-terminated string
- String that is not null-terminated
- "Label + unsigned_number" expression
- "Label - unsigned_number" expression
- "*"
- "* + unsigned_number" expression
- "* − unsigned_number" expression
- dup modifier
- equ symbol

An assembler, of course, has to be programmed to handle each of these possibilities. Evidence of the complexity of an assembler relative to a linker is given by the relative sizes of mas and lin (both programs were written in C++). The number of lines of C++ code for mas is roughly three times the number of lines of code for lin.

11.2 WRITING AN ASSEMBLER

• •

A good approach to use when writing your first assembler is to start with a version that contains minimal function. Once you have this simple version implemented and working correctly, you can then add more functionality. To reach a version comparable to **mas**, you may want to implement three or four simpler versions with progressively more functionality.

11.2.1 Specifications for a Simple Assembler

We will call our first assembler version **masv1**. It will work like **mas**, with the following exceptions:

- The command line format of **masv1** is

  masv1 *<infilename>*

  If *<infilename>* does not include an extension, then **masv1** adds ".mas" to it. **masv1** never prompts the user for any input.

- The output file name is always

  <infilename_less_extension>.mac

- **masv1** does not support list files, configuration files, the !-directive, and the &-directive.
- **masv1** treats all numbers as decimal.
- **masv1** is always case sensitive when processing labels.
- **masv1** does not support strings. Thus, none of the following statements are allowed:

  ```
          ldc   'A'
  s1:   dw    "ABC"
  s2:   dw    'ABC'
  ```

- **masv1** does not support comments or lines containing only a label. However, it allows completely blank lines.
- The operand field may contain only a label, or an integer with an optional leading sign.
- The only directive **masv1** supports is the **dw** directive.
- **masv1** supports only the instructions in the standard instruction set.
- **masv1** uses a symbol table that can hold at most 20 entries (this small upper limit makes it easy to test the code in **masv1** that handles symbol table overflow).
- **masv1** should correctly handle filenames that include "." (representing the current directory) or ".." (representing the parent directory).
- When started, masv1 should display the following message (insert your own name):

  ```
  masv1 written by . . .
  ```

  masv1, like **mas**, should return an error code of 1 on any error, and 0, otherwise. **masv1** should detect the following errors:

- Invalid operation (an item in the operation field other than a valid instruction mnemonic or **dw)**
- Ill-formed label in the label field
- Ill-formed label in operand field

- Undefined label in the operand field
- Duplicate label (two or more lines starting with the same label)
- Address or operand out of range. The operands in dw statements and the values in the x and y fields of instructions have ranges as follows:

```
dw operand:    -32768 to 65535
x field value:  0 to 4095
y field value:  0 to 255
```

For example, some *illegal* statements are

```
dw     66000
ld     4096
aloc   256
aloc   -1
```

- Symbol table overflow
- Program too big (i.e., bigger than 4096 words)
- Incorrect number of command-line arguments
- Cannot open input file
- Cannot open output file

Whenever **masv1** detects an error, it should display an error message and terminate. The error message should include the line number on which the error occurs, the input file name, the line itself, and a description of the error. Here, for example, is a typical error message:

```
ERROR on line 1 of aprog4.mas:
a?b:    ldc    5
Ill-formed label in label field
```

masv1 should not check if an instruction has the proper number of arguments. Missing operands should default to 0; extra operands should be ignored.

masv1 should use the two-pass approach that we described in Section 3.7. During pass 1, **masv1** should construct the symbol table and output the header (consisting of any required R entries followed by a T entry). During pass 2, **masv1** should construct and output each machine language instruction or data item using, as necessary, the opcode and symbol tables. Figure 11.1 shows the pseudocode (not including error handling) for **masv1**. **location_counter**, **opcode**, **operand_value**, and **machine_word** are all 16-bit variables (type **short** for Java and for most C++ systems).

A convenient way to test your version of **masv1** is to run the batch/script file **atest** in the software package. **atest** runs both **masv1** and **masv1m** (the model version in the H1 software package), and compares results. For more information on **atest**, see **sim.txt**.

11.2.2   Opcode Table

The opcode table provides the opcode for every mnemonic. The opcode table can be viewed as consisting of two columns, one containing the mnemonics and the other containing the corresponding opcodes (see Figure 11.2).

Should the opcode table also contain the length of each opcode? It could, but it is not necessary. We can determine the length of any opcode from the opcode itself. For example, all opcodes in the range F0 to FE have a length of 8 bits. Figure 11.3 shows the opcode lengths for the various ranges of opcodes.

FIGURE 11.1

```
Set location_counter to 0.
Open input file as a text file
Open output file as a binary file
// Pass 1
Loop until no more input
    +---
   |    Read one line from the input file.
   |    If the current line starts with a label,
   |        get the label and enter it and the current value
   |        of location_counter into the symbol table.
   |    Get the operand on the current line.
   |    If the operand is a label,
   |        output 'R' and the current value of
   |        location_counter to the output file.
   |    Add 1 to location_counter
    +---
Output 'T'
Reset input file to the beginning.
```

```
// Pass 2
Loop until no more input
    +---
   |    Read one line from the input file.
   |    Get the operation (a mnemonic or dw) from the current line.
   |    If the operation is a mnemonic,
   |        look up the opcode in opcode table and save it in opcode.
   |    Get the operand from the current line.
   |    If the operand is a label,
   |        look up its address in the symbol table and save
   |        it in operand_value.
   |    else                            // operand is a number
   |        convert the operand to binary
   |        and save it in operand_value.
   |    If the operation is a mnemonic,
   |        construct the machine language instruction from
   |        opcode and operand_value, and save in machine_word.
   |    else                            // operation is a dw
   |        copy operand_value to machine_word.
   |    Output machine_word.
    +---
Close files
```

FIGURE 11.2

mnemonic	opcode
"ld"	0
"st"	1
"add"	2
.	.
.	.
.	.

FIGURE 11.3

Opcodes (hex)	Length	Index Range (decimal)	Formula
0 - E	4	0 - 14	index
F0 - FE	8	15 - 29	0xF0 + (index - 15)
FF0 - FFE	12	30 - 44	0xFF0 + (index - 30)
FFF0 - FFFF	16	45 - 60	0xFFF0 + (index - 45)

If the mnemonics appear in the opcode table in opcode order, then the opcode table does not even have to contain opcodes for each mnemonic. Instead, the opcode for each mnemonic can be determined from the index (i.e., position) of the mnemonic in the table. For example, if the index of a mnemonic is less than F hex, the opcode is equal to the index. If the index is greater than or equal to F hex but less than FF hex, then the opcode is given by

```
0xF0 + (index - 15)
```

For example, the index of desp is 22 decimal. Thus, its opcode is

```
0xF0 + (22 - 15) = F7 hex
```

For each of the four ranges of opcodes, there exists a simple formula for computing the opcode from the index of its mnemonic (see Figure 11.3). With this approach, the opcode table in Java can be defined with the array in Figure 11.4. The opcode table in C++ is the same, except the array type is **char** * (or alternatively, the standard **string** class). Of course, the declaration of **opcode_table** should not have the gaps that appear in the sample declaration. **opcode_table** must be initialized with a mnemonic for every opcode. Every unused opcode (which, therefore, has no mnemonic) should be represented in **opcode_table** with a dummy mnemonic, such as "????".

One disadvantage to this implementation of the opcode table is that it requires a serial search (a slow search technique) to find an opcode. However, because the table is so small, this inefficiency has minimal impact on execution time. An alternative approach for the opcode table is to use a two-dimensional array containing mnemonic-opcode pairs presorted by mnemonic. We can then use a *binary search*—a much faster search technique, particularly for large tables—to look up opcodes. In your first implementation of **masv1**, use a serial search. Then try a binary search to see if it has any impact on execution time.

11.2.3   Symbol Table

During pass 1, the assembler records the address of every internal (i.e., local) label in a symbol table. Recall from Section 3.7 that the assembler determines the address of each label by means of an internal variable called the *location counter*. The assembler

FIGURE 11.4   `String opcode_table[] = {`

```
        "ld",        // opcode 0
        "st",        // opcode 1
        "add",       // opcode 2

            .

            .

        "desp",      // opcode F7
        "????",      // opcode F8
        "????",      // opcode F9

            .

            .

        "????",      // opcode FFF4
        "uout",      // opcode FFF5

            .

            .

        "halt"       // opcode FFFF
    };
```

initializes the location counter to zero and then increments it each time it scans a line. Thus, the location counter always contains the address of the current line. When the assembler detects a label at the beginning of a line, it enters the label and contents of the location counter (which is the address of the label) into the symbol table.

The symbol table contains two parallel arrays: one for labels and one for their corresponding addresses. For example, we can define the symbol table in Java with the class in Figure 11.5 (the C++ class is similar).

When a `SymbolTable` object is created, its constructor should allocate the **symbol** and **address** arrays (whose size is passed to the constructor function). Member functions should include an **enter** function (which enters a new label/address pair into the table) and a **search** function (which returns the address of a given label).

A program translated by **masv1** can have at most one label per location. Thus, the maximum number of labels a source program can have is 4096, one for every main memory location. By making your symbol table large enough to accommodate 4096 entries, you ensure that symbol table overflow cannot occur. A source program translated by **mas**, on the other hand, can have multiple labels per location. For example, in the following source program segment, the labels **cat**, **dog**, and **mouse** all correspond to the location containing the `ld` instruction.

```
cat:
dog:
mouse: ld    x
```

Thus, it is possible for a source program for **mas** to have more than 4096 labels. But programs with more than 4096 labels are highly unlikely. A reasonable choice, therefore, for the size of the symbol table is 4096, even for **mas**. In our initial implementation of **masv1**, however, we will use a symbol table whose size is only 20. We can then easily check if our code that tests for symbol table overflow works correctly (by assembling a program with 21 labels). After we perform this check, we can then increase the size to a more practical value, such as 4096.

FIGURE 11.5   `class SymbolTable {`

```
        private String symbol[];        // label array
        private short address[];        // address array
        private int index;             // index of next available slot

        public SymbolTable(int size)
        {
         // Constructor creates symbol and address arrays
         // and initializes index.
        }

        public void enter(String label, short address)
        {
         // Enters label/address into table.
        }

        public short search(String label)
        {
         // Returns address of label.
        }

    }
```

FIGURE 11.6

```
    1          ld      x
    2          add     y
    3          st      z
    4          halt
    5   x:     dw      2
    6   x:     dw      3
    7   z:     dw      0
```

Regardless of the size of the symbol table, the assembler should always check that there is still room in the symbol table before it adds a new entry. If symbol table overflow occurs (i.e., there is no more room), the assembler should output an error message and terminate.

Whenever the assembler enters a label into a symbol table, it should check if the label is already in the table. If it is, the assembler should generate an error message and terminate. For example, suppose the assembler is translating the program in Figure 11.6. When the assembler processes the first **dw** directive, it should enter the label **x** into the symbol table. When it processes the second **dw** directive, it should detect that **x** is already in the symbol table, and generate a "duplicate label" error message.

For symbol table lookup, the simplest technique to use is the serial search. This technique works well as long as the number of entries in the table is small; however, it is very inefficient if the number of entries is large. A faster technique for a large number of entries is *hash coding*. For your first implementation of the assembler, use the serial search technique. Then try hash coding, and see if it has any impact on execution time.

11.2.4   Using Binary Files

Files come in two basic types: text files and binary files. In a *text file*, every byte holds an ASCII code for some character. A file in which every byte does *not* hold an ASCII code is called a *binary file*. A ".mas" file is a text file. It contains the ASCII codes for the characters that make up an assembly language program. A ".mac" file, on the other hand, is a binary file. It contains binary machine language instructions as well as tables that hold binary data. It also contains some ASCII codes (for example, the strings in the P and E header entries). But a ".mac" file is not exclusively ASCII. An assembler inputs a text file and outputs a binary file. A linker inputs binary files and outputs a binary file.

Let's examine several programs in Java and C++ that illustrate the wrong and right ways to create a binary file. We will examine the output files these programs create using the **see** program in the H1 software package. **see** produces a hex/ASCII display (hex on the left, ASCII on the right) that allows us to see precisely the contents of any file. To display any file with **see**, simply enter **see** followed by the file name.

The Java program in Figure 11.7a uses **PrintWriter** to output the **short** integer in **x** (see line 8) to the file **outfile1**. With **PrintWriter**, data is always output in ASCII form. Data not already in ASCII form is first converted to ASCII before it is output. Thus, the binary number in **x** (000A in hex) is output as a sequence of ASCII codes (31 30 in hex) that represents the digits of its decimal value (10). In Figure 11.7b, we can see the hex/ASCII display of **outfile1** that **see** produces. On the left, the ASCII codes 31 and 30 (the ASCII codes for '1' and '0') appear; on the right are the corresponding characters.

Suppose we used **PrintWriter** to output the machine language instruction 000A. Unfortunately, the output file would not receive the binary instruction. Instead, it would receive 3130 hex because of the conversion to ASCII. Clearly, we cannot use **PrintWriter** to create a binary file.

In Figure 11.7c, we use **DataOutputStream** (and **FileOutputStream**) to create the file **outfile2**. The various member functions of **DataOutputStream** do not perform any conversions. Thus, line 7 outputs the binary number in **x** as is (we see this with Figure 11.7d in its hex representation 000A). This is precisely the type of output we need for our assembler. With **DataOutputStream** we can also output ASCII codes, if we need to, using the **writeByte** function. For example, line 9 outputs the ASCII code for 'C'.

To output in C++, we can use the insertion operator ($<<$) or the **write** member function in **ofstream**. The insertion operator converts data to ASCII before outputting it. Thus, we cannot use it to create a binary file. For example, line 8 in Figure 11.8a does not output the binary number in **x**. Instead, it outputs the sequence of ASCII codes (31 30) that represents the digits of its decimal value (10). In Figure 11.8b we can see these codes at the beginning of the hex display, and their character equivalents on the right. The **write** member function, on the other hand, does not convert data to ASCII. It requires two arguments: a **char** pointer that contains the address of the location from which to write, and the number of bytes to write. On line 9 in Figure 11.8a, &**x** (a **short** pointer) is cast to a **char** pointer to satisfy the requirements of the **write** function. This statement outputs

FIGURE 11.7

a)

```
 1 import java.io.*;
 2 class P1
 3 {
 4    public static void main(String[] args) throws IOException {
 5       PrintWriter outStream =
 6             new PrintWriter(new FileOutputStream("outfile1"));
 7       short x = 10;
 8       outStream.print(x);     // contents of x converted to ASCII decimal
 9       outStream.close();
10    }
11 }
```

b)

see Version x.x

```
     0:    3130                                            10
```

Input file = outfile1
List file = outfile1.see

c)

```
 1 import java.io.*;
 2 class P2
 3 {
 4    public static void main(String[] args) throws IOException {
 5    DataOutputStream outStream =
 6        new DataOutputStream(new FileOutputStream("outfile2"));
 7    short x = 10;
 8    outStream.writeShort(x); // contents of x outputed as is
 9    outStream.writeByte('C');
10    outStream.close();
11    }
12 }
```

d)

see Version x.x

```
     0:    000A 43                                    ..C
```

Input file = outfile2
List file = outfile2.see

FIGURE 11.8   a)

```
1  #include <fstream>
2 using namespace std;
3
4 int main() {
5    ofstream outStream;
6    outStream.open("outfile3");
7    short x = 10;
8    outStream << x;
9    outStream.write((char *)&x, sizeof(x));
10   outStream.close();
11   return 0;
12 }
```

b)

extra byte inserted during output

see Version x.x

```
    0:    3130  0D0A  00                        10...
```

Input file = outfile3
List file = outfile3.see

c)

```
1 #include <fstream>
2 using namespace std;
3
4 int main() {
5    ofstream outStream;
6    outStream.open("outfile4", ios::binary);
7    short x = 10;
8    outStream.write((char *)&x, sizeof(x));
9    outStream << 'C';
10   outStream.close();
11   return 0;
12 }
```

d)

see Version x.x

```
    0:  0A00  43                          ..C
```

Input file = outfile4
List file = outfile4.see

000A, the binary number in **x**. Because the file in Figure 11.8b was created on a computer that uses the *little-endian* approach (i.e., the least significant byte is first), this value appears as 0A00 in the file (see the last two bytes in the hex display in Figure 11.8b).

There is one potential problem with using the **write** function to output binary data. This problem manifests itself on a system (like Microsoft Windows) in which the end of each text line is marked by both the carriage return (0D hex) and the newline character (0A hex). On such systems, a C++ program will translate a newline character (0A hex) on output to a carriage return/newline sequence, and vice versa on input. Thus, when the **write** on line 9 in Figure 11.8a outputs 0A00 (the value of **x**), it precedes it with 0D (the carriage return character). We can see this 3-byte sequence at the end of the hex display in Figure 11.8b. To fix this problem, we simply open the file as a binary file, in which case all byte translation is inhibited. We do this on line 6 in Figure 11.8c by specifying a second argument, **ios::binary**. The **write** on line 8 then writes the binary number in **x** without preceding it with a carriage return. With binary files, we can still output ASCII codes. For example, line 9 outputs the ASCII code for 'C' using the insertion operation. The hex display in Figure 11.8d shows 0A00 (the binary number in **x**) and 43 (the ASCII code for 'C').

Opening a file as binary is necessary only on systems that do not use a single newline character to terminate text lines. In fact, on systems that use only the newline character, the C++ **open** function may not even support the **ios:binary** argument.

Now let's turn our attention to binary input files. To create an input stream in Java for a binary input file (**masv1** does not do this, but **linv1** does), use **DataInputStream** and **FileInputStream**. To read, use the **readByte** and **readShort** functions, or other functions in **DataInputStream**. For example, to read from the binary file **infile1**, use

```
DataInputStream inStream = new DataInputStream(
                         new FileInputStream("infile1"));

byte b;
short x;
b = inStream.readByte();
x = inStream.readShort();
```

In C++, create an input stream with **ifstream**, and read using its **read** function. For example, to read from the binary file **infile2**, use

```
                                          Use on systems that do not
                                          use single newline to terminate
                                          text line.

ifstream inStream;
inStream.open("infile2", ios::binary);
char b;
short x;
inStream.read(&b, sizeof(b));
inStream.read((char *)&x, sizeof(x));
```

11.2.5 Reading the Input Text File and Creating the Header

In Java we create an input stream for the input text file with

```
BufferedReader inStream = new Bufferedreader(
                         new FileReader(inFileName));
```

In C++ we use

```
ifstream inStream;
inStream.open(inFileName);
```

where **inFileName** is a string that contains the input file name. We can then read one line in Java with

```
buffer = inStream.readLine();
```

or in C++ with

```
inStream.getline(buffer, sizeof(buffer));
```

where **buffer** is a **String** variable in Java and a **char** array in C++.

masv1 does not support the **public**, **extern**, or **end** directives, so the header in the output file it creates will contain only a T entry and possibly some R entries. An R entry needs to be created for every assembly language statement in which a label appears in the operand field. The R entry for such a statement consists of the letter **R** followed by the address of the statement.

During pass 1, as the assembler scans each line, it tests if the operand field contains a label. If it does, it outputs the appropriate R entry. To output the first field of an R entry (the letter 'R'), we can use

```
outStream.writeByte('R');
```

in Java, or

```
outStream << 'R';
```

in C++. Then to output the required address (the address of the current line), we can simply output the address in the location counter with

```
outStream.writeShort(location_counter)
```

in Java, or with

```
outStream.write((char *)&location_counter, 2);
```

in C++.

At the end of pass 1, you should output the T entry that ends the header.

If you are an astute reader, you might have noticed something fishy about the statements that output 'R' or 'T': *They output only one byte.* In all the **mex** displays we have seen, a full word is used to hold the ASCII code for 'R'. This use of one word for each character in a header makes sense because one ASCII code per word is how H1 stores characters. However, all the programs in the H1 software package that process headers (**mas**, **lin**, **pic**, **mex**, and **sim**) run on computers that use only one byte per character. These programs would be awkward to write if characters in a header were stored one per word instead of one per byte. Thus, we store one character per byte in a header and write all the programs that process the header accordingly. But what about the **mex** program? Why does it show each ASCII character in a full word? The **mex** program does not show headers the way

FIGURE 11.9   (a)   (b)

```
ld   x        ld   x
     .             .
     .             .
     .             .
extern x      x:  dw   5
```

they really exist. Instead, it shows headers the way they would exist if all our software ran on a computer that, like H1, used one word per ASCII character.

Be sure to keep in mind that characters in headers are really stored one per byte when writing any program—like an assembler or a linker—that processes headers. Characters in the machine text in object, executable, and library modules, on the other hand, are stored one per word. These characters (for example, in a string defined by a **dw** directive) are copied as is into the main memory of H1, and, therefore, need to be in the form that is proper for H1.

masv1 can create and output R entries during pass 1, but only because **masv1** does not support the **extern** directive. If **extern** directives were allowed, then the assembler, in general, would not know during pass 1 if a label in an operand field of an instruction is local or external. Local labels require R entries; external labels require E entries. For example, the assembler needs to output an E entry for the reference to **x** in the `ld` instruction in Figure 11.9a. But it does not know this until it scans the **extern** directive (it is only then that it knows **x** is an external symbol). Similarly, the assembler needs to output an R entry for the `ld` instruction in Figure 11.9b, but it does not know this until is scans the definition of **x** (it is only then that it knows that **x** is a local symbol).

masv1 sets the location counter to 0 before pass 1. Then, during pass 1, **masv1** adds one to the location counter after it processes each line. Thus, the location counter always contains the address of the current line. For later versions of the assembler, the adjustment to the location counter depends on the input line. For example, a **dw** directive that defines a multiple character string requires the location counter to be incremented by the length of the string.

11.2.6 Assembling the Machine Word

Assembling a machine word from its components is conveniently handled by an **Assembler** class. The **Assembler** class should contain an **assemble** function that contructs a machine word from an operation (a mnemonic or **dw**) and an operand, and returns it to the caller. **assemble** needs both the opcode table and the symbol table. Because the opcode table is needed only by **assemble**, we can place it within the **Assembler** class; we can provide the symbol table to **assemble** via a parameter. For example, we can define **Assembler** in Java as in Figure 11.10. Alternatively, we can use a single **Tables** class that contains both the symbol and opcode tables along with the **assemble** function. Then **assemble** would have direct access to both tables.

The easiest way to construct a machine word from its components is to use the shift and bitwise OR operations. For example, suppose the variables **opcode** and **operand_value** contain, respectively, the opcode and operand values for a machine instruction. If the opcode is a 4-bit opcode, we can construct a machine instruction and assign it to **machine_word** with

```
machine_word =    (short)((opcode << 12) | operand_value);
```

FIGURE 11.10

```
class Assembler {

   private String opcodeTable[] = {
     "ld",      // opcode 0
     "st",      // opcode 1
     "add",     // opcode 2
          .

          .

          .
   }

   public short assemble(String mnemonic, String operand, SymbolTable s)
   {
     // Assembles machine word from mnemonic and operand using
     // the symbol and opcode tables.
   }

}
```

The $<<12$ operation shifts the opcode to its proper position by shifting it left 12 positions. The "$|$" (bitwise OR) operator then ORs the operand with the shifted opcode. For a **dw**, the **operand_value** contains the whole machine word, so we simply use

```
machine_word = operand_value;
```

11.2.7 Writing Machine Text to the Output File

In pass 2, the assembler again scans each line of the source program. For each line, the assembler constructs the machine word into an instruction or a data word using the information in the opcode and symbol tables. Then to output the machine word, use

```
outStream.writeShort(machine_word);
```

in Java, or

```
outStream.write((char *)&machine_word, 2);
```

in C++, where **machine_word** is the variable containing the constructed machine word.

11.2.8 Tokenizing the Input

In both pass 1 and pass 2, the assembler must break up each assembly statement into its parts (an optional label, a mnemonic, and an optional operand). We call this decomposition process *tokenizing*, and the individual statement parts it yields *tokens*. For example, on pass 2, the assembler must obtain the mnemonic and the operand on each line as individual strings, and then pass them to the **assemble** function (see Section 11.2.6).

Tokenizing is easy in Java and C++. In Java, we use the **StringTokenizer** class; in C++, we use the **strtok** function.

FIGURE 11.11

```
1 short reverseOrder(short x)
2 {
3    int y = ((int) x) & 0xffff;            // promote with no sign ext
4    return (short) (256 * (y%256) + y/256);
5 }
```

11.2.9 An Endian Problem for Java Programs

A Java program outputs binary data using the big-endian approach (i.e., the most significant byte is first). Because **sim** was written in C++, it uses the endianness of the computer on which it runs. Thus, the ".mac" files created by an assembler written in Java are incompatible with any version of **sim** that runs on a little-endian computer.

Most types of modern computers are big endian. For these computers, an endianness mismatch with Java programs does not occur. Unfortunately, PCs based on the Intel Pentium or its predecessors are all little endian. On these computers, an endianness mismatch exists with Java programs. Binary data output by a Java program cannot be used by a non-Java program. We can still mix a Java and non-Java program, however. We simply reverse the endianness of one of the programs. We can do this easily with a function **reverseOrder** that, when passed a short integer, returns that integer with its bytes reversed. We then call **reverseOrder** whenever we output a **short** integer. For example, our Java version of **masv1** can output the machine language instruction in **machine_word** with

```
outStream.writeShort(reverseOrder(machine_word));
```

instead of

```
outStream.writeShort(machine_word);
```

Figure 11.11 shows an implementation of **reverseOrder** in Java. On line 4, the division operator isolates the left byte; the modulus operator isolates the right byte. These two bytes are then combined in reverse order to form a **short** integer that is returned to the caller. This division/modulus technique works only if **y** is positive. This is the reason why the **short** integer passed to **reverseOrder** is converted to an **int** and assigned to **y** on line 3. By zeroing out the high two bytes of **y** (by ANDing it with 0xffff), we ensure that **y** is positive.

11.2.10 Adding Support for the public, extern, and end Directives

masv1 uses two passes. Pass 1 creates the symbol table and the header; pass 2 determines and outputs the machine language instructions and data. If we add support for the **public**, **extern**, and **end** directives, when should we create the header entries for these directives—in pass 1 or pass 2? Because the header precedes the machine language code in the output file, we obviously have to create the header before pass 2. Should we, therefore, create these header entries during pass 1? Unfortunately, creating header entries during pass 1 presents some major problems, as we have already seen in the preceding section. For example, consider the assembler statement

```
ld    x
```

If **x** is an internal (i.e., local) label, we have to create an R entry pointing to the instruction. On the other hand, if **x** is an external symbol, we have to create an E entry. How can the assembler know when it is scanning this instruction in pass 1 which type of entry it should create? Because the **extern** and **dw** directives can be anywhere in a program (including at the very end), it may not be until the end of pass 1 that the assembler knows if a label is internal or external. There are other problems as well. Consider the statement

```
public x
```

For this directive, the assembler has to create a P entry that contains the address of the label **x**. But because this directive can appear anywhere in a program (including at the very beginning), the assembler may not know the address of **x** at the time it is processing this directive. It is not until the end of pass 1 that the assembler definitely has the address information it needs to process the **public** directive. We have a similar situation with the **end** directive.

Our analysis shows that the header should be generated after pass 1 but before pass 2. Thus, an obvious solution is to incorporate another pass into our assembler between the two passes that already exist. In our new assembler, pass 1 would create the internal-symbol table (the usual symbol table containing every internal symbol and its address) as well as an external-symbol table that would contain every external symbol. The external-symbol table would simply be a list of every symbol specified on an **extern** directive. For example, the program in Figure 11.12 produces the internal and external symbol tables shown as comments. Pass 2 outputs the header using the information in the symbol tables. For example, when processing the statement

```
ld      x
```

in Figure 11.12 in pass 2, the assembler determines that **x** is an internal symbol because it appears in the internal-symbol table. Thus, the assembler would output an R entry containing the address of the ld instruction. When processing the statement

```
add     y
```

the assembler would determine that **y** is an external symbol because **y** appears in the external-symbol table. Thus, the assembler would output an E entry containing the address of the external reference (i.e., the address of the add instruction) and the label **y**.

The **public** and **end** directives would be handled during our new pass 2 by a simple internal-symbol table lookup. For example, when processing the statement

```
public x
```

FIGURE 11.12

		internal symbol	address	external symbol
	public x ;			
	extern y ;	---------------------------------	--------------	-------------------------------
	ld x ;	x	4	y
	add y ;	z	5	
	st z ;			
	halt ;			
x:	dw 3 ;			
z:	dw 0 ;			

the assembler looks up **x** in the internal-symbol table and outputs a P entry containing **x** and the address of **x** (obtained from the internal-symbol table). It handles an **end** directive with a label operand similarly.

Pass 3 would be identical to pass 2 of our original assembler; that is, it would output the machine language instructions and data.

11.3 WRITING A LINKER

A linker is surprisingly easy to implement. It does not have many things to do, although its actions can be somewhat confusing. If you understand the linking process described in Chapter 10, you should have no trouble implementing a simplified version of **lin**.

If you implemented **masv1** according to the specifications in Section 11.2, you will not be able to use it to create object modules for your linker to process. **masv1** does not produce linkable modules because it does not support the **public** and **extern** assembly directives. Thus, to create object modules to link, you should use **mas**.

11.3.1 Specifications for a Simple Linker

Our first version of a linker will be a simplified version of **lin** called **linv1**. It will work like **lin** with the following exceptions:

- The format of the command line is

  linv1 *<infilename> <infilename>* . . .

  If *<infilename>* does not include an extension, **linv1** adds ".mob" to it. At least one *<infilename>* must be specified. **linv1** never prompts the user for any input.
- The output file name is always

  <first_infilename_less_extension>.mac

- **linv1** is always case sensitive when processing labels.
- **linv1** does not support linking with libraries.
- **linv1** does not support list, answer, table, or cat files.
- **linv1** uses P, E, and R tables that can hold at most five entries (this small upper limit makes it easy to test the code in **linv1** that handles P, E, and R table overflow).
- linv1 should correctly handle filenames that include "." (representing the current directory) or ".." (representing the parent directory).
- When started, linv1 should display the following message (insert your own name):

  linv1 written by . . .

  linv1, like **lin**, should return an error code of 1 on any error, and 0, otherwise. If any of the following errors occur during a link, **linv1** should generate an error message and terminate:

- Unresolved external symbol
- Duplicate public symbol
- More than one starting address

- Linked program too large (greater than 4096 words)
- Unlinkable input file (i.e., a file without a valid header or text)
- P, E, or R table overflow
- Incorrect number of command-line arguments
- Cannot open input file
- Cannot open output file

Error messages should include specific information on the error whenever possible. For example, if an external symbol is unresolved, the error message should indicate which external symbol.

A convenient way to test your version of `linv1` is to run the batch/script file `ltest` in the software package. `ltest` runs both `linv1` and `linv1m` (the model version in the H1 software package), and compares results. For more information on `ltest`, see `sim.txt`.

11.3.2   Constructing the P, E, R, and S Tables

The linker operates in three phases. In the first phase it processes each input file one at a time, building tables that record the information in the headers of the object modules. During this phase, the linker also creates in memory the text part of the executable module by appending the text part of each object module to the text part in memory of the previous object module. In phase 2, the linker uses the information in the tables it built during phase 1 to resolve external references and relocate addresses. In phase 3, the linker outputs the completed executable module (including an appropriate header).

Let's examine more closely phase 1. As the linker reads in the header of each module, it places the information in the various header entries into four tables: the P table (for P entries), the E table (for E entries), the R table (for R entries), and the S table (for the s/S entry). Adjusted addresses are placed in these tables—that is, the linker adds the address of the current module (relative to the beginning of the machine code text) to the addresses in its header entries before placing these addresses in the tables.

The linker determines the address (relative to the beginning of the machine code text) of the object module it is processing by using the relationship

address of current object module

=

address of previous object module

+

size of the text in the previous object module

and stores it in a variable named `module_address`. The address of the first module, of course, is 0.

After the linker processes the header entries in the object module, it moves the text part to a buffer named `text_buffer`, immediately behind the text that is already there. `text_buffer` is used to hold the text part of the executable module. As each object module is processed, its text part is appended to the text from the previous module that is already in the text buffer. Thus, when the linker completes phase 1, the text buffer will contain the complete text for the executable module. The linker, however, needs to process this text (to resolve external references and relocate addresses), which it does in phase 2. The adjusted addresses in the P, E, R, and S tables are relative to the beginning of the text buffer.

FIGURE 11.13   a)

```
class P    // class for the P table
{
    private String symbol[];
    private short address[];
    private int index;    //index of next available slot
    private static final int maxSize = 5;

    public P()
    {
        // constructor
    }

    public int search(String s)
    {
        // finds symbol in table and returns its index
    }

    public short getAddress(int i)
    {
        // returns address of entry at index i
    }

    public String getSymbol(index i)
    {
        // returns symbol of entry at index i
    }

    public int size()
    {

        // returns current size of table
    }

    public void enter(short add, String sym)
    {

        // enters new symbol and address
    }

    public void write(DataOutputStream s)
    {
        // writes out table
    }
}
```

(continued)

FIGURE 11.13
(continued)

b)

```
class T    // class for the text buffer
{
    private final int mainMemorySize = 4096;
    private short buffer[];
    private int index;

    public T
    {
        // constructor
    }

    public void add(short x)
    {
        // add word to buffer
    }

    public void relocate(int address, int change)
    {
        // add change to word at address
    }

    public void write(DataOutputStream) throws IOException
    {
        // writes out text
    }
}
```

The P, E, R, and S tables are best implemented as classes, with each class containing the functions that handle the processing for its table. For example, one possible structure for a Java class for the P table is given in Figure 11.13a (the C++ class is similar).

The text buffer can also be a class with functions to add, relocate, and write out the text (see Figure 11.13b). Some of these classes have features in common, so be sure to take advantage of the inheritance mechanism in Java or C++.

Each R table entry contains not only the address from the R entry (appropriately adjusted), but also the address (`module_address`) of the module from which the R entries comes. `module_address` is needed during phase 2.

11.3.3 Relocating Addresses and Resolving External References

In phase 2, the linker resolves external references and relocates addresses in the text that it built in its text buffer during phase 1. The linker starts phase 2 by processing sequentially every entry in the E table. Each entry in the E table represents an external reference. Each E table entry contains an external symbol and the location of the external reference. The linker must

1. Determine the address of the external symbol. This is easy—it searches the P table for that symbol. The P table entry for that symbol has the required address.
2. Add the address of the symbol (obtained from the P table entry) to the field in the text at which the external reference occurs. The index of this field within **text_buffer** is the address in the E table entry. This addition must not over-flow into an opcode field, thereby corrupting the opcode.

If an E table entry contains a symbol that cannot be found in the P table, then the external reference cannot be resolved (assuming the linker does not support li-braries). In this case, the linker should output an "unresolved external reference" error message and terminate.

Next the linker processes every entry in the R table. Each R table entry corre-sponds to a relocatable field in the executable module text. Everything the linker needs to perform address relocation is given in the R table entries:

- The address of the relocatable field (which is the index of the relocatable field within **text_buffer**)
- The module address (contained in the **module_address** field of the R table entry), which the linker must add to the relocatable field

When every entry in the R table has been processed, phase 2 completes. The text in the text buffer is ready for output. In phase 3, the linker first outputs a com-bined header using the information in the P table, E table, and R table. The entries in the E table turn into R entries in the combined header because their references have been resolved. Next, the linker outputs the letter *T* to signal the start of the text. Finally, it outputs the text in the text buffer.

Figure 11.14 shows the pseudocode for **linv1** (not including error handling). **file_buffer** is the buffer into which a complete input file—header and text—is read. **text_buffer** is the buffer in which **linv1** builds the text for the combined program. **module_address** is a variable that keeps track of the starting address of each module relative to the beginning of **text_ buffer**. Thus, **module_address** for the first module is always 0; for the second module, it is the size of the first module; for the third module, it is the combined size of the first two modules; and so on. The addresses that are inserted into the **address** field of the S table (except for a big-S entry), P table, E table, and R table are relocated addresses (i.e., they are addresses relative to the beginning of **text_buffer**). These relocated addresses are given by

address + module_address

where **address** is the original address from the header entry. Both the input and output files must be binary files (see Section 11.2.4).

11.3.4 Adding Library Support

Adding library support to our simplified linker is not difficult. During phase 2, the linker sequentially processes each entry in the E table. If, during this process, the linker encounters an external reference that cannot be resolved with the mod-ules input up to that point, it searches the library (or libraries) for a module that will. In particular, it searches for a module that has a P entry for the external sym-bol. When the linker finds such a module, it

FIGURE 11.14

```
// Phase 1
Open output file as a binary file
Set module_address to 0
Clear text_buffer
For each file on the command line
    +---
    |    Open file as a binary file
    |    Read file into file_buffer.
    |    Loop
    |       +---
    |       |    Get header entry
    |       |    If T entry
    |       |        Move text into text_buffer following the
    |       |        text that is already there
    |       |        Set module_address to
    |       |            module_address +  size (in words) of text
    |       |        Break  from loop
    |       |    If big-S entry
    |       |        Insert 'S' and address into S table
    |       |    If small-s entry
    |       |        Insert 's' and address + module_address into S table
    |       |    If P entry
    |       |        Insert symbol and address + module_address into P table
    |       |    If E entry
    |       |        Insert symbol and address + module_address into E table
    |       |    If R entry
    |       |        Insert address + module_address and module_address
    |       |            into R table
    |       +---
    +---

// Phase 2
Process each E entry
Process each R entry

// Phase 3
Output P table entries as P header entries
Output R table entries as R header entries
Output E table entries as R header entries
Output S table entry as s/S header entry
Output 'T'
Output text_buffer
Close files
```

1. Reads in the module
2. Appends its text to the text already in the text buffer
3. Adds its P, E, R, and s/S entries with appropriately adjusted addresses to the P table, E table, R table, and S table
4. Resolves the external reference

The linker then continues with the next entry in the E table. If a library module read in by the linker contains external references, these external references will be resolved when the linker processes their entries in the E table. The linker continues in this fashion until all external references are resolved or until an external reference appears that cannot be resolved. The latter case occurs if a public symbol or an external symbol cannot be found in any of the modules linked, or in any of the specified libraries.

Once all external references are resolved, the linker proceeds in its normal fashion:

- It relocates addresses (using the information in the R table).
- It outputs the header (using the information in the P table, E table, R table, and S table). E table entries are converted to R entries.
- It outputs the text (now resolved and relocated) in the text buffer.

PROGRAMS

11.1. Perform a test to determine the endianness of the computer you plan to use to implement your assembler and linker.

11.2. Why does a C++ program reflect the endianness of the host computer but a Java program does not?

11.3. Implement **masv1**. Use a serial search for both opcode and symbol table lookup. Test your program using the batch/script file **atest**.

11.4. If your **masv1** detects an error in its input file, does it generate an empty or near empty output file? Does **mas**?

11.5. Modify **masv1** from Problem 11.3 by using a binary search for opcode table lookup and by using hash coding for symbol table lookup. Call this version **masv2**. Compare it with **masv1**. Can you detect any difference in run time?

11.6. Add support for the **public**, **extern**, and **end** directives to **masv2** from Problem 11.5. Call this version **masv3**.

11.7. Add support for strings to **masv3** (see Problem 11.6). Call this version **masv4**.

11.8. Add support for comments and blank lines to **masv4** (see Problem 11.7). Call this version **masv5**.

11.9. Enhance **masv5** (see Problem 11.8) so that it is functionally identical to **mas**.

11.10. Modify **masv1** so that it opens its output file as a text file. Does **masv1** still work correctly? Test it on several programs.

11.11. Can the header be generated by **masv3** (see Problem 11.6) during pass 1 if constraints are placed on the location of the **public**, **extern**, and **end** directives within a program? For example, suppose all such directives have to be at the very beginning of a program.

11.12. Implement **linv1**. Test your program using the batch/script file **ltest**.

11.13. Add library support to **linv1**. Call this version **linv2**.

11.14. Enhance `linv2` (see Problem 11.13) so that it is functionally equivalent to `lin`, except for the table trace.

11.15. Write a program that is functionally equivalent to `lib`.

11.16. Suggest how a module delete capability could be added to the `lib` program. How would you specify the module to be deleted?

11.17. Try linking some files that are not valid object modules. Does `lin` detect the invalid object modules?

11.18. Describe how a library should be organized to minimize search time.

11.19. Is there any reason for placing the information in an object module header at the beginning of the object module? Why not place it in a "trailer," at the end of the object module?

11.20. Write a program in C++ or Java that unassembles a ".mac" file. Your program should analyze the flow of execution so that it can avoid unassembling data words to bogus instructions.

11.21. Suppose you forget to program `masv1` to generate R entries. Would the ".mac" files it would produce still run correctly on `sim`?

Chapter Twelve

OPTIMAL INSTRUCTION SET

12.1 INTRODUCTION

In the preceding chapters, we uncovered the following shortcomings of the standard instruction set of H1:

- The amount of main memory is insufficient (see Section 2.2).
- Strings are stored inefficiently in memory (see Section 3.11).
- Immediate instructions that add and subtract are lacking (see Section 4.5).
- Index registers are lacking (see Section 4.10).
- There are too few accumulator-type registers (see Section 4.10).
- The swap instruction corrupts the sp register (see Sections 4.4 and 7.9).
- Multiply and divide instructions are lacking (see Section 7.2).
- The dual use of the sp register as a stack pointer and as a base register for the local instructions causes complications (see Sections 4.9 and 7.5).
- Obtaining the address of a variable located on the stack is difficult (see Sections 7.9 and 9.2).
- A block copy instruction is lacking (see Section 8.4).
- Calling a function given its address at run time is difficult (see Section 8.6).
- The aloc and dloc instructions are limited (see Section 8.7.1).
- Performing signed and unsigned comparisons are difficult (see Section 8.9).
- Multi-word arithmetic is difficult (see Section 8.10).
- Bit-level operations are not supported (see Section 8.11).

Fortunately, the CPU of H1 permits the easy modification of its instruction set. Within the CPU, there is a read-only memory called *microstore* whose contents—32-bit binary numbers called *microinstructions*—determine the instruction set. To modify, extend, or completely replace an instruction set, we simply replace the current microstore in H1 with a new microstore that implements a new instruction set. We call the contents of microstore *microcode* or a *microprogram*.

The *microlevel* of a computer is what we see in a computer when we study microcode—namely, the circuits and how they are controlled by microinstructions. The *machine level* of a computer is what we see when we study machine/assembly language.

In this chapter, we introduce a new instruction set for H1 that is an improved and extended version of the standard instruction set. We incorporate this new instruction set into H1 simply by replacing its current microcode. We call this new instruction set the *optimal instruction set*. The most radical change provided by the optimal instruction set is the introduction of the bp register, a separate base register distinct from sp. In the optimal instruction set, the sp register serves only as the top-of-stack pointer. One very welcome ramification of this change is the constancy of relative addresses during the execution of a function.

The optimal instruction set is optimal in the sense that it is more or less the best possible extension/modification of the standard instruction set that we can achieve, given H1's inherent limitations. The only way we might be able to significantly improve on the optimal instruction set is to start from scratch and create a completely new instruction set.

A summary of the optimal instruction set appears in Appendix A and in the file `o.txt` in the H1 software package. You may wish to print out `o.txt` and have it available as you read this chapter.

12.2 NEW AND IMPROVED INSTRUCTIONS

Before we start discussing the optimal instruction set, let's learn how to use it with `mas` and `sim`. Then as we discuss new instructions, you can experiment with them using `mas` and `sim`.

To use `mas` and `sim` with the optimal instruction set, simply insert a line containing `!o` at the beginning of your assembly language program. This !-directive tells `mas` and `sim` to use the configuration file `o.cfg` (which configures `mas` and `sim` for the optimal instruction set). It also tells `sim` to use the microcode in the file `o.hor` (this is the microcode for the optimal instruction set). `o.cfg` and `o.hor` are in the H1 software package.

A !-directive does not have to be the first line in the assembly file; it may be preceded by blank lines, comment lines, or a &-directive. A !-directive may start in any column, but it must not be preceded by any non-white space.

As you try out each new instruction, you may want to determine its *microinstruction count* (i.e., the number of microinstructions needed to fetch, decode, and execute the machine instruction). This count is a precise measure of the instruction's total execution time. To determine microinstruction counts, enter `mc` at the debugger's prompt to activate the machine-level display plus counts. In this mode, the trace of each machine instruction will show its microinstruction count in decimal.

When adding new instructions to an instruction set, we should be sensitive to four constraints:

1. The hardware, itself, imposes certain constraints. For example, if there are no available registers at the microlevel, we cannot introduce new registers at the machine level.
2. Microstore is a fixed size. On H1, it consists of 512 words. The size of our new microcode cannot exceed this limit.
3. Many opcodes are already taken by existing machine instructions. Figure 12.1 shows all the instructions in the standard instruction set and their opcodes. None of the 4-bit opcodes are available, seven 8-bit opcodes are available, all 12-bit opcodes are available, and five 16-bit opcodes are available.
4. The new microcode should support all the instructions in the standard instruction set. Then any machine program that runs with the old microcode will also run with the new microcode. Any modification to a computer with this property is said to be *backward compatible*. Although not a necessity, backward compatibility is highly desirable. Unfortunately, the standard instruction set has one

FIGURE 12.1   4-bit opcodes   8-bit opcodes   12-bit opcodes   16-bit opcodes

0	ld	F0	ret	None		FFF5	uout
1	st	F1	ldi			FFF6	sin
2	add	F2	sti			FFF7	sout
3	sub	F3	push			FFF8	hin
4	ldr	F4	pop			FFF9	hout
5	str	F5	aloc			FFFA	ain
6	addr	F6	dloc			FFFB	aout
7	subr	F7	swap			FFFC	din
8	ldc					FFFD	dout
9	ja					FFFE	bkpt
A	jzop					FFFF	halt
B	jn						
C	jz						
D	jnz						
E	call						

serious flaw (the dual use of **sp**) that requires changes that do not allow backward compatibility. Thus, programs written for the standard instruction set cannot run, as is, on H1 when H1 is microprogrammed for the optimal instruction set.

Let's now describe the new and modified instructions in the optimal instruction set.

12.2.1   mult (Hardware Multiply), m (Shift-add Multiply), div (Divide), and rem (Remainder)

Opcode (hex)	Assembly Form	Name	Description
FF3	m	Shift-add Multiply	ac = mem[sp++] * ac;
FF4	mult	Hardware multiply	ac = mem[sp++] * ac;
FF5	div	Divide	if (ac == 0) ac = sp;
			else ac = mem[sp++] / ac;
FF6	rem	Remainder	if (ac == 0) ac = ct;
			else ac = mem[sp++] % ac;

The lack of available 4-bit opcodes on H1 is a serious problem because most of the instructions that we would like to add need to specify a 12-bit address. For example, the ideal multiply instruction would multiply two numbers, one in the **ac** register and one in memory, and place the product in the **ac** register. Thus, it would naturally be a direct instruction that contains a 4-bit opcode and the 12-bit memory address of the operand. We would also like a second multiply instruction that uses relative addresses (like addr and subr); But because there are no available 4-bit opcodes, we have to take another approach. Here are two possibilities:

- The multiply instruction could use the stack exclusively: It would pop two numbers from the top of the stack, multiply them, and then push the product onto the stack. We call this the *stack-exclusive approach*.
- The multiply instruction could use both the **ac** register and the stack: It would multiply the number in the **ac** register by the number it pops from the stack, and then place the product into the **ac** register. Let's call this the *stack-**ac** approach*.

The *mult* (hardware multiply) instruction in the optimal instruction set uses the stack-ac approach because of efficiency considerations. It accesses the stack only once and, therefore, requires fewer time-consuming main memory accesses than the stack-exclusive approach. Notice that the right side of our shorthand description of the mult instruction,

```
ac = mem[sp++] * ac;
              ↑
              └──────accesses the top of the stack and then
                      increments sp (i.e., pops the stack)
```

indicates that the top of the stack is both used and popped.

With our stack-ac approach, to multiply the numbers at **x** and **y**, and store the result in **z**, we need the sequence

```
ld    y      ; get one number
push         ; push this number onto stack
ld    x      ; load the other number into the ac register
mult         ; multiply the two numbers; product goes into ac
st    z      ; save product
```

We can also use the m (shift-add multiply) instruction to multiply. It uses the stack-ac approach exactly like the mult instruction. The difference between mult and m is how they multiply: mult executes a single microinstruction that utilizes the multiplication circuit within the ALU; m, on the other hand, executes a sequence of microinstructions that performs the shift-add multiplication algorithm (we will study this algorithm in the next chapter), making it much slower than mult. Because we have the mult instruction in the optimal instruction set, it does not make sense to also have the inferior m instruction. However, we have included both instructions so that we can compare their execution times (which we will do in the next chapter).

The *div* (divide) and *rem* (remainder) instructions similarly use the stack-ac approach. These operations are not commutative, so we have to be careful about operand order when we use them. Be sure to push the dividend (the number to be divided) onto the stack, and load the divisor into the **ac** register. For example, the following sequence divides 9 by 2 and places the quotient 4 in the **ac** register:

```
ldc   9
push         ; push dividend
ldc   2      ; load ac with divisor
div          ; quotient is placed in the ac register
```

If the divisor is zero, div and rem return the contents of the sp and ct registers, respectively. Thus, div and rem are well-defined for all divisors.

12.2.2   addc (Add Constant) and subc (Subtract Constant)

Opcode (hex)	Assembly Form	Name	Description
F8	addc y	Add constant	ac = ac + y; cy = carry;
F9	subc y	Subtract constant	ac = ac - y;

Adding or subtracting a small constant from the **ac** register is a very common operation in programming. Adding or subtracting the constant 1 is particularly common. So it is no surprise that C++ and Java have operators specifically for adding or subtracting 1. For example, to add 1 to **x**, we use

x++;

An instruction set should definitely have instructions that can perform incrementations and decrementations quickly and easily. Unfortunately, the standard instruction set does not. For example, to add 1 to the **ac** register, we have to define the constant 1 with a **dw** statement, and then add or subtract it using the instructions add or sub. Thus, we need two words (the instruction and the constant). The CPU has to fetch the instruction, of course, and then fetch the constant. Thus, we also need two memory fetches. With our new instructions—*addc* (add constant) and *subc* (subtract constant)—we can increment and decrement with one word and one fetch. For example to add 1 to the **ac** register, we use

addc 1

Both addc and subc are immediate instructions. The immediate constant occupies the y-field (i.e., the rightmost 8 bits of the instruction), and, therefore, can range only from 0 to 255. Of course, it would be better if the immediate operand occupied the 12-bit x-field (like the ldc instruction), but that would require a 4-bit opcode, none of which are available.

The addc instruction also affects the cy register, a new register added to the optimal instruction set. We will discuss the **cy** register in Section 12.2.7.

12.2.3   scmp (Signed Compare)

Opcode (hex)	Assembly Form	Name	Description
FD	scmp	Signed compare	temp = mem[sp++];
			if (temp < ac) ac = -1;
			if (temp == ac) ac = 0;
			if (temp > ac) ac = 1;

The approach we have been using to compare two signed numbers is to subtract the bottom number from the top number, and then test the result. We use jz (or jnz) to test for equality, and we use jn (or jzop) to test if the top number is less than the bottom number. Both jn and jzop test only the sign bit of the result. Accordingly, we say that the `jn` and `jzop` instructions perform a *sign-only test*. Unfortunately, a sign-only test works only when overflow does not occur. If overflow occurs, then the sign of the true result is the complement of the sign of the computed result. Thus, when overflow occurs, a sign-only test indicates that the top number is less than the bottom number when it is not, and vice versa. For example, suppose the top number is 7FFF hex (32,767 decimal) and the bottom number is FFFF hex (−1 decimal). When we subtract the bottom number from the top number, overflow occurs. The result is 8000 hex (−32,768). The negative result implies incorrectly that the top number (32,767) is less than the bottom number (−1).

Recall from Section 1.15 that the correct test when comparing signed numbers is to determine if **s** XOR **v** equals 1 (**s** and **v** are, respectively, the sign and overflow flags). Unfortunately, H1 has neither flag, so it cannot perform this test. There is, however, another (although less efficient) way to compare signed numbers:

1. Subtract B from A. If the result is 0, then B equals A, and we are done.
2. If A and B have like signs, we can use the sign-only test, and we are done. The sign-only test works in this case because overflow never occurs when subtracting numbers with like signs.
3. We reach this step only if A and B have unlike signs. Thus, if A is negative, then B must be positive, implying A is less than B. If A is positive, then B must be negative, implying A is greater than B.

Our new approach to comparing signed numbers always yields the correct result, and, moreover, can be performed by H1. The *scmp* (signed compare) instruction in the optimal instruction set uses precisely this approach. Specifically, the microcode for `scmp` consists of microinstructions that perform steps 1, 2, and 3.

The `scmp` instruction uses the stack-ac approach. It compares the number it pops from the stack with the number in the **ac** register. It loads the **ac** register with −1, 0, or 1, respectively, if the number it pops from the stack is less than, equal to, or greater than the number in the **ac** register. For example, in the following sequence

```
ld    p
push
ld    q
scmp
jn    less
jz    equal
ja    greater
```

the jump to **less**, **equal**, or **greater** occurs if **p** < **q**, **p** == **q**, or **p** > **q**, respectively.

If all we need to do is test for equality (or inequality) of two signed numbers, should we use the `scmp` instruction or our usual approach (subtract and test the result with `jz` or `jnz`)? Both approaches work correctly for all cases, but the `scmp` approach is slightly less efficient, and, therefore, should be avoided. For example, the best code for

```
if (x == y)
    z = 5;
```

where **x** and **y** are global **int** variables is

```
ld    x
sub   y
jnz   @L0      ; jump over assignment statement
ldc   5        ; z = 5;
```

```
        st    z
@L0:
```

For tests other than equality and inequality, we should use the `scmp` instruction. For example, the code for

```
if (x < y)
    z = 5;
```

is

```
    ld    x
    push
    ld    y
    scmp            ; ac loaded with -1 if x < y
    jzop  @L1       ; jump over body if ac 0 or 1
    ldc   5         ; z = 5;
    st    z
@L1:
```

Most computers do not have separate compare instructions for signed and unsigned numbers. On these computers, the single compare instruction sets the carry, sign, overflow, and zero flags. The tests that are then performed on these flags determine the interpretation of the numbers—signed or unsigned.

12.2.4 `ucmp` (Unsigned Compare)

Opcode (hex)	Assembly Form	Name	Description
FE	ucmp	Unsigned compare	Same as signed compare, except with unsigned numbers

Recall from Section 1.16 that unsigned comparisons make use of a carry flag set by the CPU. Because H1 does not have a general-purpose carry flag, we have to perform unsigned comparisons on H1 with a multi-step procedure, just like we did for the `scmp` instruction. The new instruction that does this is the *ucmp* (unsigned compare) instruction. Its format is exactly like that of `scmp`. It uses the stack-ac approach, and, when executed, it loads the **ac** register with $-1, 0$, or 1, respectively, if the number it pops from the stack is less than, equal to, or greater than the number in the **ac** register.

12.2.5 `shll` (Shift Left Logical) and `shrl` (Shift Right Logical)

Opcode (hex)	Assembly Form	Name	Description
FF0	shll z	Shift left logical	ac = ac << z;
FF1	shrl z	Shift right logical	ac = ac >> z; (inject 0's)

FIGURE 12.2

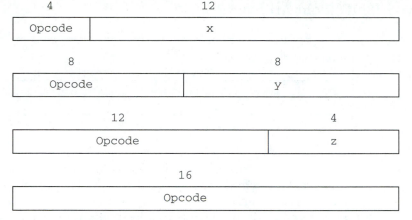

The next two instructions we want to add are the *shll* (shift left logical) and *shrl* (shift right logical). Both instructions require a 4-bit operand that specifies the number of positions to shift. For example, in the instruction

```
shrl 5
```

the operand 5 (the *shift count*) indicates that everything in the **ac** register should be shifted five positions. For both the shll and the shrl instructions, zeros are inserted into the **ac** register (into the left side for the shrl instruction, and into the right side for the shll instruction). The bits shifted out of the **ac** register are lost.

A shift count can range from 0 to 15. Thus, it can fit in the rightmost 4 bits (the *z field*) of the machine instruction, leaving 12 bits for the opcode.

We now have seen four types of instruction formats on H1 (see Figure 12.2):

4-bit opcode	12-bit x field	(like ld)
8-bit opcode	8-bit y field	(like dloc)
12-bit opcode	4-bit z field	(like shll)
16-bit opcode		(like halt)

The shift instructions are important because they allow the programmer to access individual bits. Suppose, for example, we wish to test the third bit from the left in the **ac** register. Suppose we want to jump to the label **got_one** if this bit is one, and the label **got_zero** if this bit is zero. We can use the shll instruction to make our target bit leftmost in the **ac** register. We can then use the jn instruction to test it. The required sequence is

```
shll 2      ; move the third bit from left into sign position
jn   got_one
ja   got_zero
```

Another important application of the shift instructions is in multiplication and division. Each position that the **ac** register is shifted left multiplies its contents by 2. If the **ac** register contains a positive number, each position that it is shifted right divides its contents by 2. Multiplying with the shll instruction works (assuming overflow does not occur) for positive, negative, and unsigned numbers. However, dividing with the shrl instruction works only for positive and unsigned numbers. For a negative number, the shrl instruction shifts zeros into the sign bit, making the result appear positive. For example, if 1111111111111110 (−2 in decimal) is shifted right one position with the shrl instruction, the result is not −1; instead, it is the large positive number 0111111111111111 (32,767 in decimal).

12.2.6 shra (Shift Right Arithmetic)

Opcode (hex)	Assembly Form	Name	Description
FF2	shra z	Shift right arith	ac = ac >> z; (inject sign)

The shll instruction is both a *logical* and an *arithmetic* shift. The term *logical* means that the item shifted is treated as a sequence of bits that does not necessarily represent a number; *arithmetic* means that the item shifted can be treated as a *signed* number. We use logical shift instructions to operate on unsigned numbers, and arithmetic shift instructions to operate on signed numbers.

The shll instruction is a logical shift because it can shift any sequence of bits in the **ac** register. But it is also an arithmetic shift because it performs an arithmetic operation on a signed number in the **ac** register (it multiplies it by 2 for each position shifted). The shrl instruction, on the other hand, is not an arithmetic shift. Although it does perform an arithmetic operation for positive numbers (dividing by 2 for each position shifted), it does not have the same effect on negative numbers because it inserts zeros from the left. A right *arithmetic* shift, on the other hand, inserts from the left a bit that is equal to the sign bit. Then, if a positive number is shifted right, a zero is inserted from the left; if a negative number is shifted right, a 1 is inserted from the left. Our new instruction, the shra (shift right arithmetic), works this way and, therefore, performs an arithmetic right shift. For example, if

1111111111111110

(−2 in decimal) is in the **ac** register and

shra 1

is executed, the result is 1111111111111111 (−1) because the sign bit (1) is injected from the left. Like the logical shift instructions, the shra instruction can shift up to 15 positions. For example, the instruction

shra 5

right shifts the **ac** register five positions.

Mathematics define integer division by a positive divisor in a way that requires the dividend (i.e., the number that is divided), quotient, and remainder to satisfy the following equation:

$$dividend = divisor \times quotient + remainder$$

where $0 \le remainder < divisor$.

For example, if we divide 7 by 2, the quotient and remainder are 3 and 1, respectively, because they are the values that satisfy this equation.

Let's divide −7 by 2. The remainder must be either 0 or 1. It cannot be 0 because 2 does not divide evenly into −7. Thus, it must be 1. Then, according to the equation, we have

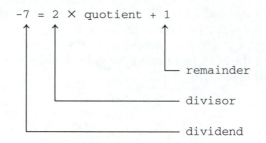

which implies the quotient must be −4. We can define division slightly different-ly, however: We can require that the remainder have the same sign as the divi-dend, and an absolute value less than that of the divisor. With this approach, −7 divided by 2 necessarily yields a remainder of −1. Plugging this remainder into our equation, we get

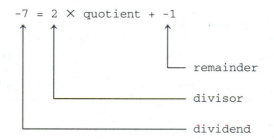

which implies the quotient must be −3. The quotient we get when we divide −7 by 2 depends on which definition of division we use. Let's see which definition Java uses. The program in Figure 12.3 performs a variety of divisions with a variety of sign combinations. When executed, this program displays

```
Dividend Divisor Quo Rem
      7       2      3    1
     -7       2     -3   -1
      7      -2     -3    1
     -7      -2      3   -1
```

Notice that the signs of the remainders equal the signs of their respective divi-dends; that is, Java uses our alternate definition of division, not the one that math-ematicians use.

FIGURE 12.3

```java
class Div {
 public static void main(String arg[])
 {
    System.out.println("Dividend Divisor Quo Rem");
    System.out.println("    7        2        " +  7/2  + "   "  + 7%2);
    System.out.println("   -7        2        " + -7/2  + "   "  + -7%2);
    System.out.println("    7       -2        " +  7/-2 + "   "  + 7%-2);
    System.out.println("   -7       -2        " + -7/-2 + "   "  + -7%-2);
 }
}
```

Our new `div` and `rem` instructions in the optimal instruction set perform the same type of division that Java does. The `shra` instruction, on the other hand, performs the other type of division. For example, if we divide −7 by 2 by shifting −7 one position with the `shra` instruction, we get −4. However, if we divide −7 by 2 with the `div` instruction, we get −3.

12.2.7 addy (Add with Carry)

Opcode (hex)	Assembly Form	Name	Description
FF7	addy	Add with carry	ac = mem[sp++] + ac + cy; cy = carry;

The add instructions (`add`, `addr`, and `addc`) can add only 16-bit numbers. We certainly want to be able to add numbers of any size. To add oversized numbers, we can use multiple words to hold the oversized numbers. We can then add two oversized numbers by adding their corresponding words. For example, in Figure 12.4, we show the addition of two 32-bit numbers, **n1** and **n2**. Each number occupies two words, one word for the high part and one word for the low part. To add the two numbers, we must add the low words for both numbers (**n1low** and **n2low**) and the high words for both numbers (**n1high** and **n2high**). The first addition yields **sumlow**, the low word of the sum; the second addition yields **sumhigh**, the high word of the sum. However, we must also add to **sumhigh** the carry, if any, coming out of the leftmost position during the addition of **n1low** and **n2low**. Ideally, we could add the carry at the same time we are adding **n1high** and **n2high**.

We need two changes to H1 to handle multiple-word addition. First, H1 needs to determine and save in a register the carry out of the leftmost position during an addition. Let's call the register for this purpose the **cy** (carry) register. In short-hand notation, **add x** would perform the operation

```
ac = ac + mem[x]; cy = carry;
```

FIGURE 12.4

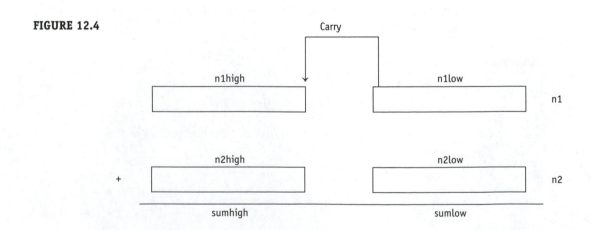

Similarly, the **addr** and **addc** instructions would save the carry. Second, we need a new instruction, addy (add with carry), that will add two numbers plus the saved carry. Because there are no available 4-bit opcodes, we will use the stack-ac approach for the addy instruction. In shorthand notation, addy performs the operation

```
ac = mem[sp++] + ac + cy; cy = carry;
```

Notice that the addy instruction not only uses the carry previously saved in the **cy** register, but also saves the carry out that occurs during the addition it performs. Thus, we can use addy again to add a third pair of numbers, and again for a fourth pair, and so on. Thus, there is no limit on the size of the multiple-word operands we can add. Here is the sequence of instructions to perform the multi-word addition in Figure 12.4:

```
ld    n1low
add   n2low    ; add low words, carry is saved in cy
st    sum1     ; save low sum
ld    n1high
push           ; get high word onto stack
ld    n2high   ; get other high word into ac register
addy           ; add high words and cy
st    sumh     ; save high sum
```

The add instruction adds the two low-order words and saves the carry out in the **cy** register. The addy instruction then adds the two high-order words and the carry in the **cy** register. The CPU in H1, unfortunately, does not output a carry bit that can be saved in the **cy** register. How, then, can H1 determine if a carry occurs? When H1 adds, it determines which of four possible cases occurs (see Figure 12.5). H1 can then tell from the case if a carry occurs. H1 can determine which case occurs by examining the sign bits of the numbers it is adding, and for cases c and d, by also examining the sign of the result. For case a, there cannot be a carry out of the leftmost column even if there is a carry in; for case b, there is always a carry out; for case c, the 1 in the most significant bit (MSB) of the result implies there was no carry in, which, in turn, implies there was no carry out; for case d, the 0 in the MSB of the result implies there was a carry in, which, in turn, implies there was a carry out. The **add, addc, addy,** and **addr** instructions in the optimal instruction set all perform this test (by executing a sequence of microinstructions that performs it) to determine if carry out occurs. They then set the **cy** register accordingly.

12.2.8   or (Bitwise Inclusive Or), xor (Bitwise Exclusive Or), and (Bitwise And), and flip (Bitwise Complement)

Opcode (hex)	Assembly Form	Name	Description
FF8	or	Bitwise or	ac = ac | mem[sp++];
FF9	xor	Bitwise excl or	ac = ac ^ mem[sp++];
FFA	and	Bitwise and	ac = ac & mem[sp++];
FFB	flip	Bitwise complement	ac = ~ac;

FIGURE 12.5

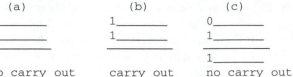
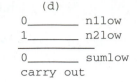

	(a)	(b)	(c)	(d)
	0_____	1_____	0_____	0_____ n1low
	0_____	1_____	1_____	1_____ n2low
	_____	_____	1_____	0_____ sumlow
	no carry out	carry out	no carry out	carry out

FIGURE 12.6

. . . 1	1	0	0	first number
. . . 1	0	1	0	second number
. . .				result

FIGURE 12.7

or

. . . 1	1	0	0
. . . 1	0	1	0
. . . 1	1	1	0

xor

. . . 1	1	0	0
. . . 1	0	1	0
. . . 0	1	1	0

and

. . . 1	1	0	0
. . . 1	0	1	0
. . . 1	0	0	0

In addition to the two logical shift instructions, three more logical instructions are important to have: the *and* (bitwise and), the *or* (bitwise inclusive or), and the *xor* (bitwise exclusive or) instructions. We call the operations these instructions perform *bitwise* because they are applied to each individual pair of corresponding bits from two operands, in isolation from the other bits. For example, consider two numbers in Figure 12.6 (we show only their rightmost four bits). We have placed one number on top of the other, thereby placing corresponding bits from the two numbers in the same column. The **or**, **xor**, and **and** instructions operate on the pair of bits (one from the first number, one from the second number) in each column. Each bit in the result depends only on the two bits above it in the same column. With the **or** instruction, the result bit is 1 if either or both bits above it are 1. With the **xor** instruction, the result bit is 1 if the two bits above it are different. A 1-output for the **or** instruction *includes* the case when both bits are 1 (hence, the name "inclusive or"); the xor instruction *excludes* this case (hence, the name "exclusive or"). With the and instruction, the result bit is 1 only if the two bits above it are both 1. Figure 12.7 shows the results when the bitwise logical operations are applied to the two numbers above. The flip instruction flips each bit in the `ac` register. Thus, if the `ac` register contained 1111111100000000, the `flip` instruction would change it to 0000000011111111.

Because of the lack of 4-bit opcodes, we use the stack-ac approach for the bitwise **or**, **and**, and **xor** instructions. One operand will be in the `ac` register; the other will be from the top of the stack. The `flip` instruction operates on only the `ac` register.

The bitwise logical instructions are important because they allow us to work with individual bits within a word. With them, we can set to 1, reset to 0, flip, or test any bit or bits within a word. Let's perform each one of these operations on bit 2 (the third bit from the right) in the word at label **x**.

To *set* (i.e., make 1) bit 2, we use

```
ld    mask4
push
ld    x
or              ; set bit 2 to 1
st    x
```

where **mask4** is defined with

```
mask4:dw    4
```

The single 1 bit in **mask4** forces its corresponding bit in the `ac` register to 1 during the `or` operation. The other bits are unchanged because they are ORed with 0 bits.

To *reset* (i.e., make 0) bit 2, we use

```
ld    maskfffb
push
ld    x
and             ; reset bit 2 to 0
st    x
```

where **maskfffb** is defined with

```
maskfffb:  dw    fffbh
```

The single 0 bit in **maskfffb** (fffbh in binary is 1111111111111011) forces its corresponding bit in the `ac` register to 0 during the `and` operation. All other bits are unchanged because they are ANDed with 1 bit in **maskfffb**.

To *flip* bit 2, we use

```
ld    mask4
push
ld    x
xor         ; flip bit 2
st    x
```

The single 1 bit in **mask4** flips its corresponding bit in the `ac` register during the xor operation. The other bits are unchanged because they are XORed with 0 bits in **mask4**. We do not use the `flip` instruction here because it flips all 16 bits.

To *test* bit 2, we use

```
ld    mask4
push
ld    x
and              ; zero all bits except bit 2
jz    is_zero
ja    is_one
```

The single 1 bit in `mask4` preserves its corresponding bit in the `ac` register. All other bits are forced to zero because they are ANDed with zero. The result of the `and` operation is zero if bit 2 in `x` is 0, and is nonzero if bit 2 is 1. Thus, the `jz` instruction jumps to the label `is_zero` if bit 2 is 0, and the `ja` instruction jumps to the label `is_one` if bit 2 is 1.

To *flip* all the bits in `x`, we use

```
ld   x
flip
st   x
```

With the exception of the shift, `addc`, and `subc` instructions, all our new instructions so far (there are more coming) could use 16-bit opcodes. However, these new instructions use 8-bit and 12-bit opcodes. The reason for using the shorter opcodes is that it saves time during the instruction decoding step that the CPU performs. During the decoding step, the CPU determines the opcode by examining each bit in serial fashion. Thus, the longer the opcode, the longer it takes the CPU to decode it.

12.2.9   `cali` (Call Indirect)

Opcode (hex)	Assembly Form	Name	Description
FFC	cali	Call indirect	mem[--sp] = pc; pc = ac12;

The next instruction we want to add to the optimal instruction set is the `cali` (call indirect) instruction. In Section 8.6, we saw that it is difficult to call a function, given its address. For example, if the `ac` register contains the address of a function that we must call, we have to use the following awkward sequence to call the function:

```
add   @call   ; adds call 0 instruction to address in ac st
st    * + 1   ; stores call instruction over next instruction
dw    0
```

where `@call` is defined with

```
@call:   call 0
```

The `add` instruction adds the `call 0` instruction (E000 in hex) to the address in the `ac` register, thereby creating a `call` instruction with the required address. The `st` instruction then stores this instruction in the word reserved by the `dw`, where it is immediately executed. We can replace this awkward three-instruction sequence with the single instruction

```
cali
```

the effect of which is to call the function whose address is currently in the `ac` register. In shorthand notation, we describe the `cali` instruction with

```
mem[--sp] = pc; pc = ac12;
```

That is, it saves the return address in the pc register (by pushing it onto the stack), and then loads the pc register with the value of the 12 rightmost bits of the ac register (denoted by the "12" in "ac12").

12.2.10 sect (Set Ct) and dect (Decrement Ct)

Opcode (hex)	Assembly Form	Name	Description
FFD	sect	Set ct register	ct = ac;
FFE	dect	Decrement ct reg	if (--ct == 0) pc++;

Because loops are so important, we need to include in the optimal instruction set two instructions that make the execution of loops more efficient. Our two new instructions for loops make use of the ct (count) register, a new register at the machine level. The *sect* (set count) instruction initializes the ct register by loading it with the contents of the ac register. The *dect* (decrement count) instruction decrements the ct register by 1, and if its new value is 0, causes the next instruction to be skipped. These two new instructions greatly simplify the setup of a count-controlled loop. For example, if we want a loop to execute 100 times, we can use the sequence

```
        ldc   100
        sect            ; set ct register to 100
start:                  ; start of loop
          .
          .             ; body of loop
          .
        dect            ; decrement ct reg; skip next inst if ct == 0
        ja    start
```

On the first 99 iterations of this loop, the dect instruction does not cause a skip. Thus, the ja instruction that follows it is executed, causing a jump back to **start**. On the 100th iteration of the loop, the ct register reaches 0, causing the dect instruction to skip over the ja instruction, thereby causing the exit from the loop. One welcome advantage of using the dect instruction to control a loop is that it leaves the ac register free for computations performed by the body of the loop.

12.2.11 sodd (Skip on Odd)

Opcode (hex)	Assembly Form	Name	Description
FFF0	sodd	Skip on odd	if (ac % 2 == 1) pc++;

We would also like to add more conditional jump instructions to our new instruction set. Here again we would like to use 4-bit opcodes but cannot because none are available. Our solution is to use a special type of conditional jump instruction called a *conditional skip instruction*, which skips over the next instruction if a condition is true. There is only one possible target address for a skip, so we do not have to specify a target address in the instruction. For example, let's suppose we want to jump to the label **even** if the contents of the **ac** register are even, and to the label **odd** if the contents are odd. We can use the *sodd* (skip on odd) instruction in the following sequence:

```
sodd
ja    even
ja    odd
```

In the odd case, the sodd instruction skips over the first ja instruction. The second ja instruction then jumps to the label **odd**. In the even case, the sodd instruction does not skip. Execution just falls through to the next instruction, the jump to the label **even**.

A number is odd if its rightmost bit is 1, and even otherwise. Thus, the sodd instruction tests the rightmost bit of the **ac** register. The jzop and jn instructions test the leftmost bit (the sign bit).

12.2.12 esba (Establish Base Address), reba (Restore Base Address), bpbp (bp to bp), pobp (Pop bp), and pbp (Push bp)

Opcode (hex)	Assembly Form	Name	Description
FA	esba	Estab base addr	mem[--sp] = bp; bp = sp12;
FB	reba	Restore base addr	sp = bp; bp = mem[sp++];
FFF1	bpbp	Bp to bp	bp = mem[bp];
FFF2	pobp	Pop bp	bp = mem[sp++];
FFF3	pbp	Push bp	mem[--sp] = bp;

Because the **sp** register is both the top-of-stack pointer and the base register for relative instructions in the standard instruction set, relative addresses change whenever a push or pop operation occurs (see Sections 4.4 and 7.5). To generate correct code, both the compiler and the assembly language programmer have the onerous task of keeping track of these changing relative addresses. Thus, the dual use of the **sp** register is a highly undesirable feature.

In the optimal instruction set, we use the **sp** register exclusively as the top-of-stack pointer. For relative instructions, we use a new register exclusively as the base register. We call this new register the **bp** (base pointer) register. For example, the instruction

```
ldr   1
```

loads the **ac** register from the memory location whose address is given by 1 plus the address in the **bp** register.

Because pushes and pops affect the **sp** register but not the **bp** register, relative addresses (which are relative to the address in **bp**) never change during the execution of a function. Thus, if the relative address of **p** is 2, the code for

```
*p = *p + 1;
```

is

```
ldr   2      ; get p
ldi          ; get *p
addc  1      ; add 1 to ac
push         ; this push does NOT increase rel address of p
ldr   2      ; get p (again use relative address 2)
sti
```

Note that the relative address of **p** remains equal to 2 in spite of the push instruction between the two ldr instructions.

To use the **bp** register, we need two new instructions: the *esba* (establish base address) and the *reba* (restore base address) instructions. The called function uses esba when it is first entered, and reba on exit (just before the ret instruction on exit). The called function allocates local variables *after* the esba instruction (see Figure 12.8). To call **f** in Figure 12.8, the calling function pushes **f**'s parameters onto the stack and then executes a call instruction. The call instruction pushes the return address on the stack (see Figure 12.9a). When the esba instruction in **f** is executed, it saves (by pushing onto the stack) the current value in the **bp** register (which is the address of the *calling* function's stack frame). It then loads the **bp** register with the address in the **sp** register, which is the address of the *called* function's stack frame (see Figure 12.9b). After the esba instruction, the called function allocates local variables on the stack (with the aloc and/or push instructions), causing the address in the **sp** register to be decremented to the address of the last variable allocated (see Figure. 12.9c).

In our shorthand notation, the effect of the esba instruction is

```
mem[--sp] = bp;   // save bp by pushing it onto the stack
bp = sp12;        // load bp with value of 12 rightmost bits
                  // of sp (the pointer to the called
                  // function's stack frame)
```

FIGURE 12.8

```
f:      esba
          .        ←——————  allocate local variables here
          .
          .
          .
        reba
        ret
```

FIGURE 12.9   a) Before esba

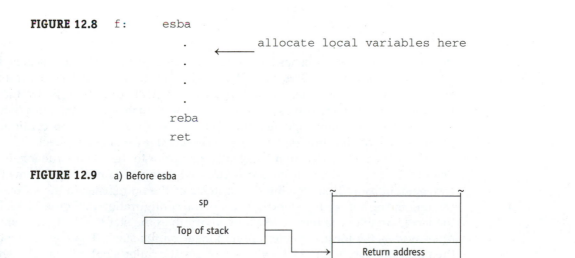

(continued)

FIGURE 12.9
(continued)

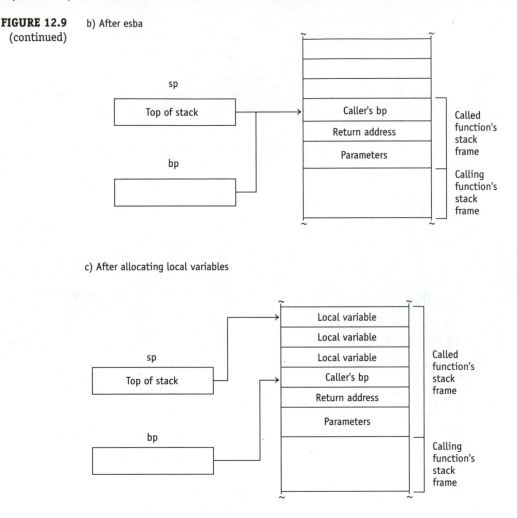

b) After esba

c) After allocating local variables

We can see it not only pushes the value in the **bp** register, but also resets **bp** with the current value in **sp**. Thus, **bp** and **sp** both point to the same location immediately after the esba instruction. Both point to the stack location in which the previous value in the **bp** register was saved. If we now push additional items onto the stack, **sp** will, of course, change, but **bp** will not. In particular, **bp** continues to point to the stack location *containing its previous value* (see Figure 12.9c).

When the reba instruction is executed just prior to the ret instruction, it both deallocates any local variables and undoes what the esba did. It performs these two operations by first copying the contents of the **bp** register to the **sp** register, causing the **bp** and **sp** registers to revert to the configuration in Figure 12.9b. Note the local variables are then lower in memory than the slot to which **sp** points; in other words, the local variables are no longer on the stack. The reba instruction then pops the top of the stack (which contains the caller's **bp**) into the **bp** register, causing the **bp** and **sp** registers to revert to the configuration in Figure 12.9a. The effect of the reba instruction is

```
sp = bp;          // deallocates local variables
bp = mem[sp++];   // pops stack into bp, restoring bp with address of
                  // the caller's stack frame
```

A simple example should clarify the use of the `esba` and `reba` instructions. Assembling the **f** function in Figure 12.10a to the *standard* instruction set, we get the code in Figure 12.10b.

FIGURE 12.10

a)

```
1 void f(int *p, int x)
2 {
3    int y;
4    y = *p + x;
5    *p = y;
6 }
```

b)

```
1               ; int y;
2 @f$pii:  aloc 1          ; allocate y
3
4               ; y = *p + x;
5               ldr  2      ; get p via relative address 2
6               ldi         ; get *p
7               addr 3      ; add x
8               str  0      ; store into y
9
10              ; *p = y;
11              ldr  0      ; get y
12              push        ; changes sp and relative addresses
13              ldr  3      ; get p via relative address 3
14              sti         ; store in *p
15
16              dloc 1      ; deallocate y
17
18              ret
19              public @f$pii
```

c)

```
1               !o
2 @f$pii:  esba            ; establish base address
3
4               ; int y
5               aloc 1
6
7               ; y = *p + x;
8               ldr  2      ; get p
9               ldi         ; get *p
```

(continued)

FIGURE 12.10
(continued)

```
10              addr 3          ; add x
11              str  -1         ; store in y (note negative rel add)
12
13              ; *p = y;
14              ldr  -1         ; get y     (note negative rel add)
15              push
16              ldr  2          ; get p
17              sti             ; store in *p
18
19              reba            ; deallocate y and restore bp
20              ret             ; return to caller
21              public @f$pii
```

FIGURE 12.11   a)

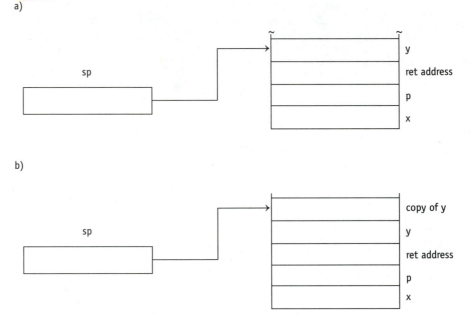

b)

The first time we access **p**, we use the relative address 2 (see Figure 12.11a). But the second time, we use 3 because the intervening push changes the **sp** register (see Figure 12.11b). If, however, we use our new instructions in the optimal instruction set, we get the code in Figure 12.10c. The first time we access **p**, we use the relative address 2 (see Figure 12.12a). The second time, we *again* use 2 because the intervening push does not change the **bp** register (see Figure 12.12b). Notice in Figure 12.12 that the relative address of **y** is −1; that is, it is one slot below the location to which **bp** points. Thus, we use the instruction

```
ldr   -1
```

to access **y**. We never had to use negative relative addresses with the standard instruction set because items on the stack are always at or above the point to which **sp** points. However, in the optimal instruction set, **bp** points to the interior of a stack frame (see Figure 12.13). Above this base point are the return address and the parameters created by the calling function (which are, therefore, accessed with

FIGURE 12.12   a)

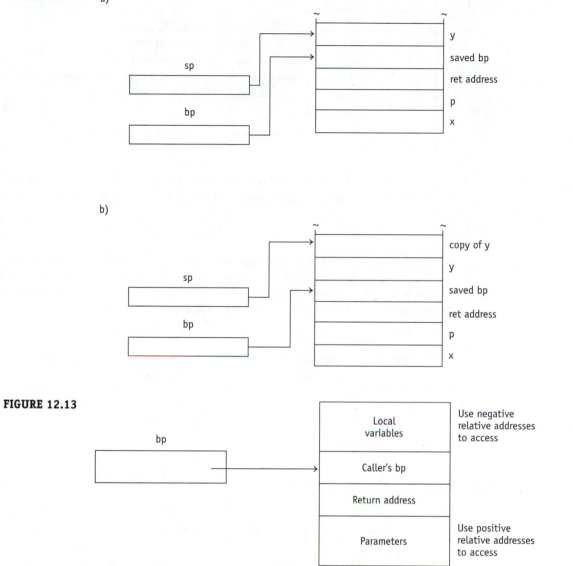

b)

FIGURE 12.13

positive relative addresses). Below this base point are the local variables (which are, therefore, accessed with negative relative addresses).

The machine instruction corresponding to the instruction

```
ldr   -1
```

is 4FFF. When executed, the CPU obtains the relative address it contains by masking out its 4-bit opcode, incorrectly extending it to 0FFF (+4095). This incorrect extension, however, does not matter because only the 12 rightmost bits are used to compute the absolute address.

Figure 12.14 shows the descriptions of the relative instructions updated to reflect the introduction of the **bp** register. Note that we are using "s" instead of "x" in the operand field in these descriptions. We do this to indicate that a relative address is a signed number (i.e., it can be positive, zero, or negative). In place of **sp**, we have **bp**.

FIGURE 12.14

Opcode (hex)	Assembly Form	Name	Description
4	ldr s	Load relative	ac = mem[bp+s];
5	str s	Store relative	mem[bp+s] = ac;
6	addr s	Add relative	ac = ac + mem[bp+s]; cy = carry;
7	subr s	Subtract relative	ac = ac - mem[bp+s];
	$-4095 \leq s \leq 4095$		

We will see in the next chapter that there is a need for an instruction that pops the top of the stack into the **bp** register; that is, we need an instruction that has the following effect:

```
bp = mem[sp++];
```

The instruction that behaves this way is the *pobp* (pop bp) instruction. We will also need an instruction that restores the **bp** register to the value to which the **bp** register currently points *without affecting the stack or the sp register*. That is, we need an instruction that has the following effect:

```
bp = mem[bp];
```

The instruction that behaves this way is the *bpbp* (bp to bp) instruction.

The esba instruction affects both the **sp** register (because it performs a push) and the **bp** register (because it loads a new value into the **bp** register). To push the contents of the **bp** register *without* affecting the value in the **bp** register, we use the *pbp* (push bp) instruction. Its shorthand description is

```
mem[--sp] = bp;
```

12.2.13   cora (Convert Relative Address)

Opcode (hex)	Assembly Form	Name	Description
FC	cora	Convert rel addr	ac = (ac + bp)12;

Because of the difficulty in obtaining the address of an item on the stack in the standard instruction set (see Section 7.9), we need the *cora* (convert relative address) instruction. The execution of a cora instruction replaces a relative address in the **ac** register with its corresponding absolute address. The shorthand description of the cora instruction is

```
ac = (bp + ac)12;
```

That is, the contents of **bp** and **ac** are added. The 12 rightmost bits of the sum (which is the absolute address) is then loaded into the **ac** register. For example, to load the **ac** register with the absolute address that corresponds to 3, we execute

```
ldc  3     ; load rel address into ac
cora       ; convert rel address in ac to an absolute address
```

In the standard instruction set, the same conversion requires the awkward sequence

```
swap               ; swap top-of-stack pointer into ac
st   @spsave       ; save top-of-stack pointer
swap               ; restore sp
ldc  3             ; get relative address
add  @spsave       ; add top-of-stack pointer to get abs address
```

As we know from Chapter 4, the `ldc` instruction is an immediate instruction that contains a constant between 0 and 4095 decimal. When executed, an `ldc` instruction loads this constant—zero-extended to 16 bits—into the **ac** register. We might expect the assembler to generate an error message for an `ldc` instruction with a negative constant, such as

```
ldc  -2
```

However, the assembler, in fact, successfully assembles it. It simply sets the immediate constant in the machine instruction to FFE hex (which equals −2). Thus, the previous `ldc` instruction would be assembled to 8FFE hex (8 is the opcode for `ldc`). When executed, this instruction loads the **ac** register with 0FFE (the immediate constant is extended on the left with four zero bits). 0FFE does *not* equal −2 (it equals 4094). However, if we use it as a relative address, we use only the 12 rightmost bits (FFE). These 12 bits are, indeed, equal to −2. Thus, it is perfectly legitimate to load negative relative addresses with the `ldc` instruction. For example, instead of using

```
ld   @_2
cora
```

where `@_2` is defined as −2 to get the absolute address for relative address −2, we can use

```
ldc  -2
cora
```

and avoid having to define the constant −2.

12.2.14 bcpy (Block Copy)

Opcode (hex)	Assembly Form	Name	Description
FFF4	bcpy	Block copy	while (ct--) mem[ac++] = mem[mem[sp]++]; sp = sp + 1;

The *bcpy* (block copy) instruction copies the block of memory pointed to by the top of the stack to the location pointed to by the **ac** register. The number of words to be moved is specified by the number in the `ct` register. During its execution, the `bcpy` instruction increments the address in the `ac` register (the *destination address*) and the address on top of the stack (the *source address*). It also decrements the count in the `ct` register. At the end of the copy, `ct` will hold 0, the `ac` register will point to the word immediately following the location to which the last word was copied, and the source address will be gone (`bcpy` pops it at the end of the copy). Before the `bcpy` instruction is executed, the source address must be on top of the stack, and destination addresses must be in the `ac` register. For example, suppose we want to copy five words from **s** to **d**, where **s** and **d** are defined with

```
s:      dw      'ABCDE'
d:      dw      '12345'
```

We first initialize the `ct` register to 5:

```
ldc     5       ; get 5
sect            ; set the ct register to 5
```

We then push the source address and load the `ac` register with the destination address:

```
ldc     s       ; get address of s
push            ; push on stack
ldc     d       ; load ac with the address of d
```

We then perform the copy:

```
bcpy
```

which copies the string 'ABCDE' on top of the string '12345'.

The `bcpy` instruction is very useful for moving large data structures that occupy a single block of memory (such as arrays and **structs**). Because the standard instruction set does not have `bcpy`, we had to resort to a word-by-word copy in Section 8.4 to copy a **struct**. For large **structs**, this word-by-word technique is very inefficient.

12.3 LINKED LISTS—AN EXAMPLE USING THE OPTIMAL INSTRUCTION SET

A linked list is a very useful data structure because its size can adjust during the execution of a program. If an executing program determines that it needs a bigger list, the list can grow; if it no longer needs some of the elements of a list, it can remove these elements, shrinking the list.

Let's examine a C++ program in Figure 12.15 that uses a linked list. This program creates a linked list and then traverses it, displaying the data in each node. The **while** loop in **main** creates the linked list. The statement on line 32

```
p = new NODE;
```

allocates a new node and assigns its address to **p**. Then, the statement

```
p -> data = x;
```

assigns the data in **x** to the data field of the node just allocated. Figure 12.16a shows the list at this point. The next step is to put this node at the beginning of the

FIGURE 12.15

```cpp
1  #include <iostream>
2  using namespace std;
3
4  struct NODE {
5    int data;
6    NODE *link;
7  };
8  //===========================================================
9  // traverse displays the data in a linked list in node order
10 void traverse(NODE *p)
11 {
12   while (p) {
13     cout << p -> data << endl;
14     p = p -> link;      // move p to next node
15   }
16 }
17 //===========================================================
18 // get_data prompts for and inputs an integer
19 void get_data(int &x)
20 {
21   cout << "enter positive int (or negative int to end)\n";
22   cin >> x;
23 }
24 //===========================================================
25 int main()
26 {
27   NODE *head, *p;
28   int x;
29   head = NULL;
30   get_data(x);
31   while (x >= 0) {          // end loop on negative number
32     p = new NODE;           // allocate new node
33     p -> data = x;
34     p -> link = head;       // new node pts to head node
35     head = p;               // head ptr pts to new node
36     get_data(x);
37   }
38   cout << "Traversing list\n";
39   traverse(head);
40   return 0;
41 }
```

FIGURE 12.16

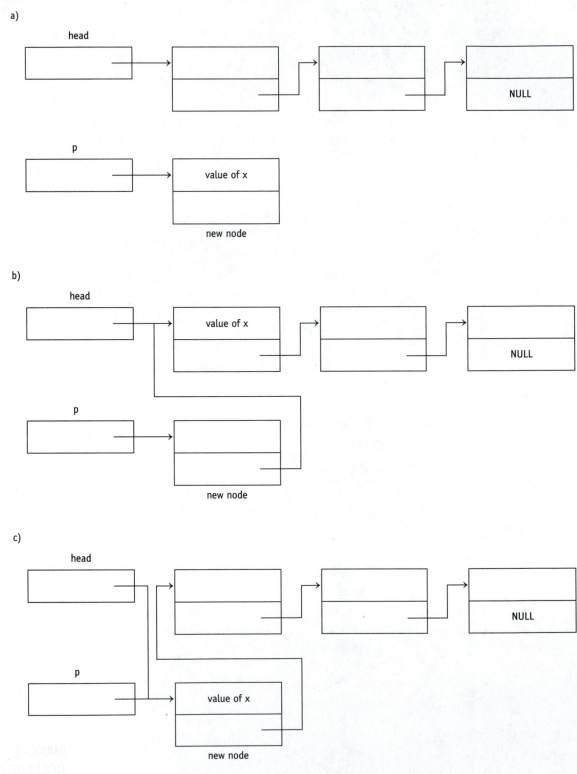

list. **head** is a pointer that points to the first node. We must do two things to put the new node on the list:

1. Get the link field of the new node to point to the node that is currently the head node (see Figure 12.16b). We do this with

```
p -> link = head;
```

2. Get **head** to point to the new node (see Figure 12.16c). We do this with

```
head = p;
```

We cannot reverse the order of lines 34 and 35 in Figure 12.15. If we did, the assignment to **head** would destroy the pointer to the node that is currently the head node. In other words, the first statement would destroy information (a pointer) we need in the second statement. In the correct order, the first statement—the assignment to the link field of the new node—simply overlays the garbage that is in the link field of the new node. Thus, we do not suffer any loss of information. Generalizing our observations here gives us an important rule to remember when programming linked structures: *Always make assignments to the fields that contain garbage first*.

The **traverse** function in Figure 12.15 traverses the linked list whose head pointer it is passed. On entry, **p** points to the first node of the list (the value parameter-passing mechanism assigns **head** to **p**). The key statement in **traverse** on line 14

```
p = p -> link;
```

moves **p** down the list to the next node. At the end of the list, this statement assigns **p** the NULL pointer in the last node. The NULL pointer in **p**, in turn, causes the exit from the **while** loop (the NULL pointer is represented by 0, and therefore evaluates to false).

The assembly code for the C++ program in Figure 12.15 appears in Figure 12.17. Most of it is a straightforward translation using the techniques that we have already studied. There is, however, one part that needs an explanation—the allocation of a new node (lines 59 to 62 in Figure 12.17) from a *heap* (a heap is a memory area from which memory is dynamically allocated). Before we examine these instructions, look at line 103, at the very end of the program. We see the **dw**

```
@avail_ptr: dw      * + 1
```

that defines a pointer that points to the next slot in memory (recall that "*" means the current address). Because **@avail_ptr** is at the end of the program, it points to the rest of main memory, all of which is available except for the command line arguments and the stack in upper memory (see Figure 12.18a). Memory that the statement

```
p = new NODE;
```

obtains comes from this available block of memory.

The code for the allocation request

```
p = new NODE;
```

FIGURE 12.17

```
 1                !o
 2                ; void traverse(NODE *p)
 3  @traverse$p4NODE:
 4                esba
 5
 6  @L0:     ldr  2           ; while (p) {
 7           jz   @L1
 8
 9           ldr  2           ; cout << p -> data << endl;
10           ldi
11           dout
12           ldc  '\n'
13           aout
14
15           ldr  2           ; p = p -> link;
16           addc 1
17           ldi
18           str  2
19
20           ja @L0
21
22  @L1:     reba
23           ret
24  ;============================================================
25  @get_data$ri:
26           esba
27
28           ldc  @m0         ; cout << "Enter positive int ...\n"
29           sout
30
31           din              ; cin >> x;
32           push
33           ldr  2
34           sti
35
36           reba
37           ret
38  ;============================================================
39  main:    esba
40
41           aloc 1           ; NODE *head;
42
43           aloc 1           ; NODE *p;
```

(continued)

FIGURE 12.17
(continued)

```
44
45              aloc 1          ; int x;
46
47              ldc   0         ; head = NULL;
48              str -1
49
50              ldc  -3         ; get_data(x);
51              cora
52              push
53              call @get_data$ri
54              dloc 1
55
56  @L2:        ldr  -3         ; while (x >= 0) {
57              jn   @L3
58
59              ld   @avail_ptr ; p = new NODE;
60              str  -2
61              addc 2
62              st   @avail_ptr
63
64              ldr  -3         ; p -> data = x;
65              push
66              ldr  -2
67              sti
68
69              ldr  -1         ; p -> link = head;
70              push
71              ldr   -2
72              addc  1
73              sti
74
75              ldr -2          ; head = p;
76              str -1
77
78              ldc -3          ; get_data(x);
79              cora
80              push
81              call @get_data$ri
82              dloc 1
83
84              ja   @L2
85
86  @L3:        ldc @m1         ;  cout << "Traversing list\n";
```

(continued)

FIGURE 12.17
(continued)

```
 87              sout
 88
 89              ldr  -1          ; traverse(head);
 90              push
 91              call @traverse$p4NODE
 92              dloc 1
 93
 94              ldc  0           ; return 0;
 95              reba
 96              ret
 97  ;============================================================
 98  @m0:   dw               "enter positive int (or negative int
                             to end)\n";
 99  @m1:   dw               "Traversing list\n";
100         public @traverse$p4NODE
101         public @get_data$ri
102         public main
103  @avail_ptr: dw   * + 1
```

is on lines 59 to 62 in Figure 12.17. The sequence first gets the value in **@avail_ptr** and stores it in **p**:

```
ld   @avail_ptr   ; get avail pointer
str  -2           ; store in p
```

Thus, the new node comes from the first two words of the available memory. Next, it adjusts **@avail_ptr** to point to the memory block that follows the two words just allocated so that the next request will come from the next two available slots (see Figure 12.18b):

```
addc 2            ; add 2 to avail pointer
st   @avail_ptr ; update @avail_ptr
```

A real C++ compiler would not generate in-line code to allocate memory as we have in Figure 12.17. Instead, it would generate a call of a function to perform the allocation. This function would maintain a data structure to keep track of available storage that is more complex than our simple **@avail_ptr**. A more complex data structure is needed to allow both the allocation of storage (with the C++ **new** operator) and its reclamation (with the C++ **delete** operator). Our simple technique using **@avail_ptr** does not allow individual blocks of memory to be reclaimed once they are allocated. Incidentally, Java programs also dynamically allocate memory from a heap. The Java system maintains a data structure that permits both memory allocation (by the **new** operator) and reclamation. Reclamation in Java, however, is automatic (done by the garbage collector). In C++, a program has to use the **delete** operator.

To create a ".mac" file from the program in Figure 12.17, we must assemble it and then link it with the start-up code in the file **sup.mob** (start-up code is a module that gets control first, performs start-up initialization, and then calls **main**). Assuming the program is in a file named **fig1217.mas**, we assemble it with

```
mas fig1217
```

FIGURE 12.18 a)

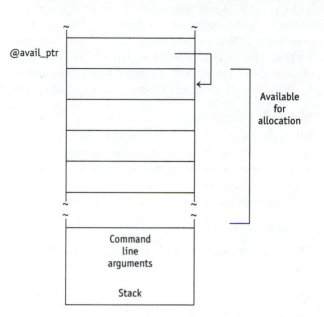

b)

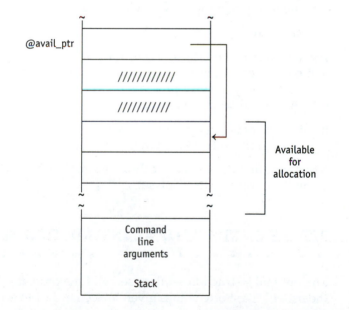

Because `fig1217.mas` contains `public` directives, `mas` assumes the file does not contain a complete program (a `public` directive makes a symbol global, and implies it will be referenced by a separately assembled module). Accordingly, `mas` outputs a ".mob" file named `fig1217.mob` instead of a ".mac" file. Next, we link `sup.mob` and `fig1217.mob` *in that order* by entering

```
lin sup fig1217 /ofig1217
```

`lin` then creates an executable file `fig1217.mac`. The output file name is specified by the `/o` command line argument (`lin` adds ".mac" to the output file name if it lacks an extension). Without the `/o` argument, `lin` would derive the output file name from the name of the first input file. Thus, if we specified `fig1217` before `sup` in the previous command, the name of the output file would be `fig1217.mac` without the `/o` command line argument. But we cannot do this here because the structure of this particular program requires that we specify `sup` first (why?).

Once we have `fig1217.mac`, we can run it on `sim` by entering

```
sim fig1217
```

Whenever `sim` runs a ".mac" file, it searches the ".mas" file with the same basename for a !-directive. Thus, in this example, `sim` will search the file `fig1217.mas` for a !-directive. Because this file contains the directive `!o`, `sim` will use the optimal instruction set.

Suppose we linked `fig1217.mob` using

```
lin sup fig1217
```

Then the output file name would default to `sup.mac`. If we then attempt to run `sup.mac` with

```
sim sup
```

sim would *not* search `fig1217.mas` for a !-directive. Instead, it would search `sup.mas`, find none, and, therefore, use the standard instruction set. To run `sup.mac` correctly, we must specify the correct microcode file with the `/m` command line argument when we invoke `sim`. To do this, enter

```
sim sup /mo
```

`/mo` tells `sim` it should use the `o.hor` microcode file (sim adds ".hor" to the file name specified by the `/m` command line argument if it lacks an extension).

Whenever you run a program on `sim` that should use the optimal instruction set, you should see the messages

```
Reading configuration file o.cfg
Reading microcode file o.hor
```

when you first invoke `sim`. If these messages do not appear, it means `sim` is *not* using the optimal instruction set.

12.4 PROGRESS REPORT ON THE OPTIMAL INSTRUCTION SET

The optimal instruction set fixes some of the problems with H1. Let's go through the list of H1's shortcomings given in Section 12.1 to see where H1 now stands.

12.4.1 An Insufficient Amount of Main Memory

This problem is intrinsic to the organization of H1. We cannot microprogram around it. Addresses are 12 bits, making 4K the maximum size of main memory.

12.4.2 Strings Are Stored Inefficiently in Memory

Because H1 still cannot easily access individual bytes within a word, using one word per character is still the most practical approach.

12.4.3 The Lack of Immediate Instructions That Add and Subtract

We now have the immediate instructions **addc** and **subc**. Because these instructions have an 8-bit immediate operand field, they can add or subtract values up to only 255. Because programs most often add or subtract small values, the limited range of these instructions minimally impacts their usefulness.

12.4.4 The Lack of an Index Register

This is a serious problem we have not fixed. Code programmed directly in assembly language typically makes extensive use of index registers. However, for compiled code, the lack of an index register is much less serious because compiled code often does not take advantage of index registers even if they exist. For example, a compiler would typically translate the assignment statement in the loop

```
for (i = 0; i < 100; i++)
    a[i] = 0;
```

where **a** and **i** are global variables, to

```
ldc   0     ; get 0
push        ; push 0 onto stack
ldc   a     ; get address of a
add   i     ; get address of a[i]
sti         ; pop zero from stack into a[i]
```

If we were to use the **sp** register as an index register and the standard instruction set, we could do the same thing with only two instructions:

```
ldc   0
str   0
```

assuming the **sp** register is initialized to the address of **a** before the start of the loop, and is incremented each time through the loop. However, it would take a very smart compiler to utilize this optimization (the compiler would have to "understand" what the **for** loop is doing).

12.4.5 Too Few Accumulator-Type Registers

We now have the **ct** register, which, with the sect and dect instructions, frees up the **ac** register within loops.

12.4.6 The swap Instruction Corrupts the sp Register

We now use swap only to initialize the **sp** register. To convert a relative address to an absolute address, we use the cora instruction, which accesses the **bp** register without corrupting it. We can also access sp without corrupting it with the div instruction (using a zero divisor).

12.4.7 The Lack of Multiply and Divide Instructions

We now have the mult, m, div, and rem instructions.

12.4.8 The Use of the `sp` Register as Both a Stack Pointer and a Base Register

The `sp` register is now exclusively a top-of-stack pointer. The new **bp** register is now the base register. Relative addresses now do not change during the execution of a function.

12.4.9 The Difficulty in Obtaining the Address of a Variable Located on the Stack

The `cora` instruction solves this problem.

12.4.10 The Lack of a Block Copy Instruction

We now have the `bcpy` instruction.

12.4.11 The Difficulty in Calling a Function, Given Its Address

We now have the `cali` instruction.

12.4.12 The Limitation of the `aloc` and `dloc` Instructions

We will solve this problem in Chapter 13 when we introduce a completely new instruction set.

12.4.13 The Difficulty in Performing Signed and Unsigned Comparisons

We now have the `scmp` and `ucmp` instructions, which correctly, although somewhat inefficiently, perform signed and unsigned comparisons.

12.4.14 The Difficulty in Performing Multi-word Addition

We now have the `add`, `addc`, `addr`, and `addy` instructions that set the carry register, and the **addy** instruction that both uses and sets the carry. Using these instructions, we can perform both multi-word addition and subtraction (to subtract, we add the two's complement of the bottom number).

12.4.15 No Support for Bit-Level Operations

We now have most of the traditional shift and bitwise instructions. We also have the `sodd` instruction, which tests the rightmost bit in the **ac** register.

Although H1 with the optimal instruction set still has some problems, it is a much improved computer. We have been able to fix problems with H1 because of the flexibility that its microprogrammed organization offers. By changing and adding microcode, we can adjust the computer at the machine level to best suit our requirements.

PROBLEMS

• •

12.1 Describe how variable length instructions can be used to circumvent the lack of 4-bit opcodes.

12.2 Why is backward compatibility so important?

12.3 Would it make sense to have shift counts greater than 15?

12.4 Write a C++ program like the Java program in Figure 12.3. Does C++ divide in the same way Java does?

12.5 If the signed number 7FFFh is multiplied by itself, how many bits are required by the product? If the unsigned number FFFFh is multiplied by itself, how many bits are required by the product?

12.6 Is the right shift operator (`>>`) signed, unsigned, or undefined in C++? In Java?

12.7 The 4-bit opcodes run from 0 hex to E hex. Why don't they run from 0 hex to F hex?

12.8 Using the optimal instruction set, write, assemble, and run on **sim** an assembly language program that
a. Prompts for and reads in a decimal number
b. Determines the number of 1 bits in the binary equivalent of the decimal number
c. Outputs in decimal the number of 1 bits

12.9 Give an algorithm that `ucmp` could use to compare unsigned numbers.

12.10 Determine the microinstruction count for every instruction in the optimal instruction set. Is there any correlation between the length of an opcode and microinstruction count?

12.11 Give a reason why the microinstruction count for `ld` should be greater than the count for `sect`. Give a reason why the microinstruction count for `sect` should be greater than the count for `ld`. What are the actual counts for these two instructions?

12.12 Using the optimal instruction set, write, assemble, and run on **sim** an assembly language program that
a. Prompts for and reads in 2 hex numbers, each containing 12 hex digits
b. Adds the two numbers
c. Outputs the sum in hex
Test your program with the numbers

```
01FFFFFFFFF0
000101230A2C
```

12.13 Same as Problem 12.12, except subtract the two numbers.

12.14 Suppose the two words at labels **x** and **y** contain a single integer of type **long** (assume **x** contains the high part and **y** contains the low part). Give the assembly code that will compute the integer's two's complement and place the result back in **x** and **y**.

12.15 H1 does not have a sign flag. What, then, do the `jzop` and `jn` instructions test? Would there be any advantage in having a sign flag?

12.16 Write a sequence of assembly language instructions that jumps to the label **all_ones** if the four leftmost bits in the **ac** register are all equal to 1. Use the bitwise instructions. Write and run a program that tests your code.

12.17 Write a sequence of assembly language instructions that sets bit 0, bit 7, and bit 15 of the **ac** register to 1 without affecting the other bits. Use the bitwise instructions. Write and run a program that tests your code.

12.18 Using the optimal instruction set, write, assemble, and run on **sim** an assembly language program that
a. Prompts for and reads in a decimal number
b. Outputs its binary equivalent

12.19 Using the optimal instruction set, write, assemble, and run on **sim** an assembly language program that

a. Prompts for and reads in a decimal number as a string (use `sin`)

b. Converts each digit to its binary equivalent

c. Using Horner's rule and the results from step 2, computes the binary number equivalent to the decimal number input in step 1

d. Converts the binary number computed in step 3 to a string of 1's and 0's, and outputs this string

12.20 Using the optimal instruction set, write, assemble, and run on **sim** an assembly language program that

a. Prompts for and reads in a binary number

b. Outputs its decimal equivalent

12.21 Using the optimal instruction set, write and run an assembly language program that prompts for and reads in an unsigned number, and then displays the value equal to three-fourths of the number read in.

12.22 Would it be useful if the `sect` instruction swapped the contents of the **ac** and **ct** registers instead of just loading the **ct** register from the **ac** register? Explain.

12.23 If you enter `lin fig1217 sup` before **sim** `fig1217` the program runs correctly for small but not large lists. Why?

12.24 Under what circumstances will the `ucmp` and `scmp` instructions yield different results? Consider three cases: both operands positive, both negative, and one positive and one negative.

12.25 Suggest an algorithm that `ucmp` can use. Hint: See Problem 12.24.

12.26 Write a sequence of assembly language instructions that has the effect of the `flip` instruction without using the `flip` instruction.

12.27 Why does the `cora` instruction set **ac** to (**ac** + **bp**)12 instead of **ac** + **bp**?

12.28 Use both `scmp` and `jz` to test for equality. Which is more efficient? By how much?

12.29 When a function returns a value, is it better to load the return value into **ac** and then execute `reba`, or vice versa? Explain.

For the following problems, translate the given program to assembly language using the optimal instruction set. Include all assembly directives that would normally appear in compiler-generated assembly code, and use mangled function names. Assemble, link with start-up code, and run on **sim**.

12.30
```
#include <iostream>
   using namespace std;
   int i = 20;
   int main()
   {
       do {
          cout << "hello\n";
          i--;
       } while (i > 0);
       return 0;
   }
```

12.31
```
#include <iostream>
   using namespace std;
int x = 18;
void f(int *p, int *q)
{
    *p = *q + 5;
}
void g(int x)
```

```
        {
            int y;
            y = x + 10;
            f(&x, &y);
            cout << x << " " << y << endl;
        }
        int main()
        {
            g(7);
            return 0;

        }
```

12.32

```
#include <iostream>
using namespace std;
void f(int a[])
{
   a[3] = 45;
}
void g(void)
{
    int z[10];
    int x = 5;
    f(z);
    cout << *(z+3) << endl;
}
int main()
{
   g();
   return 0;

}
```

Chapter Thirteen

USING, EVALUATING, AND IMPLEMENTING THE OPTIMAL AND STACK INSTRUCTION SETS

13.1 INTRODUCTION

In this chapter, we put our new optimal instruction set to use. By doing so, we will get a good sense of the adequacy of the optimal instruction set as the target language for C++. We start by considering various approaches for performing multiplication on H1 using the `mult` and `m` instructions, using assembly routines, and using C++ routines. We compare these approaches, and consider their advantages and disadvantages.

When we covered arrays in Chapter 8, we avoided two-dimensional arrays because we did not have a multiplication instruction (indexing into multi-dimensional arrays requires multiplication). With the `mult` and `m` instructions in the optimal instruction set, we can now finally look at two-dimensional arrays. There are some features of two-dimensional arrays that are often poorly understood. We will examine these features and thoroughly demystify them.

You probably already know what a C++ object is, but only from a conceptual point of view. In this chapter, we will learn what is "under the hood" of an object-oriented program. In particular, we will learn how to write assembly language programs that implement objects, inheritance, and virtual functions.

So far we have learned three parameter-passing mechanisms: call by value, call by reference, and call by value-result. Now is the time to learn call by name, a parameter-passing mechanism that is elegant and interesting, but, at the same time, complex and inefficient. It is a mechanism for which the new **bp** register in the optimal instruction set is a necessity. Call by name is no longer an important parameter-passing mechanism (modern programming languages do not support it). It is, nevertheless, important to study because it will provide us with some important insights into the architectural requirements of programming languages.

The best way to evaluate an instruction set is to compare it with another instruction set. To get a better sense of how good or bad the optimal instruction set is, we compare it with the *stack instruction set*—an instruction set in which the **ac** register is replaced by the top of the stack.

An excellent project for you to undertake when you finish this chapter is to write the microcode for the optimal and stack instruction sets. To this end, we conclude this chapter with some helpful hints on how to get started on these projects, and how to test your microcode.

13.2   MULTIPLYING ON H1

• •

In Section 10.7, we saw two special-purpose multiplication functions. One function multiplied by 15 only; the other squared a number. In this section, we will consider a variety of ways in which we can implement general-purpose multiplication on H1.

Our first approach is given by the recursive C++ function `mult_rec` in Figure 13.1 (at this point, you may wish to review the discussion of recursion in Section 8.12). Suppose `mult_rec` is invoked with

```
z = mult_rec(10, 4);
```

As the recursion in the `mult_rec` function proceeds "downward," the value of the second parameter is driven toward 0. The recursion hits "bottom" when the second parameter reaches 0. At this level `mult_rec` returns 0. Then, as the recursion proceeds "upward," `x` (which equals 10 at all levels) is added at each level to the value returned by the preceding level. On the first call, the second parameter is equal to 4, so there are a total of four levels above level 0. Thus, 10 (the value of `x`) is added to the returned value four times. That is, the function computes

$$0 + 10 + 10 + 10 + 10$$

which, of course, equals 10×4. In other words, `mult_rec` multiplies `x` by `y` by adding `y` occurrences of `x`. One problem with `mult_rec` is that it does not work if `y` is negative. However, we can easily fix this shortcoming.

The `mult_rec` function computes $x \times y$ by adding `y` occurrences of `x`. Our second approach, illustrated by the function `mult_loop` in Figure 13.2, does the same thing, except it uses a count-controlled loop instead of recursion. `mult_rec` uses the recursive approach; `mult_loop` uses the *iterative* (i.e., with a loop) approach. `mult_loop`, like `mult_rec`, does not work when the value of the second parameter is negative. However, we can easily fix this problem.

FIGURE 13.1

```
1 int mult_rec(int x, int y)
2 {
3   if (y == 0)
4       return 0;
5   return mult_rec(x, y-1) + x;
6 }
```

FIGURE 13.2

```
1 int mult_loop(int x, int y)
2 {
3     int product = 0;
4
5     while (y > 0) {
6        product = product + x;
7        y--;
8     }
9     return product;
10 }
```

FIGURE 13.3

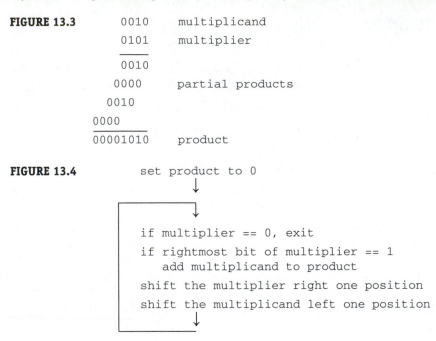

```
0010      multiplicand
0101      multiplier
────
0010
0000      partial products
0010
0000
────────
00001010  product
```

FIGURE 13.4

```
set product to 0
      ↓
      ↓
  if multiplier == 0, exit
  if rightmost bit of multiplier == 1
      add multiplicand to product
  shift the multiplier right one position
  shift the multiplicand left one position
      ↓
```

Our third approach mimics what we do when we multiply two binary numbers with pencil and paper. For example, consider the multiplication of the two 4-bit numbers shown in Figure 13.3. In multiplication, we have a bottom number and a top number. We call the bottom number (the number we are multiplying *by*) the *multiplier*. We call the top number the *multiplicand*. To compute their product, we individually multiply the multiplicand by each bit in the multiplier. Each of these computations yields a *partial product*. We align the right side of each partial product with its corresponding multiplier bit. The *product* (i.e., the final result) is the sum of these partial products.

It is very easy to determine the partial products when multiplying binary numbers. A partial product is either equal to the multiplicand (if the multiplying bit is 1) or equal to 0 (if the multiplying bit is 0). We, of course, can ignore the 0 partial products because they do not contribute to the final product. Thus, the final product is simply the sum of several instances of the multiplicand appropriately shifted, one partial product for each 1 bit in the multiplier.

Figure 13.4 gives the algorithm for computing a product by summing partial products. We call this algorithm the *shift-add algorithm* because it uses shifts and adds. Each iteration of the loop corresponds to the processing of one bit in the multiplier. When the rightmost bit in the multiplier equals 1, the multiplicand is added to the product. The multiplier is shifted right each time through the loop, so that its rightmost position receives the successive bits of the multiplier. The multiplicand is shifted left each time through the loop, so that whenever it is added to the product, it is in the appropriately shifted form.

Figure 13.4 does not indicate the type of right shift—logical or arithmetic—that is applied to the multiplier. It obviously does not matter if the multiplier is positive—both shifts inject 0's from the left. However, if the multiplier is negative, then an arithmetic right shift would inject 1's, in which case the multiplier would never go zero, regardless of the number of times it was shifted, resulting in an infinite loop. Thus, we must use a logical right shift if the algorithm is to work with negative multipliers.

FIGURE 13.5

```
 1 int mult_shift_add(int multiplicand, unsigned multiplier)
 2 {
 3   int product = 0;
 4   while (multiplier != 0) {
 5     if (multiplier & 1 == 1)              // rightmost bit == 1?
 6         product = product + multiplicand;
 7     multiplier = multiplier >> 1;         // logical shift right
 8     multiplicand = multiplicand << 1;     // shift left
 9   }
10
11   return product;
12 }
```

Figure 13.5 shows the shift-add algorithm implemented as a C++ function `mult_shift_add`. This C++ function is a straightforward implementation of the shift-add algorithm. Its only peculiarity is that the type of its second parameter—`multiplier`—is `unsigned`. By making the multiplier `unsigned`, we ensure that its right shift is logical (i.e., that 0's will be injected from the left). If `multiplier` were `int`, then the right shift would be arithmetic. Thus, a negative `multiplier` would injects 1's (the sign bit), resulting in an infinite loop (because `multiplier` would never go zero). Although the parameter `multiplier` is `unsigned`, we can still call `mult_shift_add` with `int` arguments.

Both the shift-add approach in `mult_shift_add` and the iterative approach in the `mult_loop` function use a loop. However, the shift-add approach usually works much faster because its loop usually iterates fewer times than the loop in `mult_loop`. We expect `mult_rec` to be the slowest approach, because it does everything `mult_loop` does, and, in addition, has the overhead associated with the recursive function calls. The compiler-generated assembly code for `mult_shift_add` is given in Figure 13.6.

The calling sequence for `mult_shift_add` pushes the multiplier and multiplicand (in that order) onto the stack. For example, if the multiplier and multiplicand are in two global variables, `multiplier` and `multiplicand`, then the calling sequence would be

```
ld    multiplier
push
ld    multiplicand
push
call mult_shift_add
dloc 2
```

We can also implement the shift-add algorithm on H1 directly in assembly language, in which case we could probably do better than the compiler-generated version in Figure 13.6. For example, we can translate line 13

```
if (multiplier & 1 == 1)
```

more efficiently with the following sequence:

```
ldr  3     ; get multiplier
sodd       ; skip next instruction if multiplier is odd
ja   @L2
```

FIGURE 13.6

```
 1      !o      ; directive to use optimal inst set
 2 @mult_shift_add$iui;
 3      esba
 4
 5      ; int product = 0;
 6      ldc  0
 7      push           ; allocate and initialize product to 0
 8
 9      ; while (multiplier != 0) {
10 @L0:  ldr  3         ; get multiplier
11      jz   @L1
12
13      ; if (multiplier & 1 == 1)        // rightmost bit == 1?
14      ldc  1
15      push
16      ldr  3         ; get multiplier
17      and
18      jz   @L2
19
20      ; product = product + multiplicand;
21      ldr  -1        ; get product
22      addr 2         ; add shifted multiplicand
23      str  -1        ; save produce
24 @L2:
25      ; multiplier = multiplier >> 1;
26      ldr  3         ; get multiplier
27      shrl 1
28      str  3         ; save multiplier
29
30      ; multiplicand = multiplicand << 1;
31      ldr  2         ; get multiplicand
32      shll 1         ; shift multiplicand left 1 position
33      str  2         ; save multiplicand
34      ja   @L0
35 @L1:
36      ; return product;
37      ldr  -1        ; load product into ac register
38      reba
39      ret
40      public @multi_shift_add$iui
```

instead of using the sequence on lines 14 to 18 in Figure 13.6.

Another approach we have for multiplying on H1 is to use the m instruction in our optimal instruction set. H1 executes the m instruction by performing the operations specified by the microinstructions in microstore for this instruction. These microinstructions multiply using the shift-add approach.

When H1 executes the microinstructions for the m instruction, it performs all the steps of the shift-add algorithm—the testing of the multiplier, the adding, the shifting, and the looping.

Because the shift-add algorithm is used by the m instruction, we have a choice of where to execute it: We can execute it at the microlevel by executing the m instruction, or we can execute it at the machine level by executing the machine code for `mult_shift_add` in Figure 13.6.

A final way a computer can multiply—and the fastest and most expensive—is to use a multiplier circuit. With a multiplier circuit, a computer does *not* have to execute a sequence of microinstructions implementing the shift-add algorithm. Instead, the multiplier circuit multiplies directly. The `mult` instruction multiplies in this way.

One of the principal tasks of a computer architect is to determine at what level—circuit, micro, or machine—to place a function. For example, a computer architect can place multiplication at the circuit level (with a multiplier circuit), at the microlevel (with a sequence of microinstructions in microstore), or at the machine level. Each choice has advantages and disadvantages. The circuit level is the fastest but the most expensive. The machine level is the slowest but the least expensive. The microlevel is a good cost-speed compromise.

We can characterize a function at the machine level in terms of the source language used to create it. For example, if we create a function using assembly language, we can say that the function is at the *assembly language level*; if we create a function with C++, we can say the function is at the C++ *level*. Using this characterization, we can say that multiplication on H1 can be provided

- At the C++ level (with `mult_rec`, `mult_loop`, or the C++ version of `mult_shift_add`)
- At the assembly level (with a `mult_shift_add` version written directly in assembly language)
- At the microlevel (with the m instruction)
- At the circuit level (with the `mult` instruction)

If a function is to be placed at the machine level, its machine code can be made available in a variety of ways. For example, the machine code could be a prepackaged module ready to use, such as a ROM module in main memory, an operating system module, or a C++ library function; or it could be a module that a programmer writes for a specific application that is used only in that application. The determination of the functions provided by a computer system—which functions, at what level, and how they are packaged—is a principal design problem that faces a computer architect.

We have seen a variety of approaches for multiplying on H1. We should test each one to see how fast they are. To make the comparison, we can run a program on **sim** for each approach, and then examine the machine instruction count for each program. Machine instruction counts, however, are not an accurate measure of execution time. Some machine instructions (like m) require more microinstructions and, therefore, take more time than other machine instructions. Unlike machine instructions, all microinstructions on H1 take exactly the same amount of time to execute. Thus, microinstruction counts are a precise measure of execution time. For example, a program that requires the execution of 200 microinstructions will take exactly twice the time as a program that requires 100 microinstructions.

FIGURE 13.7 Starting session. Enter h or ? for help.

```
---- [T7]  0: ld   /0 004/ enable
Microlevel enabled
---- [T7]  0: ld   /0 004/ g
  0: ld   /0 004/ ac=0000/0002
  1: add  /2 005/ ac=0002/0005
  2: st   /1 006/ m[006]=0000/0005
  3: halt /FFFF /
Machine inst count =    4 (hex) =    4 (dec)
Micro   inst count =   21 (hex) =   33 (dec)
---- [T7] q
```

FIGURE 13.8 Starting session. Enter h or ? for help.

```
---- [T7] 0: ld    /0 004/ g
  0: ld   /0 004/ ac=0000/0002
  1: add  /2 005/ ac=0002/0005
  2: st   /1 006/ m[006]=0000/0005
  3: halt /FFFF /
Machine inst count =    4 (hex) =    4 (dec)
---- [T7] s
Machinecode file  = sum.mac     Size = 7   (hex) =    7 (dec)
Microcode file    = none        Size = 93  (hex) =  147 (dec)
Config file       = none
Log file (on)     = sum.log
Answer file       = none
Simulation mode   = horizontal
Microlevel        = disabled
Shifter           = one-position
Display mode      = machine-level
Cmd line addr     = F3C    (hex) =   3900 (dec)
Load point        = 0      (hex) =      0 (dec)
Machine inst count = 4     (hex) =      4 (dec)
Micro   inst count = 21    (hex) =     33 (dec)
---- [T7] q
```

sim provides microinstruction counts whenever a program halts if **sim** runs *enabled* (i.e., if **sim** makes the microlevel visible and accessible to the user). For example, Figure 13.7 shows a debugging session in which we enable **sim** and then run a program with the **g** command. When the program halts, **sim** displays both the machine and microinstruction counts. We can see that the program requires the execution of 33 microinstructions.

Whether **sim** is enabled or not, we can always obtain microinstruction counts with the **s** (status) command. For example, in Figure 13.8, we first run the program with **sim** disabled. Because **sim** is disabled, the microinstruction count is not displayed when the program halts. So we then enter the **s** command, which displays, among other items, the microinstruction count.

FIGURE 13.9   `Starting session.  Enter h or ? for help.`

```
---- [T7] 0: ld    /0 004/ mc
Machine-level display mode + counts
---- [T7] 0: ld    /0 004/ g
  0: ld    /0 004/ ac=0000/0002   11t
  1: add   /2 005/ ac=0002/0005   11t
  2: st    /1 006/ m[006]=0000/0005   9t
  3: halt /FFFF /   2t
Machine inst count =     4 (hex) =      4 (dec)
---- [T7] mc-
Machine-level display mode
---- [T7] q
```

FIGURE 13.10   testm.mas

```
              ; multiply 3000 x 4
!o            ; configuration/microcode file to use
ldc 3000      ; get multiplier
push          ; push one number onto stack
ldc 4         ; get multiplicand
m             ; multiply using shift-add in microcode
halt
```

A third way to obtain microinstruction counts is to run **sim** in the "machine-level display mode plus counts." **sim** then displays the number of microinstructions for every machine instruction executed. For example, in Figure 13.9, we first put **sim** in this mode by entering the **mc** command. We then run the program with the **g** command. On the right of each line of the resulting trace, **sim** displays the number of microinstructions executed for the machine instruction traced on that line. For example, for the `ld` instruction, `11t` appears indicating that this instruction used 11 microinstructions. The suffix "t" at the end of each count indicates that the count is a decimal number ("t" stands for base 10). To change back to the regular machine-level display mode, enter the **mc-**command.

Let's use the machine-level display mode plus counts to determine the number of microinstructions required by the `m` instruction. Figure 13.10 shows a simple test program that multiplies 3000 and 4 using the `m` instruction.

Suppose this program is contained in the file **testm.mas**. First, we assemble **testm.mas** with **mas** by entering

mas testm

Because of the !-directive on the first line of **testm.mas**, **mas** will use the **o.cfg** configuration file when it assembles the program. The configuration file provides **mas** with information on the mnemonics for the new instructions in the optimal instruction set. Without a configuration file, **mas** would not recognize the `m` mnemonic (or any of the other new mnemonics in the optimal instruction set). Next we invoke **sim** with

sim testm

FIGURE 13.11   Reading configuration file o.cfg
Reading microcode file o.hor

```
Starting session.  Enter h or ? for help.
---- [T7] 0: ldc  /8 BB8/ mc
Machine-level display mode + counts
---- [T7] 0: ldc  /8 BB8/ g
   0: ldc  /8 BB8/ ac=0000/0BB8    8t
   1: push /F3 00/ m[FFF]=0000/0BB8  sp=0000/FFFF    13t
   2: ldc  /8 004/ ac=0BB8/0004    8t
   3: m    /FF3 0/ sp=FFFF/0000  ac=0004/2EE0    75t
   4: halt /FFFF /  2t
Machine inst count =     5 (hex) =      5 (dec)
---- [T7] q
```

to run the `testm.mac` file that `mas` creates. `sim` will automatically use the `o.cfg` configuration file and the `o.hor` microcode file. Like `mas`, `sim` needs the information in `o.cfg` on the mnemonics for the new instructions, as well as other information it contains.

Figure 13.11 shows a debugging session for the `testm` program. We first put `sim` in machine-level display mode plus counts by entering the `mc` command, and then execute the program. From the trace, we can see that the `ldc` instruction requires only 8 microinstructions. The `m` instruction, on the other hand, requires 75 microinstructions. Thus, the execution time for `m` is more than nine times the execution time for the `ldc` instruction.

13.3   TWO-DIMENSIONAL ARRAYS

• •

A useful way to view a two-dimensional array is as a one-dimensional array whose slots are arrays as well. This view is particularly useful because it is precisely how the C++ compiler views two-dimensional arrays. Let's consider an example. If we declare `d` with

```
int d[3][4];
```

we can view `d` as a one-dimensional array with three (the size of its first dimension) slots. Each of these slots is, itself, a one-dimensional array with four (the size of `d`'s second dimension) `int` slots. In the matrix representation of this array in Figure 13.12, the *entire* first row is the first slot of `d`. Similarly, the entire second and third rows are the second and third slots of `d`.

Because `d` in Figure 13.12 is a two-dimensional array, you may think that an expression using `d` with only one index does not make sense. For example, what does `d[0]` mean? `d[0]`, however, makes perfect sense if we view `d` as a one-dimensional array: `d[0]` is the first slot of `d` (which is its entire first row). Furthermore, because `d[0]` is itself an array containing four `int` slots, it makes sense to add, if we wish, an additional index to it to access these four slots. For example, we can use `d[0][0]`, `d[0][1]`, `d[0][2]`, or `d[0][3]` to reference the four `int` slots in `d[0]`.

In Section 8.7, we learned that the name of an array without square brackets is the address of the first slot of that array. Thus, if an array is an `int` array, its name is an `int` pointer that points to its first slot. Similarly, for the `d` array in Figure 13.12,

FIGURE 13.12

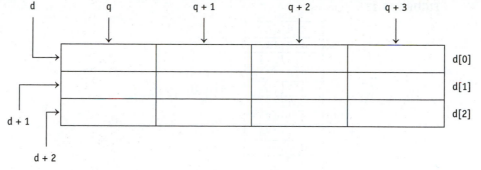

the name **d** without square brackets is the address of its first slot—that is, it is the address of (and, therefore, a pointer to) the *entire first row*. **d+1** and **d+2** are pointers to the second and third rows.

Suppose we wish to assign **d** to a pointer variable **p** with the statement

```
p = d;
```

How should we declare **p**? It should have the same type as **d** without square brackets. An **int** pointer is the wrong type because **d** without square brackets is not an **int** pointer. (**d** without square brackets is a pointer to the entire first row of the **d** array.) Thus, **p** should be a pointer to an array of four **int**'s. Accordingly, we should declare **p** with

```
int (*p)[4];
```

This declaration consists of three parts—(***p**), [4], and **int**—which should be read, respectively, as "p is a pointer," "to an array of four slots," "of type **int**." Note that **p** itself is *not* an array—it is a *single* pointer to an array.

Now consider the statement

```
q = &d[0][0];
```

How should we declare **q**? Because **d[0][0]** has type **int**, its address, **&d[0][0]**, is an **int** pointer. Thus, **q** should also be an **int** pointer. The following statement assigns to **p** the same address that the previous statement assigns to **q**:

```
p = d;
```

Both statements assign the address of the beginning of the **d** array; however, the types of **p** and **q** differ. Thus, dereferencing operations and pointer arithmetic will differ for **p** and **q**. For example, ***p** is the entire first row of the **d** array—that is, it is an **int** array containing four slots. ***q**, on the other hand, is the first **int** in the first row. Because ***p** is an array, it makes sense to index it. Thus, the expressions (***p**)[0], (***p**)[1], (***p**)[2], and (***p**)[3] are all legal. ***q**, on the other hand, cannot be similarly indexed because it designates a single **int** slot. Incidentally, when we index ***p**, we must surround it with parentheses. Otherwise, the indexing operation is applied to **p** instead of ***p** because indexing has higher precedence than dereferencing. For example, ***p[0]** would be interpreted as ***(p[0])**, and therefore, would cause a compiler time error because **p** is not an array. Pointer arithmetic also differs for **p** and **q**. **p + 1** is a pointer to the second *row* of the **d** array. **q + 1**, on the other hand, is a pointer to the second **int** in the first row of the **d** array (see Figure 13.12).

C++ maps two-dimensional arrays into memory row by row. For example, the array in Figure 13.12 appears in memory as shown in Figure 13.13. The first row occupies the first four memory locations (assuming each location can hold one

FIGURE 13.13

```
     ~              ~
    ┌──────────────┐
    │ d[0][0]      │
    ├──────────────┤
    │ d[0][1]      │
    ├──────────────┤
    │ d[0][2]      │
    ├──────────────┤
    │ d[0][3]      │
    ├──────────────┤
    │ d[1][0]      │   Main Memory
    ├──────────────┤
    │ d[1][1]      │
    ├──────────────┤
    │ d[1][2]      │
    ├──────────────┤
    │ d[1][3]      │
    ├──────────────┤
    │ d[2][0]      │
    ├──────────────┤
    │ d[2][1]      │
    ├──────────────┤
    │ d[2][2]      │
    ├──────────────┤
    │ d[2][3]      │
    └──────────────┘
     ~              ~
```

int value); the next row occupies the next four memory locations; and so on. We call this row-by-row mapping of a two-dimensional array into memory *row-major order*. Another possible mapping is column by column, which we call *column-major order*. C++ uses only row-major order.

Suppose the d array in Figure 13.12 is a global variable. It would then be declared at the assembly level with

```
d:      dw      12 dup 0
```

Let's consider the assembly code needed for the following assignment statement:

```
d[2][3] = 99;
```

d[2][3] is in row 2, so two rows (rows 0 and 1) precede it in memory. Each row contains four words. Thus, $2 \times 4 = 8$ words precede the beginning of row 2. Because d[2][3] is in column 3, three words—d[2][0], d[2][1], and d[2][2]—precede it in row 2. Therefore, a total of $8 + 3 = 11$ words in d precede d[2][3] in memory. The label d at the assembly level is the address of the beginning of the d array, so d + 11 is the address of d[2][3]. Thus, the assembly form for the assignment statement is

```
ldc   99
st    d + 11
```

When the assembler assembles this st instruction, it computes the sum of the address of d and 11. It then places this sum (which is the address of d[2][3]) into the st machine instruction. The assignment statement

```
x = 99;
```

where x is a global variable, has a similar assembly form:

```
ldc   99
st    x
```

Both sequences execute in exactly the same amount of time, reflecting the fact that the indexing operations for d[2][3] occur *before* run time. If, however, the indices are variables, then the indexing has to be performed at run time by instructions that the compiler generates. These instructions perform the same computation that the compiler and assembler perform when the indices are constants. For example, for the statement

```
d[i][j] = 99;
```

FIGURE 13.14

```
 1        ; push right-hand side of assignment statement
 2        ldc   99
 3        push
 4
 5        ; calculate i x 4 (number of words preceding ith row)
 6        ld    i
 7        push
 8        ldc   4 ; get size of second dimension
 9        mult
10
11        ; get offset to d[i][j] from beginning of array
12        add   j ; add second index to get offset of d[i][j]
13        push    ; save it on top of stack
14
15        ; get address of the beginning of d
16        ldc   d
17
18        ; get address of d[i][j]
19        addr -1 ; add top of stack (assume rel add is -1)
20        dloc  1 ; remove top of stack
21
22        sti     ; pop 99 into d[i][j]
```

the compiler generates the code in Figure 13.14. Notice that we use multiplication on line 9 to determine the number of words preceding the *i*th row. We multiply the size of the second dimension of the array (4 in this example) by the index i. In this computation, we do *not* use the size of the first dimension of the array.

As we pointed out earlier, if we execute the statement

```
p = d;
```

where p and d are as defined as shown, then *p is the one-dimensional array consisting of the entire first row of d. Because *p is an array, it makes sense to index it. For example, the statement

```
(*p)[2] = 99;
```

assigns 99 to the third slot of the first row. *p is, in effect, the name of the array consisting of the first row of d. Recall that the name of an array without square brackets is a pointer to the first slot of that array. Thus, *p (the "name" of the array consisting of the first row of d) is a pointer to the first slot in the first row. Because this slot has type int, *p is an int pointer. Now here is a very interesting observation: p and *p are both pointers, and *they both have the same value* (they both point to the beginning of the d array). p and *p differ only in type. p is a pointer to a one-dimensional array with four slots; *p is an int pointer. Because p and *p have the same value, dereferencing p does not require the usual instructions that "follow a pointer to the location to which it points." For example, if p is a global variable, the assembly code for

```
(*p)[2] = 99;
```

FIGURE 13.15

```
1 void f(int (*p)[4])
2 {
3    int i = 1, j = 2;
4    p[i][j] = 99;
6 }
7 int main()
8 {
9    int d[3][4];
10   f(d);
11   return 0;
12 }
```

is

```
ldc  99
push
ld   p      ; get address in p
addc 2      ; add 2 to this address
sti         ; pop 99 into this address
```

Observe that the assembly code does not access the location to which **p** points; it simply uses the value in **p** (which is also the value of *p). In particular, it computes 2 plus the address given by the contents of **p**, and then stores 99 at that address.

Figure 13.15 shows a program in which the two-dimensional array **d** is an argument in the call of **f**. The corresponding parameter **p** should have a matching type. Thus, we declare **p** on line 1 as a pointer to an array with four **int** slots. Equivalently, we can declare **p** on line 1 with

```
int p[][4]
```

The two declarations convey exactly the same information to the compiler—namely, that **p** is a pointer to an **int** array with four slots. You should read the three parts, **p[]**, **[4]**, and **int**, of this alternate declaration as "**p** is a pointer," "to an array of 4 slots," "of type **int**." Because **p** is a single slot, it does not make sense to specify both dimensions of **d** in the declaration of **p**. However, we *must* specify the second dimension because this dimension is needed for indexing operations (see line 8 in Figure 13.14).

13.4   OBJECT-ORIENTED PROGRAMMING IN ASSEMBLY LANGUAGE
• •

In C++, a **class** is a user-defined type that can contain both functions and data fields. Once we have defined a **class**, we can then declare variables—called *objects*—whose type is that **class**. Programs that take advantage of classes and objects are called object-oriented (OO) programs.

Not all languages support OO programming. Indeed, OO programming is relatively new, so most languages do *not* support it. C (the predecessor of C++), for example, has no support for OO programming. Some languages, such as C++ have OO capabilities but do not require the programmer to use them. Finally, some languages are pure OO languages; that is, they are designed to support only the OO style of programming. Java is an example of such a language. Because of its OO focus, Java does not have the flexibility of C++. But neither does it have the complexity of C++.

13.4.1 C++ Structs, Classes, and Objects

Before we consider classes in C++ and their corresponding objects, let's consider two programs that use structs that contain data fields only. The program in Figure 13.16 contains the definition of a **struct** named **Coordinates** on lines 4 to 7. This definition is a user-defined type that contains, in this case, two data fields, **x** and **y**. On lines 20 and 21, we use this type to create the variables **c1** and **c2**. Both **c1** and **c2** have **x** and **y** fields. On line 22, we initialize **c1** by calling the **set** function and passing it three arguments—the address of **c1**, and the two values to be used to initialize its **x** and **y** fields. On line 23, we similarly initialize **c2**. We then call the **display** function twice, passing it the address of **c1** on the first call and the address of **c2** on the second. The **display** function displays the current values in the fields

FIGURE 13.16

```cpp
1  #include <iostream>
2  using namespace std;
3
4  struct Coordinates {
5      int x;
6      int y;
7  };
8  void set(Coordinates *p, int a, int b)
9  {
10     p -> x = a;
11     p -> y = b;
12 }
13 void display(Coordinates *p)
14 {
15     cout << "x = " << p -> x << endl;
16     cout << "y = " << p -> y << endl;
17 }
18 int main()
19 {
20     Coordinates c1;
21     Coordinates c2;
22     set(&c1, 1, 2);       // access c1 through set function
23     set(&c2, 3, 4);       // access c2 through set function
24     display(&c1);         // access c1 through display function
25     display(&c2);         // access c2 through display function
26     c1.y = 22;            // access c1 directly
27     display(&c1);         // access c1 through display function
28     return 0;
29 }
```

of the `Coordinates struct` whose address it is passed. Finally, on line 26, `main` directly accesses the `y` field of `c1`, and `c1` is displayed again. The output generated by the program is

```
x = 1
y = 2
x = 3
y = 4
x = 1
y = 22
```

Figure 13.17 shows the corresponding assembly language program.

FIGURE 13.17

```
 1              !o
 2 @set$p11Coordinatesii:
 3              esba
 4
 5                          ; p -> x = a;
 6              ldr   3         ; get a
 7              push            ; push a
 8              ldr   2         ; get p
 9              sti             ; pop a to location p points to
10
11                          ; p -> y = b;
12              ldr   4         ; get b
13              push            ; push b
14              ldr   2         ; get p
15              addc  1         ; get p + 1
16              sti             ; pop b to location  p + 1 points to
17
18              reba
19              ret
20 ;==========================================================
21 @display$p11Coordinates:
22              esba
23
24                          ; cout << "x = " << p -> x << endl;
25              ldc   @m0       ; get address of @m0
26              sout            ; display string
27              ldr   2         ; get p
28              ldi             ; get *p
29              dout            ; display it
30              ldc   '\n'      ; endl
31              aout
32
33                          ; cout << "y = " << p -> y << endl;
```

(continued)

FIGURE 13.17
(continued)

```
34          ldc   @m1       ; get address of @m1
35          sout            ; display string
36          ldr   2         ; get p
37          addc  1         ; get p + 1 (address of p -> y)
38          ldi             ; get *(p + 1)
39          dout            ; display it
40          ldc   '\n'      ; endl
41          aout
42
43          reba
44          ret
45  ;========================================================
46  main: esba
47
48          aloc  2         ; Coordinates c1;
49
50          aloc  2         ; Coordinates c2;
51
52                          ; set(&c1, 1, 2);
53          ldc   2         ; get constant 2
54          push            ; push it
55          ldc   1         ; get constant 1
56          push            ; push it
57          ldc   -2        ; get relative address of c1
58          cora            ; convert to absolute address
59          push            ; push absolute address of c1
60          call @set$p11Coordinatesii
61          dloc  3         ; remove parameters from stack
62
63                          ; set(&c2, 3, 4);
64          ldc   4         ; get constant 4
65          push            ; push it
66          ldc   3         ; get constant 3
67          push            ; push it
68          ldc   -4        ; get relative address of c2
69          cora            ; convert to absolute address
70          push            ; push absolute address of c2
71          call @set$p11Coordinatesii
72          dloc  3         ; remove parameters from stack
73
74                          ; display(&c1);
75          ldc   -2        ; get relative address of c1
76          cora            ; convert to absolute address
77          push            ; push absolute address of c1
```

(continued)

FIGURE 13.17
(continued)

```
 78          call @display$p11Coordinates
 79          dloc 1        ; remove parameter from stack
 80
 81                     ; display(&c2);
 82          ldc  -4       ; get relative address of c2
 83          cora          ; convert to relative address
 84          push          ; push absolute address of c2
 85          call @display$p11Coordinates
 86          dloc 1        ; remove parameter from stack
 87
 88                     ; c1.y = 22;
 89          ldc  22       ; get constant 22
 90          push          ; push it
 91          ldc  -1       ; get relative address of c1.y
 92          cora          ; convert to absolute address
 93          sti           ; pop 22 into c1.y
 94
 95                     ; display(&c1);
 96          ldc  -2       ; get relative address of c1
 97          cora          ; convert to absolute address
 98          push          ; push absolute address of c1
 99          call @display$p11Coordinates
100          dloc 1        ; remove parameter from stack
101
102          ldc  0    ; return 0;
103          reba
104          ret
105 ;=============================================================
106 @m0:  dw    "x = "
107 @m1:  dw    "y = "
108          public @set$p11Coordinatesii
109          public @display$p11Coordinates
110          public main
```

Notice on line 2 in Figure 13.17 that the encoding of the parameters for the **set** function is **p11Coordinatesii**. The two **i**'s at the end of this name indicate, as usual, that the second and third parameters are type **int**. The first parameter, which is a pointer to a **Coordinates struct**, is encoded with **p11Coordinates**. The "p" indicates a pointer type, and "11Coordinates" is the encoding of the type **Coordinates**. The "11" here is the length of the name **Coordinates**. We need this length field to avoid ambiguity in the names of user-defined types. Suppose, for example, we encoded the parameters without this length field to get "pCoordinatesii". Then this mangled name could represent three parameters, the last two of which are type **int**. But it could also represent other parameter lists, such as a single parameter that is a pointer to a user-defined type **Coordinatesii** (**Coordinatesii** is a perfectly legal name for a user-defined type). With the length field 11,

FIGURE 13.18

```
1 #include <iostream>
2 using namespace std;
3
4 struct Coordinates {
5     int x;
6     int y;
7 };
8 void set(Coordinates &c, int a, int b)
9 {
10     c.x = a;
11     c.y = b;
12 }
13 void display(Coordinates &c)
14 {
15     cout << "x = " << c.x << endl;
16     cout << "y = " << c.y << endl;
17 }
18 int main()
19 {
20     Coordinates c1, c2;
21     set(c1, 1, 2);          // access c1 through set function
22     set(c2, 3, 4);          // access c2 through set function
23     display(c1);            // access c1 through display function
24     display(c2);            // access c2 through display function
25     c1.y = 22;              // access c1 directly
26     display(c1);            // access c1 through display function
27     return 0;
28 }
```

however, the type name is unambiguous: It must be the 11 characters that follow the length field—namely **Coordinates**.

In the calls of **set** and **display**, the first argument is a pointer to a **struct**. Within these functions, this pointer has to be dereferenced to access the data fields of the pointed-to **struct**. For example on lines 27 to 29 in Figure 13.17, we dereference this pointer (located at relative address 2) to access the value in the **x** field.

A second approach to our **Coordinates** program is given in Figure 13.18. In this version, we use the reference parameter mechanism to pass the **struct** to the **set** and **display** functions. As we explained in Chapter 8, we can view the argument corresponding to a reference parameter as replacing the reference parameter during the function call. Thus, when we call **display** on line 23 with

```
display(c1);
```

c1, the argument, replaces the corresponding reference parameter **c** in the called function. Thus, when line 15 in the **display** function,

```
cout << "x = " << c.x << endl;
```

is executed, it is as if it reads

```
cout << "x = " << c1.x << endl;
```

with the argument `c1` replacing the parameter `c`. As we know from Chapter 8, this replacement is only a conceptual view of the reference mechanism. What really happens is that the pointer to the argument `c1` is passed when the call

```
display(c1);
```

is executed, and this pointer (contained in the parameter `c`) is automatically dereferenced when

```
cout << "x = " << c.x << endl;
```

is executed in the `display` function. Thus, the assembler code for the program in Figure 13.18 (which uses the reference mechanism) is almost identical to the assembler code for the program in Figure 13.16 (which explicitly uses the address and dereferencing operators). The *only* difference is in the mangled names of the functions: The encoding of the **struct** parameters becomes **r11Coordinates**. The "p" (indicating pointer) in Figure 13.17 (on lines 2, 21, 60, 71, 78, 85, 99, 108, and 109) becomes "r" (indicating reference parameter).

A third approach to a **Coordinates** program is given in Figure 13.19. Here we are using classes instead of structs. An *object* is a variable that, in general, contains both data and functions. The functions and variables within an object are called, respectively, *member functions* and *member variables*. A *class* is a user-defined type that specifies the make-up of an object. When we declare an object using a **class**, we say we are *instantiating* the object. This word simply means we are creating an object as specified by the class definition. For example, on line 24 in Figure 13.19, we are instantiating two objects, `c1` and `c2`, using the class **Coordinates**. The definition of the **Coordinates** class appears on lines 4 to 11. We can see that the **Coordinates** class consists of two variables (`x` and `y`) and two member functions (**set** and **display**). On line 8, the data variables are flagged as **private**, indicating that they can be accessed only by member functions within the class (i.e., by **set** and **display**). The member functions, however, are flagged as **public**, indicating that they can be accessed (i.e., called) from outside the class as well as from within.

A class definition typically contains function prototypes rather than function definitions, in which case the corresponding function definitions appear outside the class. Different classes can use the same function names, so a function definition outside its class must specify not only its name, but also the class to which it belongs. For example, on line 12 in Figure 13.19, we see at the start of the definition of the **set** function both the class name (**Coordinates**) and the function name (**set**) separated by the scope resolution operator (`::`).

Figure 13.20a shows a conceptual picture of the objects `c1` and `c2`. Notice that each object contains a **set** and **display** function, in addition to the data in `x` and `y`. The two **set** functions are identical, but have a different effect: The **set** function in `c1` sets the data in `c1`; the **set** function in `c2` sets the data in `c2`.

To call the **set** function, we have to indicate which **set** function—the one in `c1` or the one in `c2`—to call. We do this by specifying both the object and the func-

FIGURE 13.19

```
1 #include <iostream>
2 using namespace std;
3
4 class  Coordinates {
5    public:
6        void set(int a, int b);        // function prototype
7        void display();                // function prototype
8    private:
9        int x;
10       int y;
11 };
12 void Coordinates::set(int a, int b)    // function definition
13 {
14    x = a;
15    y = b;
16 }
17 void Coordinates::display()            // function definition
18 {
19    cout << "x = " <<  x << endl;
20    cout << "y = " <<  y << endl;
21 }
22 int main()
23 {
24    Coordinates c1, c2;
25    c1.set(1, 2);          // access c1 through set function
26    c2.set(3, 4);          // access c2 through set function
27    c1.display();          // access c1 through display function
28    c2.display();          // access c2 through display function
29 // c1.y = 22;            // illegal--y is private
30    return 0;
31 }
```

tion name in a call, separating the two with the dot (.) operator. For example, to call the **set** function in **c2**, we use

```
c2.set();
```

One advantage of an object over a **struct** variable without member functions is that an object can limit access to its data variables. In Figure 13.19, the **x** and **y** data fields can be accessed only from within the class (i.e., they can be accessed only by the **set** and **display** functions). We cannot access them from outside the class. For example, if we attempt to change the **y** field of **c1** with

```
c1.y = 22;
```

outside the class, we would get a compile-time error. This statement, however, is legal with our **struct** approach (see line 25 in Figure 13.18).

FIGURE 13.20   a)

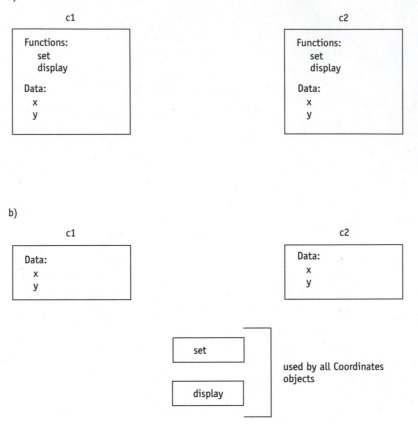

As with reference parameters, our conceptual view of objects (as containing both data and functions) is quite different from its actual implementation at the assembly level. In particular, when we create objects with a statement such as

```
Coordinates c1, c2;
```

we are, in fact, *not* creating physical objects that contain both data and functions as we depicted in Figure 13.20a. Instead, we are only allocating storage for the member data. Member functions are physically separate. Moreover, there is only one copy of each member function, and this copy is shared by all the objects of that class (see Figure 13.20b). The address of an object is the address of its data area. It is *not* the address of any of its member functions. Thus, if `cp` is a **Coordinates** pointer, then

```
cp = &c1;
```

assigns to `cp` the address of the data area for `c1`.

The name of a member function at the assembly level consists of its name at the C++ level prefixed with its class name, and postfixed with its parameter-list encoding. In this composite name, the class name is delimited with the "@" sign, and the parameter list encoding is prefixed by the "$" sign. For example, the assembly-level name of the **set** function in the **Coordinates** class is

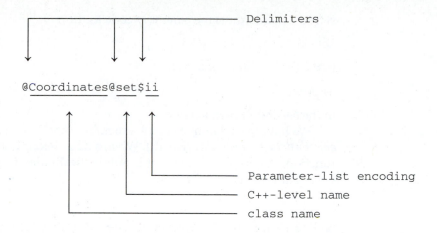

Thus, the C++ statements

```
c1.set(1, 2);
```

and

```
c2.set(3, 4);
```

at the assembly level are both calls to the *same* function whose name is **@Coordinates@set$ii**. Notice the obvious similarity of this assembly-level name to the C++-level name in the definition of the **set** function on line 12 of Figure 13.19:

```
void Coordinates::set(int a, int b)
```

Here is an important question: If

```
c1.set(1, 2);
```

and

```
c2.set(3, 4);
```

both call the *same* function, how can these two calls affect *different* data (the first call affects the data in **c1**; the second call affects the data in **c2**)? The answer is simple: In each call, the address of the calling object's data is passed to the **set** function (in addition to the two arguments specified inside the parentheses). This address is an *implicit argument* (i.e., it is implied) because it does not appear within the parentheses in the function call. The **set** function dereferences this address to access the member variables of the calling object. Thus, in the call

```
c1.set(1, 2);
```

three arguments are passed: the address of **c1**, 1, and 2. This call, in fact, is translated to the same assembly code as the call

```
set(&c1, 1, 2);
```

in the first **struct** version of this program (Figure 13.16), or

```
set(c1, 1, 2);
```

in the second **struct** version (Figure 13.18). Similarly, the call

```
c2.set(3, 4);
```

is translated to the same assembly code as the call

```
set(&c2, 3, 4);
```

in the first **struct** version, or

```
set(c2, 3, 4);
```

in the second **struct** version.

We have seen that in a call of a member function in an object, *the address of an object's data is an implied argument*. When a data field is referenced within a member function, this implied argument is automatically dereferenced to access that data field. Thus, the statement

```
y = b;
```

on line 15 in Figure 13.19 generates the assembly code

```
ldr  4        ; get b
push          ; push b
ldr  2        ; get implied parameter (address of object)
addc 1        ; add offset of y field to get its address
sti           ; pop b into y
```

This is precisely the code generated for the corresponding statements

```
p -> y = b;
```

or

```
c.y = b;
```

in our two **struct** versions. In fact, the assembly code for the object version of our program is virtually identical to the assembly code for the two **struct** versions. The only difference is in the name mangling. In the object version, the mangled function names have the type of implied argument as part of the function name instead of as part of the parameter list encoding. For example, the name of the **set** function within the **Coordinates** class is **@Coordinates@set$ii**. Contrast this with the mangled names **@set$p11Coordinatesii** and **@set$r11Coordinatesii** in our two **struct** versions. For the object case, we do not need a length field because the user-defined type name is delimited by a pair of "@" signs. Compare the code in Figure 13.21 for the object version with the code in Figure 13.17. The two versions are essentially identical.

FIGURE 13.21

```
1       !o
2  @Coordinates@set$ii:
3          esba
4
5                      ; x = a;
6       ldr  3         ; get a
7       push           ; push it
8       ldr  2         ; get address of x
9       sti            ; pop a into x
10
```

(continued)

FIGURE 13.21
(continued)

```
11                        ; y = b;
12          ldr  4        ; get b
13          push          ; push it
14          ldr  2        ; get address of x
15          addc 1        ; get address of x + 1 (i.e., of y)
16          sti           ; pop b into  y
17
18          reba
19          ret
20  ;========================================================
21  @Coordinates@display$v:
22          esba
23
24                  ; cout << "x = " << x << endl;
25          ldc  @m0      ; get address of @m0
26          sout          ; display string
27          ldr  2        ; get address of x
28          ldi           ; dereference address of x
29          dout          ; display it
30          ldc  '\n'     ; endl
31          aout
32
33                  ; cout << "y = " << y << endl;
34          ldc  @m1      ; get address of @m1
35          sout          ; display string
36          ldr  2        ; get address of x
37          addc 1        ; get address of x + 1 (i.e., of y)
38          ldi           ; dereference address of y
39          dout          ; display it
40          ldc  '\n'     ; endl
41          aout
42
43          reba
44          ret
45  ;========================================================
46  main: esba
47
48          aloc 2     ; Coordinates c1;
49
50          aloc 2     ; Coordinates c2;
51
52                     ; c1.set(1, 2);
53          ldc  2        ; get constant 2
```

(continued)

FIGURE 13.21
(continued)

```
54          push            ; push it
55          ldc  1          ; get constant 1
56          push            ; push it
57          ldc  -2         ; get relative address of c1
58          cora            ; convert to absolute address
59          push            ; push absolute address of c1
60          call @Coordinates@set$ii
61          dloc 3          ; remove parameters from stack
62
63                      ; c2.set(3, 4);
64          ldc  4          ; get constant 4
65          push            ; push it
66          ldc  3          ; get constant 3
67          push            ; push it
68          ldc  -4         ; get relative address of c2
69          cora            ; convert to absolute address
70          push            ; push absolute address of c2
71          call @Coordinates@set$ii
72          dloc 3          ; remove parameters from stack
73
74                      ; c1.display();
75          ldc  -2         ; get relative address of c1
76          cora            ; convert to absolute address
77          push            ; push absolute address of c1
78          call @Coordinates@display$v
79          dloc 1          ; remove parameter from stack
80
81                      ; c2.display();
82          ldc  -4         ; get relative address of c2
83          cora            ; convert to relative address
84          push            ; push absolute address of c2
85          call @Coordinates@display$v
86          dloc 1          ; remove parameter from stack
87
89          ldc  0     ; return 0;
90          reba
91          ret
92 ;=================================================
93 @m0:  dw    "x = "
94 @m1:  dw    "y = "
95          public @Coordinates@set$ii
96          public @Coordinates@display$v
97          public main
```

Objects are similar to reference parameters in that both hide their underlying implementation, providing the programmer with a conceptual view that is easier to work with. Objects, however, provide another important service: They allow the control of data access. In particular, by making data fields `private`, we can restrict their access to the member functions in the same class. This control is a very good feature. The data fields are much less likely to be corrupted if all accesses are through carefully designed and tested member functions. Member functions typically include checks to ensure data integrity. For example, suppose a field is supposed to contain the minutes of the current time. Because the range of values for minutes is 0 to 59, a member function can check that any change to this field does not produce a value outside this range.

Notice in Figure 13.21 that the data fields of the objects `c1` and `c2` at the assembly level can be accessed from outside the member functions (for example, from `main`). However, a compiler will never generate such code because we declared the data fields in these objects `private`. The compiler will respond to any attempt to do so at the C++ level with an error message.

13.4.2   Inheritance

Suppose a C++ class exists that is almost perfect for an application that we are writing. We only need to add a few new functions and variables and make a few modifications to its existing functions. Of course, we could rewrite the whole class, making the required modifications and extensions. However, a much easier and practical approach is to use the inheritance mechanism in C++ to create our required class. *Inheritance* in C++ is a mechanism we can use to define new classes from classes that already exist. With inheritance, our new class (called the *derived class*) "inherits" (i.e., automatically includes) all the members of a specified existing class (called the *base class*). Consider the program in Figure 13.22, which illustrates the inheritance mechanism. `A` is the class from which a new class `B` is derived. Thus, `A` is the base class and `B` is the derived class. Line 19 is where we specify that `B` is derived from `A` (by appending ": public A" to the name of class `B`).

The use of inheritance in a program establishes a hierarchy: The derived class is lower in this hierarchy; the base class is higher. Thus, in the program in Figure 13.22, `A` is "above" `B` in this inheritance hierarchy.

`A` contains the `set` and `display_x` functions and the variable `x` (see lines 4 to 10). Thus, the derived class `B` also contains these members. However, `B` also contains its own `set` function, a `display_y` function, and the variable `y` (see lines 19 to 25).

The object `a` (line 37) is type `A`, and, therefore, contains only the `set` and `display_x` functions and the variable `x` (see Figure 13.23a). On lines 38 and 39, we

FIGURE 13.22

```
1 #include <iostream>
2 using namespace std;
3
4 class A {                    // A is the base class
5     public:
```

(continued)

FIGURE 13.22
(continued)

```
 6         void set();
 7         void display_x();
 8    protected:           // allows derived class to access x
 9        int x;
10 };
11 void A::set()
12 {
13    x = 1;
14 }
15 void A::display_x()
16 {
17    cout << x << endl;
18 }
19 class B: public A {    // B is derived from A
20    public:
21        void set();       // redefines set() from A
22        void display_y();
23    private:
24        int y;
25 };
26 void B::set()           // sets both x and y
27 {
28    x = 2;               // illegal if x is private
29    y = 3;
30 }
31 void B::display_y()
32 {
33    cout << y << endl;
34 }
35 int main()
36 {
37    A a;
38    a.set();
39    a.display_x();        // displays 1
40 // a.display_y();        // illegal--display_y not in a
41    B b;
42    b.set();              // invoke set from B
43    b.display_x();        // displays 2
44    b.display_y();        // displays 3
45    b.A::set();           // explicitly invoke set in from A
46    b.display_x();        // displays 1
47 // a.B::set();           // illegal--B-level set not in a
48    return 0;
49 }
```

FIGURE 13.23 a)

```
                            a

        ┌─────────────────────────────────┐
        │  Functions:                     │
        │    set                          │
        │    display_x                    │
        │                                 │
        │  Data:                          │
        │    x                            │
        │                                 │
        │                                 │
        └─────────────────────────────────┘
```

b)

```
                            b

        ┌─────────────────────────────────┐
        │  Functions:                     │
        │    set (from A)                 │
        │    set (from B)                 │
        │    display_x (from A)           │
        │    display_y (from B)           │
        │                                 │
        │  Data:                          │
        │    x (from A)                   │
        │    y (from B)                   │
        │                                 │
        └─────────────────────────────────┘
```

invoke the two functions in the object **a**. Of course, we cannot invoke the **display_y** function via **a** because there is no **display_y** function in **a** (see line 40).

The object **b** is type **B**, and, therefore, contains the **set** and **display_y** functions and the **y** variable from class **B**. In addition, it contains everything in class **A**—namely, the **A**-level **set** function, **display_x**, and the **x** variable (see Figure 13.23b).

Although **b** contains two **set** functions, the one defined in class **B** essentially replaces the one from class **A**. Accordingly, whenever we invoke the **set** function via **b**, we invoke the **set** function from class **B** (see line 42). We say that the **B** class *redefines* the **set** function. This redefinition does not occur if the function in the derived class has a different parameter list as its corresponding function in the base class. For example, suppose that the **set** function in class **B** used one integer parameter. Then in **b**, both functions would coexist with the overloaded name **set**. Then the call

```
b.set();
```

would invoke the **set** from **A**, but

```
b.set(2);
```

would invoke the **set** from **B**.

The inheritance that we used in the program in Figure 13.22 makes for a complex hierarchial structure at the C++ level. However, at the assembly level, this program is quite straightforward. Unlike the C++ level, all functions have unique names at the assembly level (recall that each function name is prefixed with the name of the class in which it is defined). Because the compiler knows the members of the **A** and **B** classes, it can generate the appropriate code for each call of a member function. For example, for the C++ statement

```
a.set();
```

the compiler generates the code

```
ldc  -1          ; get relative address of a
cora             ; convert to absolute address
push
call @A@set$v    ; call set function in A
dloc 1           ; remove parameter from stack
```

which calls the function **@A@set$v** (the **A**-level **set** function), passing it the address of the data area of the object **a**. For the call

```
b.set();
```

the compiler generates a similar sequence, but calls **@B@set$v** (the **B**-level set function) because it knows that the class **B** has its own **set** function that redefines the **set** function from class **A**:

```
ldc  -3          ; get relative address of b
cora             ; convert to absolute address
push
call @B@set$v
dloc 1           ; remove parameter from stack
```

When we call the **set** function via the **b** object, we normally call the **B**-level **set** function. We can, however, call the **A**-level **set** function (the other **set** function in the object **b**) by explicitly specifying it. For example, in the call

```
b.A::set();
```

we have qualified the **set** function name with the class name **A** using the scope resolution operator (**::**). Accordingly, the compiler generates the following code that calls the **A**-level **set** function:

```
ldc  -3              ; get relative address of b
cora                 ; convert to absolute address
push
call @A@set$v
dloc 1               ; remove parameter from stack
```

We, of course, can explicitly request a function via an object only if it is in that object. For example, the call

```
a.B::set();
```

is illegal because the **B**-level set function is not in the object **a**.

The complete assembly code for the program in Figure 13.22 is given in Figure 13.24.

13.4.3   Calling Member Functions via Pointers

In the program in Figure 13.22, **a** and **b** are declared as follows:

```
A a;
B b;
```

FIGURE 13.24

```
 1                  !o
 2 @A@set$v:
 3              esba
 4
 5                                    ; x = 1;
 6              ldc   1               ; get constant 1
 7              push                  ; push it
 8              ldr   2               ; get address of x into ac
 9              sti                   ; pop 1 from stack into x
10
11              reba
12              ret
13 ;=====================================================
14 @A@display_x$v:
15              esba
16
17                                    ; cout << x << endl;
18              ldr   2               ; get address of x
19              ldi                   ; get x
20              dout                  ; output x
21              ldc   '\n'            ; endl
22              aout
23
24              reba
25              ret
26 @B@set$v:
27              esba
28
29                                    ; x = 2;
30              ldc   2               ; get constant 2
31              push                  ; push it
32              ldr   2               ; get address of x
33              sti                   ; pop 2 from stack into x
34
35                                    ; y = 3;
36              ldc   3               ; get constant 3
37              push                  ; push it
38              ldr   2               ; get address of x
39              addc  1               ; add 1 to get address of y
40              sti                   ; pop 3 from stack into y
41
42              reba
43              ret
```

(continued)

FIGURE 13.24
(continued)

```
44  ;=========================================================
45  @B@display_y$v:
46              esba
47
48                              ; cout << y << endl;
49              ldr  2          ; get address of x
50              addc 1          ; add 1 to get address of y
51              ldi             ; get y
52              dout            ; display it
53              ldc  '\n'       ; endl
54              aout
55
56              reba
57              ret
58  ;=========================================================
59  main:       esba
60
61                              ; A a;
62              aloc 1          ; allocate x field in a
63
64                              ; a.set();
65              ldc  -1         ; get relative address of a
66              cora            ; convert to absolute address
67              push            ; create implicit parameter
68              call @A@set$v   ; call set function in A
69              dloc 1          ; remove parameter from stack
70
71                              ; a.display_x();
72              ldc  -1         ; get relative address of a
73              cora            ; convert to absolute address
74              push            ; create implicit parameter
75              call @A@display_x$v
76              dloc 1          ; remove parameter from stack
77
78                              ; B b;
79              aloc 2          ; allocate x, y fields in b
80
81                              ; b.set();
82              ldc  -3         ; get relative address of b
83              cora            ; convert to absolute address
84              push            ; create implicit parameter
85              call @B@set$v
86              dloc 1          ; remove parameter from stack
```

(continued)

FIGURE 13.24
(continued)

```
87
88                              ; b.display_x();
89          ldc  -3             ; get relative address of b
90          cora                ; convert to absolute address
91          push                ; create implicit parameter
92          call @A@display_x$v
93          dloc 1              ; remove parameter from stack
94
95                              ; b.display_y();
96          ldc  -3             ; get relative address of b
97          cora                ; convert to absolute address
98          push                ; create implicit parameter
99          call @B@display_y$v
100         dloc 1              ; remove parameter from stack
101
102                             ; b.A::set();
103         ldc  -3             ; get relative address of b
104         cora                ; convert to absolute address
105         push                ; create implicit parameter
106         call @A@set$v
107         dloc 1              ; remove parameter from stack
108
109                             ; b.display_x();
110         ldc  -3             ; get relative address of b
111         cora                ; convert to absolute address
112         push                ; create implicit parameter
113         call @A@display_x$v
114         dloc 1              ; remove parameter from stack
115
116         ldc  0              ; return 0;
117         reba
118         ret
119 ;=======================================================
120         public @A@set$v
121         public @A@display_x$v
122         public @B@set$v
123         public @B@display_y$v
124         public main
```

a is type **A**; b is type **B**. Because the class **B** is derived from the class **A**, it contains everything in class **A**, plus some extra members (the **display_y** function and the **y** variable). Because **b** contains everything in **A**, we can also, quite correctly, view **b** as a type **A** object, as well as a type **B** object. To understand this better, consider the following analogy: **a** is like a toolbox, and **b** is like a toolbox with something extra—let's say a cheese sandwich (see Figure 13.25).

FIGURE 13.25   a) `toolbox <-> class A`

```
┌─────────────────────────────┐
│                             │
│   Tools                     │
│                             │
└─────────────────────────────┘
```

b) `toolbox with a cheese sandwich <-> class B`

```
┌─────────────────────────────┐
│                             │
│   Tools                     │
│   Cheese sandwich           │
│                             │
└─────────────────────────────┘
```

Clearly, **b**—a toolbox with a cheese sandwich—is also a toolbox. Analogously, **b**—a **B** object—is also an **A** object. On the other hand, **a**—a toolbox (without a cheese sandwich)—is *not* also a toolbox with a cheese sandwich. Therefore, **a**—an **A** object—is *not* also a **B** object (it does not have `display_y` or **y**), but a **B** object is also an **A** object. In other words, an object of a derived class is also an object of the base class, but not vice versa.

Now suppose we have two pointers defined as follows:

```
A* aptr;
B* bptr;
```

It would, of course, make sense to assign to **aptr** and **bptr**, respectively, the address of **a** and the address of **b**:

```
aptr = &a;
bptr = &b;
```

Then **aptr**, an **A**-level pointer, would point to an **A** object, and **bptr**, a **B**-level pointer, would point to a **B** object. But it also makes sense to assign **aptr** the address of **b**:

```
aptr = &b;
```

because, as we just observed, *b is also an A-level object*. However, it does *not* make sense to assign **bptr** the address of **a**, because a is *not* a **B**-level object:

```
bptr = &a;   // illegal
```

The statement

```
aptr = &a;
```

causes **aptr** (an **A**-level pointer) to point *across* to an object at its own level in the inheritance hierarchy, and the statement

```
aptr = &b;
```

causes **aptr** to point *down* to an object *lower* in the inheritance hierarchy. Both statements are legal, so we can say *object pointers can point across or down*. The *illegal* statement

```
bptr = &a;
```

attempts to make **bptr** point *up* to an object higher in the inheritance hierarchy. Because this statement is illegal, we can say *object pointers cannot point up*.

Let's consider the program in Figure 13.26, which illustrates the use of object pointers.

FIGURE 13.26

```
1 #include <iostream>
2 using namespace std;
3
4 class A {                    // A is the base class
5     public:
6         void set();
7         void display_x();
8     protected:               // allows derived class to access x
9         int x;
10 };
11 void A::set()
12 {
13     x = 1;
14 }
15 void A::display_x()
16 {
17     cout << x << endl;
18 }
19 class B: public A {          // B is derived from A
20     public:
21         void set();          // redefines set() from A
22         void display_y();
23     private:
24         int y;
25 };
26 void B::set()                // sets both x and y
27 {
28     x = 2;                   // illegal if x is private
29     y = 3;
30 }
31 void B::display_y()
32 {
33     cout << y << endl;
34 }
35 int main()
36 {
37     A a;
38     A* aptr;
39     B b;
40     B* bptr;
```

(continued)

FIGURE 13.26
(continued)

```
41
42      aptr = &a;
43      aptr -> set();         // invokes set in A
44      aptr -> display_x();   // invokes display_x in A--displays 1
45
46      aptr = &b;
47      aptr -> set();         // invokes set in A
48      aptr -> display_x();   // invokes display_x in A--displays 1
49
50      bptr = &b;
51      bptr -> set();         // invokes set in B
52      bptr -> display_x();   // invokes display_x in A--displays 2
53      bptr -> display_y();   // invokes display_y in B--displays 3
54
55      bptr ->A::set();       // invokes set in A
56      bptr -> display_x();   // invokes display_x in A--displays 1
57
58 // bptr = &a;              // illegal--bptr cannot point "up"
59      return 0;
60 }
```

Because **aptr** initially points to **a** (see line 42), we can access the public members of **a** via **aptr** in exactly the same way we can access **struct** fields via a pointer to that **struct**. For example, to invoke the **set** function via **aptr** (see line 43), we use the statement

```
aptr -> set();
```

Line 46 in Figure 13.26,

```
aptr = &b;
```

makes **aptr** point down to **b**. Recall that **b** has two **set** functions: one inherited from class **A** and one from class **B**. A very important question, then, is which **set** function will the call on line 47,

```
aptr -> set();
```

invoke? Because **aptr** is pointing to a **b** object, it is reasonable to expect that the **B**-level **set** function will be invoked. But this is not the case. This statement, in fact, invokes the **A**-level **set** function. The reason for this behavior becomes clear when we consider the translation of the statement by the compiler. At compile time, the program has not yet run. Neither **aptr** nor the **b** object are in existence. The compiler, at *compile time*, does not know what **aptr** will point to at *run time*. Moreover, because **aptr** is an **A**-level pointer, the compiler simply assumes it is pointing to an **A**-level object, and generates a call to the **A**-level **set** function (which initializes only **x** in **b**).

For the program in Figure 13.26, a compiler could conceivably determine at compile time that **aptr** on line 47 will point to a **B**-level object at run time by examining the previous statement (line 46), which assigns **aptr** the address of **b**.

However, a compiler could not do this, in general. For example, suppose the following code,

```
cin >> x;
if (x == 1)
    aptr = &a;
else
    aptr = &b;
```

precedes the statement,

```
aptr -> set();
```

Then, it would be impossible for the compiler to determine what **aptr** would contain at run time because the contents of **aptr** depend on the value input into **x** at run time. A further complication is illustrated by the following loop:

```
for (int i = 1; i <= 10; i++) {
   if (i % 2 == 0)
       aptr = &a;
   else
       aptr = &b;

   // aptr points to a when i = 2, 4, 6, 8, 10
   // aptr points to b when i = 1, 3, 5, 7, 9
   aptr -> set();
}
```

When the statement

```
aptr -> set();
```

in this loop is executed, **aptr** points to either **a** or **b**, depending on the iteration. How then should the compiler translate this statement? Notice that the object that **aptr** points to necessarily contains the **A**-level **set** function (because both **a** and **b** contain the **A**-level **set** function). However, the pointed-to object contains the **B**-level set function only if the object is **b**. Clearly, the easiest approach for the compiler to take for this statement is to generate code that calls the **A**-level **set** function, passing it the address in **aptr** (which is the address of the object's data). In other words, *the compiler generates code according to the level of the pointer, and not of the object pointed to.* Thus, because **aptr** is an **A**-level pointer, the compiler generates a call to the **A**-level **set** function. Figure 13.27 shows the assembly code for the program in Figure 13.26. The calls of the **set** function via **aptr** on lines 78 and 95 are both translated to

```
ldr  -2       ; get aptr (address of object)
push          ; create parameter
call @A@set$v  ; A-Level set function
dloc 1        ; remove parameter
```

even though at run time **aptr** contains the address of **b** for the call on line 95. In both calls, **@A@set$v**, the **A**-level **set** function, is called.

13.4.4 Virtual Functions and Polymorphism

In the program in Figure 13.26, the function call

```
aptr -> set();
```

FIGURE 13.27

```
 1              !o
 2  @A@set$v:
 3          esba
 4
 5                              ; x = 1;
 6          ldc   1            ; get constant 1
 7          push               ; push it1
 8          ldr   2            ; get address of x
 9          sti                ; pop 1 from stack into x
10
11          reba
12          ret
13  ;=========================================================
14  @A@display_x$v:
15          esba
16
17                              ; cout << x << endl;
18          ldr   2            ; get address of x
19          ldi                ; get x
20          dout               ; display it
21          ldc   '\n'         ; endl
22          aout
23
24          reba
25          ret
26  ;=========================================================
27  @B@set$v:
28          esba
29
30                              ; x = 2;
31          ldc   2            ; get constant 2
32          push               ; push it
33          ldr   2            ; get address of x
34          sti                ; pop 2 from stack into x
35
36                              ; y = 3;
37          ldc   3            ; get constant 3
38          push               ; push it
39          ldr   2            ; get address of x
40          addc  1            ; add 1 to get address of y
41          sti                ; pop 3 from stack into y
42
43          reba
```

(continued)

FIGURE 13.27
(continued)

```
44          ret
45  ;=========================================================
46  @B@display_y$v:
47          esba
48
49                          ; cout << y << endl;
50          ldr  2          ; get address of x
51          addc 1          ; add 1 to get address of y
52          ldi             ; get y
53          dout            ; display it
54          ldc  '\n'        ; endl
55          aout
56
57          reba
58          ret
59  ;=========================================================
60  main:   esba
61
62          aloc 2          ; A a;
63
64          aloc 1          ; A* aptr
65
66          aloc 3          ; B b;
67
68          aloc 1          ; B* bptr;
69
70                          ; aptr = &a;
71          ldc  -1         ; get relative address of a
72          cora            ; convert to absolute address
73          str  -2         ; store in aptr
74
75                          ; aptr -> set();
76          ldr  -2         ; get aptr (address of object)
77          push            ; create parameter
78          call @A@set$v   ; A-level set function
79          dloc 1          ; remove parameter
80
81                          ; aptr -> display_x();
82          ldr  -2         ; get aptr (address of object)
83          push            ; create parameter
84          call @A@display_x$v  ; displays 1
85          dloc 1          ; remove parameter
86
```

(continued)

FIGURE 13.27
(continued)

```
 87                                       ; aptr = &b;
 88              ldc   -4                  ; get relative address of b
 89              cora                      ; convert to absolute address
 90              str   -2                  ; store in aptr
 91
 92                                        ; aptr -> set();
 93              ldr   -2                  ; get aptr (address of object)
 94              push                      ; create parameter
 95              call  @A@set$v            ; A-level set function
 96              dloc  1                   ; remove parameter
 97
 98                                        ; aptr -> display_x();
 99              ldr   -2                  ; get aptr (address of object)
100              push                      ; create parameter
101              call  @A@display_x$v      ; displays 1
102              dloc  1                   ; remove parameter
103
104                                        ; bptr = &b;
105              ldc   -4                  ; get relative address of b
106              cora                      ; convert to absolute address
107              str   -5                  ; store in bptr
108
109                                        ; bptr -> set();
110              ldr   -5                  ; get bptr (address of object)
111              push                      ; create parameter
112              call  @B@set$v
113              dloc  1                   ; remove parameter
114
115                                        ; bptr -> display_x();
116              ldr   -5                  ; get bptr (address of object)
117              push                      ; create parameter
118              call  @A@display_x$v      ; displays 2
119              dloc  1                   ; remove parameter
120
121                                        ; bptr -> display_y();
122              ldr   -5                  ; get bptr (address of object)
123              push                      ; create parameter
124              call  @B@display_y$v      ; displays 3
125              dloc  1                   ; remove parameter
126
127                                        ; bptr ->A::set();
128              ldr   -5                  ; get bptr (address of object)
129              push                      ; create parameter
```

(continued)

FIGURE 13.27
(continued)

```
130            call @A@set$v
131            dloc 1              ; remove parameter
132
133                               ; bptr -> display_x();
134            ldr  -5             ; get bptr (address of object)
135            push                ; create parameter
136            call @A@display_x$v  ; displays 1
137            dloc 1              ; remove parameter
138
139            ldc  0             ; return 0;
140            reba
141            ret
142 ;============================================================
143            public @A@set$v
144            public @A@display_x$v
145            public @B@set$v
146            public @B@display_y$v
147            public main
```

calls the **A**-level **set** function, **@A@set$v**, even if **aptr** points to an object of type **B**. It is the level of the pointer—**aptr** in this case—and not the level of the object pointed to that determines the **set** function called. Accordingly, because **aptr** is an **A**-level pointer, the **A**-level **set** function is called.

Now let's make one small change to the program in Figure 13.26: Change line 6 from

```
void set();
```

to

```
virtual void set();
```

The inclusion of the keyword **virtual** causes the **set** function in class **A** to become a *virtual* function. It also causes any **set** function with the same signature (i.e., with the same name and parameter list) defined in any derived class to be virtual as well. Thus, the two **set** functions in class **B** (one inherited from **A**, one defined in **B**) both become virtual. Because making the **A**-level set function virtual automatically makes the **B**-level set function virtual, we don't have to similarly add **virtual** to the prototype of the **B**-level **set** function (line 21), although it would be legal and sensible to do so.

With a virtual function, it is the object, not the pointer, that determines at which level the function is called. For example, if the **set** function is virtual, and **aptr** points to an **A**-level object, then the call

```
aptr -> set();
```

calls the **A**-level **set** function. If, on the other hand, **aptr** points to a **B**-level object, then this call calls the **B**-level **set** function. Thus,

```
aptr = &a;      // a is an A-level object
aptr -> set();
```

calls `@A@set$v` (the A-level `set` function), but

```
aptr = &b;        // b is a B-level object
aptr -> set();
```

calls `@B@set$v` (the B-level `set` function).

Without the **virtual** keyword on line 6, the program in Figure 13.26 displays

```
1
1
2
3
1
```

With the **virtual** keyword, it displays

```
1
2
2
3
1
```

The difference in the second line of the display comes from lines 46 to 48 in Figure 13.26. When the `set` function is not virtual, its call via `aptr` (line 47) invokes the A-level `set` function, which sets `x` to 1. However, when `set` is virtual, this call calls the B-level `set` function, which sets `x` to 2 (and `y` to 3). Thus, `display_x` in the former case displays 1; in the latter case, it displays 2.

In Section 13.4.3, we learned that it is impossible for the compiler *at compile time* to generate code for

```
aptr -> set();
```

that calls the `set` function at the level of the object pointed to. However, this behavior—calling the function at the level of the object pointed to—is precisely what happens when `set` is a virtual function. How, then, is this accomplished? The answer is simple: For this statement, the compiler generates code that at *run time* determines the appropriate `set` function to call. If at run time `aptr` is pointing to an A-level object, then this code will call the A-level `set` function; if `aptr` is pointing to a B-level object, then this code will call the B-level `set` function. What cannot be done at compile time (determining the type of the object pointed to) can be done easily at run time, at the cost of a few extra instructions.

To understand how virtual functions are handled, let's first examine the underlying data structures in effect for the program in Figure 13.26 as is (i.e., without the **virtual** keyword on line 6). After line 42,

```
aptr = &a;
```

is executed, `aptr` points to the data area for `a`, which consists of a single field `x` (see Figure 13.28a). After line 46,

```
aptr = &b;
```

is executed, `aptr` points to the data area for `b`, which consists of the `x`- and `y`-fields (see Figure 13.28b). The code for the call

```
aptr -> set();
```

FIGURE 13.28

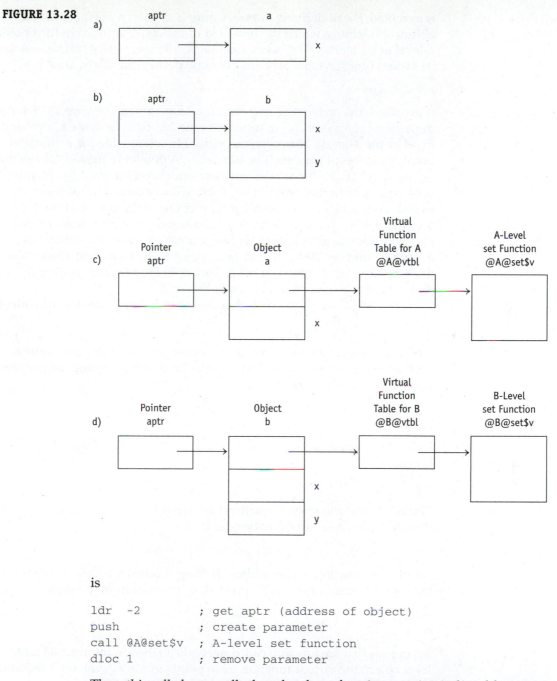

is

```
ldr  -2         ; get aptr (address of object)
push            ; create parameter
call @A@set$v   ; A-level set function
dloc 1          ; remove parameter
```

Thus, this call always calls the **A**-level **set** function, passing it the address in **aptr**. When **aptr** is pointing to **a**, the **A**-level set function sets the **a**'s **x**-field; if **aptr** is pointing to **b**, the **A**-level **set** function similarly sets **b**'s **x**-field.

Now let's consider the case when the **set** function is virtual. Then the data area for both the objects **a** and **b** contain an extra field that is located at the very beginning of the data area. This extra field points to a *virtual function table*, which in turn points to the virtual functions for that object. For example, after

```
aptr = &a;
```

is executed, the underlying data structure is as shown in Figure 13.28c. The virtual function table to which the first field of the object **a** points in turn points to the **A**-level **set** function. The object **a** contains only one virtual function. Accordingly, its virtual function table contains only one pointer. Similarly, after

```
aptr = &b;
```

is executed, the underlying data structure is as shown in Figure 13.28d. Recall that the **b** object contains two **set** functions (one inherited from the **A**-level and one defined at the **B**-level). However, the virtual function table for **B** contains only one pointer—to the **B**-level function, **@B@set$v**. A pointer to the **A**-level **set** function is not needed because the **A**-level function is never called when the pointed-to object is of type **B**. If, on the other hand, there were another virtual function in class **A** with a name and/or parameter list different from the **set** function, then the **A** and **B** virtual tables would each have an additional pointer for this additional virtual function. For example, if the **display_x** function were also virtual, then the **A** and **B** virtual function tables would both point to this function (both tables would point to the *same* function, if, as in Figure 13.26, **display_x** were not redefined with a **display_x** function in class **B**).

Now let's examine the code that the compiler generates for the statement

```
aptr -> set();
```

when **set** is a virtual function. Let's assume **aptr** is at relative address −3. First, the address in **aptr** is pushed onto the stack, thereby creating the parameter to be accessed by the called function:

```
ldr   -3        ; get aptr (address of object)
push            ; create parameter
```

Next, this address is dereferenced to load into **ac** the address of the virtual function table:

```
ldi             ; get pointer to virt function table
```

The address of the virtual function table, in turn, is dereferenced to load **ac** with the address of the function to be called:

```
ldi             ; get address of virt function
```

Finally, the function whose address is in **ac** is called via the cali instruction, and then the parameter, previously pushed, is removed from the stack:

```
cali            ; call virtual function
dloc 1          ; remove parameter
```

We can see that the function called depends on the virtual function table. For an **A**-level object, the virtual function table points to the **A**-level **set** function; for a **B**-level object, its virtual function table points to the **B**-level **set** function.

The virtual function tables are created with **dw** statements:

```
@A@vtbl:   dw    @A@set$v  ; virtual function table for A
@B@vtbl:   dw    @B@set$v  ; virtual function table for B
```

In response to the declaration of an object variable that contains virtual functions, the compiler must generate code to create the underlying data structure for that object. For example, for

```
A a;
```

the compiler generates code that allocates on the stack the data area for **a**:

```
aloc 2          ; allocate data area for a
```

and then initializes the first field of this data area to point to the appropriate virtual function table:

```
ldc  @A@vtbl    ; get address of virtual function table for A
str  -2         ; store this address in data area for a
```

where -2 is the relative address of the data area of **a**. For the statement,

```
aptr = &a;
```

the compiler generates code that assigns the address of the data area of **a** to **aptr**. If the relative addresses of **a** and **aptr** are -2 and -3, respectively, the compiler generates:

```
ldc  -2         ; get relative address of a
cora            ; convert to absolute address
str  -3         ; store in aptr
```

after which the underlying data structure is as shown in Figure 13.28c.

Figure 13.29 gives the complete assembly language for the program in Figure 13.26 with **virtual** added.

FIGURE 13.29

```
 1                !o
 2 @A@set$v:
 3             esba
 4
 5                      ; x = 1;
 6             ldc  1       ; get constant 1
 7             push         ; push it
 8             ldr  2       ; get address of object's data
 9             addc 1       ; get address of x
10             sti          ; pop 1 from stack into x
11
12             reba
13             ret
14 ; ======================================================
15 @A@display_x$v:
16             esba
17
18                      ; cout << x << endl;
19             ldr  2       ; get address of object's data area
20             addc 1       ; get address of x
21             ldi          ; get x
22             dout         ; display it
23             ldc  '\n'    ; endl
24             aout
```

(continued)

FIGURE 13.29
(continued)

```
25
26          reba
27          ret
28  ; ================================================================
29  @B@set$v:
30          esba
31
32                     ; x = 2;
33          ldc   2        ; get constant 2
34          push           ; push it
35          ldr   2        ; get address of object's data area
36          addc  1        ; get address of x
37          sti            ; pop 2 from stack into x
38
39                     ; y = 3;
40          ldc   3        ; get constant 3
41          push           ; push it
42          ldr   2        ; get address of object's data area
43          addc  2        ; add 2 to get address of y
44          sti            ; pop 3 from stack into y
45
46          reba
47          ret
48  ; ================================================================
49  @B@display_y$v:
50          esba
51
52                     ; cout << y << endl;
53          ldr   2        ; get address of object's data area
54          addc  2        ; add 1 to get address of y
55          ldi            ; get y
56          dout           ; display it
57          ldc   '\n'     ; endl
58          aout
59
60          reba
61          ret
62  ; ================================================================
63  main:   esba
64
65                     ; A a;
66          aloc  2        ; allocate data area for a
67          ldc  @A@vtbl ; get add of virt function table for A
```

(continued)

FIGURE 13.29
(continued)

```
68          str  -2         ; store this address in data area for a
69
70                          ; A* aptr;
71          aloc 1          ; allocate aptr
72
73                          ; B b;
74          aloc 3          ; allocate for data for b
75          ldc  @B@vtbl    ; get add of virt function table for B
76          str  -6         ; store this address in data area for b
77
78                          ; B* bptr;
79          aloc 1          ; allocate bptr
80
81                          ; aptr = &a;
82          ldc  -2         ; get relative address of a
83          cora            ; convert to absolute address
84          str  -3         ; store in aptr
85
86                          ; aptr -> set();
87          ldr  -3         ; get aptr (address of object)
88          push            ; create parameter
89          ldi             ; get pointer to virt function table
90          ldi             ; get address of virt function
91          cali            ; call virtual function
92          dloc 1          ; remove parameter
93
94                          ; aptr -> display_x();
95          ldr  -3         ; get aptr (address of object)
96          push            ; create parameter
97          call @A@display_x$v ; displays 1
98          dloc 1          ; remove parameter
99
100                         ; aptr = &b;
101         ldc  -6         ; get relative address of b
102         cora            ; convert to absolute address
103         str  -3         ; store in aptr
104
105                         ; aptr -> set();
106         ldr  -3         ; get aptr (address of object)
107         push            ; create parameter
108         ldi             ; get pointer to virt function table
109         ldi             ; get address of virt function
110         cali            ; call virtual function
```

(continued)

FIGURE 13.29
(continued)

```
111          dloc 1          ; remove parameter
112
113                          ; aptr -> display_x();
114          ldr  -3         ; get aptr (address of object)
115          push            ; create parameter
116          call @A@display_x$v ; displays 2
117          dloc 1          ; remove parameter
118
119                          ; bptr = &b;
120          ldc  -6         ; get relative address of b
121          cora            ; convert to relative address
122          str  -7         ; store in bptr
123
124                          ; bptr -> set();
125          ldr  -7         ; get bptr (address of object)
126          push            ; create parameter
127          ldi             ; get pointer to virt function table
128          ldi             ; get address of virtual function
129          cali            ; call virtual function
130          dloc 1          ; remove parameter
131
132                          ; bptr -> display_x();
133          ldr  -7         ; get bptr (address of object)
134          push            ; create parameter
135          call @A@display_x$v  ; displays 2
136          dloc 1          ; remove parameter
137
138                          ; bptr -> display_y();
139          ldr  -7         ; get bptr (address of object)
140          push            ; create parameter
141          call @B@display_y$v;  ; displays 3
142          dloc 1          ; remove parameter
143
144                          ; bptr ->A::set();
145          ldr  -7         ; get bptr (address of object)
146          push            ; create parameter
147          call @A@set$v
148          dloc 1          ; remove parameter
149
150                          ; bptr -> display_x();
151          ldr  -7         ; get bptr (address of object)
152          push            ; create parameter
153          call @A@display_x$v  ; displays 1
```

(continued)

FIGURE 13.29
(continued)

```
154          dloc 1        ; remove parameter
155
156          ldc  0     ; return 0;
157          reba
158          ret
159 ; ========================================================
160 @A@vtbl: dw        @A@set$v  ; virtual function table for A
161 @B@vtbl: dw        @B@set$v  ; virtual function table for B
162          public @A@set$v
163          public @A@display_x$v
164          public @B@set$v
165          public @B@display_y$v
166          public main
```

We have just seen that if we call a virtual function via an object *pointer*, the calling code accesses the object's virtual function table to obtain the function's address. However, if we call a virtual function via an *object*, the calling code calls the function directly via its name, exactly as it would if the function were not virtual. For example, if the relative address of **a** and **b** are -2 and -6, respectively, the call

```
a.set();
```

generates the code

```
ldc  -2          ; get relative address of a
cora             ; convert to absolute address
push             ; create parameter
call @A@set$v
dloc 1           ; remove parameter
```

whether or not the **set** function is virtual. Similarly, the call

```
b.set();
```

generates

```
ldc  -6          ; get relative address of b
cora             ; convert to absolute address
push             ; create parameter
call @B@set$v
dloc 1           ; remove parameter
```

We have seen that if the **set** function in Figure 13.26 is **virtual**, then the effect of the statement

```
aptr -> set();
```

depends on the type of object that **aptr** points to. Here we have a *single* item (a function call) that has *multiple* possible effects. This "single item/multiple effects" feature is called *polymorphism*.

We can find other examples of polymorphism in C++. For example, in the statement

```
x = y + z;
```

the effect of the operator + depends of the type of the operands. If **y** and **z** are of type `int`, then + causes an integer addition. If, on the other hand, **y** and **z** are of type `float`, then + causes a floating point addition. Here the *single* symbol + has *multiple* possible effects that depend on the type of its operands. Another similar example of polymorphism occurs with function name overloading. For example, in the program in Figure 8.11 in Chapter 8, the overloaded function name `fol` invokes different functions in the calls

```
fol(10);
fol();
fol(2, 3);
```

Here, the *single* identifier, `fol`, has *multiple* possible effects depending on the type, number, and order of the arguments used in the function calls.

13.5 CALL BY NAME

• •

Call by name is the Rolls-Royce of parameter-passing mechanisms: It's too costly to be practical, but it is certainly elegant and worthy of our attention. Call by name has some significant *disadvantages*:

- Programs that use call by name can be difficult to understand.
- The mechanism involves a great deal of run-time overhead (more than call by reference).
- Implementing call by name is a major task.

Given the complexity of call by name, it is not surprising that it is not supported by modern programming languages. Nevertheless, it is important to study because it will provide us with some important insights into the architectural requirements of programming languages.

We will add support for call by name to C++ using the same approach that we used to add support for call by value-result. In particular, we will use the pound sign (#) to signal that a parameter is a name parameter. For example, in line 5 of Figure 13.30, the parameter **x** is prefixed with #. This pound sign signals that **x** is a name parameter. In the call-by-name mechanism, the argument in a function call is *not* evaluated by the calling sequence for the function. Instead, the argument is evaluated *every* time its corresponding parameter is *used* in the called function. For example, in the program in Figure 13.30, the calling sequence for the call of n on line 19 does *not* evaluate **p** + **q**. Instead, **p** + **q** is evaluated every time its corresponding parameter **x** in the function n is *used*. Thus, **p** + **q** is evaluated when the assignment statement on line 9 is executed. **y** is assigned 3 (the value of **p** + **q** at this point). The argument **p** + **q** is evaluated again when the assignment statement on line 12 is executed. This time, the value of **p** + **q** is 8 because the intervening assignment statement on line 11 increases **p** by 5. Thus, **y** is assigned 8.

A good way to conceptualize the call-by-name mechanism is that it substitutes the argument itself (not the value of the argument) for the parameter. Thus, the assignment statement

```
y = x;
```

FIGURE 13.30

```
1  #include <iostream>
2  using namespace std;
3
4  int p = 1;
5  void n(int #x)              // # signals the name mechanism
6  {
7      int y;
8
9      y = x;
10     cout << y << endl;
11     p = p + 5;
12     y = x;
13     cout << y << endl;
14 }
15
16 int main()
17 {
18     int q = 2;
19     n(p + q);               // argument is p + q
20     n(q);                   // argument is q
21     return 0;
22 }
```

on line 9 becomes

```
y = p + q;
```

when the argument **p + q** in the first call is substituted for the parameter **x**. In the second call (in which the argument is **q**), the same assignment statement becomes

```
y = q;
```

when the argument **q** is substituted for the parameter **x**. Using this conceptual view, it is easy to determine that the program in Figure 13.30 displays

```
3
8
2
2
```

Note that if the argument **q** were passed using call by reference instead of call by name, the effect would be the same. Call by name and call by reference have the same effect when the argument is a simple variable.

In the call-by-name mechanism, an argument is evaluated each time its corresponding parameter is used. Let's see how this evaluation is performed. For each name argument, the compiler automatically generates a function that evaluates it. The compiler then translates each use of a name parameter to a call of the function that evaluates its corresponding argument. For example, in Figure 13.30, each use of the parameter **x** on the first call of **n** is translated to a call of a function that evaluates the argument **p + q**. We call these functions that the compiler generates to

FIGURE 13.31

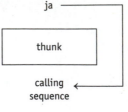

evaluate call-by-name arguments *thunks*. In call by name, we have three types of functions in operation: the *calling function*, the *called function*, and the *thunk* (which is called by the called function wherever the name parameter is referenced).

Where are thunks located? Because a thunk evaluates the argument in a function call, it makes sense that the calling sequence has attached to it the thunks needed to evaluate the arguments used in that call. For example, suppose we call the **n** function in Figure 13.30 four times:

```
n(p + q);
n(p);
n(p + p);
n(q + q);
```

Each call has a different argument, and therefore requires a different thunk. Each calling sequence would have attached to it the thunk for its argument. For example, the calling sequence for the first call above would have attached to it a thunk that evaluates **p + q**.

The most natural location for a thunk is right before the calling sequence, in which case the thunk needs to be preceded with a ja instruction that jumps over the thunk (see Figure 13.31). The ja instruction is necessary to prevent the execution of the thunk prior to the execution of the calling sequence. A thunk should be executed only when it is called—that is, only when its corresponding parameter is used in the called function.

What should the calling sequence pass to the called function? The called function has to call the thunk, so the calling sequence *must pass the thunk's address*. The called function can then call the thunk by means of this address.

How should the thunk return the value of the argument it is evaluating? Putting the value of the argument in the **ac** register seems to be a reasonable approach. However, we will see shortly that this approach is flawed. It is necessary to return the *address* of a memory location that contains the value of the argument.

Figure 13.32 is the assembly code for the program in Figure 13.30. Let's examine lines 53 to 66. These lines contain the calling sequence and the embedded thunk for the call

```
n(p + q);
```

The embedded thunk (lines 56 to 61) computes the value of **p + q** and then places the sum in an implicit local variable. The address of (*not the value in*) this implicit variable is then returned to the caller via the **ac** register. **@L0** and **@L1** are names the compiler generates for labels. Notice on lines 63 and 64 that the calling sequence passes the address of the beginning of the thunk (i.e., the address of **@L1**) to the called function **n**.

When we implement call by name on H1, we will run into a major problem: How does the thunk access variables on the stack? If an argument in the call contains

FIGURE 13.32

```
1                !o
2 @n$ni:    esba
3
4                      ; int y;
5          aloc 1      ; allocate y
6
7                      ; y = x;
8          ldr  2      ; get x (address of thunk)
9          pbp         ; save bp on stack
10         bpbp        ; restore thunk's bp
11         cali        ; call thunk
12         pobp        ; restore current bp
13
14         ldi         ; get value computed by thunk
15         str  -1     ; store value in y
16
17                     ; cout << y << endl;
18         ldr  -1     ; get y
19         dout        ; display it
20         ldc  '\n'   ; endl
21         aout
22
23                     ; p = p + 5;
24         ldc  5      ; get constant 5
25         add  p      ; add p
26         st   p      ; store back in p
27
28                     ; y = x;
29         ldr  2      ; get x (address of thunk)
30         pbp         ; save bp on stack
31         bpbp        ; restore thunk's bp
32         cali        ; call thunk
33         pobp        ; restore current bp
34         ldi         ; get value computed by thunk
35         str  -1     ; store value in y
36
37                     ; cout << y << end;
38         ldr  -1     ; get y
39         dout        ; display it
40         ldc  '\n'   ; endl
41         aout
42
43         reba
```

(continued)

FIGURE 13.32
(continued)

```
44              ret
45  ; ==========================================================
46  main:       esba
47
48                      ; int q = 2;
49              ldc  2       ; allocate and initialize q
50              push
51
52                      ; n(p + q);
53              aloc 1       ; create implicit variable
54              ja   @L0     ; jump over thunk
55                           ; start of thunk ─────────┐
56  @L1:        ld   p       ; get p                    │
57              addr -1      ; add q                     │
58              str  -2      ; store sum in implicit var │
59              ldc  -2      ; get rel add of implicit var│
60              cora         ; convert to absolute address│
61              ret          ; return this address       │
62                           ; end of thunk ─────────────┘
63  @L0:        ldc  @L1     ; get address of thunk
64              push         ; create parm with this address
65              call @n$ni
66              dloc 2       ; dloc parm and implicit var
67
68
69                      ; n(q);
70              ja   @L2     ; jump over thunk
71
72  @L3:        ldc  -1      ; thunk simply returns
73              cora         ; address of q
74              ret
75
76  @L2:        ldc  @L3     ; get address of thunk
77              push         ; create parm with this address
78              call @n$ni
79              dloc 1       ; dealloc parm
80
81              ldc  0       ; return 0;
82              reba
83              ret
84  ; ==========================================================
85  p:          dw   1
86              public @n$ni
87              public main
```

FIGURE 13.33   a)

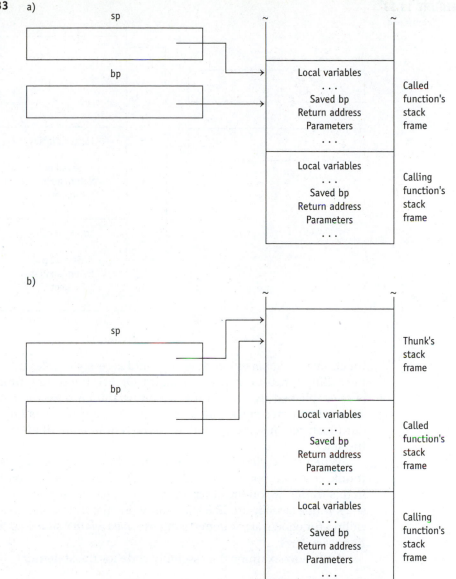

b)

items from the calling function that are on the stack (dynamic local variables or parameters), these items—because they are on the stack—are accessed via relative instructions. Relative instructions, of course, require an appropriate value in the **bp** register. But the **bp** register changes as the calling function calls the called function (see Figure 13.33a) and, perhaps, again when the called function calls the thunk (see Figure 13.33b). What, then, are the correct relative addresses to use in the relative instructions in the thunk to access the stack items that are in the stack of the calling function? The best (and easiest) way to handle this problem is to reset the **bp** register so that it points to the stack frame of the calling function while the thunk is executing. Then the thunk can use the same relative addresses that the calling function uses (see Figure 13.33c). The resetting of the **bp** register makes good sense: The arguments that have to be evaluated by a thunk are from the calling function. Thus, the thunk should execute in the calling

FIGURE 13.33
(continued)

c)

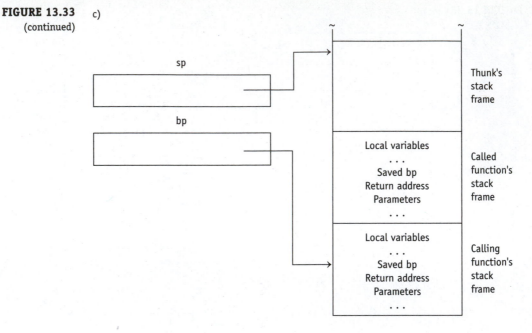

function's *environment*—that is, it should access variables in exactly the same way the calling function accesses variables. On H1, the calling function's environment is reestablished by temporarily resetting the **bp** register so that it points to the calling function's stack frame. Note that this approach is impossible for the standard instruction set: The dual use of **sp** requires that it always point to the top of the stack.

When the called function calls the thunk, a stack frame is created for the thunk, consisting of a return address and other items. **sp** points to the lowest item in this frame. **bp**, on the other hand, is reset so that it points to the *calling function's* stack frame (see Figure 13.33c). Thus, when the thunk is executing it can access the calling function's stack items using the *same relative addresses* that the calling function uses.

Let's now examine the assembly code for the statement

```
y = x;
```

on lines 7 to 15 in Figure 13.32. Because **x** is a name parameter, **x** must be evaluated by calling the thunk provided by the calling function. To do this, **n** executes

```
ldr   2
```

to load the parameter **x** (which is a pointer to the thunk that evaluates its corresponding argument). The number 2 is the relative address of **x**. Then it executes

```
pbp
```

to save the current **bp** register contents on the stack, followed by

```
bpbp        ; set bp to point to main's stack frame
```

to restore **bp** with the caller's **bp** value. Next, it executes

```
cali
```

which calls the thunk via its address in the `ac` register (loaded there by the `ldr` instruction in the above sequence). Because the `bpbp` instruction resets **bp** to point to **main**'s stack frame, the thunk accesses **main**'s stack frame with the same relative addresses that **main** uses. This is good news for the compiler, because it means that the compiler translates the statements within the thunks in **main** the same way it translates the other statements in **main**. It does not have to treat thunks in a special way.

When the thunk returns to **n**, **n** immediately executes

```
pobp
```

to restore **bp** using the value it previously saved on the stack. Thus, **bp** again points to **n**'s stack frame, allowing **n** to again access its parameter **x** and its local variable **y** that are located in its stack frame. Recall that a thunk always returns the address of the computed value—not the value itself. Thus, when the thunk returns, **n** accesses the value computed by the thunk by dereferencing the value's address in the `ac` register using an `ldi` instruction:

```
ldi        ; get value computed by thunk
```

To complete the assignment to **y**, **n** executes

```
str  -1    ; store result in y
```

to store the value that the thunk computes (now in `ac`) into **y**.

When the compiler mangles function names, it encodes name parameters with the prefix "n". Because **x** is a name parameter of type **int** in the program in Figure 13.30, it is encoded with "ni". Thus, the mangled name of **n** is **@n$ni**.

To understand why a thunk should return the address of the value of the argument rather than the value itself, consider the program in Figure 13.34. In this program, the name parameter **x** appears on both the left and right sides of assignment statements. Because the argument in the function call

```
name_test(t);
```

is a variable, an implicit variable is not needed by the thunk to hold its value. The thunk for this argument can simply return the address of **t** with the following sequence:

```
ldc  t
ret
```

FIGURE 13.34

```
1  int t = 10, q;
2  void name_test(int #x)
3  {
4      q = x;    // name parameter is on right side
5      x = 5;    // name parameter is on left side
6  }
7  int main()
8  {
9      name_test(t);
10     return 0;
11 }
```

When the first assignment statement

```
q = x;      // name parameter is on right side
```

is executed, the thunk is called and it returns the address of t. This address is then dereferenced to obtain the value of t that is assigned to q. It would certainly be simpler if the thunk returned the value in t and not its address. However, if the thunk were to return the value in t, what would happen during the execution of the second assignment statement:

```
x = 5;
```

Recall that the name mechanism, in effect, substitutes the argument for the parameter. Thus, this assignment statement should have the same effect as

```
t = 5;
```

But if the called function is passed the value of t, how can the called function place 5 into t? It must have the address of t to do this. Thus, the thunk *must* return the address of t, and the called function must be set up to receive this address.

The position of a name parameter in an assignment statement—left side or right side—does not affect the way the thunk is called. However, it does affect what happens after the thunk returns. When a name parameter is on the right side, a value is *loaded* from the address returned by the thunk. When the name parameter is on the left side, a value is *stored* at the address returned by the thunk. In the former case, we use an `ldi` instruction; in the latter case, we use an `sti` instruction.

13.6   A STACK-ORIENTED ARCHITECTURE

13.6.1   Architecture versus Organization

The structure of a computer at the circuit level—the types of circuits and how they are connected—is a computer's *organization*. The characteristics of a computer that we see at the machine level—the registers, the instruction set, main memory, and so on—are a computer's *architecture*. A computer's organization is essentially fixed. To change it requires a redesign of the computer. However, a computer's architecture depends on its microcode (assuming it uses a microcoded rather than a hardwired control section), and microcode can be changed without redesigning the computer. Thus, it is possible to give H1 a radically different architecture simply by changing its microcode.

H1 as it appears with the standard or optimal instruction sets has a *register-oriented architecture*. It is register-oriented in the sense that operations usually involve a register. For example, the `add` instruction adds a memory operand to a register; the `dout` and `shll` instructions operate on numbers in the **ac** register. In a *stack-oriented architecture*, operations involve operands on the stack. For example, the `add` instruction adds the top two operands on the stack and places the sum back on the stack. The `dout` instruction pops and displays the number on top of the stack. The `shll` instruction shifts the number on top of the stack. In a stack architecture, there is no **ac** register.

Most architectures today are register-oriented. There is, however, one very notable exception: the Java Virtual Machine (JVM) is stack-oriented. JVM is the machine on which all compiled Java programs run. To run an H1 program on your computer, you have to use the `sim`—a program that makes your computer behave like H1. Similarly, to run a Java program on your computer, you have to use the *Java interpreter*—a program that makes your computer behave like the JVM.

When almost all modern architectures are register-oriented, why did the designers of the JVM go with a stack architecture? To properly answer this question, we must first examine a stack architecture. We will examine a stack architecture for H1 whose instruction set is comparable in function to the optimal instruction set. We call this new instruction set the *stack instruction set*.

To use the stack instruction set on `sim`, you should include a `!k` directive in your assembly language programs. You will also have to link your object modules with `ksup.mob` (the start-up code for the stack instruction set) instead of `sup.mob`. A summary of the stack instruction set appears in Appendix A and in the file `k.txt` in the H1 software package.

13.6.2 Using the Top of the Stack Instead of the `ac` Register

For our register-oriented instruction sets, an essential operation is the loading of the `ac` register. For this operation, we have three instructions, one direct (`ld`), one relative (`ldr`), and one immediate (`ldc`). Here are some examples of their use:

```
ld   100     ; load from location 100
ld   x       ; load from location x
ldr  -2      ; load relative from relative address -2
ldc  5       ; load constant 5
ldc  x       ; load address of x
```

In a register-oriented architecture, the target of a load operation is a register; in a stack-oriented architecture, the target is the stack (in particular, the top of the stack). In other words, a load operation in the stack instruction set takes an operand and places it on top of the stack. Thus, a *load operation is simply a push*.

Corresponding to the `ld` instruction in the register-oriented instruction sets, we have the `p` (push) instruction in the stack instruction set. For example,

```
p    100
```

pushes the operand at location 100 onto the stack. Note that this instruction does *not* push 100 onto the stack—it pushes the operand at location 100. The instruction

```
p    x
```

pushes the operand at **x**.

Corresponding to `ldr`, we have the `pr` (push relative) instruction, which pushes the memory operand at the specified relative address. For example,

```
pr   -2
```

pushes the memory operand at relative address −2 (relative to the base address in the **bp** register) onto the stack.

Corresponding to `ldc`, we have the `pc` (push constant) instruction, which pushes the immediate constant in the instruction onto the stack. For example,

```
pc   5
```

pushes 5 onto the stack. Just as `ldc` can load addresses, so can `pc`. For example,

```
ldc  x
```

loads the address of **x**. Similarly,

```
pc   x
```

pushes the address of **x** onto the stack. For both of these instructions, the assembler produces a machine instruction whose immediate constant is the absolute address of **x** (recall that the assembler replaces symbolic addresses like **x** with their corresponding absolute addresses). Thus, when the `ldc` or `pc` instructions are executed, the address of **x** is loaded or pushed, respectively.

The store instructions in the stack instruction set require that the top two items on the stack be the value to be stored and the target address of the store. For example, if we execute the sequence,

```
pc   x      ; push address of x
pc   5      ; push value 5
```

then the top two items on the stack are the value 5 and the address of **x** (see Figure 13.35a). If we then execute the *stav* (store address/value) instruction,

```
stav      ; store value at address and double pop
```

FIGURE 13.35

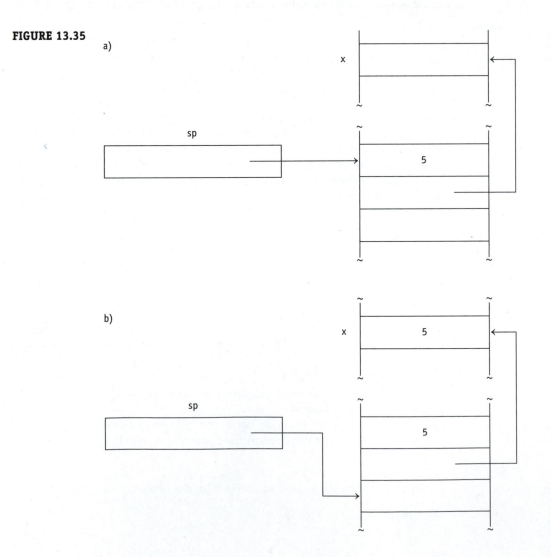

the top of the stack (the value) is stored at the target address given by the second item on the stack. In addition, both the value and the address on the stack are popped. Thus, the `stav` instruction in this example causes 5 to be stored at **x** (see Figure 13.35b), and double pops the stack.

If we push the address and value in reverse order (i.e., if we push the value first), then to perform a store we should use the *stva* (store value/address) instruction instead of the `stav` instruction. The `stav` instruction expects the address to be pushed first; the `stva` instruction expects the value to be pushed first. For example, in the following sequence, we use the `stva` instruction because we are pushing the value first:

```
pc    5     ; push value 5 first
pc    x     ; push address of x
stva        ; store value at address and double pop
```

The stack instruction set has one more load-type instruction. This instruction is actually called the *load* instruction. It replaces the top of the stack with the memory operand that the top of the stack is currently pointing to. For example, the instruction

```
pc    x     ; push address of x
```

pushes the address of **x** onto the stack (see Figure 13.36a). If we then execute

```
load      ; replace top of stack with what it is pointing to
```

it replaces the address of **x** on top of the stack with the contents of **x** (see Figure 13.36b).

FIGURE 13.36

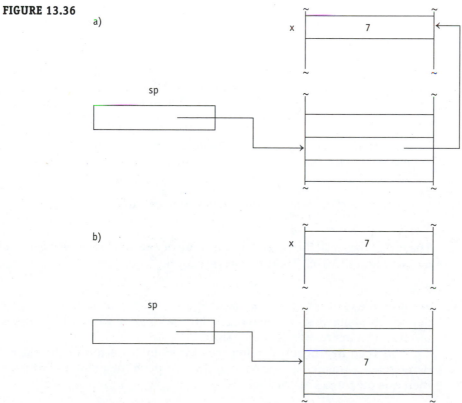

FIGURE 13.37   a)

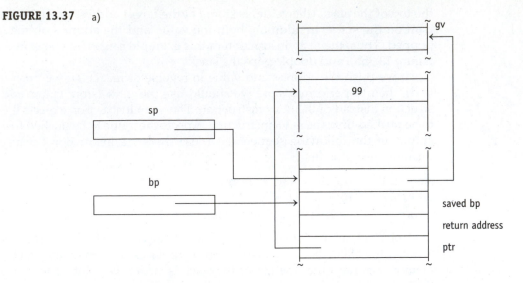

The `pc/load` sequence can be replaced by a single p instruction:

```
p    x
```

which pushes the contents of **x** onto the stack. However, we often cannot use a p instruction because it requires us to specify the address of the operand to be pushed. This address may be unavailable until run time. Consider, for example, the code for the assignment statement in the following C++ function:

```
int gv;
void f(int *ptr)
{
     gv = *ptr;
}
```

We cannot use a p instruction to access ***ptr** because the address in the p instruction would have be equal to the address in **ptr**, but the latter address is not known until run time. Thus, to perform the assignment, we first push the address of **gv** with

```
pc    gv
```

(see Figure 13.37a). Next, we push the pointer **ptr** (which has the relative address 2) onto the stack with

```
pr    2     ; 2 is the relative address of ptr
```

(see Figure 13.37b) and then dereference it by executing

```
load
```

The top of the stack then contains the value of ***ptr**, below which is the address of **gv** (see Figure 13.37c). Thus, by next executing

```
stav
```

we store the value of ***ptr** in **gv** (see Figure 13.37d). Alternatively, we could have dereferenced **ptr** first and then pushed the address of **gv**, in which case we would use the `stva` instruction to do the store.

The `load` instruction dereferences the pointer on top of the stack. Thus, to dereference a pointer, all we have to do is to push the pointer onto the stack and then execute a `load` instruction.

FIGURE 13.37
(continued)

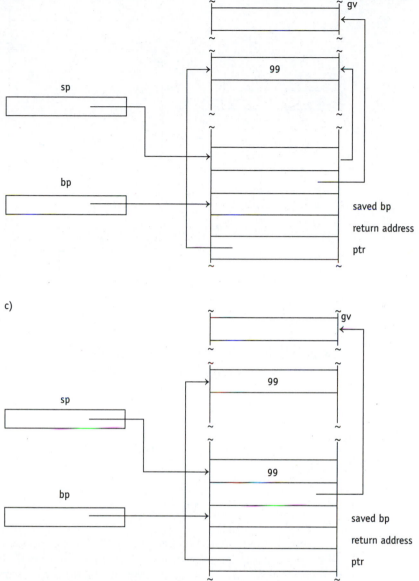

13.6.3 Availability of 4-Bit Opcodes

In the optimal instruction set we were forced to use different instruction formats for the arithmetic instructions because of a lack of 4-bit opcodes. However, in the stack instruction set, we do not have a similar problem. All the arithmetic instructions (except for the immediate types) work in exactly the same way. They all pop and operate on the top two operands on the stack and push the result. For example to add 2 and 3, we use

```
pc    2
pc    3
add
```

FIGURE 13.37   d)
(continued)

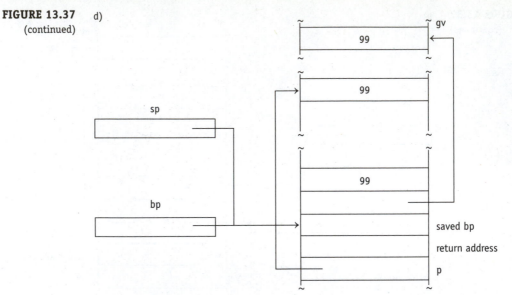

To multiply, we use

```
pc   2
pc   3
mult
```

We also do not need a pair of instructions—direct and relative—for each operation. For example, to add two items at the labels **x** and **y**, we use

```
p    x
p    y
add
```

And to add two items at relative addresses −1 and −2, we also use the add instruction:

```
pr   -1
pr   -2
add
```

Because the *arithmetic instructions do not use 4-bit opcodes*, there are many more 4-bit opcodes available for other types of instructions than in the optimal instruction set. For example, we have jump instructions (*jodd* and *jcnt*) in place of the awkward sodd and dect instructions in the optimal instruction set. We also have new jump instructions that test for the greater than zero (*jp*) and the zero or negative (*jzon*) conditions.

All the conditional jump instructions, except for jcnt (jcnt decrements and tests the **ct** register), test and pop the top of the stack. For example, the code for

```
if (x < 0)     // assume x is global
    x++
```

is

```
p     x          ; push value of x first time
jzop  @L0        ; pops the value of x
p     x          ; push value of x second time
pc    1          ; push 1
```

```
add                    ; add
pc      x              ; push address of x
stva                   ; double pop and store sum into x @L0:
```

Notice we have to push the value of **x** a second time because `jzop` pops, tests, and discards the value from the first push.

The conditional jump instructions are convenient for making comparisons with zero, as the previous example illustrates. For other comparisons, use the *scmp* (for signed comparisons) or *ucmp* (for unsigned comparisons) instruction. These instructions work as they do in the optimal instruction set, except that they use the stack exclusively. For example, the code for

```
if (x < y)       // assume x and y are global signed ints
    x = 3;
```

is

```
        p      x          ; push value of x
        p      y          ; push value of y
        scmp              ; double pop and compare
        jzop @L1          ; jump if x >= y

        pc     x          ; x = 3;
        pc     3
        stav

@L1:
```

In the optimal instruction set, the `aloc` and `dloc` instructions subtract and add an immediate constant to the **sp** register. Unfortunately, because of a lack of 4-bit opcodes, the immediate operand can be at most 255. Thus, to allocate or deallocate a large array on the stack, we may have to use a multiple number of `aloc` or `dloc` instructions. In the stack instruction set, however, we have the *aspc* (add to sp constant) instruction that has a 12-bit immediate operand. We can use this one instruction to either allocate or deallocate up to 4095 words. For example, to allocate a 2000-word array, we use

```
aspc -2000
```

To deallocate the array, we use

```
aspc 2000
```

Taking advantage of the availability of 4-bit opcodes in the stack instruction set, we have been able to improve the `cora` instruction. `cora` now uses a 4-bit opcode, which allows the relative address it has to convert to fit in the instruction itself. For example, to convert the relative address -4 to an absolute address, we execute

```
cora -4
```

The relative address -4 is in the `cora` instruction itself (in its 12 rightmost bits). In contrast, in the optimal instruction set, the `cora` instruction uses an 8-bit opcode. The address to convert has to be provided by the **ac** register. Thus, we have to do two things: Load the **ac** register and execute the `cora` instruction. For example, to convert the relative address -4, we have to execute

```
ldc  -4
cora
```

13.6.4 Special Stack Operations

Sometimes the top two items on the stack are in the wrong order. If that is the case, it is easy to switch them to the reverse order by using the *rev* (reverse) instruction. For example, after the execution of

```
pc   1
pc   2    ; 2 is on top of 1
```

2 is on top of the stack with 1 below it. If we then execute

```
rev       ; 1 is now on top of 2
```

1 and 2 switch locations in the stack. 1 ends up on top of the stack with 2 below it. Similar to rev is the *rot* (rotate) instruction. It moves the second item on the stack to the top, the third item to the second position, and the top to the third position. For example, suppose the stack from top down contains 1, 2, 3. After a rot instruction, it would contain 2, 3, 1.

Many instructions in the stack instruction set pop (and thereby destroy) the value on top of the stack. To preserve this value, simply use the *dupe* instruction to duplicate the value on top of the stack. Do this before you use a top-destroying instruction. Then one instance of the value will remain on the stack after the instruction destroys the other instance.

At this point, you may feel that the stack instruction set is complex and difficult to use. However, once you start using it, you will quickly find that it is, in fact, quite easy. It fact, it may even be easier to use than the register-oriented instruction sets.

13.6.5 Simpler Compiling

One of the benefits of the stack architecture is that the stack can easily function as a convenient temporary storage area. For example, consider the following assignment statement:

```
x = a + b + c;
```

When a compiler translates this statement to the optimal instruction set, it has to scan and remember the left side of the statement (**x**), generate code to evaluate the right side, and then generate code to store the result in the left side's variable (which it previously scanned and remembered). If all the variables are global, the code for this statement is

```
ld    a
add   b
add   c
st    x
```

x is the first item the compiler scans, but it is not until the end of the statement that the compiler generates code using **x**. Thus, the compiler must remember **x** until it completes the right side of the statement. However, with the stack instruction set the compiler does not have to do this. When the compiler scans the left side, it simply generates code that saves the left side's address on the stack. It then scans and generates code evaluating the right side. Finally, it generates a stav instruction that stores the value of the right side into the address previously saved on the stack (i.e., the address of **x**). Here is the code:

```
pc   x       ; save address of x
p    a
```

```
p    b
add
p    c
add
stav            ; now store result in saved address
```

With the stack instruction set, the compiler does not have to remember the left side's variable—it simply generates code as it scans the statement. We use the stack to remember the left side (specifically its address), but this occurs at run time, not at compile time. A similar simplification for the compiler occurs when processing expressions in which higher precedence operators appear to the right of lower precedence operators. For example, for the statement

```
x = a + b*c;
```

the compiler scans **a** before **b*c**, but in a register-oriented instruction set, it has to generate code for **b*c** first because it uses a higher precedence operator. Thus, the compiler has to remember **a**, generate code for **b*c**, and then generate code using **a**. The resulting code is

```
ld   b   ; compiler must remember x and a
push
ld   c
mult
add  a   ; use a here
st   x   ; use x here
```

In the stack instruction set, the compiler simply generates code as it scans the statement left to right. It does not have to remember **x** or **a**:

```
pc   x   ; push address of x
p    a   ; push a
p    b   ; push b
p    c   ; push c
mult     ; multiply b and c
add      ; add value of a
stav     ; store result in x
```

13.6.6 Returning Values

With the register-oriented instructions, we use the **ac** register to return a value from a called function. However, we cannot do this with the stack instruction set because it does not have an **ac** register. Obviously, we have to use the stack instead, and therein lies a problem. For example, suppose a C++ function contains a **return** statement that returns 5:

```
return 5;
```

At the assembly level, we can attempt to return 5 by pushing it on the stack with

```
pc   5
```

Figure 13.38a shows the stack at this point. If we then execute the standard return linkage consisting of

```
reba
ret
```

FIGURE 13.38   a)

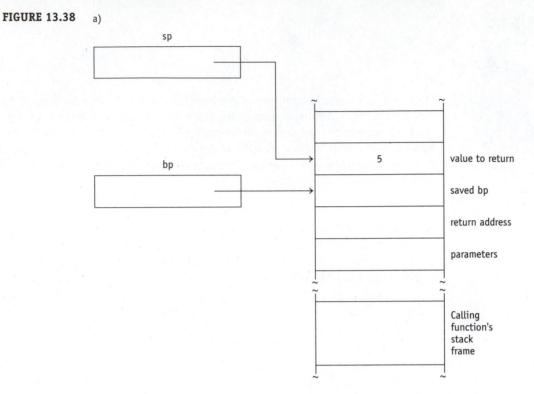

the `reba` instruction restores **bp** to the caller's value and, unfortunately, pops 5 off the stack by resetting **sp** to point above the saved **bp** (see Figure 13.38b). Thus, on return to the calling function, the return value is no longer on the stack. Recall our discussion in Section 4.4 that on real computers interrupts can occur during the execution of a program. Once an item is off the stack, it may be immediately overlaid by the data pushed by the interrupt mechanism. Thus, once an item is off the stack, we should assume *it is no longer available*.

The correct way to return a one-word value is for the caller to allocate a return area on the stack just before it creates the parameters for the call. The called function then returns a value by placing it in this return area. When the called function returns to the caller, the caller pops the parameters, leaving the returned value on top of the stack. For example, the code for

```
sum = ret_sum(5, 7);
```

is

```
pc    sum          ; push address of sum
aspc  -1           ; allocate return area
pc    7            ; create 2nd parameter
pc    5            ; create 1st parameter
call  $ret_sum@ii
aspc  2            ; remove parameters
stav               ; place return value in sum
```

The first aspc instruction allocates the return area on the stack, after which the two pc instructions create two parameters on the stack. On return from **ret_sum**, the second aspc instruction pops the two parameters, leaving the return value on top of the stack. The stav instruction that follows then stores the return value in **sum**,

FIGURE 13.38
(continued)

b) After the reba

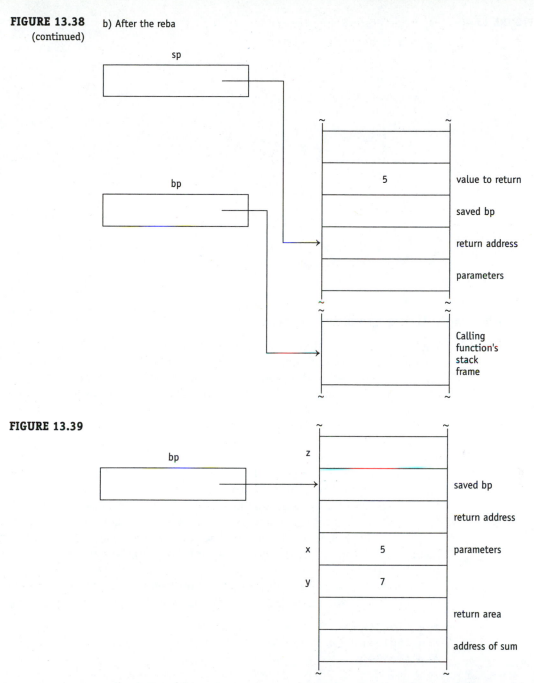

FIGURE 13.39

and pops both the return value and the address of the **sum**. Within **ret_sum**, the relative address of the return area is 4 (see Fig. 13.39). Thus, to return a value that is on top of the stack, **ret_sum** first pushes the address of the return area with

```
cora 4
```

and then stores the return value in the return area with

```
stva
```

to store the return value in the return area.

FIGURE 13.40

```
 1  #include <iostream>
 2  using namespace std;
 3
 4  int sum;
 5  int ret_sum(int x, int y)
 6  {
 7      int z;
 8      z = x + y;
 9      return z;
10  }
11  int main() {
12      sum = ret_sum(5, 7);
13      cout << sum << endl;
14      return 0;
15  }
```

13.6.7 An Example Using the Stack Instruction Set

We have not yet covered every instruction in the stack instruction set; however, we do not need to. Those that remain are either identical to their counterparts in the optimal instruction set or differ only in their use of the top of the stack in place of the **ac** register. So let's now examine assembly code that uses the stack instruction set for the simple C++ program in Figure 13.40. Its assembly code is given in Figure 13.41.

Figure 13.39 shows the state of the stack when the assignment statement within **ret_sum** is executed. The relative addresses of **x**, **y**, and **z** are, respectively, 2, 3, and −1. The code for this assignment statement first pushes the absolute address of **z** (see line 7 in Figure 13.41). It then pushes (lines 8 and 9) and adds (line 10) the values of **x** and **y**, and stores the result in **z** (line 11).

The code for the **return** statement is exactly as we described earlier: The return value is stored in a return area whose address is an implicit parameter on the stack.

The **cout** statement is translated to a `dout-aout` sequence at the assembly level. Note that these instructions output (and pop) the value on top of the stack (lines 30 and 32).

To run the program in Figure 13.41, you first have to assemble it, then link it with **ksup.mob** (the start-up code for the stack instruction set). To do this, enter

```
mas fig1341
lin fig1341 ksup
sim fig1341
```

13.6.8 Comparing the Optimal and Stack Instruction Sets

Our examination of the stack instruction set has revealed several advantages:

- Its instructions have a consistent format. For example, the instructions to add, subtract, multiply, and divide all work the same way.
- It does not have a shortage of 4-bit opcodes because none of the arithmetic instructions use them. Thus, it is able to have a richer set of instructions, which includes a full complement of jump instructions, a more powerful allocate/deallocate instruction (`aspc`), and an improved `cora` instruction.
- Compiling programs to a stack architecture is simpler.

FIGURE 13.41

```
 1              !k          ; use the stack instruction set
 2 @ret_sum$ii:
 3         esba
 4
 5         aspc -1    ; int z;
 6                    ; z = x + y;
 7         cora -1       ; push address of z
 8         pr   2        ; push x
 9         pr   3        ; push y
10         add           ; compute x + y
11         stav          ; store sum in z
12                    ; return z;
13         pr   -1       ; push value of z
14         cora 4        ; push address of return area
15         stva          ; save return value in return area
16         reba
17         ret
18 ; =======================================================
19 main:     esba
20                    ; sum = ret_sum(5, 7);
21         pc   sum      ; push address of sum
22         aspc -1       ; allocate return area
23         pc   7        ; create parameters
24         pc   5
25         call @ret_sum$ii
26         aspc 2        ; deallocate parameters
27         stav          ; store return value in sum
28
29         p    sum      ; cout << sum << endl;
30         dout
31         pc   '\n'
32         aout
33                    ; return 0;
34         cora 4        ; push address of return area
35         pc   0        ; push 0
36         stav          ; store return value in return area
37         reba
38         ret
39 ; =======================================================
40 sum:      dw   0       ; int sum;
41         public @ret_sum$ii
42         public main
```

We have yet to address the most important issue, however: How will a program written with the optimal instruction set perform compared with a program written with the stack instruction set. Which program will be faster? Which program will be smaller? By testing and analyzing a variety of programs using the optimal and stack instruction sets, we may be able answer this question quickly.

One major factor in the execution speed of programs using a given instruction set is the quality of the microcode implementing that instruction set. Thus, if the microcode for the stack instruction set were very efficient but that for the optimal instruction set were not, then we would expect the optimal instruction set to perform relatively poorly. This poor performance would be a reflection more of its microcode than of any inherent disadvantages of its architecture. We can discount this variable in our present investigation, however, because the microcode in **o.hor** and **k.hor** is of the same quality.

A theoretical analysis of the two instruction sets clearly suggests that the register-oriented architecture should out-perform the stack architecture. There are two reasons for this conclusion. First, each computation in the stack instruction set involves three memory accesses: The two stack operands must be fetched, and the result placed back on the stack. In contrast, for the optimal instruction set, computations involve at most two memory accesses (one to load the **ac** register with one operand, and a second to access the other operand), and if one operand is already in the **ac** register, then we do not need the load operation. Second, with the stack instruction set, the two operands in a computation have to be placed on the stack, requiring up to four more memory accesses. For comparison purposes, let's add the values in two global variables, **x** and **y**, and put the result in a third global variable, **z**. For the optimal instruction set we have

```
ld   x    ; requires one memory access
add  y    ; requires one memory access
st   z    ; requires one memory access
```

which requires three memory accesses plus three more to access the three instructions. For the stack instruction set we have

```
pc   z    ; requires one memory access
p    x    ; requires two memory accesses
p    y    ; requires two memory accesses
add       ; requires three memory accesses
stav      ; requires three memory accesses
```

which requires 11 memory accesses plus five more to access the five instructions for a total of 16 accesses. Six accesses versus 16 is quite a difference. The number of memory accesses in a code sequence is not the only factor in execution speed, but it is an important one. So we would expect the run times for these code segments to be in line with the number of memory accesses they perform. Let's run these two segments on **sim** to determine the microinstruction counts for each instruction. Figure 13.42 shows the results (recall that the **mc** command sets the display mode that displays microinstruction counts). For the optimal instruction set, the total microinstruction count is 37; for the stack instruction set, 77. The ratio of microinstruction counts is 77 to 37 = 2.1. The ratio for memory accesses is in the same ballpark: 16 to 6 = 2.7. Let's try one more comparison, this time using the code for the C++ program in Figure 13.40. Its stack instruction set version (Figure 13.41) executes 349 microinstructions; its optimal instruction set version executes 246 microinstructions, for a ratio of 1.4. Again, the optimal instruction set significantly outperforms the stack instruction set.

FIGURE 13.42

```
                        Optimal Instruction Set
0: ld    /0 004/ ac=0000/0002    10t
1: add   /2 005/ ac=0002/0005  cy=0000/0000    17t
2: st    /1 006/ m[006]=0000/0005    8t
3: halt /FFFF /    2t
                 Stack Instruction Set
0: pc    /1 008/ m[FFF]=0000/0008  sp=0000/FFFF    10t
1: p     /0 006/ m[FFE]=0000/0002  sp=FFFF/FFFE    12t
2: p     /0 007/ m[FFD]=0000/0003  sp=FFFE/FFFD    12t
3: add   /F1 00/ m[FFE]=0002/0005  sp=FFFD/FFFE  cy=0000/0000    24t
4: stav  /F3 00/ m[008]=0000/0005  sp=FFFE/0000    17t
5: halt /FFFF /    2t
```

Should we conclude that stack instruction sets are no good and avoid them? There are several reasons we should *not* do this. First, it is always dangerous to make sweeping generalizations based on a few test cases. Second, a stack architecture can result in simpler, more straightforward code. Thus, it is certainly possible that for some languages this characteristic of a stack architecture would be so pronounced that it would make the stack architecture superior for those languages. Algol and Pascal, for example, are languages that require complex manipulations of a run-time stack. An architecture designed specifically to perform these manipulations might outperform other architectures. (This was the design philosophy of the Burroughs B5000 and B6000 series of computers.) Third, we might be able to minimize or eliminate the principal bottleneck for a stack architecture—accessing the top of the stack—through ingenious computer design. For example, we might incorporate in our computer high-speed registers to hold the top items on the stack. Stack operation would then access these fast registers rather than the slower main memory. We could then enjoy the elegance of a stack architecture without seriously sacrificing performance.

13.6.9 Some Observations on the Java Virtual Machine

Let's now return to the question that we posed at the beginning of this chapter: Why did the designers of the JVM choose a stack architecture? A stack architecture certainly has some advantages, but the performance penalty would seem to outweigh these advantages. This conclusion, however, is incorrect. It is based on a faulty assumption—namely, that a performance differential between two architectures implemented in hardware also exists if the two architectures are simulated. Performance differentials, in fact, often evaporate when architectures are simulated, precisely because they are simulations. To understand why this is so, consider the ac register in H1. The **sim** program (a C++ program) simulates it with a **short int** variable. Thus, when the simulated H1 loads the ac register, the **sim** program is actually storing a value in this variable (which is located in memory as part of the **sim** program). In other words, *a register access on a real H1 is really a memory access in the simulated H1*. Thus, the performance advantage of accessing registers in a register-oriented architecture versus the stack in main memory in a stack architecture does not exist for simulated machines—all accesses are main memory accesses on simulated machines. JVM, like H1, is a simulated machine. Although it has been implemented as a real machine for some special applications, its most common form is as a simulated machine. Thus, its architecture correctly should not be evaluated in the same way as the architecture of a real machine.

One of the outstanding features of the JVM is the compactness of its *bytecode* (i.e., its machine code). For example, the executable form for the C++ version of the `linv1` linker described in Chapter 11 contains 36,864 bytes. Its Java version contains only 10,179 bytes. One of the reasons for the compactness of JVM's byte-code is its use of many one-byte instructions. Not only are all its arithmetic instructions one byte, but many of its load and store instructions are also one byte. For example, the `icont_5` instruction (a one-byte instruction) loads 5 (i.e., it pushes 5 onto the stack). `istore_2` (another one-byte instruction) stores into local variable 2 (i.e., it pops the top of the stack into local variable 2). Each of these special-purpose instructions requires an opcode. Opcodes are available for them on the JVM because of its stack architecture, which, as we saw earlier, consumes fewer opcodes than a register-oriented architecture with the same functionality.

13.7 MICROCODING THE OPTIMAL AND STACK INSTRUCTION SETS

• •

If you have studied Chapter 6, an excellent project for you to do at this point is to write the microcode for the optimal instruction set. To do this, first copy **s.has** to a new file **os.has** ("os" stands for *o*ptimal instruction set, *s*tudent version). Then add support for each new or modified instruction in the optimal instruction set to your **os.has** file. On completing **os.has**, assemble it with

has os

has will assemble **os.has** using the configuration file **os.cfg** in the H1 software package. Next, run the test program **osprog.mac** in the software package on **sim** by entering

sim osprog /z

The argument **/z** causes **osprog** to run with no trace. **osprog.mas** contains the !-directive !os so **sim** will automatically use your **os.hor** microcode. It will also use the **os.cfg** configuration file in the H1 software package. **sim** will respond with either

```
Simulator Version x.x
Reading configuration file os.cfg
Reading microcode file os.hor
No errors detected in optimal instruction set
```

if no errors are detected, or with

```
Simulator Version x.x
Reading configuration file os.cfg
Reading microcode file os.hor
ERROR detected in optimal instruction set at loc XXXX hex
```

where *XXXX* is the hex location at which an error is detected. Suppose the error-detection location is 001D. Then run **osprog** on **sim** again but without the **/z** argument. Enter with **b1d** (to set a breakpoint at the error-detection location 1D) and then **g** to go (i.e., execute) to that location:

```
---- [T7] 0: ldc  /8 000/ b1d
Machine-level breakpoint set at 1D
```

```
---- [T7] 0: ldc  /8 000/ g
  0: ldc  /8 000/ ac=0000/0000
  1: swap /F7 00/ sp=0000/0000  ac=0000/0000
                .
                .
                .
 19: sub  /3 2F9/ ac=0002/0000
 1A: st   /1 308/
 1B: ld   /0 308/ ac=0000/0005
 1C: jz   /C 01E/
Machine-level breakpoint at 1D
---- [T7] 1D: call /E 288/
```

The `call` instruction at location 1D calls the code that generates the error message. The preceding `jz` instruction jumps over this call if *no* error is detected in this test sequence. Thus, the `ac` register should contain zero at this point. But we can see from the `ld` instruction at location 1B that it contains 5 instead. By carefully examining the instructions leading up to the `ld`, we can spot an error in the `st` instruction at location 1A: It does not store anything into main memory (it should store the contents of the `ac` register).

The next step is to reset the program with **o** (do over), set a breakpoint at the `st` instruction (location 1A), and go until the breakpoint (i.e., the `st` instruction) is reached:

```
---- [T7] 1D: call /E 288/ o
Starting session.  Enter h or ? for help.
---- [T7] 0: ldc  /8 000/ b1a
Machine-level breakpoint set at 1A
---- [T7] 0: ldc  /8 000/ g
  0: ldc  /8 000/ ac=0000/0000
  1: swap /F7 00/ sp=0000/0000  ac=0000/0000
                .
                .
                .
 19: sub  /3 2F9/ ac=0002/0000
Machine-level breakpoint at 1A
---- [T7] 1A: st   /1 308/
```

Now enable **sim**, set the micro display mode, and trace one machine instruction. The trace then shows all the microlevel activity corresponding to the `st` instruction:

```
---- [T7] 1A: st   /1 308/ enable
Microlevel enabled
---- [T7] 1A: st   /1 308/ m
Microlevel display mode
---- [T1] 0: pc = 1 + pc; mar = pc; / ←hit ENTER
  0: pc = 1 + pc; mar = pc;
     mar=2F9/01A  pc=001A/001B
  1: rd;
     Rd from m[01A] mdr=0002/1308  1A: st   /1 308/
  2: ir = mdr; if (s) goto 7;
     ir=32F9/1308
  3: dc = left(ir); if (s) goto B;
     dc=97C8/2610
```

```
 4: dc = left(dc); if (s) goto 11;
    dc=2610/4C20
 5: dc = left(dc); if (s) goto 54;
    dc=4C20/9840
54: mdr = ac; mar = ir;
    mar=01A/308  mdr=1308/0000
55: goto 0;
---- [T1] 0: pc = 1 + pc; mar = pc; /
```

The microcode at locations 0 to 5 are decoding instructions; the microcode for the execution of the st instruction is at locations 54 and 55. The microinstruction at 54 is correct (it loads the **mar** and **mdr** registers). However, the microinstruction at location 55 is missing a **wr**.

Now that we have identified our bug, we can exit **sim** and fix the symbolic microcode in **os.has**. However, before we do this, let's make a temporary fix right in **sim** to see if our proposed fix works. We'll assemble the correct microinstruction into location 55 with the **a** command:

```
---- [T1] 0: pc = 1 + pc; mar = pc; / a55
55:  goto 0; / wr; goto 0
56:  mar = ir; /              ←hit ENTER to exit assembly mode
---- [T1] 0: pc = 1 + pc; mar = pc; /
```

Next we enter **o#** to do over. The **#** suffix on this command prevents **sim** from reinitializing microstore (which would overlay our fix):

```
---- [T1] 0: pc = 1 + pc; mar = pc; / o#
Starting session.  Enter h or ? for help.
---- [T1] 0: pc = 1 + pc; mar = pc; /
```

Finally, we enter **K** (in uppercase) to kill the previously set machine-level breakpoint, followed by **n** and **g** to see if **osprog** now succeeds:

```
---- [T1] 0: pc = 1 + pc; mar = pc; / K
Machine-level breakpoint killed
---- [T1] 0: pc = 1 + pc; mar = pc; / n
No display mode
---- [T7] g
No errors detected in optimal instruction set
```

Now **osprog** correctly runs to completion.

If you prefer an easier first step than writing **os.has**, you can write the microcode for a subset of the optimal instruction set that does not support the cy register, addy, mod, mult, scmp, shra, and ucmp. If you do this, you should create the microcode in a file named **osl.has** ("osl" stands for *o*ptimal instruction set, *s*tudent version, *l*ess the difficult instructions), and test your program with the test program **oslprog.mac** and the configuration file **osl.cfg** (both are in the H1 software package).

Because the microcode in the H1 software package for the optimal instruction set is encrypted, you cannot compare it with your own. However, you can get a sense of how your microcode matches up with the encrypted code by running the test cases with the **mc** command (machine-level display plus counts). You can then compare the microinstruction counts for your microcode with those for the encrypted microcode. For example, you can invoke **sim** with

sim osprog

and then enter `mc` and `g` to see the counts for your own microcode (`osprog.mac` uses your microcode in `os.hor`). Then run `sim` again with

`sim oprog`

and similarly enter `mc` and `g` to see the counts for the encrypted microcode (`oprog.mac` uses the encrypted microcode in `o.hor`). `osprog.mac` and `oprog.mac` are identical except for the microcode they use.

The H1 software package contains test files for the stack instruction set that parallel those of the optimal instruction set. For example, to test your microcode for the optimal instruction set, you should run `osprog.mac` or `oslprog.mac`. Similarly, to test your microcode for the stack instruction set, you should run `ksprog.mac` or `kslprog.mac`.

13.8 CHALLENGE OF MICROPROGRAMMING

Our optimal instruction set is considerably better than the standard instruction set. It is sufficiently powerful that we have been able to use it in this chapter as the target language for some fairly complicated C++ programs. The stack instruction set in some respects is even better, but it suffers a performance penalty.

Through the flexibility provided by microcode, we have been able fix most of H1's problems. However, we cannot fix every problem with H1. H1 has limited resources with which the microcode must work. For example, the main memory is limited to 4096 words, and all the opcodes are in use so we cannot add any more instructions (unless we use multiple-word instructions).

The optimal and stack instruction sets are about as good and they can be, given their general approach. We, of course, could try a completely new approach, and perhaps produce even better instruction sets. For example, using some two-word instructions, we might be able to further improve the optimal instruction set. Of course, two-word instructions incur a penalty: the CPU has to fetch two words instead of one, and instructions occupy more memory. However, the added power of a two-word instruction might easily compensate for this penalty.

Let's consider using a two-word format for the `mult` instruction in the optimal instruction set. Fig. 13.43a shows a program that multiplies 7 and 11 using the present form of the `mult` instruction which uses the stack-ac approach (the object code appears as comments). With a two-word `mult` instruction, we do not have to use the stack-ac approach. Instead, we can use its second word to hold the address of the second operand (see Figure 13.43b). Using the two-word `mult` instruction seems better: we do not need the initial `ld` and `push` instructions to prepare the stack for the multiply. Although the new `mult` instruction requires slightly more time (for two additional microinstructions to fetch its second word), the execution time for the entire program is substantially less (21 fewer microinstructions are executed); and even its size is less (by one word). You can try out these two programs yourself—they are both in the H1 software package (`fig1343a.mas` and `fig1343b.mas`).

Two-word instructions are also useful for combining instructions, thereby freeing opcodes. For example, we can combine `addc` and `subc` into a single two-word `addc` instruction, in which the second word contains the constant. With the 16-bit constant in the second word, we can represent values from -32768 to 65535. Thus, our two-word `addc` instruction can subtract (by adding negative constants) as well as add. Its range (-32768 to 65535) is also much greater than the range of the

FIGURE 13.43   a)

```
1                  !o
2                  ld    x      ; 0005
3                  push         ; F300
4                  ld    y      ; 0006
5                  mult         ; FF40
6                  halt         ; FFFF
7 x:               dw    7      ; 0007
8 y:               dw    11     ; 000B
```

b)

```
1                  !o2
2                  ld    x      ; 0004
3                  mult  y      ; FF40 0005   (two-word instruction)
4                  halt         ; FFFF
5 x:               dw    7      ; 0007
6 y:               dw    11     ; 000B
```

present `addc` and `subc` instructions (-255 to 255). An added benefit is that it frees up the opcode for `subc`.

For a more radical change to the optimal instruction set, we could make all opcode fields eight bits followed by an eight-bit operand field. For instructions with operands requiring more than eight bits, we could use a two-word format. We would then have 24 bits (eight from the first word and 16 from the second) for an operand.

The preceding proposals for improving the optimal instruction set certainly suggest that our optimal instruction set is hardly optimal. There are, in fact, better instruction sets for H1.

Microcode can almost always be improved; and with each improvement comes a better instruction set. To write microcode that is truly optimal, or close to it, is the challenge of microprogramming.

PROBLEMS

• •

13.1.   Implement the optimal instruction set less the difficult instructions (see Section 13.7). Test your microcode against `oslprog.mac`.

13.2.   Implement the stack instruction set less the difficult instructions (see Section 13.7). Test your microcode against `kslprog.mac`.

13.3.   Implement the optimal instruction set. Test your microcode against `osprog.mac`.

13.4.   Implement the stack instruction set. Test your microcode against `ksprog.mac`.

13.5.   Evaluate the relative speed of the six methods for multiplication corresponding to `mult_rec`, `mult_loop`, `mult_shift_add`, `mult_shift_add` (optimized), the mult instruction, and the m instruction. Use microinstruction counts as a measure of run-time. Compute 2×2, 127×127, and 128×128 in your test. Tabulate your results. What accounts for the difference in run-time between the various methods?

13.6.   Modify the program in Figure 13.10 so that 3000 and 4 are still multiplied but with 4 on the stack and 3000 in the `ac` register. Is the instruction count for the m instruction the same?

13.7. Does the shift-add multiplication algorithm work correctly when the two numbers to be multiplied are

- Both positive
- Both negative
- Multiplier positive, multiplicand negative
- Multiplier negative, multiplicand positive
- Both unsigned

Experiment with the following two cases:

a. Two 16-bit numbers are multiplied; the product fits into 16 bits.
b. Two 16-bit numbers are multiplied; the product requires more than 16 bits.

13.8. Would it be better if the reba instruction did only this:

```
bp = mem[bp];
```

13.9. Determine the microinstruction count for the instructions in the standard instruction set and also in the optimal instruction set. Is there any instruction in both that has different counts in the two instruction sets?

13.10. What is your "wish list" for H1? Specifically, what three instructions would you most like to see added to the optimal instruction set? Justify your choices.

13.11. Describe a shift-subtract algorithm to divide two positive integers.

13.12. Why is a function implemented in microcode on H1 faster than if it were implemented with machine language?

13.13. Would it be better if the cora instruction in the stack instruction set worked like this:

```
mem[sp] = (bp + mem[sp])12;
```

13.14. Implement a hardware stack containing up to 32 16-bit slots. Hint: Use 16 32-bit bidirectional shift registers.

13.15. Why does fast, inexpensive memory make a hardwired control section a more likely choice than a microprogrammed control section?

13.16. Without using call by name, implement the same function as in Figure 13.30. Hint: Pass to **n** a pointer to a function that computes the value of the argument.

13.17. Change the **set** member function in Figure 13.19 so that it checks for data integrity. Assume each field must be between 0 and 99. Modify the program in Figure 13.21 to reflect your changes.

13.18. Assuming **set**, **display_x**, and **display_y** are **virtual**, translate the program in Figure 13.26 to assembly language, assemble, and run on **sim**. Draw pictures of the data structures that **aptr** and **bptr** point to.

13.19. Add a class **c** to the program in Figure 13.26. The class **c** should contain a **set** function that sets **x** and **y** to 10 and 20, respectively. Add the following statements to **main**:

```
C c;              // C subclass of B
aptr = &c;
aptr -> set();
c.display_x();
c.display_y();
```

Assuming **set** (but not **display_x** or **display_y**) is **virtual**, translate to assembly language, assemble, and run on **sim**. Draw pictures of the data structures that **aptr** and **bptr** point to (see Figure 13.28).

13.20. Suppose an object's data area points directly to its virtual functions (instead of pointing to the virtual function table, which in turn points to the virtual functions). Compare this approach with the virtual table approach. What are the advantages and disadvantages of each approach?

13.21. C++ supports virtual member functions, but not virtual member variables. Is this a serious limitation?

13.22. How can 32-bit multiplication be performed using 16-bit multiplication. Can it be done with the `mult` instruction in the optimal instruction set?

13.23. Show the proper way to declare a three-dimensional array parameter.

13.24. Give a formula for determining the offset of `d[i][j]` from the beginning of `d`, where `d` is a two-dimensional array with R rows and C columns.

13.25. Give a formula for determining the offset of `d[i][j][k]` from the beginning of `d`, where `d` is a three-dimensional array whose dimensions are R, C, and D.

13.26. Suppose `z` is declared as follows:

```
int z[100][200];
```

If `z` were used as a value argument, show two ways to define its corresponding parameter.

13.27. Why might you want to change the ldr instruction to use an eight-bit opcode and the stack-ac approach?

13.28. Translate the program in Figure 12.15 to the stack instruction set. Run on **sim**. Compare its size and microinstruction count with its optimal instruction set version.

13.29. Translate the program in Figure 13.30 to the stack instruction set. Run on **sim**. Compare its size and microinstruction count with its optimal instruction set version.

13.30. An alternative to having a thunk pass the address of the argument is to have two thunks for each argument, one returning the value of the argument and the other returning the address of the value of the argument. The called function would call whichever thunk was appropriate. Using this approach, translate to assembly language, link, and run the program in Figure 13.34.

13.31. Implement the following JVM-like instruction set in microcode. Each instruction consists of a *one-word* opcode followed in some cases by a *one-word* operand.

```
Mnemonic  Operand      Description

icm1                   mem[--sp] = -1
ic0                    mem[--sp] = 0;
ic1                    mem[--sp] = 1;
ic2                    mem[--sp] = 2;
push       w           mem[--sp] = w;
ild0                   mem[--sp] = mem[bp + 0];
ild1                   mem[--sp] = mem[bp + 1];
ild2                   mem[--sp] = mem[bp + 2];
ild        w           mem[--sp] = mem[bp + w];
ist0                   mem[bp + 0] = mem[sp++];
ist1                   mem[bp + 1] = mem[sp++];
ist2                   mem[bp + 2] = mem[sp++];
ist        w           mem[bp + w] = mem[sp++];
call       w           mem[--sp] = pc; pc = w;
aspc       w           sp = sp + w;
iadd                   like add in the stack instruction set
isub                   like sub in the stack instruction set
imul                   like mult in the stack instruction set
idiv                   like div in the stack instruction set
ret                    like ret in the stack instruction set
esba                   like esba in the stack instruction set
reba                   like reba in the stack instruction set
```

Using this instruction set, translate and run on `sim`:

```
void f(int x) {
    int a,b,c,d;
    a = -1;
    b = 1;
    c = 2;
    d = 3;
    a = b + x;
    b = x - 1;
    c = c * 5;
    d = d / 2;
    cout << a << end;
    cout << b << end;
    cout << c << end;
    cout << d << end;
}
int main()
{
    f();
    return 0;
}
```

13.32. What serious problem results if we replace the `mult` instruction in the optimal instruction set with the two-word instruction described in Section 13.8?

13.33. How would you make the optimal instruction set better using two-word instructions? Be sure to avoid making it worse (see Problem 13.32). Implement your instruction set, and prepare a test program (like `oprog.mas`) and a ".txt" file (like o.txt). Note: to specify a two-word instruction to `mas` and `sim`, place 2 on its corresponding line in part 1 of the configuration file to the right of the number of operands (see the `mult` instruction in `o2.cfg`).

    a. For the following problems, translate the given program to assembly language using the optimal instruction set. Include all assembly directives that would normally appear in compiler-generated assembly code, and use mangled function names. Assemble, link with start-up code, and run on `sim`.

    b. Same as a, but use the stack instruction set.

13.34.
```
include <iostream>
using namespace std;
int main (int argc, char *argv[])
{
    int i = 0;
    while (argc--)
        cout << argv[i++] << endl;
    return 0;
}
```

13.35.
```
include <iostream>
 using namespace std;
void f()
{
    int x;
    x = 1;
```

```
        int y;
        y = 2;
        cout << x << " " << y << endl;
    }
    int main()
    {
        f();
        return 0;
    }
```

13.36.
```
    include <iostream>
    using namespace std;
    int a;
    class  C {
        public:
            void f(int a, int &b);
            int x;
            int y;
    };
    void C::f(int a, int &b)
    {
        x = a;
        y = a;
        b = x + y;;
    }
    int main()
    {
        C c;
        c.f(10, a);
        cout << a << endl;
        c.f(20, a);
        cout << a << endl;
        c.x = 30;
        cout << c.x << endl;
        return 0;
    }
```

13.37.
```
    include <iostream>
    using namespace std;
    class A {
        public:
            virtual void f();
    };
    void A::f()
    {
        cout << "f in A\n";
    }
    class B: public A {
    };
    class C: public B {
        public:
            void f();
    };
    void C::f() {
```

```
            cout << "f in C\n";
        }
        int main()
        {
            A* ap;
            B b;
            C c;

            ap = &b;
            ap -> f();
            ap = &c;
            ap -> f();
            return 0;
        }
```

13.38.
```
        include <iostream>
        using namespace std;
        class A {
            public:
                int x;
        };
        class B: public A {
            public:
                int x;
        };
        int main()
        {
            A* ap;
            B b;
            b.A::x = 1;    // access A-level x
            b.x = 2;       // access B-level x

            ap = &b;
            ap -> x = 3;
            cout << b.A::x << endl;
            cout << b.x << endl;
            return 0;
        }
```

13.39.
```
        include <iostream>
        using namespace std;
        int table[2][3];
        int (*p)[3];
        int main()
        {
            p = table + 1;
            table[0][1] = 3;
            table[1][2] = 4;
            cout << table[0][1] << endl;
            cout << table[1][2] << endl;
            cout << p[0][2] << endl;
            cout << (*p)[2] << endl;
            return 0;
        }
```

13.40.
```
include <iostream>
using namespace std;
int table[5][5][5];
int i = 1, j = 2, k = 3;
int main()
{
    table[0][1][2] = 2;
    table[i][j][k] = 3;
    cout << table[0][1][2] << endl;
    cout << table[i][j][k] << endl;
    return 0;
}
```

13.41.
```
include <iostream>
using namespace std;
int a = 100;
void f(int #x)
{
    x = x + 5;
}
int main()
{
    cout << "a = " << a << endl;
    f(a);
    cout << "a = " << a << endl;
    return 0;
}
```

13.42.
```
include <iostream>
using namespace std;
int a = 100;
void f(int #x)
{
    a = x + 5;
}
void g(int z)
{
    int y = 1;
    f(y + 20);
    cout << "a = " << a << endl;
    cout << "y = " << y << endl;
    f(z + 20);
    cout << "a = " << a << endl;
    cout << "y = " << y << endl;
}
int main()
{
    g(7);
    return 0;
}
```

13.43.
```
include <iostream>
using namespace std;
```

```
        int a = 5, b = 6;
        void f(int #x, int &r)
        {
            a = x;
            r = 25;
            b = x;
        }
        int main()
        {
            int y = 10;
            f(y, y);
            cout << "a = " << a << endl;
            cout << "b = " << b << endl;
            cout << "y = " << y << endl;
            return 0;
        }
```

13.44.
```
        include <iostream>
        using namespace std;
        int table[3][3];
        void f(int a[][3])
        {
            int i = 2, j = 2;
            a[1][1] = 11;
            a[i][j] = 22; }
        int main()
        {
            f(table);
            cout << table[1][1] << endl;
            cout << table[2][2] << endl;
            return 0;
        }
```

13.45.
```
        include <iostream>
        using namespace std;
        void f(int n)
        {
            if (n > 0) {
                cout << n << endl;
                f(n - 1);
                cout << "goodbye\n";
            }
            else
                cout << "hello\n";
        }
        int main()
        {
            f(3);
            return 0;
        }
```

Chapter Fourteen

MEMORY SYSTEMS

14.1   INTRODUCTION

• •

We can view a computer system as a collection of resources that form a functional computing device. Some of the resources that make up a computer system are the CPU, main memory, I/O devices, interconnecting buses, programs, and data files. For a computer to do as much work as possible, it must use its resources—particularly, the CPU and main memory—efficiently.

In Chapter 2, we learned that the CPU cannot do anything unless it can obtain machine instructions from main memory. If at any time the CPU cannot obtain the instructions it needs, it cannot do useful work. Because of this dependency of the CPU on main memory, main memory is a critical factor in the performance of any computer system. Ideally, we want a main memory system that can provide the CPU with machine instructions at all times, allowing the CPU to keep busy 100 percent of the time.

In this chapter, we will learn how to structure a computer so that memory use is more efficient. We will examine several memory systems of varying degrees of complexity, starting with the simple (and inefficient) memory system in H1. We will then look at a slightly more complicated system that uses a *relocation register* (a register that simplifies program relocation). Next, we will examine *simple paging* (which divides a program into fixed length blocks called pages), *demand paging* (which is a generalization of the simple paging technique), and *segmentation with paging* (which divides a program into segments that are, in turn, divided into pages). We will also learn how to make main memory faster using *cache memory* (a small, fast memory used in conjunction with main memory).

One of the concepts that we have encountered throughout this book is that of the address. In Chapter 3, we learned that the assembly process determines the addresses of labels, and inserts these addresses into machine instructions. In Chapter 7, we learned that some types of addresses (addresses of globals and static locals) can be determined at assembly time, but others (addresses of stack items) cannot. Each type of address requires a particular type of machine instruction: direct for globals and static locals, and relative for stack items. In Chapter 10, we learned that addresses have to be relocated (i.e., adjusted) when a program is loaded into a nonzero location, and that the linking mechanism is almost exclusively involved in the manipulation of addresses. It is no surprise, then, that addresses are central to this chapter as well. To understand various main memory systems, we need to understand addresses—when they are determined, how they are generated, how they propagate, and how they map to specific locations in main memory.

14.2   PROPAGATION OF ADDRESSES

• •

Let's examine the program in Figure 14.1 with respect to the addresses it contains and manipulates. The `ldc` instruction at location 0 loads the **ac** register with the address of **x**. The `st` instruction that follows it then stores this address in **y**. Thus, after the execution of the `st` instruction, both the **ac** register and **y** hold the address of **x**. The remainder of the program accesses and displays what the **ac** register and **y** are pointing to (which is **x**). Thus, the program outputs "5", the value of **x**, twice.

Assuming the executable version of the program in Figure 14.1 is in the file `fig1401.mac`, we can run it with

sim fig1401

in which case it is loaded into memory starting at location 0. Alternatively, we can run it with

sim /p400 fig1401

in which case it is loaded into memory starting at location 400 hex. In either case, the program outputs "5" twice; however, in the latter case, the operating system (i.e., **sim**) has to relocate all the addresses in the program to accommodate the nonzero load point before the program can be executed. For this example, it has to add 400 hex (the load point) to each address in the machine code text. In Chapter 10, we learned that the information that **sim** needs to relocate addresses is provided by the header in the `fig1401.mac` file. Figure 14.2 shows the formatted display of this header. The header contains three R entries, one for each address that has to be relocated. The address field in each R entry contains the location in the machine code text of an address that has to be relocated. Thus, these R entries

FIGURE 14.1

```
          LOC       OBJ    SOURCE
          hex*dec

          0   *0    800C           ldc   x       ; ac now contains an address
          1   *1    100D           st    y       ; y now contains an address
          2   *2    F100           ldi           ; get what ac is pointing to
          3   *3    FFFD           dout          ; display it
          4   *4    800A           ldc   '\n'
          5   *5    FFFB           aout
          6   *6    000D           ld    y       ; get address in y
          7   *7    F100           ldi           ; get what y is pointing to
          8   *8    FFFD           dout          ; display it
          9   *9    800A           ldc   '\n'
          A   *10   FFFB           aout
          B   *11   FFFF           halt
          C   *12   0005   x:      dw    5
          D   *13   000A   y:      dw    0
          E   *14   ================== end of program ======================
```

FIGURE 14.2

Type	Address	Symbol
R	0000	
R	0001	
R	0006	
T		

tell us that our program has addresses at locations 0, 1, and 6 that have to be relocated for nonzero load points. By examining the source program in Figure 14.1, we can see that we do, indeed, have addresses (of **x**, **y**, and **y**, respectively) at these locations.

Now let's perform a mental experiment. Suppose we load the program in Figure 14.1 into location 0 and then start executing it. Suppose after the first two instructions execute, we stop the program, relocate it to location 400 hex, and restart its execution from this new location. Would the program work correctly? It would if we relocate all its addresses to reflect its new load point. Is this relocation easy to do? You might think that it is, as long as the header information is still available. The header specifies the locations of the addresses that have to be relocated. So we simply relocate each of these addresses to accommodate the new load point. Unfortunately, our analysis neglects one important fact: Once a program starts executing, addresses can propagate to new locations. If we relocate only the addresses specified by the header, we will not relocate (as we must) any of the propagated addresses. For example, after the first two instructions in the program in Figure 14.1 execute, addresses propagate to both the **ac** register and **y**. If we move the program at this point to a new location, we must relocate the addresses in the **ac** register and **y**, in addition to the locations specified by the header.

By tracing through the program in Figure 14.1, we can track the propagation of addresses so that if we want to relocate the program in mid-execution, we can do so correctly (by relocating all its addresses—both original and propagated). However, an operating system certainly cannot do this. It would have to understand and monitor the execution of every instruction in a program. Thus, we come to the following conclusion: *For a computer system like H1, a program cannot be moved in memory once it starts executing.*

14.3 MULTIPROGRAMMING

A natural question to ask about the preceding section is why would anyone want to move a program in mid-execution? For a system like H1, in which only one program at a time is in memory, there is no reason to move a program once it is loaded. We call systems with one program in memory at a time *uniprogramming systems*. However, for *multiprogramming systems*—systems in which more than one program can be in memory at a time—*dynamic program relocation* (i.e., moving programs at mid-execution) can be useful, as we shall now see.

Figure 14.3 shows main memory in a typical multiprogramming system. The operating system resides in low main memory. Above it are several user programs. If a computer system has only one CPU, only one program can execute at a time. However, if the program that is currently executing enters a *wait state*

FIGURE 14.3   Main Memory

Operating System
Program 1
Program 2
Program 3
Program 4

(i.e., it stops executing because it has to wait for something), the operating system can give control to one of the other user programs. As long as at least one of the user programs is ready to run, the operating system can keep the CPU doing useful work. In contrast, in a uniprogramming system, whenever the user program waits, the CPU ceases doing useful work.

14.4   DIRECT MEMORY ACCESS

A program usually enters a wait state when it issues an I/O request. For example, suppose an input request in a program is followed immediately by instructions that use the data to be input (this pattern is typically the case). Then, obviously, after issuing the I/O request, a program must wait until the input is available before it can continue executing. Thus, it has to enter a wait state.

When a program waits for I/O in a multiprogramming system, the operating system gives control to another program in memory. Thus, while an I/O operation for one program occurs, the CPU executes another. We call this concurrent activity *CPU-I/O overlap*.

I/O operations require a controlling processor. If the CPU performs this function, then CPU-I/O overlap—an essential capability of a multiprogramming system—is not possible. The CPU cannot at the same time both control I/O for one program and execute another program. To allow CPU-I/O overlap, I/O subsystems on computers typically include a *direct memory access (DMA)* controller to handle I/O transfers. When a program enters a wait state because of an I/O request, the DMA controller can perform the requested I/O operation. At the same time, the CPU can execute another program in memory.

During CPU-I/O overlap, both the CPU and the DMA controller share main memory. Because the CPU is the principle user of main memory, the use of main memory by the DMA controller is called *cycle stealing* (it "steals" memory access cycles from the CPU).

14.5   TIMESHARING

A *timesharing system* is a type of multiprogramming system in which each user program is under the control of the user at a terminal. The operating system gives control to each user program that is ready, one after another, but only for a few

FIGURE 14.4

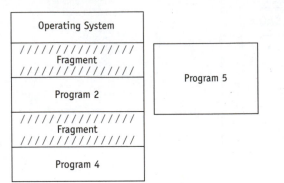

FIGURE 14.5

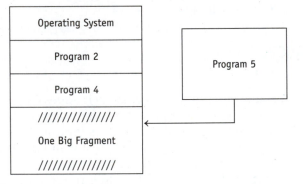

milliseconds at a time. Thus, each user program gets a small period of time (called a *timeslice*) at regular intervals in which it can run. The operating system distributes timeslices in some equitable way, such as round-robin, so that all programs can advance in their execution.

Now let's consider what happens to memory in a multiprogramming system in which four programs are currently in main memory (see Figure 14.3). Suppose programs 1 and 3 terminate, leaving two *fragments* (i.e., available blocks) in main memory. If we now want to load program 5, whose size is bigger than either fragment, we cannot do it. It will not fit (see Figure 14.4), even though the total amount of available memory is large enough for program 5. However, if the operating system first compacts memory by moving programs 2 and 4 down (i.e., to low main memory), it creates one big fragment in high main memory consisting of all the available space. This big fragment can now accommodate a big program, such as program 5 (see Figure 14.5). By performing this compaction, the operating system is moving programs 2 and 4 *in mid-execution.*

Having as many programs in memory as possible is important in a multiprogramming system. With many programs in memory, we increase the likelihood that at any given time at least one is ready to run, allowing the CPU to perform useful work. By allowing more programs in memory, moving programs in mid-execution has the potential to permit greater utilization of the CPU.

FIGURE 14.6

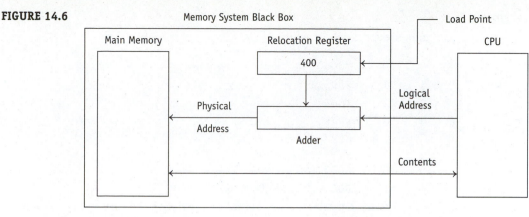

14.6   RELOCATION REGISTER

• •

In Section 14.2, we concluded that a program cannot be relocated in memory once it starts execution. How, then, can memory compaction (which moves programs in mid-execution) be performed in a multiprogramming system? We can easily do it if we add a *relocation register* to our memory system (see Figure 14.6). In a simple memory system, the address from the CPU goes directly to main memory. With the incorporation of a relocation register, however, the address from the CPU (the *logical address*) goes, instead, to an adder where the contents of the relocation register are added to it. The resulting address (the *physical address*) then goes to main memory. Main memory responds by returning the memory contents at the physical address. We call this type of address adjustment *dynamic address translation* because it occurs while the program is running ("dynamic" here means at run time).

Suppose the relocation register contains 400. Then every address the CPU sends to main memory has 400 added to it. Thus, the address 0 maps to cell number 400, 1 maps to cell number 401, and so on. The action of the relocation register is to change *how addresses map to cells in main memory*. This mapping depends on the contents of the relocation register. For example, if we load the relocation register with 100, then address 0 would map to cell number 100 rather than 400.

When the operating system loads a user program into main memory that uses a relocation register, it also loads the relocation register with the load point of the program. For example, if it loads the user program into main memory starting at cell number 400, it also loads 400 into the relocation register. By loading the load point into the relocation register, the operating system makes the address 0 map to the load point. Thus, from the program's point of view, it has been loaded into address 0, and, therefore, requires *no adjustment of its addresses*.

With the addition of a relocation register, moving a program in mid-execution is simple: The operating system simply moves the user program to a new location and loads the relocation register with the new load point, making the new load point correspond to address 0. Thus, from the program's point of view, it has not moved at all—it is still at address 0.

Let's look at a simple example of a relocation register in action. Suppose the operating system initially loads the program in Figure 14.7 into main memory starting at cell number 0. Then it would also load the relocation register with 0.

FIGURE 14.7

```
           LOC        OBJ           SOURCE
           hex*dec

           0    *0    0004          ld   x
           1    *1    2005          add  y
           2    *2    1006          st   z
           3    *3    FFFF          halt

           4    *4    0002   x      dw   2
           5    *5    0003   y:     dw   3
           6    *6    0000   z:     dw   0
           7    *7    ==================== end of fig1407.mas ==================
```

When the ld instruction is executed, the logical address 4 (the address in the ld instruction) is sent to the memory system. The adder there adds 0 to it, yielding 4 as the physical address, which then goes to main memory. Main memory responds with the contents of location 4 (where **x** currently resides). Suppose the operating system now moves the program to cell number 100 and loads the relocation register with 100. Then when the add instruction is executed, 5 (the address in the add instruction) is sent to the memory system, where it is translated to the physical address 105. Main memory responds with 3, the contents of cell number 105 (where **y** currently resides). If the operating system now moves the program to cell number 200 and loads the relocation register with 200, 6 (the address in the st instruction) maps to cell number 206. Thus, the **ac** register is stored in cell number 206 (where **z** currently resides). From the program's point of view, its starting address is fixed at 0 during its entire execution. Thus, the addresses in its instructions (004 in the ld, 005 in the add, and 006 in the st instruction) should not be relocated, regardless of the program's load point.

When the program in Figure 14.7 executes, it appears to occupy addresses 0 to 6, regardless of its load point. If its load point is 200, the program actually occupies the memory cells 200 to 206. We have two sets of addresses here: one set from the program's point of view (0 to 6), and another from the main memory's point of view (200 to 206). The former is called the *logical address space* of the program; the latter is called the *physical address space*.

Let's now consider a completely different explanation of the action of a relocation register. We can view the addresses that an executing program generates as *offsets* from the beginning of the program. For example, we can view the 004 in the ld instruction in Figure 14.7 as the offset of **x** from the beginning of the program rather than the absolute address of **x**. To get the absolute address of **x**, we must add its offset and the load point of the program. This conversion is precisely what the relocation register mechanism does: It converts offsets that an executing program generates to the absolute addresses that main memory requires. Moreover, because offsets are relative to the beginning of a program, *they do not depend on its load point*. Thus, regardless of the load point, a program is loaded *as is* into memory. If the program is subsequently moved, it is moved *as is* to the new load point. As long as the relocation register contains the current load point, the offsets from the program are converted to the correct absolute addresses.

A relocation register permits the mid-execution relocation of programs. Thus, a system with a relocation register can easily perform memory compaction, thereby solving the memory fragmentation problem. Unfortunately, compaction involves a considerable amount of overhead. During compaction, the CPU must execute instructions that move user programs to new locations in memory. While the CPU is doing this, it cannot execute user programs. Because programs can be large, moving programs can be a time-consuming process. The result is that the advantage of compaction (allowing more programs to fit into memory so that the CPU can keep busy) is largely offset by the overhead it requires.

In the next section we will consider *paging*, another system for solving the memory fragmentation problem. Paging systems do not move programs around in memory, and, therefore, are potentially superior to systems that use compaction.

14.7 VIRTUAL MEMORY

Virtual memory is a memory management system that gives a computer the appearance of having more main memory than it really has (hence the name "virtual," which means not real). Virtual memory has two important advantages:

1. Main memory is used more efficiently. In particular, only those portions of an executing program that are in use occupy main memory. For example, a 20-megabyte word processing program with only 128 kilobytes in use would occupy only 128 kilobytes of main memory.
2. Programs that are bigger than main memory can still be executed.

At one point, some computer architects thought that computers would eventually have so much main memory that virtual memory would be unnecessary. Main memory sizes have, indeed, dramatically increased, but so has the size of programs. Thus, main memory continues to be a critical resource that has to be used efficiently.

Virtual memory is implemented in one of three ways: demand paging, segmentation, or, most commonly, a combination of segmentation and paging.

We start our study of virtual memory with the examination of simple paging. Simple paging does not provide virtual memory; however, as you shall see, it can easily be extended to support virtual memory.

14.7.1 Simple Paging

In a *simple paging system*, we view user programs as consisting of fixed length blocks called *pages*. For example, the user program in Figure 14.8 consists of four pages, numbered 0 to 3 (we number pages starting from 0). Each page has the same length, typically a power of 2, such as $2^{10} = 1024 = 1K$, $2^{11} = 2048 = 2K$, or $2^{12} = 4096 = 4K$. The lines separating consecutive pages in Figure 14.8 are imaginary. Within the program there is no marker of any sort dividing one page from the next.

Suppose our computer uses 16-bit addresses. Then each address can be represented with four hex digits. Further suppose that the page size for the program in Figure 14.8 is 4K. Then the addresses of page 0 run from 0000 to 0FFF hex (0 to 4095 decimal). Figure 14.9 summarizes the address range for each page. Notice in Figure 14.9 that the leftmost hex digit always equals the page number of the page at that address. For example, the address 1FFF whose leftmost hex digit is 1 is in page 1. The three rightmost hex digits in an address specify the displacement into

FIGURE 14.8   User Program

```
                    ┌──────────────┐ 0
                    │              │
                    │   Page 0     │
                    │              │
                    │              │ 0FFF
                    ├──────────────┤ 1000
                    │              │
                    │   Page 1     │
                    │              │
                    │              │ 1FFF
                    ├──────────────┤ 2000
                    │              │
                    │   Page 2     │
                    │              │
                    │              │ 2FFF
                    ├──────────────┤ 3000
                    │              │
                    │   Page 3     │
                    │              │
                    │              │ 3FFF
                    └──────────────┘
```

FIGURE 14.9   Page   Address Range (hex)

```
    0            0000 to 0FFF

    1            1000 to 1FFF

    2            2000 to 2FFF

    3            3000 to 3FFF
```

FIGURE 14.10

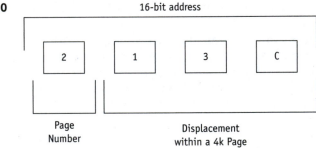

16-bit address

Page Number   Displacement within a 4k Page

the page. For example, the address 213C in a byte-addressable memory system is 13C bytes into page 2. In a paging system, we always view addresses as consisting of two components: the page number and the displacement into that page (see Figure 14.10).

The displacement component of an address has to be big enough to hold any displacement within a page. Thus, for a 2^{12}-byte (4K) page size, the displacement field has to hold displacements up to $2^{12} - 1$ (displacements start from 0, so the maximum displacement is one less that 2^{12}). Because the number $2^{12} - 1$ in binary consists of 12 1-bits, a 2^{12} page size requires a 12-bit (3 hex digit) displacement field. Generalizing, we get that a page size of 2^n requires an n-bit displacement field.

The page-number component of an address contains all the bits in the address to the left of the displacement component. For example, in a 32-bit address with a 12-bit displacement field, the leftmost 20 bits make up the page number field.

FIGURE 14.11

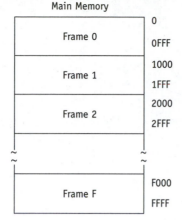

Main Memory

Frame 0	0 ... 0FFF
Frame 1	1000 ... 1FFF
Frame 2	2000 ... 2FFF
Frame F	F000 ... FFFF

FIGURE 14.12

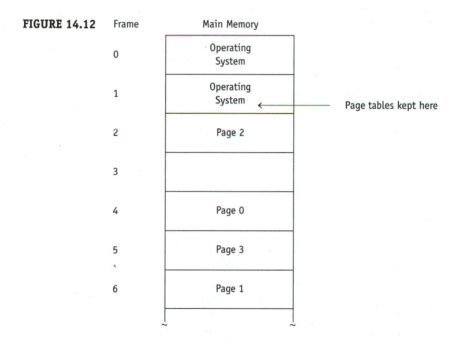

Frame   Main Memory

Frame	Main Memory
0	Operating System
1	Operating System
2	Page 2
3	
4	Page 0
5	Page 3
6	Page 1

Page tables kept here

In a paging system, we view main memory as consisting of fixed-length blocks. However, to distinguish them from the fixed-length pages that make up programs, we call the blocks of main memory *frames* (see Figure 14.11).

In a paging system, when an operating system loads a user program into memory, it loads each page into *any* available frame. The pages do not have to appear in consecutive frames, nor do they have to appear in their normal order. Thus, page 2 can be loaded below or above page 1. For example, the operating system might load pages 0, 1, 2, and 3 of the program in Figure 14.8 into frames 4, 6, 2, and 5, respectively (see Figure 14.12). Typically, the operating system resides in the frames in low main memory, so these frames are not available for user programs. To keep the diagram in Figure 14.12 simple, we have shown the operating system as occupying only two frames. In reality, operating systems are large programs that would occupy many frames in low main memory.

FIGURE 14.13   Page Table

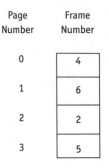

Page Number	Frame Number
0	4
1	6
2	2
3	5

FIGURE 14.14   Memory System Black Box

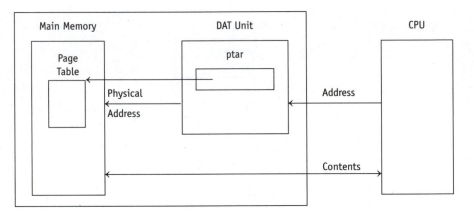

As in systems with a relocation register, a paging operating system does *not* relocate the addresses in the user program when loading the program into main memory.

Because pages and frames are the same size, any page can go into any available frame. Thus, the memory fragmentation problem that can occur with nonpaging systems can never occur in a paging system.

As the operating system loads pages of a user program into memory, it keeps track of the location of each page by building a page table for that program. A *page table* is a one-dimensional array in main memory (in the operating system's area) that contains a slot for every page in the corresponding user program. Thus, for a user program that contains four pages, the operating system would build a page table containing four slots. Suppose the operating system loads frame 4 with page 0. Then it would record this by placing 4 into slot 0 of the page table. In a page table, each index represents a page number, and the corresponding slot contains the frame number for that page. For example, the page table in Figure 14.13 shows that pages 0, 1, 2, and 3 are in frames 4, 6, 2, and 5, respectively.

When a program executes in a paging system, the addresses the CPU sends to main memory first go to a *dynamic address translation unit (DAT unit)* where they are translated to physical addresses. To do this translation, the DAT unit accesses frame numbers from the page table for the program currently executing (see Figure 14.14).

FIGURE 14.15

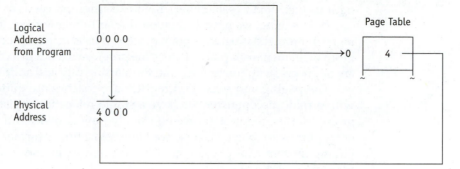

Use left hex digit as index into page table

Logical Address from Program   0 0 0 0

Physical Address   4 0 0 0

Page Table

0   4

FIGURE 14.16

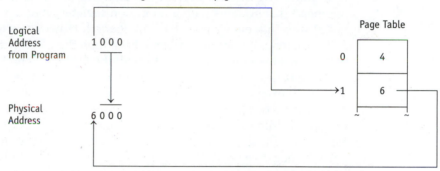

Use left hex digit as index into page table

Logical Address from Program   1 0 0 0

Physical Address   6 0 0 0

Page Table

0   4

1   6

Let's examine how the translation works. Suppose the program corresponding to the page table in Figure 14.13 is about to execute. Before it passes control to the program, the operating system loads the `ptar` *(page table address register)* in the DAT unit with the address of the page table of the program that is about to execute. Assume the program's start address is 0000. To pass control to the program, the operating system loads the address 0000 into the `pc` register, causing the CPU to fetch the instruction at this address. In the fetch process, the CPU sends the address 0000 to the memory system. The DAT unit takes the left hex digit of this address (the page number) and uses it as an index into the page table pointed to by the `ptar`, obtaining 4 (the frame for page 0). It then substitutes 4 (the frame number) for the left hex digit (the page number) in the address to get the physical address 4000 (see Figure 14.15). 4000 is the physical address of page 0 in main memory. The DAT unit then sends this physical address to main memory, which responds by returning the instruction at the beginning of page 0.

Let's jump ahead in the execution of our program to the point at which the last instruction in page 0 is about to execute. Assume that this instruction is 2 bytes in length and starts at 0FFE. Thus, the `pc` at this point contains the address 0FFE. In the fetch process, the CPU sends 0FFE to the memory system, where it is translated to the physical address 4FFE. The `pc` register is incremented by the instruction length (to 1000) and the fetched instruction is executed. When the CPU repeats its fetch-increment-execute cycle, it uses the address 1000 (the address now in the `pc` register). This time, however, the DAT unit accesses the page table using the index 1 (the left hex digit of the address), and receives frame number 6, the number of the frame holding page 1 (see Figure 14.16). Thus, the physical address is

6000 (the address of page 1 in main memory). Although pages 0 and 1 are not contiguous (i.e., next to each other), their execution proceeds as if they were.

With paging, we have a situation similar to that with systems using a relocation register: From the program's point of view, it resides in memory starting at address 0. From main memory's point of view, the program resides in a collection of frames that are not necessarily contiguous, and the starting physical address is not necessarily 0.

The paging and relocation register approaches are quite similar. In a system with a relocation register, we have a single relocation register for the whole program. In a paging system, we effectively have a relocation register (a page table entry) for every page. Because we have relocation information for each page in a paging system, the placement of each page in memory is independent of the placement of the other pages.

Simple paging nicely eliminates the memory fragmentation problem in a multiprogramming system. Moreover, paging systems do not have the compaction overhead that systems with a relocation register have. Specifically, programs are not moved in memory once they are loaded. However, paging systems do suffer from a potentially serious problem. Each time the CPU fetches an item from memory, *two* read operations are performed: the first to obtain the frame number from the page table (which is located in main memory), and the second to obtain the desired item from main memory at the computed physical address. The CPU can execute instructions no faster than it can get them from main memory. Thus, by increasing the access time for main memory (by requiring two reads), paging forces the CPU to execute instructions at a slower rate. If this problem were unfixable, the negative impact of paging on execution time would be worse than its positive effect on memory fragmentation. However, we will see in the next section that by carefully designing the DAT unit, we can eliminate virtually all of the slowdown associated with the address translation mechanism in a paging system.

14.7.2   Associative Memory

The obvious solution to the problem with paging—two reads performed every time the CPU fetches an item from memory—is to keep a copy of the page table in a local memory area within the DAT unit (see Figure 14.17). Then each time the

FIGURE 14.17

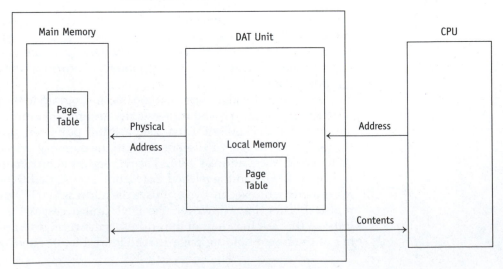

Memory System Black Box

FIGURE 14.18

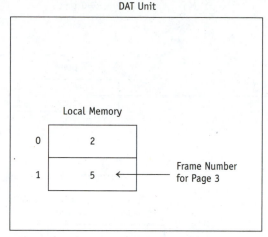

DAT Unit

Local Memory

0 | 2

1 | 5 ← Frame Number for Page 3

DAT unit translates an address from that program, it can get the frame number it needs very quickly from its local memory. If this local memory is very fast, the translation of addresses can also be very fast. Because the local memory within the DAT unit can hold information from only one page table at a time, the operating system still must maintain a page table in main memory for every user program currently in the system. Whenever the executing program goes into a wait state or terminates, the page table for the next program to execute is loaded into the DAT unit's local memory.

Because the local memory within the DAT unit has to be very fast, it is very expensive. A super-fast local memory that is large enough to hold the largest possible page would be too expensive. Because of cost considerations, the local memory within a DAT unit typically has only a few slots. Then it can be made fast and yet still be inexpensive because of its small size. But what happens when the page table is too big to fit into local memory? Let's consider a simple example. Suppose the four-page program corresponding to the page table in Figure 14.13 is currently executing, and local memory in the DAT unit has only two slots. Although the whole page table cannot fit, local memory can hold the page table entries for those pages that are active at any given time, assuming no more than two pages are ever active at any time. For example, if only pages 2 and 3 are active, we can keep their frame numbers (2 and 5) in local memory (see Figure 14.18). The absence of the other two entries from local memory has no negative impact, as long as their corresponding pages remain inactive.

There is, however, a serious problem with Figure 14.18. The index into local memory is now *not* the page number, as it is for the full page table. For example, at index 1, we have the frame number for page 3. How, then, does the DAT unit know which page corresponds to each entry? It cannot, unless we store in every slot of local memory *both* the page number and its corresponding frame number. Figure 14.19 gives a correct picture of local memory. Each slot contains a page number and its corresponding frame number. In addition, each slot has a *valid bit* (a single bit) that, if equal to 1, indicates that its slot is valid (i.e., contains a valid page and frame number).

Let's examine how the DAT unit translates a logical address using the local memory in Figure 14.19. It takes the left hex digit from the logical address (this is the page number) and inputs it to the local memory. Local memory then searches for a slot that contains this page number. When it finds it, it outputs the frame

FIGURE 14.19

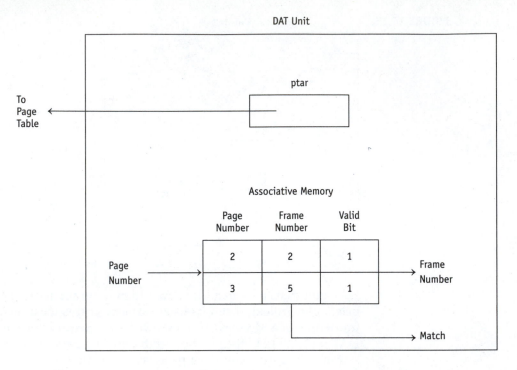

DAT Unit

number in that slot, and sets the *match output* to 1 to indicate a successful search. For example, for Figure 14.19, if the DAT unit inputs 3, it gets back 5; if it inputs 2, it gets back 2. For both of these cases it would also set the match output to 1. If, however, the DAT unit inputs 0, then the match output is set to 0, indicating an unsuccessful search for page number 0.

The memory in Figure 14.19 is very unusual in two respects. First, unlike most memory units (which input an *address* and output the *contents* at that address), the memory in Figure 14.19 inputs the *contents* of a subfield of one of its slots. It then outputs the *contents* of another subfield of the same slot. Thus, we can describe the memory in Figure 14.19 as *contents-in/contents-out* memory. In contrast, regular memory is *address-in/contents-out* memory. A common name for the memory in Figure 14.19 is *content-addressable*. This name makes sense because we "address" a slot by the contents of a subfield of that slot. Another common name—the one that we use in this book—is *associative* memory. This name also makes sense because a subfield of a slot is addressed by the data in a subfield with which it is "associated." To distinguish the associative memory in the DAT unit from associative memory that may be used elsewhere in a computer system, we call the associative memory in the DAT unit the *translation lookaside buffer (TLB)*.

The second respect in which the associative memory in Figure 14.19 is unusual is that it searches *in parallel* every slot for the input page number. For example, if we input 3, it searches the first slot for 3 and, *at the same time*, it searches the second slot for 3. If a serial search were used here, it would take too long. Remember, address translation has to be virtually instantaneous.

When an operating system loads a program into memory, it sets all the valid bits in the TLB to 0 (a machine instruction does this). It also loads the `ptar` with the address of the page table for the program that is about to execute. To translate the first address, the DAT unit supplies the page number in the address to the

TLB. The TLB responds with a 0 on the match output (because all entries are not valid initially). Thus, the DAT unit, for this address, has to access the page table in main memory pointed to by the `ptar`. After it obtains the frame number from the page table, it enters this frame number and the page number into the TLB and sets the valid bit for that entry to 1. Thus, subsequent address translations for the same page use the data in the TLB. Similarly, if, during the execution of a program, a page becomes active that was previously inactive, its page and frame number will not be in the TLB. Thus, on the first address translation for such a page, the match output will be 0. The unsuccessful search forces the DAT unit to get the frame number from the page table pointed to by the `ptar`. It then enters the page and frame numbers into the TLB, overlaying an entry for a page that hopefully has become inactive. Thus, only the first access of a page whose frame number is not in the TLB requires the DAT unit to access the page table in memory. As long as there are enough slots in the TLB to hold the page information for all the active pages at a given time, the system works quite well. Typical sizes for the TLB run from 32 to 1024 slots.

The dynamic address translation that the DAT unit performs is a *hardware* function. The operating system (which is software) does perform some necessary initialization (creating the page table in memory, setting the valid bits in the TLB to 0, and loading the `ptar`); however, once program execution starts, the address translation mechanism (searching the TLB, accessing the page table in memory on an unsuccessful search, updating the TLB, and constructing the physical address) is all hardware. If any of these functions were performed by software, address translation would take too long.

14.7.3 Interrupts

Although H1 is not a real computer, it has most of the features found in real computers. However, one important feature found in virtually all computers that is *not* in H1 is an interrupt mechanism. The memory system that we are to examine next (demand paging) uses interrupts. So before we get to demand paging, we should first study interrupts.

Suppose a user program is executing and we want to stop it, execute some other code, and then later on, restart it from where it was stopped. What would we have to save in order to restart it from the point at which it was stopped? Of course, we would have to save the address of the instruction to be executed next (i.e., the contents of the `pc` register). In fact, we would need to save all the user-level registers, the `flags` register that holds status bits like the overflow and carry flags, and those system-level registers that contain information specifically for the executing program. Without this information, we could not re-establish the state of the computer as it was when the program was stopped.

Let's call the information that is needed to restart a program the *execution state* of the program. The interrupt mechanism performs four actions:

1. It saves the most critical parts of the execution state (typically the contents of the `pc` and `flags` registers).
2. It changes the CPU mode from *user mode* to *supervisor mode*. Whenever a user program runs, the CPU has to be in the user mode; whenever the operating system runs, the CPU has to be in the supervisor mode. (We will learn more about these two modes in Section 14.7.7.)
3. It causes a jump to an *interrupt handler* (a machine code routine usually in the operating system).

4. The interrupt handler immediately saves the rest of the execution state, and then proceeds to "handle" the interrupt; that is, it performs the task that is appropriate for the type of interrupt that occurred.

The first three actions—saving the most critical state information, switching modes, and jumping to the interrupt handler—are hardware mechanisms. The fourth—the interrupt handler—is software.

After the interrupt handler finishes whatever it has to do, there are several possible actions it can take:

- It can restart the interrupted program by restoring the execution state, including the CPU mode in effect at the time the interrupt.
- It can terminate the interrupted program. This action is taken when the interrupt occurs because the program performed some illegal action.
- It can give control to some other program by re-establishing the execution state of that program. Such a switch from one program to another involves saving the execution state of the former and re-establishing the execution state of the latter. We call this change of state a *context switch* ("context" here means execution state).
- It can put the computer in a *wait state* (an idle state in which instructions are not executed) if no program is ready to run.

Figure 14.20 shows how memory can be structured to handle interrupts. *Interrupt vectors* (special locations in low main memory) contain the addresses of the interrupt handlers. These vectors are initialized when the computer is booted. Each type of interrupt has its own vector, which points to the interrupt handler for that

FIGURE 14.20

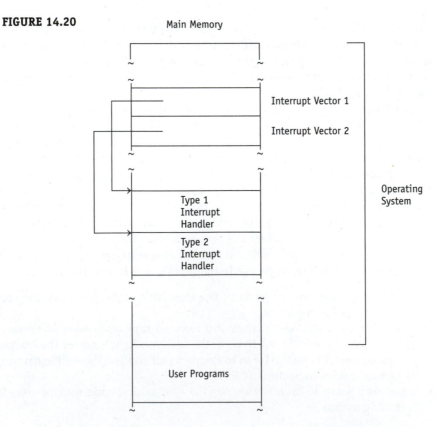

Main Memory

Interrupt Vector 1

Interrupt Vector 2

Type 1
Interrupt
Handler

Type 2
Interrupt
Handler

Operating
System

User Programs

type of interrupt. When an interrupt occurs, the CPU automatically saves the `pc` and, perhaps, some other registers, on the stack in memory, and then jumps to the location to which its corresponding interrupt vector points. The first thing the interrupt handler does is to save whatever state information the hardware interrupt mechanism itself did not save. For example, if the hardware interrupt mechanism saves only the contents of the `pc` and **flags** registers, then the interrupt handler would save the contents of the other registers.

One type of interrupt that can occur is a timer interrupt. In a timesharing system, the operating system sets a timer before it gives control to a user program. The timer functions like an alarm clock. When the timer goes off (signaling the end of the timeslice for the current program), it causes an interrupt. The timer interrupt handler then gets control, saves the state of the current program, resets the timer, and gives control to the next ready program. If this next program was previously interrupted, the interrupt handler gives it control simply by restoring the state information that the interrupt handler saved at the time the program was last interrupted.

Another type of interrupt occurs when a program performs an illegal operation. For example, suppose a program in a multiprogramming system tries to store data on top of another program in memory. The hardware will detect this illegal memory reference and generate a program-error interrupt. In this case, the interrupt handler terminates the offending program.

Interrupts can occur at any time. Whenever they occur, state information is stored on the stack. Thus, once an item is popped from the stack, its residual copy in memory can be overlaid at any time with state information from an interrupt, even if the executing program does not overlay it. For example, suppose the following sequence of instructions is executed in a multiprogramming system:

```
ldc   5
push
pop
aloc 1
```

This sequence pushes and then pops 5, after which the 5 is still on the stack below the point to which the **sp** register is pointing (see Figure 14.21a).

FIGURE 14.21   a)

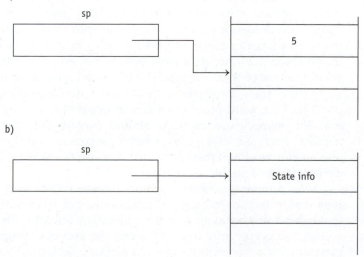

The `aloc` instruction then decrements the **sp** register so that it points again to the 5. Are we guaranteed that the **sp** register is pointing to 5? No, because, if an interrupt occurs between the `pop` and `aloc` instructions, state information overlays the 5 on the stack. Then when the program is restarted and the `aloc` instruction is executed, the 5 is no longer there (see Figure 14.21b).

The **sp** register should never be in a corrupted state when an interrupt occurs. If it were, the interrupt mechanism would save state information at the location specified by the corrupted **sp** register, possibly overlaying critical data and/or instructions. Recall that the `swap-st-swap` sequence that we used in Chapters 7 and 8 to determine the address of stack items corrupts the **sp** register for a short period of time. If H1 had interrupts, we would have to either avoid this sequence, or, alternatively, *disable* interrupts (i.e., prevent them from occurring) during its execution.

When one module of a user program wants to pass control to another of its modules, it executes a call, return, or jump instruction. However, to pass control to the operating system, these instructions are never used. Instead, the interrupt mechanism is used.

Some interrupts are forced on a user program. For example, a timer interrupt at the end of a program's timeslice forces control back to the operating system. Other interrupts, however, are *requested* by the user program. For example, if a user program wants the operating system to perform a service, it requests an interrupt by executing an instruction whose function is to trigger an interrupt. The interrupt passes control to the operating system, which performs the service and then returns to the user program. We call these interrupt-triggering instructions *programmed-interrupt instructions* (because they are programmed into the executable code), *supervisor call instructions* (because they call the "supervisor"), or *trap instructions* (because they "trap" the executing program and force it to go to the operating system).

14.7.4 Demand Paging

Now that we understand interrupts, let's examine a generalization of the simple paging system that we studied in Section 14.7.1.

Although simple paging solves the memory fragmentation problem, a memory system using it is still very inefficient. When a program executes, generally only a small portion of its code is executing at any given time. For example, when we use a word processor to simply enter data into a file, we do not use that portion of the word processor that performs spell-checking. A sophisticated word processor might contain 20 megabytes of code, but at any given time it may need only a small fraction of that. Suppose, for example, it needs at most 1 megabyte at any given time. Then 19 megabytes of memory—the memory used to hold the unused portion of the word processor—is memory that is serving no useful purpose. For efficient memory use, memory should contain only the code that is currently needed. Then our 20-megabyte word processor would never occupy more than one megabyte of real memory. This "loading on demand" is the concept that underlies demand paging.

Most programs generate memory references that tend to cluster in small localities within the program. We call this behavior the *locality of reference*. Programs that exhibit this behavior can run with only a subset of its pages in memory—the subset that is currently in use. We call this subset of pages the *working set* of the program. As a program executes, its working set typically changes, and, therefore,

FIGURE 14.22

Page Number	Frame Number	Valid Bit
0	0	0
1	0	0
2	2	1
3	5	1

the pages that have to be in memory also change. Keeping the working set in memory as a program executes is the job of a demand paging system.

Demand paging works like regular paging with a few additional twists. In demand paging, each page table entry contains two parts: the frame number and a valid bit. The valid bit indicates if the corresponding page is in memory. For example, the page table in Figure 14.22 shows that pages 2 and 3 are in frames 2 and 5, respectively. Pages 0 are 1 are not in memory (we know this because their valid bits are 0 in the page table).

When the operating system in a demand paging system is about to give control to a program for the first time, it allocates a page table in memory, but it neither loads the program nor loads the page table with frame numbers. Instead, it sets all the valid bits in both the page table and the TLB to 0 (it executes machine instructions to do this), and it loads the **ptar** with the address of the page table. It then gives control to the program by loading the **pc** register with the program's start address. When the DAT unit translates this start address, its search of the TLB fails, of course, because the TLB is initially empty. When the search fails, the DAT unit then attempts to access a frame number from the page table pointed to by the **ptar**, using the page number in the start address as an index. For example, suppose the start address is 0000 and its left hex digit is the page number. Thus, the DAT unit would use 0, its left hex digit (the page number), as an index into the page table. But because the valid bit for this page table entry is 0 initially (indicating the page is not in memory), this access fails. We call this situation—a page is needed that is not in memory—a *page fault*. Whenever a page fault occurs, the DAT unit generates a *page-fault interrupt*, causing the page fault interrupt handler in the operating system to get control. This interrupt handler loads into memory the page that is needed from an I/O device, enters its frame number into its page table and sets its valid bit to 1, and then restarts the program that caused the interrupt. This time, the DAT unit finds a valid page entry in the page table, so it can complete the address translation and update the TLB with the page and frame number. Thus, subsequent accesses of this page now proceed with no delay.

The reading in of a page during a page-fault interrupt is called a *page-in* operation. The I/O device that is used to hold the pages of an executing program in a demand paging system is called the *paging device*.

A page fault requires the intervention of the operating system to load the needed page into memory and update the page table accordingly. This process is time-consuming because it involves the execution of an interrupt handler containing many machine instructions. Thus, in a demand paging system, we want to keep page faults to a minimum. Some page faults are necessary, and cannot be avoided; however, sometimes an excessive number of page faults occur, causing the system to spend most of its time performing paging operations instead of executing user programs. When this happens, we say the system is *thrashing*.

14.7.5 Page Replacement Policies for Demand Paging

When the operating system performs a page-in operation, it has to select a frame in which to load the page. If all the frames are occupied, it has to overlay a page in some frame with a new page. If the page to be overlaid has changed since it was paged in, its current state obviously must be saved. This is accomplished by writing it out to the paging device before the new page is paged in. We call this operation a *page-out* operation. The operating systems can determine if a page-out operation is necessary by examining the *dirty bit* attached to the frame holding the page to be replaced. The operating system sets this bit to 0 when a page is first paged in. The dirty bit is then automatically set to 1 by the hardware whenever the page is subsequently written to. Thus, if the dirty bit for a page to be replaced is 1, it must be paged out before a new page can overlay it.

When the operating system selects a page for replacement, it attempts to select one that will not be needed again in the near future, or even better, not at all. One possible page replacement policy is *first-in-first-out (FIFO)*. With FIFO, the oldest page in memory is selected for replacement. The oldest page, however, is often one that is still in use, making it a bad choice for replacement. For example, many programs have a controlling routine that calls the various subroutines of the program. The controlling routine is needed during the execution of the entire program. The page containing the controlling routine is often the oldest (it typically executes first), and, therefore, would be selected for replacement by the FIFO policy.

FIFO is a policy that is easy to implement. It does not require special hardware support. Because page-in operations are performed by the operating system, the operating system can easily keep track of the time-in-memory order of the pages in memory. When a page must be replaced, the operating system simply uses the time-in-memory information it maintains to identify the oldest page. Because this order changes relatively infrequently (only on a page-in operation), maintaining the time-in-memory order of pages involves a minimal amount of overhead.

The ideal page-replacement policy would select a page whose next reference is the least imminent. With stock funds, past performance is no guarantee of future gains. However, because most programs exhibit the locality-of-reference behavior, past activity of a program is, in fact, a good predictor of future activity. An active page will probably continue to be active, and an inactive page will probably continue to be inactive. Of course, an active page might suddenly become inactive, and vice versa, but these shifts occur relatively infrequently. These observations suggest that a *least recently used (LRU)* policy—a policy that selects the page that has gone unused for the longest period of time—should work well. LRU requires that software and/or hardware keep track of the time-of-last-use order of the pages in memory. Because this order can change very frequently (it can change each time an instruction is executed), keeping track of it has to be essentially a hardware function. Consider what would occur if it were done purely in software: On *every* memory reference, a software routine would have to get control to update the page order. Clearly, a purely software approach would involve an exorbitant amount of overhead.

To minimize the hardware costs associated with LRU, computer designers typically implement a policy that only approximates true LRU. An LRU approximation does not necessarily select the least recently used page. However, it does select one that has not been used recently. We call LRU approximations *not used recently* (NUR) policies. One approach for implementing an NUR policy is to attach a reference bit to each frame in main memory (in addition to the dirty bit). Reference bits are automatically set to 1 whenever their corresponding frames are referenced. By periodically setting all the reference bits to 0 and then later examining them, the operating system can identify which pages have not been used recently.

Demand paging can dramatically increase the capabilities of a computer system. Suppose memory in a system without demand paging is big enough to hold five complete programs. With demand paging, the same memory could hold, perhaps, as many as 50 programs because only a fraction of every program is in memory at any given time.

Demand paging also allows a program that is too big to fit into memory to execute. For example, suppose a program contains 20 megabytes but memory has only 4 megabytes. Without demand paging we could not load and run the program. But with demand paging, the 20 megabyte program can run because only its active portion needs to be in memory at any given time. With demand paging, we can run a program of any size, up to the addressing capabilities of the computer. For example, if a computer uses 32-bit addresses, we could run programs whose size is as large as 2^{32} bytes.

14.7.6 Page Size Considerations

Which is better in a demand paging system, a small page size or a large page size? Let's examine the advantages and disadvantages of both sizes.

The length of a user program is usually not an exact multiple of the page size. Thus, the last page for most programs is partially unused. The last page, however, always occupies a complete frame when loaded into memory. Thus, its unused portion occupies, and thereby wastes, main memory. We call this waste *internal page fragmentation* because it is "internal" to a page.

The unused portion of the last page of a program is, on the average, one half of a page. Thus, the smaller the page size, the less memory is wasted due to internal page fragmentation. Our conclusion: A small page size is better.

Suppose a program consists of two pages. If we reduce page size by a factor of 8, the same program would consist of 9 to 16 pages (only 9 pages are needed if our two-page program occupies only a small portion of its second page). As page size decreases, the size and, therefore, memory requirements of page tables increase. Our conclusion: A large page size is better.

Suppose a program executes from top to bottom and then terminates. Assume that with large pages, the program consists of 2 pages, and with small pages, the program consists of 16 pages. Then, in the large page case, only 2 page faults occur; in the small page case, 16 page faults occur. Our conclusion: A large page size is better.

Suppose a four-page program is executing that contains a loop covering pages 0 and 2 (see Figure 14.23a) that iterates 100,000 times. If memory contains only two frames, then only two page faults (to load pages 0 and 2) occur during the execution of the loop. If, instead, we use pages double in size and the same amount of memory (see Figure 14.23b), only one page can fit into memory at a time. Thus, each iteration of the loop generates two page faults (to load page 0, and then to load page 1, overlaying page 0), for a total of 200,000 page faults (compared with only 2 for the small page size)! Our conclusion: A small page size is better.

FIGURE 14.23 a)

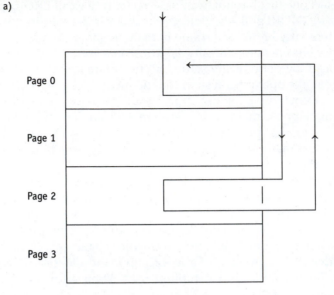

Page 0

Page 1

Page 2

Page 3

b)

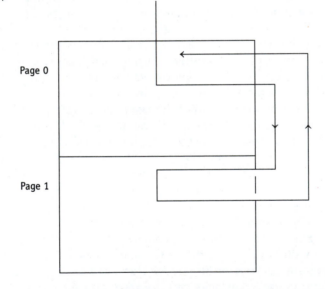

Page 0

Page 1

We have just seen some scenarios in which large pages are better, and other scenarios in which small pages are better. Because of the conflicting results, it is impossible to conclude from our analysis what is the optimal page size. This uncertainty is often the case when analyzing computer systems. Most proposed new designs have pros and cons. Thus, it is often hard to predict how well a new design will work.

Sometimes an analysis clearly implies a new design is great (or terrible), and when the new design is implemented and tested, the analysis turns out to be completely wrong. Computer systems are difficult to analyze accurately because they are complex, interactive systems. Most analyses, on the other hand, are based on simple models (like the execution patterns in Figure 14.23), which may yield different results than the actual system.

Computer scientists debated the virtues of various page sizes for several years. The final consensus, which is based principally on tests performed on actual systems, is that large page sizes are better.

14.7.7 Supervisor/User Modes

To ensure the integrity of a multiprogramming computer system, a user program must not be allowed to execute certain instructions. For example, a user program should not be allowed to execute machine instructions that perform I/O. Otherwise, it could read from or write to any location on any I/O device. One user could then access and/or corrupt the data of another user. Thus, in a multiprogramming system, the operating system—not the user program—must perform all I/O. If a user program needs I/O, it simply passes a request to the operating system. The set timer instruction is another example of an instruction whose use is restricted to the operating system. If a user program could set the timer in a time-sharing system, it could "hog" the CPU by setting the timer to a large value, thereby increasing its timeslice. In general, a computer system must prevent user programs from doing anything that could adversely affect either the operating system or another user program. We call machine instructions that a user program is not allowed to execute *privileged instructions*.

Privileged instructions are implemented by means of two CPU running modes: a *supervisor mode* and a *user mode*. When in supervisor mode, the CPU can execute any instruction. However, when in user mode, the CPU cannot execute any privileged instruction. Any attempt to do so results in an immediate program-error interrupt and the termination of the offending program. For this two-mode approach to work correctly, the CPU obviously must be in supervisor mode whenever the operating system is running, and in user mode whenever a user program is running. Thus, whenever control passes from the operating system to a user program, or vice versa, a mode change must also occur.

It is easy for the operating system to effect a mode change when passing control to a user program. It simply executes an instruction that changes mode. However, this instruction cannot be used for the reverse direction because it is a privileged instruction (i.e., it can be executed only when the CPU is already in the supervisor mode). If it were not privileged, a user program could execute it to put the CPU in supervisor mode, and then do anything it wanted. Thus, to change to the supervisor mode, the interrupt mechanism is used. An interrupt changes mode, but it also necessarily passes control back to the operating system. Thus, it is impossible for a user program to use an interrupt to change to supervisor mode, and, at the same time, retain control of the CPU.

The necessity of changing to supervisor mode when control returns to the operating system is the reason why the call, return, and jump instructions cannot be used. These instructions transfer control but do not change mode.

14.7.8 Memory Protection

User programs obviously have to be able to load from and store to memory. Thus, load and store instructions cannot be privileged. What, then, keeps a user program from accessing memory belonging to the operating system or another user?

FIGURE 14.24

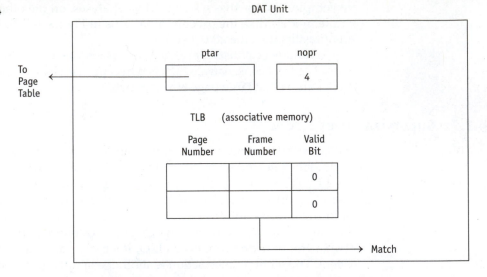

Clearly, a computer system must have a *memory protection mechanism*—a mechanism to enforce proper use of memory.

With paging it is easy to provide a memory protection mechanism. The DAT unit simply monitors the page numbers in the addresses it translates. If a page number is out of bounds, the DAT unit generates a program-error interrupt, resulting in the termination of the program. For example, suppose a user program has only four pages. Then the only valid page numbers are 0, 1, 2, and 3. If the program generates an address with some other page number, then the DAT unit generates a program-error interrupt.

To detect out-of-bounds addresses, the DAT unit must know how many pages are in a program. An easy way to provide this information is to incorporate a *number-of-pages register* (`nopr`) within the DAT unit to hold the number of pages in the current program. Before passing control to a program, the operating system loads the `nopr` with the number of pages in the program, in addition to loading the `ptar` and setting the valid bits in the TLB to 0. With the `nopr` within the DAT unit, the DAT unit has immediately available the information it needs for address checking (see Figure 14.24).

Without paging, memory protection is more difficult to implement. Here is a typical approach. When the operating systems loads a user program into memory, it assigns it a unique number called a *tag*. It also assigns the same tag to every block of memory that belongs to the program. When the program runs, the memory hardware checks every memory reference it makes. If the tag of the memory block that the program references does not match the tag of the executing program (which means the program is referencing memory that is not its own), the memory hardware generates a program-error interrupt, resulting in the termination of the program.

14.7.9 Segmentation with Paging

Because a stack grows downward, it makes sense to put a stack in high memory and the program code and data in low main memory. That way, the space into which the stack can grow is maximized. In a demand paging system, we can put the stack at the top of its logical address space. For example, a system with 32-bit addresses has a 4-gigabyte address space. We can put our stack at the top of this address space and our program code and data at the bottom. Although this configuration makes the total size of the program enormous (4 gigabytes), it still can be executed on a demand paging system. The unused gap between the program code and data on the bottom and the stack at the top would never be paged in, and therefore would never occupy real memory. But we do have one major problem with this configuration: It requires a page table that is too big. For example, for a page size of 4K, the page table would have $2^{32}/2^{12} = 2^{20}$ entries.

To solve the problem of page tables that are excessively large because they map unused gaps in the logical address space, we can divide our program into functional segments. For example, we might divide our program into a code segment, a data segment, and a stack segment, each having its own page table. Each page table would be sufficiently large to map only its corresponding segment. The unused gap in the address space would not be represented by any page table. Thus, the combined size of all the page tables would be minimized. We call this approach of dividing a program into separate segments, each of which is separately paged, *segmentation with paging*.

In addition to minimizing page table size, segmentation with paging has other advantages:

- It allows the specification of a *privilege level* (the level of memory protection) and an *access mode* (i.e., permissible accesses, such as read/write, read-only, execute, etc.) for each segment that is tailored to that segment. For example, the code segment of the operating system could be marked as privilege level 0 (most protected) and "execute only." We cannot easily do this in a pure paging system because pages do not correspond to logical units of a program. A single page, for example, could contain both program code and data.
- Because each segment has, in effect, its own virtual memory, it simplifies the mechanics of dynamically increasing or decreasing the size of a segment.
- Because segments are logical units of a program, sharing of segments among users is simplified. For example, multiple users executing a C++ compiler can share its code segment. Each user, however, would have its own data and stack segments.

14.8   CACHE MEMORY

Suppose you have a desk on which you can keep 10 books, and a bookcase in your basement that can hold an additional 1000 books. It would make sense to keep the 10 books that you are currently using on your desk. Then you would not have to go to the basement every time you wanted to use one of these books. If you ever needed a book that was in the basement, you could switch a book from your desk (ideally, one that you were no longer using) with the new book you need from the basement. You would then have the new book immediately available on your desk. With this approach you have the storage capacity for a total of 1010 books, but most of the time when you need a book, it would be immediately available from among the 10 books on your desk. Thus, the *desk/bookcase* technique provides both *large capacity and quick access*.

We have already seen this technique used in several places in a computer system:

- For efficient code, an assembler language programmer or a compiler keeps the most active variables (such as a running sum or a loop count) in a register, allowing quick access.
- The TLB holds the page and frame numbers of only the active pages. For inactive pages, frame numbers are kept in the page table in main memory.
- In a demand paging system, only the active pages are in memory, where they can be quickly accessed by the CPU. Inactive pages reside on an I/O device from which they can be paged in if needed.

Cache memory is one more area in which the desk/bookcase technique is used. Cache memory is very fast memory that holds the most active items from main memory. When the CPU needs something from main memory, most of the time it can obtain it from the cache rather than the slower main memory. The effect of cache memory is to greatly reduce the average time for a memory access. Because modern CPUs are so fast, a main memory without a cache is usually not fast enough for the CPU, and, therefore, would create a major bottleneck in the execution of instructions.

Modern CPUs are designed with small, built-in cache memories. Because the built-in cache is small, most modern computers supplement it with a larger external cache memory. The typical personal computer has 512K of external cache memory. Internal and external caches are often referred to as *L1* (i.e., level 1) and *L2* (i.e., level 2) caches, respectively.

Cache memory is expensive on a per-byte basis because it has to be fast. However, the total amount needed to significantly improve memory performance is small, and, therefore, its total cost is small. The improved performance of a computer system with cache memory is usually well worth the additional cost of the cache.

14.8.1 Replacement Policies for Cache Memory

When the CPU requests data from a cached memory system, it is provided from the cache if it is there. Otherwise, it is provided from the slower main memory. We call the former case a *hit*; the latter, a *miss*. The *hit ratio*—hits divided by the sum of hits and misses—is a measure of cache performance. A well-designed cache can have a hit ratio close to 1.

Cache is organized into fixed-length blocks called *lines*. On a miss, the block of main memory containing the fetched item and its neighbors is loaded into a line of the cache. Because most programs exhibit the property of locality of reference, there is a high likelihood that there will be more fetches from this block. Thus, loading this block into cache increases the chances that subsequent fetches will be from cache rather than main memory.

Cache systems do not necessarily allow new blocks to be placed anywhere in cache. In fact, some systems do not allow any choice. For example, with direct mapping (see Section 14.8.3), the line to which a block is mapped is completely determined by the block's address.

Those systems that allow at least some choice with respect to the placement of new blocks in cache must implement a policy to determine that choice. A policy that works well, but can be difficult to implement, is least recently used (LRU). *Random* is the policy in which the cache line for replacement is selected at random. This policy works almost as well as LRU, but is easier to implement. First-in-first-out (FIFO) is the policy in which the oldest entry is selected for replacement. Like random, it is easy to implement; however, because the oldest entry is often an active entry, FIFO generally does not perform as well as random or LRU.

14.8.2 Write Policies

When the CPU requests a write to a memory block that is also in cache, we say that a *write hit* has occurred. A write hit provides two possible policies for updating the cache and main memory. With the *write-through policy*, both the cache line and the memory block are updated. With the *write-back policy*, however, only the cache is immediately updated. Memory is updated later, when a new block is to be loaded into the cache line. At that time, the entire cache line is written to memory before the new block is loaded. With the write-back policy, a *dirty bit* is maintained for each cache line. This bit is set whenever a write to the cache line occurs. Thus, the dirty bit indicates whether the contents of the cache line match the corresponding block in memory. When a cache line is loaded with a new block, its contents are first written to memory if its dirty bit is set.

When the CPU requests a write to a memory block that is *not* also in cache, we say that a *write miss* has occurred. As with a write hit, there are two possible policies for updating the cache and main memory. With *write-no-allocate*, only a write to main memory occurs. With *write-allocate*, main memory is first updated, and then a cache line is "allocated" (i.e., selected) into which the updated memory block is loaded.

Both the write-through and write-back policies run into problems on systems in which main memory is shared by multiple processors, each with its own cache. Suppose, for example, a write by one processor updates only its own cache. Then subsequent reads by other processors might access out-of-date data from their own individual caches. One solution to this problem is to cache only nonsharable memory. This approach, unfortunately, partially defeats the purpose of caching. Another solution, albeit complex in its implementation, is to update all caches on any write operation.

14.8.3 Memory-to-Cache Mapping Schemes

To keep our examples simple, let's devise caching schemes for a word-addressable main memory with only 4096 words (like the memory in H1). For caching purposes, let's divide memory into 256 16-word blocks (see Figure 14.25a). Our cache will consist of 16 lines, each containing 16 words. Although these sizes are not typical, they are adequate for illustrating various caching mechanisms. Notice in Figure 14.25a that the first two hex digits of each address are equal to the block number for that address. The third digit is the displacement within the block. For example, the address 104 corresponds to the word in block 10 whose displacement is 4 (see Figure 14.25b).

In a cache system that uses *associative mapping*, any block of memory can be loaded into any line of cache. When a block is loaded into cache, both the data in the block and the block number are loaded. The data goes into a line of the cache; the block number goes into the *tag* attached to that line. For example, Figure 14.26 shows the cache with block 2 in line 0. Because the block number subfield of a 12-bit address goes into the tag attached to a cache line, this subfield itself is often called a *tag*.

In addition to the tag, attached to each cache line is a valid bit. The *valid bit* indicates whether the line contains valid data. When a computer is first started, all the valid bits are set to 0 (indicating that the cache is empty). They are also set to 0 on a context switch in a virtual memory system.

FIGURE 14.25 a)

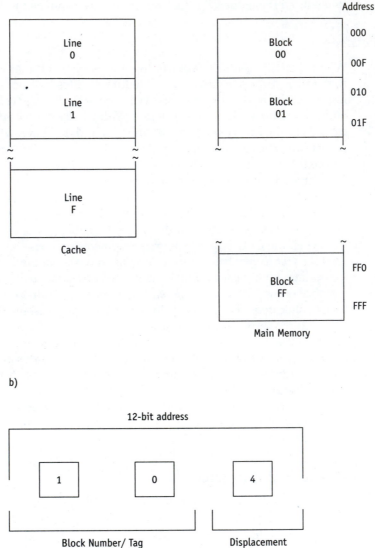

Cache

Main Memory

b)

12-bit address

Block Number/ Tag

Displacement
within 16-Word Block

On a read operation, the cache system obtains the block number from the first two hex digits of the address, and then searches the tags for this number. Because speed is critical, all the tags have to be searched in parallel. This requirement means that the cache has to be implemented with associative memory. Because of the high cost of associative memory, associative mapping is practical for only small cache memories.

With associative mapping, the random replacement policy probably provides the best cost/performance trade-off. It can be implemented cheaply, but performs almost as well as LRU.

With *direct mapping*, the cache line to which a memory block is mapped is fixed. We have 256 memory blocks and 16 cache lines, so 16 blocks will map to each cache line. Which blocks should map to which lines? One possible approach—a bad one—is to map the first 16 blocks to line 0, the next 16 to line 1, and so on. However,

FIGURE 14.26   Associative Mapping

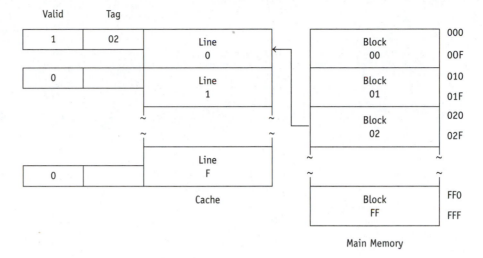

because of locality of reference, this approach makes it likely that the active blocks will have to contend for the same line of cache. For example, suppose the first 16 blocks contain a loop. Ideally, all 16 blocks of the loop should be in the cache. But if they all map to line 0, only one block at a time can be in the cache. Thus, as the loop executes, misses would continually occur, each causing a block to overlay the previous block in the cache. A better approach is to map successive memory blocks to successive cache lines. Each group of 16 successive blocks would map to cache lines 0 to F. With this approach, a 16-block loop would cause misses on only the first pass, after which the entire loop would be in cache. Subsequent passes would then be executed from the cache without any misses.

Let's consider which blocks map to line 0 when we map successive blocks to successive lines of cache. Block 00 to block 0F map to lines 0 to F. Thus, block 10 (the next block) has to map to line 0. Every sixteenth block—blocks 00, 10, 20, . . . , F0—maps to line 0. Similarly, blocks 01, 11, 21, . . . , F1 map to line 1. Notice that the right hex digit of the block number indicates the line to which it maps. The left hex digit, the *tag*, distinguishes among the 16 possible blocks that can map to the indicated line. With direct mapping, we can view a 12-bit address as consisting of three parts: a tag, a line number (the two digits that make up the block number), and a displacement (see Figure 14.27a). For example, the address 104 hex consists of a tag, line number, and displacement equal to 1, 0, and 4, respectively.

With direct mapping, the cache line to which a block maps is specified by the middle digit of the block's address. The left digit is loaded into the tag attached to that cache line. For example, Figure 14.27 shows the cache loaded with the block that corresponds to the address 104 hex. The middle digit of this address, 0, specifies the line to which the block maps. The left digit, 1, is the value that distinguishes this block from the other blocks that map to line 0. It is stored in the tag attached to line 0.

With direct mapping, it is easy for the cache system to access an item in the cache, given the item's memory address. The middle digit of the address specifies the cache line number. Thus, the cache system can go directly to this line. We do not need the associative search that we need with associative mapping. The cache system can then compare the tag field in the address with the tag on the specified cache line. A match indicates that the item is in that cache line at a displacement given by the right digit of its address.

FIGURE 14.27

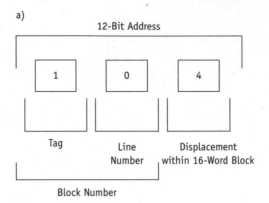

Direct Mapping

a)

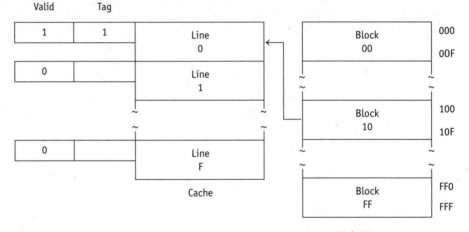

b)

Although associative mapping is more flexible than direct mapping, it requires an expensive associative memory. It also has to support a replacement algorithm that dynamically selects lines for replacement. A compromise approach—one that is more flexible than direct mapping but less complex than associative mapping—is *set-associative mapping*. This mapping maps memory blocks to cache lines in exactly the same way that direct mapping does. However, with set-associative mapping, each cache line consists of a set of storage areas, each of which can hold one memory block. Thus, multiple blocks that map to the same cache line can coexist in cache. For example, in Figure 14.28, both blocks 00 and 10 are in cache line 0. Because each line contains two blocks in this example, we call it a *two-way set-associative cache*. Set-associative caches are typically two- or four-way.

With a set-associative cache, to determine if an item is in the cache, given the item's address, the cache system goes to the cache line specified by the item's address (the middle digit in our example). It then searches the tags on that line for a match with the tag field in the address (the left digit in our example). As with associative mapping, the search of the tags has to be performed in parallel. However,

FIGURE 14.28   Set-Associative Mapping

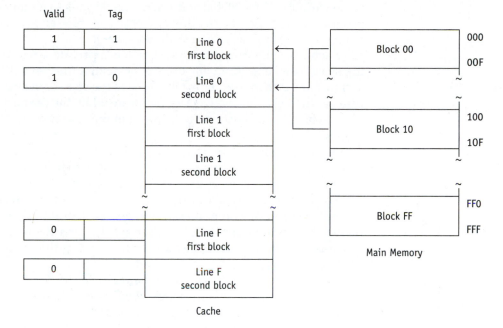

Cache

because so few tags are involved (only two in Figure 14.28), the cost to implement this search is not excessive.

LRU, in general, is an expensive replacement policy to implement. However, because the size of each set in set-associative mapping is small (typically two or four), the cost of LRU is not prohibitive with this mapping. For example, with two-way set-associative mapping, LRU can be implemented with only a single extra bit in each cache line. This extra bit would indicate which block was less recently used.

14.9   SHARABLE PROGRAMS

• •

In a timesharing system, multiple user programs can be in memory at the same time. The operating system gives control to each program in some systematic fashion, giving each program a short timeslice in which to execute.

Suppose several users in a timesharing system are executing a compiler program, each compiling a different C++ program. Each user, of course, could have a separate copy of the C++ compiler in memory. An alternative approach is to have a single copy of the compiler that is simultaneously shared by all the users performing a compilation.

The technical term to describe a sharable program is *reentrant*. The term *reentrant* denotes the capability of a sharable program to be reentered by additional users before the current user is finished with the program. Thus, a reentrant program can be executed *concurrently* (i.e., in parallel) by multiple users.

A program must be designed in a specific way to make it reentrant. In particular, it cannot share memory to which it writes among multiple users. For example, suppose a program writes to a global or static local variable. Then whatever one user stores in the variable would be corrupted by the next user who writes to the same variable. Thus, global and static local variables cannot be used in a reentrant program unless they are read-only. Local variables and parameters, on the other hand, are permissible, as you shall now see.

Each user in a timesharing system has a private stack. Whenever the operating system switches from one user to the next, it first saves the current user's execution state. It then restores the machine to the state of the next user. Specifically, it restores the registers and flags as they were when the next user was last executing. Thus, when the next user gets control from the operating system, the stack register points to that user's private stack area. Because dynamic local variables and parameters for each user are located in that user's private stack area, these items are distinct for each user. Thus, what one user does to its dynamic local variables and parameters does not affect the corresponding variables for the other users.

Dynamic memory allocation is also permissible in a reentrant program. For example, a reentrant program can use the **new** operator. Whenever memory is dynamically allocated to a user, that user gets the private use of that memory. Thus, each user's use of dynamic memory will not affect the dynamic memory belonging to other users.

In Chapters 7 and 8, our use of **@spsave** in the swap-st-swap sequence that computes the address of a stack item would not be permissible in a reentrant program. **@spsave** maps to a single memory slot, and, therefore, would be used by multiple users. A use of **@spsave** by one user would be corrupted by the next user if the switch to the next user occurred while **@spsave** was in use by the first user. Thus, the cora instruction introduced in Chapter 12, which makes **@spsave** unnecessary, is important for two reasons: It not only permits a more efficient computation of the address of stack item, but also allows programs to perform this computation without violating the requirements for reentrancy.

In a timesharing or multiprogramming environment, we can have multiple users each executing a different program. However, we can also have multiple users concurrently executing a single reentrant program. In the latter case, there are *multiple* executing entities for *one* program, each having its own stack and execution state. It is also possible for a single user executing a program to spawn multiple executing entities that concurrently execute that program. We call these executing entities *processes*, *tasks*, or *threads*.

PROBLEMS

· ·

14.1. Write a simple assembly language program that contains a field that is initially relocatable, but becomes nonrelocatable during execution.

14.2. Determine the number of page faults using LRU for the following sequence of page references:

```
0, 1, 0, 2, 0, 3, 0, 4, 0, 5, 0, 6, 0, 7, 0
```

Assume only two frames are available. Determine the number for FIFO as well.

14.3. Same as Problem 14.2, but for

```
0, 1, 2, 3, 4, 5, 6, 0, 1, 2, 3, 4, 5, 6, 0
```

14.4. Same as Problem 14.2, but use MRU (most recently used).

14.5. Same as Problem 14.3, but use MRU (most recently used).

14.6. Give an example of a sequence of page references in which LRU outperforms FIFO. Give another example in which FIFO outperforms LRU.

14.7. Suppose main memory and cache memory have access times of 100 and 10 nanoseconds, respectively. If 90 percent of memory accesses are from cache memory, what is the average access time?

14.8. If a cache memory costs $100 per 512 kilobytes, and main memory costs $200 per 512 megabytes, what is the average cost per byte? What is the cost of 512 megabytes of cache-type memory?

14.9. In a multiprogramming system that is not a timesharing system, does the operating system set the timer before giving control to a user program?

14.10. Suppose a paging system has 32-bit addresses. If the page size is 4K, how many bits are in the displacement portion of a logical address? How many bits are in the page number portion of a logical address?

14.11. What is the difference between a logical address and a physical address?

14.12. Write a simple assembly language program that has only one address in memory initially but has exactly five when it terminates.

14.13. Why should anything in memory just below the top of the stack be regarded as garbage?

14.14. When a user program wishes to pass control to the multiprogramming operating system, it never uses a jump or call instruction. Why not?

14.15. If RAM becomes very cheap, will demand paging become unnecessary?

14.16. Is there any advantage if the operating system loads pages in page order; that is, if pages with higher numbers go into higher memory locations?

14.17. Propose a system that would allow an operating system to keep track of free frames in a paging system.

14.18. Under what circumstances must the page that is being overlaid in a page-in operation be paged out?

14.19. In what way is NUR (not used recently) better than LRU?

14.20. Is thrashing more likely if a demand paging system uses a poor page-replacement policy? Why?

14.21. Design a two-word associative memory in which each word contains a 2-bit page number, a 2-bit frame number, and a 1-bit valid bit.

14.22. Why must the DAT mechanism have an off/on switch?

14.23. What are the symptoms of a timesharing system that is thrashing?

14.24. If a timesharing system is thrashing, what are the easiest ways to stop the thrashing?

14.25. Should a user program be able to modify its own page table? Explain.

14.26. Should the machine instruction that sets memory tags be privileged? Explain.

14.27. In a demand paging system, can a page initially be executed in one frame, and then later on in a different frame? Explain.

14.28. Is the tag checking performed in a memory protection system that uses tags done by the hardware or software?

14.29. Are "timesharing" and "multiprogramming" synonymous?

14.30. What is a possible advantage of using a reentrant compiler in a timesharing system?

14.31. Suppose a program is to be *serially reusable*; that is, shared by multiple users in a serial fashion. Each user finishes execution before the next user executes it. Can any program be shared in this way? Or must a program be structured in a certain way? How are global and static local variables initialized in a serially reusable program? Is a reentrant program necessarily serially reusable? Is a serially reusable program necessarily reentrant?

14.32. A static local variable is initialized at the assembly level with **dw** statements. Show how you can force an additional one-time-only initialization of static locals at the beginning of program execution. In what type of program would you want this type of initialization?

14.33. Why would you expect programs to exhibit the locality-of-reference property?

14.34. Does the row-major representation of multi-dimensional arrays have any advantages over column-major?

14.35. If we increase the size of memory by a factor of 10, should we also increase the size of cache by the same factor to maintain the same hit ratio?

14.36. Assume a 32-bit address, a 64-byte block, and a cache with 8192 lines. Show the decomposition of an address into its component fields (see Figures 14.25 and 14.27). Consider associative, direct, and two-way set-associative mapping.

14.37. Give a scenario in which write-back is faster than write-through. Give a scenario in which write-through is faster than write-back.

14.38. Which is worse, demand paging without a TLB or a main memory without a cache?

14.39. Can the three approaches for caches—associative, direct, and set-associative—also be applied to the TLB?

14.40. Which is better with write-back: write-no-allocate or write-allocate?

14.41. Propose a hardware/software implementation of a page replacement policy that approximates LRU. Assume the hardware supports reference bits.

14.42. Propose an implementation of a FIFO cache replacement policy.

14.43. Give one scenario in which a small cache block size is better than a large block size, and one in which a large block size is better than a small block size. Assume a constant total storage capacity for the cache.

14.44. Why does the hardware not save the entire execution state at the time of an interrupt?

14.45. In a demand paging system, does it make sense to preload a program before it starts running?

14.46. Suppose five programs in memory each are in a wait state 10 percent of the time. What percent of time, on the average, will all five be in the wait state?

14.47. During CPU-I/O overlap, contention for which resource is likely to occur?

14.48. What is the advantage of multithreading in a Java program? Assume your computer has only one CPU.

Chapter Fifteen

SOME MODERN ARCHITECTURES

15.1 INTRODUCTION

Now that we have thoroughly studied the structure and operation of H1, we are well prepared to study some modern computer architectures. In this chapter, we will examine the SPARC, the architecture of the Sun Microsystems workstations, and the Intel Pentium, the processor used in most personal computers. The SPARC and Pentium are representative, respectively, of the *reduced instruction set computer (RISC)* and *complex instruction set computer (CISC)* approaches, and, therefore, nicely complement each other in our study of computer architectures. Of course, we cannot comprehensively cover these two architectures in just one chapter; however, we can get a good sense of their most salient features and provide a foundation for further study.

15.2 CISC VS. RISC

CISC and RISC represent opposite philosophies in computer design. A CISC is characterized by a large, complex instruction set that supports a variety of addressing modes. Because of the complexity of its instruction set, a CISC usually has a microprogrammed control section. In contrast, a RISC is characterized by an instruction set designed for speed. It typically has fewer and less complex instructions and addressing modes than a CISC, a large number of general-purpose registers, and a hardwired control section. The CISC approach attempts to enhance performance by minimizing the *semantic gap*—the gap between the high-level language in which we write programs and machine language. The RISC approach attemps to enhance performance by making machine language simple but fast, and to let sophisticated compilers handle the semantic gap.

A RISC does not provide the array of complex machine instructions that a CISC does. For example, a RISC typically does not have an instruction to perform a block copy. To perform a block copy, a RISC executes a loop of machine instructions that copies only one unit of memory (e.g., a byte or a word) per iteration. On a CISC, a block copy is typically performed by a single machine instruction. This instruction is implemented in the control section with a loop of microinstructions that copies one unit of memory per iteration. Thus, on both a RISC and a CISC, a block copy is performed by a loop that copies one unit of memory per iteration. However, on a RISC, this loop is at the *machine level*; on a CISC, it is at the *microlevel*.

A RISC typically has fewer instructions than a CISC; however, it does not necessarily have a small instruction set. Indeed, some RISCs have more than 200 instructions. The distinguishing characteristic of a RISC is not so much the number of instructions, but the less complex and more uniform nature of its instructions.

Although the arguments in favor of the RISC philosophy are compelling, it is by no means an accepted conclusion that RISC is better than CISC. To justify such a conclusion would be difficult. Suppose, for example, a RISC outperforms a "comparable" CISC. Can we conclude with any certainty that the RISC approach is superior? Probably not. The performance differential may have nothing to do with the RISC versus CISC dichotomy. It might be due to a better cache, a more efficient I/O system, better compilers, the test suite, or a hundred other variables. Another complicating factor is the "impurity" of most computer designs; that is, they are neither pure RISC nor pure CISC. Thus, a RISC system might perform particularly well because of its CISC features, and vice versa. The optimal design point is likely somewhere between RISC and CISC, and this point may continually change as technology progresses.

The RISC philosophy emerged in the 1980s in response to three important developments. The first was the drop in access time and cost of RAM memory systems. Faster and cheaper memory made the implementation of function in machine code a reasonable alternative to its implementation in microcode. The second was the development of compiler technology that could handle the special requirements of a RISC. The third was the discovery that compiler-generated code for CISCs often under-utilized complex machine instructions. Thus, the advantages that these instructions were supposed to provide were not being realized.

If a CISC has a complex instruction set that performs a high-level operation, why would a compiler not use it? To answer this question, let's look at a simple example using the optimal instruction set of H1. Consider the `for` loop in Figure 15.1a. It executes 10 times, displaying "hello\n" on each iteration. An efficient translation of this loop using the `dect` instruction is given in Figure 15.1b. The `dect` instruction is in the optimal instruction set precisely to support count-controlled loops. However, most compilers would not use it here because it does not correspond to a literal translation of the loop in Figure 15.1a. The C++ loop specifies the initialization and incrementation of a local variable **x**, but **x** is nowhere represented in the assembler code in Figure 15.1b. Thus, a compiler is likely to translate the C++ loop to the inefficient but more literal form in Figure 15.1c. This form creates and initializes a local variable **x**. It then uses the `scmp` instruction on each iteration to compare **x** and 10. Compilers will usually not use a machine language instruction that does not exactly match the semantics of the high-level construct. Because an exact match is the exception rather than the rule, compilers often avoid powerful machine language instructions that could result in more efficient code.

15.3 SPARC—A RISC ARCHITECTURE

The *SPARC (Scalable Processor Architecture)* is a RISC architecture that was first introduced by Sun Microsystems in 1987. The term "Scalable" in SPARC's title means that the architecture can be implemented at different performance levels, with the cost varying roughly linearly with the level of performance.

FIGURE 15.1   a) C++ code

```
        for (int x = 0; x < 10; x++)
            cout << "hello\n";
```

b) Efficient assembler code (optimal instruction set)

```
        ldc   10
        sect          ; load 10 into ct register
    @L0:

            .
            .         ; body of loop
            .

        dect          ; decrement ct, skip next inst if ct == 0
        ja @L0
```

c) Inefficient assembler code (optimal instruction set)

```
        ldc   0       ; allocate and initialize x
        push          ; assume relative address of x is -1

@L0:    ldr   -1      ; exit test
        push
        ldc   10
        scmp          ; compare x and 10
        jzop @L1      ; jump if x >= 10

            .
            .         ; loop body
            .

        ldc   1       ; increment x
        addr  -1
        str   -1

        ja    @L0
@L1:    dloc 1        ; deallocate x
```

The original version of SPARC had 32-bit registers, and no hardware multiply and divide. The latest version has a variety of enhancements, including 64-bit registers, hardware multiply and divide, 128-bit floating-point operations, faster context switching, and new machine instructions.

15.3.1   Overlapping Register Windows

A program executing on a SPARC has at any given time access to 32 integer registers and 64 floating-point registers. The integer registers are numbered 0 to 31 (see Figure 15.2). In a SPARC machine instruction, an integer register is specified with a 5-bit binary number (5 bits are needed to hold a value from 0 to 31).

The 32 integer registers form four groups: *global* (registers 0 to 7), *out* (registers 8 to 15), *local* (registers 16 to 23), and *in* (registers 24 to 31). Register 0 is permanently set to zero. The name of each group suggests how the registers in that group might be used (*global* for global variables, *out* for outgoing arguments in

FIGURE 15.2   Integer Registers

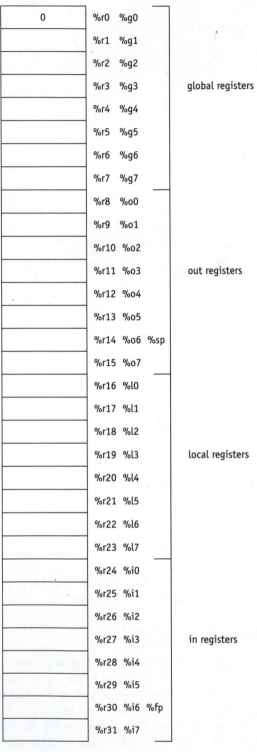

a function call, `local` for local variables, and `in` for incoming parameters in a function call). Actual use, however, often varies from these nominal uses. For example, the `out` registers are often used to hold local variables.

In an assembly instruction, we specify a register with "%r" followed by the register's decimal number. For example, to specify register 31, we use `%r31` instead of the number `31` by itself. We can also specify a register using its group name and number. For example, the group name of `%r24` (the first register in the `in` group) is `%i0`. A group name consists of "%", followed by the group identifier ("g", "o", "l", or "i"), followed by the number of the register within its group. Be sure to avoid misreading the `local` group identifier (the letter "l") as the digit "1". For example, `%l2` is `local` register 2, not register 12.

Register 14 is the *stack pointer*. Accordingly, we can specify it in an assembly instruction with the name `%sp` (or with its synonyms, `%r14` or `%o6`). Register 30 is the *frame pointer* (this register functions like the `bp` register in H1—it is used to access the stack frame of the executing function). We can specify it with `%fp` (or with `%r30` or `%i6`).

By keeping variables in registers, we can avoid the overhead of accessing variables in main memory. Our programs will then run faster. There is, however, a potential penalty with this use of registers. When a function calls another function, the called function will naturally want to keep its variables in registers. However, if it does so, it will corrupt the calling function's variables that are in registers. To avoid this problem, the called function has to save to main memory the contents of any registers it plans to use. Then, just before returning to the caller, the called function has to restore these registers with the values it previously saved. Unfortunately, the time penalty involved in saving and restoring registers to and from memory during a function call can be considerable. As a result, the advantage of a large number of registers can be largely negated by the save-restore overhead that it requires.

SPARC uses a unique technique to avoid most of the save-restore overhead during function calls. When a called function first gets control, it executes a `save` instruction. This instruction causes the system to switch to a new set of `out`, `local`, and `in` registers. Thus, the called function can use its registers (the new set) without affecting the calling function's registers (the old set). Just before the called function returns, it executes the `restore` instruction. This instruction causes the system to revert back to the caller's register set. The save and restore instructions do not transfer data between registers and memory; they simply switch the active register set. Thus, they execute quickly (far more quickly than saving and restoring registers to and from memory).

We can describe the integer register system on SPARC using a window metaphor. Suppose we visualize all the register sets in the form of a circle with a "window" over the accessible registers. A SPARC may have as few as 3 and as many as 32 register sets. Figure 15.3 shows a register circle containing eight sets numbered 7 to 0 with the window over set 6. The executing program "sees" (i.e., can access) only the registers that are "visible" through the window (i.e., set 6). On a chain of function calls, the window moves clockwise on each call, thereby providing a new set of registers at each level. As each function in the chain returns to its caller, the window moves counter-clockwise, thereby reactivating the caller's registers.

Please understand that the "window" in this description is only a metaphor—there is no physical window that moves in a circle. There is, however, a machine register `cwp` (current window pointer) that determines which register set is in use.

FIGURE 15.3   REGISTER WINDOW

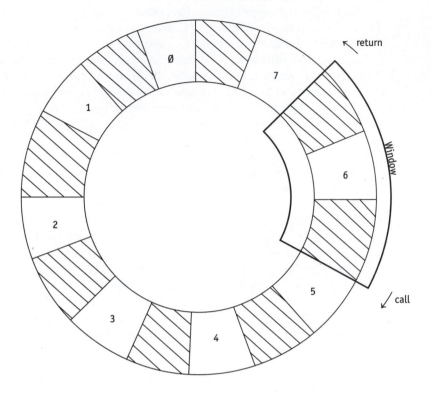

It holds the number of the active register set. When a save instruction is executed at the beginning of a called function, cwp is decremented, causing the hardware to activate a new register set. When the restore instruction is executed at the end of the called function, cwp is incremented, causing the hardware to reactivate the caller's register set.

In Chapter 7, we learned that parameters for a function call are created by pushing items onto the stack. The called function can then access the parameters on the stack using relative instructions. Instead of passing parameters on a stack, suppose we pass them in registers. We then avoid the overhead of accessing the stack (which is in memory). Obviously, we cannot pass parameters in registers if the called function is provided with a new set of registers. If, however, there were some overlap between successive sets of registers, the shared registers could be used to pass parameters. This approach is precisely what the SPARC uses. Specifically, the calling function's out registers and the called function's in registers are the same eight registers. For example, %o0 in the calling function is the same register as %i0 in the called function. Figure 15.4 shows the register window when cwp is 7 and when it is 6. Notice that the two windows overlap: The out registers when cwp is 7 and the in registers when cwp is 6 are the same set of registers.

With overlapping register windows on a SPARC, a calling function passes parameters by placing them into its out registers, and then executing a call. The called function can then access these parameters in its in registers. Neither %o6 nor %o7 are available for parameter passing (%o6 is the stack pointer register;

FIGURE 15.4   OVERLAPPING REGISTER WINDOWS

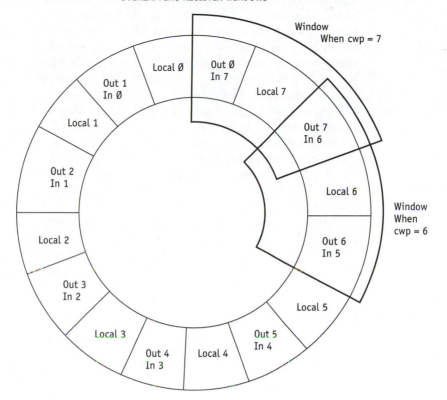

%o7 is the register that receives the link address when a call is executed). Thus, we have only six **out** registers (%o0 to %o5) for parameter passing. If we have to pass more than six parameters, the first six can be in **out** registers. However, the remaining parameters have to be passed on the stack. Although a limit of six registers for parameters may seem inadequate, studies have shown that function calls with more than six parameters are rare, occurring in about only 1 percent of all calls.

In a chain of function calls, each function gets a new set of registers. Obviously, if the chain is long enough, the system will run out of register sets. On a function call, if no new registers are available, *window overflow* occurs. Window overflow triggers a *trap* (i.e., an internally generated interrupt), which *spills* (i.e., saves) the contents of a register set onto the stack in a *register spill area*, thereby freeing a register set for use by the called function. On return to a function whose register set was previously spilled, a *window underflow occurs*. A window underflow triggers a trap that restores the register set with its original values from its spill area on the stack.

To better understand window overflow and underflow, let's consider a specific example. To keep our example simple, assume that the SPARC system has only three register sets. Suppose we execute a program that is composed of four functions—**fa**, **fb**, **fc**, and **fd**—in the form of a chain; that is, **fa** calls **fb**, **fb** calls **fc**, and **fc** calls **fd**. On each call, the register window moves clockwise to the next register set. Assume **cwp** is 2 when **fa** is executing, and sets 1 and 0 are available. The call of **fb** decrements **cwp** to 1. When **fb** calls **fc**, **cwp** is decremented to 0. The **out** registers of the active register set (set 0) are also the `in` registers of the next set (set 2). Because set 2 is already in use (by `fa`), window overflow occurs at this time. Figure 15.5a shows what happens at this point: The trap that occurs saves the `in` and `local` registers of set 2 to the stack, which frees up the set 0. `fc` can then execute using register set 0. When `fc` calls `fd`, `cwp` wraps around to 2. Because set 2 shares registers with set 1, and set 1 is in use (by `fb`), window overflow occurs again. The subsequent trap saves the `in` and `local` registers of set 1, freeing up set 2 (see Figure 15.5b). `fd` can then execute using register set 2. When `fd` returns to `fc`, `cwp` wraps back down to 0. When `fc` returns to `fb`, `cwp` is incremented to 1, at which point window underflow occurs (recall `fd` previously used the `in` registers for `fb` in set 1). The trap that occurs restores set 1 using the values previously saved on the stack so that `fb` can execute. Similarly, when `fb` returns to `fa`, another window underflow occurs. The trap that occurs restores set 0 so `fa` can execute.

Suppose in the preceding example that `fc` calls `fd` and `fd` returns to `fc` many times before `fc` ultimately returns to `fb`. Then, during this period when execution is oscillating between `fc` and `fd`, no window overflows or underflows occur (except for the window overflows when `fc` and `fd` are invoked for the first time). Thus, the call-return overhead is at a minimum. If, however, the oscillation involves three levels, `fb`, `fc`, and `fd`, there would be an overflow each time `fd` is called and an underflow each time `fc` returned to `fb`. Thus, with three register sets, we incur a significant increase in call-return overhead if the oscillations cover three or more levels. For a SPARC with eight register sets, we start incurring this overhead when the oscillations cover eight or more levels. A key point to under-

FIGURE 15.5   WINDOW OVERFLOW

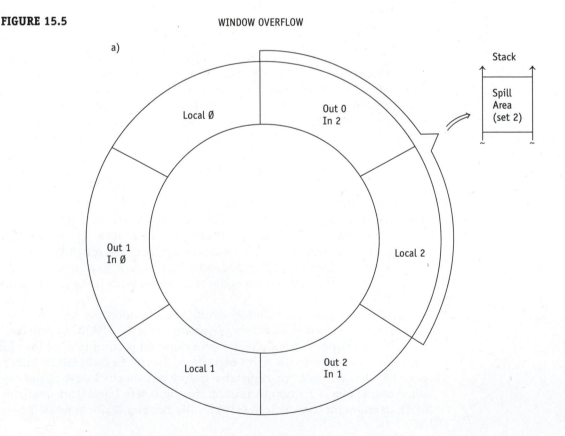

a)

FIGURE 15.5

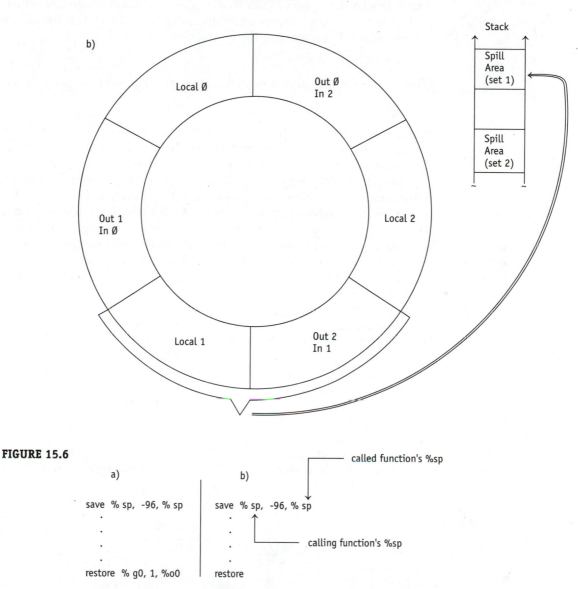

WINDOW OVERFLOW

FIGURE 15.6

stand here is that the principal factor in call-return overhead is not necessarily the length of a chain of function calls. For oscillating calls, it is the number of levels the oscillations cover when the chain executes.

15.3.2 Save and Restore Instructions

Figure 15.6 shows examples of the two common forms of functions in SPARC assembly language. For both forms, the function starts with the save instruction (which decrements **cwp**) and ends with the restore instruction (which increments **cwp**). Both the save and restore instructions perform an addition depending on the operands they provide. The first two operands are added and the result is placed in the third operand. For example, the `restore` instruction in Figure 15.6a adds the contents of `%g0` (which is always 0) and 1. It then places the result in `%o0`, but *only after the register switch* to the calling function's registers. Thus, after the return to the calling function, `%o0` (the caller's `%o0`) contains the return value 1. This instruction implements the C++ statement

```
return 1;
```

The `restore` instruction in Figure 15.6b is shorthand for

```
restore %g0, %g0, %g0
```

Because the third operand is `%g0`, the addition has no effect (the value in `%g0` is permanently set to 0). This form of the `restore` instruction corresponds to the C++ return statement in which no value is returned.

Let's now consider the `save` instruction as it appears in Figure 15.6. This instruction adds the contents of `%sp` (the *calling function's* stack pointer register) and −96 (thus, effectively subtracting 96). It then places the result back in `%sp`, but *only after the register switch* to the called function's registers. In other words, it places the result in the *called function's* stack pointer. Thus, when the called function executes, its stack pointer points to a location that is 96 bytes lower in memory than the location to which the calling function's stack pointer points. Moreover, because of register overlap, the calling function's stack pointer is also `%fp` register in the called function's register set. Thus, when the called function executes, `%fp` (the frame pointer) points to the base of the caller's stack frame, and `%sp` (the stack pointer) points to the base of the called function's stack frame (see Figure 15.7). The called function can access its stack frame using `%sp` with positive displacements, or using `%fp` with negative displacements. It can also access the calling function's stack frame using `%fp` with positive displacements.

Figure 15.8 shows the typical format of a stack frame (the format may vary depending on the compiler). With only the required elements, the stack frame size is 92 bytes. However, because a stack frame should always start on a double word boundary (i.e., a boundary whose address is divisible by 8), 4 bytes of padding are

FIGURE 15.7

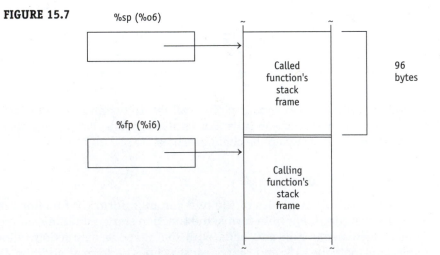

FIGURE 15.8

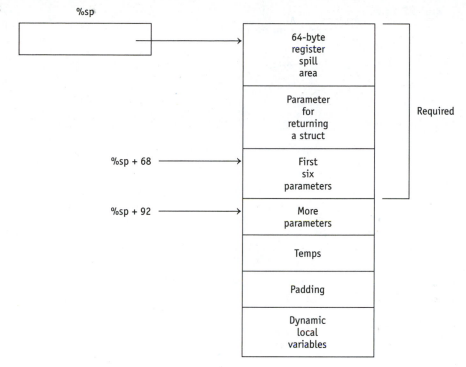

needed, making the minimum frame size 96 (which is divisible by 8). If a function has dynamic local variables that are not in registers, or if it calls another function with more than the six parameters, the save instruction has to reserve more than 96 bytes for these additional requirements.

Suppose the stack frame in Figure 15.8 is for the function f. If f contains one local dynamic variable x, the compiler would likely use a register to hold it. However, if f contains the statement,

```
p = &x;
```

then x would have to be in memory (in the stack frame) because the address operator, &, requires the memory address of x. We have a similar situation with parameters. Suppose f passes the function g a parameter in a register. If g wants the address of that parameter, the parameter must be in memory. This possibility is the reason why space is reserved in the f stack frame for the first six parameters, even if f passes parameters in registers. This space is for *outgoing parameters*—that is, for parameters that f passes *out* to functions it calls.

A stack frame for a function is created by the save instruction at the beginning of the function. For the compiler to generate this instruction with the correct value for its middle operand, it has to know the total storage requirements of the function. But to do this, it first has to scan the entire function. Thus, the compiler can generate the save instruction only after it has made at least one pass over the function.

The first 64 bytes in each stack frame is a spill area that is utilized on a window overflow. For example, suppose a save instruction decrements **cwp** to 0. On a system with three register sets, a trap is triggered if set 2 is already in use

FIGURE 15.9

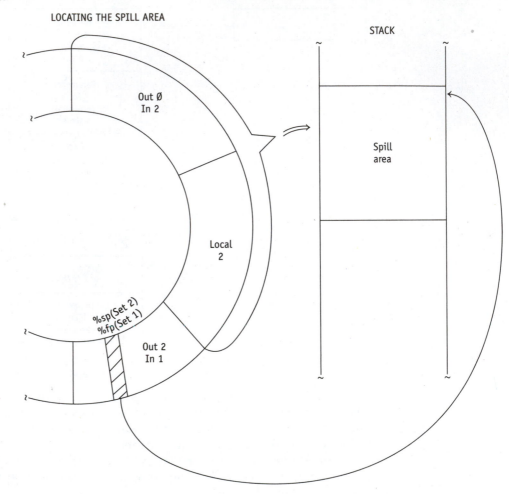

LOCATING THE SPILL AREA

(because the `out` registers of set 0 overlap the `in` registers of set 2). The trap then saves the `in` and `local` registers of set 2 in the spill area pointed to by the stack pointer for this set (see Figure 15.9). Later, the register window will ultimately move back to set 2 from set 1, causing a window underflow trap. This trap then restores set 2 from the spill area pointed to by the stack pointer for this set.

Now consider the following potential "dog-chasing-tail" problem. To locate the spill area for set 2 during a window underflow, we need the stack pointer for this set. But if the stack pointer for this set is in the spill area, we will not be able to access it because we do not know the location of the spill area. In other words, to find the spill area, we first have to get the stack pointer. But to get the stack pointer, we first have to find the spill area. This problem, in fact, does not exist. Only the `in` and `local` registers are in the spill area. The stack pointer (`%o6`) is an `out` register. Thus, the stack pointer for set 2 is *not* in the spill area for set 2. Where, then, is it? Because of register overlap, the stack pointer for set 2 is in `%fp` (`%i6`) for set 1. Thus, when the window underflow trap for set 2 occurs, the pointer to the spill area for set 2 is available in `%fp` of set 1.

15.3.3   Load and Store Instructions

The SPARC is a *load/store architecture*—an architecture in which only the `load` and `store` instructions access main memory. All the arithmetic instructions in a load/store architecture operate on values in registers or immediate values, and place the result back in a register. They do not access main memory. Thus, to add two values that are in memory and place the result back in memory, we have to

1. Load the first value into a register.
2. Load the second value into a register.
3. Add the two registers and place the result in a register.
4. Store the result back into memory.

In contrast, in an architecture that has an `add` instruction for which one of the operands is in memory (like the `add` instruction on H1), we have to

1. Load the first value into a register.
2. Add the second value in memory to the register containing the first value.
3. Store the result back into memory.

For H1, we have one fewer instruction than in the load/store case. However, step 2 for H1 performs essentially the same operations that steps 2 and 3 together perform in the load/store case. Thus, the total work done for both cases is essentially the same. Moreover, if we keep values in registers, we can avoid load and store operations altogether, in which case there is no instruction-count disadvantage for the load/store architecture.

A load/store architecture has three important advantages. First, it makes for a smaller instruction set (we do not need all the arithmetic instructions that access memory). Second, it minimizes contention for main memory because fewer instructions access main memory (an important consideration for instruction pipelining—see Section 15.3.5). Third, it makes for a more uniform instruction set with respect to instruction execution time (also an important consideration for instruction pipelining).

Let's examine the `ld` (load) instruction in the assembly language for the SPARC. Its first operand field specifies the memory operand address; the second, the destination register. For example, the instruction

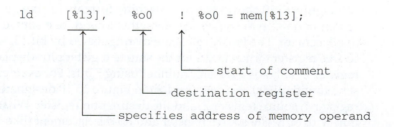

```
ld      [%13],    %o0    ! %o0 = mem[%13];
```

start of comment
destination register
specifies address of memory operand

loads the word pointed to by `%13` into `%o0`. The square brackets signal that the operand is in memory—that is, the operand is in the location to which the enclosed register points. Note that a comment starts with "!" in SPARC assembly language.

The memory pointer in an `ld` instruction can be provided by a single register, by two registers, or by one register and a displacement. For example, in the instruction

```
ld   [%sp],  %o0
```

FIGURE 15.10   a) Two source registers

31 30	29 25	24 19	18 14	13	12 5	4 0
op	rd	op3	rs1	0	---	rs2

b) One source register plus a displacement

31 30	29 25	24 19	18 14	13	12 0
op	rd	op3	rs1	1	simm13

op: opcode, 11 for both ld and st

rd: destination register

op3:   opcode, 00000 for ld, 00100 for st

rs1:   source register 1

rs2:   source register 2

simm13:   13-bit signed immediate value (holds displacement for load and store instructions)

the memory address is the contents of **%sp**. However, in

```
ld  [%sp + %13], %o0
```

the memory address is the sum of the contents of **%sp** and **%13**, and in

```
ld [%sp + 68], %o0
```

it is the sum of the contents of **%sp** and the displacement 68. This displacement is held in the machine instruction in a 13-bit signed field. Thus, its value can vary from −4096 to +4095. In the preceding instructions, **%sp** and **%i3** are *source* registers because they are associated with the "source" (i.e., the operand to be loaded). **%o0** is the *destination* register because it is the destination of the load. Like all assembly language instructions on the SPARC, the ld instruction specifies its source operands to the left of the destination operands (the Pentium assembly language we discuss in section 15.4 uses the opposite convention).

Figure 15.10 shows the two machine formats for the ld instruction. The first accommodates two source registers; the second, one source register and a 13-bit displacement. The two formats are distinguished by bit 13, which is 0 for the two source register format and 1 for the source register plus displacement format. Each register field holds a register number using 5 bits. For example, **%o0** (**%r8**) is represented with 01000. **rs1**, **rs2**, and **rd** in Figure 15.10 designate, respectively, source register 1, source register 2, and the destination register. What about an ld instruction with only one source register and no displacement (like ld [%13], %o0)? We can use either the first format in Figure 15.10 with **rs2** set to 000000 (**%g0**), or the second format with the displacement set to zero. In either case, the address of the source is given by **rs1** alone.

On a SPARC with 64-bit registers, the ld instruction loads the memory operand into the lower half of the register and zeros out the upper half. In other words, it treats the operand as a 32-bit unsigned word. (If it were to treat the word it loads as a signed word, it would sign extend it.) Accordingly, an alternative mnemonic for this instruction on 64-bit machines is `lduw` (load unsigned word). Other load instructions available on both 32- and 64-bit machines are `ldub` (load unsigned byte), `ldsb` (load signed byte), `lduh` (load unsigned half), `ldsh` (load signed half), `ldx` (load extended, which loads a doubleword into a register), and `ldd` (load double, which loads two consecutive words into an even-odd pair of registers). The unsigned versions use zero-extension; the signed versions use sign-extension.

Memory operands to be loaded must be appropriately aligned in memory. For example, the operand in a halfword load must be on a halfword boundary (i.e., the operand's address must be divisible by 2). Similarly, a word load and a double-word load require a word and doubleword alignment, respectively, corresponding to addresses divisible by 4 and 8. C++ compilers always place integer data in memory on the required boundary. However, if a program processes integer data in an input buffer, it is possible to run into a boundary problem. For example, suppose **p** is a character pointer that points to a field in an input buffer that contains a binary integer. To load the integer into the integer variable **x**, we might use

```
x = *(int *)p;
```

This instruction first casts the pointer to an **int** pointer and then dereferences it to access the word to which it points. However, this statement will work only if the integer is on a word boundary. If it is not, a Sun Workstation responds with the cryptic error message "Bus Error." This error message occurred when **lin** (the H1 linker) was ported from a Pentium machine to the Sun SPARC Workstation. The Pentium does not require any boundary alignments for its load instructions. Thus, it does not object to the previous statement (which appeared in the C++ code for **lin**). To fix this problem, the C++ statement was replaced with

```
memcpy(x, p, sizeof(int));
```

The **memcpy** function performs a byte-by-byte copy and does not, therefore, require any boundary alignment.

An `st` (store) instruction can specify a memory location in the same ways that an `ld` instruction can: It can use one register, two registers, or a register and a 13-bit signed displacement. The following instructions illustrate the three variations:

```
st   %o0, [%sp]          ! mem[%sp]        = %o0;
st   %o0, [%sp + %l3]     ! mem[%sp + %l3] = %o0;
st   %o0, [%sp + 68]      ! mem[%sp + 68]  = %o0;
```

The store instructions on the SPARC include `stb` (store byte), `sth` (store half), `st` or `stw` (store word), `stx` (store extended, which stores the doubleword in a register), and `std` (store double, which stores the two lower words in a even/odd register pair).

By now you may be quite comfortable with the load and store instructions on the SPARC, but we still have some outstanding concerns. For example, where is the instruction that loads one register from another? And where is the instruction that loads a register with an immediate constant? Both operations are possible on the SPARC using the `or` instruction. For example, consider the instruction

```
or   %g0, %i3, %i5        ! %i5 = %i3;
```

FIGURE 15.11

Instruction	Machine Code					
	31 30	29 25	24 19	18 14	13	12 0
	op	rd	op3	rs1	1	simm13
ld [%i0 + 4], %o0	11	01000	000000	11001	1	0000000000100
or %i0, 4, %o0	10	01000	000010	11001	1	0000000000100

%o0 (%r8)

%i0 (%r25)

4

This instruction ORs the contents of the first two registers, and places the result in the third register. Because %g0 contains 0, the result of the OR operation is equal to the value of the middle operand (the contents of %i3). Thus, the effect of this instruction is to copy the value in %i3 to %i5. To load an immediate constant, we also use an or instruction. For example, the instruction

```
or %g0, 50, %i5            ! %i5 = 50;
```

ORs **%g0** with 50, and places the result in **%i5**. Here again, the result of the OR is equal to the value of the middle operand (the immediate operand 50) because **%g0** is the first operand. Thus, the effect of this instruction is to load 50 into **%i5**. Because the immediate constant occupies a signed 13-bit field, its value can range from −4096 to +4095.

The or instruction has two formats that are very much like the two formats for the ld instruction in Figure 15.10. The only difference is in the use of the **simm13** field. In an or instruction, **simm13** is an immediate operand. In a load or store, it is an address displacement. For example, the ld and or instructions in Figure 15.11 have identical machine code except for the opcode bits. In the ld instruction, the contents of **%i0** plus 4 is the address of the memory operand (thus, "4" is a displacement). In the or instruction, the contents of **%i0** and 4 are the two operands that are ORed together (thus, "4" is an immediate operand). Both instructions in machine language form contain the 4 in the **simm13** field.

Like the or instruction, all the logical and arithmetic instructions can have a second operand that is either a register or a 13-bit signed value. In addition, they all have two versions: one that sets the condition code and one that does not. Mnemonics of instructions that set the condition code end in "cc". For example, both of the following instructions copy **%i3** to **%i5**:

```
orcc   %g0, %i3, %i5     ! sets condition code
or     %g0, %i3, %i5     ! does not set condition code
```

However, the *orcc* (or and modify condition code) instruction also sets the condition code according to the result of the operation.

FIGURE 15.12

```
        .section ".text"                ! text section
                .
                .
                .

        sethi  %hi(x), %i0              ! load high 22 bits into %i0
        or     %i0,  %lo(x),  %i0       ! or 10 low bits into %i0
                .
                .
                .

        .section ".data"                ! data section
        .align 4
x:      .word  7
```

One more concern remains regarding loads and stores: How do we load and store from a symbolic label? For example, can we use the instruction

```
ld  x, %i0        ! no such instruction
```

to load the word at the label **x** into **%i0**? The corresponding machine instruction would have to contain the absolute address of **x**. But there is no field in the ld instruction for an absolute address. This instruction does not exist. Incidentally, if there were such a field, it would have to contain at least 30 bits (it does not need the two lowest bits in a 32-bit *word* address because they are always 0).

One way to load **%i0** from **x** is to load the 32-bit address of **x** into a register, and then use this address to access **x**. Unfortunately, loading the address of **x** is complicated on the SPARC. There is no immediate instruction that can load a complete address. We cannot use the or instruction because its 13-bit immediate field is too small to hold an address (remember we need at least 30 bits to hold a word address). However, we can load the address of **x** in two parts: The sethi instruction can load its high 22 bits, and the or instruction can load the remaining 10 low bits. Figure 15.12 shows the required sequence. Instructions and data have to be in separate sections in an assembly language program. Accordingly, Figure 15.12 shows the sethi and or instructions in the ".text" section, and the data word **x** in the ".data" section. The ".text" section is a read-only area. The assembler directive **.section** flags the start or reactivation of the specified section; **.align** 4 forces a full-word boundary; and **.word** defines a word.

The sethi and or instructions in Figure 15.12 both hold immediate data that together make up the address of **x**. The sethi instruction loads the high 22 bits of the destination register with the high 22 bits of the address of **x**. It also zeros out the low 10 bits of the destination register. The or instruction then ORs in the low 10 bits.

The expression %hi(x) is shorthand for high 22 bits of the address of **x**. This 22-bit value is held in an immediate field in the sethi instruction (see Figure 15.13a). When the sethi instruction in Figure 15.12 is executed, this value is loaded into the *high* 22 bits of **%i0** (the destination register). In addition, the low 10 bits of **%i0** are zeroed out.

The expression %lo(x) is shorthand for the 10 low bits of **x**. These bits, extended on the left with three zeros, are held in the 13-bit immediate field of the or instruction (see Figure 15.13b). When the or instruction in Figure 15.12 is executed, the value in this immediate field is ORed into **%i0** (the destination register). The effect of

FIGURE 15.13   a) sethi

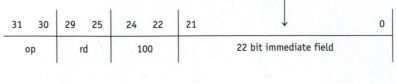

b) or   (low 10 bits of address of x)

31 30	29 25	24 19	18 14	13	12 ↓ 0
op	rd	op3	rs1	1	simm13

the `sethi`/`or` sequence in Figure 15.12 is to load **%i0** with a 32-bit address of **x**. Once the address of **x** is in **%i0**, we can either load or store at this address. For example,

```
ld   [%i0], %o0          ! %o0 = mem[%i0];
```

loads **x** into **%o0**, and

```
st   %o0, [%i0]          ! mem[%i0] = %o0;
```

stores **%o0** into **x**.

A more efficient sequence for accessing **x** is possible if the `ld` or `st` instruction combines the two parts of the address of **x**. We can then eliminate the `or` instruction. For example, we can use

```
sethi  %hi(x),   %i0
```

to load the high 22 bits of the address of **x** into **%i0**. We can then use

```
ld   [%i0 + %lo(x)], %o0
```

to load from **x** or

```
st   %o0, [%i0 + %lo(x)]
```

to store into **x**. The `ld` instruction first computes the address of **x** (by summing the contents of **%i0** with the `%lo(x)` value in its **simm13** field). It then loads **%o0** with the word at this address (which is **x**). Similarly, the `st` instruction first computes the address of **x** and then stores **%o0** at this address.

The sequence in Figure 15.12 is useful if we have to assign the address of **x** to a variable. For example, the code for

```
p = &x;
```

is

```
sethi  %hi(x),   %i0             ! get address of x
or     %i0,  %lo(x),   %i0

sethi  %hi(p),   %i1             ! store address in p
st     %i0, [%i1 +  %lo(p)]
```

Most instructions on the SPARC do not contain addresses, and, therefore, have no relocatable fields. However, the `sethi` and `or` instructions in Figure 15.12 each contain a portion of the address of **x**. Thus, these instructions have relocatable fields that have to be adjusted to reflect the actual address of **x** when the program is linked or loaded into memory.

Recall that the `or` instruction can load immediate values, but only within the range of -4096 to $+4095$. However, with a `sethi/or` sequence, we can load any 32-bit constant into a register. For example, to load 0x12345678 into `%o0`, we use

```
sethi  %hi(0x12345678), %o0        ! load high 22 bits
or     %o0, %lo(0x12345678), %o0   ! or in low 10 bits
```

15.3.4 Branch, `call`, and `jmpl` Instructions

A 32-bit SPARC has two sets of condition codes: one for floating-point operations (`fcc`) and one for integer operations (`icc`). A 64-bit SPARC has three sets: one for floating-point operations (`fcc`), one for 32-bit integer operations (`icc`), and one for 64-bit integer operations (`xcc`). The `icc` and `xcc` sets each have four bits: **N** (negative), **Z** (zero), **V** (signed overflow), and **C** (carry). These bits are set as we discussed in Chapter 1 (the **N** bit in the SPARC corresponds to the **s** bit in Chapter 1).

On a 64-bit SPARC, the `icc` and `xcc` sets reflect, respectively, the results of 32-bit and 64-bit operations. For example, suppose we add two numbers on a 64-bit machine. **Z** in `icc` would indicate if the low word of the result is zero; **Z** in `xcc` would indicate if the entire 64-bit result is zero.

Figure 15.14 lists the branch instructions on the SPARC. Note that some branch instructions come in pairs, one for signed operations, one for unsigned.

FIGURE 15.14   Branch instructions

Opcode	Cond	Mnemonic	Name (test)
00	1000	ba	Branch always
00	0000	bn	Branch never
00	0001	be	Branch equal (Z == 1)
00	0010	ble	Branch less or equal ((N ^ V) == 1 || Z == 1)
00	0100	bleu	Branch less or equal unsigned (C == 1 || Z == 1)
00	0011	bl	Branch less ((N ^ V) == 1)
00	0101	bcs	Branch carry set (C == 1)
		blu	Branch less unsigned (C == 1)
00	0110	bneg	Branch negative (N == 1)
00	1001	bne	Branch not equal (Z == 0)
00	1010	bg	Branch greater (Z == 0 && N ^ V == 0)
00	1100	bgu	Branch greater unsigned (Z == 0 && C == 0)
00	1011	bge	Branch greater or equal (N ^ V == 0)
00	1101	bcc	Branch carry clear (C == 0)
		bgeu	Branch greater or equal unsigned (C == 0)
00	1110	bpos	Branch positive (N == 0)
00	0111	bvs	Branch signed overflow (V == 1)
00	1111	bvc	Branch no signed overflow (V == 0)

For example, `bl` (branch less) and `blu` (branch less unsigned) are for signed and unsigned operations, respectively. The conditional branch instructions test the result of the instruction that most recently set the condition code. For example, in the sequence,

```
subcc   %i0, %i1, %g0
bl      xxx
```

the branch to **xxx** occurs if the result of the *subcc* (subtract and modify condition code) instruction is less than zero, or equivalently, if the contents of `%i0` are less than the contents of `%i1`. The type of comparison performed depends on the test that the conditional branch performs. `bl` performs the "S XOR V = 1" test that we discussed in Section 1.15. Thus, it performs a signed comparison test. `blu` performs the "C = 1" test. Thus, it performs an unsigned comparison test. Let's not forget the `bneg` (branch negative) instruction. It performs the "S == 1" test. It determines if the *computed* result is less than zero. In contrast, `bl` determines if the *true* result is less than zero. Recall from Section 1.15 that these two results differ if overflow occurs. Incidentally, the subcc instruction is, in effect, a *compare instruction* (an instruction that sets the condition code based on the result of a comparison). It sets the condition code, and then the `bl` instruction tests the condition code to determine if the contents of `%i0` are less than the contents of `%i1`. Because the subcc instruction uses the destination register `%g0` (which is permanently set to 0), its only effect is to set the condition code.

The machine code for a branch instruction contains a signed number that is a word displacement. The target address is given by this displacement plus the address of the branch instruction itself. For example, if the displacement in a branch instruction is 20 then the target byte address is the location 20 words beyond the location of the branch instruction. It is computed by adding the address in the **pc** register (which is the address of the branch instruction) and the displacement extended with two zeros on its right (to convert it to a byte displacement).

In assembly language, we specify the target address for a branch in the usual way. For example, to branch always to the label **xxx**, we use

```
ba    xxx
```

To translate this instruction, the assembler computes the word displacement from the branch instruction to the label **xxx**. It then places this displacement into the branch machine instruction.

The 64-bit machines have all the integer branch instructions that the 32-bit machines do. Let's call these instructions the "old" branch instructions. The old integer branch instructions test the **icc** set of condition codes. The 64-bit machines have an additional set of branch instructions that can test either **icc** or **xcc**, depending on the setting of certain bits in their machine instructions. Let's call these instructions the "new" branch instructions. The old and new branch instructions have different formats at the machine level (see Figure 15.15). If we specify a condition code set in an assembly language branch instruction, we get a new branch instruction. Otherwise, we get an old instruction. For example, we get an old branch instruction for

```
ba    xxx                ! old
```

but we get a new branch instruction for

```
ba    %icc, xxx          ! new--use icc
ba    %xcc, xxx          ! new--use xcc
```

FIGURE 15.15

a) Old branch instruction

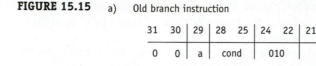

31	30	29	28	25	24	22	21	0
0	0	a	cond		010		disp22	

b) New branch instruction

31	30	29	28	25	24	22	21	20	19	18	0
0	0	a	cond		001		cc		p	disp19	

c) Call instruction

31	30	29	0
0	1	disp30	

a:	annul bit
cond:	condition
cc:	condition code set (00: icc, 10: xcc)
p:	prediction bit
disp19:	19-bit signed word displacement
disp22:	22-bit signed word displacement
disp30:	30-bit signed word displacement

The `call` instruction contains a 30-bit field (see Figure 15.15c) that holds the high 30 bits of a 32-bit signed word displacement. Instructions are always on a word boundary, so the 32-bit displacement to any instruction will necessarily have its two lowest bits equal to 0. Thus, the 30-bit field in a `call` instruction provides a complete 32-bit displacement. Unlike the branch instructions (which have only a 22- or 19-bit word displacement field), a `call` instruction can jump to any location in a 32-bit address space. Because the branch instructions are intra-module transfers, they do not need the 32-bit range of the `call` instruction.

When a `call` instruction is executed, it does *not* save the return address. Instead, it saves its own address in `%o7`. We call this address the *link address*. The called function has to compute the appropriate return address from the link address stored by the `call` instruction (we will see examples of this in Section 15.3.6).

The `jmpl` (jump and link) instruction is similar in function to the `call` instruction. Let's look at some examples. The instruction

```
jmpl    %i7, %o7          ! jump to address in %i7
```

saves its own address (the link address) in the register specified in the second operand (`%o7` in this example). It then transfers control to the address specified by the first operand (`%i7` in this example). The first operand can also be two registers, as in

```
jmpl    %i6 + %i7, %o7    ! jump to address given by %i6 + %i7
```

or one register and a signed displacement, as in

```
jmpl    %i7 + 8,   %o7    ! jump to address given by %i7 + 8
```

Note that a `jmpl` instruction specifies the register to receive its address. A `call` cannot (it always uses `%o7`). The `jmpl` instruction has the same format as the `load` and `store` instructions (see Figure 15.10). The **rs1**, **rs2**, and **simm13** fields in the machine instruction set specify the target address. The **rd** field specifies the register that receives the link address.

We now have seen the three basic machine instruction formats on the SPARC. We have *format one* (branch/`sethi` instructions), *format two* (the `call` instruction format), and *format three* (a format that is used by many types of instructions including the `load` and `store` instructions). The format of a machine instruction can be identified by its **op** field (the instruction's first 2 bits). **op** is 00 for branch instructions, 01 for the `call` instruction, and 10 or 11 for format three instructions. A 64-bit SPARC also has a *format four*—a variation of format three—that is used for some new instructions. The **op** field for format four instructions is 11.

15.3.5   Instruction Pipelining

To increase the rate at which a computer executes instructions, we might try adding a second CPU. To avoid contention for memory, we should also add a second memory unit so that each CPU has its own unit. We then have essentially two computers that together can certainly execute more instructions per unit time than our original computer. But we also have a far more expensive computer. A more cost-effective approach is to use an *instruction pipeline*. In a pipeline, the sequence of operations necessary to fetch and execute an instruction are performed by a sequence of stages. An instruction is executed as it passes through and is processed by these stages, very much like a car is built as it passes through the stages of a factory assembly line. Each stage of a pipeline can be working on a different instruction. Thus, a pipeline allows instructions to be executed in parallel.

Figure 15.16a shows successive snapshots of a pipeline as it executes the instructions `I1`, `I2`, `I3`, and `I4`, in that order. `I1` enters the pipeline first. When `I1` moves from stage 1 to stage 2, `I2` enters stage 1. Thus, in the second snapshot, the pipeline is simultaneously processing both `I1` and `I2`. Each time the instructions in the pipeline progress to the next stage, a new instruction enters stage 1. Thus, the pipeline fills up as new instructions enter. In the last snapshot, the pipeline is simultaneously processing all four instructions. The matrix in Figure 15.16b is an alternative representation of the pipeline activity in Figure 15.16a. It shows the location in the pipeline of each instruction as a function of time. For example, the fourth line of the matrix shows that `I4` is in `S1` (i.e., stage 1) at time = 3.

Suppose each stage in Figure 15.16 requires one clock cycle. Then the execution time for each instruction is four cycles. The instruction execution rate, however, is one per cycle, assuming the pipeline is full. Without pipelining, each instruction would have to complete before the next one could start. The execution rate would be one instruction every four cycles—one-fourth that of the pipelined case. If full, a four-stage pipeline provides a four-fold increase in the execution rate.

Pipelining requires some extra hardware (for buffering between stages, and for detecting and handling dependencies between instructions), but its cost is modest relative to the increase in execution rate that it provides. We, of course, can increase execution rate without pipelining by buying multiple computers. Clearly, a pipeline is a far more cost-effective approach.

In a pipeline, execution time depends on the sum of the times required by each stage. Execution rate, on the other hand, depends on the time required by the slowest stage because it sets the pace for the pipeline. For example, in a four-stage pipeline, with three stages requiring one cycle and one stage requiring five cycles, execution time is $1 + 1 + 1 + 5 = 8$. The execution rate is one instruction every

FIGURE 15.16   a) Snapshots of a four-stage pipeline

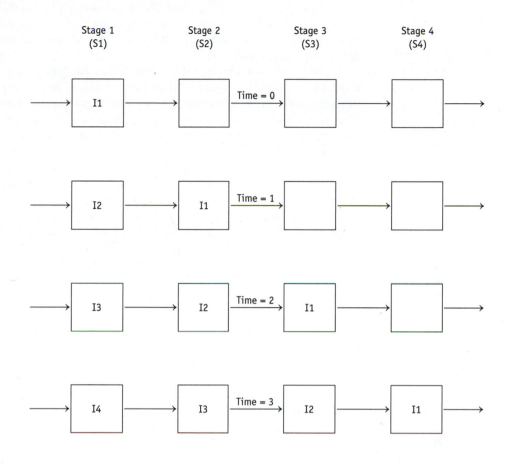

b) Instruction vs. time representation

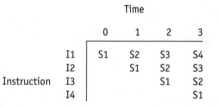

		0	1	2	3
	I1	S1	S2	S3	S4
	I2		S1	S2	S3
Instruction	I3			S1	S2
	I4				S1

five cycles. Pipelining in this example is not much better than the nonpipelined case. To remedy the slow execution rate here, we can break up the slowest stage into five substages, each requiring one cycle. Then execution time would still be 8 cycles, but the execution rate would increase to one instruction per cycle.

Dependencies between instructions in a pipeline cause problems. If an instruction in one stage needs information that is not yet available from an instruction in another stage, the pipeline is forced to *stall* (i.e., some stage goes idle) until the required information becomes available.

Suppose when we are designing a computer, we have to choose between a four-stage pipeline in which each stage requires two cycles or an eight-stage pipeline in which each stage requires one cycle. A four-stage pipeline multiplies the execution rate by up to four, but the eight-stage pipeline multiplies it by up to eight. Should we, therefore, use the eight-stage pipeline? Not necessarily. The eight-stage pipeline is more likely to have dependencies. Thus, the advantage of more stages may be cancelled out by both the added cost and the stalls the additional dependencies force.

A load/store architecture is well-suited for pipelining for several reasons. First, the simplicity of this architecture minimizes dependencies between instructions that can cause stalls. Second, the execution requirements of instructions in a load/store architecture tend to be uniform across the instruction set. This uniformity makes it possible to design a pipeline that is a good "fit" for most of the instructions in the instruction set. Third, by limiting the number of instructions that access memory, a load/store architecture minimizes contention for memory.

A pipeline increases the instruction execution rate by permitting the parallel execution of instructions. To increase the execution rate even further, we can use multiple pipelines. With a single pipeline, we can *issue* (i.e., start executing) one instruction every cycle. With multiple pipelines, we can issue multiple instructions every cycle, with each instruction entering a different pipeline. We call this mode of instruction execution *superscalar execution*. As you would expect, dependencies become an even greater problem for superscalar execution. However, if superscalar execution is well designed, it can provide a cost-effective improvement in execution rates.

Let's now examine in detail a four-stage pipeline for the SPARC. Although the implementation of pipelining on a SPARC can vary (the architecture specification for the SPARC does not include an implementation for the instruction pipeline), our four-stage pipeline will reveal general principles that apply to any implementation.

Our pipeline consists of the following stages:

1. Fetch: Fetch instruction.
2. Decode: Decode the opcode, access operands, compute the effective address for load and store instructions, and compute the target address for branch.
3. Execute: Perform the ALU operation for an arithmetic or logical instruction and access the cache on a load or store.
4. Write back: Update registers.

Suppose we execute the following sequence:

```
ld    [%l0], %o0
ld    [%l1], %o1
or    %o0, %o1, %o2
```

Figure 15.17a shows the corresponding activity in the pipeline, assuming no stalls occur. There is no dependency between the two ld instructions, so they execute without any complications. However, there is a *data dependency* between the or instruction and second ld instruction. Specifically, the or instruction needs the values that are loaded by the ld instructions. These values becomes available in the CPU only after the ld instructions complete the execute stage. Thus, the or instruction cannot complete the decode stage until *after* the ld instructions complete the execute stage. But Figure 15.17a shows that this requirement is violated (the or instruction completes the decode stage at the *same time* that the second ld instruction completes the execute stage). Thus, for this instruction sequence, our assumption that stalls do not occur is wrong. A stall has to occur to allow time for the second ld instruction to provide the value needed by the or instruction (see Fig-

FIGURE 15.17 a)

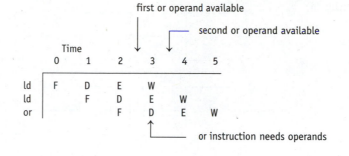

b)

ure 15.17b). We call the idle period that results from a stall a *bubble*. This bubble propagates down the pipeline on successive cycles (see Figure 15.17c). One way to avoid dependency stalls is to reorder the instructions so that the dependency no longer exists. Instruction reordering does not sound easy to do correctly, and it is not (any reordering must not affect the results of the program). However, it is one of the important tasks a good compiler for a pipelined computer should perform. Incidentally, the arithmetic and logical instructions on the SPARC come in pairs (one sets the condition code and one does not) to allow more flexibility in instruction reordering.

A data dependency is not the only kind of dependency that can cause a pipeline to stall. In a *structural dependency*, two instructions contend for a hardware resource (such as memory). In a *control dependency*, the availability of an instruction depends on another. Control dependencies are associated with transfer-of-control instructions (i.e., branch, `call`, and `jmpl` instructions). Particularly troublesome are the conditional branch instructions. These instructions require a condition test that causes their outcome (i.e., to branch or not to branch) to be known late in the execution process.

Let's see how a control dependency can cause a stall. In our discussion, we will refer to three instructions:

1. The *control instruction* (an instruction that conditionally or unconditionally transfers control to a new location). Control instructions include the branch, `call`, and `jmpl` instructions.
2. The *fall-through instruction* (the instruction that physically follows the control instruction in memory).
3. The *target instruction* (the instruction at the location to which the control instruction transfers control if the transfer occurs).

FIGURE 15.17
(continued)

c)

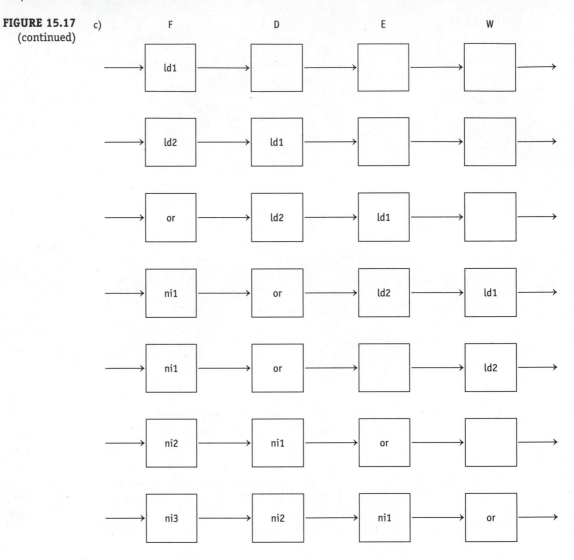

When a control instruction enters the decode stage, the fall-through instruction enters the pipeline. This instruction, however, should not be executed if the control instruction ultimately transfers control to a new location. After the control instruction completes the decode stage, the decision of whether to transfer control is known. If the transfer is not to occur, the fall-through instruction proceeds through the pipeline. If, however, the transfer is to occur, the fall-through instruction (which is in the pipeline) is discarded and the target instruction fetched (see Figure 15.18a). Unfortunately, as the target instruction is fetched, the decode stage is idle because the instruction ahead of it in the pipeline (the fall-through instruction) was discarded. This bubble then propagates to the E and W stages on the next two cycles.

Because control instructions occur frequently in programs, the stalls they cause can significantly impact the efficiency of the pipeline. A simple way to avoid

FIGURE 15.18   a) Without delayed branching

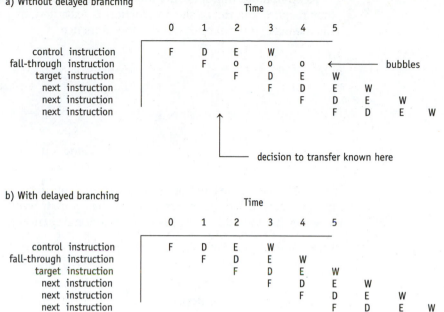

decision to transfer known here

b) With delayed branching

these stalls is to allow the fall-through instruction to execute whether or not the transfer of control occurs (the SPARC uses this technique). For the no-transfer case, we get the sequence

control instruction
fall-through instruction

and for the transfer case, we get

control instruction
fall-through instruction
target instruction

We call this technique *delayed branching* because it delays the branch (i.e., the transfer of control) until after the fall-through instruction is executed. We call the fall-through instruction the *delay-slot instruction*, and the position it occupies the *delay slot*. Figure 15.18b shows the pipeline activity using delayed branching when a transfer occurs. Because the delay-slot instruction is executed, the pipeline does not stall.

With delayed branching, we can usually place the instruction that would logically precede the control instruction after the control instruction. For example, if we want to pass 5 via %o0 to a function sub, we can code

```
call sub
or   %g0, 5, %o0      ! load 5 into %o0
```

Although the or instruction follows the call instruction in the pipeline, it completes its execution before the actual transfer to sub. Thus, on entry into sub, %o0 contains 5.

Keep in mind that it is only the actual transfer of control that is delayed. In all other respects the delay-slot instruction is executed *after* the control instruction. This means that we cannot reorder the sequence

```
ld     [%l0], %o2
subcc  %o0, %o1, %g0        ! compare %o0 with %o1
bl     xxx                  ! branch based on result of subcc
```

to

```
ld     [%i0], %o2
bl     xxx                  ! branch based on result of subcc
subcc  %o0, %o1, %g0        ! compare %o0 with %o1
```

If we did, the `bl` instruction would test the condition code *before* the `subcc` instruction sets it. However, we can put the `ld` instruction into the delay slot (because neither the `subcc` nor the `bl` instruction depend on it) to get

```
subcc  %o0, %o1, %g0        ! compare %o0 with %o1
bl     xxx                  ! branch based on result of subcc
ld     [%i0], %o2
```

Sometimes, because of dependencies in an instruction sequence that lead up to a control instruction, no instruction can be moved into the delay slot. For example, in the sequence,

```
ld   [%l0], %o0
ld   [%l1], %o1
subcc %o0, %o1, %g0        ! depends on ld instruction
bl     xxx                  ! branch based on result of compare
nop                         ! fill in delay slot with nop
```

the `ld` instructions have to precede the `subcc` which, in turn, has to precede the `bl`. Thus, to fill the delay slot, we use a *nop* (a no-operation instruction). A nop does no useful work, so we should avoid it if possible. A possible alternative to a nop is to move the target instruction into the delay slot (assuming the `bl` instruction is the only path to the target instruction). Unfortunately, this approach does not work because the delay slot instruction is always executed, even when the `bl` instruction does not transfer control. However, if we replace the previous `bl` instruction with

```
bl,a   xxx
```

then the delay instruction is executed only if the transfer of control occurs. With this form of the `bl` instruction, the target instruction can correctly be moved into the delay slot. The ",a" suffix on a branch mnemonic sets the **a** bit (the *annul bit*) in the machine instruction to 1 (see Figure 15.15). When **a** is 1, the delay-slot instruction is executed only when the transfer of control occurs. If, on the other hand, the **a** bit is 0 (which occurs if the ",a" suffix is omitted), the delay-slot instruction is always executed.

The new branch instructions have a **p** (prediction) bit in addition to an **a** bit (see Figure 15.15). The **p** bit tells the hardware either that a branch is likely to occur (if **p** = 1) or that it is not likely to occur (if **p** = 0). The two alternatives are specified at the assembly level by suffixing ",pt" (predict taken) or ",pn" (predict not taken) to the mnemonic of the instruction. For example, the **p** bit for

```
ble,nt   xxx
```

is 0, but it is 1 for

```
ble,pt  xxx
```

The conditional branch instruction at the bottom of a loop is a good candidate for **p** = 1. Most loops iterate many times. Thus, the likelihood that this branch occurs is high. On the other hand, a conditional branch to an infrequently used error routine is a good candidate for **p** = 0.

The **p** bit can help the hardware minimize the delays associated with conditional branch instructions. If **p** = 0, the hardware can proceed as if there were no branch; if **p** = 1, it can proceed as if the branch were unconditional. In either case, delays are minimized if the prediction is correct. If, however, the prediction is incorrect, the processing of the incorrect instruction sequence must be undone. In some designs, the hardware itself predicts the likelihood that a conditional branch instruction branches using the previous outcomes for that instruction. We call this technique *dynamic branch prediction*.

15.3.6 Linkage Instructions

Figure 15.19 shows the instructions for calling and returning from a function. The `call` instruction in the calling function is followed by a delay-slot instruction. We typically use this instruction to load an argument into an **out** register. For example, the assembly code for

```
sub(1,2);
```

is

```
or %g0, 1, %o0    ! load 1 into %o0
call sub
or %g0, 2, %o1    ! load 2 into %o1
```

Here, the first `or` instruction loads the argument 1 into **%o0**. The second `or` instruction loads the argument 2 into **%o1**. Because this instruction is in the delay slot, it is executed before the `call` instruction transfers control to **sub**.

SPARC assembly language does not have a directive that is comparable to the **extern** directive in H1 assembly language. Any undefined symbol is simply assumed to be external. Thus, if the two functions in Figure 15.19 are separately assembled, the assembler will assume **sub** is external. Global symbols, on the

FIGURE 15.19

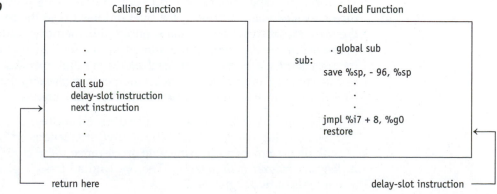

other hand, have to be explicitly identified with the `.global` directive (which is comparable to the **public** directive in H1 assembly language). Thus, in the called function in Figure 15.19, the label **sub** must appear in a `.global` directive.

When a `call` instruction is executed, the address of the `call` instruction itself is saved in `%o7`. When the `save` instruction at the beginning of the called function switches register sets, this register becomes `%i7`. The called function should not, of course, return to the address in `%i7` (this is the address of the `call` instruction). Nor should it return to the address given by `%i7 + 4` (this is the address of the delay-slot instruction that has already been executed). The correct return address is given by `%i7 + 8` (the address of the instruction following the delay-slot instruction). Thus, the instruction to return to the caller is

```
jmpl   %i7 + 8, %g0
```

This instruction jumps to the address given by `%i7 + 8`, and then saves its link address (i.e., the address of the `jmpl`) in the register specified by the second operand. We use `%g0` as the second operand because we do not need this link address.

The `restore` instruction that restores the caller's registers appears in the delay slot that follows the `jmpl` instruction. It is executed before `jmpl` jumps back to the calling function. However, the `jmpl` instruction reads its registers before the register switch occurs. Thus, the previous `jmpl` instruction accesses `%i7` of the *called* function (which contains the caller's link address), not `%i7` of the *calling* function. Suppose instead of the `jmpl`/`restore` sequence in Figure 15.19, we used

```
restore
jmpl    %i7 + 8,   %g0        ! accessing caller's %i7
nop
```

When the `jmpl` instruction in this sequence is executed, the register switch triggered by the `restore` instruction has already occurred. Thus, the `jmpl` instruction incorrectly accesses `%i7` of the *calling* function for the link address (the link address is in `%o7` of the calling function). To fix this problem, we simply use `%o7` in the `jmpl` instruction:

```
restore
jmpl    %o7 + 8,   %g0        ! accessing caller's %o7
nop
```

15.3.7 Addressing Modes

The three principal modes of addressing operands are immediate, direct, and indirect. In *immediate addressing*, the operand itself is in the instruction. In *direct addressing*, the instruction contains either the memory address of the operand (*memory direct addressing*) or the number of the register that contains the operand (*register direct addressing*). In *indirect addressing*, the operand address is either in a register (*register indirect addressing*) or in memory (*memory indirect addressing*). Register indirect addressing has three common extensions:

1. *Register indirect with displacement*: The operand address is given by the contents of a register plus a displacement. The relative instructions on H1 use register indirect with displacement addressing with an assumed indirect register (either **sp** or **bp**).
2. *Register indirect with indexing*: The operand address is given by the sum of the contents of two registers.

FIGURE 15.20

Addressing mode	Example
register direct/immediate	add %o0, 5, %o2
register direct	add %o0, %o1, %o2
memory direct	ld [40], %o0
register indirect	ld [%i0], %o0
register indirect with displacement	ld [%i0 + 8], %o0
register indirect with indexing	ld [%i0 + %i1], %o0

FIGURE 15.21

```
 1           ! assume address of table is in %i0
 2       or    %g0, %g0, %i1      ! zero out index reg
 3       or    %g0, 10, %i2       ! set count to 10
 4
 5 loop:  ld    [%i0 + %i1], %o0   ! access element from table
 6              .
 7              .
 8              .
 9       subcc %i2, 1, %i2        ! decrement count
10       bne   loop               ! branch if count not zero
11       add   %i1, 4, %i1        ! add 4 to index reg
```

3. *Register indirect with displacement and indexing*: The operand address is given by the sum of the contents of two registers plus a displacement.

Figure 15.20 summarizes the addressing modes supported by the SPARC.

Memory direct addressing on the SPARC is very limited because the memory address has to fit into the 13-bit **simm13** field of the load and store instructions. Thus, the maximum address is 4095 decimal.

Register indirect with displacement addressing on the SPARC is well-suited for accessing data members of a **struct**, **class**, or stack frame. We simply use the indirect register to hold the address of the **struct**, **class**, or stack frame. Then use the displacement of each field to access that field. For example, if %i0 holds the address of a **struct**, then

```
ld [%i0 + 4] , %o0
```

accesses the item that is 4 bytes into that **struct**.

To access the elements of an array on a SPARC, we can use register indirect with index addressing. In this type of addressing, two registers together hold the operand address. Use the first register to hold the address of the array, and the second (the "index register") to hold the index into the array. For example, the code in Figure 15.21 shows a loop that sequentially accesses the 10 elements of a word array table. Each time through the loop, the index register (%i1) is incremented by the size of one element (see line 11). When the count in %i2 reaches 0, the loop terminates.

15.3.8 A Simple Assembly Language Program

Let's now examine a simple assembly language program for the SPARC that adds 1 and 15, and then stores and displays the sum.

Before we look at the code for this program, let's review the C++ function **printf** (we call it from our assembly language program). When **printf** is called, its first argument (the *control string*) is displayed. However, before this string is displayed, any conversion codes it contains are replaced with the values of the succeeding arguments in the call. A conversion code starts with "%" followed by one or more characters that specify the type of conversion requested. For example, if **sum** contains 16, and we call **printf** with

```
printf("sum = %d\n", sum);
```

printf will first replace the conversion code %d with the decimal value in **sum** ("%d" specifies a conversion to decimal). **printf** then displays the resulting string:

```
sum = 16
```

Recall from Section 9.5 that a C++ compiler uses the address of a string constant wherever that string constant appears. Thus, the previous **printf** call passes two arguments: the *address* of the control string and the value of the argument 16.

We are now ready to examine the program in Figure 15.22. Our program is optimized for clarity rather than efficiency. It consists of three sections: a ".text" section for instructions, a ".data" section for initialized data, and a ".bss" section for uninitialized data. The ".text" section is read-only. The other two sections are read and write. The program uses a variety of assembler directives:

- **.section** (lines 1, 28, 34) specifies the type of section that follows.
- **.global** (line 2) flags the listed identifiers as global.
- **.asciz** (line 29) creates a null-terminated ASCII string.
- **.align** (line 30) forces a boundary alignment.
- **.word** (line 31) defines a word.
- **.skip** (line 36) reserves the indicated number of bytes.

The code on lines 7 to 16 access and add **x** and **y**, and then store the result in **sum**. Lines 18 to 23 implement a call to the **printf** function. The two arguments are passed in **%o0** and **%o1**. Lines 18 and 19 load the first argument (the address of the control string) into **%o0**; lines 21 and 23 load the second argument (the value of **sum**) into **%o1**. Line 22 then calls **printf**. Note that the instructions on lines 23 and 26 are in delay slots.

The executable file for the program in Figure 15.22 contains the **x**, **y**, and **cs** constants. However, it does not contain any space for the items in the ".bss" section. Space is provided for the ".bss" section when the operating system loads the program into memory. Before the program starts executing, this space is zeroed out. Thus, the ".bss" section is appropriate for global data with no explicit initial value (recall that uninitialized global variables in C++ must default to zero).

Instead of using the jmpl/restore sequence on lines 25 and 26 in Figure 15.22, we can terminate the program with the sequence

```
or   %g0, 1, %g1        ! load 1 (terminate program) into %g1
ta   0                  ! trap to operating system
```

The *ta* instruction (trap always) is, in effect, passing a request to the operating system by means of an interrupt. The value in **%g1** indicates the specific request. The

FIGURE 15.22

```
 1              .section ".text"              ! text section
 2              .global main
 3    main:
 4              save  %sp, -96, %sp           ! create called functions frame
 5                                            ! and switch regs
 6
 7              sethi  %hi(x), %l7            ! get x
 8              ld [%l7 + %lo(x)], %o0
 9
10              sethi %hi(y), %l7             ! get y
11              ld [%l7 + %lo(y)], %o1
12
13              add   %o0, %o1, %o0           ! add x and y
14
15              sethi  %hi(sum), %l7          ! store result in sum
16              st    %o0, [%l7 + %lo(sum)]
17
18              sethi %hi(cs), %o0            ! get high part of address of cs
19              or    %o0, %lo(cs), %o0       ! get low part of address of cs
20
21              sethi %hi(sum), %l7           !get high part of address of sum
22              call printf
23              ld [%l7 + %lo(sum)],%o1       ! load sum into % 01
24
25              jmpl  %i7 + 8, %g0            ! return to caller
26              restore                       ! switch to caller's regs
27    !================================================================
28              .section ".data"             ! initialized data section
29    cs:       .asciz    "sum = %d\n"        ! null-terminated string
30              .align  4                     ! force full-word boundary
31    x:        .word   1                     ! integer word
32    y:        .word   15                    ! integer word
33    !================================================================
34              .section ".bss"              ! uninitialized data section
35              .align  4
36    sum:      .skip   4
```

operating system has been programmed to interpret 1 as a program termination request. Thus, for this sequence, the operating system terminates the program.

In addition to passing control to the operating system, trap instructions decrement the **cwp**, change the CPU from *user mode* to *supervisor mode*, and disable further interrupts. When the CPU is in user mode, the executing program cannot adversely affect any other user program or the operating system. For example, if the executing program attempts to execute a *privileged instruction* (an instruction only the operating system should execute) or access another user's memory, an interrupt occurs that forces the termination of the offending program.

The `jmpl/restore` sequence on lines 25 and 26 in Figure 15.22 does not return directly to the operating system. Instead, it returns to a *start-up module* that then executes the `or/ta` sequence to return control to the operating system. The start-up module gets control first from the operating system (hence, the name "start-up module"), it calls **main**, and on return from **main**, it executes the `or/ta` sequence. Because a separate module (i.e., the start-up module) calls **main** module, the label **main** must be global (see line 2 in Figure 15.22).

For each branch instruction, there is a corresponding trap instruction. For example, corresponding to `ble` (branch on less or equal) there is `tle` (trap on less or equal). Unlike the branch instructions, trap instructions are not followed by delay slots.

15.3.9   Synthetic Instructions

To compare the values in **%i0** and **%i1**, we can use the assembly instruction

```
cmp     %i0, %i1
```

When the assembler processes this instruction, it cannot translate it to a compare machine instruction because there is no such instruction. Instead, it translates it to the machine instruction for

```
subcc   %i0, %i1, %g0
```

which, when executed, has no effect other than to set the condition code based on the values in **%i0** and **%i1**. This is precisely what a compare instruction would do. Thus, this particular `subcc` instruction is, in effect, a compare instruction. The `cmp` instruction is not a real instruction. It is just shorthand for another instruction (the `subcc`), which performs a compare operation. Because `cmp` is not a real instruction, we call it a *synthetic* (i.e., artificial) instruction.

Synthetic instructions make reading and writing assembly language programs easier. For example, when we see a `cmp` instruction in a program, we know immediately its intent (to compare two numbers). This is not the case when we see a `subcc` instruction that performs a compare operation. For a `subcc` instruction, we have to study its operands before its intent becomes clear.

One of the principal goals of this chapter is to understand the instruction set of the SPARC. Because the synthetic instructions tend to obscure the true nature of the instruction set, we have refrained from using them. However, they do improve program readability, and for this reason, we will use them from now on.

Four synthetic instructions (`ret`, `retl`, `mov`, and `set`) are particularly important to know. We use *ret* and *retl* to return from functions (we will discuss how they are used later). We use *mov* to load a register from another register, or to load a constant from −4096 to +4095 into a register. For example,

```
mov   %i0, %o0
```

loads the contents of **%i0** into **%o0**, and

```
mov    7, %o0
```

loads 7 into **%o0**. To load a 32-bit value into a register, we use *set*. For example,

```
set 0x12345678, %o0
```

FIGURE 15.23

Synthetic Instruction	Real Instruction	Function
`btst  reg1/immed, reg2`	`andcc reg1, reg2/immed, %g0`	bit test
`bset  reg1/immed, reg2`	`or    reg1, reg2/immed, reg1`	bit set
`bclr  reg1/immed, reg2`	`andn  reg1, reg2/immed, reg1`	bit clear
`btog  reg1/immed, reg2`	`xor   reg1, reg2/immed, reg1`	bit toggle
`clr   reg`	`or    %g0, %g0, reg`	clear
`clr   [address]`	`st    %g0, [address]`	clear
`clrh  [address]`	`sth   %g0, [address]`	clear half
`clrb  [address]`	`stb   %g0, [address]`	clear byte
`cmp   reg1, reg2/immed`	`subcc reg1, reg2/immed, %g0`	compare
`dec   reg`	`sub   reg, 1, reg`	decrement
`dec   immed, reg`	`sub   reg, immed, reg`	decrement
`deccc reg`	`sub   reg, 1, reg`	decrement
`deccc immed, reg`	`subcc reg, immed, reg`	decrement
`inc   reg`	`add   reg, 1, reg`	increment
`inc   immed, reg`	`add   reg, immed, reg`	increment
`inccc reg`	`addcc reg, 1, reg`	increment
`inccc immed, reg`	`addcc reg, immed, reg`	increment
`mov   reg1/immed, reg2`	`or    %g0, reg1/immed, reg2`	move
`neg   reg`	`sub   %g0, reg, reg`	negate
`nop`	`sethi 0, %g0`	no operation
`ret`	`jmpl  %i7 + 8, %g0`	return
`retl`	`jmpl  %o7 + 8, %g0`	ret from leaf
`If 4096 <= value < 4096`		
`      set value, reg`	`or    %g0, value, reg`	set to value
`If value & 0x3ff == 0`		
`      set value, reg`	`sethi %hi(value), reg`	set to value
`If value neither`		
`      set value, reg`	`sethi %hi(value), reg`	set to value
	`or    reg, %lo(value), reg`	

loads 0x12345678 into `%o0`. This synthetic instruction is unusual in that it translates to two real instructions:

```
sethi %hi(0x12345678), %o0
or    %g0, %lo(0x12345678), %o0
```

Similarly,

```
set  x, %o0
```

translates to the `sethi/or` sequence in Figure 15.12 that loads the address of **x** into **%o0**.

Figure 15.23 lists the real instruction equivalences for these and other common synthetic instructions. Because the `set` synthetic instruction can expand to a `sethi/or` sequence, we may get unexpected results if we place it in a delay slot. For example, suppose we load the argument 0x12345678 into %o0 and then call **sub** using

```
call sub
set  0x12345678, %o0
```

This sequence, in reality, is

```
call sub
sethi %hi(0x12345678), %o0
or    %o0, %lo(0x12345678), %o0
```

Because only the `sethi` instruction is in the delay slot, only it will be executed before the call of **sub**. The `or` instruction will be executed after the return from **sub**. Thus, the value passed to **sub** in %o0 will not be 0x12345678.

15.3.10   Compiler-Generated Code

The assembler code for H1 that we examined in previous chapters is reasonably efficient even though it was generated by a "dumb" (i.e., nonoptimizing) compiler. If we had used an optimizing compiler, the assembly code would have been better, but not by much. The principal benefit of an optimizing compiler for H1 would be derived from a more intelligent use of the **ac** register. In particular, by keeping track of the contents of the **ac** register, an optimizing compiler would avoid generating a load instruction for a value already in the **ac** register (for an example of this, see Section 7.2). However, this optimization would occur relatively infrequently, and, therefore, have little overall impact on the efficiency of the code generated.

The extent of the difference between optimized and nonoptimized code depends on the system. For a system like H1 with very few registers, the difference is minimal. However, for a system like the SPARC, the difference is dramatic. With its many general-purpose registers, how its registers are managed has a large impact on the efficiency of the code generated.

Generating code that uses registers efficiently is not easy. Indeed, assembly language programmers often do a poor job managing registers in their own programs. Because a good compiler can perform an extensive analysis of a program's structure to determine register usage, it can often do a better job managing registers than an assembly language programmer. Let's look at several examples in which a structural analysis of a program is important for code optimization:

- Suppose a compiler determines that **m** is used in only the first half of a program, and **n** in only the second half. Then the compiler can map **m** and **n** to the same register. If, instead, it mapped **m** and **n** to different registers, there would be one less register available to hold other variables.
- Suppose **m** and **n** are used throughout a program, but an analysis reveals that **m** will be accessed more often than **n**. If only one register is available, the compiler should map **m**, not **n**, to that register.
- Suppose the following sequence appears in a program:

```
a = p -> q -> r -> x;
cout << a;
c = p -> q -> r -> y;
```

For the first assignment statement, the compiler has to generate code for the expression p -> q -> r that follows the chain of pointers from **p** to **q** to **r**. **r** contains the address of the structure that contains **x**. If the compiler generates code that retains this address in a register, it does not have to generate code to recompute it for the second assignment statement. It simply generates code to access **y** using the retained address. However, if any component of the expression p -> q -> r can change between the two assignment statements, the compiler must not use the value of the first instance of the expression. For example, suppose

```
p++;
```

is between the two assignment statements. Because this statement affects the value of p -> q -> r, the compiler must generate code to recompute p -> q -> r in the second assignment statement. One complicating factor with this type of optimization is that it is often difficult (or impossible) for a compiler to determine if a component of an expression can change. For example, if the statement between the two earlier assignment statements is a function call, the compiler has to analyze the called function to determine if it can change any component of p -> q -> r. The compiler has to perform similar detective work if an intervening statement is

```
(*t)++;
```

Here, the compiler needs to determine if **t** can point to any component of the expression p -> q -> r. This is not an easy task, particularly in C++ where pointers can be manipulated so freely.

To better understand the complexities of generating optimized code, let's examine a C++ program and its compiler-generated assembler equivalent for the SPARC. Our program is a "do-nothing" program whose only function is to illustrate the actions of a compiler (the **gcc** compiler).

In Figure 15.24a, we have a C++ program with both global and local variables. **main** calls **fa**, passing it three arguments, one global and two local. Recall from

FIGURE 15.24 a) C++ code

```
1 int gv1, gv2 = 5;
2 int fa(int x, int y, int z)
3 {
4    return x + y + z;
5 }
6 int main()
7 {
8    int lv1, lv2 = 7;
9
10   lv1 = 11;
11   gv1 = fa(gv2, lv1, lv2);
12
13   return 0;
14 }
```

FIGURE 15.24 (continued)

b) SPARC code

```
1                .section ".text"
2                .global  fa_iii
3
4 fa_iii:  add     %o0, %o1, %o0          ! return x + y + z;
5.         retl
6          add     %o0, %o2, %o0
7
8                .global  main
9 main:    save    %sp, -96, %sp
10
11               sethi   %hi(gv2), %o0         ! gv1 = fa(gv2, lv1, lv2);
12               ld      [%o0+%lo(gv2)], %o0
13               mov     11, %o1               ! lv1 = 11;
14               call    fa_iii
15               mov     7, %o2                ! int lv2= 7;
16               sethi   %hi(gv1), %o1         ! store ret value in gv1
17               st      %o0,[%o1 + %lo(gv1)]
18
19               ret
20               restore %g0, 0, %o0
21 !================================================================
22               .section ".data"
23               .global  gv2                  ! int gv2 = 5;
24               .align   4
25 gv2:          .word    5
26 !================================================================
27               .section ".bss"
28               .global  gv1
29               .align   4
30 gv1:          .skip    4
```

Section 15.3.1 that the registers associated with a function call are spilled to a spill area in the stack only when a function call in a chain *below it* needs registers in its set. Thus, a *leaf function* (i.e., a function that does not contain any function calls) will never have its registers spilled, and, therefore, does not require the save/restore sequence to allocate and deallocate a spill area. fa in Figure 15.24a is a leaf function, and is so simple that it does not require a spill area or anything else in a stack frame that a save instruction would create. Nor does it need its own register set. Thus, the compiler here wisely refrains from generating an unnecessary save/restore sequence in its corresponding assembler function **fa_iii** (see Figure 15.24b). Because there is no register set switch when **fa_iii** is called, the link address is in **%o7** instead of **%i7**. Thus, **fa_iii** returns to its caller with the retl (return from leaf) synthetic instruction (line 5 in Figure 15.24b), which corresponds to the actual instruction

```
jmpl   %o7 + 8, %g0
```

main, on the other hand, has a `save/restore` sequence. Thus, its link address is in **%i7**. Accordingly, it returns to its caller with the `ret` synthetic instruction (line 19 in Figure 15.24b), which corresponds to

```
jmpl   %i7 + 8, %g0
```

The global variables **gv1** and **gv2** are mapped to memory locations (see lines 22 to 30 in Figure 15.24b). Why not map them to `global` registers? Using `global` registers has some disadvantages. First, a global variable in a register requires the overhead of a run-time initialization; that is, it requires the execution of instructions when the program executes. In contrast, a global variable in memory is initialized at assembly time. Thus, it does not require initializing instructions that are executed at run time. Furthermore, using `global` registers presents a complication for a program consisting of separately compiled modules. For example, suppose a compiler maps a global variable to **%g1** in one module. How does it know this when it compiles another module that also references the same global variable? To ensure a mapping that is consistent across all modules, we would somehow have to instruct the compiler to map each global variable to a particular `global` register. But if we did this, it might constrain the compiler in a way that would defeat some of its optimization strategies. The result could easily be less efficient code.

The call of **fa_iii** in Figure 15.24b starts on line 11 where a `sethi` and `ld` instruction load the value of **gv1** (the first argument) into **%o0**. On line 13, a `mov` instruction moves 11 into **%o1**. This is the code that corresponds to the assignment of 11 to **lv1** on line 11 of Figure 15.24a. By using **%o1** to hold **lv1**, the compiler does not have to generate another instruction to load **%o1** for the call of **fa_iii** (a very nice optimization). Similarly, the compiler uses **%o2** for **lv2**, making unnecessary an instruction to load **%o2** for the call of **fa_iii**. Although the `local` registers are nominally for local variables, the compiler here uses **out** registers instead because it results in more efficient code.

Let's now examine compiler-generated code for the SPARC for some additional programs that illustrate special cases. Our next program (see Figure 15.25) illustrates what happens on a SPARC when a function call has more than six arguments. Because only six **out** registers are available for parameter passing, the seventh argument in the call of **fb** on line 9 in Figure 15.25a has to be passed via the stack. In the corresponding assembler code in Figure 15.25b, we can see on line 24 that the seventh argument is stored in the stack. Recall from Figure 15.8 that 92 bytes above the start of a stack frame is the space for any parameters beyond the sixth. Thus, line 24 stores the value of the seventh parameter at the address given by **%sp** + 92. **fb_iiiiiii** adds all the values in **%o0** to **%o5** plus the word at **%sp** + 92 (for this program, no padding is needed). It then returns the sum in **%o0**. In the C++ version, the return value is assigned to the global variable **gv**. However, because **gv** is not referenced again, the compiler does not generate code to do this. In fact, it even does not allocate **gv**. If the call of **fb_iii** had even more parameters, the `save` instruction on line 15 in Figure 15.25b would reserve additional space for these additional parameters. For example, for nine parameters, the `save` instruction would be

```
save   %sp, -104, %sp
```

FIGURE 15.25

a)

```
 1 int gv;
 2 int fb(int t, int u, int v, int w, int x, int y, int z)
 3 {
 4    return t + u + v + w + x + y + z;
 5 }
 6 int main()
 7 {
 8    gv = fb(1, 2, 3, 4, 5, 6, 7);
 9    return 0;
10 }
```

b)

```
 1              .section ".text"
 2              .global  fb_iiiiiii
 3 fb_iiiiiii:
 5              add     %o0, %o1,  %o0    !return t + u + v + w + x + y + z;
 6              add     %o0, %o2,  %o0
 7              add     %o0, %o3,  %o0
 8              add     %o0, %o4,  %o0
 9              add     %o0, %o5,  %o0
 4              ld      [%sp+92],   %g1
10              retl
11              add     %o0, %g1,    %o0
12
13              .global main
14 main:        save    %sp, -96, %sp
15
16              mov     1, %o0                ! gv = g(1, 2, 3, 4, 5, 6, 7);
17              mov     2, %o1
18              mov     3, %o2
19              mov     4, %o3
20              mov     5, %o4
21              mov     6, %o5
22              mov     7, %g1
23              call    fb_iiiiiii
24              st      %g1, [%sp+92]
25
26              ret                           ! return 0;
27              restore %g0, 0, %o0
```

Figure 15.26 illustrates what happens when a local variable has to be in memory. The call of **fc** in Figure 15.26a on line 8 passes the address of **lv**. Thus, **lv** has to be in memory. The compiler maps **lv** to the high end of the stack frame for **main** (see Figure 15.8). Because this program does not use any temps in memory, or

FIGURE 15.26   a)

```
1 void fc(int *p)
2 {
3     *p = 99;
4 }
5 int main()
6 {
7     int lv;
8     fc(&lv);
9     return 0;
10 }
```

b)

```
1              .section ".text"
2              .global fc_pi
3 fc_pi:    mov    99, %g1        ! *p = 99;
4              retl
5              st     %g1, [%o0]
6
7              .global main
8 main:      save   %sp, -96, %sp
9
10            call   fc_pi          !  fc(&lv);
11            add    %sp, 92, %o0
12
13            ret                   ! return 0;
14            restore %g0, 0, %o0
```

more than six parameters, **lv** maps to the address given by **%sp** + 92. Accordingly, the add instruction on line 11 in Figure 15.26b places the value of **%sp** + 92 into **%o0**. **fc_pi** then stores 99 at this address.

In all the preceding examples of compiler-generated SPARC code, the called function was a leaf function, and, therefore, was able to avoid using a save/restore sequence. In our final example (Figure 15.27), the called function, **fd**, itself calls a function, **fnull**. The call of **fnull** forces the compiler to generate a save/restore sequence for **fd** (which is the only reason for **fnull** in this program). Let's take a look at the assembler code in Figure 15.27b for this program. The local variable **lv** in **main** resides in **%o0** and is passed to **fd_i** via the same register (see line 24). Thus, **%i0** in **fd_i** (which is **%o0** in **main**) corresponds to the parameter **x**. There is also space for **x** in the stack frame for **main**, the address of which is given by **%sp** + 68 (see Figure 15.8). Because **%sp** in **main** is **%fp** in **fd_i**, the memory address of **x** within **fd_i** is **%fp** + 68.

Within **fd_i**, **x** simultaneously has two locations: **%i0** and on the stack at **%fp** + 68. When **fp_i** needs the value of **x**, it uses the value in **%i0** (see line 13 in Figure 15.27b); when it needs its address, it uses **%fp** + 68 (see line 10). If **fd_i** did not require the address of **x**, **main** would, nevertheless, reserve space for it on the stack.

FIGURE 15.27

a)

```
 1 int *gpv;
 2 void fnull()
 3 {}
 4 void fd(int x)
 5 {
 6    gpv = &x;
 7    *gpv = x + 3;
 8    fnull();          // forces fd to save/restore
 9 }
10 int main()
11 {
12    int lv = 7;
13
14    fd(lv);
15
16    return 0;
17 }
```

b)

```
 1                 .section ".text"
 2                 .global  fnull_v
 3 fnull_v:   retl
 4                 nop
 5
 6                 .global  fd_i
 7 fd_i:      save      %sp, -96, %sp
 8
 9                 sethi     %hi(gpv), %o1        ! gpv = &x;
10                 add       %fp, 68, %o0
11                 st        %o0, [%o1+%lo(gpv)]
12
13                 mov       %i0, %o0             ! *gpv = x + 3;
14                 add       %o0, 3, %o0
15                 call      fnull_v              ! fnull();
16                 st        %o0, [%fp+68]
17
18                 ret
19                 restore
29
20                 .global  main
21 main:      save      %sp, -96, %sp
22
```

(continued)

FIGURE 15.27 (continued)

```
23                   call    fd_i                        ! fd(lv);
24                   mov     7, %o0
25
26                   ret
27                   restore
28  !================================================================
29                   .section  ".bss"
30                   .global   gpv
31                   .align    4
32  gpv:             .skip     4
```

15.3.11   Memory-Mapped I/O

The SPARC does not have instructions explicitly for I/O. To perform I/O on a SPARC, we use the load and store instructions. By loading and storing to the addresses associated with an I/O device, we read and write from that I/O device. Because this type of I/O maps memory addresses to I/O devices, we call it *memory-mapped I/O.*

Each I/O device typically has several addresses associated with it (for commands, status information, and data). Status information indicates the state of the I/O device or operation (ready, busy, error, data available, etc.). For example, suppose an input device uses addresses 0xfffffff0, 0xfffffff1, and 0xfffffff2 for commands, status, and data, respectively. Then to send the read command (assume it is 1) to a device, we would use

```
set   0xfffffff0, %o0
mov   1, %i0
stb   %i0, [%o0]          ! send read command
```

To get status, we would use

```
ldb [%o0 + 1], %i0        ! get status
```

When the status byte indicates that data is available, we would then read the data with

```
ldb  [%o0 + 2], %i0       ! get data
```

Memory-mapped I/O does not use special I/O instructions, each of which would require an opcode. Thus, more opcodes are available for other instructions. It does, however, reduce the address space available for memory. Any address associated with an I/O device cannot be used to access main memory.

I/O devices are typically shared among users. Thus, there is a danger that one user might access or corrupt another user's data. To prevent this possibility, a user program is not allowed to perform its own I/O. Instead, it passes an I/O request to the operating system. If the request is legal, the operating system performs the I/O operation for the user.

With memory-mapped I/O, a user is prevented from performing its own I/O by the memory-protect mechanism (obviously the load and store instructions cannot be privileged). If a user attempts to access an I/O device, the memory-protect mechanism generates an interrupt that results in the termination of the offending program.

The program in Figure 15.22 performs I/O by calling the `printf` function. The `printf` function itself, however, cannot perform I/O because it is part of the user program. It, instead, passes an I/O request to the operating system using a `trap` instruction. When the I/O operation is complete, the operating system returns to the user program using the `rett` (return from trap) instruction. A `rett` instruction does the reverse of a `trap` instruction: It returns to the user, increments the `cwp`, changes the CPU from supervisor to user mode, and enables further interrupts.

For most I/O requests, the operating system initiates the I/O operation, and, in addition, places the user program in a *wait state*. It then gives control to another program, which executes while the I/O operation for the first program progresses. When the I/O operation completes, the I/O device triggers an interrupt that causes control to return to the operating system. The operating system then provides the I/O to the requesting program, and changes its state to ready, at which time the requesting program is eligible to continue its execution. We call this approach to I/O that uses the interrupt mechanism to signal the completion of an I/O operation *interrupt-driven I/O*. The alternative approach in which the CPU repeatedly checks the status of an I/O device is called *program-controlled I/O*.

15.4   THE PENTIUM: A CISC ARCHITECTURE

The latest processors in Intel's IA-32 product line are the Pentium series. "IA-32" stands for "Intel Architecture: 32 bit." The 80386 was the first IA-32 processor. Introduced in 1985, the 80386 was succeeded by the 80486 in 1989, and then by the first of the Pentium series in 1993.

The Pentium has a CISC architecture, although it utilizes some techniques typically associated with a RISC. For example, it uses hardwired control for its simpler instructions. This approach allows it to achieve high performance with its simpler instructions in the same way a RISC does, and, at the same time, cost-effectively implement in microcode its complex instructions. It uses pipelining, superscalar execution, and dynamic branch prediction. Starting with the Pentium Pro (1995), the processor itself can reorder instructions, allowing the parallel execution of more instructions. Support for vector operations on floating-point data was added with the Pentium III (1999). A *vector operation* is one in which a single instruction can operate on multiple data items. We call an instruction with this capability an *SIMD* instruction (single instruction multiple data). One of the remarkable features of the Pentium (and an essential factor in its success) is its compatibility extending all the way back to the 8086 processor Intel introduced in 1978. This backward-compatibility is also responsible for the Pentium's complex structure. It is several generations of processors rolled up into one.

15.4.1   Register Structure

The Pentium is a descendant of earlier Intel processors whose word size is 2 bytes. Thus, the term "word" historically has meant a 2-byte item for Intel's processors. For consistency's sake, Intel carried over this terminology to the Pentium. Thus,

FIGURE 15.28 Principal Registers on the Pentium

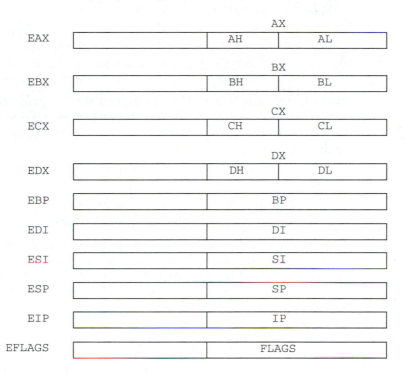

a word on a Pentium is 2 bytes, even though its register and address sizes are 4 bytes. Intel calls a 4-byte item a *doubleword*.

The Pentium has 4-byte registers that are extensions of the 2-byte registers found on earlier processors. For example, the Intel 8088 (the processor on the early IBM PCs) has a 2-byte register called **ax**. The Pentium has a 4-byte register called **eax** (extended **ax**). For backward compatibility, the lower halves of the Pentium's extended registers function like the 2-byte registers of the earlier processors, and are designated with the same names. For example, the **ax** register on a Pentium is the lower half of the **eax** register. The **ax** register, in turn, consists of 2-byte registers, **ah** and **al** (see Figure 15.28). Most registers on the Pentium have a specific function. They are not as general purpose as the registers on the SPARC. For example, **EDI** and **ESI** are the "destination index" and the "source index" registers that are used by the block copy instruction. There are also considerably fewer registers on the Pentium than on the SPARC.

15.4.2   Assembly Language

In the Pentium assembly language we will use, the direction of a mov instruction is from right to left. For example, the instruction

```
mov     ebp, esp
```

moves the contents of **esp** to **ebp**. The mnemonic mov represents a whole class of instructions. In addition to a register-to-register move like the previous instruction, a mov instruction can move an immediate value into a register, load from memory, and store into memory; it can perform these operations with a variety of data lengths. For example, the mov instructions

```
mov    eax, 3              ; load eax with 4-byte integer 3
mov    ax, 3               ; load ax with 2-byte integer 3
mov    eax, [ebp-8]        ; load eax from memory
mov    [ebp-8], eax        ; store eax into memory
```

move immediate (4 bytes), move immediate (2 bytes), load from memory, and store to memory, respectively. Square brackets signal a memory operand. For example, in the last instruction, **[ebp-8]** specifies the address given by the contents of the **ebp** register minus 8.

Both of the following mov instructions store the contents of a register in the same memory location:

```
mov    [ebp-8], eax        ; store 4 bytes
mov    [ebp-8], ax         ; store 2 bytes
```

However, they differ in the number of bytes they store. The first mov stores 4 bytes; the second, stores 2 bytes. Because **eax** is a 4-byte register, the assembler knows it has to assemble the first instruction to the instruction that stores 4 bytes. Similarly, because **ax** is a 2-byte register, the assembler knows it has to translate the second instruction to the instruction that stores 2 bytes. Now consider the following mov instruction:

```
mov    [ebp-8], 7
```

This instruction stores 7 into the location specified by the first operand. However, it does not specify if the address specified by its first operand is a byte, word, or doubleword address. Thus, this instruction is ambiguous. It does not specify the data width. To make this instruction acceptable to the assembler, we have to qualify its address operand as a byte, word, or doubleword address. To do this, we precede the address operand in the assembly instruction with "byte ptr", "word ptr", or "dword ptr". For example,

```
mov    byte ptr [ebp-8], 7
```

stores a single byte containing 7 into the location given by [ebp-8]. Similarly,

```
mov    word ptr [ebp-8], 7
```

stores a word containing 7, and

```
mov    dword ptr [ebp-8], 7
```

stores a doubleword containing 7.

15.4.3 Compiler-generated Code

Figure 15.29 shows the Pentium version of the C++ program in Figure 15.24a. Because assembler code for the Pentium and H1 are so similar you should not have much trouble understanding this program.

main in Figure 15.29 is both a called function (it is called by start-up code) and a calling function (it calls **@fa$iii**). **main** and **@fa$iii** both start with the two-instruction sequence

```
push ebp                   ; save ebp on the stack
mov  ebp, esp              ; move in called fn's frame address
```

FIGURE 15.29

```
Intel Pentium code
 1 .code
 2          public  @fa$iii
 3 @fa$iii: push    ebp
 4          mov     ebp, esp
 5
 6          mov     eax, [ebp+8]            ; return x + y + z;
 7          add     eax, [ebp+12]
 8          add     eax, [ebp+16]
 9
10          pop     ebp
11          ret
12
13          public  main
14 main:    push    ebp
15          mov     ebp, esp
16
17          add     esp,-8                  ; int lv1, lv2 = 7;
18          mov     dword ptr [ebp-8], 7
19
20          mov     dword ptr [ebp-4], 11 ; lv1 = 11;
21
22          push    dword ptr [ebp-8]       ; gv1 = fa(gv2, lv1, lv2);
23          push    dword ptr [ebp-4]
24          push    dword ptr [gv2]
25          call    @fa$iii
26          add     esp,12
27          mov     [gv1], eax
28
29          xor     eax, eax                ; return 0;
30          mov     esp, ebp
31          pop     ebp
32          ret
33 ;=============================================================
34 .data
35          public gv1
36 gv1      dd      ?                       ; reserve 4 bytes
37          public gv2
38 gv2      dd      5                       ; define constant 5
```

FIGURE 15.30   a) Before push/mov sequence (right after call instruction)

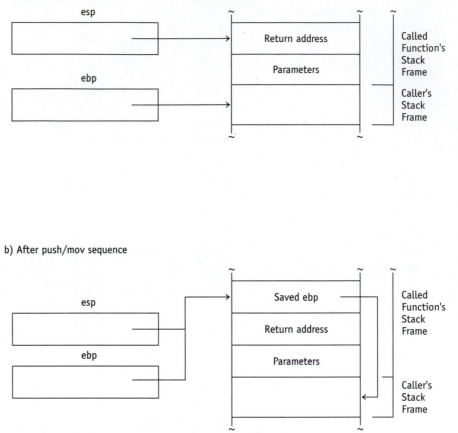

b) After push/mov sequence

This sequence has exactly the same effect as a single esba instruction in the optimal and stack instruction sets for H1. Figure 15.30a shows the stack configuration just before this sequence is executed. **esp** (the top-of-stack pointer) points to the return address (pushed by the call instruction just executed by the caller), and **ebp** (the base pointer) points to the caller's stack frame. The push instruction saves the caller's base pointer by pushing it onto the stack (see Figure 15.30b). The mov instruction then loads **ebp** with the address in **esp** (which is the base pointer for the called function). Thus, the items in the called function stack frame can now be accessed via **ebp**. For example, the instruction

```
mov     eax, [ebp+8]
```

accesses the doubleword (the parameter **x**) 8 bytes above the location pointed to by **ebp**.

The start of the exit sequence in **main** (lines 30 and 31),

```
mov     esp, ebp
pop     ebp
```

has exactly the same effect as a reba instruction in the optimal and stack instruction sets. The mov removes the called function's local variables from the stack; the pop reestablishes the caller's base pointer by popping the top of the stack (the saved base pointer) into the `ebp` register. If the called function has no local variables, the `mov` instruction is unnecessary because `esp` would already equal `ebp`. That is why the exit sequence for `@fa$iii` (line 10) omits the `mov` instruction. After this sequence is executed, the stack reverts back to the configuration in Figure 15.30a. The `ret` instruction (lines 11 and 32) then returns control to the calling function.

The `add` instruction on line 17 allocates the local variables `lv1` and `lv2` by adding −8 to the stack pointer `esp`. The `push` instructions on lines 22 to 24 push the values of the arguments that are passed to `@fa$iii`. `@fa$iii` adds these values and returns their sum to `main` via the `eax` register.

The Pentium code in Figure 15.29 is not optimized. If we keep `lv1` and `lv2` in registers, we can eliminate the instruction on line 17 that allocates these variables on the stack. Then the instructions on lines 18, 20, 22, and 23 can be replaced with instructions that make one fewer memory references. With these optimizations, the program consists of 21 instructions with 14 referencing memory (remember to count any instruction that performs a push or a pop). The corresponding SPARC program (Figure 15.24b) has 13 instructions with only 2 referencing memory. For this program, the SPARC is clearly the winner. By using registers effectively, the SPARC program has roughly half the complexity of the Pentium program.

High-powered compilers are particularly important for RISC systems. There are two reasons for this. First, RISC systems typically have a large number of registers. To generate efficient code, the compiler must manage these registers well. Second, RISC systems are pipelined. To maintain high pipeline efficiency, the compiler must generate code sequences that minimize pipeline dependencies. For a CISC like the Pentium, a high-powered compiler is less critical.

15.4.4 I/O Instructions

Unlike the SPARC, the Pentium has instructions dedicated to I/O. The **IN** instructions perform input; the **OUT** instructions perform output. The width of the data transfer depends on the register specified in the I/O instruction. For example,

```
IN AL,DX     ; read one byte
```

reads 1 byte (because AL is a 1-byte register) from the I/O device whose *port number* (i.e., address) is in DX, but

```
IN AX,DX     ; read two bytes
```

reads 2 bytes (because **AX** is a 2-byte register). I/O instructions can specify the port number in two ways: directly with an 8-bit constant, or indirectly with the DX register. For example, in the instruction

```
IN AL,61H  ; port number address is 61H
```

the port number is specified directly, but in

```
IN  AL,DX   ; port number is in DX register
```

it is specified indirectly. With the direct approach, the port number is limited to 8 bits; with the indirect approach it is limited to 16 bits. Figure 15.31 summarizes the I/O instructions on the Pentium.

FIGURE 15.31   I/O Instructions on the Pentium

```
IN      AL,DX
IN      AX,DX
IN      EAX,DX
IN      AL,<8-bit port number>
IN      AX,<8-bit port number>
IN      EAX,<8-bit port number>

OUT     DX,AL
OUT     DX,AX
OUT     DX,EAX
OUT     <8-bit port number>,AL
OUT     <8-bit port number>,AX
OUT     <8-bit port number>,EAX
```

FIGURE 15.32

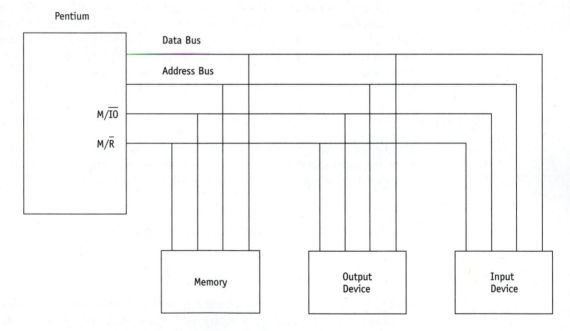

The Pentium has two control lines for data bus transfers (see Figure 15.32). One control line (M/$\overline{\text{IO}}$) indicates if the transfer is with memory or with an I/O device; the other control line (W/$\overline{\text{R}}$) indicates if the transfer is a write or a read. Because of the M/$\overline{\text{IO}}$ control line on the Pentium, a memory location and an I/O device can have the same address without interfering with each other. On a memory operation, only memory responds because M/$\overline{\text{IO}}$ is 1. On an I/O operation, only an I/O device responds because M/$\overline{\text{IO}}$ is 0. The M/$\overline{\text{IO}}$ control line creates two separate address spaces: one for memory and one for I/O devices.

With memory-mapped I/O, the I/O instructions are "free": We use the load and store instructions. But it forces memory to share its address space with the I/O devices. With dedicated I/O instructions, we have two separate address spaces. But the I/O instructions consume valuable opcodes that could have been used for other instructions.

FURTHER READING

Bryant, R., and O'Hallaron, D. *Computer Systems: A Programmer's Perspective.* Upper Saddle River, NJ: Prentice-Hall, 2003.

Irvine, K. *Assembly Language for Intel-Based Computers*, 4th ed. Upper Saddle River, NJ: Prentice-Hall, 2003.

Paul, R. *SPARC Architecture, Assembly Language Programming, and C*, 2nd ed. Upper Saddle River, NJ: Prentice-Hall, 2000.

Weaver, D., and Germond, T. *The SPARC Architecture Manual.* Englewood Cliffs, NJ: PTR Prentice-Hall, 1994.

PROBLEMS

15.1. Using `sp` as the base pointer in the standard instruction set of H1 causes complications. But using `%sp` as a base pointer on a SPARC does not cause similar complications. Why not?

15.2. Why is pipelining more cost-effective than buying multiple computers?

15.3. Why does the displacement field in a SPARC `call` instruction have more bits than the displacement field in a branch instruction?

15.4. Why are global variables usually not kept in global registers on the SPARC?

15.5. Why are two sets of integer condition code bits used on a 64-bit SPARC? Why not have just the `xcc` set?

15.6. What is the advantage of having more register sets on a SPARC? Are there any disadvantages?

15.7. Give a circumstance in which the `andn` instruction on the SPARC would be useful (see Appendix D).

15.8. Give a circumstance in which the `orn` instruction on the SPARC would be useful (see Appendix D).

15.9. With a 16-bit address space, which makes more sense: memory-mapped I/O or dedicated I/O instructions? With a 32-bit address space? With a 64-bit address space?

15.10. A trap on the SPARC decrements the `cwp`, thereby causing the trap handling code to use the next register set. It also disables further traps, including window overflow traps. Is there potential here that the trap handling code will corrupt some users' registers? What must the trap handling code do to avoid this?

15.11. What are the three principal functions of the `rett` instruction on the SPARC?

15.12. Propose a way to reduce the overhead associated with a context switch on a SPARC.

15.13. Why does the SPARC require boundary alignments for operands that are loaded and stored?

15.14. Why is a longer pipeline not necessarily better than a shorter one?

15.15.   What is the potential advantage of a longer pipeline?

15.16.   Most of the load instructions on the SPARC come in signed and unsigned pairs. Why do the store instructions not also come in pairs?

15.17.   Which of the following sequences at the end of a called function on a SPARC correctly returns control to the calling function? Assume the called function executed a `save` instruction on entry.

```
restore            restore
ret                retl
nop                nop
```

15.18.   A nop instruction on a SPARC is translated to a `sethi` instruction. Why not use

```
add    %g0, %g0, %g0
```

instead of a `sethi`?

15.19.   Propose two simpler alternatives to interrupt-driven I/O that do not allow concurrent I/O activity with program execution.

15.20.   What tests do `bge` and `bpos` perform on the condition code on a SPARC? Do they perform the same tests?

15.21.   Does `%r14` have to be the stack pointer? Could we use another register without changing any aspect of the SPARC architecture?

15.22.   Remove the dependency in the following SPARC sequence without affecting what it does:

```
ld    [%l0], %o0
ld    [%l1], %o1
or    %o0, %o1, %o2
```

15.23.   Is

```
mov %o0 + 7, %o1
```

a legal synthetic instruction on a SPARC?

15.24.   Is

```
mov 5000, %o1
```

a legal synthetic instruction on a SPARC?

15.25.   Translate Figure 15.27a with line 7 appearing twice in succession to SPARC assembly code.

15.26.   Write and run a SPARC assembly language program that adds 10 numbers in a table in memory, and displays the sum. Use 33, 11, −4, 73, 1000, −123456, 15, −1, 11, and 7.

15.27.   Write and run a SPARC assembly language program that displays all prime numbers less than 5000.

15.28.   Write and run a SPARC assembly language program that displays a large capital letter *I* that spans 40 lines. Use multiple copies of the character @ to form the letter.

15.29.   Same as Problem 15.28, but for the letter Z.

15.30.   Write and run a SPARC assembly language program that displays itself in hex.

15.31.   Write and run a SPARC assembly language program that prompts the user for two numbers, reads in the numbers as strings, converts the strings to binary numbers, adds the binary numbers, converts the sum to a string, and then displays this final string.

15.32. Write and run the SPARC assembly language program specified in Problem 4.24.

15.33. Translate the C++ code in Figure 15.24a to H1 assembly language.

15.34. Optimize the Pentium program in Figure 15.29.

15.35. The SPARC uses two program counters, `pc` and `npc`. Why?

15.36. Why does `@fa$iii` in Figure 15.29 not end with

```
mov     esp, ebp
pop     ebp
ret
```

15.37. Use `%fp` instead of `%sp` in `fb_iiiiiii` in Figure 15.25b.

15.38. Rewrite the program in Figure 15.24b with `lv1` and `lv2` in local registers. How much worse is the resulting code?

15.39. How is the starting point specified in a SPARC assembler program? Hint: Examine Figure 15.22.

15.40. Why does the SPARC compiler reserve stack space for parameters even when it is not needed?

15.41. What problem can occur because of the way function names are mangled in Figure 15.24b? What is the solution if the problem occurs?

15.42. Suppose an expression is repeated in a program with an intervening function call. What must the compiler do to determine if the value for the first instance of the expression can be used for the second instance?

15.43. Is

```
sethi x >> 10, %o0
```

a legal assembler instruction on a SPARC, where `x` is a label on a constant in the ".data" section? What about

```
sethi 0x12345678 >> 10, %o0
```

15.44. Define a data word in the ".text" section of a SPARC program. Does the program assemble without error? Can the program load from the word? Can it store in the word?

15.45. What is the difference between `ldx` and `ldd` on a SPARC?

15.46. When an overflow trap on a SPARC spills a register set to a spill area, how does it know where the spill area is for that set of registers?

15.47. If a SPARC has five register sets, how long can a function chain be without causing a window overflow?

15.48. Propose a simple implementation of dynamic branch prediction.

15.49. Which is more likely to do a better job in branch prediction: the compiler or the hardware? Justify your answer.

15.50. Suppose the hardware assumed that a branch instruction would always branch (in which case if a branch did not occur, the processing of the target sequence would have to be undone). Would this approach likely improve or degrade the execution rate?

15.51. Draw a diagram like that in Figure 15.17c for the pipeline activity shown in Figure 15.18b and in Figure 15.18c.

15.52. What additional hardware is required to implement a pipeline?

15.53. Can a called function access the calling function's stack frame using `%sp` as a base address on a SPARC?

15.54. What determines instruction execution rate on a pipelined computer?

15.55.   Hand assemble the following SPARC instructions. Give your answers in hex.

```
ld  [%sp], %o0
ld  [%fp+8], %r15
ld  [%i2+%l3], %g0
st  %o0, [%sp], %o0
st  %r15, [%fp+8],%r15
st  %g0, [%i2+%l3], %g0
```

15.56.   What benefit can be derived from the **p** bit on a SPARC?

15.57.   Why is the type of addressing used by branch and `call` instructions on the SPARC called pc-relative addressing?

15.58.   What is the advantage of the relative addressing used by the `call` and branch instructions on the SPARC?

15.59.   Why do some instructions on the SPARC come in pairs: one sets the condition code and one does not?

15.60.   Explain why having pairs of arithmetic and logical instructions (one sets the condition code and one does not) on the SPARC allows more flexibility in instruction reordering. Give a specific example.

15.61.   Translate the program in Figure 15.25 to Pentium assembly language. How does your answer compare with the SPARC assembly code?

15.62.   Translate the program in Figure 15.26 to Pentium assembly language. How does your answer compare with the SPARC assembly code?

15.63.   Translate the program in Figure 15.27 to Pentium assembly language. How does your answer compare with the SPARC assembly code?

15.64.   Write a C++ program that requires fewer assembler instructions on a Pentium than on a SPARC.

15.65.   How is **%g1** used in Figure 15.25b?

15.66.   For what type of C++ statements does the SPARC handle significantly better than the Pentium?

15.67.   We set **p** to 0 by suffixing ",nt" to a branch mnemonic in SPARC assembly language, but we do not suffix anything to set **a** to 0. Why?

15.68.   Why are distinct sections used for initialized and uninitialized global variables in a SPARC assembly language program?

15.69.   If an expression consists of local variables exclusively, can the call and execution of a function change the value of the expression?

15.70.   Give the nonsynthetic assembler instructions that correspond to the following SPARC synthetic instructions:

```
mov  7,%o0
mov  %i0, %o7
nop
ret
retl
set  5, %o0
set  5000, %o9
inc  %i0
clr  %i0
clr  [%i0]
```

15.71.   Hand assemble the code in Figure 15.22. Give your answer in hex.

15.72.   Hand assemble the code in Figure 15.24b. Give your answer in hex.

15.73. Hand assemble the code in Figure 15.25b. Give your answer in hex.

15.74. Hand assemble the code in Figure 15.26b. Give your answer in hex.

15.75. Hand assemble the code in Figure 15.27b. Give your answer in hex.

15.76. Add the line

```
cout << gv1 << endl;
```

betweens lines 11 and 12 in Figure 15.24a. Translate to the stack instruction set and run on **sim**.

For the following problems, translate the given program to H1, SPARC, and Pentium assembly code.

15.77.
```
#include <cstdio>
using namespace std;
void f(int x)
{
    if (x == 0) return;
    printf("%d\n", x);
    f(x - 1);
}
int main()
{
    f(10);
    return 0;
}
```

15.78.
```
#include <cstdio>
using namespace std;
void f(int &x)
{
    x = 5;
}
int main()
{
    int y = 8;
    f(y);
    printf("%d\n", y);
    return 0;
}
```

15.79.
```
#include <cstdio>
using namespace std;
int gv;
void f(int a,int b,int c,int d,int e,int f,int g,int h)
{
    gv = a + b + c + d + e + f + h + g + 1;
}
int main()
{
    printf("%d\n", gv);
    return 0;
}
```

15.80.
```cpp
#include <cstdio>
using namespace std;
void f(int x)
{
    int *p;
    printf("%d\n", x);
    p = &x;
    *p = 99;
    printf("%d\n", x);
}
int main()
{
    f(5);
    return 0;
}
```

15.81.
```cpp
#include <cstdio>
using namespace std;
int gv = 55;
int f(int x, int y)
{
    return gv + x + y;
}
int main()
{
    int y = 3, z;
    z = f(y + 18, 44);
    printf("%d\n", z);
    return 0;
}
```

15.82.
```cpp
#include <cstdio>
using namespace std;
struct S {
    int x, y;
};
int main()
{
    S a;
    a.x = 5;
    a.y = 6;
    printf("%d %d\n", a.x, a.y);
    return 0;
}
```

15.83.
```cpp
#include <cstdio>
using namespace std;
struct S {
    int x, y;
};
S f()
{
```

```
        S a;
        a.x = 1;
        a.y = 2;
        return a;
    }
    int main()
    {
        S b;
        b = f();
        printf("%d %d\n", b.x, b.y);
        return 0;
    }
```

Chapter Sixteen

JAVA VIRTUAL MACHINE

16.1   INTRODUCTION

Most compilers translate programs to the machine code of the computer on which they run. The translated programs can then run on those computers. For example, a C++ compiler for a PC outputs PC machine code that can run on a PC. Java compilers, however, are different. Regardless of the computer on which they run, Java compilers translate Java programs to *bytecode*, the machine code for the Java Virtual Machine (JVM). To execute bytecode on a PC, we have to run a program—the Java interpreter—on that PC to make it look like the JVM. For example, suppose the file `Simple.java` contains a Java program. To compile it with the Sun Java SDK system, we enter

```
javac Simple.java
```

`javac` (the Java compiler) translates `Simple.java` and outputs the translated program to the file `Simple.class`. To run `Simple.class`, we enter

```
java Simple
```

`java` (the Java interpreter) then simulates the JVM and runs the bytecode in `Simple.class` on this simulated machine.

The two principle advantages of compiling to bytecode are portability and security. A translated Java program can run on any computer for which a Java interpreter is available. Moreover, running Java programs is relatively safe. The Java interpreter places limits on what bytecode can do, thereby protecting the host system. On the negative side, Java programs tend to be slow, principally for these reasons:

1. The interpretation of bytecode can involve a considerable amount of overhead. Each bytecode instruction interpreted by the JVM requires the JVM to execute 10 or more machine instructions on the host computer. Thus, a Java program may run 10 or more times slower than an equivalent program in *native code* (code in the machine language of the host computer). Some JVMs use *just-in-time (JIT)* compiling to speed up program execution. In this technique, bytecode instructions are compiled to native code on an as-needed basis. The native code can then be used in place of the bytecode.
2. The JVM *dynamically* links classes; that is, it loads and combines classes into a single program *at run time*. Thus, linking overhead contributes to execution time *every* time a Java program executes. In contrast, C++ programs are generally linked only once, before execution.
3. The JVM performs checks during loading and linking (this process is called *verification*), and during the execution of bytecode to ensure the safety of the host

system. Run-time checks include tests for invalid array bounds, invalid reference casts, and object references using a `null` reference. Although these checks are important, they all increase the execution time of Java programs.

Many Web pages have embedded *applets*—Java programs *automatically* downloaded and executed on your computer whenever you visit one of these pages with your Web browser. These applets execute on the JVM that is part of your Web browser. Clearly, applets have to be portable (so they can run on all the different types of computers connected to the Web). Even more important, applets must be safe to run; that is, they must be prevented from performing any inappropriate action (like erasing your hard disk or transmitting your confidential files). Java applets running on the JVM in your Web browser meet both of these requirements. In contrast, compiled C++ programs are neither portable nor safe. Thus, although C++ programs are, in general, faster than comparable Java programs, they are ill-suited as a substitute for Java applets.

We are already familiar with many of the concepts underlying the JVM. For example, in Chapter 13, we learned how objects are implemented at the assembly level. Although we addressed C++ objects specifically, the basic concepts that we learned also apply to Java. In the same chapter, we also studied a stack architecture whose basic structure is similar to that of the JVM.

Let's now investigate some of the instructions and features of the JVM. We cannot cover every instruction in a single chapter (there are 202 standard instructions). However, we can cover enough of them to get a clear picture of the structure and operation of the JVM.

16.2　STRUCTURE OF THE JVM

The four principal parts of the JVM are the **execution engine**, the **method area**, the **Java stack**, and the **heap** (see Figure 16.1).

The *execution engine* is the CPU of the JVM. It contains the **pc** register as well as other implementation-dependent registers. The **pc** holds a 32-bit address. Thus, the JVM has a 2^{32} = 4 gigabyte address space.

The *method area* (sometimes called the *class area*) contains the information on each class provided by its ".class" file. This includes not only the bytecode for each method (in Java, functions are called *methods*), but also additional information needed for verification and linking. Also associated with the method area are static variables. A Java *static variable* is a variable that is shared by all the objects of a class. Only one copy exists. In contrast, an *instance variable* is not shared—each object has its own copy.

Whenever a method is called, a *frame* for that method is pushed onto the top of the *Java stack*. Whenever that method returns to its caller, its frame is popped from the Java stack and discarded. Thus, the top frame always is for the currently executing method.

A frame consists of two distinct items: a local variable array and an operand stack. A *local variable array* contains the parameters and local variables associated with a method call. The *operand stack* is a holding area for operands and results. For example, the `iadd` instruction pops the top two integers from the operand stack, adds them, and pushes the result back onto the operand stack. Be careful not to confuse the *Java stack* (the structure that holds frames) with the *operand*

FIGURE 16.1   Java Virtual Machine

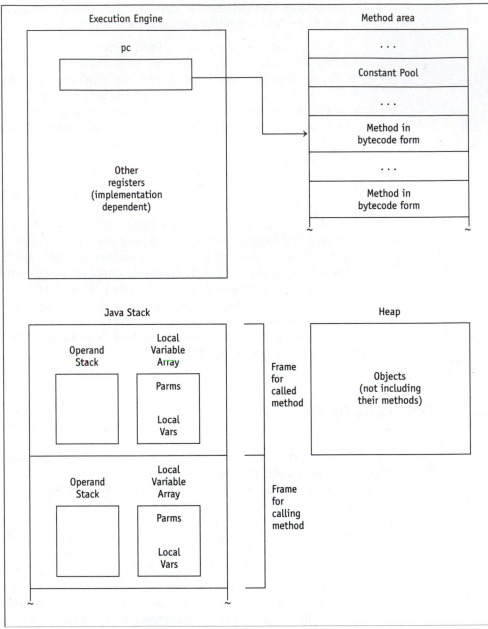

stack (the stack within a single frame). Because of the central role of the operand stack during the execution of bytecode, we say that the JVM has a *stack-oriented architecture*.

Each slot in the operand stack and the local variable array holds 4 bytes. The operand stack and the local variable array can hold any of Java's primitive types (`byte, short, int, long, float, double,` and `char`), as well as object and array references. `byte` and `short` items are sign extended to 4 bytes when they are pushed onto the operand stack or stored in the local variable array; `char` items are zero extended to 4 bytes; and `double` and `long` items use two consecutive slots.

The *heap* contains objects. Whenever an object is created, an area for it is dynamically allocated in the heap. The heap contains the data fields of objects but not their methods. One set of methods for each class appears in the method area, and is shared by all objects of that class. Periodically, the *garbage collection* mechanism in the JVM determines which objects are no longer referenced. These objects are deallocated so the storage they occupy in the heap can be reused.

16.3 SOME COMMON OPERATIONS THAT USE THE OPERAND STACK

The JVM has a variety of instructions that operate on the operand stack and the local variable array. For the sake of clarity, we will represent the opcodes of these instructions with their mnemonics, and their operands with decimal numbers. You, of course, should understand that bytecode consists of binary numbers.

Many of the mnemonics for instruction start with the first letter of the data type on which the instruction operates. For example, the initial "i" in the mnemonic `iadd` indicates an integer operation. The `iadd` instruction adds two integers. To represent a reference, the mnemonics use the letter "a".

Most bytecode instructions are only 1 byte long and contain only an opcode. For example, to push the integer constant 0 onto the operand stack, we use the 1-byte instruction `iconst_0`. There are similar 1-byte instructions that push $-1, 2, 3,$ 4, and 5. Their mnemonics also start with "iconst_", but are suffixed with "m1", "2", "3", "4", and "5", respectively. For example `iconst_5` pushes 5. If we want to push a constant for which no 1-byte instruction exists, we have to use a multiple-byte instruction. For example, to push 6, we use a *bipush* instruction (byte integer push):

```
bipush 6
```

This instruction consists of a 1-byte opcode (10 hex) followed by a 1-byte operand field containing 6. When executed, it converts the 6 to a 4-byte **int** (by sign extension), and then pushes it onto the operand stack. To push an integer whose value requires 2 bytes, we use the *sipush* instruction (short integer push). Its operand field is 2 bytes long and, therefore, can accommodate integers from -32768 to 32767.

Let's say we wish to add 3, 6, and 130. One possible instruction sequence is

```
iconst_3              ; push 3
bipush    6           ; push 6
iadd                  ; pop 6 and 3, add, and push sum (9)
sipush    130         ; push 130
iadd                  ; add 130 and 9, add, and push sum
```

The instructions, like `iadd`, that perform a binary operation pop the top two items from the operand stack, operate on them, and then push the result back onto the operand stack. The JVM has a variety of arithmetic instructions. For example, it has *fadd* (float add), *ladd* (long add), and *dadd* (double add), in addition to `iadd`. There are similar instructions for subtraction, multiplication, division, and remainder. (For a complete list of JVM instructions, see Appendix E.)

Values in the local variable array can be pushed onto the operand stack. (The instructions that do this are called *load instructions*.) One-byte instructions are used for the more common load operations; for example, to load an integer from local variable 0 (i.e., from the first slot in the local variable array), we use

```
iload_0
```

Other single-byte `iload` instructions are `iload_1`, `iload_2`, and `iload_3`. To load from local variable 4 and above, we have to use the multiple-byte `iload` instruction. For example,

```
iload 4
```

is a 2-byte instruction that pushes the value in local variable 4.

The *store instructions* do the reverse of the load instructions; that is, they store the value popped from the operand stack into the local variable array. For example,

```
istore_0
```

pops and stores the value on top of the operand stack in local variable 0. Other `istore` instructions include `istore_1`, `istore_2`, and `istore_3`. There are similar sets of load and store instructions for `float`, `long`, `double`, and reference types. For example `aload_2` loads a reference from local variable 2 ("a" stands for "reference"); `astore_2` stores a reference into local variable 2.

The `putstatic` and `getstatic` instructions transfer values between the top of the operand stack and static variables. The `putstatic` instruction pops the value on top of the operand stack and stores it in a static variable; the `getstatic` instruction pushes the value in a static variable onto the operand stack. The operand field in the `putstatic` and `getstatic` instructions specify the static variable to use. This field contains an index into the *constant pool* where there are pointers to the variable's class and name, from which its location can be determined. For example, in the instruction

```
getstatic 2
```

the operand 2 is an index into the constant pool. We will examine the structure of the constant pool in Section 16.8.

16.4 INVOKING AND RETURNING FROM METHODS

• •

An invoke instruction calls a method. The type of invoke instruction to use depends on the type of method called. To call a static method (a *static method* in Java is one that can be called via its class), we use the *invokestatic* instruction. The operand field in the `invokestatic` instruction specifies the method to call. Like the `putstatic` and `getstatic` instructions, this operand is an index into the constant pool. For example, in the instruction

```
invokestatic 3
```

the operand 3 is an index into the constant pool. The *invokevirtual* instruction calls instance methods (i.e., methods in objects). The *invokespecial* instruction calls special methods, such as the superclass's constructor. The sequence for call-

FIGURE 16.2

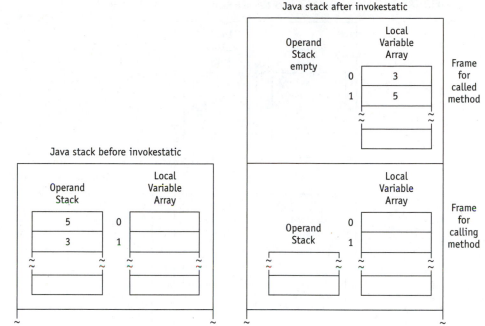

ing a method first pushes the arguments to be passed onto the operand stack. The invoke instruction then performs several functions:

- It creates a frame for the called method and pushes it onto the Java stack.
- It pops the arguments from the caller's operand stack and places them in the called method's local variable array. If the called method is static, the arguments are placed in the local variable array starting with local variable 0. For nonstatic methods, the arguments start at local variable 1. In the latter case, local variable 0 is loaded with the reference to the object that contains the called method. Figure 16.2 shows the before and after pictures of the Java stack for an invokestatic instruction that passes two arguments, 3 and 5. Notice that 3, the left argument (which is pushed first by the caller), ends up in local variable 0.
- It transfers control to the called method.

A *return* instruction returns control to the calling method. Its execution pops the frame of the called method, uncovering the frame of the caller. The specific return instruction to use depends on whether a value is returned, and if one is, its type. For example, the *return* instruction simply returns to the caller. The *ireturn* instruction (integer return), on the other hand, returns the integer on top of the called method's operand stack. For example, suppose the called method executes

```
icont_3      ; push 3
ireturn      ; return 3
```

The icont_3 instruction pushes 3 onto the operand stack. Then the ireturn instruction pops this value and pushes it onto the *caller's* operand stack, pops the called method's frame, and finally returns control to the caller (see Figure 16.3.). Other types have corresponding return instructions. For example, there is a *freturn* instruction (float return) that returns a float value.

FIGURE 16.3

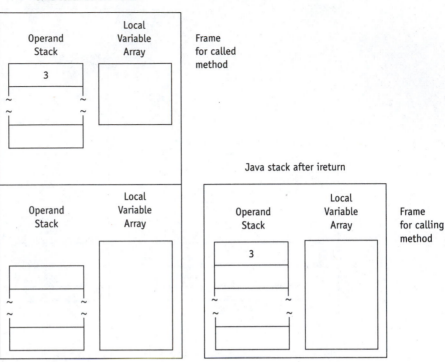

Java stack before ireturn

Java stack after ireturn

16.5 IMPLEMENTATION OF THE EXECUTION ENGINE

The execution engine of the JVM repeatedly performs the four steps that a CPU typically performs:

1. Fetch the instruction.
2. Increment the **pc**.
3. Decode the opcode.
4. Execute the instruction.

Figure 16.4 shows the implementation of these steps in C++ code. This code assumes that the variable **sp** points to the top of the operand stack. Thus, ***sp** (or equivalently **sp**[0]) accesses the top item, and ***(sp+1)** (or equivalently **sp**[1]) accesses the operand stack item just below the top. The code also assumes that the variable, **ap** points to first local variable in the local variable array. Thus, ***ap** (or **ap**[0]) accesses this variable, and ***(ap+1)** (or **ap**[1]) accesses the next, and so on. In the fetch step, only the opcode is fetched. If an instruction contains additional bytes, they are fetched during the execution step. At that time, the **pc** is again incremented so that it ends up pointing to the beginning of the next instructions (see lines 9 and 10 in Figure 16.4).

Figure 16.4 illustrates how easy it is to implement the execution engine. The fetch and increment steps are simple C++ statements. The decoding function is performed by a **select** statement, each case of which executes one instruction.

FIGURE 16.4

```
Action                    C++ Code
-------------------------------------------------------------------
 1 Fetch          | opcode =
 2               |    (unsigned char)*pc;   // zero extend *pc
 3               |
 4 Increment pc  | pc++;                    // move pc over opcode
 5               |
 6 Decode        | select (opcode) {
 7 Opcode        |
 8               |    case 16:              // bipush opcode is 16
 9               |      sp--;               // make room for push
10               |      sp[0] = (int)*pc;   // fetch and push operand
11               |      pc++;               // move pc over operand
12               |      break;
13               |
14               |    case 27:              // iload_1 opcode is 27
15               |      sp--;               // make room for push
16               |      sp[0] = ap[1];      // push loc var 1
17               |      break;
18 Execute       |
19               |    case 96:              // iadd opcode is 96
20               |      sp[1] =             // slot below top
21               |      sp[0] + sp[1];      // sum of top 2 slots
22               |      sp++;               // now pop top
23               |      break;
24               |
25               |    // other cases
26               |  }
```

16.6 THE WISDOM OF USING A STACK ARCHITECTURE FOR THE JVM

Register-oriented architectures tend to be faster than stack-oriented architectures. By keeping operands in registers, a register-oriented architecture minimizes the number of time-consuming memory references that occur as a program executes. In contrast, a stack-oriented architecture keeps operands on the stack (i.e., in memory). Thus, operations on these operands necessarily involve memory references. Does the inferior performance of a stack architecture mean it was a bad choice for the JVM?

The JVM is a *virtual machine*; that is, it is typically implemented with a program that simulates its behavior. In a simulated machine, registers are represented by variables. For example, the `pc` "register" in Figure 16.4 is really a variable in C++ that would likely be in memory at run time. Thus, register accesses in a simulated machine are really memory accesses. A register-oriented architecture with a significant performance advantage over a stack architecture may have absolutely no advantage when both architectures are implemented in software.

Thus, from a performance point of view, a stack architecture was *not* a bad choice for the JVM. Moreover, a stack architecture provides a significant benefit for the JVM—its instructions are short (most bytecode instructions are only 1 byte) because they do not need extra fields to specify the locations of operands.

16.7 A SIMPLE EXAMPLE

• •

Let's now examine the simple Java program in Figure 16.5. We have commented each statement with its relative byte location, its bytecode (in hex and symbolic form), and its effect. We have boldfaced the Java source code so that it is easily discernible among all the comments. Note that there are two methods in addition to **main** and **fa** created by the Java compiler: **<init>** (the default constructor) and **<clinit>** (the class initializer). For this program, the class variables **gv1** and **gv2** are represented by constant pool indices 4 and 2, respectively (see lines 19, 23, and 39). **lv1** and **lv2** in **main** appear in local variables 1 and 2, respectively, for **main** (see lines 13, 16, 20, and 21). Parameters **x**, **y**, and **z** appear in local variables 0, 1, and 2, respectively, for **fa** (see lines 29, 30, and 32). Our program contains bytecode for four meth-

FIGURE 16.5

```
1  class Simple {
2  static int gv1, gv2 = 5;
3
4  // <init> method              ; default constructor
5  // 0  2A      aload_0         ; get object's reference
6  // 1  B70001 invokespecial 1  ; invoke <init> in superclass
7  // 4  B1      return
8  //=============================================================
9  public static void main(String arg[])
10 {
11   int lv1,
12   lv2 = 7;        // 0  1007   bipush 7     ; push 7
13                   // 2  3D     istore_2     ; store in lv2
14
15   lv1 = 11;       // 3  100B   bipush 11    ; push 11
16                   // 5  3C     istore_1     ; store in lv1
17
18   gv1 = fa(gv2, lv1, lv2);
19                   // 6  B20002 getstatic 2  ; push gv2
20                   // 9  1B     iload_1      ; push lv1
21                   // 10 1C     iload_2      ; push lv2
22                   // 11 B80003 invokestatic 3 ; call fa
23                   // 14 B30004 putstatic 4  ; pop into gv1
24                   // 17 B1     return
25 }
```

(continued)

FIGURE 16.5 (continued)

```
26  //===========================================================
27  public static int fa(int x, int y, int z)
28  {
29    return x + y + z; // 0   1A  iload_0        ; push x
30                      // 1   1B  iload_1        ; push y
31                      // 2   60  iadd           ; pop/pop/add/push
32                      // 3   1C  iload_2        ; push z
33                      // 4   60  iadd           ; pop/pop/add/push
34                      // 5   AC  ireturn        ; pop and return
35  }
36  //===========================================================
37  // <clinit> method            ; class initializer
38  // 0   08      iconst_5        ; push 5
39  // 1   B30002  putstatic 2     ; pop into gv2
40  // 4   B1      return
41  }
```

ods: **main**, **fa**, and two initialization methods, **<init>** and **<clinit>**. **<init>** calls the constructor for the superclass **java.lang.Object**; **<clinit>** initializes **gv2** to 5.

16.8   CONSTANT POOL

Figure 16.6. shows a formatted display of the constant pool for the program in Figure 16.5 (all numbers are decimal in this display). Each entry in the constant pool consists of a 1-byte *tag* (which identifies the type of entry) followed by some information that depends on the type of entry. For example, the tag 10 identifies a Methodref entry. This type of entry holds the constant pool indices of the Class and NameAndType entries for some method. Other tags are 1 (UTF8), 3 (Integer), 4 (Float), 5 (Long), 6 (Double), 7 (Class), 9 (Fieldref), 11 (InterfaceMethodref), and 12 (NameAndType). UTF8 entries contain a string preceded by a 2-byte length field. (We don't show these length fields in Figure 6.6.)

By following the arrows in Figure 16.6, we can trace how the operand of the invokestatic instruction on line 22 in Figure 16.5 identifies the **fa** method. For example, the following chain of entries exist

```
3 -> 5 -> 25 "Simple"
```

which yields "Simple", the class name of the method. Similarly, the chains

```
3 -> 23 -> 16 "fa"
3 -> 23 -> 17 "(III)I"
```

yield the name and descriptor of the method. The descriptor, "(III)I", is an encoding of the parameters and the return value of **fa**. The three I's within the parentheses indicate that **fa** has three integer parameters. The item following the parentheses indicates the return type. Here "I" indicates that **fa** returns an integer. Starting at index 1 in the constant pool, there are similar chains for **<init>**. Its

FIGURE 16.6

```
3      (operand in the invokestatic instruction on line 22 in Fig. 16.5)
```

Constant Pool

Index	Tag		Information			
1:	10	(Methodref)	6	(Class Index);	21	(NameAndType Index)
2:	9	(Fieldref)	5	(Class Index);	22	(NameAndType Index)
3:	10	(Methodref)	5	(Class Index);	23	(NameAndType Index)
4:	9	(Fieldref)	5	(Class Index);	24	(NameAndType Index)
5:	7	(Class)	25			
6:	7	(Class)	26			
7:	1	(UTF8)	"gv1"			
8:	1	(UTF8)	"I"			
9:	1	(UTF8)	"gv2"			
10:	1	(UTF8)	"<init>"			
11:	1	(UTF8)	"()V"			
12:	1	(UTF8)	"Code"			
13:	1	(UTF8)	"LineNumberTable"			
14:	1	(UTF8)	"main"			
15:	1	(UTF8)	"([Ljava/lang/string;)V"			
16:	1	(UTF8)	"fa"			
17:	1	(UTF8)	"(III)I"			
18:	1	(UTF8)	"<clinit>"			
19:	1	(UTF8)	"SourceFile"			
20:	1	(UTF8)	"Simple.java"			
21:	12	(NameAndType)	10	(Name Index);	11	(Descriptor Index)
22:	12	(NameAndType)	9	(Name Index);	8	(Descriptor Index)
23:	12	(NameAndType)	16	(Name Index);	17	(Descriptor Index)
24:	12	(NameAndType)	7	(Name Index);	8	(Descriptor Index)
25:	1	(UTF8)	"Simple"			
26:	1	(UTF8)	"java/lang/Object"			

descriptor, "()V", at index 11 indicates **<init>** takes no parameters and returns void. The descriptor for **main** also appears in the constant pool (at index 15). The "L" in this descriptor indicates that everything that follows it up to the semicolon is a full class name. The "[" that precedes the "L" indicates an array type. Thus, the descriptor "([Ljava/lang/String;)V" specifies a single String array parameter and a void return value. Note that within the JVM, the components of a class name are separated with slashes rather than periods.

The constant pool also contains chains to static variables. For example, the chain that starts at index 4 leads to **gv1**:

```
4 -> 24 -> 7 "gv1"
```

Notice that constant pool chains lead to symbolic references, not actual addresses. For example, the index 4 leads to the string "gv1", not the address of **gv1**. At some point, the JVM has to determine the addresses corresponding to the symbolic references in the constant pool. This process is called *constant pool resolution*. Symbol references are usually resolved on as-needed basis (*late resolution*) as bytecode executes. Alternatively, they can be resolved *en masse* at class load time (*early resolution*).

16.9 CLASS FILE FORMAT

Figure 16.7 shows the hex display in boldface of the complete **Simple.class** file. The items not in boldface—the line numbers, indices, and comments—have been added to make the display more readable. This display shows several areas that contain an *attribute*. The first 2 fields of an attribute are always the constant pool index of its name, and its length. What then follows depends on the type of attribute. For example, we find a *SourceFile attribute* at the bottom of the file consisting of

0013	Attribute name index ("SourceFile")
00000002	Attribute length (length of what follows this field)
0014	Name index ("Simple.java")

FIGURE 16.7

Hex Display of Simple.class

```
1            CAFE BABE    Magic number (signature for class files)
2            0003         Minor version number of JVM
3            002D         Major version number of JVM
4       ----------------------------------------------------------
5  Constant pool
6
7            001B         Constant pool count
8  Index    Tag
9   01:     0A  0006 0015
10  02:     09  0005 0016
11  03:     0A  0005 0017
12  04:     09  0005 0018
13  05:     07  0019
14  06:     07  001A
15  07:     01  0003 6776 31              "gv1"
16  08:     01  0001 49                   "I"
17  09:     01  0003 6776 32              "gv2"
18  0A:     01  0006 3C69 6E69 743E       "<init>"
19  0B:     01  0003 2829 56              "()V"
```

(continued)

FIGURE 16.7 (continued)

```
20  0C:    01  0004 436F 6465                              "Code"
21  0D:    01  000F 4C69 6E65 4E75 6D62 6572 5461 626C 65
22                                                         "LineNumberTable"
23  0E:    01  0004 6D61 696E                              "main"
24  0F:    01  0016 285B 4C6A 6176 612F 6C61 6E67 2F53 7472 696E 673B 2956
25                                                         "([Ljava/lang/String;)V"
26  10:    01  0002 6661                                   "fa"
27  11:    01  0006 2849 4949 2949                         "(III)I"
28  12:    01  0008 3C63 6C69 6E69 743E                    "<clinit>"
29  13:    01  000A 536F 7572 6365 4669 6C65               "SourceFile"
30  14:    01  000B 53 696D 706C 652E 6A61 7661            "Simple.java"
31  15:    0C  000A 000B
32  16:    0C  0009 0008
33  17:    0C  0010 0011
34  18:    0C  0007 0008
35  19:    01  0006 5369 6D70 6C65                         "Simple"
36  1A:    01  0010 6A61 7661 2F6C 616E 672F 4F62 6A65 6374
37                                                         "java/lang/Object"
38  ------------------------------------------------------------
39  0020     Access flags (0020 indicates that JVM should
40              use newer version of invokespecial instruction)
41  0005     This class index ("Simple")
42  0006     Super class index ("java/lang/Object")
43  0000     Interfaces count
44  0002     Fields count
45  ------------------------------------------------------------
46  gv1
47  0008     Access flags (0008 indicates static)
48  0007     Name index ("gv1")
49  0008     Descriptor index ("I")
50  0000     Attributes count
51  ------------------------------------------------------------
52  gv2
53  0008     Access flags (0008 indicates static)
54  0009     Name index ("gv2")
55  0008     Descriptor index ("I")
56  0000     Attributes count
57  ------------------------------------------------------------
58  0004     Number of methods
59  ------------------------------------------------------------
60  <init>
61  0000     Access flags (0000 indicates default access)
62  000A     Name index of method ("<init>")
63  000B     Descriptor index     ("()V")
64  0001     Attributes count
```

(continued)

FIGURE 16.7 (continued)

```
65
66  000C        Attribute name index ("Code")
67  0000001D    Attribute length
68  0001        Max stack
69  0001        Max locals
70  00000005    Code length
71  2A B70001 B1    Bytecode                              Code
72  0000        Exceptions count                          Attribute
73  0001        Attributes count
74
75  000D        Attribute Name Index ("LineNumberTable")  Line
76  00000006    Attribute length                          Number
77  0001        LineNumberTable length                    Table
78  0000 0001   Location/line number                      Attribute
79
80  ------------------------------------------------------------
81 main
82  0009        Access flags (0009 indicates public and static)
83  000E        Name index of method ("main")
84  000F        Descriptor index ("([Ljava/lang/String;)V")
85  0001        Attribute count
86
87  000C        Attribute name index ("Code")
88  00000036    Attribute length
89  0003        Max stack
90  0003        Max locals
91  00000012    Code length
92  1007 3D 100B 3C B20002 1B 1C B80003 B30004 B1    Bytecode    Code
93  0000        Exceptions count                                 Attribute
94  0001        Attribute count
95
96  000D        Attribute name index ("LineNumberTable")  Line
97  00000012    Attribute length                          Number
98  0004        LineNumberTable length                    Table
99  0000 000C   Location/line number                      Attribute
100 0003 000F   Location/line number
101 0006 0012   Location/line number
102 0011 0019   Location/line number
103
104 ------------------------------------------------------------
105 fa
106 0009        Access flags (0009 indicates public and static)
107 0010        Name index of method ("fa")
108 0011        Descriptor index ("(III)I")
109 0001        Attribute count
```

(continued)

FIGURE 16.7 (continued)

```
110
111  000C      Attribute name index ("Code")                          ⌐
112  0000001E  Attribute length                                       │
113  0002      Max stack                                              │
114  0003      Max locals                                             │
115  00000006  Code length                                            │
116  1A 1B 60 1C 60 AC    Bytecode                          Code      │
117  0000      Exceptions count                             Attribute │
118  0001      Attribute count                                        │
119                                                                   │
120  000D      Attribute name index ("LineNumberTable")   Line    ⌐   │
121  00000006  Attribute length                            Number  │  │
122  0001      LineNumberTable length                      Table   │  │
123  0000 001D Location/line number                        Attribute⌐ │
124                                                                └  ┘
125  ------------------------------------------------------------
126 <clinit>
127  0008      Access flags (0008 indicates static)
128  0012      Name index of method ("<clinit>")
129  000B      Descriptor index ("()V")
130  0001      Attribute count
131                                                                   ⌐
132  000C      Attribute name index ("Code")                          │
133  0000001D  Attribute length                                       │
134  0001      Max stack                                              │
135  0000      Max locals                                             │
136  00000005  Code length                                            │
137  08 B30002 B1         Bytecode                          Code      │
138  0000      Exceptions count                             Attribute │
139  0001      Attribute count                                        │
140                                                                   │
141  000D      Attribute name index ("LineNumberTable")   Line    ⌐   │
142  00000006  Attribute length                            Number  │  │
143  0001      LineNumberTable length                      Table   │  │
144  0000 0002 Location/line number                        Attribute│  │
145                                                                └  ┘
146  ------------------------------------------------------------
147  0001      Attributes count
148                                                                   
149  0013      Attribute name index ("SourceFile")     SourceFile ⌐
150  00000002  Attribute length                         Attribute │
151  0014      Name index ("Simple.java")                        ┘
```

The first field gives the name index of the attribute (0013 is the constant pool index of "SourceFile"). The second gives the byte length of the variable portion of the attribute (i.e., the portion that follows this length field). The last field gives the name index of the source file (0014 is the constant pool index of "Simple.java").

Each method is represented in a class file with several fields, the principle of which is a Code attribute. For example, in Figure 16.7, the **main** method is represented by lines 82 to 102, the last 16 of which are the Code attribute for **main**. Among the fields within a Code attribute are *max stack* (the maximum number of words that can appear on the operand stack), *max locals* (the size of the local variable array), *code length*, and the *bytecode* for the method. The max stack and max locals subfields provide information to the JVM that allow it to allocate an operand stack and local variable array of the correct size when a method is invoked.

The *LineNumberTable* is an attribute within the Code attribute. It provides the correspondence between bytecode locations and their corresponding source code line numbers. For example, the second entry in the LineNumberTable for **main** (0003 000F) on line 100 indicates that line number F (15 decimal) starts at location 3 (confirm this from Figure 16.5). The LineNumberTable allows the JVM to generate an error message with the source code line number of the offending Java instruction. For example, if an error occurs at location 3 in **main**, the JVM would generate an error message flagging line 15 in the source program. The LineNumberTable is also used by debuggers that have the capability of stepping through the source code one line at a time.

The *interfaces count* field (line 43) is 0 because this class does not implement any interfaces. Similarly, the *exceptions count* fields (72, 93, 117, and 138) are 0 because none of the methods catch exceptions.

16.10 SPACE EFFICIENCY OF BYTECODE

The program in Figure 16.5 is comparable to the SPARC program in Figure 15.24 and the Pentium program in Figure 15.29. Let's compare the number of bytes in the three versions of this program. The table in Figure 16.8 shows the results. We can see that bytecode is very space efficient relative to the SPARC and the Pentium. Space efficiency is an important property for Web programs—the smaller they are, the more quickly they can be sent over the Internet.

16.11 CONTROL STATEMENTS

Bytecode instructions that jump from one point to another within a method use **pc**-relative addressing; that is, the target address is given by the offset in the instruction plus the value in the **pc** register (which is the address of the executing

FIGURE 16.8

	SPARC	Pentium	Bytecode
main	40	52	18
fa	12	14	6
<init>	-	-	5
<clinit>	-	-	5
Total bytes	52	66	34

instruction). For example, the bytecode instruction A70006 (goto 6) on line 10 in Figure 16.9 consists of the opcode A7 and the offset 0006. When executed, it jumps to 6 bytes beyond its location (to the iload_1 instruction on line 14).

The goto instruction is an unconditional jump instruction—it always jumps to the target address. The instructions on lines 16 and 20, on the other hand, are conditional jump instructions—they transfer control only if a certain condition is true. The *if_icmplt* instruction (integer compare less than) on line 16 pops the top two items (10 and the value of **x**) from the operand stack (they must be integers) and compares them. If the second integer popped is less than the first, the jump occurs. The *if_icmpge* instruction (integer compare greater than or equal) on line 20 operates in the same way, except that it performs a greater than or equal test. The JVM also has conditional jump instructions that pop only one value from the operand stack, and compare it with zero. For example, the *iflt* instruction (if less than) jumps if the value it pops from the operand stack is less than zero. A third type of conditional jump instruction on the JVM compares references (for equality or inequality). These instructions (*if_acmpeq* and *if_acmpne*) compare references, not the objects referenced. What about conditional jump instructions for **long**, **float**, and **double** types? *There are none.* What, then, would be the bytecode for the program in Figure 16.9 if we were to change the type of **x** and **y** to **long**, **float**, or **double**? You will answer this question in Problem 16.20.

The **while** loop starting on line 10 has its exit test at the physical *end* of the loop (on lines 14–16). **while** loops are supposed to have leading exit tests, and al-

FIGURE 16.9

```
1 class Control {
2 public static void main(String arg[])
3 {
4     int x = 3,        // 0   06          iconst_3  ; push 3
5                       // 1   3C          istore_1  ; pop into x
6
7         y = 4;        // 2   07          iconst_4  ; push 4
8                       // 3   3D          istore_2  ; pop into y
9
10    while (x < 10 )   // 4   A7 0006     goto 6    ; goto loc 4+6
11
12      x++;            // 7   84 01 01    iinc 1 1  ; add 1 to 1
13
14  // (x < 10)             10  1B          iload_1   ; push x
15  // exit test            11  10 0A       bipush 10 ; push 10
16  // is here              13  A1 FFFA     if_icmplt -6 ; goto loc 13-6
17
18    if (x < y)        // 16  1B          iload_1   ; push x
19                      // 17  1C          iload_2   ; push y
20                      // 18  A2 0009     if_icmpge 9 ; goto 18+9
21
22      x = 20;         // 21  10 14       bipush 20 ; push 20
23                      // 23  3C          istore_1  ; store in x
24
25    else              // 24  A7 0006     goto 6    ; goto 24+6
```

(continued)

FIGURE 16.9   (continued)

```
26
27          x = 30;        // 27 10 1E      bipush 30   ; push 30
28                         // 29 3C         istore_1    ; pop into x
29
30  }                      // 30 B1         return      ; return to caller
31  }
```

though it's not obvious, this one does have one. The goto instruction at the beginning of the loop (line 10) jumps directly to the exit test. Thus, the exit test is executed before the loop body.

The 16-bit offset in control instructions permits jumps in a range of 32K in either direction. For longer jumps, we have to use the *goto_w* instruction (goto wide). This instruction contains an offset 32 bits wide, and can jump to any point in the JVM's 32-bit address space, as long as the jump is legal (the target address has to be the address of the beginning of an instruction within the same method).

The *iinc* instruction (integer increment) is an unusual instruction in that it contains 2 operand fields, each 1 byte long: a local variable number (from 0 to 255) and an increment (from -128 to 127). For example, the iinc instruction on line 12 increments local variable 1 (**x**) by 1.

16.12   UNASSEMBLING CLASS FILES

An assembler converts its symbolic input to binary. An *unassembler* (or *disassembler*) does the opposite—it converts a program from binary to symbolic form (i.e., to assembly language). We can unassemble Java class files using the **javap** unassembler in the Sun Java SDK system. For example, to unassemble **Simple.class** (the class file in Figure 16.7), enter

```
javap -c Simple
```

Figure 16.10 shows the output **javap** produces (in boldface), to which line numbers and a few comments have been added. We see exactly the same bytecode that appears in Figure 16.5. Notice, however, that **<init>** (the default constructor starting on line 11) has been renamed to **Simple()**. This change makes sense because, at the Java level, we use the class name as the constructor name. The class initializer, **<clinit>**, has also been renamed (see line 36). It is now a no-name static initializer (which is also a Java-level construct).

From the information in **Simple.class**, **javap** is able to reconstruct the contents of the **Simple** class, including the names and types of its members (see lines 2–9). For any bytecode instruction containing a constant pool index, it displays not only the index (prefixed with "#"), but also symbolic information obtainable via that index from the constant pool. For example, the getstatic instruction on line 21 includes 2 (the constant pool index in the actual instruction) and <Field int gv2> (the corresponding constant pool information). Confirm this from the actual constant pool in Figure 16.6.

Suppose we wanted to create an assembly language for the JVM. We could simply use the form illustrated by Figure 16.10, with one modification: We would

FIGURE 16.10

```
 1 Compiled from Simple.java
 2 class Simple extends java.lang.Object {
 3    static int gv1;
 4    static int gv2;
 5    Simple();
 6    public static void main(java.lang.String[]);
 7    public static int fa(int, int, int);
 8    static {};
 9 }
10
11 Method Simple()        ←<init> method
12   0 aload_0
13   1 invokespecial #1 <Method java.lang.Object()>
14   4 return
15
16 Method void main(java.lang.String[])
17   0 bipush 7     ┌── constant pool index
18   2 istore_2        ┌── symbolic info obtained via constant
19   3 bipush 11       │                     pool index 2
20   5 istore_1  ↓     ↓
21   6 getstatic #2 <Field int gv2>
22   9 iload_1
23  10 iload_2
24  11 invokestatic #3 <Method int fa(int, int, int)>
25  14 putstatic #4 <Field int gv1>
26  17 return
27
28 Method int fa(int, int, int)
29   0 iload_0
30   1 iload_1
31   2 iadd
32   3 iload_2
33   4 iadd
34   5 ireturn
35
36 Method static {}     ←<clinit> method
37   0 iconst_5
38   1 putstatic #2 <Field int gv2>
39   4 return
```

not specify constant pool indices because we would not know them. For example, for the getstatic instruction on line 21, we would write

```
getstatic <Field int gv2>
```

omitting the constant pool index. The assembler would then figure out the correct index, and insert it in the bytecode instruction it outputs. This task is something the assembler can do because it also constructs the constant pool.

FIGURE 16.11   a)

```
1 class IRTest {
2    public static void main(String arg[])
3    {
4       int y;
5       y = sum(1, 2);
6    }
7    static int sum(int m, int n)
8    {
9       return m + n;
10   }
11 }
```

b)

```
1 Method void main(java.lang.String[])
2    0 iconst_1              ; push 1
3    1 iconst_2              ; push 2
4    2 invokestatic #2 <Method int sum(int, int)>
5    5 istore_1              ; save value returned on stack in loc var 1
6    6 return
7
8 Method int sum(int, int)
                            ; return m + n;
9    0 iload_0              ; get 1st parameter from loc var 0
10   1 iload_1              ; get 2nd parameter from loc var 1
11   2 iadd                 ; pop/pop/add/push
12   3 ireturn              ; return value on top of stack
```

Assembly languages have, in fact, been created for the JVM (see, for example, Engel, 1999; Meyer and Downing, 1997). They can be handy if you want to modify a class file for which you do not have the Java source. To do this, you simply unassemble the class to your assembly language, modify the class in its assembly form, and then assemble it back into a class file.

Let's now use **javap** to confirm that our description in Section 6.4 of the invoke/return mechanism is correct. Figure 16.11 shows a Java class and the **javap** output for its two methods. Notice on lines 2 and 3 in Figure 16.11b, **main** pushes 1 and 2 onto its *operand stack*. **sum**, however, accesses these parameters from its *local variables* 0 and 1 (see lines 9 and 10). The iadd instruction on line 11 pushes the sum of the two parameters onto **sum**'s operand stack. But on return to **main**, the return value is obtained from the top of **main**'s operand stack (see line 5).

16.13   OBJECTS AND ARRAYS

Any discussion of the JVM would not be complete without an examination of its mechanisms for object and array creation and access. Let's look at the example in Figure 16.12, which uses objects and arrays.

FIGURE 16.12   a)

```
 1 class OATest {
 2  public static void main(String arg[])
 3  {
 4     O o;
 5     int a[];
 6     o = new O();
 7     o.x = 6;
 8     o.f();
 9     a = new int[7];
10     a[5] = 3;
11  }
12 }
```

b)

```
 1 Method void main(java.lang.String[])
 2    0 new #2 <Class O>                    ;  o = new O();
 3    3 dup                                   ; duplicate reference
 4    4 invokespecial #3 <Method O()>
 5    7 astore_1                             ; save reference
 6
 7    8 aload_1                         ;  o.x = 6;
 8    9 bipush 6
 9   11 putfield #4 <Field int x>
10
11   14 aload_1                         ;  o.f();
12   15 invokevirtual #5 <Method void f()>
13
14   18 bipush 7                        ;  a = new int[7];
15   20 newarray int
16   22 astore_2                             ; save reference
17
18   23 aload_2                         ;  a[5] = 3;
19   24 iconst_5
20   25 iconst_3
21   26 iastore
22
23   27 return
```

What is most interesting about this example is how few bytecode instructions it uses to create an object. In fact, it uses *only one* instruction—the *new* instruction on line 2 in Figure 16.12b. In contrast, the creation of an object in a C++ program requires the execution of dozens of machine instructions. This difference does not mean that Java programs create objects faster than C++ programs. The Java interpreter has to execute dozens of machine instructions to interpret a single new instruction. Thus, the actual execution time to create an object in Java is as long as in C++ (or even longer because of the overhead of the interpretation process). Thus, the significance of these high-level bytecode instructions is not *speed*—it is *size*. These high-level instructions make for small programs, which, therefore, can be transmitted quickly over the Internet.

The `new` instruction allocates storage for objects from the heap (see Figure 16.1). There is no bytecode instruction to undo what the `new` instruction does; that is, there is no instruction to deallocate storage in the heap. Deallocation is handled automatically by the garbage collection mechanism of the JVM.

The *dup* instruction (line 3) duplicates the reference to the new object returned by `new`. The `invokespecial` instruction (line 4) removes one reference from the operand stack. Without the `dup` instruction, there would be no reference on the operand stack for the `astore_1` instruction (line 5). The `invokespecial` instruction (line 4) calls method `O()` (i.e., the **<init>** constructor in the new object). Finally the `astore_1` instruction (line 7) stores the original reference in local variable 1.

The *putfield* instruction (line 9) assigns a new value to the **x** field. Before it is executed, the object reference and the new value have to be pushed (lines 7 and 8). The **x** field is specified by the instruction itself (its second byte contains the constant pool index of **x**).

The *newarray* instruction (line 15) creates an **int** array with seven elements. Before it is executed, the array size has to be pushed (line 14). The array type is specified by the instruction itself (its second byte contains a code representing the array type). **javap**, however, displays the type rather than the actual numeric code (for **int**, the code is 10).

An assignment to an **int** array is handled by *iastore* (line 21). Here, the "a" in the mnemonic means "array," not "reference," as in `astore_1`. The computation associated with array indexing is not performed by bytecode instructions. Instead, it is performed by the JVM when it interprets the `iastore` instruction. Like the `new` instruction, `newarray` is a high-level instruction in a low-level language.

16.14   JVM—AN ABSTRACT MACHINE

The JVM is an *abstract machine*; that is, its specification leaves out many implementation details. For example, when the `invokestatic` instruction is executed, the return address has to be saved (the **pc** register has to be loaded with this address when the called method returns to its caller). The JVM specification does not indicate *how* or *where* this return address should be saved. It specifies only *what* should happen—namely, that the **pc** register should be loaded with a method's address when the method is called, and with the return address when the method executes a return. The JVM specification leaves the details concerning the saving and restoring of the **pc** register to the implementer of the JVM.

FURTHER READING

Engel, J. *Programming for the Java Virtual Machine.* Reading, MA: Addison-Wesley, 1999.

Harold, E. *Java Secrets.* Forster City, CA: IDG Books Worldwide, 1997.

Lindholm, T. and Yellin, F. *The Java Virtual Machine Specification.* Reading, MA: Addison-Wesley, 1997.

Meyer, J. and Downing, T. *Java Virtual Machine.* Sebastopol, CA: O'Reilly, 1997.

Venners, B. *Inside the Java Virtual Machine.* New York: McGraw-Hill, 1998.

PROBLEMS

• •

16.1. Compile the program in Figure 16.5. Display the ".class" with **see**. In the hex display, locate the constant pool. What is in the 2 bytes immediately preceding the constant pool entry with index 1?

16.2. Why is interpreting bytecode slower than executing native machine code?

16.3. Give two reasons why Java programs tend to be slower than C++ programs.

16.4. What is in local variable 0 when **main** in Figure 16.5 is executing?

16.5. Why does the JVM have no I/O instructions?

16.6. Do different compilers translate the same Java program to exactly the same bytecode?

16.7. From the constant pool, determine the class and method names of the method call by the invokespecial instruction on line 6 in Figure 16.5.

16.8. When are **<init>** and **<clinit>** in Figure 16.5 executed?

16.9. Compare the execution time of the SPARC, Pentium, and bytecode programs in Figure 15.24, Figure 15.29, and Figure 16.5. Assume each instruction requires one unit of time. (Is this a good assumption?)

16.10. What is the maximum size of a Java method?

16.11. Why are implementation details not included in the JVM specification?

16.12. Add the case for fadd (its opcode is 98 decimal) to Figure 16.4.

16.13. If the putstatic instruction on line 23 in Figure 16.5 were to execute twice, why might it execute faster the second time?

16.14. What types should **opcode, pc, sp**, and **ap** in Figure 16.4 have?

16.15. The primitive types in Java have uniform sizes across all platforms. How might this uniformity impact the execution time of Java programs?

16.16. What is the reason for the unusual position of the exit test in the **while** loop in Figure 16.9?

16.17. Propose a mechanism for supporting recursion other than a stack.

16.18. Using a hex editor, change the putstatic instruction in **main** in **Simple.class** to three icont_1 instructions (04 hex). Run the program. What happens?

16.19. Determine how to create an array of objects (newarray creates arrays for primitive types only).

16.20. Change the type of **x** and **y** in Figure 16.9 to **float**. Compile and unassemble the class file. How are the **float** comparisons performed?

16.21. How can unsigned integer comparisons be performed in bytecode?

16.22. How large can a local variable array be?

16.23. Does the JVM support global variables?

16.24. Create a display like that in Figure 16.7 for the class in Figure 16.9.

16.25. JVM has some very high-level bytecode instructions. Does it make sense to have similar instructions on all computers?

16.26. When does the JVM check if the operands for iadd are of the correct type? At run time?

16.27. Write a Java program that will cause the overflow of the operand stack. When does the JVM detect a problem with the program?

16.28. Write a Java method whose max stack field in its class file contains 10.

16.29. Write a Java method whose max locals field in its class file contains 10.

16.30. How does UTF8 differ from ASCII?

16.31. Write a program that outputs a formatted display of the constant pool in a class file.

16.32. Write a program that outputs in hex the bytecode for each method in a class file.

16.33. Write a program that is functionally equivalent to **javap**.

16.34. How does your Java compiler handle

```
x = 1 + 2;
```

Does the bytecode add 1 and 2, or does it simply use 3 directly?

16.35. How does your Java compiler handle

```
x = 1 + y + 2;
```

Does the bytecode add 1 and 2, or does it simply use 3 directly?

16.36. How does your Java compiler handle

```
x = a + (b + (c + d));
```

Does it ignore the parentheses?

16.37. How does your Java compiler handle

```
d = (double)(i + l + f);
```

where d, i, l, and f are type double, int, long, and float, respectively.

16.38. By comparing the programs in Figure 15.24 and Figure 16.5, determine the reason for the space efficiency of bytecode relative to the SPARC.

Translate the following classes to bytecode in symbolic form. Use the **javap** format (see Figure 16.10), omitting constant pool indices.

16.39.
```
class X {
    public static void main(String arg[]) {
        int x;
        x = 1;
        x = 5;
    }
}
```

16.40.
```
class X {
    static int x;
    public static void main(String arg[])
    {
        x = 1;
        x = 5;
    }
}
```

16.41.
```
class X {
    public static void main(String arg[])
    {
        f(3);
    }
    public static void f(int a)
    {
        a = 1;
    }
}
```

16.42.
```
class X {
    static int a = 1, b = 2;
    public static void main(String arg[])
    {
        int x = 3, y = 4, z;
```

```
            z = f(a, b, x, y);
        }
        public static int f(int a, int b, int x, int y)
        {
            ireturn (a + a + b + x - y);
        }
    }
```

16.43.
```
class X {
    public static void main(String arg[])
    {
        int a[][];
        a = new[2][3];
        a[1][2] = 5;
    }
}
```

16.44.
```
class X {
    public static void main(String arg[])
    {
        int i, x = 0;
        for (i = 0; i < 5; i++)
            x++;
    }
}
```

16.45.
```
class X {
    public static void main(String arg[])
    {
        int x;
        if (x >= 0)
            x++;
    }
}
```

16.46.
```
class X {
    public static void main(String arg[])
    {
        O o,p;
        o = new O();
        p = new O();
        o.x = 5;
        p.x = 6;
        if (o == p)
            p = null;
    }
}
class O {
    int x;
}
```

INSTRUCTION SET SUMMARIES
(from s.txt, b.txt, o.txt, k.txt)

STANDARD INSTRUCTION SET (s.has, s.hor, s.vas, s.ver, s.cfg)

Opcode (hex)	Assembly Form	Name	Description
0	ld x	Load	ac = mem[x];
1	st x	Store	mem[x] = ac;
2	add x	Add	ac = ac + mem[x];
3	sub x	Subtract	ac = ac - mem[x];
4	ldr x	Load relative	ac = mem[sp+x];
5	str x	Store relative	mem[sp+x] = ac;
6	addr x	Add relative	ac = ac + mem[sp+x];
7	subr x	Subtract relative	ac = ac - mem[sp+x];
8	ldc x	Load constant	ac = x;
9	ja x	Jump always	pc = x;
A	jzop x	Jump zero or pos	if (ac >= 0) pc = x;
B	jn x	Jump negative	if (ac < 0) pc = x;
C	jz x	Jump zero	if (ac == 0) pc = x;
D	jnz x	Jump nonzero	if (ac != 0) pc = x;
E	call x	Call procedure	mem[--sp] = pc; pc = x;
F0	ret	Return	pc = mem[sp++];
F1	ldi	Load indirect	ac = mem[ac];
F2	sti	Store indirect	mem[ac] = mem[sp++];
F3	push	Push onto stack	mem[--sp] = ac;
F4	pop	Pop from stack	ac = mem[sp++];
F5	aloc y	Allocate	sp = sp - y;
F6	dloc y	Deallocate	sp = sp + y;
F7	swap	Swap ac, sp	temp = ac; ac = sp; sp = temp;
FFF5	uout	Unsigned out	Output number in ac reg as unsigned decimal number
FFF6	sin	String input	Input string to address in ac
FFF7	sout	String output	Output string pointed to by ac

FFF8	hin	Hex input	Input hex number to ac register
FFF9	hout	Hex output	Output number in ac in hex
FFFA	ain	ASCII input	Input ASCII char to ac register
FFFB	aout	ASCII output	Output ASCII char in ac register
FFFC	din	Decimal input	Input decimal number (signed or unsigned) to ac register
FFFD	dout	Decimal output	Output number in ac reg as a signed decimal number
FFFE	bkpt	Breakpoint	Trigger breakpoint
FFFF	halt	Halt	Trigger halt

Instruction Fields

x:	12	rightmost bits of instruction,	$0 <= x <= 4095$	(FFF hex)
y:	8	rightmost bits of instruction,	$0 <= y <= 255$	(FF hex)
z:	4	rightmost bits of instruction,	$0 <= z <= 15$	(F dec)

Registers

pc:	program counter register
sp:	stack pointer register
ac:	accumulator register
temp:	designates a work register within the CPU

BASIC INSTRUCTION SET (b.has, b.hor, b.vas, b.ver, b.cfg)

• •

Opcode (hex)	Assembly Form	Name	Description
0	ld x	Load	ac = mem[x];
2	st x	Store	mem[x] = ac;
4	shll z	Shift left log	ac << z;
6	shrl z	Shift right log	ac >> z;
8	addc x	Add constant	ac = ac + x;
A	flip	Flip ac	ac = ~ac;
C	mult x	Multiply	ac = ac * mem[x];
E	jn x	Jump on negative	if (ac < 0) pc = x;
FFF5	uout	Unsigned out	Output number in ac reg as unsigned decimal number
FFF6	sin	String input	Input string to address in ac
FFF7	sout	String output	Output string pointed to by ac
FFF8	hin	Hex input	Input hex number to ac register
FFF9	hout	Hex output	Output number in ac in hex

FFFA	ain	ASCII input	Input ASCII char to ac register
FFFB	aout	ASCII output	Output ASCII char in ac register
FFFC	din	Decimal input	Input decimal number (signed or unsigned) to ac register
FFFD	dout	Decimal output	Output number in ac reg as a signed decimal number
FFFE	bkpt	Breakpoint	Trigger breakpoint
FFFF	halt	Halt	Trigger halt

!-directive: b

Instruction Fields

x:	12	rightmost bits of instruction,	0 <= x <= 4095	(FFF hex)
z:	4	rightmost bits of instruction,	0 <= z <= 15	(F dec)

Registers

pc: program counter register

ac: accumulator register

OPTIMAL INSTRUCTION SET (o.hor, o.cfg)

• •

Opcode (hex)	Assembly Form	Name	Description
0	ld x	Load	ac = mem[x];
1	st x	Store	mem[x] = ac;
2	add x	Add	ac = ac + mem[x]; cy = carry;
3	sub x	Subtract	ac = ac - mem[x];
4	ldr s	Load relative	ac = mem[bp+s];
5	str s	Store relative	mem[bp+s] = ac;
6	addr s	Add relative	ac = ac + mem[bp+s]; cy = carry;
7	subr s	Subtract relative	ac = ac - mem[bp+s];
8	ldc x	Load constant	ac = x;
9	ja x	Jump always	pc = x;
A	jzop x	Jump zero or pos	if (ac >= 0) pc = x;
B	jn x	Jump negative	if (ac < 0) pc = x;
C	jz x	Jump zero	if (ac == 0) pc = x;
D	jnz x	Jump nonzero	if (ac != 0) pc = x;
E	call x	Call procedure	mem[--sp] = pc; pc = x;
F0	ret	Return	pc = mem[sp++];

F1	ldi	Push indirect	ac = mem[ac];
F2	sti	Store indirect	mem[ac] = mem[sp++];
F3	push	Push onto stack	mem[--sp] = ac;
F4	pop	Pop from stack	ac = mem[sp++];
F5	aloc y	Allocate	sp = sp - y;
F6	dloc y	Deallocate	sp = sp + y;
F7	swap	Swap ac, sp	temp = ac; ac = sp; sp = temp;
F8	addc y	Add constant	ac = ac + y; cy = carry;
F9	subc y	Subtract constant	ac = ac - y;
FA	esba	Estab base addr	mem[--sp] = bp; bp = sp12;
FB	reba	Restore base addr	sp = bp; bp = mem[sp++];
FC	cora	Convert rel addr	ac = (ac + bp)12;

FD	scmp	Signed compare	temp = mem[sp++];
			if (temp < ac) ac = -1;
			if (temp == ac) ac = 0;
			if (temp > ac) ac = 1;

FE	ucmp	Unsigned compare	Same as scmp except unsigned comparison
FF0	shll z	Shift left logical	ac = ac << z; (inject 0's)
FF1	shrl z	Shift right logical	ac = ac >> z; (inject 0's)
FF2	shra z	Shift right arith	ac = ac >> z; (inject sign)
FF3	m	Shift-add multiply	ac = mem[sp++] * ac;
FF4	mult	Hardware multiply	ac = mem[sp++] * ac;
FF5	div	Divide	if (ac == 0) ac = sp; else ac = mem[sp++] / ac;
FF6	rem	Remainder	if (ac == 0) ac = ct; else ac = mem[sp++] % ac;
FF7	addy	Add with carry	ac = mem[sp++] + ac + cy; cy = carry;
FF8	or	Bitwise or	ac = ac | mem[sp++];
FF9	xor	Bitwise excl or	ac = ac ^ mem[sp++];
FFA	and	Bitwise and	ac = ac & mem[sp++];
FFB	flip	Bitwise complement	ac = ~ac;
FFC	cali	Call indirect	mem[--sp] = pc; pc = ac12;
FFD	sect	Set ct register	ct = ac;
FFE	dect	Decrement ct reg	if (--ct == 0) pc++;
FFF0	sodd	Skip on odd	if (ac % 2 == 1) pc++;
FFF1	bpbp	Bp to bp	bp = mem[bp];
FFF2	pobp	Pop bp	bp = mem[sp++];
FFF3	pbp	Push bp	mem[--sp] = bp;

FFF4	bcpy	Block copy	while (ct--)
			mem[ac++] = mem[mem[sp]++];
			sp = sp + 1;

FFF5	uout	Unsigned out	Output number in ac reg as unsigned decimal number
FFF6	sin	String input	Input str to address in ac
FFF7	sout	String output	Output str pointed to by ac
FFF8	hin	Hex input	Input hex number to ac reg
FFF9	hout	Hex output	Output number in ac in hex
FFFA	ain	ASCII input	Input ASCII char to ac reg
FFFB	aout	ASCII output	Output ASCII char in ac reg
FFFC	din	Decimal input	Input decimal number (signed or unsigned) to ac register
FFFD	dout	Decimal output	Output number in ac reg as a signed decimal number
FFFE	bkpt	Breakpoint	Trigger breakpoint
FFFF	halt	Halt	Trigger halt

!-directive: o

Instruction Fields

s:	12 rightmost bits of instruction, -4095 <= s <= 4095 (FFF hex)
x:	12 rightmost bits of instruction, 0 <= x <= 4095 (FFF hex)
y:	8 rightmost bits of instruction, 0 <= y <= 255 (FF hex)
z:	4 rightmost bits of instruction, 0 <= z <= 15 (F dec)

Registers

pc:	program counter register
sp:	stack pointer register
ac:	accumulator register
ct:	count register
cy:	carry register
bp:	base pointer register
temp:	designates a work register within the CPU

Note: An item followed by "12" in the instruction set descriptions denotes the 12 rightmost bits of that item. Main memory references (i.e., wherever "mem[. . .]" appears) use only the 12 rightmost of the address specified.

STACK INSTRUCTION SET (k.hor, k.cfg)

• •

Opcode (hex)	Assembly Form	Name	Description
0	p x	Push	mem[--sp] = mem[x];
1	pc x	Push constant	mem[--sp] = x;
2	pr s	Push relative	mem[--sp] = mem[bp + s];

3	cora s	Convert rel addr	mem[--sp] = (bp + s)12;
4	aspc s	Add to sp constant	sp = (sp + s)12;
5	call x	Call	mem[--sp] = pc; pc = x;
6	ja x	Jump always	pc = x;
7	jcnt x	Jump count	if (--ct) pc = x;
8	jp x	Jump positive	if (mem[sp++] > 0) pc = x;
9	jn x	Jump negative	if (mem[sp++] < 0) pc = x;
A	jz x	Jump zero	if (mem[sp++] == 0) pc = x;
B	jnz x	Jump nonzero	if (mem[sp++] != 0) pc = x;
C	jodd x	Jump odd	if (mem[sp++] % 2 == 1) pc = x;
D	jzon x	Jump zero or neg	if (mem[sp++] <= 0) pc = x;
E	jzop x	Jump zero or pos	if (mem[sp++] >= 0) pc = x;
F0	ret	Return	pc = mem[sp++];

F1	add	Add	temp = mem[sp++];
			mem[sp] = mem[sp] + temp;
			cy = carry;

F2	sub	Subtract	temp = mem[sp++]; mem[sp] = mem[sp] - temp;
F3	stav	Store addr/value	temp = mem[sp++]; mem[mem[sp++]] = temp;
F4	stva	Store value/addr	temp = mem[sp++]; mem[temp] = mem[sp++];
F5	load	Load	mem[sp] = mem[mem[sp]];
F6	addc y	Add constant	mem[sp] = mem[sp] + y; cy = carry;
F7	subc y	Subtract constant	mem[sp] = mem[sp] - y;
F8	dupe	Dupe top of stack	temp = mem[sp]; mem[--sp] = temp;
F9	esba	Estab base addr	mem[--sp] = bp; bp = sp12;
FA	reba	Restore base addr	sp = bp; bp = mem[sp++];
FB	zesp	Zero sp	sp = 0;

FC	scmp	Signed compare	temp1 = mem[sp++];
			temp2 = mem[sp];
			if (temp2 < temp1) mem[sp] = -1;
			if (temp2 == temp1) mem[sp] = 0;
			if (temp2 > temp1) mem[sp] = 1;

FD	ucmp	Unsigned compare	Same as scmp except unsigned comparison

FE	rev	Reverse	temp1 = mem[sp++];
			temp2 = mem[sp];
			mem[sp--] = temp1;
			mem[sp] = temp2;

FF0	shll z	Shift left logical	mem[sp] << z; (inject 0's)
FF1	shrl z	Shift right logical	mem[sp] >> z; (inject 0's)
FF2	shra z	Shift right arith	mem[sp] >> z; (inject sign)
FF3	m	Shift-add multiply	temp = mem[sp++]; mem[sp] = mem[sp] * temp;
FF4	mult	Hardware multiply	temp = mem[sp++]; mem[sp] = mem[sp] * temp;

FF5	div	Divide	temp1 = mem[sp++];
			temp2 = sp;
			if (temp1 == 0) mem[--sp] = temp2;
			else mem[sp] = mem[sp] / temp;

FF6	rem	Remainder	temp = mem[sp++];
			if (temp == 0) mem[--sp] = ct;
			else mem[sp] = mem[sp] % temp;

FF7	addy	Add with carry	temp = mem[sp++];
			mem[sp] = mem[sp] + temp + carry;
			cy = carry;

FF8	or	Bitwise incl or	mem[sp] = mem[sp++] | mem[sp];
FF9	xor	Bitwise excl or	mem[sp] = mem[sp++] ^ mem[sp];
FFA	and	Bitwise and	mem[sp] = mem[sp++] & mem[sp];
FFB	flip	Bitwise complement	mem[sp] = ~mem[sp];
FFC	cali	Call indirect	temp = mem[sp]; mem[sp] = pc; pc = temp12;
FFD	sect	Set ct	ct = mem[sp++];
FFE	rot	Rotate	Rotate up top 3 stack items
FFF0	psp	Push sp	temp = sp; mem[--sp] = temp;
FFF1	bpbp	Bp to bp	bp = mem[bp];
FFF2	pobp	Pop bp	bp = mem[sp++];
FFF3	pbp	Push bp	mem[--sp] = bp;

FFF4	bcpy	Block copy	while (ct--)
			   mem[mem[sp+1]++]
			    = mem[mem[sp]++];
			sp = sp + 2;

FFF5	uout	Unsigned out	Output mem[sp++] as unsigned decimal number
FFF6	sin	String input	Input str to mem[sp++]
FFF7	sout	String output	Output str pointed to by mem[sp++]
FFF8	hin	Hex input	Input hex number to mem[--sp]
FFF9	hout	Hex output	Output number in mem[sp++]

FFFA	ain	ASCII input	Input ASCII char to mem[--sp]
FFFB	aout	ASCII output	Output ASCII char in mem[sp++]
FFFC	din	Decimal input	Input decimal number (signed or unsigned) to mem[--sp]
FFFD	dout	Decimal output	Output number in mem[sp++] as a signed decimal number
FFFE	bkpt	Breakpoint	Trigger breakpoint
FFFF	halt	Halt	Trigger halt

!-directive: k

Instruction Fields

s:	12	rightmost bits of instruction, -4095 <= s <= 4095	(FFF hex)
x:	12	rightmost bits of instruction,	0 <= x <= 4095	(FFF hex)
y:	8	rightmost bits of instruction,	0 <= y <= 255	(FF hex)
z:	4	rightmost bits of instruction,	0 <= z <= 15	(F dec)

Registers

pc:	program counter register
sp:	stack pointer register
ct:	count register
cy:	carry register
bp:	base pointer register
temp:	designates a work register within the CPU
temp1:	designates a work register within the CPU
temp2:	designates a work register within the CPU

Note: An item followed by "12" in the instruction set descriptions denotes the 12 rightmost bits of that item. Main memory references (i.e., wherever "mem[. . .]" appears) use only the 12 rightmost of the address specified.

MICROLEVEL SUMMARY (from mic.txt)

MICROLEVEL REGISTERS

• •

Number	Name	Contents	Usage			
0	0	0000	constant 0			
1	1	0001	constant 1			
2	xmask	0FFF	x-field mask		read	not
3	ymask	00FF	y-field mask		only	renameable
4	zmask	000F	z-field mask			
5	mdr		memory data register			
6	pc		program counter			
7	sp		stack pointer			
8	ac		accumulator			
9	ir		instruction register		read/	renameable
A	dc		decoding register		write	
B	ct		count register			
C	cy		carry register			
D	bp		base pointer			
E	e					
F	f					
.	.					
.	.					
.	.					
1F	1f					

Note: Usage of registers 6 to 1F depends on the microcode.

H1: HORIZONTAL MICRO

• •

Microinstruction format:

C	A	B	ALU	MAR	RD	WR	COND	ADDR	
5	5	5	3	1	1	1	2	9	width (bits)

A:	Register number of register driving the A bus
B:	Register number of register driving the B bus
C:	Register number of register loaded from the C bus

ALU

0:	A (left input straight through)
1:	~A (bitwise complement)
2:	A & B (bitwise AND)
3:	A * B
4:	A + B
5:	A - B
6:	Shift left one position
7:	Shift right one position

MAR

0:	Do not load mar
1:	Load mar from B bus

RD

0:	Do not read
1:	Read from mem[mar]

WR

0:	Do not write
1:	Write mdr to mem[mar]

COND

0:	No branch
1:	Branch if S = 1
2:	Branch if Z = 1
3:	Always branch

ADDR: Branch-to address

V1: VERTICAL MICRO

• •

Instruction formats:

OPCODE	C	A	B	
4	5	5	5	width (bits)

OPCODE	C	A	FILL	
4	5	5	5	width (bits)

OPCODE	FILL	B			
4	10	5		width (bits)	

OPCODE	FILL	A	FILL		
4	5	5	5	width (bits)	

OPCODE	FILL	ADDR		
4	6	9		width (bits)

OPCODE	FILL		
4	15		width (bits)

OPCODE: see table below

A:	Register number of register driving the A bus
B:	Register number of register driving the B bus
C:	Register number of register loaded from the C bus
ADDR:	Branch-to address
FILL:	Don't care

Assembly format:

Opcode (hex)	Assembly Form		Name	Description
0	add	rc ra rb	Add	rc = ra + rb; set sz;
1	sub	rc ra rb	Subtract	rc = ra - rb; set sz;
2	mult	rc ra rb	Multiply	rc = ra * rb; set sz;
3	and	rc ra rb	Bitwise and	rc = ra & rb; set sz;
4	flip	rc ra	Flip bits	rc = ~ra; set sz;
5	move	rc ra	Move register	rc = ra; set sz;
6	left	rc ra	Left shift	rc = left(ra); set sz;
7	right	rc ra	Right shift	rc = right(ra); set sz;
8	mar	rb	Load mar	mar = rb;
9	sz	ra	Set sz	set sz (with ra);
A	ba	addr	Branch always	mpc = addr;
B	bn	addr	Branch if neg	if (n) mpc = addr;
C	bz	addr	Branch if zero	if (z) mpc = addr;
D	rd	Read	mdr = mem[mar];	
E	wr	Write	mem[mar] = mdr;	

ra:	Register number in A field
rb:	Register number in B field
rc:	Register number in C field
addr:	Address in ADDR field

MICROCODE FOR THE STANDARD INSTRUCTION SET (from s.has)

```
/ Standard Instruction Set Horizontal Microcode  s.has

/ The label indicates the opcode decoded up to that point.
/ Each hex digit in a label represents 4 bits.  0 or 1 in a
/ label represents the bits 0 and 1.  For example, the
/ label LF_01 corresponds to opcode bits 1111 01; the label
/ LF_2 corresponds to opcode bits 1111 0010.

/***************************************************************/
/      Fetch instruction and increment pc register            /
/***************************************************************/
fetch:      mar = pc; pc = pc + 1;
            rd;
            ir = mdr;
/***************************************************************/
/            Decode opcode                                    /
/***************************************************************/
            dc = ir; if(s) goto L1;
L0:         dc = left(dc); if (s) goto L01;
L00:        dc = left(dc); if (s) goto L001;
L000:       dc = left(dc); if (s) goto L0001;
            goto L0000;
L1:         dc = left(dc); if (s) goto L11;
L10:        dc = left(dc); if (s) goto L101;
L100:       dc = left(dc); if (s) goto L9;
            goto L8;
L01:        dc = left(dc); if (s) goto L011;
L010:       dc = left(dc); if (s) goto L5;
            goto L4;
L11:        dc = left(dc); if (s) goto L111;
L110:       dc = left(dc); if (s) goto LD;
            goto LC;
L001:       dc = left(dc); if (s) goto L3;
            goto L2;
L011:       dc = left(dc); if (s) goto L7;
            goto L6;
L101:       dc = left(dc); if (s) goto LB;
            goto LA;
L111:       dc = left(dc); if (s) goto LF;
            goto LE;

LF:         dc = left(dc); if (s) goto LF_1;
LF_0:       dc = left(dc); if (s) goto LF_01;
LF_00:      dc = left(dc); if (s) goto LF_001;
LF_000:     dc = left(dc); if (s) goto LF_0001;
            goto LF_0000;
LF_1:       dc = left(dc); if (s) goto LF_11;
```

```
LF_10:      dc = left(dc); if (s) goto LF_101;
LF_100:     dc = left(dc); if (s) goto LF_9;
            goto LF_8;
LF_01:      dc = left(dc); if (s) goto LF_011;
LF_010:     dc = left(dc); if (s) goto LF_5;
            goto LF_4;
LF_11:      dc = left(dc); if (s) goto LF_111;
LF_110:     dc = left(dc); if (s) goto LF_D;
            goto LF_C;
LF_001:     dc = left(dc); if (s) goto LF_3;
            goto LF_2;
LF_011:     dc = left(dc); if (s) goto LF_7;
            goto LF_6;
LF_101:     dc = left(dc); if (s) goto LF_B;
            goto LF_A;
LF_111:     dc = left(dc); if (s) goto LF_F;
            goto LF_E;


LF_F:       dc = left(dc); if (s) goto LF_F_1;
LF_F_0:     dc = left(dc); if (s) goto LF_F_01;
LF_F_00:    dc = left(dc); if (s) goto LF_F_001;
LF_F_000:   dc = left(dc); if (s) goto LF_F_0001;
            goto LF_F_0000;
LF_F_1:     dc = left(dc); if (s) goto LF_F_11
LF_F_10:    dc = left(dc); if (s) goto LF_F_101;
LF_F_100:   dc = left(dc); if (s) goto LF_F_9;
            goto LF_F_8;
LF_F_01:    dc = left(dc); if (s) goto LF_F_011;
LF_F_010:   dc = left(dc); if (s) goto LF_F_5;
            goto LF_F_4;
LF_F_11:    dc = left(dc); if (s) goto LF_F_111
LF_F_110:   dc = left(dc); if (s) goto LF_F_D;
            goto LF_F_C;
LF_F_001:   dc = left(dc); if (s) goto LF_F_3;
            goto LF_F_2;
LF_F_011:   dc = left(dc); if (s) goto LF_F_7;
            goto LF_F_6;
LF_F_101:   dc = left(dc); if (s) goto LF_F_B;
            goto LF_F_A;
LF_F_111:   dc = left(dc); if (s) goto LF_F_F;
            goto LF_F_E;


LF_F_F:     dc = left(dc); if (s) goto fetch
LF_F_F_0:   dc = left(dc); if (s) goto LF_F_F_01
LF_F_F_00:  dc = left(dc); if (s) goto LF_F_F_001
LF_F_F_000: dc = left(dc); if (s) goto LF_F_F_0001;
            goto LF_F_F_0000;
LF_F_F_001: dc = left(dc); if (s) goto LF_F_F_3
            goto LF_F_F_2;
LF_F_F_01:  dc = left(dc); if (s) goto fetch;
LF_F_F_010: dc = left(dc); if (s) goto fetch;
            goto LF_F_F_4;


/****************************************************************/
/          Microcode for each instruction                      /
/****************************************************************/


L0000:      /----------------------- LD ----------------------
            mar = ir;
            rd;
            ac = mdr; goto fetch;
```

```
L0001:          /----------------------- ST ----------------------
                mar = ir; mdr = ac;
                wr; goto fetch;
L2:             /----------------------- ADD ----------------------
                mar = ir;
                rd;
                ac = ac + mdr; goto fetch;
L3:             /----------------------- SUB ----------------------
                mar = ir;
                rd;
                ac = ac - mdr; goto fetch
L4:             /----------------------- LDR ----------------------
                f = ir + sp;
                mar = f;
                rd;
                ac = mdr; goto fetch;
L5:             /----------------------- STR ----------------------
                f = ir + sp;
                mar = f; mdr = ac;
                wr; goto fetch:
L6:             /----------------------- ADDR ----------------------
                f = ir + sp;
                mar = f;
                rd;
                ac = mdr + ac; goto fetch;
L7:             /----------------------- SUBR ----------------------
                f = ir + sp;
                mar = f;
                rd;
                ac = ac - mdr; goto fetch;
L8:             /----------------------- LDC ----------------------
                ac = ir & xmask; goto fetch;
L9:             /----------------------- JA ----------------------
                pc = ir & xmask; goto fetch;
LA:             /----------------------- JZOP ----------------------
                0  = ac; if (s) goto fetch;
                pc = ir & xmask; goto fetch;
LB:             /----------------------- JN ----------------------
                0  = ac; if (s) goto dojn;
                goto fetch;
dojn:           pc = ir & xmask; goto fetch;
LC:             /----------------------- JZ ----------------------
                0  = ac; if (z) goto dojz;
                goto fetch;
dojz:           pc = ir & xmask; goto fetch;
LD:             /----------------------- JNZ ----------------------
                0  = ac; if (z) goto fetch;
                pc = ir & xmask; goto fetch;
LE:             /----------------------- CALL ----------------------
                sp = sp - 1;
                mar = sp; mdr = pc;
                pc = ir & xmask; wr; goto fetch;
LF_0000:        /----------------------- RET ----------------------
                mar = sp; sp = sp + 1;
                rd;
                pc = mdr; goto fetch;
LF_0001:        /----------------------- LDI ----------------------
                mar = ac;
                rd;
                ac = mdr; goto fetch;
```

```
LF_2:          /--------------------------- STI ----------------------
               mar = sp; sp = sp + 1;
               rd;
               mar = ac;
               wr; goto fetch;
LF_3:          /----------------------- PUSH ---------------------
               sp = sp - 1;
               mar = sp; mdr = ac;
               wr; goto fetch;
LF_4:          /----------------------- POP ----------------------
               mar = sp; sp = sp + 1;
               rd;
               ac = mdr; goto fetch;
LF_5:          /----------------------- ALOC ---------------------
               f = ir & ymask;
               sp = sp - f; goto fetch;
LF_6:          /----------------------- DLOC ---------------------
               f = ir & ymask;
               sp = sp + f; goto fetch;
LF_7:          /----------------------- SWAP ---------------------
               f = ac;
               ac = sp;
               sp = f; goto fetch;
/*****************************************************************/
/              Available Opcodes                                /
/*****************************************************************/
LF_8:          /-------------------------------------------------
LF_9:          /-------------------------------------------------
LF_A:          /-------------------------------------------------
LF_B:          /-------------------------------------------------
LF_C:          /-------------------------------------------------
LF_D:          /-------------------------------------------------
LF_E:          /-------------------------------------------------
LF_F_0000:     /-------------------------------------------------
LF_F_0001:     /-------------------------------------------------
LF_F_2:        /-------------------------------------------------
LF_F_3:        /-------------------------------------------------
LF_F_4:        /-------------------------------------------------
LF_F_5:        /-------------------------------------------------
LF_F_6:        /-------------------------------------------------
LF_F_7:        /-------------------------------------------------
LF_F_8:        /-------------------------------------------------
LF_F_9:        /-------------------------------------------------
LF_F_A:        /-------------------------------------------------
LF_F_B:        /-------------------------------------------------
LF_F_C:        /-------------------------------------------------
LF_F_D:        /-------------------------------------------------
LF_F_E:        /-------------------------------------------------
LF_F_F_0000:/----------------------------------------------------
LF_F_F_0001:/----------------------------------------------------
LF_F_F_2:      /-------------------------------------------------
LF_F_F_3:      /-------------------------------------------------
LF_F_F_4:      /-------------------------------------------------
               goto fetch;
```

SPARC SUMMARY (from sparc.txt)

Format 1

Old branch instructions

31	30	29	28	25	24	22	21	0
0	0	a	cond		010		disp22	

sethi

31	30	29	25	24	22	21	0
0	0	rd		100		disp22	

New branch instructions

31	30	29	28	25	24	22	21	20	19	18	0
0	0	a	cond		001		cc		p	disp19	

Format 2

Call instruction

31	30	29	0
0	1	disp30	

Format 3

Two source registers

31	30	29	25	24	19	18	14	13	12	5	4	0
op		rd		op3		rs1		0	---		rs2	

One source register plus a displacement

31	30	29	25	24	19	18	14	13	12	0
op		rd		op3		rs1		1	simm13	

a:	annul bit
cc:	condition code set (00: icc, 10: xcc)
cond:	condition
disp19:	19-bit signed word displacement
disp22:	22-bit signed word displacement
disp30:	30-bit signed word displacement
op:	opcode, 10 or 11 for format three instructions

p: prediction bit

rd: destination register

op3:   opcode

rs1:   source register 1

rs2:   source register 2

simm13:   13-bit signed immediate value (holds displacement for load and store instructions)

Arithmetic instructions (format 3)

Op/op3	Mnemonic	Name
10/000000	add	Add
10/010000	addcc	Add and modify cc
10/001000	addx	Add extended
10/011000	addxcc	Add extended and modify cc
10/000100	sub	Subtract
10/010100	subcc	Subtract and modify cc
10/001100	subx	Subtract extended
10/011100	subxcc	Subtract extended and modify cc

Branch instructions (format 1)

Op	cond		
00	1000	ba	Branch always
00	0000	bn	Branch never
00	0001	be	Branch equal (Z == 1)
00	0010	ble	Branch less or equal ((N ^ V) == 1 || Z == 1)
00	0100	bleu	Branch less or equal unsigned (C == 1 || Z == 1)
00	0011	bl	Branch less ((N ^ V) == 1)
00	0101	bcs	Branch carry set (C == 1)
		blu	Branch less unsigned (C == 1)
00	0110	bneg	Branch negative (N == 1)
00	1001	bne	Branch not equal (Z == 0)
00	1010	bg	Branch greater (Z == 0 && N ^ V == 0)
00	1100	bgu	Branch greater unsigned (Z == 0 && C == 0)
00	1011	bge	Branch greater or equal (N ^ V == 0)
00	1101	bcc	Branch carry clear (C == 0)
		bgeu	Branch greater or equal unsigned (C == 0)
00	1110	bpos	Branch positive (N == 0)
00	0111	bvs	Branch signed overflow (V == 1)
00	1111	bvc	Branch no signed overflow (V == 0)

Load and Store Instructions (format 3)

Op/op3	Mnemonic	Name
11/000001	ldub	Load unsigned byte
11/001001	ldsb	Load signed halfword
11/000010	lduh	Load unsigned halfword

11/001010	ldsh	Load signed halfword
11/000000	ld/lduw	Load/load unsigned word
11/001000	ldsw	Load signed word
11/001011	ldx	Load extended
11/000011	ldd	Load double
11/000101	stb	Store byte
11/000110	sth	Store halfword
11/000100	st/stw	Store/store word
11/001110	stx	Store extended
11/000111	std	Store double
11/001111	swap	Swap

Logical Instructions (format 3)

Op/op3	Mnemonic	Name
10/000001	and	And
10/010001	andcc	And and modify cc
10/000101	andn	And with complement
10/010101	andncc	And with complement and modify cc
10/000010	or	Or
10/010010	orcc	Or and modify cc
10/000110	orn	Or with complement
10/010110	orncc	Or with complement and modify cc
10/000011	xor	Exclusive or
10/010011	xorcc	Exclusive or and modify cc
10/000111	xnor	Complement of exclusive or
10/010111	xnorcc	Complement of exclusive or and modify cc

Multiply (format 3)

Op/op3	Mnemonic	Name
10/100100	mulsc	Multiply shift and modify cc
10/101000	rdy	Read %y register
10/110000	wry	Write %y register

Shift Instructions (format 3)

Op/op3	Mnemonic	Name
10/100101	sll	Shift left logical
10/100110	srl	Shift right logical
10/100111	sra	Shift right arithmetic

Trap Instructions (format 3)

Op/op3	rd (cond)	Mnemonic	Name
10/111010	x1000	ta	Trap always
10/111010	x0000	tn	Trap never
10/111010	x0001	te	Trap equal (Z == 1)

10/111010	x0010	tle	Trap less or equal ((N ^ V) == 1 || Z == 1)
10/111010	x0100	tleu	Trap less or equal unsigned (C == 1 || Z == 1)
10/111010	x0011	tl	Trap less ((N ^ V) == 1)
10/111010	x0101	tcs	Trap carry set (C == 1)
		tlu	Trap less unsigned (C == 1)
10/111010	x0110	tneg	Trap negative (N == 1)
10/111010	x1001	tne	Trap not equal (Z == 0)
10/111010	x1010	tg	Trap greater (Z == 0 && N ^ V == 0)
10/111010	x1100	tgu	Trap greater unsigned (Z == 0 && C == 0)
10/111010	x1011	tge	Trap greater or equal (N ^ V == 0)
10/111010	x1101	tccu	Trap carry clear (C == 0)
		tgeu	Trap greater or equal unsigned (C == 0)
10/111010	x1110	tpos	Trap positive (N == 0)
10/111010	x0111	tvs	Trap signed overflow (V == 1)
10/111010	x1111	tvc	Trap no signed overflow (V == 0)

x = ignored

Window Instructions (format 3)

Op/op3	Mnemonic	Name
10/111100	save	Save
10/111101	restore	Restore

Control

Op/op3	Mnemonic	Name
01	call	call (format 1)
10/111000	jmpl	jump and link (format 2)
10/111001	rett	return from trap (format 2)

Miscellaneous

Op/op3	Mnemonic	Name
00/	sethi	Set high (format 1)

Others (not discussed)

floating point instructions

tagged integer subtraction

new instructions for the 64-bit SPARC

Synthetic Instruction		Real instruction		Function
btst	reg1/immed, reg2	andcc	reg1, reg2/immed, %g0	bit test
bset	reg1/immed, reg2	or	reg1, reg2/immed, reg1	bit set
bclr	reg1/immed, reg2	andn	reg1, reg2/immed, reg1	bit clear
btog	reg1/immed, reg2	xor	reg1, reg2/immed, reg1	bit toggle
clr	reg	or	%g0, %g0, reg	clear
clr	[address]	st	%g0, [address]	clear
clrh	[address]	sth	%g0, [address]	clear half

clrb	[address]	stb	%g0, [address]	clear byte
cmp	reg1, reg2/immed	subcc	reg1, reg2/immed, %g0	compare
dec	reg	sub	reg, 1, reg	decrement
dec	immed, reg	sub	reg, immed, reg	decrement
deccc	reg	sub	reg, 1, reg	decrement
deccc	immed, reg	subcc	reg, immed, reg	decrement
inc	reg	add	reg, 1, reg	increment
inc	immed, reg	add	reg, immed, reg	increment
inccc	reg	addcc	reg, 1, reg	increment
inccc	immed, reg	addcc	reg, immed, reg	increment
mov	reg1/immed, reg2	or	%g0, reg1/immed, reg2	move
neg	reg	sub	%g0, reg, reg	negate
nop		sethi	0, %g0	no operation
ret		jmpl	%i7 + 8, %g0	return
retl		jmpl	%o7 + 8, %g0	ret from leaf
If 4096 <= value < 4096				
set value, reg		or	%g0, value, reg	set to value
If value & 0x3ff == 0				
set value, reg		sethi	%hi(value), reg	set to value
If value neither				
set value, reg		sethi	%hi(value), reg	set to value
		or	reg, %lo(value), reg	

Integer Registers

%r0	%g0	
.	.	Global
%r7	%g7	
%r8	%o0 return-value register	
.	.	Out
%r14	%o7 %sp	
%r15	%o7 link register	
%r16	%l0	
.	.	Local
%r23	%l7	
%r24	%i0	
.	.	In
%r30	%i6 %fp	
%r31	%i7	
%y		Multiply/divide register

Floating Point Registers

%f0	
.	Single-precision
%f31	

%f0		
%f2		
.		Double-precision
%f62		

%f0		
%f4		
.		Quad-precision
%f60		

Directive		Description
.align	n	Forces alignment
.asciz	<double_quote_string>	Define null-terminated string
.byte		Define byte
.global	<label>	Declares label global
.half		Define halfword
.section	".text"	Start/continuation of code
.section	".data"	Start/continuation of init data
.section	".bss"	Start/continuation of uninit data
.skip	n	Reserve n bytes
.word	<operand>	Define word
main:		Marks starting point

JAVA VIRTUAL MACHINE BYTECODE SUMMARY
(from jvm.txt)

Mnemonic Conventions

	Meaning		Example
2	double word	dup2	(dup doubleword on top of stack)
2	"to"	i2f	(int to float)
a	reference	aload	(load reference from loc var)
a	array	aaload	(load reference from array)
b	byte	i2b	(int to byte)
b	boolean	bastore	(byte or boolean array store)
c	char	caload	(char array load)
const	push constant	iconst_0	(push int const 0)
d	double	dadd	(double add)
f	float	fadd	(float add)
i	int	iadd	(int add)
l	long	ladd	(long add)
load	push	iload	(int load)
_m1	minus 1	iconst_m1	(push int const -1)
_w	wide index (2 bytes)	ldc_w	(load constant wide)
_w	wide address (4 bytes)	goto_w	(goto wide)
_<n>	0, 1, 2, 3	iload_3	
_<d>	0, 1	dconst_1	
_<f>	0, 1, 2	fconst_2	
_<i>	0, 1, 2, 3, 4, 5	iconst_5	

Opcode (hex)	Mnemonic	Instruction Operands
32	aaload	
53	aastore	
01	aconst_null	
19	aload	local variable index (1 byte)
2A-2D	aload_<n>	
BD	anewarray	constant pool index (2 bytes)
B0	areturn	
BE	arraylength	
3A	astore	local variable index (1 byte)
4B-4E	astore_<n>	
BF	athrow	
33	baload	

54	bastore	
10	bipush	constant (1 byte)
34	caload	
55	castore	
C0	checkcast	constant pool index (2 bytes)
90	d2f	
83	d2i	
8F	d2l	
63	dadd	
31	daload	
52	dastore	
98	dcmpg	
97	dcmpl	
0E-0F	dconst_<d>	
6F	ddiv	
18	dload	local variable index (1 byte)
26-29	dload_<n>	
6B	dmul	
77	dneg	
73	drem	
AF	dreturn	
39	dstore	local variable index (1 byte)
47-4A	dstore_<n>	
67	dsub	
59	dup	
5A	dup_x1	
5B	dup_x2	
5C	dup2	
5D	dup2_x1	
5E	dup2_x2	
8D	f2d	
8B	f2i	
8C	f2l	
62	fadd	
30	faload	
51	fastore	
96	fcmpg	
95	fcmpl	
0B-0D	fconst_<f>	
6E	fdiv	
17	fload	local variable index (1 byte)
22-25	fload_<n>	
6A	fmul	
76	fneg	
72	frem	
AE	freturn	
38	fstore	local variable index (1 byte)

43-46	fstore_<n>	
66	fsub	
B4	getfield	constant pool index (2 bytes)
B2	getstatic	constant pool index (2 bytes)
A7	goto	pc-relative address (2 bytes)
C8	goto_w	pc-relative address (4 bytes)
91	i2b	
92	i2c	
87	i2d	
86	i2f	
85	i2l	
93	i2s	
60	iadd	
2E	iaload	
7E	iand	
4F	iastore	
03-08	iconst_<i>	
02	iconst_m1	
6C	idiv	
A5	if_acmpeq	pc-relative address (2 bytes)
A6	if_acmpne	pc-relative address (2 bytes)
9F	if_icmpeq	pc-relative address (2 bytes)
A2	if_icmpge	pc-relative address (2 bytes)
A3	if_icmpgt	pc-relative address (2 bytes)
A4	if_icmple	pc-relative address (2 bytes)
A1	if_icmplt	pc-relative address (2 bytes)
A0	if_icmpne	pc-relative address (2 bytes)
99	ifeq	pc-relative address (2 bytes)
9C	ifge	pc-relative address (2 bytes)
9D	ifgt	pc-relative address (2 bytes)
9E	ifle	pc-relative address (2 bytes)
9B	iflt	pc-relative address (2 bytes)
9A	ifne	pc-relative address (2 bytes)
C7	ifnonnull	pc-relative address (2 bytes)
C6	ifnull	pc-relative address (2 bytes)
84	iinc	local variable index (1 byte), increment (1 byte)
15	iload	local variable index (1 byte)
1A-1D	iload_<n>	
68	imul	
74	ineg	
C1	instanceof	constant pool index (2 bytes)
B9	invokeinterface	constant pool index (2 bytes), number of args (1 byte) , 0 (1 byte)
B7	invokespecial	constant pool index (2 bytes)
B8	invokestatic	constant pool index (2 bytes)
B6	invokevirtual	constant pool index (2 bytes)
80	ior	
70	irem	

AC	ireturn	
78	ishl	
7A	ishr	
36	istore	local variable index (1 byte)
3B-3E	istore_<n>	
64	isub	
7C	iushr	
82	ixor	
A8	jsr	pc-relative address (2 bytes)
C9	jsr_w	pc-relative address (4 bytes)
8A	l2d	
89	l2f	
88	l2i	
61	ladd	
2F	laload	
7F	land	
50	lastore	
94	lcmp	
09-0A	lconst_<l>	
12	ldc	constant pool index (1 byte)
13	ldc_w	constant pool index (2 bytes)
14	ldc2_w	constant pool index (2 bytes)
6D	ldiv	
16	lload	local variable index (1 byte)
1E-21	lload_<n>	
69	lmul	
75	lneg	
AB	lookupswitch	pad (0-3 bytes), default (4 bytes), number of pairs (4 bytes), pairs (8 bytes each pair)
81	lor	
71	lrem	
AD	lreturn	
79	lshl	
7B	lshr	
37	lstore	local variable index (1 byte)
3F-42	lstore_<n>	
65	lsub	
7D	lushr	
83	lxor	
C2	monitorenter	
C3	monitorexit	
C5	multianewarray	constant pool index (2 bytes), dimensions (1 byte)
BB	new	constant pool index (2 bytes)
BC	newarray	type code (1 byte)
00	nop	
57	pop	
58	pop2	

B5	putfield	constant pool index (2 bytes)
B3	putstatic	constant pool index (2 bytes)
A9	ret	local variable index (1 byte)
B1	return	
35	saload	
56	sastore	
11	sipush	constant (2 bytes)
5F	swap	
AA	tableswitch	pad (0-3 bytes), default (4 bytes), low (4 bytes), high (4 bytes), jump table offsets (4 bytes each)
C4	wide	opcode (1 byte), local variable index (2 bytes)
		or
		iinc opcode (1 byte), local variable index (2 bytes), increment (2 bytes)

ASCII SUMMARY (from ascii.txt)

Hex	Decimal		Hex	Decimal		Hex	Decimal	
20	32	<blank>	41	65	A	61	97	a
21	33	!	42	66	B	62	98	b
22	34	"	43	67	C	63	99	c
23	35	#	44	68	D	64	100	d
24	36	$	45	69	E	65	101	e
25	37	%	46	70	F	66	102	f
26	38	&	47	71	G	67	103	g
27	38	'	48	72	H	69	104	h
28	40	(	49	73	I	69	105	i
29	41	)	4A	74	J	6A	106	j
2A	42	*	4B	75	K	6B	107	k
2B	43	+	4C	76	L	6C	108	l
2C	44	,	4D	77	M	6D	109	m
2D	45	-	4E	78	N	6E	110	n
2E	46	.	4F	79	O	6F	111	o
2F	47	/	50	80	P	70	112	p
30	48	0	51	81	Q	71	113	q
31	49	1	52	82	R	72	114	r
32	50	2	53	83	S	73	114	s
33	51	3	54	84	T	74	116	t
34	52	4	55	85	U	75	117	u
35	53	5	56	86	V	76	118	v
36	54	6	57	87	W	77	119	w
37	55	7	58	88	X	78	120	x
38	56	8	59	89	Y	79	121	y
39	57	9	5A	90	Z	7A	122	z
3A	58	:	5B	91	[	7B	123	{
3B	59	;	5C	92	\	7C	124	|
3C	69	<	5D	93	]	7D	125	}
3D	61	=	5E	94	^	7E	126	~
3E	62	>	5F	95	_			
3F	63	?	60	96	`			
40	64	@						

Control Characters

Hex	Decimal	Abbreviation	Meaning
00	0	NUL	Nul
01	1	SOH	Start of header
02	2	STX	Start of text
03	3	ETX	End of text
04	4	EOT	End of transmission
05	5	ENQ	Enquiry
06	6	ACK	Acknowledge
07	7	BEL	Bell
08	8	BS	Backspace
09	9	HT	Horizontal tab
0A	10	LF	Line feed (i.e., newline)
0B	11	VT	Vertical tab
0C	12	FF	Form feed (i.e., new page)
0D	13	CR	Carriage return
0E	14	SO	Shift out
0F	15	SI	Shift in
10	16	DLE	Data link escape
11	17	DC1	Device control 1
12	18	DC2	Device control 2
13	19	DC3	Device control 3
14	20	DC4	Device control 4
15	21	NAK	Negative Acknowledge
16	22	SYN	Synchronous idle
17	23	ETB	End of transmission block
18	24	CAN	Cancel
19	25	EM	End of medium
1A	26	SUB	Substitute
1B	27	ESC	Escape
1C	28	FS	File separator
1D	29	GS	Group separator
1E	30	RS	Record separator
1F	31	US	Unit separator
7F	127	DEL	Delete

NUMBER CONVERSION SUMMARY
(from number.txt)

Dec	Binary	Hex	HEX TABLE	POWERS OF 2
0	0000	0	0 * 16 = 0	2 to the 0 = 1
1	0001	1	1 * 16 = 16	" " 1 = 2
2	0010	2	2 * 16 = 32	" " 2 = 4
3	0011	3	3 * 16 = 48	" " 3 = 8
4	0100	4	4 * 16 = 64	" " 4 = 16
5	0101	5	5 * 16 = 80	" " 5 = 32
6	0110	6	6 * 16 = 96	" " 6 = 64
7	0111	7	7 * 16 = 112	" " 7 = 128
8	1000	8	8 * 16 = 128	" " 8 = 256
9	1001	9	9 * 16 = 144	" " 9 = 512
10	1010	A	10 * 16 = 160	" " 10 = 1024 = 1 K
11	1011	B	11 * 16 = 176	" " 11 = 2048
12	1100	C	12 * 16 = 192	" " 12 = 4096
13	1101	D	13 * 16 = 208	" " 13 = 8192
14	1110	E	14 * 16 = 224	" " 14 = 16,384
15	1111	F	15 * 16 = 240	" " 15 = 32,768
			16 * 16 = 256	" " 16 = 65,536
				" " 20 = 1,048,576 = 1 M
				" " 30 = 1,073,741,824 = 1 G

Range of unsigned 1-byte numbers: 0   to 255
Range of signed 1-byte numbers: -128   to 127
Range of unsigned 2-byte numbers: 0   to 65,535
Range of signed 2-byte numbers: -32,768 to 32,767
Range of unsigned 4-byte numbers: 0   to 4G - 1
Range of signed 4-byte numbers: -2G   to 2G - 1

HELP WITH C++ FOR JAVA PROGRAMMERS

Every C++ program must consist of at least the `main` function. The `cin` object handles input from the standard input device (i.e., the keyboard); the `cout` object handles output to the standard output device (i.e., the display monitor). Both `cin` and `cout` require the inclusion of the `iostream` include file. `endl` represents "\n". The insertion operator `<<` inserts an item into the output stream (i.e., it outputs); the extraction operator `>>` extracts an item from the input stream (i.e., it inputs).

The `using` statement is similar in function to the `import` statement in Java. Without it, we would have to use the fully qualified names of `cout`, `cin`, and `endl` (which are `std::cout`, `std::cin`, and `std::endl`, respectively).

```
1   // Sample Program 1
2   #include <iostream>            // required by cin, cout
3   using namespace std;          /* now do not have to
4                                     qualify names of cin,
5                                     cout, and endl */
6   int main()
7   {
8       int x;
9
10      cout << "Enter integer\n"; // display "Enter integer"
11      cin >> x;                  // read integer into x
12      cout << x << " squared = " // display "3 squared ="
13           << x*x << endl;
14      return 0;
15  }
```

Sample session:

```
Enter integer
3                   ←3 entered by the user
3 squared = 9
```

===
A pointer is an address. A pointer variable holds an address. The statement

```
int x, y;
```

declares the `int` variables `x` and `y`. The statement

```
int *p, *q;
```

declares the `int` pointer variables `p` and `q`. The statement

```
y = x;
```

assigns the value of **x** to **y**. The statement

```
p = &x;
```

assigns the address of **x** to **p** (**&** in this context means "address of"). ***p** is the location to which **p** points. Thus, the statement

```
*p = 5;
```

assigns 5 to the location to which **p** points. It does *not* assign 5 to **p**. To *dereference a pointer* means to follow it to the location to which it points. For example, we are dereferencing **p** in both of these statements:

```
*p = 5;
y = *p;
```

In the first, we are placing 5 into the location to which **p** points; in the second, we are placing the value in the location to which **p** points into **y**.

Arithmetic operations can be performed on pointers. For example, suppose an **int** pointer **p** points to the first element of an **int** array. Then the statement

```
p = p + 1;
```

changes **p** so that it points to the next element of the array. Thus, adding 1 to **p** in a C++ statement actually increases the address in **p** by the size of one array element. If the size of an **int** is 4 bytes, this statement actually adds 4 to the contents of **p**.

The name of an array without square brackets is interpreted as a pointer to (i.e., the address of) the *first* slot of that array. For example, suppose **a** is an **int** array, and **p** is an **int** pointer. Then

```
p = a;
```

assigns the address of **a[0]** to **p**. Alternatively, we can use the equivalent (but longer) statement

```
p = &a[0];
```

A pointer to an array can be used like the name of that array. For example, if **p** points to an array **a**, we can use **p** as the array name. For example, in place of

```
a[2] = 3;
```

we can use

```
p[2] = 3;       // use p as the array name
```

We can also use **p** as a pointer:

```
*(p + 2) = 3;  // or use p as a pointer
```

These three statements all have the same effect.

Arrays can be created with the **new** operator. For example,

```
p = new int[3];
```

allocates an **int** array consisting of three slots, and assigns its address to **p**. We can then use **p** as the name of this array. For example, to assign 5 to the second slot of this dynamically allocated array, we can use

```
p[1] = 5;
```

Arrays can also be created with global or local declarations. For example, the declaration

```
int a[] = { 1, 2, 3 };
```

within a function declares a local array **a** containing 1, 2, and 3 in its three slots.

```
1   // Sample Program 2
2   #include <iostream>
3   using namespace std;
4
5   int main()
6   {
7       int a[] = { 1, 2, 3 };        // local array
8       int x;
9       int *p;                       // p is an int pointer
10
11      p = &x;                       // p now points to x
12      *p = 5;                       // assign 5 to x
13      cout << "x = " << x << endl;      // display "x = 5"
14      p = a;                        // p now points to a[0]
15      cout << *p << endl;           // display a[0]
16      p = p + 2;                    // p now points to a[2]
17      cout << *p << endl;           // display a[2]
18      p = new int[3];               // p assigned add of array
19      p[1] = 5;                     // assign 5 to 2nd slot
20      *(p + 1) = 6;                 // assign 6 to 2nd slot
21      cout << p[1] << endl;         // display 2nd slot
22      return 0;
23  }
```

Output:

```
x = 5;
1
3
6
```

```
===================================================================
```

A global variable is declared outside a function. It is created and initialized at assembly time. A global variable whose declaration does not specify an initial value is guaranteed to have the initial value 0.

A dynamic local variable is a variable declared within a function without the keyword **static**. It is created on entry to the function, and is destroyed on exit. Unless explicitly initialized, the value of a dynamic local variable is undefined.

A function call must be preceded by either the function's definition or its prototype. A function prototype is like the first line of a function definition, terminated with a semicolon.

```
1   // Sample Program 3
2   #include <iostream>
3   using namespace std;
4
5   void f(int z);                    // prototype for f
```

```
 6  int gv1;                        // global, initial value is 0
 7  int gv2 = 5;                    // global, initial value is 5
 8
 9  int main()
10  {
11      f(2); f(3);
12      return 0;
13  }
14  void f(int z)                   // z is a parameter
15  {
16      int x;                      // created on each call
17                                  // value of x undefined
18      x = z;                      // now value of x defined
19      cout << "x = " << x << endl;
20      cout << "gv1 = " << gv1 << endl;
21      cout << "gv2 = " << gv2 << endl;
22      gv1++; gv2++;               // increment gv1, gv2
23  }
```

Output:

```
x = 2
gv1 = 0
gv2 = 5
x = 3
gv1 = 1
gv2 = 6
```

==

Function calls pass the value of their arguments unless reference parameters are used (see Sample Program 5). If &**y** is an argument in a function call, the address of **y** is passed.

```
 1  // Sample Program 4
 2  #include <iostream>
 3  using namespace std;
 4
 5  void f(int x, int *p)           // x gets 5; p points to y
 6  {
 7    *p = x;                       // assign x to y
 8  }
 9  int main()
10  {
11    int y;
12
13    f(5, &y);                     // pass 5 and address of y
14    cout << "y = " << y << endl;
15    return 0;
16  }
```

Output:

```
y = 5
```

==

A reference parameter receives the address of its corresponding argument. This address is automatically dereferenced wherever the parameter is used. An **&** preceding the name of a parameter in the parameter list of a function definition identifies the parameter as a reference parameter.

```
1   // Sample Program 5
2   #include <iostream>
3   using namespace std;
4
5   void f(int x, int &r)            // r is ref parm, r points to y
6   {
7     r = x;                        // r dereferenced
8   }
9   int main()
10  {
11    int y;
12    f(5, y);                      // pass 5 and address of y
13    cout << "y = " << y << endl;
14    return 0;
15  }
```

Output:

```
y = 5
```

===

A **struct** and a **class** are almost identical. The only difference is that in a **struct**, members default to **public**, but in a **class**, members default to **private**.

An instance of a **struct** or a **class** can be created with the **new** operator or with an ordinary declaration. For example, suppose κ is a class and **q** is declared with

```
K *q;
```

Then the statement

```
q = new K;
```

assigns the address of a newly created κ object to **q**. The object can then be accessed through **q**. For example, if the object has a public **int** field **x**, we can assign 5 to this field with

```
(*q).x = 5;
```

(*q) is the object **q** points to. Thus, (*q).**x** is the **x** field of this object. We can also write this statement equivalently with

```
q -> x = 5;
```

Objects can also be created with declarations. For example, the declaration

```
K k;
```

creates an object **k** of type κ. **k** denotes the object itself—not its address. This object can be accessed directly through the name **k** using the dot operator. For example, if **k** has an **int** field **x**, we can assign it 5 with

```
k.x = 5:
```

A **class** declaration usually contains only the prototypes of its member functions. The definitions of member functions appear outside the class. These definitions start with

```
<return type> <class name>::<function name>(parameter list)
```

A semicolon should follow the closing brace of a **struct** or **class** definition.

```
 1   // Sample Program 6
 2   #include <iostream>
 3   using namespace std;
 4
 5   class K {
 6   public:
 7     int x;
 8     void f(int a);             // prototype for f
 9   };                           // remember the ";"
10   void K::f(int a)             // definition of f
11   {
12     x = a;
13   }
14
15   int main()
16   {
17     K k, *p, *q;               /* k is a K object
18                                   p, q are K-object ptrs */
19     p = &k;                    // assign p the address of k
20     k.f(1);                    // invoke f thru k
21     (*p).f(1);                 // another way to invoke f
22     p -> f(1);                 // another way to invoke f
23     cout << k.x << endl;       // display x thru k
24     cout << (*p).x << endl;    // display x via ptr p
25     cout << p -> x << endl;    // display x via ptr p
26     q = new K;                 // agn add of new obj to q
27     (*q).f(2);                 // invoke f via ptr q
28     q -> f(2);                 // invoke f via ptr q
29     cout << (*q).x << endl;    // display x via ptr q
30     cout << q -> x << endl;    // display x via ptr q
31     return 0;
32   }
```

Output:

```
1
1
1
2
2
```

GLOSSARY

Absolute address The address of an item in main memory relative to the beginning of main memory.

Activation record A block dynamically allocated on a stack during a function call containing the parameters, local variables, and other information for that call.

ALU Arithmetic/logic unit. Performs arithmetic and logical operations.

Applet A Java program embedded in a Web page.

Argument An item passed to a function during a function call.

ASCII American Standard Code for Information Interchange. A 7-bit (usually extended to 8 bits) code for representing character data.

Assembler A program that translates assembly language.

Assembler directive A command in an assembly language program that directs the assembler to perform some function.

Associative memory Memory in which each slot includes a key. Each slot is accessed via its key.

Backward compatible The ability of a computer to run programs written for earlier models.

Big endian The storage of multiple-byte numbers with the most significant byte in the lower memory location.

Bit A symbol—0 or 1—in the binary system.

Black box A model of a device that does not reveal its internal structure.

Boolean algebra An algebra of two-state variables.

Boolean function A function with two-state inputs and outputs.

Boot The initial loading of main memory that occurs when a computer is powered up.

Branch prediction The process of predicting the next instruction to be executed after a conditional branch instruction to minimize the occurrence of a pipeline stall.

Bubble A stall in a pipeline.

Bus A group of wires that carries data from one location to another.

Byte A grouping of 8 bits.

Byte-addressable An addressing scheme in which consecutive bytes are given consecutive addresses.

Bytecode Machine language for the Java Virtual Machine.

Cache A high-speed memory that holds a subset of the contents of main memory.

Call by name A function call mechanism that causes the evalution of an argument every time its corresponding parameter is referenced.

Call by reference A function call mechanism that passes the address of the argument.

Call by value A function call mechanism that passes the value of the argument.

Call by value-result A function call mechanism that passes the value of the argument, and on return from the called function, updates the argument with the final value of its corresponding parameter.

Capacitance The property of electrical circuits that resists a change in voltage.

Chip A block of a semiconductor material on which an electrical circuit has been deposited.

CISC Complex Instruction Set Computer. A computer whose instruction set contains high-level instructions with a variety of addressing modes.

Class A programming type that contains both data and functions.

Class file The file the Java compiler creates for each class in a program.

Clock frequency The number of pulses generated by a clock per second.

Combinational circuit A circuit whose output depends only on its current input.

Compiler A program that translates a high-level language to machine language.

Computational section The section in the CPU that contains the ALU and associated circuitry.

Computer architecture   The features of a computer that an assembly language programmer "sees."

Computer organization   The structures of a computer that implement its architecture.

Constant pool   A collection of constants in a Java ".class" file.

Content-addressable memory   Same as *associative memory.*

Context switch   A switch from the execution of one program or process to another.

Control dependency   A dependency in which the availability of one instruction depends on another instruction.

Control section   The section within the CPU that generates control signals.

CPU   Central processing unit. The unit that contains the computational and control sections.

CPU-I/O overlap   The execution of instructions by the CPU in parallel with an I/O operation.

Cycle stealing   The temporary pause in memory utilization by the CPU to allow access of memory by an I/O device.

Data dependency   A dependency in which the data produced by one instruction is required by another instruction.

Datapath   The register bank, CPU, associated circuitry, and interconnecting buses.

Decoder   A circuit that indicates the value of a binary number.

Direct addressing   An addressing mode in which the instruction contains the absolute address of the operand.

Direct mapping   An address mapping technique in which the location to which an address is mapped is determined exclusively by the address.

Dirty bit   A bit that, when set, indicates that its associated block of memory has been altered.

DMA   Direct memory access. Accessing memory without the utilization of the CPU.

Dynamic variable   A variable that is created during program execution.

Encoder   A circuit that produces a different code on its outputs for each of its inputs.

EEPROM   Electrically erasable PROM.

EPROM   Erasable PROM.

Excess-*n*   A numbering scheme in which a number's representation is obtained by adding a constant to its normal representation.

Executable file   A file that is a complete program in runable form.

External reference   A reference in one module to an item in another separately assembled or compiled module.

Fall-through instruction   The instruction immediately following a conditional branch instruction.

FIFO   First-in-first-out.

Fixed point   A number representation scheme in which the radix point is fixed in the rightmost position.

Flash memory   A type of electrically alterable ROM.

Flip-flop   A circuit that can switch between two states.

Floating point   A number representation scheme that allows numbers with fractional parts to be represented.

Full adder   A circuit that adds three bits.

Gate   A simple combinational circuit that performs a logical operation, such as AND, OR, or NOT.

Global variable   A variable whose scope covers the entire program.

Half adder   A circuit that can add two bits.

Heap   A block of memory from which memory is dynamically allocated to executing programs.

Hertz   One cycle per second.

Hit   A memory access for which the desired item is in the cache.

Hit rate   Percentage of memory accesses that are hits.

Horizontal microcode   Microcode that uses a minimum of decoding circuits. It is characterized by fewer but longer microinstructions than vertical microcode.

Horner's method   An efficient algorithm for evaluating polynomials.

Hypertext   Documents that are connected to other documents by embedded links.

Immediate addressing   An addressing mode in which the operand is in the instruction.

Indexed addressing   An addressing mode in which the contents of a register provides an index (i.e., an offset to the operand).

Indirect addressing   An addressing mode in which the instruction contains bits that indicate the location of the address of the operand.

Inductance   The property of electrical circuits that resists a change in current.

IC   Integrated circuit. A complete circuit on a single block of semiconductor material.

Inheritance   A feature of object-oriented languages that permits the derivation of one class from another.

Internal fragmentation   In a paging system, the unused portion of the memory frame that holds the last page of a program.

Interpreter   A program that executes a program at the source level.

Interrupt handler   A routine that gets control when an interrupt first occurs.

ISA   Instruction set architecture. The characteristics of a computer's instruction set.

JIT compiling   Just-in-time compiling. Compiling code on an as-needed basis during the interpretation of a program.

JVM   Java Virtual Machine.

L1 cache   Cache built into the microprocessor chip.

L2 cache   Cache external to the microprocessor chip.

Library   A file containing a collection of functions in machine code form.

LIFO   Last-in-first-out.

Linker   A program that combines separately assembled or compiled modules.

Little endian   The storage of multiple-byte numbers with the least significant byte in the lower memory location.

Loader   A routine that loads an executable program into main memory.

Load point   The address at which a program is loaded.

Load/store architecture   An architecture in which only load and store instructions access main memory.

Locality of reference   The tendency of executing programs to make memory accesses that cluster in small localities of memory.

Local variable   A variable whose scope is limited to the program block in which it appears.

Logical address   An address of an item from the executing program's point of view.

LRU   Least recently used.

Machine language   The programming language that the machine (i.e., the computer) can understand directly.

Memory address bus   The bus that carries addresses to main memory.

Memory data bus   The bus that carries data to and from main memory.

Method   Object-oriented terminology for a function.

Microinstruction   A binary number whose bits propagate to various circuits via control lines.

Microprogram   A sequence of microinstructions that performs a useful task.

Microstore   The ROM in which microinstructions are stored.

Miss   A memory access for which the desired item is not in the cache.

Multiplexer   A circuit that selects exactly one of its inputs for output.

Multiprogramming   A system in which multiple programs simultaneously in main memory compete for the CPU.

Native code   Machine language code for the computer on which it is located.

Object   A variable whose type is a class.

One's complement   A binary number system in which a number is negated by flipping its bits.

Opcode   The portion of a machine instruction that specifies the operation.

Operating system   A program that controls a computer system and interfaces with the user.

Overclocking   Running the system clock faster than normal.

Overflow   A situation in which the result of a computation cannot fit in the allotted space.

Page fault   A reference to a page that is not in main memory.

Page table   A table indicating the memory location of a program's pages.

Paging   The system that allows fixed length parts (pages) of a program to be loaded into main memory noncontiguously and in any order.

Parameter   A variable in a function that receives the argument passed by the calling function.

PC-relative addressing   An addressing mode in which the instruction contains the offset from itself to the target location.

Physical address   The actual address of an item in memory.

Pipelining   A technique that allows multiple instructions to be executed simultaneously.

Pointer   The address of an item in main memory.

Polymorphism   A feature of object-oriented languages that permits a single operator to behave differently depending on the types of its operands.

PROM   A high school dance. A programmable ROM.

Radix point   The point in a positional numbering system that divides the whole part from the fractional part.

RAM   Random access memory. Memory whose slots each can be accessed without first accessing its predecessors. By convention, "RAM" implies read and write random access memory.

Register   A circuit that can hold a single binary item.

Register addressing   An addressing mode in which a register contains the operand.

Register indirect addressing   A type of indirect addressing in which a register contains the address of the operand.

Register-oriented architecture   An architecture in which most operations involve a register.

Register window   A system in which at a given time only a subset of registers can be accessed—namely, those registers "under the window."

Relocation   Changing the starting point of a module or a program.

Resolution   The process of replacing an item's symbol with the item's address.

RISC   Reduced instruction set computer. A computer with an instruction set containing fewer and less complex instructions than a CISC.

ROM   Read-only memory.

Scope   The range of a program in which an identifier is defined.

Segmentation   A system that allows logical parts of a program to be loaded into memory noncontiguously and in any order.

Semantic gap   The gap between high-level languages and machine language.

Semiconductor   A material whose conductivity lies between a conductor and an insulator.

Sequential circuit   A circuit with memory.

Signed magnitude   A number representation in which the sign and the magnitude of a number are stored.

Silicon   An element from which integrated circuits are fabricated.

Stack   A LIFO data structure.

Stack frame   Same as *activation record*.

Stack-oriented architecture   An architecture in which most instructions operate on the stack.

Stall   A situation in a pipeline that forces a stage to go idle.

Start-up code   Initialization code that is part of an executable file.

Static variable   A variable whose slot is part of the executable file (C++). A variable accessed via its class (Java).

Sticky bit   A bit whose value is set to 1 if any of the group of bits it represents is 1.

Structural dependency   A dependency in which two instructions contend for the same hardware resource.

Superscalar   Using multiple pipelines.

Supervisor mode   A running mode of a computer for which privileged operations are permitted.

Symbol table   A table containing symbols and their corresponding addresses built by an assembler and other programs.

Synthetic instruction   Nonexistent instructions that can be mapped to existing instructions.

Thrashing   Excessive paging activity that occurs when memory is over-committed.

Thunk   A function that evaluates arguments in call by name.

Timesharing   A system that permits the simultaneous use of a computer by multiple users.

Timeslice   A short period of time in a timesharing system during which a program or process is allowed to use the CPU.

TLB   Translation lookaside buffer. An associative memory for dynamic address translation.

Two's complement   A binary numbering system in which a number is negated by flipping its bits and adding one.

Unassembler   A program that converts a machine language program to assembly language.

Underflow   A situation in a floating-point computation in which the magnitude of the result is too small to be represented.

User mode   A running mode of a computer system during which certain privileged operations are not allowed.

UTF8   A coding scheme for representing 16-bit Unicode characters that uses only 8 bits for the ASCII characters.

Vector operation   A computation involving one operation on multiple data items.

Vertical microcode   Microcode using microinstructions whose length is minimized by means of decoding circuits.

Virtual memory   A system that creates the illusion of more memory than actually exists.

Volatile memory   Memory whose contents are lost if power is not maintained.

Von Neumann architecture   The architecture characterized by an executing program stored in main memory.

INDEX